A Commentary
to
Kant's 'Critique of Pure Reason'

A Commentary to Kant's 'Critique of Pure Reason'

by
Norman Kemp Smith
Sometime Professor of Logic and Metaphysics
University of Edinburgh

with a new introduction by
Sebastian Gardner
Department of Philosophy
University College London

palgrave
macmillan

First edition published in 1918 by The Macmillan Press Ltd.
Second revised and enlarged edition 1923
Reprinted 1979
This edition 2003
PALGRAVE MACMILLAN
Houndmills, Basingstoke, Hampshire RG21 6XS and
175 Fifth Avenue, New York, N.Y. 10010
Companies and representatives throughout the world

PALGRAVE MACMILLAN is the global academic imprint of the Palgrave
Macmillan division of St. Martin 's Press, LLC and of Palgrave Macmillan Ltd.
Macmillan® is a registered trademark in the United States, United Kingdom
and other countries. Palgrave is a registered trademark in the European
Union and other countries.

ISBN 978-1-4039-1504-7   ISBN 978-0-230-59596-5 (eBook)
DOI 10.1057/9780230595965

This book is printed on paper suitable for recycling and
made from fully managed and sustained forest sources.
Logging, pulping and manufacturing processes are
expected to conform to the environmental regulations
of the country of origin.

A catalogue record for this book is available from the British Library.

Library of Congress Cataloging-in-Publication Data
Smith, Norman Kemp, 1872–1958.
    A commentary to Kant's Critique of pure reason / by Norman Kemp
Smith ; with a new introduction by Sebastian Gardner.—2nd ed.
        p. cm.
    Includes bibliographical references and index.

    1. Kant, Immanuel, 1724–1804. Kritik der reinen Vernunft. I. Title.

B2779.S5 2003
121—dc21

                                                                2003051780

Tansferred to Digital Printing 2008

CONTENTS

INTRODUCTION

THE CRITIQUE OF PURE REASON[1]

[1] Headings not in Kant's Table of Contents are printed in italics.

vii

CONTENTS

CONTENTS

NOTE

In all references to the *Kritik der Reinen Vernunft* I have given the original pagings of both the first and second editions. References to Kant's other works are, whenever possible, to the volumes thus far issued in the new Berlin edition. As the *Reflexionen Kant's zur Kritik der reinen Vernunft* had not been published in this edition at the time when the *Commentary* was completed, the numbering given is that of B. Erdmann's edition of 1884.

ABBREVIATIONS

Berlin edition of Kant's works W
Pagings in the first edition of the *Kritik der reinen Vernunft* A
Pagings in the second edition B
Adickes' edition of the *Kritik der reinen Vernunft* (1889) K

KEMP SMITH'S READING OF KANT'S
CRITIQUE OF PURE REASON

Norman Kemp Smith's *A Commentary to Kant's 'Critique of Pure Reason'* appeared in 1918, eleven years before his translation of Kant's philosophical masterpiece, and it provided the essential context out of which the translation emerged. Just as the translation has endured, so the *Commentary* belongs, alongside H. J. Paton's equally detailed *Kant's Metaphysics of Experience* (2 vols, 1936) and A. C. Ewing's succinct *A Short Commentary on Kant's 'Critique of Pure Reason'* (1938), to a small number of English-language works on the *Critique of Pure Reason* written in the first half of the twentieth century that have stood the test of time and become classics of Kant scholarship. The historical period to which Kemp Smith belongs, and which is reflected in his approach to Kant, is of course distinguished from our own in many important respects, but the historical distance has done nothing to dissociate the questions that Kemp Smith raises about Kant from the ones that are raised now, and it remains standard practice to consult Kemp Smith for his view of the matters debated by contemporary Kant commentators.

It goes without saying that a short discussion can hope to give an idea of, but not to do justice to, the richness and fineness of the *Commentary*. What I wish to show here is that the distance at which the contemporary reader stands from the philosophical world in which Kemp Smith composed his *Commentary*, far from reducing the work's relevance, gives it a special value, over and above that which it possesses intrinsically by virtue of its detailed and acute scholarship, and the striking clarity and elegance of Kemp Smith's prose.

British philosophy at the end of the nineteenth century, when Kemp Smith began his philosophical studies, was characterised by the predominance of various forms of idealism that bore a Hegelian stamp: the varied but ultimately unified outlook defended by T. H. Green, F. H. Bradley, J. M. McTaggart and Bernard Bosanquet was at the height of its influence.[1] North American philosophy also included important proponents of idealism, such as Josiah Royce. Despite this circumstance of idealism's predominance, Kemp Smith did not find himself in a context of well-developed knowledge and discussion of Kant. Kant's ideas had not at any time settled in a stable form in Britain: throughout the nineteenth century the native tradition of empiricism had offered strong resistance, and from the days of its initial reception[2] right up to the era of British idealism, Kant's philosophy had been prone to appear through the lenses of Fichte, Schelling and Hegel, either subject to their criticisms or partially merged with their doctrines, and no movement comparable to neo-Kantianism in Germany had attempted to retrieve Kant's philosophy by disentangling it from the arguable disfigurements to which his successors had subjected it. To take two important instances: the extensive study of Kant published by Edward Caird in 1889, which comprehensively exposits and reviews the entire Critical system, concludes that Kant's 'fundamental error' was to misunderstand his own philosophical method, which 'is already in itself the dialectical method of Fichte and Hegel', as a consequence of which Kant fails to see that by way of the unity of self-consciousness 'we can go beyond phenomena to their noumenal reality'.[3] Similarly, John Watson's defence of Kant against his nineteenth-century empiricist rivals and detractors, published in the same decade, declares that the *Critique*'s distinction of a 'given manifold' and 'originated forms' is incoherent: it 'has not only no proper justification' but is 'inconsistent with the spirit of the Critical philosophy itself', yields merely 'relative knowledge' and so 'no knowledge at all', 'the great imperfection' in Kant's theory being ultimately 'his want of the idea of development' as it is found in Fichte, Schelling and Hegel.[4]

It is also relevant for an appreciation of the originality of Kemp Smith's undertaking, that the motive for historical study had in any case waned. Although one of the most important steps in the formation of British idealism had consisted in a study of Hegel – James Stirling's *The Secret of Hegel* (1865) – by the late nineteenth century British idealism had become sufficiently established and well developed for its historical origins in Hegel, let alone Kant, to have faded from view: Bradley, McTaggart *et al.* offered their own proofs of idealism; it was not felt, as it surely is now, that the case for absolute idealism is best made through an examination of its great historical proponents.

Thus, although a tradition of study of Kant did exist in the Scottish universities[5] where, excepting a period at Princeton and some visits to Germany, Kemp Smith spent all of his professional life – he studied at St Andrews, held a position at Glasgow and occupied the Chair of Logic and Metaphysics in Edinburgh from 1919 to 1945 – no body of English-language Kant scholarship remotely comparable in quantity or complexity to that which now surrounds us had yet been produced, a fact reflected in Kemp Smith's multiple references in his *Commentary* to German secondary literature, in place of sources in English. The *Commentary*, if it did not quite inaugurate systematic scholarship on Kant in the English-speaking world, had little precedent. The Appendix on Kant's *Opus Postumum*, added in the second edition of 1923, on posthumous writings of Kant's that have begun to receive thorough attention in the anglophone world only very recently, again showed Kemp Smith to be a pioneer.

Kemp Smith did not himself subscribe to any of the prevalent 'absolute', Hegelian forms of idealism; he wrote articles on the nature of universals in which he criticised the strongly holistic and monistic idealism of Bradley and Bosanquet.[6] The effect of his contemporary philosophical climate was nonetheless to impress upon him the deep explanatory power of idealist thinking, and to make it possible for him to endorse Kant's claim to have effected an irreversible revolution in metaphysics and philosophical method, and to identify the core of this revolution with idealism. Though well aware of the reaction against idealism represented by his contemporaries Bertrand Russell and G. E. Moore, and acquainted with the developments gathering pace in early analytic philosophy, Kemp Smith did not recognise in this new movement a serious rival, either substantial or methodological, to the idealist position. Russell and Moore's reasons for rejecting Hegelian idealism, which reflected a general opposition to, or at any rate a minimalist orientation in metaphysics, had little in common with Kemp Smith's criticisms of that position. The contemporaries who engaged Kemp Smith's interest and admiration were instead A. N. Whitehead, Henri Bergson and William James, philosophers who, though not in any sense adherents of German idealism, remained in key respects attuned to its philosophical programme. The exact form of the idealism that should be regarded as issuing from Kant's revolution was in Kemp Smith's view a matter of uncertainty and open to enquiry, and in pursuing his study of Kant, Kemp Smith's aim was twofold: it was in part to rediscover and clarify through historical labour the rationale for the contemporary idealist outlook which he regarded as fundamentally correct, but also and more importantly, he sought to determine precisely what form of idealism should be accepted.[7]

Separating Kemp Smith from the situation of contemporary anglophone Kant commentators is therefore the fact that Kemp Smith had not undergone the sequence of historical experiences that analytic philosophy passed through in the course of the twentieth century, the net effect of which has been, while allowing some aspects of Kant to be highlighted, to reduce the accessibility of Kant's transcendental idealism. Kemp Smith did not have to negotiate his way past the obstacles supplied by positivism's attack on metaphysical propositions, the linguistic turn, and the powerful American-led, pragmatically-orientated forms of philosophical naturalism, in order to take a fundamentally sympathetic view of Kant: for better or worse, he was not under pressure to incorporate into his defence of Kant's achievement an account of how Kant might be read as having anticipated the criticisms implied by logical positivism, linguistic philosophy and pragmatist naturalism. Kemp Smith's historical relation to Kant was in short, in the respects mentioned, more direct than our own.

Kemp Smith's interpretation of Kant is embedded in, and inseparable from, a broader view that he takes of the development of modern philosophy. Kemp Smith made detailed historical studies of Descartes,

Locke, Hume and other modern figures as well as of Kant,[8] and his view of Kant's early modern ancestry is – as the plethora of references to these figures in the *Commentary* shows – essential for understanding why he interprets Kant as he does.

Philosophy made, Kemp Smith believes, a new start with Descartes, by virtue of the fact that the doctrine of the heterogeneity of mind and matter created a new problem of knowledge:[9] How can mind, which is essentially unextended, stand in a cognitive relation to matter, which is essentially extended? This problem was in fact, Kemp Smith holds, a product of a long historical development running up from the Greek stoics' inward turn and discovery of subjectivity, and their institution of an antagonism of man and nature. Augustine had already formulated the doctrine of representative perception propounded by Descartes – the notion that our immediate awareness is restricted to ideas in our minds, which must then, in order for other knowledge to be possible, be determined to bear some appropriate relation, of causality or similitude, to independently existing objects. But the problem had changed between Augustine and Descartes, on account of the new view of matter implied by the results of modern natural science: once matter had been wholly despiritualised and dehumanised, and reduced to a single substance exhibiting only diversified events of motion, it had ceased to be intelligible that we should receive from matter even mere sensations, let alone full-fledged perceptions. The problematic doctrine of representative perception is at the centre of early modern philosophy, on Kemp Smith's interpretation: it is this problem, and not the cogito, which on his view provides the starting point for Descartes' philosophical system. Descartes' solution had however, according to Kemp Smith, aggravated the problem, by fallaciously treating thoughts as, along with perceptions, further *objects* of awareness. Kant does not make this mistake: he accords a quite different role to thought, in the context of a radical recasting of the problem of knowledge.

What Kant's revolution amounts to, in Kemp Smith's view, will be considered shortly. Its effect in any case, Kemp Smith considers, has been to establish the supremacy of idealism over the other two perennial types of philosophy, naturalism and scepticism.[10] Idealism is not therefore, on Kemp Smith's view, a specifically modern invention: he in fact regards idealism – which he defines as a concern to show 'spiritual values' transcend the natural environment, 'have a more than merely human significance' and 'stand on the same plane of objectivity' as empirical truths – as having changed less since classical times than naturalism and scepticism, and as the standpoint that emerges more naturally from philosophical reflection. Though idealism has achieved supremacy, it has not done so independently of its competitors: interaction with naturalism and scepticism has been highly fruitful for the development of idealism, as the case of Kant demonstrates. Nor, Kemp Smith allows, has idealism quite displaced its rivals. Scepticism, after enjoying a period where it flourished in the nineteenth century, in the positivism of Comte and his successors, has either retired or passed into naturalism, but naturalism has, Kemp Smith concedes, received a new impetus: developments in the human sciences since the nineteenth century have allowed the sphere of values, which was previously accorded due recognition only by idealism, to fall potentially into the orbit of naturalism, which now presents itself as explaining our 'idealistic tendencies' in terms of our 'instinctive equipment' and suchlike, and which may now even grant a degree of validity to human values. Though willing to recognise the existence in *some* sense of values of several sorts, naturalism claims that 'the intellectual values stand apart by themselves': that is to say, in Kantian terms, that naturalism claims the greater and more fundamental reality of theoretical reason in its empirical employment. What finally allows idealism to meet this challenge and to nevertheless maintain its edge over naturalism is, Kemp Smith supposes, here invoking Kant's argument in the *Critique* for the dependence of empirical knowledge on *a priori* conditions, '*the fact that science exists at all*': the fact of scientific knowledge, and that of knowledge in general, is unaccountable naturalistically. This consideration, '*when taken with the other achievements of the human spirit*, in the arts, in the moral, social and religious life', 'outweighs in philosophical significance' the conclusions of naturalistic enquiry, and is enough 'to render intelligible the objective claims of aesthetics and morals': their possession of 'absoluteness' is no more or less mysterious than the fact of theoretical knowledge. On this basis the idealist is justified in retorting that naturalists ultimately 'keep their eyes off the human values': because they 'approach them only through the study of our natural and economic setting', the result is that 'they do not study them at all'.[11]

What this brief summary of Kemp Smith's broader historical and philosophical view shows – revealing a substantial difference from many contemporary anglophone approaches to Kant's theoretical philosophy – is the manner in which Kemp Smith regards idealism, not essentially as a position in theoretical philosophy that may be argued to have axiological pay-offs, but as a position formed essentially by axiological concerns. The motivation for Kant's transcendental analysis of knowledge is bound up from the start with consciousness of value.[12]

The present situation in philosophy being, in Kemp Smith's view, the one described above, the question arises how the *Critique* manages to secure idealism's hegemony. What does Kant's revolution in theoretical philosophy consist in?

One position which may, according to Kemp Smith, be found in the *Critique*, remains within the basic methodological and doctrinal bounds set by Descartes: knowledge is to be accounted for in terms of the subjective contents of individual consciousness, where the criterion for the individuation of subjects is that of an ordinary empirical judgement of personal identity, and the contents in question are prised apart from the existence of the objects which they purport to represent. This position (summarised on pp. 272–3) accepts the dogmatic assumption that the materials of knowledge are atomic sensations. It infers that space and time, and the categories, since they are not derivable from such data, are supplied by the mind. Mind remains conceived in Cartesian manner as a separate, object-independent entity which precedes knowledge and renders it possible.

This position improves on Cartesian rationalism, Kemp Smith thinks, at least to the extent of substituting for innate ideas the merely empty forms of thought, and of treating the distinction of sense and thought as two elements of, rather than as two modes of, knowledge. Otherwise Kant's position resembles the subjective idealism of Berkeley: each individual creates empirical reality afresh by construction out of sensation, the criterion for objectivity being intersubjective sameness, in a merely qualitative sense of 'same'. The subjectivist outlook is reflected in statements of Kant's such as that 'all objects with which we can occupy ourselves, are one and all in me, that is, are determinations of my identical self' (A129).

There is however also present in the *Critique*, Kemp Smith argues, a quite different position, which contradicts subjectivism by locating the grounds for knowledge outside the consciousness of individual subjects. Kemp Smith calls this – perhaps not altogether felicitously, in view of the reductionist connotation that the term has (now, at any rate) in the philosophy of perception – phenomenalism.[13] Kant's phenomenalism is most clearly located, and distinguished from his subjectivism, in the Transcendental Deduction, especially in its second edition version, and it also comes to the fore in the Refutation of Idealism. The essence of this position is that:

> the generative conditions of experience [...] must fall outside the field of consciousness, and as activities dynamically creative cannot be of the nature of ideas or contents. They are not subconscious ideas but non-conscious processes. They are not the submerged content of experience, but its conditioning grounds. Their most significant characteristic has still, however, to be mentioned. They must no longer be interpreted in subjectivist terms, as originating in the separate existence of an individual self. In conditioning experience they generate the only self for which experience can vouch [...]. (p. 273)

On this view, subject and object are correlative, mutually necessary elements in the unity of experience, from which it follows, Kemp Smith argues, that the self can exist only as an immediately object-conscious being, thereby undermining the doctrine of representative perception. Since it is then as true to assert that nature makes the self possible as that the self creates nature, both mentalistic and materialistic explanations of experience are ruled out. We are thus left with an attitude towards experience that is in one sense purely analytical – we find it to be composed of qualitatively distinct, necessarily interconnected formal and contentual elements – but *not* in another: Kemp Smith goes beyond the analytic thesis of Strawson's descriptive metaphysics by affirming that what the latter calls our 'conceptual scheme' – for Kemp Smith, the form 'fixed for all experience' (p. xli) – has 'generative', synthetic, trans-phenomenal grounds which in some sense explain it.[14] Our knowledge of these grounds is however circumscribed: Kant's phenomenalism denies, importantly, that philosophical reason is able to penetrate cognition so far as to uncover its complete explanation (that being the thesis of absolute idealism). The conditions of experience are 'in their real nature unknowable by us': we cannot affirm that the transcendental unity of apperception is the source of synthetic processes, nor that these processes are the activities of a noumenal self, and their very characterisation as mental rests on an analogy that may, for all we know, reflect the limitation of our cognitive power (pp. 277–8). Kant's rationalism is thus highly moderate, in comparison with either his Leibnizian predecessors or his idealist successors: he holds that the only grounds of knowledge determinable by us are 'brute conditions' that cannot be shown to possess 'intrinsic necessity' (p. xlii).

The result is a set of double doctrines and systematic ambiguities: the *Critique* contains a 'twofold view' (p. 272) of many central topics, including inner sense, causality, apperception, the scope of the categories, the existence of things in themselves, the status of appearance, and the relation of objects to representations (which the subjectivist Kant identifies and the phenomenalist Kant distinguishes).

It is not entirely clear whether Kemp Smith regards the subjectivist position as free from contradiction or as answering the sceptic. What is certain in any case is that Kant's subjectivism is in Kemp Smith's view inferior to his phenomenalism, in which lies the genuine Copernican revolution: the subjectivist position is not strictly pre-Critical – it is a progressive development within Descartes' framework and it amounts to one 'development of the Critical standpoint' (p. 263) – but it leaves that framework intact, whereas the phenomenalist position reconceptualises human knowledge in a way that places us beyond it.

Why should the *Critique* have this dual character? Kemp Smith explains it, in part, in terms of 'the tentative and experimental character of Kant's own final solutions':

The arguments of the deduction are only intelligible if viewed as an expression of the conflicting tendencies to which Kant's thought remained subject. He sought to allow due weight to each of the divergent aspects of the experience which he was analysing; and in so doing proceeded, as it would seem, simultaneously along the parallel lines of what appeared to be the possible, alternative methods of explanation. (p. 272)

There is no doubt that Kemp Smith's discernment of phenomenalism as a position present in the *Critique*, and his perception of a sharp and crucial contrast between it and Kant's subjectivism, were enabled and conditioned by his intimate knowledge of the post-Kantian idealist position and his intention to challenge the prevalent Hegelian view, exemplified by Caird and Watson, that Kant's philosophy is an altogether one-sided subjective idealism to which the *only* alternative is absolute idealism. As he writes in *Prolegomena to an Idealist Theory of Knowledge* (p. 8):

Since the time of Kant, and largely through his influence, the uncompromising Berkeleian thesis, that 'material' Nature is mind-dependent, has, indeed, been displaced by what, initially at least, is the more modest, though also usually much less definite, claim that Mind and Nature stand in relations of mutual implication. But even this claim has frequently been urged, especially by thinkers of the Hegelian type, in forms much more ambitious than the needs of an idealist orientation towards life and towards the Universe would seem to demand.

The position located between subjective and absolute idealism which Kemp Smith claims to find in the *Critique*, raises of course many questions, and Kemp Smith does not pretend that Kant gave it final or definitive form (pp. 283–4). One question is whether the position ascribed by Kemp Smith to Kant is not better described as a form of realism.[15] The issue here, of whether idealism once rendered non-subjective ceases to count as idealism, is one that recurs again and again in the interpretation – and self-interpretation – of the post-Kantian idealists: a sign not that Kemp Smith has collapsed the distinction between Kantian and post-Kantian idealism, but an indication of how little further bearing is provided by the labels 'idealist' and 'realist' once the basic Copernican move has established idealism in a basic, foundational sense.

Kemp Smith's characterisation of Kant's method in the *Critique* deserves clarificatory comment, for it may seem to combine two different ways of construing his argument which are often regarded as exclusive. The 'transcendental method', Kemp Smith says, 'is really identical in general character with the hypothetical method of the natural sciences' (p. xliv): we begin by taking knowledge to be something actual, and ask what conditions can account for it; philosophical reflection takes the fact of knowledge as an explanandum and looks for its best explanation. This suggests that Kemp Smith interprets Kant, as some have done, as reaching only *conditional* conclusions, to the effect that, *if* certain (ordinary empirical and/or scientific) knowledge claims are accorded objective validity, *then* certain (transcendental, *a priori*) conditions, which are coherent and in the light of which those knowledge claims would be validated, may, or must, be accepted as their presuppositions. In fact Kemp Smith does not regard this (as Kant refers to it) 'analytic' or 'regressive' method – which, it is often pointed out, leaves the sceptic unanswered in the respect that the antecedent of the conditional has not been shown to be necessary – as exhausting the *Critique*'s stock of argument. The text is also seen by Kemp Smith (pp. 44–8) as exhibiting a ('synthetic' or 'progressive') form of argument that proceeds from a claim to knowledge that, though neither expressing a logical truth nor deducible from any other proposition, cannot be controverted. This form of argument – 'transcendental arguments', in the sense attributed to Kant by P. F. Strawson and many other interpreters – reaches conclusions that are, if the argument is sound, *unconditional*. The favoured candidate for the premise of Kant's transcendental argumentation, in the reconstructions of Strawson and many others, is some proposition that concerns the self – the claim that I have awareness of myself as a thinker or subject of mental states. Kemp Smith's view (reflecting his interest in Bergson's philosophy) is different: the ultimate premise of the transcendental argumentation that he locates in the *Critique* – most clearly visible in the Analytic of Principles – is mere consciousness of time (see pp. xli, 241–4). The objective validity of space and the categories is deduced as a condition for this ultimate, irrepudiable fact. Kemp Smith's view is therefore that the given 'factual experience' (pp. 238–9) from which the transcendental method sets out consists not of particular and determinate ordinary empirical or scientific cognitions but of a highly general and abstract claim arrived at through their analysis.

I have discussed Kemp Smith so far without mentioning the so-called 'patchwork' theory of the *Critique* (pp. xxviii–xxxiii), which is salient in his *Commentary* and with which his name – along with that of his German predecessor, Hans Vaihinger, whose monumental *Kommentar zur Kritik der reinen Vernunft* (2 vols, Stuttgart, 1882–92) Kemp Smith was profoundly influenced by and refers to frequently – is strongly associated. Because the patchwork theory has come to be rejected and Kemp Smith's adherence to it (which drew heavy criticism early on from his contemporary H. J. Paton) is not generally viewed as doing him any favours, it is important to emphasise how little difference rejection of the patchwork theory makes to the value of his *Commentary*.

The term 'patchwork theory' is used commonly to encompass three claims: one concerning the text as an articulation of a philosophical position, one that concerns its process of composition, and one that defines the proper method of its interpretation. The philosophical claim is that the *Critique of Pure Reason* contains deep inconsistencies which no amount of exegetical ingenuity can remove or palliate, and which need to be interpreted as reflecting directly two different and conflicting philosophical positions, as explained above. The compositional claim is that the co-existence of these two positions in the one work is to be explained in part by the circumstances of Kant's authorship: namely the rapidity with which Kant – responding to the urgings of friends and perhaps with a sense of urgency derived from awareness of his own numbered days – welded into a single document the numerous manuscripts and drafts of different sections which had been composed over a very long period – well over a decade – in the course of which his views had developed and altered substantially. The methodological claim is that one does best to read the *Critique* with a view to assigning different sections and passages within sections to different phases of composition, as a palimpsest.

The compositional claim is not convincing, if for no other reason than that the evidence of all Kant's other writings, including those of his final years, when the pressure of mortality was certainly on his mind, counts against imputing to Kant the literary disposition implied by Kemp Smith's conjecture. In addition, the fact that the long interval between the first and second editions of the *Critique* gave Kant the opportunity to straighten out its doctrines but did not do so – Kemp Smith regards the second edition as giving more prominence to the proper Critical view, but he does not align his subjectivist and phenomenalist Kants with the first and second editions respectively – speaks against the hypothesis. The basis for the third, methodological claim – which is in any case undermined by the difficulty, which is greater than Kemp Smith supposes, of assigning dates to passages – is thereby removed.

The philosophical claim, however, is the one that really matters for the lasting interest of Kemp Smith's *Commentary*, and it is independent of the compositional and methodological claims. Kemp Smith does not, after all, dispute that Kant did regard the *Critique* as expressing a unified philosophical whole, and he has, as we have seen, an explanation for why Kant was mistaken in thinking this which does not rely on his compositional conjecture. Kemp Smith's supposition is that the only way of according to Kant a position that improves significantly upon subjective idealism, yet which will not slide into absolute idealism, is by drawing a line within the text between an earlier and inferior, and a later and superior position; this partial truncation is the price to be paid for Kant's philosophical stability. To anyone who rejects Kemp Smith's policy, his dual-position reading of Kant stands as an open challenge: to provide an interpretation of Kant which shows the *Critique* to be a finished philosophical whole that is neither merely the closing chapter of the early modern philosophical story, nor merely the seed of late modern systems.[16]

SEBASTIAN GARDNER
LONDON

Notes

1. A good idea of the situation can be got from Peter Robbins, *The British Hegelians 1875–1925* (New York: Garland, 1982), and Peter Hylton, *Russell, Idealism, and the Emergence of Analytic Philosophy* (Oxford: The Clarendon Press, 1990), Part I.
2. The early years of British Kant reception are documented in Guiseppe Micheli, 'The early reception of Kant's thought in England 1785–1805', in George MacDonald Ross and Tony McWalter eds, *Kant and His Influence* (Bristol: Thoemmes, 1990), and René Wellek, *Immanuel Kant in England 1793–1838* (Princeton, NJ: Princeton University

Press, 1931). Wellek concludes (pp. 260–1): 'we cannot help noticing one common trait which seems to characterize the England of the early nineteenth century: all the thinkers who had a positive relation to Kant, somehow managed to put him back into the framework of English tradition and English orthodoxy. With none of them Kant succeeded in breaking or changing their traditional turn of mind'.

3. *The Critical Philosophy of Kant*, 2 vols (Glasgow: Macleshose, 1889), vol. 2, pp. 640–1, 643.

4. *Kant and His English Critics: A Comparison of Critical and Empiricist Philosophy* (Glasgow: Macleshose, 1881), pp. 331, 337, 341. T. H. Green's 'Lectures on the Philosophy of Kant' (in *Works*, 3rd edn, ed. R. L. Nettleship (London: Longman, 1893), vol. 2, pp. 2–155) were published in 1886 but tend, like Caird and Watson, to a critical Hegelian view of Kant. William Wallace's *Kant* (Edinburgh: Blackwood, 1882) belongs also to the period but is mainly biographical, containing only two short chapters on the first *Critique*. One notable voice of dissent – a source of loosely Kantian criticism of Hegel – was A. S. Pringle-Pattison, Kemp Smith's predecessor at Edinburgh. Pringle-Pattison did not however clarify Kant's doctrines significantly.

5. The special relation of Scotland with Kant is attributable to, first, the earlier development of the Scottish universities than the English, and second, the two-way relation of influence between Scottish common sense realism and Germany from the mid-eighteenth century: see Manfred Kuehn, *Scottish Common Sense in Germany, 1768–1800: A Contribution to the History of Critical Philosophy* (Kingston: McGill–Queen's University Press, 1987), and 'Hamilton's reading of Kant: a chapter in the early Scottish reception of Kant's thought', in Ross and McWalter eds, *Kant and His Influence*.

6. 'The nature of universals', I, II and III, in *The Credibility of Divine Existence: The Collected Papers of Norman Kemp Smith*, ed. A. J. D. Porteous, R. D. MacLennon and G. E. Davie (London: Macmillan, 1967).

7. Kemp Smith did not publish a full statement of his own idealism. His *Prolegomena to an Idealist Theory of Knowledge* (London: Macmillan, 1924) deals only with perception of the outer world. The papers collected in *The Credibility of Divine Existence* give indications of his more general position, sketched in the essay in that volume by G. E. Davie, 'The significance of the philosophical papers'. For whatever reason, Kemp Smith appears to have chosen overall to remain within the sphere scholarship: see A. J. D. Porteous, 'Biographical sketch', in op. cit., pp. 26–7.

8. Norman Kemp Smith, *Studies in the Cartesian Philosophy* (London: Macmillan, 1902), *The Philosophy of Hume: A Critical Study of its Origins and Central Doctrines* (London: Macmillan, 1941), *New Studies in the Philosophy of Descartes* (London: Macmillan, 1952), and 'John Locke', in *The Credibility of Divine Existence*.

9. See *Studies in the Cartesian Philosophy*, esp. Chs 1, 7. Kemp Smith's historical view here bears a marked resemblance to John McDowell's diagnosis of the role played by science's 'disenchantment' of nature in forming our present epistemological predicament, in *Mind and World* (Cambridge, MA: Harvard University Press, 1994).

10. See Norman Kemp Smith, 'The present situation in philosophy', Inaugural Lecture, University of Edinburgh 1919 (Edinburgh: James Thin, 1919).

11. Op. cit., pp. 19, 27–8.

12. See p. xxxix. Kemp Smith pursued this view with respect to other figures, arguing in the case of Hume that the key to his philosophy lies not in the empiricist tenets announced at the opening of the *Treatise* but in his Hutchesonian view of ethical consciousness as based on feeling, and that the true Locke, as opposed to the Locke refashioned by the French Enlightenment, gave epistemological priority to the absolute cognition of ethics and natural theology. Also note in this connection the

(neo-Kantian) claim, on pp. lix–lx, that, for Kant, philosophy as such deals with problems of value, the *Critique* being concerned specifically with 'the logical values'.

13. Alternative appellations considered by Kemp Smith are 'Critical idealism' and 'objective idealism' (p. 274).

14. Clarifying the issue which separates these two views of what transcendental philosophy must claim, see Mark Sacks, *Objectivity and Insight* (Oxford: Oxford University Press, 2000), Ch. 6.

15. A. C. Ewing suggests as much in the Introduction to his *Idealisms: A Critical Survey* (London: Methuen, 1934). The same question arises regarding the position Kemp Smith takes on perception in his *Prolegomena to an Idealist Theory of Knowledge*, where he seeks to incorporate into idealism the naturalistic idea of a causal relation due to an independently existing object. Kemp Smith is classified by some as a 'Critical realist', alongside Robert Adamson, his mentor at Glasgow.

16. As an illustration of how the issue with which Kemp Smith's reading of Kant is most intensely preoccupied remains central to Kant scholarship, and as an index of Kemp Smith's continuing relevance, see Frederick Beiser's recent, ground-breaking work, *German Idealism: The Struggle Against Subjectivism 1871–1801* (Cambridge, MA: Harvard University Press, 2002), Part I. Beiser discusses Kemp Smith on pp. 58–9, 164–5, 209.

Publisher's Note

In the main body of the text, page numbers in Roman numerals refer to those of the 1923 edition.

PREFACE TO THE SECOND EDITION

I AM indebted to Baron von Hügel, Professor Joachim, and Professor Ward for a large number of corrections and criticisms. These have enabled me to make many needed revisions. Use has also been made of Professor Adickes' elaborate and valuable work, *Kants Opus Postumum dargestellt und beurteilt*, published in 1920. As it sets Kant's views during the period 1797–1803 in quite a new light, I have added an Appendix in which they are discussed in their bearing upon his teaching in the *Critique of Pure Reason*.

NORMAN KEMP SMITH.

EDINBURGH, *June* 1923.

PREFACE TO THE FIRST EDITION

THE *Critique of Pure Reason* is more obscure and difficult than even a metaphysical treatise has any right to be. The difficulties are not merely due to defects of exposition; they multiply rather than diminish upon detailed study; and, as I shall endeavour to show in this *Commentary*, are traceable to two main causes, the composite nature of the text, written at various dates throughout the period 1769–1780, and the conflicting tendencies of Kant's own thinking.

The *Commentary* is both expository and critical; and in exposition no less than in criticism I have sought to subordinate the treatment of textual questions and of minor issues to the systematic discussion of the central problems. Full use is made of the various selections from Kant's private papers that have appeared, at intervals, since the publication of his *Lectures on Metaphysics* in 1821. Their significance has not hitherto been generally recognised in English books upon Kant. They seem to me to be of capital importance for the right understanding of the *Critique*.

Some apology is perhaps required for publishing a work of this character at the present moment. It was completed, and arrangements made for its publication, shortly before the outbreak of war. The printers have, I understand, found in it a useful stop-gap to occupy them in the intervals of more pressing work; and now that the type must be released, I trust that in spite of, or even because of, the overwhelming preoccupations of the war, there may be some few readers to whom the volume may be not unwelcome. That even amidst the distractions of actual campaigning metaphysical speculation can serve as a refuge and a solace is shown by the memorable example of General Smuts. He has himself told us that on his raid into Cape Colony in the South African War he carried with him for evening reading the *Critique of Pure Reason*. Is it surprising that our British generals, pitted against so unconventional an opponent, should have been worsted in the battle of wits?

The *Critique of Pure Reason* is a philosophical classic which marks a turning-point in the history of philosophy, and no interpretation, even though now attempted after the lapse of a hundred years, can hope to be adequate or final. Some things are clearer to us than they were to Kant's contemporaries; in other essential ways our point of view has receded from his, and the historical record, that should determine our judgments, is far from complete. But there is a further difficulty of an even more serious character. The *Critique* deals with issues which are still controversial, and their interpretation is possible only from a definite standpoint. The limitations of this standpoint and of the philosophical *milieu* in which it has been acquired unavoidably intervene to distort or obscure our apprehension of the text. Arbitrary and merely personal judgments I have, however, endeavoured to avoid. My sole aim has been to reach, as far as may prove feasible, an unbiased understanding of Kant's great work.

Among German commentators I owe most to Vaihinger, Adickes, B. Erdmann, Cohen, and Riehl, especially to the first named. The chief English writers upon Kant are Green, Caird, and Adamson. In so far as Green and Caird treat the Critical philosophy as a half-way stage to the Hegelian standpoint I find myself frequently in disagreement with them; but my indebtedness to their writings is much greater than my occasional criticisms of their views may seem to imply. With Robert Adamson I enjoyed the privilege of personal discussions at a time when his earlier view of Kant's teaching was undergoing revision in a more radical manner than is apparent even in his posthumously published University lectures. To the stimulus of his suggestions the writing of this *Commentary* is largely due.

My first study of the *Critique* was under the genial and inspiring guidance of Sir Henry Jones. With characteristic kindliness he has read through my manuscript and has disclosed to me many defects of exposition and argument. The same service has been rendered me by Professor G. Dawes Hicks, whose criticisms have been very valuable, particularly since they come from a student of Kant who on many fundamental points takes an opposite view from my own.

I have also to thank my colleague, Professor Oswald Veblen, for much helpful discussion of Kant's doctrines of space and time, and of mathematical reasoning.

Mr. H. H. Joachim has read the entire proofs, and I have made frequent modifications to meet his very searching criticisms. I have also gratefully adopted his revisions of my translations from the *Critique*. Similar acknowledgments are due to my colleague, Professor A. A. Bowman, and to my friend Dr. C. W. Hendel.

I have in preparation a translation of the *Critique of Pure Reason*, and am responsible for the translations of all passages given in the present work. In quoting from Kant's other writings, I have made use of the renderings of Abbott, Bernard, and Mahaffy; but have occasionally allowed myself the liberty of introducing alterations.

Should readers who are already well acquainted with the *Critique* desire to use my *Commentary* for its systematic discussions of Kant's teaching, rather than as an accompaniment to their study of the text, I may refer them to those sections which receive italicised headings in the table of contents.

NORMAN KEMP SMITH.

LONDON, *January* 1918.

INTRODUCTION

I. TEXTUAL

KANT'S METHOD OF COMPOSING THE 'CRITIQUE OF PURE REASON'

SELDOM, in the history of literature, has a work been more conscientiously and deliberately thought out, or more hastily thrown together, than the *Critique of Pure Reason*. The following is the account which Kant in a letter to Moses Mendelssohn (August 16, 1783) has given of its composition:

"[Though the *Critique* is] the outcome of reflection which had occupied me for a period of at least twelve years, I brought it to completion in the greatest haste within some four to five months, giving the closest attention to the content, but with little thought of the exposition or of rendering it easy of comprehension by the reader—a decision which I have never regretted, since otherwise, had I any longer delayed, and sought to give it a more popular form, the work would probably never have been completed at all. This defect can, however, be gradually removed, now that the work exists in a rough form."[1]

These statements must be allowed the greater weight as Kant, in another letter (to Garve, August 7, 1783), has given them in almost the same words:

"I freely admit that I have not expected that my book should meet with an immediate favourable reception. The exposition of the materials which for more than twelve successive years I had been carefully maturing, was not composed in a sufficiently suitable manner for general comprehension. For the perfecting of its exposition several years would have been required, whereas I brought it to completion in some four to five months, in the fear that, on longer delay, so prolonged a labour might finally become burdensome, and that my increasing years (I am already in my sixtieth year) would perhaps incapacitate me, while I am still the sole possessor of my complete system."[2]

The twelve years here referred to are 1769–1780; the phrase "at least twelve years" indicates Kant's appreciation of the continuity of his mental development. Hume's first influence upon Kant is probably to

---

[1] *W.* x. p. 323.
[2] *W.* x. p. 316.

be dated prior to 1760. The choice, however, of the year 1769 is not arbitrary; it is the year of Kant's adoption of the semi-Critical position recorded in the *Inaugural Dissertation* (1770).[1] The "four to five months" may be dated in the latter half of 1780. The printing of the *Critique* was probably commenced in December or January 1780–1781.

But the *Critique* is not merely defective in clearness or popularity of exposition. That is a common failing of metaphysical treatises, especially when they are in the German language, and might pass without special remark. What is much more serious, is that Kant flatly contradicts himself in almost every chapter; and that there is hardly a technical term which is not employed by him in a variety of different and conflicting senses. As a writer, he is the least exact of all the great thinkers.

So obvious are these inconsistencies that every commentator has felt constrained to offer some explanation of their occurrence. Thus Caird has asserted that Kant opens his exposition from the non-Critical standpoint of ordinary consciousness, and that he discloses the final position, towards which he has all along been working, only through repeated modifications of his preliminary statements. Such a view, however, cannot account either for the specific manner of occurrence or for the actual character of the contradictions of which the *Critique* affords so many examples. These are by no means limited to the opening sections of its main divisions; and careful examination of the text shows that they have no such merely expository origin. The publication of Kant's *Reflexionen* and *Lose Blätter*, and the devoted labours of Benno Erdmann, Vaihinger, Adickes, Reicke and others, have, indeed, placed the issue upon an entirely new plane. It can now be proved that the *Critique* is not a unitary work, and that in the five months in which, as Kant tells us, it was "brought to completion" (*zu Stande gebrachf*), it was not actually written, but was pieced together by the combining of manuscripts written at various dates throughout the period 1769–1780.

Kant's correspondence in these years contains the repeated assertion that he expected to be able to complete the work within some three or six months. This implies that it was already in great part committed to writing. In 1780 Kant must therefore have had a large body of manuscript at his disposal. The recently published *Lose Blätter* are, indeed, part of it. And as we shall have constant occasion to observe, the *Critique* affords ample evidence of having been more or less mechanically constructed through the piecing together of older manuscript, supplemented, no doubt, by the insertion of connecting links, and modified by occasional alterations to suit the new context. Kant, it would almost seem, objected to nothing so much as the sacrifice of an argument once consecrated by committal to paper. If it could be inserted, no matter at what cost of repetition, or even confusion, he insisted upon its insertion. Thus the *Subjective* and *Objective Deductions* of the first edition can, as we shall find, be broken up into at least four distinct

---

[1] Cf. Kant's letter to Lambert, September 2, 1770: *W.* x. p. 93.

layers, which, like geological strata, remain to the bewilderment of the reader who naturally expects a unified system, but to the enlightenment of the student, once the clues that serve to identify and to date them have been detected. To cite another example: in the *Second Analogy*, as given in the first edition, the main thesis is demonstrated in no less than five distinct proofs, some of which are repetitions; and when Kant restated the argument in the second edition, he allowed the five proofs to remain, but superimposed still another upon them. Kant does, indeed, in the second edition omit some few passages from various parts of the *Critique*; but this is in the main owing to his desire to protect himself against serious misunderstanding to which, as he found, he had very unguardedly laid himself open. The alterations of the second edition are chiefly of the nature of additions.

Adickes' theory[1] that Kant in the "four to five months" composed a brief outline of his entire argument, and that it was upon the framework of this outline that the *Critique* was elaborated out of the older manuscript, may possibly be correct. It has certainly enabled Adickes to cast much light upon many textual problems. But his own supplementary hypothesis in regard to the section on the *Antinomies*, namely, that it formed an older and separate treatise, may very profitably be further extended. Surely it is unlikely that with the expectation, continued over many years, of completion within a few months, Kant did not possess, at least for *the Aesthetic, Dialectic,* and *Methodology*, a general outline, that dated further back than 1780. And doubtless this outline was itself altered, patched, and recast, in proportion as insight into the problems of the *Analytic*, the problems, that is to say, which caused publication to be so long deferred, deepened and took final form.

The composite character of the *Critique* is largely concealed by the highly elaborate, and extremely artificial, arrangement of its parts. To the general plan, based upon professedly logical principles, Kant has himself given the title, architectonic; and he carries it out with a thoroughness to which all other considerations, and even at times those of sound reasoning, are made to give way. Indeed, he clings to it with the unreasoning affection which not infrequently attaches to a favourite hobby. He lovingly elaborates even its minor detail, and is rewarded by a framework so extremely complicated that the most heterogeneous contents can be tidily arranged, side by side, in its many compartments. By its uniformity and rigour it gives the appearance of systematic order even when such order is wholly absent.

But we have still to consider the chief reason for the contradictory character of the contents of the *Critique*. It is inseparably bound up with what may perhaps be regarded as Kant's supreme merit as a philosophical thinker, especially as shown in the first *Critique*,—namely, his open-minded recognition of the complexity of his problems, and of the many difficulties which lie in the way of any solution which he is

---

[1] Embodied in his edition of the *Kritik* (1889).

himself able to propound. Kant's method of working seems to have consisted in alternating between the various possible solutions, developing each in turn, in the hope that some midway position, which would share in the merits of all, might finally disclose itself. When, as frequently happened, such a midway solution could not be found, he developed his thought along the parallel lines of the alternative views.

"You know that I do not approach reasonable objections with the intention merely of refuting them, but that in thinking them over I always weave them into my judgments, and afford them the opportunity of overturning all my most cherished beliefs. I entertain the hope that by thus viewing my judgments impartially from the standpoint of others some third view that will improve upon my previous insight may be obtainable. . . . Long experience has taught me that insight into a subject which I am seeking to master is not to be forced, or even hastened, by sheer effort, but demands a fairly prolonged period during which I return again and again to the same concepts, viewing them in all their aspects and in their widest possible connections, while in the intervals the sceptical spirit awakens, and makes trial whether my conclusions can withstand a searching criticism."[1] "In mental labour of so delicate a character nothing is more harmful than preoccupation with extraneous matters. The mind, though not constantly on the stretch, must still, alike in its idle and in its favourable moments, lie uninterruptedly open to any chance suggestion which may present itself. Relaxations and diversions must maintain its powers in freedom and mobility, so that it may be enabled to view the object afresh from every side, and so to enlarge its point of view from a microscopic to a universal outlook that it adopts in turn every conceivable standpoint, verifying the observations of each by means of all the others."[2] "I am not of the opinion of the well-meaning writer who has recommended us never to allow doubts in regard to a matter upon which we have once made up our minds. In pure philosophy that is not feasible. Indeed the understanding has in itself a natural objection to any such procedure. We must consider propositions in all their various applications; even when they may not seem to require a special proof, we must make trial of their opposites, and in this way fight for delay, until the truth becomes in all respects evident."[3]

That these are no mere pious expressions of good intention, but represent Kant's actual method of working, is amply proved by the contents of the *Critique*. We find Kant constantly alternating between opposed standpoints, to no one of which he quite definitely commits himself, and constantly restating his principles in the effort to remove the objections to which, as he recognises, they continue to lie open. The *Critique*, as already stated, is not the exposition of a single unified system, but is the record of Kant's manifold attempts to formulate and to solve his many-sided problems. Even those portions of the *Critique* which embody his latest views show that Kant is still unwilling to sacrifice insight to consistency. When he is guilty of special pleading— for he cannot be altogether absolved even from that charge—it is in the interests of his logical architectonic, for which, as I have said, he

---

[1] From letter to Marcus Herz, June 7, 1777: *W.* x. pp. 116–17.
[2] From letter to Marcus Herz, February 21, 1772: *W.* x. p. 127.
[3] *Reflexionen* ii. 5.

cherishes a quite unreasoning affection, and not of his central principles. So far from concealing difficulties, or unduly dwelling upon the favouring considerations, Kant himself emphasises the outstanding objections to which his conclusions remain subject. If his teaching is on certain points very definite, it is in other hardly less important respects largely tentative.

The value of Kant's *Critique* as an introduction to modern philosophy is greatly enhanced by this method of procedure. The student who has steeped himself in the atmosphere of the *Critique*, however dissatisfied he may perhaps be with many of its doctrines, has become familiar with the main requirements which a really adequate metaphysics must fulfil, or at least will have acquired a due sense of the complexity of the problems with which it deals.

Recognition of the composite nature of the text will safeguard us in two ways. In the first place, citation of single passages is quite inconclusive. Not only must all the relevant passages be collated; they must be interpreted in the light of an historical understanding of the various stages in Kant's development. We must also be prepared to find that on certain main questions Kant hesitates between opposed positions, and that he nowhere definitively commits himself to any quite final expression of view.

Secondly, we cannot proceed on the assumption that Kant's maturest teaching comes where, had the *Critique* been a unitary work, composed upon a definite and previously thought out plan, we should naturally expect to find it, namely, in its concluding portions. The teaching of much of the *Dialectic*, especially in its account of the nature of the phenomenal world and of its relation to the knowing mind, is only semi-Critical. This is also true of Kant's *Introduction* to the *Critique*. Introductions are usually written last; and probably Kant's *Introduction* was written after the completion of the *Aesthetic*, of the *Dialectic*, and of the *Analytic* in its earlier forms. But it bears all the signs of having been composed prior to the working out of several of his most characteristic doctrines in the central parts of the *Analytic*.

Thus both Kant's introductory statements of the aims and purposes of the *Critique*, and his application of his results in the solution of metaphysical problems, fail to represent in any adequate fashion the new and revolutionary principles to which he very gradually but successfully worked his way. The key to the *Critique* is given in the central portions of the *Analytic*, especially in the *Deduction of the Categories*. The other parts of the *Critique* reveal the Critical doctrines only as gradually emerging from the entangling influence of pre-Critical assumptions. Their teaching has to be radically remodelled before they can be made to harmonise with what, in view both of their intrinsic character and of the corresponding alterations in the second edition, must be regarded as Kant's maturest utterances.

This was a task which Kant never himself attempted. For no sooner had he attained to comparative clearness in regard to his new Critical principles and briefly expounded them in the *Analytic* of the first edition, than he hastened to apply them in the spheres of morality, aesthetics, and teleology. When the *Critique* appeared in 1781 he was fifty-seven years of age; and he seems to have feared that if he allowed these purely theoretical problems, which had already occupied his main attention for "at least twelve years," to detain him longer, he would be debarred from developing and placing on permanent record the new metaphysics of ethics which, as the references in the first *Critique* show, had already begun to shape itself in his mind. To have expended further energy upon the perfecting of his theoretical philosophy would have endangered its own best fruits. Even the opportunity in 1787 of a second edition of the *Critique* he used very sparingly, altering or adding only where occasional current criticism—his puzzled contemporaries having still for the most part maintained a discreet silence—had clearly shown that his modes of exposition were incomplete or misleading.

II. HISTORICAL

KANT'S RELATION TO HUME AND TO LEIBNIZ

Kant's manner of formulating his fundamental problem—How are synthetic *a priori* judgments possible?—may well seem to the modern reader to imply an unduly scholastic and extremely rationalistic method of approach. Kant's reasons for adopting it have, unfortunately, been largely obscured, owing to the mistaken interpretation which has usually been given to certain of his personal utterances. They have been supposed to prove that the immediate occasion of the above formula was Hume's discussion of the problem of causality in the *Enquiry into the Human Understanding*. Kant, it is argued, could not have been acquainted with Hume's earlier and more elaborate *Treatise on Human Nature*, of which there was then no translation; and his references to Hume must therefore concern only the later work.

Vaihinger has done valuable service in disputing this reading of Kant's autobiographical statements. Kant does not himself make direct mention of the *Enquiry*, and the passages in the *Critique* and in the *Prolegomena*[1] in which Hume's teaching is under consideration seem rather to point to the wider argument of the *Treatise*. This is a matter of no small importance; for if Vaihinger's view can be established, it will enable us to appreciate, in a manner otherwise impossible, how Kant should have come to regard the problem of *a priori synthesis* as being the most pressing question in the entire field of speculative philosophy.

The essential difference between the *Treatise* and the *Enquiry*, from the standpoint of their bearing upon Critical issues, lies in the wider scope and more radical character of the earlier work. The *Enquiry*

---

[1] These passages are by no means unambiguous, and are commented upon below, p. 61 ff.

discusses the problem of causality only in the form in which it emerges in *particular* causal judgments, *i.e.* as to our grounds for asserting that this or that effect is due to this or that cause. In the *Treatise*, Hume raises the broader question as to our right to postulate that events must always be causally determined. In other words, he there questions the validity of the *universal* causal principle, that whatever begins to exist must have a cause of existence; and he does so on the explicit ground that it demands as necessary the connecting of two concepts, that of an event and that of an antecedent cause, between which *no connection of any kind* can be detected by the mind. The principle, that is to say, is not self-evident; it is synthetic. The concept of an event and the concept of a cause are quite separate and distinct ideas. Events can be conceived without our requiring to think antecedent events upon which they are dependent. Nor is the principle capable of demonstration. For if it be objected that in questioning its validity we are committing ourselves to the impossible assertion that events arise out of nothing, such argument is only applicable if the principle be previously granted. If events do not require a cause, it is as little necessary to seek their source in a generation out of nothing as in anything positive. Similarly, when it is argued that as all the parts of time and space are uniform, there must be a cause determining an event to happen at one moment and in one place rather than at some other time or place, the principle is again assumed. There is no greater difficulty in supposing the time and place to be fixed without a cause than in supposing the existence to be so determined. The principle, Hume concludes, is non-rational in character. It is an instrument useful for the organisation of experience; and for that reason nature has determined us to its formation and acceptance. Properly viewed, it expresses a merely instinctive belief, and is explicable only in the naturalistic manner of our other propensities, as necessary to the fulfilling of some practical need. "Nature has determined us to judge as well as to breathe and feel."

From this naturalistic position Hume makes a no less vigorous attack upon the empirical philosophies which profess to establish general principles by inductive inference from the facts of experience. If the principles which lie at the basis of our experience are non-rational in character, the same must be true of our empirical judgments. They may correctly describe the uniformities that have hitherto occurred in the sequences of our sensations, and may express the natural expectations to which they spontaneously give rise; but they must never be regarded as capable of serving as a basis for inference. In eliminating *a priori* principles, and appealing exclusively to sense-experience, the empiricist removes all grounds of distinction between inductive inference and custom-bred expectation. And since from this standpoint the possibility of universal or abstract concepts—so Hume argues—must also be denied, deductive inference must likewise be eliminated from among the possible instruments at the disposal of the mind. So-called inference is never the source of our beliefs; it is our fundamental natural beliefs, as determined by the constitution of our nature in its reaction upon external influences, that generate those expectations which, however they may masquerade in logical costume, have as purely natural a source as our sensations and feelings. Such, briefly and dogmatically stated, is the sum and substance of Hume's teaching.[1]

Now it was these considerations that, as it would seem, awakened Kant to the problem of *a priori* synthesis. He was, and to the very last remained, in entire agreement with Hume's contention that the principle of causality is neither self-evident nor capable of logical demonstration, and he at once realised that what is true of this principle must also hold of all the other principles fundamental to science and philosophy. Kant further agreed that inductive inference from the data of experience is only possible upon the prior acceptance of rational principles independently established; and that we may not, therefore, look to experience for proof of their validity. Thus with the rejection of self-evidence as a feature of the *a priori*, and with the consequent admission of its synthetic character, Kant is compelled to acquiesce in the inevitableness of the dilemma which Hume propounds. Either Hume's sceptical conclusions must be accepted, or we must be able to point to some criterion which is not subject to the defects of the rationalist and empirical methods of proof, and which is adequate to determine the validity or invalidity of general principles. Is there any such alternative ? Such is Kant's problem as expressed in the formula: How are synthetic *a priori* judgments possible?

It is a very remarkable historical fact that notwithstanding the clearness and cogency of Hume's argument, and the appearance of such competent thinkers as Thomas Reid in Scotland, Lambert and Crusius in Germany, no less than thirty years should have elapsed before Hume found a single reader capable of appreciating the teaching of the *Treatise* at its true value.[2] Even Kant himself was not able from his reading of the *Enquiry* in 1756–1762 to realise the importance and bearing of the main problem.[3] Though in the *Enquiry* the wider issue regarding the general principle of causality is not raised, the bearing of Hume's discussion, when interpreted in the light of Kant's own teaching, is sufficiently clear; and accordingly we cannot be absolutely certain that it was not a re-reading of the *Enquiry* or a recalling of its argument[1] that

---

[1] For justification of this interpretation of Hume I must refer the reader to my articles on "The Naturalism of Hume" in *Mind*, vol. xiv. N.S. pp. 149–73, 335–47.

[2] To this fact Kant himself draws attention: "But the perpetual hard fate of metaphysics would not allow Hume to be understood. We cannot without a certain sense of pain consider how utterly his opponents, Reid, Oswald, Beattie, and even Priestley, missed the point of the problem. For while they were ever assuming as conceded what he doubted, and demonstrating with eagerness and often with arrogance what he never thought of disputing, they so overlooked his inclination towards a better state of things, that everything remained undisturbed in its old condition."—*Prolegomena*, p. 6; Mahaffy and Bernard's trans, p. 5.

[3] Sulzer's translation of Hume's *Essays* (including the *Enquiries*) appeared in 1754–56.

suggested to Kant the central problem of his Critical philosophy. The probability, however, is rather that this awakening took place only indirectly through his becoming acquainted with the wider argument of the *Treatise* as revealed in James Beattie's extremely crude and unsympathetic criticism of Hume's philosophy.[2] Beattie had great natural ability, and considerable literary power. His prose writings have a lucidity, a crispness, and a felicity of illustration which go far to explain their widespread popularity in the latter half of the eighteenth century. Their literary quality is, however, more than counterbalanced by the absence of any genuine appreciation of the deeper, speculative implications and consequences of the problems discussed. And this being so, he is naturally at his worst in criticising Hume. In insisting, as he does, upon the absurd practical results[3] that would follow from the adoption of Hume's sceptical conclusions, he is merely exploiting popular prejudice in the philosophical arena. That, however, may be forgiven him, if, as would seem to be the case, the quotations which he gives verbatim from Hume's *Treatise* really first revealed to Kant the scope and innermost meaning of Hume's analysis of the causal problem.

The evidence in support of this contention is entirely circumstantial. The German translation of Beattie's *Essay on the Nature and Immutability of Truth* was published at Easter 1772, *i.e.* in the year in which Kant, in the process of his own independent development, came, as is shown by his famous letter to Herz,[4] to realise the mysterious, problematic character of *a priori* knowledge *of the independently real*. He was then, however, still entirely unconscious of the deeper problem which at once emerges upon recognition that *a priori* principles, quite apart from all question of their objective validity, are synthetic in form. We know that Kant was acquainted with Beattie's work; for he twice refers to Beattie's

---

[1] The word which Kant uses is *Erinnerung* (cf. below, p. xxix, *n.* 4). There are two main reasons for believing that Kant had not himself read the *Treatise*. He was imperfectly acquainted with the English language, and there was no existing German translation. (Jakob's translation did not appear till 1790–91. On Kant's knowledge of English, cf. Erdmann: *Archiv für Geschichte der Philosophie*, Bd. i. (1888) pp. 62 ff., 216 ff.; and K. Groos: *Kant-Studien*, Bd. v. (1900) p. 177 ff.: and below, p. 156.) And, secondly, Kant's statements reveal his entire ignorance of Hume's view of mathematical science as given in the *Treatise*.

[2] Cf. Vaihinger, *Commentary*, i. p. 344 ff. Beattie does, indeed, refer to Hume's view of mathematical science as given in the *Treatise*, but in so indirect and casual a manner that Kant could not possibly gather from the reference any notion of what that treatment was. Cf. Beattie's *Essay on the Nature and Immutability of Truth* (sixth edition), pp. 138, 142, 269.

[3] These Hume had himself pointed out both in the *Treatise* and in the *Enquiry*, and because of them he rejects scepticism as a feasible philosophy of life. Kant's statement above quoted that Hume's critics (among whom Beattie is cited) "were ever assuming what Hume doubted, and demonstrating with eagerness and *often with arrogance* what he never thought of disputing," undoubtedly refer in a quite especial degree to Beattie.

[4] *Werke*, x. p. 123 ff. It is dated February 21, 1772. Cf. below, pp. 219–20.

criticism of Hume.[1] What more probable than that he read the translation in the year of its publication, or at least at some time not very long subsequent to the date of the letter to Herz? The passages which Beattie quotes from the *Treatise* are exactly those that were necessary to reveal the full scope of Hume's revolutionary teaching in respect to the general principle of causality. There seems, indeed, little doubt that this must have been the channel through which Hume's influence chiefly acted. Thus at last, by a circuitous path, through the quotations of an adversary, Hume awakened philosophy from its dogmatic slumber,[2] and won for his argument that appreciation which despite its cogency it had for thirty years so vainly demanded.

Let us now turn our attention to the rationalist philosophy in which Kant was educated. Hume's contention that experience cannot by itself justify any inductive inference forms the natural bridge over which we can best pass to the contrasting standpoint of Leibniz. Hume and Leibniz find common ground in denouncing empiricism. Both agree in regarding it as the mongrel offspring of conflicting principles. If rationalism cannot hold its own, the alternative is not the finding of firm foothold in concrete experience, but only such consolation as a sceptical philosophy may afford.[3] The overthrow of rationalism means the destruction of metaphysics in every form. Even mathematics and the natural sciences will have to be viewed as fulfilling a practical end, not as satisfying a theoretical need. But though Leibniz's criticism of empiricism is, in its main contention, identical with that of Hume, it is profoundly different both in its orientation and in the conclusions to which it leads. While Hume maintains that induction must be regarded as a non-rational process of merely instinctive anticipation, Leibniz argues to the self-legislative character of pure thought. Sense-experience reveals reality only in proportion as it embodies principles derived from the inherent character of thought itself. Experience conforms to *a priori* principles, and so can afford an adequate basis for scientific induction.

There is a passage in Hume's *Enquiry* which may be employed to illustrate the boldly speculative character of Leibniz's interpretation of the nature and function of human thought. "Nothing . . . [seems] more unbounded than the thought of man, which not only escapes all human

---

[1] In *Prolegomena*, p. 6 (above quoted, p. xxviii, *n*. I), and p. 8 (trans, p. 6): "I should think Hume might fairly have laid as much claim to sound sense as Beattie, and besides to a critical understanding (such as the latter did not possess)."

[2] Cf. *Prolegomena*, p. 8: "I honestly confess that my recollection of David Hume's teaching (*die Erinnerung des David Hume*) was the very thing which many years ago [Kant is writing in 1783] first interrupted my dogmatic slumber, and gave my investigations in the field of speculative philosophy quite a new direction." Kant's employment of the term *Erinnerung* may perhaps be interpreted in view of the indirect source of his knowledge of Hume's main position. He would bring to his reading of Beattie's quotations the memory of Hume's other sceptical doctrines as expounded in the *Enquiry*.

[3] Kant, it should be noted, classifies philosophies as either dogmatic (= rationalistic) or sceptical. Empiricism he regards as a form of scepticism.

power and authority, but is not even restrained within the limits of nature and reality. . . . While the body is confined to one planet, along which it creeps with pain and difficulty, the thought can in an instant transport us into the most distant regions of the universe. . . . What never was seen, or heard of, may yet be conceived; nor is anything beyond the power of thought, except what implies an absolute contradiction." This passage in which Hume means to depict a false belief, already sufficiently condemned by the absurdity of its claims, expresses for Leibniz the wonderful but literal truth. Thought is the revealer of an eternal unchanging reality, and its validity is in no way dependent upon its verification through sense. When Voltaire in his *Ignorant Philosopher* remarks that "it would be very singular that all nature, all the planets, should obey eternal laws, and that there should be a little animal, five feet high, who, in contempt of these laws, could act as he pleased, solely according to his caprice,"[1] he is forgetting that this same animal of five feet can contain the stellar universe in thought within himself, and has therefore a dignity which is not expressible in any such terms as his size may seem, for vulgar estimation, to imply. Man, though dependent upon the body and confined to one planet, has the sun and stars as the playthings of his mind. Though finite in his mortal conditions, he is divinely infinite in his powers.

Leibniz thus boldly challenges the sceptical view of the function of reason. Instead of limiting thought to the translating of sense-data into conceptual forms, he claims for it a creative power which enables it out of its own resources to discover for itself, not only the actual constitution of the material world, but also the immensely wider realm of possible entities. The real, he maintains, is only one of the many kingdoms which thought discovers for itself in the universe of truth. It is the most comprehensive and the most perfect, but still only one out of innumerable others which unfold themselves to the mind in pure thought. Truth *is* not the abstracting of the universal aspects in things, not a copy of reality, dependent upon it for meaning and significance. Truth is wider than reality, is logically prior to it, and instead of being dependent upon the actual, legislates for it. Leibniz thus starts from the possible, as discovered by pure thought, to determine in an *a priori* manner the nature of the real.

This Leibnizian view of thought may seem, at first sight, to be merely the re-emergence of the romantic, rationalistic ideal of Descartes and Malebranche. So to regard it would, however, be a serious injustice. It was held with full consciousness of its grounds and implications, and reality was metaphysically reinterpreted so as to afford it a genuine basis. There was nothing merely mystical and nothing undefined in its main tenets. Leibniz differs from Malebranche in being himself a profound mathe-

---

[1] Quoted by Beattie (*op. cit.*, sixth edition, p. 295), who, however incapable of appreciating the force of Hume's arguments, was at least awake to certain of their ultimate consequences.

matician, the co-discoverer with Newton of the differential calculus. He also differs from Descartes in possessing an absorbing interest in the purely logical aspects of the problem of method; and was therefore equipped in a supreme degree for determining in genuinely scientific fashion the philosophical significance and value of the mathematical disciplines.

Hume and Leibniz are thus the two protagonists that dwarf all others. They realised as neither Malebranche, Locke, nor Berkeley, neither Reid, Lambert, Crusius, nor Mendelssohn ever did, the really crucial issues which must ultimately decide between the competing possibilities. Each maintained, in the manner prescribed by his general philosophy, one of what then appeared to be the only two possible views of the function of thought. The alternatives were these: (*a*) Thought is merely a practical instrument for the convenient interpretation of our human experience; it has no objective or metaphysical validity of any kind; (*b*) Thought legislates universally; it reveals the wider universe of the eternally possible; and prior to all experience can determine the fundamental conditions to which that experience must conform. Or to interpret this opposition in logical terms: (*a*) The fundamental principles of experience are synthetic judgments in which no relation is discoverable between subject and predicate, and which for that reason can be justified neither *a priori* nor by experience; (*b*) all principles are analytic, and can therefore be justified by pure thought.

The problem of Kant's *Critique*, broadly stated, consists in the examination and critical estimate of these two opposed views. There is no problem, scientific, moral, or religious, which is not vitally affected by the decision which of these alternatives we are to adopt, or what reconciliation of their conflicting claims we hope to achieve. Since Kant's day, largely owing to the establishment of the evolution theory, this problem has become only the more pressing. The naturalistic, instrumental view of thought seems to be immensely reinforced by biological authority. Thought would seem to be reduced to the level of sense - affection, and to be an instrument developed through natural processes for the practical purposes of adaptation. Yet the counter-view has been no less powerfully strengthened by the victorious march of the mathematical sciences. They have advanced beyond the limits of Euclidean space, defining possibilities such as no experience reveals to us. The Leibnizian view has also been reinforced by the successes of physical science in determining what would seem to be the actual, objective character of the independently real. Kant was a rationalist by education, temperament, and conviction. Consequently his problem was to reconcile Leibniz's view of the function of thought with Hume's proof of the synthetic character of the causal principle. He strives to determine how much of Leibniz's belief in the legislative power of pure reason can be retained after full justice has been done to Hume's damaging criticisms. The fundamental principles upon which all experience and all knowledge ultimately rest are *synthetic* in nature:

how is it possible that they should also be *a priori*? Such is the problem that was Kant's troublous inheritance from his philosophical progenitors, Hume and Leibniz.[1]

III. GENERAL

In indicating some of the main features of Kant's general teaching, I shall limit myself to those points which seem most helpful in preliminary orientation, or which are necessary for guarding against the misunderstandings likely to result from the very radical changes in terminology and in outlook that have occurred in the hundred and thirty years since the publication of the *Critique*. Statements which thus attempt to present in outline, and in modern terms, the more general features of Kant's philosophical teaching will doubtless seem to many of my readers dogmatic in form and highly questionable in content. They must stand or fall by the results obtained through detailed examination of Kant's *ipsissima verba*. Such justification as I can give for them will be found in the body of the *Commentary*.

I. THE NATURE OF THE *A PRIORI*

The fundamental presupposition upon which Kant's argument rests— a presupposition never itself investigated but always assumed—is that universality and necessity cannot be reached by any process that is empirical in character. By way of this initial assumption Kant arrives at the conclusion that the *a priori*, the distinguishing characteristics of which are universality and necessity, is not given in sense but is imposed by the mind; or in other less ambiguous terms, is not part of the matter of experience but constitutes its form. The matter of experience is here taken as equivalent to sensation; while sensation, in turn, is regarded as being the non-relational.

The explanation of Kant's failure either to investigate or to prove this assumption has already been indicated. Leibniz proceeds upon the assumption of its truth no less confidently than Hume, and as Kant's main task consisted in reconciling what he regarded as being the elements of truth in their opposed philosophies, he very naturally felt secure in rearing his system upon the one fundamental presupposition on which they were able to agree. It lay outside the field of controversy, and possessed for Kant, as it had possessed for Hume and for Leibniz, that authoritative and axiomatic character which an unchallenged preconception tends always to acquire.

---

[1] For a more detailed statement of Kant's relation to his philosophical predecessors, cf. below, Appendix B, p. 583 ff.

The general thesis, that the universal and necessary elements in experience constitute its form, Kant specifies in the following determinate manner. The form is fixed for all experience, that is to say, it is one and the same in each and every experience, however simple or however complex. It is to be detected in consciousness of duration no less than in consciousness of objects or in consciousness of self. For, as Kant argues, consciousness of duration involves the capacity to distinguish between subjective and objective succession, and likewise involves recognition[1] with its necessary component self-consciousness. Or to state the same point of view in another way, human experience is a temporal process and yet is always a consciousness of meaning. As temporal, its states are ordered successively, that is, externally to one another; but the consciousness which they constitute is at each and every moment the awareness of some single unitary meaning by reference to which the contents of the successive experiences are organised. The problem of knowledge may therefore be described as being the analysis of the consciousness of duration, of objectivity, and of self-consciousness, or alternatively as the analysis of our awareness of meaning. Kant arrives at the conclusion that the conditions of all four are one and the same.[2]

Kant thus teaches that experience in all its embodiments and in each of its momentary states can be analysed into an endlessly variable material and a fixed set of relational elements. And as no one of the relational factors can be absent without at once nullifying all the others, they together constitute what must be regarded as the determining form and structure of every mental process that is cognitive in character. Awareness, that is to say, is identical with the act of judgment, and therefore involves everything that a judgment, in its distinction from any mere association of ideas, demands for its possibility.

Kant's position, when thus stated, differs from that of Leibniz only in its clearer grasp of the issues and difficulties involved, and consequently in the more subtle, pertinacious, and thoroughgoing character of the argument by which it is established. Its revolutionary character first appears when Kant further argues, in extension of the teaching of Hume, that the formal, relational elements are of a *synthetic* nature. The significance and scope of this conclusion can hardly be exaggerated. No other Kantian tenet is of more fundamental importance.[3] With it the main consequences of Kant's Critical teaching are indissolubly bound up.

---

[1] The term "recognition" is employed by Kant in its widest sense, as covering, for instance, recognition of the past as past, or of an object as being a certain kind of object.

[2] Consciousness of time, consciousness of objects in space, consciousness of self, are the three modes of experience which Kant seeks to analyse. They are found to be inseparable from one another and in their union to constitute a form of conscious experience that is equivalent to an act of judgment—*i.e.* to be a form of awareness that involves relational categories and universal concepts.

[3] As we have noted (above, pp. xxvi–xxvii), it was Hume's insistence upon the synthetic, non-self-evident character of the causal axiom that awakened Kant from his dogmatic slumber. Cf. below, pp. 61 ff., 593 ff.

As the principles which lie at the basis of our knowledge are synthetic, they have no intrinsic necessity, and cannot possess the absolute authority ascribed to them by the rationalists. They are prescribed to human reason, but cannot be shown to be inherently rational in any usual sense of that highly ambiguous term. They can be established only as brute conditions, verifiable in fact though not demonstrable in pure theory (if there be any such thing), of our actual experience. They are conditions of *sense-experience*, and that means of our knowledge of appearances, never legitimately applicable in the deciphering of ultimate reality. They are valid within the realm of experience, useless for the construction of a metaphysical theory of things in themselves. This conclusion is reinforced when we recognise that human experience, even in its fundamental features (*e.g.* the temporal and the spatial), might conceivably be altogether different from what it actually is, and that its presuppositions are always, therefore, of the same contingent character. Even the universality and necessity which Kant claims to have established for his *a priori* principles are of this nature. Their necessity is always for us extrinsic; they can be postulated only if, and so long as, we are assuming the occurrence of human sense-experience.

Thus Kant is a rationalist of a new and unique type. He believes in, and emphasises the importance of, the *a priori*. With it alone, he contends, is the *Critique* competent to deal. But it is an *a priori* which cannot be shown to be more than relative. It does, indeed, enable us to conceive the known as relative, and to entertain in thought the possibility of an Absolute; but this it can do without itself possessing independent validity. For though the proof of the *a priori* is not empirical in the sense of being inductive, neither is it logical in the sense of being deduced from necessities of thought. Its "transcendental" proof can be executed only so long as experience is granted as actual; and so long as the fundamental characteristics of this experience are kept in view.

Lastly, the *a priori* factors are purely relational. They have no inherent content from which clues bearing on the supersensible can be obtained. Their sole function is to serve in the interpretation of contents otherwise supplied.

The *a priori*, then, is merely relational, without inherent content; it is synthetic, and therefore incapable of independent or metaphysical proof; it is relative to an experience which is only capable of yielding appearances. The *a priori* is as strictly factual as the experience which it conditions.

Even in the field of morality Kant held fast to this conviction. Morality, no less than knowledge, presupposes *a priori* principles. These, however, are never self-evident, and cannot be established by any appeal to intuition. They have authority only to the extent to which they can be shown to be the indispensable presuppositions of a moral consciousness that is undeniably actual.[1]

---

[1] Cf. below, pp. lvi, 571 ff.

That the *a priori* is of this character must be clearly understood. Otherwise the reader will be pursued by a feeling of the unreality, of the merely historical or antiquarian significance, of the entire discussion. He may, if he pleases, substitute the term formal or relational for *a priori*. And if he bears in mind that by the relational Kant is here intending those elements in knowledge which render possible the relations constitutive of *meaning*, he will recognise that the Critical discussion is by no means antiquated, but still remains one of the most important issues in the entire field of philosophical enquiry.

2. KANT'S CONTRIBUTION TO THE SCIENCE OF LOGIC

The above conclusions have an important bearing upon logical doctrine. Just as modern geometry originates in a sceptical treatment of the axiom of parallels, so modern, idealist logic rests upon Kant's demonstration of the revolutionary consequences of Hume's sceptical teaching. If principles are never self-evident, and yet are not arrived at by induction from experience, by what alternative method can they be established? In answer to this question, Kant outlines the position which is now usually entitled the *Coherence* theory of truth.[1] That theory, though frequently ascribed to Hegel, has its real sources in the *Critique of Pure Reason*. It expresses that modification in the Leibnizian rationalism which is demanded by Hume's discovery of the synthetic character of the causal axiom. Neither the deductive methods of the Cartesian systems nor the inductive methods of the English philosophies can any longer be regarded as correctly describing the actual processes of scientific proof.

General principles are either presuppositions or postulates. If *a priori*, they are presupposed in all conscious awareness; as above indicated, they have a *de facto* validity within the experience which they thus make possible. If more special in nature, they are the postulates to which we find ourselves committed in the process of solving specific problems; and they are therefore discovered by the method of trial and failure.[2] They are valid in proportion as they enable us to harmonise appearances, and to adjudicate to each a kind of reality consistent with that assigned to every other.

Proof of fact is similar in general character. The term fact is eulogistic, not merely descriptive; it marks the possession of cognitive significance in regard to some body of knowledge, actual or possible. It can be applied to particular appearances only in so far as we can determine their conditions, and can show that as thus conditioned the mode of their existence is relevant to the enquiry that is being pursued. The convergence of parallel lines is fact from the standpoint of psychological

---

[1] Cf. below, pp. 36–7.
[2] Cf. below, p. 543 ff.

investigation; from the point of view of their physical existence it is merely appearance. Ultimately, of course, everything is real, including what we entitle appearance;[1] but in the articulation of human experience such distinctions are indispensable, and the criteria that define them are prescribed by the context in which they are being employed.

Thus facts cannot be established apart from principles, nor principles apart from facts. The proof of a principle is its adequacy to the interpretation of all those appearances that can be shown to be in any respect relevant to it, while the test of an asserted fact, *i.e.* of our description of a given appearance, is its conformity to the principles that make insight possible.

Though the method employed in the *Critique* is entitled by Kant the "transcendental method," it is really identical in general character with the hypothetical method of the natural sciences. It proceeds by enquiring what conditions must be postulated in order that the admittedly given may be explained and accounted for.[2] Starting from the given, it also submits its conclusions to confirmation by the given. Considered as a method, there is nothing metaphysical or high-flying about it save the name. None the less, Kant is in some degree justified in adopting the special title. In view of the unique character of the problem to be dealt with, the method calls for very careful statement, and has to be defended against the charge of inapplicability in the philosophical field.

The fundamental thesis of the Coherence theory finds explicit formulation in Kant's doctrine of the judgment: the doctrine, that awareness is identical with the act of judging, and that judgment is always complex, involving both factual and interpretative elements. Synthetic, relational factors are present in *all* knowledge, even in knowledge that may seem, on superficial study, to be purely analytic or to consist merely of sense-impressions. Not contents alone, but contents interpreted in terms of some specific setting, are the sole possible objects of human thought. Even when, by forced abstraction, particulars and universals are held mentally apart, they are still being apprehended through judgments, and therefore through mental processes that involve both. They stand in relations of mutual implication within a *de facto* system; and together they constitute it.

This is the reason why in modern logic, as in Kant's *Critique*, the theory of the judgment receives so much more attention than the theory of reasoning. For once the above view of the judgment has been established, all the main points in the doctrine of reasoning follow of themselves as so many corollaries. Knowledge starts neither from sense-data nor from general principles, but from the complex situation in which the human race finds itself at the dawn of self-consciousness. That situation is organised in terms of our mental equipment; and this

[1] Cf. below, pp. liii–iv.
[2] Cf. below, pp. 45, 238–43.

already existing, rudimentary system is what has made practicable further advance; to create a system *ab initio* is altogether impossible. The starting-point does not, however, by itself alone determine our conclusions. Owing to the creative activities of the mind, regulative principles are active in all consciousness; and under their guidance the experienced order, largely practical in satisfaction of the instinctive desires, is transformed into a comprehended order, controlled in view of Ideal ends. Logic is the science of the processes whereby this transformation is brought about. An essentially metaphysical discipline, it cannot be isolated from the general body of philosophical teaching; it is not formal, but transcendental; in defining the factors and processes that constitute knowledge, its chief preoccupation is with ultimate issues.

In calling his new logic "transcendental" Kant, it is true, also intends to signify that it is supplementary to, not a substitute for, the older logic, which he professes to accept.[1] Moreover his intuitional theory of mathematical science, his doctrine of the "pure concept," his attributive view of the judgment—all of them survivals from his pre-Critical period[2]—frequently set him at cross-purposes with himself. His preoccupation, too, with the problem of the *a priori* leads him to underestimate the part played in knowledge by the strictly empirical. But despite all inconsistencies, and notwithstanding his perverse preference for outlandish modes of expression, he succeeds in enforcing with sufficient clearness the really fundamental tenets of the Coherence view.

3. THE NATURE OF CONSCIOUSNESS

I shall now approach Kant's central position from another direction, namely, as an answer to the problem of the nature of consciousness. We are justified, I think, in saying that Kant was the first in modern times to raise the problem of the nature of awareness, and of the conditions of its possibility. Though Descartes is constantly speaking of consciousness, he defines it in merely negative terms, through its opposition to matter; and when he propounds the question how material bodies can be known by the immaterial mind, his mode of dealing with it shows that his real interest lies not in the nature of consciousness but in the character of the existences which it reveals. His answer, formulated in terms of the doctrine of representative perception, and based on the supposed teaching of physics and physiology, is that material bodies through their action on the sense-organs and brain generate images or duplicates of themselves. These images, existing not in outer space but only in consciousness, are, he asserts, mental in nature; and being mental they are, he would seem to conclude, immediately and necessarily apprehended by the mind. Thus Descartes gives us, not an analysis

[1] Cf. below, pp. 33–6, 181, 183–6.
[2] Cf. below, pp. 33–42, 394–5, 398.

of the knowing process, but only a subjectivist interpretation of the nature of the *objects* upon which it is directed.

Quite apart, then, from the question as to whether Descartes' doctrine of representative perception rests on a correct interpretation of the teaching of the natural sciences—Kant was ultimately led to reject the doctrine—it is obvious that the main epistemological problem, *i.e.* the problem how awareness is possible, and in what it consists, has so far not so much as even been raised. Descartes and his successors virtually assume that consciousness is an ultimate, unanalysable form of awareness, and that all that can reasonably be demanded of the philosopher is that he explain what objects are actually presented to it, and under what conditions their presentation can occur. On Descartes' view they are conditioned by antecedent physical and physiological processes; according to Berkeley they are due to the creative activity of a Divine Being; according to Hume nothing whatsoever can be determined as to their originating causes. But all three fail to recognise that even granting the objects to be of the character asserted, namely, mental, the further problem still remains for consideration, how they come to be consciously apprehended, and in what such awareness consists.

Certain interpretations of the nature of the knowing process are, of course, to be found in the writings of Descartes and his successors. But they are so much a matter of un-examined presupposition that they never receive exact formulation, and alternate with one another in quite a haphazard fashion. We may consider three typical views.

1. There is, Descartes frequently seems to imply—the same assumption is evident throughout Locke's *Essay*—a self that stands behind all mental states, observing and apprehending them. Consciousness is the power which this self has of contemplating both itself and its ideas. Obviously this is a mere ignoring of the issue. If we assume an observer, we *ipso facto* postulate a process of observation, but we have not explained or even defined it.

2. There is also in Descartes a second, very different, view of consciousness, namely, as a diaphanous medium analogous to light. Just as light is popularly conceived as revealing the objects upon which it falls, so consciousness is regarded as revealing to us our inner states. This view of consciousness, for reasons which I shall indicate shortly, is entirely inadequate to the facts for which we have to account. It is no more tenable than the corresponding view of light.

3. In Hume we find this latter theory propounded in what may at first sight seem a more satisfactory form, but is even less satisfactory. Sensations, images, feelings, he argues, are *states* of consciousness, one might almost say *pieces* of consciousness, *i.e.* they are conceived as carrying their own consciousness with them. Red, for instance, is spoken of as a sensation, and is consequently viewed both as being a sense-content, *i.e.* something sensed or apprehended, and also at the same time as the sensing or awareness of it. This view is unable to withstand criticism. There is really no more ground for asserting that red colour

carries with it consciousness of itself than for saying that a table does. The illegitimacy of the assertion is concealed from us by the fact that tables appear to exist when there is no consciousness present, whereas redness cannot be proved to exist independently of consciousness—it may or may not do so. Many present-day thinkers, continuing the tradition of the English associationists, hold to this pre-Kantian view. Sensations, feelings, etc., are, it is implied, pieces of consciousness, forms of awareness; through their varying combinations they constitute the complex experiences of the animal and human mind.

Kant's teaching is developed in direct opposition to all such views. If we discard his antiquated terminology, and state his position in current terms, we find that it amounts to the assertion that *consciousness is in all cases awareness of meaning.* There is no awareness, however rudimentary or primitive, that does not involve the apprehension of meaning. Meaning and awareness are correlative terms; each must be studied in its relation to the other. And inasmuch as meaning is a highly complex object of apprehension, awareness cannot be regarded as ultimate or as unanalysable. It can be shown to rest upon a complexity of generative conditions and to involve a variety of distinct factors.

There are thus, from the Kantian standpoint, two all-sufficient reasons why the diaphanous view of consciousness, *i.e.* any view which treats consciousness merely as a medium whereby the existent gets itself reported, must be regarded as untenable. In the first place, as already remarked, it is based on the false assumption that consciousness is an ultimate, and that we are therefore dispensed from all further investigation of its nature. Kant claims to have distinguished successfully the many components which go to constitute it; and he also professes to have shown that until such analysis has been made, there can be no sufficient basis for a philosophical treatment either of the problems of sense-perception or of the logical problems of judgment and inference. The diaphanous view, with its mirror-like mode of representation, might allow of the side-by-sideness of associated contents; it can never account for the processes whereby the associated contents come to be apprehended.

Secondly, the diaphanous view ignores the fundamental distinction between meaning and existence. Existences rest, so to speak, on their own bottom; they are self-centred even at the very moment of their reaction to external influences. Meaning, on the other hand, always involves the interpretation of what is given in the light of wider considerations that lend it significance. In the awareness of meaning the given, the actually presented, is in some way transcended, and this transcendence is what has chiefly to be reckoned with in any attempt to explain the conscious process. Kant is giving expression to this thesis when he contends that all awareness, no matter how rudimentary or apparently simple, is an act of judgment, and therefore involves the relational categories. *Not passive contemplation but active judgment, not mere conception but synthetic interpretation, is the fundamental form, and the only form, in which our consciousness exists.* This, of course, commits Kant to the assertion that there is no mode of cognition that can be described as immediate or un-reflective. There is an immediate *element* in all knowledge, but our consciousness of it is always conditioned and accompanied by interpretative processes, and in their absence there can be no awareness of any kind.

By way of this primary distinction between existence and meaning Kant advances to all those other distinctions which characterise our human experience, between appearance and reality, between the real and the Ideal, between that which is judged and the criteria which control and direct the judging process. Just because all awareness is awareness of meaning, our human experience becomes intelligible as a purposive activity that directs itself according to Ideal standards.

The contrast between the Kantian and the Cartesian views of consciousness can be defined in reference to another important issue. The diaphanous view commits its adherents to a very definite interpretation of the nature of relations. Since they regard consciousness as passive and receptive, they have to maintain that relations can be known only in so far as they are apprehended in a manner analogous to the contents themselves. I do not, of course, wish to imply that this view of relational knowledge is in all cases and in all respects illegitimate. Kant, as we shall find, has carried the opposite view to an impossible extreme, assuming without further argument that what has been shown to be true of certain types of relation (for instance, of the causal and substance-attribute relations) must be true of all relations, even of those that constitute space and time. It cannot be denied that, as William James and others have very rightly insisted, such relations as the space-relations are *in some degree or manner* presentational. This does not, however, justify James in concluding, as he at times seems inclined to do, that all relations are directly experienced. Such procedure lays him open to the same charge of illegitimate reasoning. But even if we could grant James's thesis in its widest form, the all-important Critical question would still remain: in what does awareness, whether of presented contents or of presented relations, consist, and how is it possible? In answering this question Kant is led to the conclusion that consciousness must be regarded as an activity, and as determining certain of the conditions of its own possibility. Its contribution is of a uniform and constant nature; it consists, as already noted, of certain relational factors whose presence can be detected in each and every act of awareness.

There is one other respect in which Kant's view of consciousness differs from that of his Cartesian predecessors.[1] Consciousness, he maintains, does not reveal itself, but only its objects. In other words, there is no awareness of awareness. So far as our mental states and processes can be known at all, they are known in the same objective manner in which

---

[1] With the sole exception of Malebranche, who on this point anticipated Kant.

we apprehend existences in space.[1] Now if this be so, a very important consequence follows. If there is no awareness of awareness, but only of meanings all of which are objective, there can be no consciousness of the generative, synthetic processes that constitute consciousness *on its subjective side*. For consciousness, being an *act* of awareness in which *meaning* is apprehended, has a twofold nature, and must be very differently described according to the aspect which at any one time we may have in view. When we regard it on its *objective* side as awareness of *meaning*, we are chiefly concerned with the various factors that are necessary to meaning and that enter into its constitution. That is to say, our analysis is essentially logical. When, on the other hand, we consider consciousness as an *act* of awareness, our problem is ontological or as it may be entitled (though the term is in this reference somewhat misleading, since the enquiry as defined by Kant is essentially metaphysical) psychological in character. Between these two aspects there is this very important difference. The logical factors constitutive of meaning can be exhaustively known; they are elements in the meanings which consciousness reveals; whereas the synthetic processes are postulated solely in view of these constituent factors, and in order to account for them. The processes, that is to say, are known only through that which they condition, and on Kant's teaching we are entirely ruled out from attempting to comprehend even their possibility.[2] They must be thought as occurring, but they cannot be known, *i.e.* their nature cannot be definitely specified. The postulating of them marks a gap in our knowledge, and extends our insight only in the degree that it discloses our ignorance. As consciousness rests upon, and is made possible by, these processes, it can never be explained in terms of the objective world to which our sense-experience, and therefore, as Kant argues, our specific knowledge, is exclusively limited. The mind can unfold its contents in the sunshine of consciousness, only because its roots strike deep into a soil that the light does not penetrate. These processes, thus postulated, Kant regards as the source of the *a priori* elements, and as the agency through which the synthetic connections necessary to all consciousness are brought about.

According to Kant's Critical teaching, therefore, consciousness, though analysable, is not such as can ever be rendered completely comprehensible. When all is said, it remains for us a strictly *de facto* form of

---

[1] This is the position that Kant endeavours to expound in the very unsatisfactory form of a doctrine of "inner sense." Cf. below, pp. i–ii, 291 ff.

[2] This was Kant's chief reason for omitting the so-called "subjective deduction of the categories" from the second edition. The teaching of the subjective deduction is, however, preserved in almost unmodified form throughout the *Critique* as a whole, and its "transcendental psychology" forms, as I shall try to show, an essential part of Kant's central teaching. In this matter I find myself in agreement with Vaihinger, and in complete disagreement with Riehl and the majority of the neo-Kantians. The neo-Kantian attempt to treat epistemology in independence of all psychological considerations is bound to lead to very different conclusions from those which Kant himself reached. Cf. below, pp. 237 ff., 263–70.

existence, and has to be taken just for what it presents itself as being. It is actually such as to make possible the logical processes of judgment and inference. It is actually such as to render possible a satisfactory proof of the scientific validity, within the field of sense-experience, of the principle of causality, and of such other principles as are required in the development of the positive sciences. It is also such as to render comprehensible the controlling influence of Ideal standards. But when we come to the question, how is consciousness of this type and form possible, that is, to the question of its metaphysical significance and of the generative conditions upon which it rests, we find, Kant maintains, that we have no data sufficient to justify any decisive answer.

The ontological, creative, or dynamical aspect of consciousness, I may further insist, must be constantly borne in mind if the Critical standpoint is to be properly viewed. The logical analysis is, indeed, for the purposes of the central portions of the *Critique* much the more important, and alone allows of detailed, exhaustive development; but the other is no less essential for an appreciation of Kant's attitude towards the more strictly metaphysical problems of the *Dialectic*.

Hegel and his disciples have been the chief culprits in subordinating, or rather in entirely eliminating, this aspect of Kant's teaching. Many of the inconsistencies of which they accuse Kant exist only if Kant's teaching be first reduced to a part of itself. To eliminate the ontological implications of his theory of consciousness is, by anticipation, to render many of his main conclusions entirely untenable, and in particular to destroy the force of his fundamental distinction between appearance and reality. If consciousness knows itself in its ultimate nature—and such is Hegel's contention—one half of reality is taken out of the obscurity in which, on Kant's reading of the situation, it is condemned to lie hidden. Man is more knowable than nature, and is the key to nature; such is Hegel's position, crudely stated. Contrast therewith the teaching of Kant. We can know nature more completely (though still very incompletely) than we can ever hope to comprehend the conditions which make possible and actual man's spiritual life. The moral consciousness is an autonomously acting source of independent values, and though a standing miracle, must be taken for all that on independent and separate enquiry it is found to be. Hegel, in his endeavour to establish an intellectual monism, does violence to some of the highest interests which he professes to be safeguarding. Kant, while outlining in Idea a Kingdom of Ends, remains satisfied with a pluralistic distinction between the intellectual and the moral categories. The antithesis of the two philosophies is in some degree the ancient opposition between Aristotle and Plato, restated in modern terms.

4. PHENOMENALISM, KANT'S SUBSTITUTE FOR SUBJECTIVISM

The revolutionary character of the above conclusions is shown by the difficulty which Kant himself found in breaking away from many of the presuppositions that underlie the views which he was renouncing; and this is nowhere more evident than in his constant alternation throughout the *Critique* between a *subjectivism*[1] that is thoroughly Cartesian—we might almost, allowing for his rationalism, say Berkeleian—in character, and a radically different position which may be entitled *phenomenalism*. The latter is alone genuinely Critical, and presents Kant's teaching in its maturest form. For though first formulated only in those portions of the *Analytic* that are late in date of writing, and in those passages of the second edition which supplement them, it would seem to be the logical outcome of Kant's other main doctrines.

I have especially in mind Kant's fundamental distinction between appearance and reality; it has an all-important bearing upon the Cartesian opposition between the mental and the material, and especially upon the question as to what view ought to be taken of our so-called *subjective* experiences. The objective is for the Cartesians the independently real; the subjective is asserted to have an altogether different kind of existence in what is named the field of consciousness. Kant's phenomenalist restatement of this distinction is too complex and subtle to be made intelligible in the brief space available in this *Introduction*—it is expounded in the body of the *Commentary*[2]—but its general character I may indicate in a few sentences. All subjectivist modes of stating the problem of knowledge, such as we find in Hume and in Leibniz no less than in Descartes, Locke, and Berkeley, are, Kant finally concluded, illegitimate and question-begging. Our so-called subjective states, whether they be sensations, feelings, or desires, are *objective* in the sense that they are *objects* for consciousness.[3] Our mental states do not run parallel with the system of natural existences; nor are they additional to it. They do not constitute our consciousness of nature; they are themselves part of the natural order which consciousness reveals. They compose the empirical self which is an objective existence, integrally connected with the material environment in terms of which alone it can be understood. The subjective is not opposite in nature to the objective, but a sub-species within it. While, however, the psychical is thus to be regarded as a class of known appearances, and as forming together with the physical a single system of nature, this entire order is, in Kant's view, conditioned by an underlying realm of noumenal existence; and when the question of the possibility of the *knowing*, that is, of the *experiencing* of such a comprehensive natural system, is raised, it is to this noumenal sphere that we are referred. Everything experienced, even a sensation or feeling, is an event, but the experiencing of

[1] This subjectivism finds expression in Kant's doctrine of the "transcendental object" which, as I shall try to prove, is a doctrine of early date and only semi-Critical. That doctrine is especially prominent in the section on the Antinomies. See below p. 204 ff.

[2] Cf. pp. 270 ff., 298 ff., 308–21, 373–4, 414–17.

[3] That this statement holds of feelings and desires, and therefore of all the emotions, as well as of our sense-contents, is emphasised by Kant in the *Critique of Practical Reason*. Cf. below, pp. 276, 279–80, 312, 384–5.

it is an act of awareness, and calls for an explanation of an altogether different kind.

Thus the problem of knowledge, stated in adequate Critical terms, is not how we can advance from the merely subjective to knowledge of the independently real,[1] but how, if everything known forms part of a comprehensive natural system, consciousness and the complex factors which contribute to its possibility are to be interpreted. On this latter question, as already indicated, Kant, though debarring both subjectivism and materialism, otherwise adopts a non-committal attitude. So long as we continue within the purely theoretical domain, there are a number of alternatives between which there are no sufficient data for deciding. To debar subjectivism is not to maintain the illusory or phenomenal character of the individual self; and to rule out materialism is not to assert that the unconscious may not generate and account for the conscious. In other words, they are ruled out not for any ulterior reasons derived from their supposed metaphysical consequences, but solely because they are based on palpable misinterpretations of the cognitive situation that generates those very problems to which they profess to be an answer.

5. THE DISTINCTION BETWEEN HUMAN AND ANIMAL INTELLIGENCE

The inwardness of Kant's Critical standpoint may perhaps be made clearer by a brief consideration of his view of animal intelligence. We are accustomed nowadays to test a psychology of human consciousness by its capacity to render conceivable an evolution from lower forms. How does Kant's teaching emerge from such a test?

It may at once be admitted that Kant has made no special study of animal behaviour, and was by no means competent to speak with authority in regard to its conditions. Indeed it is evident that anything which he may have to say upon this question is entirely of the nature of a deduction from results obtained in the human sphere. But when this has been admitted, and we are therefore prepared to find the problems approached from the point of view of the difference rather than of the kinship between man and the animals, we can recognise that, so far as the independent study of human consciousness is concerned, there is a certain compensating advantage in Kant's pre-Darwinian standpoint. For it leaves him free from that desire which exercises so constant, and frequently so deleterious an influence, upon many workers in the field of psychology, namely, to maintain at all costs,

---

[1] The connection of this teaching with Kant's theory of consciousness may be noted. If consciousness in all its forms, however primitive, is *already* awareness of meaning, its only possible task is to define, modify, reconstruct, and develop such meaning, never to obtain for bare contents or existences objective or other significance. Cf. above, pp. xli–ii, xliv.

in anticipation of conclusions not yet by any means established, the fundamental identity of animal and human intelligence. This besetting desire all too easily tends to the minimising of differences that may perhaps with fuller insight be found to involve no breach of continuity, but which in the present state of our knowledge cannot profitably be interpreted save in terms of their differentiating peculiarities.

The current controversy between mechanism and vitalism enforces the point which I desire to make. Biological problems, as many biologists are now urging, can be most profitably discussed in comparative independence of ultimate issues, entirely in view of their own domestic circumstances. For only when the actual constitution of organic compounds has been more completely determined than has hitherto been possible can the broader questions be adequately dealt with. In other words, the differences must be known before the exact nature and degree of the continuity can be defined. They cannot be anticipated by any mere deduction from general principles.

The value of Kant's analysis of human consciousness is thus closely bound up with his frank recognition of its inherent complexity. Not simplification, but specification, down to the bedrock of an irreducible minimum of correlated factors, is the governing motive of his Critical enquiries. His results have therefore the great advantage of being inspired by no considerations save such as are prescribed by the actual subject-matter under investigation. As already noted, Kant maintains that human consciousness is always an awareness of meaning, and that consequently it can find expression only in judgments which involve together with their other factors the element of recognition or self-consciousness.

This decides for Kant the character of the distinction to be drawn between animal and human intelligence. As animals, in his view, cannot be regarded as possessing a capacity of self-consciousness, they must also be denied all awareness of meaning. However complicated the associative organisation of their ideas may be, it never rises to the higher level of logical judgment. For the same reason, though their ideas may be schematic in outline, and in their bearing on behaviour may therefore have the same efficiency as general concepts, they cannot become universal in the logical sense. "Animals have apprehensions, but not apperceptions, and cannot, therefore, make their representations universal."[1] In support of this position Kant might have pointed to the significant fact that animals are so teachable up to a certain point, and so unteachable beyond it. They can be carried as far as associative suggestion will allow, but not a step further. To this day it remains true— at least I venture the assertion—that no animal has ever been conclusively shown to be capable of apprehending a sign as a sign. Animals may seem to do so owing to the influence of associated ideas, but are, as it would appear, debarred from crossing the boundary line

---

[1] *Reflexionen zur Anthropologie*, 207.

which so sharply distinguishes associative suggestion from reflective knowledge.

But Kant is committed to a further assertion. If animals are devoid of all awareness of meaning, they must also be denied anything analogous to what we must signify by the term consciousness. Their experience must fall apart into events, that may, perhaps, be described as mental, but cannot be taken as equivalent to an act of awareness. "*Apprehensio bruta* without consciousness,"[1] such is Kant's view of the animal mind. Its mental states, like all other natural existences, are events in time, explicable in the same naturalistic fashion as the bodily processes by which they are conditioned; they can not be equated with that human consciousness which enables us to reflect upon them, and to determine the conditions of their temporal happening.

The distinction which Kant desires to draw is ultimately that between events and consciousness of events. Even if events are psychical in character, consisting of sensations and feelings, there will still remain as fundamental the distinction between what is simply a member of the causal series of natural events and the consciousness through which the series is apprehended. Kant's most explicit statements occur in a letter to Herz.[2] He is referring to data of the senses which cannot be self-consciously apprehended:

"I should not be able to know that I have them, and they would therefore be for me, as a cognitive being, absolutely nothing.

They might still (if I conceive myself as an animal) exist in me (a being unconscious of my own existence) as representations . . . , connected according to an empirical law of association, exercising influence upon feeling and desire, and so always disporting themselves with regularity, without my thereby acquiring the least cognition of anything, not even of these my own states."[3]

As to whether Kant is justified in maintaining that the distinction between animal and human consciousness coincides with the distinction between associative and logical or reflective thinking, I am not concerned to maintain. This digression has been introduced solely for the purpose of defining more precisely the central tenets of Kant's Critical teaching.

6. THE NATURE AND CONDITIONS OF SELF-CONSCIOUSNESS

We have still to consider what is perhaps the most serious of all the misunderstandings to which Kant has laid himself open, and which is in large part responsible for the widespread belief that his Critical

---

[1] In sketch of a letter (summer 1792) to Fürst von Beloselsky (*W.* xi. p. 331).

[2] May 26, 1789 (*W.* xi. p. 52).

[3] That Kant has not developed a terminology really adequate to the statement of his meaning, is shown by a parenthesis which I have omitted from the above quotation.

principles, when consistently developed, must finally eventuate in some such metaphysics as that of Fichte and Hegel. I refer to the view that Kant in postulating synthetic processes as conditioning consciousness is postulating a noumenal self as exercising these activities, and is therefore propounding a *metaphysical explanation* of the synthetic, *a priori* factors in human experience.[1]

Kant's language is frequently ambiguous. The Leibnizian spiritualism, to which in his pre-Critical period he had un-questioningly held, continued to influence his terminology, and so to prevent his Critical principles from obtaining consistent expression. This much can be said in support of the above interpretation of Kant's position. But in all other respects such a reading of his philosophy is little better than a parody of his actual teaching. For Kant is very well aware that the problem of knowledge is not to be solved in any such easy and high-handed fashion. In the *Critique* he teaches quite explicitly that to profess to explain the presence of *a priori* factors in human experience by means of a self assumed for that very purpose would be a flagrant violation, not only of Critical principles, but even of the elementary maxims of scientific reasoning. In the first place, explanation by reference to the activities of such a self would be explanation by faculties, by the unknown; it is a cause that will explain anything and everything equally well or badly.[2] Self-consciousness has, indeed, to be admitted as a fact;[3] and from its occurrence Kant draws important conclusions in regard to the conditions which make experience possible. But, in so doing, Kant never intends to maintain that we are justified in postulating as part of those conditions, or as condition of those conditions, a noumenal self. The

---

[1] This interpretation of Kant appears in a very crude form in James's references to Kant in his *Principles of Psychology*. It appears in a more subtle form in Lotze and Green. Caird and Watson, on the other hand, have carefully guarded themselves against this view of Kant's teaching, and as I have maintained (pp. xliii–v), lie open to criticism only in so far as they tend to ignore those aspects of Kant's teaching which cannot be stated in terms of logical-implication.

[2] It may be objected that this is virtually what Kant is doing when he postulates synthetic activities as the source of the categories. Kant would probably have replied that he has not attempted to define these activities save to the extent that is absolutely demanded by the known character of their products, and that he is willing to admit that many different explanations of their nature are possible. They *may* be due to some kind of personal or spiritual agency, but also they may not. On the whole question of the legitimacy of Kant's general method of procedure, cf. below, pp. 235–9, 263 ff., 273–4, 277 ff., 461–2, 473–7.

[3] Cf. *Concerning the Advances made by Metaphysics since Leibniz and Wolff* (Werke (Hartenstein), viii. 530–1): "I am conscious to myself of myself—this is a thought which contains a twofold I, the I as subject and the I as object. How it should be possible that I, the I that thinks, should be an object ... to myself, and so should be able to distinguish myself from myself, it is altogether beyond our powers to explain. It is, however, an undoubted fact ... and has as a consequence the complete distinguishing of us off from the whole animal kingdom, since we have no ground for ascribing to animals the power to say I to themselves."

conditions which make experience possible, whatever they may be, are also the conditions which make self-consciousness possible. Since the self is known only as appearance, it cannot be asserted to be the conditioning ground of appearance.

This first objection is not explicitly stated by Kant, but it is implied in a second argument which finds expression both in the *Deduction of the Categories* and in the chapter on the *Paralogisms*. The only self that we know to exist is the *conscious* self. Now, as Kant claims to have proved, the self can be thus conscious, even of itself, only in so far as it is conscious of objects. Consequently we have no right to assume that the self can precede such consciousness as its generating cause. That would be to regard the self as existing prior to its own conditions, working in darkness to create itself as a source of light.

But there is also a third reason why Kant's Critical solution of the problem of knowledge must not be stated in spiritualist terms. Self-consciousness, as he shows, is itself *relational* in character. It is a fundamental factor in human experience, not because the self can be shown to be the agency to which relations are due, but solely because, itself a case of recognition, it is at the same time a necessary condition of recognition, and recognition is indispensably presupposed in all consciousness of meaning.[1] Awareness of meaning is the fundamental mystery, and retains its profoundly mysterious character even when self-consciousness has been thus detected as an essential constituent. For self-consciousness does not explain the possibility of meaning; it is itself, as I have just remarked, only one case of recognition, and so is itself only an instance, though indeed the supreme and most important instance, of what we must intend by the term meaning. All awareness, not excepting that of the knowing self, rests upon noumenal conditions whose specific nature it does not itself reveal. Only on moral grounds, never through any purely theoretical analysis of cognitive experience, can it be proved that the self is an abiding personality, and that in conscious, personal form it belongs to the order of noumenal reality.

7. KANT'S THREEFOLD DISTINCTION BETWEEN SENSIBILITY, UNDERSTANDING, AND REASON

Even so summary a statement of Critical teaching as I am attempting in this *Introduction* would be very incomplete without some reference to Kant's threefold distinction between the forms of sensibility, the categories of the understanding, and the Ideas of Reason.

On investigating space and time Kant discovers that they cannot be classed either with the data of the bodily senses or with the concepts of the understanding. They are sensuous (*i.e.* are not abstract but concrete, not ways of thinking but modes of existence), yet at the same time are

[1] Cf. above, p. xxxiv; below, pp. 250–3, 260–3, 285–6.

a priori. They thus stand apart by themselves. Each is unique in its kind, is single, and is an infinite existence. To describe them is to combine predicates seemingly contradictory. Viewed as characterising things in themselves, they are, in Kant's own phrase, monstrosities (*Undinge*). To them, primarily, are due those problems which have been a standing challenge to philosophy since the time of Zeno the Eleatic, and which Kant has entitled "antinomies of Reason."

In contrast to sensibility Kant sets the intellectual faculties, understanding and Reason. In the understanding originate certain pure concepts, or as he more usually names them, categories. The chief of these are the categories of "relation "—substance, causality and reciprocity. They combine with the forms of sensibility and the manifold of sense to yield the consciousness of an empirical order, interpretable in accordance with universal laws.

To the faculty of Reason Kant ascribes what he entitles Ideas. The Ideas differ from space, time, and the categories in being not "constitutive" but "regulative." They demand an *unconditionedness* of existence and a *completeness* of explanation which can never be found in actual experience. Their function is threefold. In the first place, they render the mind dissatisfied with the haphazard collocations of ordinary experience, and define the goal for its scientific endeavours. Secondly, they determine for us the criteria that distinguish between truth and falsity.[1] And thirdly, in so doing, they likewise make possible the distinction between appearance and reality, revealing to us an irreconcilable conflict between the ultimate aims of science and the human conditions, especially the spatial and temporal conditions under which these aims are realised. The Ideas of Reason are the second main factor in the "antinomies."

The problem of the *Critique*, the analysis of our awareness of meaning, is a single problem, and each of the above elements involves all the others. Kant, however, for reasons into which I need not here enter, has assigned part of the problem to what he entitles the *Transcendental Aesthetic*, and another part to the *Transcendental Dialectic*. Only what remains is dealt with in what is really the most important of the three divisions, the *Transcendental Analytic*, But as the problem is one and indivisible, the discussions in all three sections are condemned to incompleteness save in so far as Kant, by happy inconsistency, transgresses the limits imposed by his method of treatment. The *Aesthetic* really does no more than prepare the ground for the more adequate analysis of space and time given in the *Analytic* and *Dialectic*, while the problem of the *Analytic* is itself incompletely stated until the more comprehensive argument of the *Dialectic* is taken into account.[2] Thus the

---

[1] Cf. A 651 = B 679: "The law of Reason, which requires us to seek for this unity, is a necessary law, as without it we should have no Reason at all, and without Reason no coherent employment of the understanding, and in the absence of this no sufficient criterion of empirical truth." Cf. also below, pp. 390–1, 414–17, 429–31, 519–21. 558–61.

[2] Regarding a further complication, due to the fact that the *Dialectic* was written before the teaching of the *Analytic* was properly matured, cf. above, p. xxiv.

statement in the *Aesthetic* that space and time are *given* to the mind by the sensuous faculty of receptivity is modified in the *Analytic* through recognition of the part which the syntheses and concepts of the understanding must play in the construction of these forms; and in the *Dialectic* their apprehension is further found to involve an Idea of Reason. Similarly, in the concluding chapter of the *Analytic*, in discussing the grounds for distinguishing between appearance and reality, Kant omits all reference to certain important considerations which first emerge into view in the course of the *Dialectic*. Yet, though no question is more vital to Critical teaching, the reader is left under the impression that the treatment given in the *Analytic* is complete and final.

Partly as a consequence of this, partly owing to Kant's inconsistent retention of earlier modes of thinking, there are traceable throughout the *Critique* two opposed views of the nature of the distinction between appearance and reality. On the one view, this distinction is mediated by the relational categories of the understanding, especially by that of causality; on the other view, it is grounded in the Ideas of Reason. The former sets appearance in opposition to reality; the latter regards the distinction in a more tenable fashion, as being between realities less and more comprehensively conceived.[1]

A similar defect is caused by Kant's isolation of immanent from transcendent metaphysics.[2] The former is dealt with only in the *Analytic*, the latter only in the *Dialectic*. The former, Kant asserts, is made possible by the forms of sensibility and the categories of the understanding; the latter he traces to an illegitimate employment of the Ideas of Reason. Such a mode of statement itself reveals the impossibility of any sharp distinction between the immanent and the transcendent. If science is conditioned by Ideals which arouse the mind to further acquisitions, and at the same time reveal the limitations to which our knowledge is for ever condemned to remain subject; if, in other words, everything known, in being correctly known, must be apprehended as appearance (*i.e.* as a subordinate existence within a more comprehensive reality), the distinction between the immanent and the transcendent falls within and not beyond the domain of our total experience. The meaning which our consciousness discloses in each of its judgments is an essentially metaphysical one. It involves the thought, though not the knowledge, of something more than what the experienced can ever itself be found to be. The metaphysical is immanent in our knowledge; the transcendent is merely a name for this immanent factor when it is falsely viewed as capable of isolation and of independent treatment. By Kant's own showing, the task of the *Dialectic* is not merely to refute the pretensions of transcendent metaphysics, but to develop the above general thesis, in confirmation of the positive conclusions established in the *Analytic*. The *Critique* will then supply the remedy for certain evils to which the human mind has hitherto been subject.

[1] Cf. below, pp. 331, 390–1, 414–17.
[2] Cf. below, pp. 22, 33, 56, 66 ff.

"*The Critique of Pure Reason* is a preservative against a malady which has its source in our rational nature. This malady is the opposite of the love of home (the home-sickness) which binds us to our fatherland. It is a longing to pass out beyond our immediate confines and to relate ourselves to other worlds."[1]

8. THE PLACE OF THE *CRITIQUE OF PURE REASON* IN KANT'S PHILOSOPHICAL SYSTEM

The positive character of Kant's conclusions cannot be properly appreciated save in the wider perspectives that open to view in the *Critique of Practical Reason* and in the *Critique of Judgment*. Though in the *Critique of Pure Reason* a distinction is drawn between theoretical and moral belief, it is introduced in a somewhat casual manner, and there is no clear indication of the far-reaching consequences that follow in its train. Unfortunately also, even in his later writings, Kant is very unfair to himself in his methods of formulating the distinction. His real intention is to show that scientific knowledge is not coextensive with human insight; but he employs a misleading terminology, contrasting knowledge with faith, scientific demonstration with practical belief.

As already indicated, the term knowledge has, in the Critical philosophy, a much narrower connotation than in current speech. It is limited to *sense-experience*, and to such inferences therefrom as can be obtained by the only methods that Kant is willing to recognise, namely, the mathematico-physical. Aesthetic, moral and religious experience, and even organic phenomena, are excluded from the field of possible knowledge.

In holding to this position, Kant is, of course, the child of his time. The absolute sufficiency of the Newtonian physics is a presupposition of all his utterances on this theme. Newton, he believes, has determined in a quite final manner the principles, methods and limits of scientific investigation. For though Kant himself imposes upon science a further limitation, namely, to appearances, he conceives himself, in so doing, not as weakening Newton's natural philosophy, but as securing it against all possible objections. And to balance the narrow connotation thus assigned to the term knowledge, he has to give a correspondingly wide meaning to the terms faith, moral belief, subjective principles of interpretation. If this be not kept constantly in mind, the reader is certain to misconstrue the character and tendencies of Kant's actual teaching.

But though the advances made by the sciences since Kant's time have rendered this mode of delimiting the field of knowledge altogether untenable, his method of defining the sources of *philosophical insight* has proved very fruitful, and has many adherents at the present day. What Kant does—stated in broad outline—is to distinguish between the problems of *existence* and the problems of *value*, assigning the former to

---

[1] *Reflexionen* (B. Erdmann's edition) ii. 204.

science and the latter to philosophy.[1] Theoretical philosophy, represented in his system by the *Critique of Pure Reason*, takes as its province the logical values, that is, the distinction of truth and falsity, and defining their criteria determines the nature and limits of our theoretical insight. Kant finds that these criteria enable us to distinguish between truth and falsity only on the empirical plane. Beyond making possible a distinction between appearance and reality, they have no applicability in the metaphysical sphere.

The *Critique of Practical Reason* deals with values of a very different character. The faculty of Reason, which, as already noted,[2] renders our consciousness a purposive agency controlled by Ideal standards, is also, Kant maintains, the source of the moral sanctions. But whereas in the theoretical field it subdues our minds to the discipline of experience, and restrains our intellectual ambitions within the limits of the empirical order, it here summons us to sacrifice every natural impulse and every secular advantage to the furtherance of an end that has absolute value. In imposing duties, it raises our life from the "pragmatic "[3] level of a calculating expediency to the higher plane of a categorical imperative.

The categorical imperative at once humbles and exalts; it discloses our limitations, but does so through the greatness of the vocation to which it calls us.

"This principle of morality, just on account of the universality of the legislation which makes it the formal supreme determining principle of our will, without regard to any subjective differences, is declared by the Reason to be a law for all rational beings. . . . It is, therefore, not limited to men only, but applies to all finite beings that possess Reason and Will; nay, it even includes the Infinite Being as the Supreme Intelligence."[4]

Consequently, in employing moral ends in the interpretation of the Universe, we are not picturing the Divine under human limitations, but are discounting these limitations in the light of the one form of value that is known to us as absolute.

"*Duty!* . . . What origin is worthy of thee and where is to be found the root of thy noble descent . . . a root to be derived from which is the indispensable condition of the only worth that men can give themselves."[5]

In his earlier years Kant had accepted the current, Leibnizian view that human excellence consists in intellectual enlightenment, and that it is therefore reserved for an *élite*, privileged with the leisure and endowed with the special abilities required for its enjoyment. From this arid intellectualism he was delivered through the influence of Rousseau.

---

[1] For an alternative and perhaps more adequate method of describing Kant's general position, cf. below, p. 571 ff.

[2] Above, pp. xxxviii–ix, xlii, xliv.

[3] Cf. below, p. 577.

[4] *Critique of Practical Reason, W.* v. p. 32; Abbott's trans, pp. 120–1.

[5] *Op. cit.* p. 86; Abbott's trans, p. 180.

"I am by disposition an enquirer. I feel the consuming thirst for knowledge, the eager unrest to advance ever further, and the delights of discovery. There was a time when I believed that this is what confers real dignity upon human life, and I despised the common people who know nothing. Rousseau has set me right. This imagined advantage vanishes. I learn to honour men, and should regard myself as of much less use than the common labourer, if I did not believe that my philosophy will restore to all men the common rights of humanity."[1]

These common rights Kant formulates in a purely individualist manner. For here also, in his lack of historic sense and in his distrust alike of priests and of statesmen, he is the child of his time. In the education and discipline of the soul he looks to nothing so artificial and humanly limited—Kant so regards them—as religious tradition and social institutions. Human rights, he believes, do not vary with time and place; and for their enjoyment man requires no initiation and no equipment beyond what is supplied by Nature herself. It is from this standpoint that Kant adduces, as the twofold and sufficient inspiration to the rigours and sublimities of the spiritual life, the starry heavens above us and the moral law within. They are ever-present influences on the life of man. The naked eye reveals the former; of the latter all men are immediately aware. In their universal appeal they are of the very substance of human existence. Philosophy may avail to counteract certain of the hindrances which prevent them from exercising their native influence; it cannot be a substitute for the inspiration which they alone can yield.

Thus the categorical imperative, in endowing the human soul with an intrinsic value, singles it out from all other natural existences, and strengthens it to face, with equanimity, the cold immensities of the cosmic system. For though the heavens arouse in us a painful feeling of our insignificance as animal existences, they intensify our consciousness of a sublime destiny, as bearers of a rival, and indeed a superior, dignity.

In one fundamental respect Kant broke with the teaching of Rousseau, namely, in questioning his doctrine of the natural goodness and indefinite perfectibility of human nature.[2] Nothing, Kant maintains, is

---

[1] *Fragmente aus item Nachlasse* (*Werke* (Hartenstein), viii. p. 624). Cf. below, pp. 577–8. Kant claims for all men equality of political rights, and in his treatise on *Perpetual Peace* maintains that wars are not likely to cease until the republican form of government is universally adopted. He distinguishes, however, between republicanism and democracy. By the former he means a genuinely representative system; the latter he interprets as being the (in principle) unlimited despotism of majority rule. Kant accordingly contends that the smaller the staff of the executive, and the more effective the representation of minorities, the more complete will be the approximation to the ideal constitution. In other words, the less government we can get along with, the better.

[2] *On the Radical Evil in Human Nature, W,* vi. p. 20; Abbott's trans, p. 326. "This opinion [that the world is constantly advancing from worse to better] is certainly not founded on experience if what is meant is *moral* good or evil (not civilisation), for the history of all times speaks too powerfully against it. Probably it is merely a good-natured hypothesis . . . designed to encourage us in the unwearied cultivation of the germ of good that perhaps lies in us. . . ."

good without qualification except the good will; and even that, perhaps, is never completely attained in any single instance. The exercise of duty demands a perpetual vigilance, under the ever-present consciousness of continuing demerit.

"I am willing to admit out of love of humanity that most of our actions are indeed correct, but if we examine them more closely we everywhere come upon the dear self which is always prominent. . . ."[1] "Nothing but moral fanaticism and exaggerated self-conceit is infused into the mind by exhortation to actions as noble, sublime and magnanimous. Thereby men are led into the delusion that it is not duty, that is, respect for the law, whose yoke . . . they *must* bear, whether they like it or not, that constitutes the determining principle of their actions, and which always humbles them while they *obey* it. They then fancy that those actions are expected from them, not from duty, but as pure merit. . . . In this way they engender a vain high-flying fantastic way of thinking, flattering themselves with a spontaneous goodness of heart that needs neither spur nor bridle, nor any command. . . ."[2]

In asserting the goodness and self-sufficiency of our natural impulses Rousseau is the spokesman of a philosophy which has dominated social and political theory since his day, and which is still prevalent. This philosophy, in Kant's view, is disastrous in its consequences. As a reading of human nature and of our moral vocation, it is hardly less false than the Epicurean teaching, which finds in the pursuit of pleasure the motive of all our actions. A naturalistic ethics, in either form, is incapacitated, by the very nature of its controlling assumptions, from appreciating the distinguishing features of the moral consciousness. Neither the successes nor the failures of man's spiritual endeavour can be rightly understood from any such standpoint. The human race, in its endurance and tenacity, in its dauntless courage and in its soaring spirit, reveals the presence of a *prevenient* influence, *non-natural* in character; and only if human nature be taken as including this higher, directive power, can it assume to itself the eulogy which Rousseau so mistakenly passes upon the natural and undisciplined tendencies of the human heart. For as history demonstrates, while *men* are weak, *humanity* is marvellous.

"There is one thing in our soul which, when we take a right view of it, we cannot cease to regard with the highest astonishment, and in regard to which admiration is right and indeed elevating, and that is our original moral capacity in general. . . . Even the incomprehensibility of this capacity,[3] a capacity which proclaims a Divine origin, must rouse man's spirit to enthusiasm and strengthen it for any sacrifices which respect for his duty may impose on him."[4]

---

[1] *Foundations of the Metaphysics of Morals*, W. iv. p. 407; Abbott's trans, p. 24.

[2] *Critique of Practical Reason*, W. v. pp. 84–5; Abbott's trans, pp. 178–9.

[3] Cf. *Foundations of the Metaphysics of Morals*, W. iv. p, 463; Abbott's trans, p. 84: "While we do not comprehend the practical unconditional necessity of the moral imperative, we yet comprehend its *incomprehensibility*, and this is all that can be fairly demanded of a philosophy which strives to carry its principles up to the very limit of human reason."

[4] *On the Radical Evil in Human Nature*, W. vi. pp. 49–50; Abbott's trans, pp. 357–8.

We are not here concerned with the detail of Kant's ethical teaching, or with the manner in which he establishes the freedom of the will, and justifies belief in the existence of God and the immortality of the soul. In many respects his argument lies open to criticism. There is an unhappy contrast between the largeness of his fundamental thesis and the formal, doctrinaire manner in which it is developed. Indeed, in the *Critique of Practical Reason* the individualist, deistic, rationalistic modes of thinking of his time are much more in evidence than in any other of his chief writings; and incidentally he also displays a curious insensibility—again characteristic of his period—to all that is specific in the religious attitude. But when due allowances have been made, we can still maintain that in resting his constructive views upon the supreme value of the moral personality Kant has influenced subsequent philosophy in hardly less degree than by his teaching in the *Critique of Pure Reason.*[1]

The two *Critiques*, in method of exposition and argument, in general outcome, and indeed in the total impression they leave upon the mind, are extraordinarily different. In the *Critique of Pure Reason* Kant is meticulously scrupulous in testing the validity of each link in his argument. Constantly he retraces his steps; and in many of his chief problems he halts between competing solutions. Kant's sceptical spirit is awake, and it refuses to cease from its questionings. In the *Critique of Practical Reason*, on the other hand, there is an austere simplicity of argument, which advances, without looking to right or left, from a few simple principles direct to their ultimate consequences. The impressiveness of the first *Critique* consists in its appreciation of the *complexity* of the problems, and in the care with which their various, conflicting aspects are separately dealt with. The second *Critique* derives its force from the fundamental conviction upon which it is based.

Such, then, stated in the most general terms, is the manner in which Kant conceives the *Critique of Pure Reason* as contributing to the establishment of a humanistic philosophy. It clears the ground for the practical Reason, and secures it in the autonomous control of its own domain. While preserving to the intellect and to science certain definitely prescribed rights, Kant places in the forefront of his system the moral values; and he does so under the conviction that in living up to the opportunities, in whatever rank of life, of our common heritage, we obtain a truer and deeper insight into ultimate issues than can be acquired through the abstruse subtleties of metaphysical speculation.

I may again draw attention to the consequences which follow from Kant's habitual method of isolating his problems. Truth is a value of universal jurisdiction, and from its criteria the judgments of moral and other values can claim no exemption. Existences and values do not constitute independent orders. They interpenetrate, and neither can be adequately dealt with apart from the considerations appropriate to the

---

[1] Cf. Pringle-Pattison: *The Idea of God in the Light of Recent Philosophy*, p. 25 ff.

other. In failing to co-ordinate his problems, Kant has over-emphasised the negative aspects of his logical enquiries and has formulated his ethical doctrines in a needlessly dogmatic form.

These defects are, however, in some degree remedied in the last of his chief works, the *Critique of Judgment*. In certain respects it is the most interesting of all Kant's writings. The qualities of both the earlier *Critiques* here appear in happy combination, while in addition his concrete interests are more in evidence, to the great enrichment of his abstract argument. Many of the doctrines of the *Critique of Pure Reason*, especially those that bear on the problems of teleology, are restated in a less negative manner, and in their connection with the kindred problems of natural beauty and the fine arts. For though the final decision in all metaphysical questions is still reserved to moral consid-erations, Kant now takes a more catholic view of the field of philosophy. He allows, though with characteristic reservations, that the *empirical* evidence obtainable through examination of the broader features of our total experience is of genuinely philosophical value, and that it can safely be employed to amplify and confirm the independent convic-tions of the moral consciousness. The embargo which in the *Critique of Pure Reason*, in matters metaphysical, is placed upon all tentative and probable reasoning is thus tacitly removed; and the term knowledge again acquires the wider meaning very properly ascribed to it in ordinary speech.

A COMMENTARY TO KANT'S "CRITIQUE OF PURE REASON"

TITLE: KRITIK DER REINEN VERNUNFT

THE term critique or criticism, as employed by Kant, is of English origin. It appears in seventeenth and eighteenth century English, chiefly in adjectival form, as a literary and artistic term—for instance, in the works of Pope, who was Kant's favourite English poet. Kant was the first to employ it in German, extending it from the field of aesthetics to that of general philosophy. A reference in Kant's *Logic*[1] to Home's *Elements of Criticism*[2] would seem to indicate that it was Home's use of the term which suggested to him its wider employment. "Critique of pure reason," in its primary meaning, signifies the passing of critical judgments upon pure reason. In this sense Kant speaks of his time as "the age of criticism (*Zeitalter der Kritik*)." Frequently, however, he takes the term more specifically as meaning a critical investigation leading to positive as well as to negative results. Occasionally, especially in the *Dialectic*, it also signifies a discipline applied to pure reason, limiting it within due bounds. The first appearance of the word in Kant's writings is in 1765 in the *Nachricht*[3] of his lectures for the winter term 1765–1766. Kant seldom employs the corresponding adjective, critical (*kritisch*). His usual substitute for it is the term transcendental.

Pure (rein) has here a very definite meaning. It is the absolutely *a priori*. Negatively it signifies that which is

---

[1] *Einleitung,* i.

[2] Henry Home, Lord Kames, published his *Elements of Criticism* in 1762.

[3] *W.* ii. p. 311. In referring to his course in logic, Kant states that he will consider the training of the power of sound judgment in ordinary life, and adds that "in the *Kritik der Vernunft* the close kinship of subject-matter gives occasion for casting some glances upon the *Kritik des Geschmacks, i.e.* upon *Aesthetics.*" This passage serves to confirm the conjecture that the term *Kritik* was borrowed from the title of Home's work.

independent of experience.   Positively it signifies that which originates from reason itself, and which is characterised by universality and necessity.[1] By "pure reason" Kant therefore means reason in so far as it supplies out of itself, independently of experience, *a priori* elements that as such are characterised by universality and necessity.

Reason (*Vernunft*) is used in the *Critique* in three different meanings.   In the above title it is employed in its widest sense, as the source of all *a priori* elements.   It includes what is *a priori* in sensibility as well as in understanding (*Verstand*). In its narrowest sense it is distinct even from understanding, and signifies that faculty which renders the mind dissatisfied with its ordinary and scientific knowledge, and which leads it to demand a completeness and unconditionedness which can never be found in the empirical sphere.   Understanding conditions science ; reason generates metaphysics.   Understanding has categories ; reason has its Ideas.   Thirdly, Kant frequently employs understanding and reason as synonymous terms, dividing the mind only into the two faculties, sensibility and spontaneity.   Thus in A 1-2, understanding and reason are used promiscuously, and in place of *reine Vernunft* we find *reiner Verstand*.   As already stated, the term reason, as employed in Kant's title, ought properly to be taken in its widest sense.   Sensibility falls within reason in virtue of the *a priori* forms which it contains.   Kant does not himself, however, always interpret the title in this strict sense.   The triple use of the term is an excellent example of the looseness and carelessness with which he employs even the most important and fundamental of his technical terms.   Only the context can reveal the particular meaning to be assigned in each case.

The phrase "*of* pure reason" (*der reinen Vernunft*) has, as Vaihinger points out,[2] a threefold ambiguity.   (1) Sometimes it is a genitive objective.   The critical enquiry is directed upon pure reason as its object.   This corresponds to the view of the *Critique* as merely a treatise on method. (2) Sometimes it is a genitive subjective.   The critical enquiry is undertaken by and executed through pure reason.   This expresses the view of the *Critique* as itself a system of pure rational knowledge.   (3) At other times it has a reflexive meaning.   Pure reason is subject and object at once.   It is both subject-matter and method or instrument.   Through the *Critique* it attains to self-knowledge.   The *Critique* is the critical examination of pure reason by itself.   The first view

[1] For Kant's other uses of the term *pure*, cf. below, p. 55.
[2] *Commentar zu Kants Kritik der reinen Vernunft*, i. pp. 117-20.

would seem to be the original and primary meaning of the title. The second view very early took its place alongside it, and appears in many passages. The third view must be taken as representing Kant's final interpretation of the title; it is on the whole the most adequate to the actual content and scope of the *Critique*. For the *Critique* is not merely a treatise on method; it is also a system of pure rational knowledge. It professes to establish, in an exhaustive and final manner, the *a priori* principles which determine the possibility, conditions, and limits of pure rational knowledge.[1]

---

[1] For a definition, less exclusively titular, and more adequate to the actual scope of the *Critique*, cf. below, p. 56. Reason, when distinguished from understanding, I shall hereafter print with a capital letter, to mark the very special sense in which it is being employed.

MOTTO

DE nobis ipsis silemus: De re autem, quae agitur, petimus: ut homines eam non opinionem, sed opus esse cogitent; ac pro certo habeant, non sectae nos alicuius, aut placiti, sed utilitatis et amplitudinis humanae fundamenta moliri. Deinde ut suis commodis aequi . . . in commune consulant . . . et ipsi in partem veniant. Praeterea ut bene sperent, neque instauratonem nostram ut quiddam infinitum et ultra mortale fingant, et animo concipiant; quum revera sit infiniti erroris finis et terminus legitimus.

This motto, which was added in the second edition, is taken from the preface to Bacon's *Instauratio Magna*, of which the *Novum Organum* is the second part. As the first part of the *Instauratio* is represented only by the later, separately published, *De Augmentis Scientiarum*, this preface originally appeared, and is still usually given, as introductory to the *Novum Organum*.

The complete passage (in which I have indicated Kant's omissions) is rendered as follows in the translation of Ellis and Spedding:[1]

"Of myself I say nothing; but in behalf of the business which is in hand I entreat men to believe that it is not an opinion to be held, but a work to be done; and to be well assured that I am labouring to lay the foundation, not of any sect or doctrine, but of human utility and power. Next, I ask them to deal fairly by their own interests [and laying aside all emulations and prejudices in favour of this or that opinion], to join in consultation for the common good; and [being now freed and guarded by the securities and helps which I offer from the errors and impediments of the way] to come forward themselves and take part [in that which remains to be done]. Moreover, to be of good hope, nor to imagine that this Instauration of mine is a thing infinite and beyond the power of man, when it is in fact the true end and termination of infinite error."

---

[1] *Philosophical Works of Francis Bacon* (edited by J. M. Robertson, 1905), p. 247.

4

The opening sentence of Bacon's preface might also have served as a fitting motto to the *Critique* :

"It seems to me that men do not rightly understand either their store or their strength, but overrate the one and underrate the other."

Or again the following :

"I have not sought nor do I seek either to enforce or to ensnare men's judgments, but I lead them to things themselves and the concordances of things, that they may see for themselves what they have, what they can dispute, what they can add and contribute to the common stock. . . . And by these means I suppose that I have established for ever a true and lawful marriage between the empirical and the rational faculty, the unkind and ill-starred divorce and separation of which has thrown into confusion all the affairs of the human family."

DEDICATION

TO

FREIHERR VON ZEDLITZ

KARL ABRAHAM, FREIHERR VON ZEDLITZ had been en-
trusted, as Minister (1771–1788) to Frederick the Great, with
the oversight and direction of the Prussian system of education. He held Kant in the highest esteem.[1] In February
1778 we find him writing to thank Kant for the pleasure he
had found in perusing notes of his lectures on physical
geography, and requesting the favour of a complete copy.[2]
A week later he invited Kant to accept a professorship of
philosophy in Halle,[3] which was then much the most important university centre in Germany. Upon Kant's refusal
he repeated the offer, with added inducements, including the
title of Hofrat.[4] Again, in August of the same year, he writes
that he is attending, upon Mendelssohn's recommendation
(and doubtless also in the hope of receiving from this indirect
source further light upon Kant's own teaching in a favourite
field), the lectures on anthropology of Kant's disciple and
friend, Marcus Herz. The letter concludes with a passage
which may perhaps have suggested to Kant the appropriate-
ness of dedicating his *Critique* to so wise and discerning a
patron of true philosophy.

"Should your inventive power extend so far, suggest to me the
means of holding back the students in the universities from the
bread and butter studies, and of making them understand that their
modicum of law, even their theology and medicine, will be immensely

---

[1] For Zedlitz's severe strictures (Dec. 1775) upon the teaching in Königsberg
University, and his incidental appreciative reference to Kant, cf. Schubert's
edition of Kant's *Werke*, xi. pt. ii. pp. 59-61.
[2] Cf. *W.* x. p. 207.　　　　　　　　　　[3] *Op. cit.* pp. 212-13.
[4] Cf. *op. cit.* pp. 208-9.

more easily acquired and safely applied, if they are in possession of more philosophical knowledge. They can be judges, advocates, preachers and physicians only for a few hours each day; but in these and all the remainder of the day they are men, and have need of other sciences. In short, you must instruct me how this is to be brought home to students. Printed injunctions, laws, regulations— these are even worse than bread and butter study itself." [1]

A Minister of Education who thus ranks philosophy above professional studies, and both as more important than all academic machinery, holds his office by divine right.

[1] *Op. cit.* p. 219.

PREFACE TO THE FIRST EDITION

DETAILED discussion of the *Prefaces* is not advisable. The problems which they raise can best be treated in the order in which they come up in the *Critique* itself. I shall dwell only on the minor incidental difficulties of the text, and on those features in Kant's exposition which are peculiar to the *Prefaces*, or which seem helpful in the way of preliminary orientation. I shall first briefly restate the argument of the *Preface* to the first edition, and then add the necessary comment.

Human reason is ineradicably metaphysical. It is haunted by questions which, though springing from its very nature, none the less transcend its powers. Such a principle, for instance, as that of causality, in carrying us to more and more remote conditions, forces us to realise that by such regress our questions can never be answered. However far we recede in time, and however far we proceed in space, we are still no nearer to a final answer to our initial problems, and are therefore compelled to take refuge in postulates of a different kind, such, for instance, as that there must be a first unconditioned cause from which the empirical series of causes and effects starts, or that space is capable of existing as a completed whole. But these assumptions plunge reason in darkness and involve it in contradictions. They are the sources of all the troubles of the warring schools. Error lies somewhere concealed in them—the more thoroughly concealed that they surpass the limits of possible experience. Until such error has been detected and laid bare, metaphysical speculation must remain the idlest of all tasks.

In the latter part of the eighteenth century metaphysics had fallen, as Kant here states, into disrepute. The wonderful success with which the mathematical and natural sciences were being developed served only to emphasise by contrast the ineffectiveness of the metaphysical disciplines. Indifference to philosophy was the inevitable outcome, and was due, not to levity, but to the matured judgment of the age, which refused to be any longer put off with such pretended

8

knowledge. But since the philosophical sciences aim at that knowledge which, if attainable, we should be least willing to dispense with, the failure of philosophy is really a summons to reason to take up anew the most difficult of all its tasks. It must once and for all determine either the possibility or the impossibility of metaphysics. It must establish

" . . . a tribunal which will assure to reason its lawful claims, and which will also be able to dismiss all groundless pretensions, not by despotic decrees, but in accordance with its own eternal and unalterable laws. This tribunal is no other than the *Critique of Pure Reason*." [1] "Our age is, in especial degree, the age of criticism (*Kritik*), and to such criticism everything must submit. Religion, through its sanctity, and law-giving, through its majesty, may seek to exempt themselves from it. But they then awaken just suspicion, and cannot claim the sincere respect which reason accords only to that which has been able to sustain the test of free and open examination." [2]

As has already been emphasised in the preceding historical sketch, Kant had learnt to trust the use of reason, and was a rationalist by education, temperament, and conviction. He here classifies philosophies as dogmatic and sceptical; and under the latter rubric he includes all empirical systems. 'Empiricism' and 'scepticism' he interprets as practically synonymous terms. The defect of the dogmatists is that they have not critically examined their methods of procedure, and in the absence of an adequate distinction between appearance and reality have interpreted the latter in terms of the former. The defect of the empiricists and sceptics is that they have misrepresented the nature of the faculty of reason, ignoring its claims and misreading its functions, and accordingly have gone even further astray than their dogmatic opponents. All knowledge worthy of the name is *a priori* knowledge. It possesses universality and necessity, and as such must rest on pure reason. Wherever there is science, there is an element of pure reason. Whether or not pure reason can also extend to the unconditioned is the question which decides the possibility of constructive metaphysics. This is what Kant means when he declares that the *Critique* is a criticism of the power of reason, in respect of all knowledge after which it may strive independently of experience. Pure reason is the subject-matter of the enquiry; it is also the instrument through which the enquiry is made.[3] Nothing empirical or merely hypothetical has any place in it, either as subject-matter or as method of argument.

From this position Kant draws several important conse-

[1] A v.-vi.　　　[2] A v. *n.*　　　[3] Cf. above on title, pp. 2-3.

quences. First, since pure reason means that faculty whereby we gain knowledge independently of all experience, it can be isolated and its whole nature exhaustively determined. Indeed pure reason (Kant seeks to prove) is so perfect a unity that if " its principle " should be found insufficient to the solution of a single one of all the questions which are presented to it by its own nature, we should be justified in forthwith rejecting it as also incompetent to answer with complete certainty any one of the other questions. In metaphysics it must be either all or nothing,[1] either final and complete certainty or else absolute failure.

"While I am saying this I can fancy that I detect in the face of the reader an expression of indignation mingled with contempt at pretensions seemingly so arrogant and vainglorious ; and yet they are incomparably more moderate than the claims of all those writers who on the lines of the usual programme profess to prove the simple nature of the soul or the necessity of a first beginning of the world."[2]

In so doing they pretend to define realities which lie beyond the limits of possible experience ; the *Critique* seeks only to deal with that faculty of reason which manifests itself to us within our own minds. Formal logic shows how completely and systematically the simple acts of reason can be enumerated. Aristotle created this science of logic complete at a stroke. Kant professes to have established an equally final metaphysics ; and as logic is not a science proper, but rather a propaedeutic to all science, metaphysics, thus interpreted, is the only one of all the sciences which can immediately attain to such completeness.

" For it is nothing but the inventory of all our possessions through pure reason, systematically arranged. In this field nothing can escape us. What reason produces entirely out of itself cannot lie concealed, but is brought to light by reason itself immediately the common principle has been discovered."[3]

Secondly, the *Critique* also claims certainty. With the removal of everything empirical, and the reduction of its subject-matter to pure reason, all mere opinion or hypothesis is likewise eliminated. Probabilities or hypotheses can have no place in a *Critique of Pure Reason*.[4] Everything must be derived according to *a priori* principles from pure conceptions in which there is no intermixture of experience or any special intuition.

This *Preface* to the first edition, considered as introductory

[1] Cf. below, pp. 543, 576-7. [2] A vii.-viii.
[3] A xiv. [4] Cf. below, pp. 543 ff.

to the *Critique*, is misleading for two reasons. First, because in it Kant is preoccupied almost exclusively with the problems of metaphysics in the strict ontological sense, that is to say, with the problems of the *Dialectic*. The problems of the *Analytic*, which is the very heart of the *Critique*, are almost entirely ignored. They are, it is true, referred to in A x-xi, but the citation is quite externally intercalated; it receives no support or extension from the other parts of the *Preface*. This results in a second defect, namely, that Kant fails to indicate the more empirical features of his new Critical standpoint. Since ultimate reality is supersensuous, metaphysics, as above conceived, can have no instrument save pure reason. The subjects of its enquiry, God, freedom, and immortality, if they are to be known at all, can be determined only through *a priori* speculation. This fact, fundamental and all-important for Kant, was completely ignored in the popular eclectic philosophies of the time. They professed to derive metaphysical conclusions from empirical evidence. They substituted, as Kant has pointed out,[1] "a physiology of the human understanding" for the Critical investigation of the claims of reason, and anthropology for ethics. They were blind to the dogmatism of which they are thereby guilty. They assumed those very points which most call for proof, namely, that reason is adequate to the solution of metaphysical problems, and that all existence is so fundamentally of one type that we can argue from the sensuous to the supersensuous, from appearance to reality. When they fell into difficulties, they pleaded the insufficiency of human reason, and yet were all the while unquestioningly relying upon it in the drawing of the most tremendous inferences. Such, for instance, are the assumptions which underlie Moses Mendelssohn's contention that since animals as well as men agree in the apprehension of space, it must be believed to be absolutely real.[2] These assumptions also determine Priestley's assertion that though every event has its cause, there is one causeless happening, namely, the creative act to which the existence of the world is due.[3] On such terms, metaphysics is too patently easy to be even plausible. "Indifference, doubt, and, ir final issue, severe criticism, are truer signs of a profound habit of thought."[4] The matter of experience affords no data for metaphysical inference. In the *a priori* forms of experience, and there alone, can meta-

[1] Cf. A 86 = B 118-19.
[2] Morgenstunden; *Gesammelte Schriften*, 1863 edition, ii. pp. 246, 288. Cf. below, pp. 160-1.
[3] Cited by R. A. Sigsbee, *Philosophisches System Joseph Priestleys* (1912), p. 33.
[4] A v. *n.*

physics hope to find a basis, if any basis is really discoverable.

This is Kant's reason for so emphatically insisting that the
problem of the *Critique* is to determine "how much we can
hope to achieve by reason, when all the material and assistance
of experience is taken away."[1]   But in keeping only this one
point in view Kant greatly misrepresents the problems and
scope of the *Critique*.   Throughout the *Preface* he speaks the
language of the *Aufklärung*.   Even in the very act of limiting
the scope of reason, he overstresses its powers, and omits
reference to its empirical conditions.   It is well to contrast
this teaching with such a passage as the following :

"The position of all genuine idealists from the Eleatics to Berkeley
is contained in this formula : 'All cognition through the senses and
experience is nothing but mere illusion, and only in the ideas of
pure understanding and Reason is there truth.'   The fundamental
principle ruling all my idealism, on the contrary, is this : 'All cognition of things solely from pure understanding or pure Reason is
nothing but mere illusion, and only in experience is there truth.'"[2]

But that passage is equally inadequate as a complete expression
of Kant's Critical philosophy.   The truth lies midway between
it and the teaching of the *Preface* to the first edition.   Pure
reason is as defective an instrument of knowledge as is factual
experience.   Though the primary aim of metaphysics is to
determine our relation to the absolutely real, and though that
can only be done by first determining the nature and possible
scope of *a priori* principles, such principles are found on
investigation to possess only empirical validity.   The central
question of the *Critique* thus becomes the problem of the
validity of their *empirical* employment.   The interrelation of
these two problems, that of the *a priori* and that of experience, and Kant's attitude towards them, cannot be considered
till later.   The defects of the *Preface* to the first edition are
in part corrected by the extremely valuable *Preface* substituted
in the second edition.   But some further points in this first
Preface must be considered.

Prescribed by the very nature of reason itself.[3]—Metaphysics
exists as a "natural disposition," and its questions are not
therefore merely artificial.

"As natural disposition (*Naturanlage*) . . . metaphysics is real.
For human reason, without being moved merely by the idle desire for
extent and variety of knowledge, proceeds impetuously, driven on by

---

[1] A viii.   [2] *Prolegomena, Anhang,* Trans. of Mahaffy and Bernard, p. 147.
[3] A 1.

an inward need, to questions such as cannot be answered by any empirical employment of reason, or by principles thence derived. Thus in all men, as soon as their reason has become ripe for speculation, there has always existed and will always continue to exist some kind of metaphysics." [1]

Hence results what Kant entitles *transcendental illusion.*

"The cause of this transcendental illusion is that there are fundamental rules and maxims for the employment of Reason, subjectively regarded as a faculty of human knowledge, and that these rules and maxims have all the appearance of being objective principles. We take the subjective necessity of a connection of our concepts, *i.e.* a connection necessitated for the advantage of the understanding, for an objective necessity in the determination of things in themselves. This is an illusion which can no more be prevented than we can prevent the sea from appearing higher at the horizon than at the shore, since we see it through higher light rays ; or to cite a still better example, than the astronomer can prevent the moon from appearing larger at its rising, although he is not deceived by this illusion. . . . There exists, then, a natural and unavoidable dialectic of pure Reason, not one in which a bungler might entangle himself through lack of knowledge, or one which some sophist has artificially invented to confuse thinking people, but one which is inseparable from human Reason, and which, even after its deceiving power has been exposed, will not cease to play tricks with it and continually to entrap it into momentary aberrations that will ever and again call for correction." [2]

Dogmatism. [3]—According to Kant there are three possible standpoints in philosophy—the dogmatic, the sceptical, and the critical. All preceding thinkers come under the first two heads. A dogmatist is one who assumes that human reason can comprehend ultimate reality, and who proceeds upon this assumption. He does not, before proceeding to construct a metaphysics, enquire whether it is possible. Dogmatism expresses itself (to borrow Vaihinger's convenient mode of definition [4]) through three factors—*rationalism, realism,* and *transcendence.* Descartes and Leibniz are typical dogmatists. As rationalists they hold that it is possible to determine from pure *a priori* principles the ultimate nature of God, of the soul, and of the material universe. They are realists in that they assert that by human thought the complete nature of objective reality can be determined. They also adopt the attitude of transcendence. Through pure thought they go out beyond the sensible and determine the supersensuous.

---

[1] B 21. Cf. *Prolegomena,* § 60 ff., and below, pp. 427-9, 552.
[2] A 297-8 = B 353-5. Cf. below, pp. 427-9.   [3] A iii.   [4] i. p. 50.

Scepticism (Kant, as above stated,[1] regards it as being in effect equivalent to empiricism) may similarly be defined through the three terms, *empiricism, subjectivism, immanence.* A sceptic can never be a rationalist. He must reduce know-ledge to sense-experience. For this reason also his knowledge is infected by subjective conditions; through sensation we cannot hope to determine the nature of the objectively real. This attitude is also that of immanence; knowledge is limited to the sphere of sense-experience. Criticism has similarly its three constitutive factors, *rationalism, subjectivism, im-manence.* It agrees with dogmatism in maintaining that only through *a priori* principles can true knowledge be obtained. Such knowledge is, however, subjective[2] in its origin, and for that reason it is also only of immanent application; knowledge is possible only in the sphere of sense-experience. Dogmatism claims that knowledge arises independently of experience and extends beyond it. Em-piricism holds that knowledge arises out of sense-experience and is valid only within it. Criticism teaches that knowledge arises independently of particular experience but is valid only for experience.

The following passages in the *Methodology* give Kant's view of the historical and relative values of the two false methods:

"The sceptic is the taskmaster who constrains the dogmatic reasoner to develop a sound critique of the understanding and reason. When the latter has been made to advance thus far, he need fear no further challenge, since he has learned to distinguish his real possessions from that which lies entirely beyond them, and to which he can therefore lay no claim. . . . Thus the sceptical procedure cannot of itself yield any satisfying answer to the questions of reason, but none the less it prepares the way by awakening its circumspection, and by indicating the radical measures which are adequate to secure it in its legitimate possessions."[3] "The first step in matters of pure reason, marking its infancy, is *dogmatic*. The second step is *sceptical*, and indicates that experience has rendered our judgment wiser and more circumspect. But a third step, such as can be taken only by fully matured judgment, is now necessary. . . . This is not the censorship but the critique of reason, whereby not its present bounds but its determinate [and necessary] limits, not its ignorance on this or that point, but in regard to

---

[1] P. 9.
[2] This statement, as we shall find, calls for modification. Kant's Critical position is more correctly described as phenomenalism than as subjectivism. Cf. above, pp. xlv-vii; below, p. 270 ff.
[3] A 769 = B 797.

all possible questions of a certain kind, are demonstrated from principles, and not merely arrived at by way of conjecture. Scepticism is thus a resting-place for human reason, where it can reflect upon its dogmatic wanderings and make survey of the region in which it finds itself, so that for the future it may be able to choose its path with more certainty. But it is no dwelling-place for permanent settlement. That can be obtained only through perfect certainty in our knowledge, alike of the objects themselves and of the limits within which all our knowledge of objects is enclosed."[1]

Locke.[2]—Cf. A 86 = B 119; A 270 = B 327; B 127.

On the unfavourable contrast between mathematics and metaphysics.[3]—Cf. *Ueber die Deutlichkeit der Grundsätze* (1764), *erste Betrachtung*, and below, pp. 40, 563 ff.

The age of criticism.[4]—Kant considered himself as contributing to the further advance of the eighteenth century Enlightenment.[5] In view, however, of the contrast between eighteenth and nineteenth century thought, and of the real affiliations and ultimate consequences of Kant's teaching, it seems truer to regard the Critical philosophy as at once completing and transcending the *Aufklärung*. Kant breaks with many of its most fundamental assumptions.

The Critique of Pure Reason.[6]—Kant here defines the *Critique* as directed upon pure reason.[7] Further it is a criticism of knowledge which is "independent of all experience," or, as Kant adds "free from all experience." Such phrases, in this context, really mean *transcendent*. The *Critique* is here taken as being a Critical investigation of transcendent metaphysics, of its sources, scope, and limits.[8]

Opinion or hypothesis not permissible.[9]—Cf. below, p. 543 ff.

I know no enquiries, etc.[10]—The important questions raised by this paragraph are discussed below, p. 235 ff.

Jean Terrasson (1670–1750).[11]—The quotation is from his work posthumously published (1754), and translated from the French by Frau Gottsched under the title *Philosophie nach ihrem allgemeinen Einflusse auf alle Gegenstände des Geistes und der Sitten* (1762). Terrasson is also referred to by Kant in his *Anthropologie*, §§ 44 and 77. Terrasson would seem to be the author of the *Traité de l'infini créé* which has been falsely ascribed to Malebranche. I have translated this latter treatise in the *Philosophical Review* (July 1905).

Such a system of pure speculative reason.[12]—The relation in

1 A 761 = B 789-90. Cf. Sections I.-III. in the *Methodology.*
2 A iii.　　　　　3 A v. *n.*　　　　4 A v. *n.*
5 Cf. Kant's *Beantwortung der Frage: Was heist Aufklärung?* 1784.
6 A v.　　　　7 Cf. above, pp. 2-3.
8 Cf. above, pp. xliv-v; below, pp. 19, 33, 56, 66 ff.
9 A ix.　　10 A x.-xi.　　11 A xii.-xiii.　　12 A xv.

which this system would stand to the *Critique* is discussed below, pp. 71-2.   Speculative does not with Kant mean transcendent, but merely theoretical as opposed to practical. Cf. B 25, A 15 = B 29, A 845 = B 873.

Under the title : Metaphysics of Nature.[1]—No such work, at least under this title, was ever completed by Kant.   In the Kantian terminology " nature " signifies " all that is."   Cf. below, p. 580.

[1] A xv.   Cf. below, p. 66-7.

PREFACE TO THE SECOND EDITION

I SHALL again give a brief explanatory paraphrase, before proceeding to detailed comment. The main points of the preface of the first edition are repeated. "Metaphysics soars above all teaching of experience, and rests on concepts only. In it reason has to be her own pupil."[1] But Kant immediately proceeds to a further point. That logic should have attained the secure method of science is due to its limitation to the *a priori* form of knowledge. For metaphysics security of method is far more difficult, since it *"has to deal not with itself alone, but also with objects."*[2]

The words which I have italicised form a very necessary correction of the first edition preface, according to which the *Critique* would seem to "treat only of reason and its pure thinking." A further difference follows. The second edition preface, in thus emphasising the objective aspect of the problem, is led to characterise in a more complete manner the method to be followed in the Critical enquiry. How can the *Critique*, if it is concerned, as both editions agree in insisting, only with the *a priori* which originates in human reason, solve the specifically metaphysical problem, viz. that of determining the independently real? How can an idea in us refer to, and constitute knowledge of, an object? The larger part of the preface to the second edition is devoted to the Critical solution of this problem. The argument of the *Dialectic* is no longer emphasised at the expense of the *Analytic*.

Kant points out that as a matter of historical fact each of the two rational sciences, mathematics and physics, first entered upon the assured path of knowledge by a sudden revolution, and by the adoption of a method which in its general characteristics is common to both. This method consists, not in being led by nature as in leading-strings, but in interrogating nature in accordance with what reason

---

[1] B xiv.   [2] B ix.

produces on its own plan. The method of the geometrician does not consist in the study of figures presented to the senses. That would be an empirical (in Kant's view, sceptical) method. Geometrical propositions could not then be regarded as possessing universality and necessity. Nor does the geometrician employ a dogmatic method, that of studying the mere conception of a figure. By that means no new knowledge could ever be attained. The actual method consists in interpreting the sensible figures through conceptions that have been rigorously defined, and in accordance with which the figures have been constructively generated. The first discovery of this method, by Thales or some other Greek, was "far more important than the discovery of the passage round the celebrated Cape of Good Hope."[1]

Some two thousand years elapsed before Galileo formulated a corresponding method for physical science. He relied neither on mere observation nor on his own conceptions. He determined the principles according to which alone concordant phenomena can be admitted as laws of nature, and then by experiment compelled nature to answer the questions which these principles suggest. Here again the method is neither merely empirical nor purely dogmatic. It possesses the advantages of both.

Metaphysics is ripe for a similar advance. It must be promoted to the rank of positive science by the transforming power of an analogous method. The fundamental and distinguishing characteristic of mathematical and physical procedure is the legislative power to which reason lays claim. Such procedure, if generalised and extended, will supply the required method of the new philosophy. Reason must be regarded as self-legislative in all the domains of our possible knowledge. *Objects must be viewed as conforming to human thought, not human thought to the independently real.* This is the "hypothesis" to which Kant has given the somewhat misleading title, "Copernican."[2] The *method of procedure* which it prescribes is, he declares, analogous to that which was followed by Copernicus, and will be found to be as revolutionary in its consequences. In terms of this hypothesis a complete and absolutely certain metaphysics, valid now and for all time, can be created at a stroke. The earliest and oldest enterprise of the human mind will achieve a new beginning. Metaphysics, the mother of all the sciences, will renew her youth, and will equal in assurance, as she surpasses in dignity, the offspring of her womb.

From this new standpoint Kant develops phenomenalism

[1] B xi.   [2] Cf. below, pp. 22-5.

on rationalist lines. He professes to prove that though our knowledge is only of appearances, it is conditioned by *a priori* principles. His "Copernican hypothesis," so far from destroying positive science, is, he claims, merely a philosophical extension of the method which it has long been practising. Since all science worthy of the name involves *a priori* elements, it can be accounted for only in terms of the new hypothesis. Only if objects are regarded as conforming to our forms of intuition, and to our modes of conception, can they be anticipated by *a priori* reasoning. Science can be *a priori* just because, properly understood, it is not a rival of metaphysics, and does not attempt to define the absolutely real.

But such a statement at once suggests what may at first seem a most fatal objection. Though the new standpoint may account for the *a priori* in experience and science, it can be of no avail in metaphysics. If the *a priori* concepts have a mental origin, they can have no validity for the independently real. If we can know only what we ourselves originate, things in themselves must be unknown, and metaphysics must be impossible. But in this very consequence the new hypothesis first reveals its full advantages. It leads to an interpretation of metaphysics which is as new and as revolutionary[1] as that which it gives to natural science. Transcendent metaphysics is indeed impossible, but in harmony with man's practical and moral vocation, its place is more efficiently taken by an immanent metaphysics on the one hand, and by a metaphysics of ethics on the other. Together these constitute the new and final philosophy which Kant claims to have established by his Critical method. Its chief task is to continue "that noblest enterprise of antiquity,"[2] the distinguishing of appearances from things in themselves. The unconditioned is that which alone will satisfy speculative reason; its determination is the ultimate presupposition of metaphysical enquiry. But so long as the empirical world is regarded as true reality, totality or unconditionedness cannot possibly be conceived—is, indeed, inherently self-contradictory. On the new hypothesis there is no such difficulty. By the proof that things in themselves are unknowable, a sphere is left open within which the unconditioned can be sought. For though this sphere is closed to speculative reason, the unconditioned can be determined from data yielded by reason in its practical activity. The hypothesis which at first seems to destroy metaphysics proves on examination to be its necessary presupposition. The "Copernican hypothesis" which conditions science will also account for metaphysics properly conceived.

---

[1] Cf. above, p. lvi; below, p. 571 ff.   [2] *Dissertation*, § 7.

Upon this important point Kant dwells at some length. Even the negative results of the *Critique* are, he emphasises, truly positive in their ultimate consequences. The dogmatic extension of speculative reason really leads to the narrowing of its employment, for the principles of which it then makes use involve the subjecting of things in themselves to the limiting conditions of sensibility. All attempts to construe the unconditioned in terms that will satisfy reason are by such procedure ruled out from the very start. To demonstrate this is the fundamental purpose and chief aim of the *Critique*. Space and time are merely forms of sensuous intuition; the concepts of understanding can yield knowledge only in their connection with them. Though the concepts in their purity possess a quite general meaning, this is not sufficient to constitute knowledge. The conception of causality, for instance, necessarily involves the notion of time-sequence; apart from time it is the bare, empty, and entirely unspecified conception of a sufficient ground. Similarly, the category of substance signifies the permanent in time and space; as a form of pure reason it has a quite indefinite meaning signifying merely that which is always a subject and never a predicate. In the absence of further specification, it remains entirely problematic in its reference. The fact, however, that the categories of the understanding possess, in independence of sensibility, even this quite general significance is all-important. Originating in pure reason they have a wider scope than the forms of sense, and enable us to conceive, though not to gain knowledge of, things in themselves.[1] Our dual nature, as being at once sensuous and supersensuous, opens out to us the apprehension of both.

Kant illustrates his position by reference to the problem of the freedom of the will. As thought is wider than sense, and reveals to us the existence of a noumenal realm, we are enabled to reconcile belief in the freedom of the will with the mechanism of nature. We can recognise that within the phenomenal sphere everything without exception is causally determined, and yet at the same time maintain that the whole order of nature is grounded in noumenal conditions. We can assert of one and the same being that its will is subject to the necessity of nature and that it is free— mechanically determined in its visible actions, free in its real supersensible existence. We have, indeed, no knowledge of the soul, and therefore cannot assert on theoretical grounds that it possesses any such freedom. The very possibility of freedom transcends our powers of comprehension. The

---

[1] All these assertions call for later modification and restatement.

proof that it can at least be conceived without contradiction
is, however, all-important. For otherwise no arguments from
the nature of the moral consciousness could be of the least
avail; before a palpable contradiction every argument is
bound to give way. Now, for the first time, the doctrine of
morals and the doctrine of nature can be independently
developed, without conflict, each in accordance with its own
laws. The same is true in regard to the existence of God
and the immortality of the soul. By means of the Critical
distinction between the empirical and the supersensible worlds,
*these conceptions are now for the first time rendered possible of
belief.* "I had to remove *knowledge*, in order to make room
for *belief*."[1] "This loss affects only the *monopoly of the schools*,
in no respect the *interests of humanity*."[2]

Lastly, Kant emphasises the fact that the method of the
Critique must be akin to that of dogmatism. It must be
rational *a priori*. To adopt any other method of procedure
is "to shake off the fetters of *science* altogether, and thus
to change work into play, certainty into opinion, philosophy
into philodoxy."[3] And Kant repeats the claims of the preface
of the first edition as to the completeness and finality of his
system. "This system will, as I hope, maintain through the
future this same unchangeableness."[4]

Logic.[5]—For Kant's view of the logic of Aristotle as complete and perfect, cf. below, pp. 184-5. Kant compares metaphysics to mathematics and physics on the one hand, and to
formal logic on the other. The former show the possibility of
attaining to the secure path of science by a sudden and single
revolution; the latter demonstrates the possibility of creating
a science complete and entire at a stroke. Thanks to the
new Critical method, metaphysics may be enabled, Kant
claims, to parallel both achievements at once.

Theoretical and practical reason.[6]—Such comment as is
necessary upon this distinction is given below. Cf. p. 569 ff.

**Hitherto it has been supposed that all knowledge must conform
to the objects.**[7]—This statement is historically correct. That
assumption did actually underlie one and all of the pre-
Kantian philosophies. At the same time, it is true that Kant's
phenomenalist standpoint is partially anticipated by Hume,
by Malebranche and by Leibniz, especially by the first named.
Hume argues that to condemn knowledge on the ground that
it can never copy or truly reveal any external reality is to
misunderstand its true function. Our sense perceptions
and our general principles are so determined by nature

---

[1] B xxx.   [2] B xxxii.   [3] B xxxvii.   [4] B xxxviii.
[5] B vii.   [6] B viii.   [7] B xvi.

as to render feasible only a practical organisation of life. When we attempt to derive from them a consistent body of knowledge, failure is the inevitable result.[1]   Malebranche, while retaining the absolutist view of conceptual knowledge, propounds a similar theory of sense-perception.[2]   Our perceptions are, as he shows, permeated through and through, from end to end, with illusion.   Such illusions justify themselves by their practical usefulness, but they likewise prove that theoretical insight is not the purpose of our sense-experience.   Kant's Copernican hypothesis consists in great part of an extension of this view to our conceptual, scientific knowledge.   But he differs both from Malebranche and from Hume in that he develops his phenomenalism on rationalist lines.   He professes to show that though our knowledge is only of the phenomenal, it is conditioned by *a priori* principles.   The resulting view of the distinction between appearance and reality has kinship with that of Leibniz.[3] The phenomena of science, though only appearances, are none the less *bene fundata*.   Our scientific knowledge, though not equivalent to metaphysical apprehension of the ultimately real, can be progressively developed by scientific methods.

The two "parts" of metaphysics.[4]—Kant is here drawing the important distinction, which is one result of his new standpoint, between *immanent* and *transcendent* metaphysics.   It is unfortunate that he does not do so in a more explicit manner, with full recognition of its novelty and of its far-reaching significance.   Many ambiguities in his exposition here and elsewhere would then have been obviated.[5]

The unconditioned which Reason postulates in all things by themselves, by necessity and by right.[6]—Points are here raised the discussion of which must be deferred.   Cf. below, pp. 429-31, 433-4, 558-61.

The Critique is a treatise on method, not a system of the science itself.[7]—Cf. A xv.; B xxxvi.; and especially A 11 = B 24, below pp. 71-2.

The Copernican hypothesis.[8]—Kant's comparison of his new hypothesis to that of Copernicus has generally been misunderstood.   The reader very naturally conceives the Copernican revolution in terms of its main ultimate consequence, the reduction of the earth from its proud position of central pre-eminence.   But that does not bear the least

---

[1] Cf. above, pp. xxvi-vii; below, pp. 594-5.
[2] Cf. "Malebranche's Theory of the Perception of Distance and Magnitude," in *British Journal of Psychology* (1905), i. pp. 191-204.
[3] Cf. below, pp. 143 ff., 604.   [4] B xviii.-xix.   [5] Cf. below, pp. 33, 56, 66 ff.
[6] B xx.   [7] B xxii.   [8] B xvi.; B xxii. *n.*

analogy to the intended consequences of the Critical philosophy.   The direct opposite is indeed true.   Kant's hypothesis is inspired by the avowed purpose of neutralising the
naturalistic implications of the Copernican astronomy.   His
aim is nothing less than the firm establishment of what
may perhaps be described as a Ptolemaic, anthropocentric
metaphysics.   Such naturalistic philosophy as that of Hume
may perhaps be described as Copernican, but the Critical
philosophy, as humanistic, has genuine kinship with the Greek
standpoint.

Even some of Kant's best commentators have interpreted
the analogy in the above manner.[1]   It is so interpreted by
T. H. Green[2] and by J. Hutchison Stirling.[3]   Caird in his
Critical Philosophy of Kant makes not the least mention of the
analogy, probably for the reason that while reading it in the
same fashion as Green, he recognised the inappropriateness
of the comparison as thus taken.   The analogy is stated in
typically ambiguous fashion by Lange[4] and by Höffding.[5]
S. Alexander, while very forcibly insisting upon the Ptolemaic
character of the Kantian philosophy, also endorses this
interpretation in the following terms :

"It is very ironical that Kant himself signalised the revolution
which he believed himself to be effecting as a Copernican revolution.
But there is nothing Copernican in it except that he believed it to be
a revolution. If every change is Copernican which reverses the
order of the terms with which it deals, which declares A to depend
on B when B had before been declared to depend on A, then Kant
—who believed that he had reversed the order of dependence of mind
and things—was right in saying that he effected a Copernican revolution. But he was not right in any other sense. For his revolution,
so far as it was one, was accurately anti-Copernican."[6]

As the second edition preface is not covered by the
published volumes of Vaihinger's *Commentary*, the point has
not been taken up by him.

Now Kant's own statements are entirely unambiguous and
do not justify any such interpretation as that of Green and
Alexander.   As it seems to me, they have missed the real
point of the analogy.   The misunderstanding would never
have been possible save for our neglect of the scientific

---

[1] Watson's *The Philosophy of Kant Explained* (p. 37) is the only work in
which I have found correct and unambiguous indication of the true interpretation
of Kant's analogy.

[2] *Prolegomena to Ethics*, bk i. ch. i. § 11.

[3] *Text-Book to Kant* (1881), p. 29.

[4] *History of Materialism*, Eng. transl., ii. pp. 156, 158, 237.

[5] *Geschichte der neueren Philosophie* (1896), ii. p. 64.

[6] *Hibbert Journal*, October 1909, p. 49.

classics. Kant must have had first-hand acquaintance with Copernicus' *De Revolutionibus*, and the comparison which he draws assumes similar knowledge on the part of his readers. Copernicus by his proof of the "hypothesis" (his own term) of the earth's motion sought only to achieve a more harmonious ordering of the Ptolemaic universe. And as thus merely a simplification of the traditional cosmology, his treatise could fittingly be dedicated to the reigning Pope. The sun upon which our terrestrial life depends was still regarded as uniquely distinct from the fixed stars; and our earth was still located in the central region of a universe that was conceived in the traditional manner as being single and spherical. Giordano Bruno was the first, a generation later, to realise the revolutionary consequences to which the new teaching, consistently developed, must inevitably lead. It was he who first taught what we have now come to regard as an integral part of Copernicus' revolution, the doctrine of innumerable planetary systems side by side with one another in infinite space.

Copernicus' argument starts from the Aristotelian principle of relative motion. To quote Copernicus' exact words:

"All apprehended change of place is due to movement either of the observed object or of the observer, or to differences in movements that are occurring simultaneously in both. For if the observed object and the observer are moving in the same direction with equal velocity, no motion can be detected. Now it is from the earth that we visually apprehend the revolution of the heavens. If, then, any movement is ascribed to the earth, that motion will generate the appearance of itself in all things which are external to it, though as occurring in the opposite direction, as if everything were passing across the earth. This will be especially true of the daily revolution. For it seems to seize upon the whole world, and indeed upon everything that is around the earth, though not upon the earth itself. . . . As the heavens, which contain and cover everything, are the common locus of things, it is not at all evident why it should be to the containing rather than to the contained, to the located rather than to the locating, that a motion is to be ascribed."[1]

The apparently objective movements of the fixed stars and of the sun are mere appearances, due to the projection of our own motion into the heavens.

"The first and highest of all the spheres is that of the fixed stars, self-containing and all-containing, and consequently immobile, in short the locus of the universe, by relation to which the motion and position of all the other heavenly bodies have to be reckoned."[2]

---

[1] *De Revolutionibus*, I. v.   [2] *Ibid.* I. x.

Now it is this doctrine, and this doctrine alone, to which Kant is referring in the passages before us, namely, Copernicus' hypothesis of a subjective explanation of apparently objective motions. And further, in thus comparing his Critical procedure to that of Copernicus, he is concerned more with the positive than with the negative consequences of their common hypothesis. For it is chiefly from the point of view of the *constructive* parts of the *Aesthetic, Analytic,* and *Dialectic* that the comparison is formulated. By means of the Critical hypothesis Kant professes on the one hand to account for our scientific knowledge, and on the other to safeguard our legitimate metaphysical aspirations. The spectator projects his own motion into the heavens; human reason legislates for the domain of natural science. The sphere of the fixed stars is proved to be motionless; things in themselves are freed from the limitations of space and time. "Copernicus dared, in a manner contradictory of the senses but yet true, to seek the observed movements, not in the heavenly bodies, but in the spectator."[1]

In view of Kant's explicit elimination of all *hypotheses* from the *Critique*[2] the employment of that term would seem to be illegitimate. He accordingly here states that though in the *Preface* his Critical theory is formulated as an hypothesis only, in the *Critique* itself its truth is demonstrated *a priori.*

Distinction between knowing and thinking.[3]—Since according to Critical teaching the limits of sense-experience are the limits of knowledge, the term knowledge has for Kant a very limited denotation, and leaves open a proportionately wide field for what he entitles thought. Though things in themselves are unknowable, their existence may still be recognised in thought.

---

[1] B xxii. *n.*   [2] Cf. below, p. 543 ff.
[3] B xxvi. Cf. above, pp. lv-vi, 20; below, pp. 290-1, 331, 342, 404 ff.

INTRODUCTION

I SHALL first[1] give a restatement, partly historical and partly explanatory, of Kant's main argument as contained in the enlarged *Introduction* of the second edition.

There were two stages in the process by which Kant came to full realisation of the Critical problem. There is first the problem as formulated in his letter of 1772 to Herz: how the *a priori* can yield knowledge of the independently real.[2] This, as he there states it, is an essentially metaphysical problem. It is the problem of the possibility of transcendent metaphysics. He became aware of it when reflecting upon the function which he had ascribed to intellect in the *Dissertation*. Then, secondly, this problem was immeasurably deepened, and at the same time the proper line for its treatment was discovered, through the renewed influence which Hume at some date subsequent to February 1772 exercised upon Kant's thought.[3] Hume awakened Kant to what may be called the *immanent* problem involved in the very conception of *a priori* knowledge as such. The primary problem to be solved is not how we advance by means of *a priori* ideas to the independently real, but how we are able to advance beyond a subject term to a predicate which it does not appear to contain. The problem is indeed capable of solution, just because it takes this *logical* form. Here as elsewhere, ontological questions are viewed by Kant as soluble only to the extent to which they can be restated in logical terms. Now also the enquiry becomes twofold: how and in what degree are *a priori* synthetic judgments possible, first in their employment within the empirical sphere (the problem of immanent metaphysics) and secondly in their application to things in themselves (the problem of transcendent metaphysics). The outcome of the Critical enquiry is to establish

[1] This restatement will continue up to p. 33. In pp. 33-43 I shall then give general comment on the *Introduction* as a whole. In p. 43 ff. I add the necessary detailed treatment of special points. [2] Cf. below, p. 219 ff.

[3] Cf. above, p. xxv ff.; below, pp. 61 ff., 593 ff.

the legitimacy of immanent metaphysics and the impossibility of all transcendent speculation.

The argument of Kant's *Introduction* follows the above sequence. It starts by defining the problem of metaphysical knowledge *a priori*, and through it leads up to the logical problem of the *a priori* synthetic judgment. In respect of time all knowledge begins *with* experience. But it does not therefore follow that it all arises *from* experience. Our experience may be a compound of that which we receive through impressions, and of that which pure reason supplies from itself.[1] The question as to whether or not any such *a priori* actually exists, is one that can be answered only after further enquiry. The two inseparable criteria of the *a priori* are necessity and universality. That neither can be imparted to a proposition by experience was Kant's confirmed and unquestioned belief. He inherited this view both from Leibniz and from Hume. It is one of the presuppositions of his argument. Experience can reveal only co-existence or sequence. It enables us only to assert that so far as we have hitherto observed, there is no exception to this or that rule. A generalisation, based on observation, can never possess a wider universality than the limited experience for which it stands. If, therefore, necessary and universal judgments can anywhere be found in our knowledge, the existence of an *a priori* that originates independently of experience is *ipso facto* demonstrated.[2]

The contrast between empirical and *a priori* judgments, as formulated from the dogmatic standpoint, is the most significant and striking fact in the whole range of human knowledge. *A priori* judgments claim absolute necessity. They allow of no possible exception. They are valid not only for us, but also for all conceivable beings, however different the specific conditions of their existence, whether they live on the planet Mars or in some infinitely remote region of stellar space, and no matter how diversely their bodily senses may be organised. Through these judgments a creature five feet high, and correspondingly limited by temporal conditions, legislates for all existence and for all time. Empirical judgments, on the other hand, possess only a hypothetical certainty. We recognise that they may be

---

[1] This statement is first made in the *Introduction* to the second edition. It is really out of keeping with the argument of the *Introduction* in either edition. Cf. below, pp. 39-40, 57, 85, 168, 222, 245 ff. (especially pp. 278, 288).

[2] This is the argument of the *Introduction* to the second edition. In the first edition Kant assumes without question the existence of the *a priori*. He enquires only whether it is also valid in its metaphysical employment beyond the field of possible experience

overturned through some addition to our present experience, and that they may not hold for beings on other planets or for beings with senses differently constituted. Whereas the opposite of a rational judgment is not even conceivable, the opposite of an empirical judgment is always possible. The one depends upon the inherent and inalienable nature of our thinking; the other is bound up with the contingent material of sense. The one claims absolute or metaphysical truth: the other is a merely tentative *résumé* of a limited experience.

The possibility of such *a priori* judgments had hitherto been questioned only by those who sought to deny to them all possible objective validity. Kant, as a rationalist, has no doubt as to their actual existence. In the *Introduction* to the second edition he bluntly asserts their *de facto* existence, citing as instances the propositions of mathematics and the fundamental principles of physical science. Their possibility can be accounted for through the assumption of *a priori* forms and principles.[1] But with equal emphasis he questions the validity of their *metaphysical* employment. For that is an entirely different matter. We then completely transcend the world of the senses and pass into a sphere where experience can neither guide nor correct us. In this sphere the *a priori* is illegitimately taken as being at once the source of our professed knowledge and also the sole criterion of its own claims.

This is the problem, semi-Critical, semi-dogmatic, which is formulated in the letter of 1772 to Herz.[2] What right have we to regard ideas, which as *a priori* originate from within, as being valid of things in themselves? In so doing we are assuming a pre-established harmony between our human faculties and the ultimately real; and that is an assumption which by its very nature is incapable of demonstration. The proofs offered by Malebranche and by Leibniz are themselves speculative, and consequently presuppose the conclusion which they profess to establish.[3] As above stated, Kant obtained his answer to this problem by way of the logical enquiry into the nature and conditions of *a priori* judgment.

One of the chief causes, Kant declares, why hitherto metaphysical speculation has passed unchallenged among those who practise it, is the confusion of two very different kinds of judgment, the analytic and the synthetic. Much the greater portion of what reason finds to do consists in the analysis of our concepts of objects.

---

[1] The argument of the first edition, though briefer, is substantially the same.
[2] Quoted below, pp. 219-20.   [3] Cf. below, pp. 114, 290, 590.

"As this procedure yields real knowledge *a priori*, which progresses in secure and useful fashion, reason is so far misled as surreptitiously to introduce, without itself being aware of so doing, assertions of an entirely different order, in which reason attaches to given concepts others completely foreign to them—and moreover attaches them *a priori*. And yet one does not know how reason comes to do this. This is a question which is never as much as thought of."[1]

The concepts which are analytically treated may be either empirical or *a priori*. When they are empirical, the judgments which they involve can have no wider application than the experience to which they give expression; and in any case can only reveal what has all along been thought, though confusedly, in the term which serves as subject of the proposition. They can never reveal anything different in kind from the contents actually experienced. This limitation, to which the analysis of empirical concepts is subject, was admitted by both empiricists and rationalists. The latter sought, however, to escape its consequences by basing their metaphysics upon concepts which are purely *a priori*, and which by their *a priori* content may carry us beyond the experienced. But here also Kant asserts a *non possibile*. A *priori* concepts, he seeks to show, are in all cases purely logical functions without content, and accordingly are as little capable as are empirical concepts of carrying us over to the supersensible. This is an objection which holds quite independently of that already noted, namely, that their objective validity would involve a pre-established harmony.

What, then, is the nature and what are the generating conditions of synthetic judgments that are also *a priori*? In all judgments there is a relation between subject and predicate, and that can be of two kinds. Either the predicate B belongs to the subject A, or B lies outside the sphere of the concept A though somehow connected with it. In the former case the judgment is analytic; in the latter it is synthetic. The one simply unfolds what has all along been conceived in the subject concept; the other ascribes to the concept of the subject a predicate which cannot be found in it by any process of analysis. Thus the judgment 'all bodies are extended' is analytic. The concept of body already contains that of extension, and is impossible save through it. On the other hand, the judgment 'all bodies are heavy' is synthetic. For not body as such, but only bodies which are in interaction with other bodies, are found to develop this

---

[1] A 6 = B 10.   I here follow the wording of the second edition.

property. Bodies can very well be conceived as not influencing one another in any such manner.

There is no difficulty in accounting for analytic judgments. They can all be justified by the principle of contradiction. Being analytic, they can be established *a priori*. Nor, Kant here claims, is there any difficulty in regard to synthetic judgments that are empirical. Though the predicate is not contained in the subject concept, they belong to each other (though accidentally) as parts of a given empirical whole. Experience is the *x* which lies beyond the concept A, and on which rests the possibility of the synthesis of B with A. In regard, however, to synthetic judgments which are likewise *a priori*, the matter is very different. Hitherto, both by the sensationalists and by the rationalists, all synthetic judgments have been regarded as empirical, and all *a priori* judgments as analytic. The only difference between the opposed schools lies in the relative value which they ascribe to the two types of judgment. For Hume the only really fruitful judgments are the synthetic judgments *a posteriori*; analytic judgments are of quite secondary value; they can never extend our knowledge, but only clarify its existing content. For Leibniz, on the other hand, true knowledge consists only in the analysis of our *a priori* concepts, which he regards as possessing an intrinsic and fruitful content; synthetic judgments are always empirical, and as such are purely contingent.[1]

Thus for pre-Kantian philosophy analytic is interchangeable with *a priori*, and synthetic with *a posteriori*. Kant's Critical problem arose from the startling discovery that the *a priori* and the synthetic do not exclude one another. A judgment may be synthetic and yet also *a priori*. He appears to have made this discovery under the influence of Hume, through study of the general principle of causality—every event must have a cause.[2] In that judgment there seems to be no connection of any kind discoverable between the subject (the conception of an event as something happening in time) and the predicate (the conception of another event preceding it as an originating cause); and yet we not merely ascribe the one to the other but assert that they are necessarily connected. We can conceive an event as sequent upon a preceding empty time; none the less, in physical enquiry, the causal principle is accepted as an established truth. Here, then, is a new and altogether unique type of judgment, of thoroughly

---

[1] Kant's view of the *a priori* differs from that of Leibniz in *two* respects. For Kant *a priori* concepts are merely logical functions, *i.e.* empty; and secondly, are always synthetic. Cf. above, pp. xxxiii-vi, 186, 195-6, 257-8, 290-1, 404 ff.

[2] Cf. above, pp. xxv-vii; below, pp. 61 ff., 593 ff.

paradoxical nature. So entirely is it without apparent basis, that Hume, who first deciphered its strange character, felt constrained to ascribe our belief in it to an unreasoning and merely instinctive, 'natural' habit or custom.

Kant found, however, that the paradoxical characteristics of the causal principle also belong to mathematical and physical judgments. This fact makes it impossible to accept Hume's sceptical conclusion. If even the assertion $7 + 5 = 12$ is both synthetic and *a priori*, it is obviously impossible to question the validity of judgments that possess these characteristics. But they do not for that reason any the less urgently press for explanation. Such an enquiry might not, indeed, be necessary were we concerned only with scientific knowledge. For the natural sciences justify themselves by their practical successes and by their steady unbroken development. But metaphysical judgments are also of this type; and until the conditions which make *a priori* synthetic judgment possible have been discovered, the question as to the legitimacy of metaphysical speculation cannot be decided. Such judgments are plainly mysterious, and urgently call for further enquiry.

The problem to be solved concerns the ground of our ascription to the subject concept, as necessarily belonging to it, a predicate which seems to have no discoverable relation to it. What is the unknown x on which the understanding rests in asserting the connection? It cannot be repeated experience; for the judgments in question claim necessity. Nor can such judgments be proved by means of a logical test, such as the inconceivability of the opposite. The absence of all apparent connection between subject and predicate removes that possibility. These, however, are the only two methods of proof hitherto recognised in science and philosophy. The problem demands for its solution nothing less than the discovery and formulation of an entirely novel method of proof.

The three main classes of *a priori* synthetic judgments are, Kant proceeds, the mathematical, the physical, and the metaphysical. The synthetic character of mathematical judgments has hitherto escaped observation owing to their being proved (as is required of all apodictic certainty) according to the principle of contradiction. It is therefrom inferred that they rest on the authority of that principle, and are therefore analytic. That, however, is an illegitimate inference; for though the truth of a synthetic proposition can be thus demonstrated, that can only be if another synthetic principle is first presupposed. It can never be proved that its truth, as a separate judgment, is demanded by the principle of contradiction. That 7 + 5 must equal 12 does not follow analytically from the conception of the sum of seven and five. This conception contains nothing beyond the union of both numbers into one; it does not tell us what is the single number that combines both. That five should be added to seven is no doubt implied in the conception, but not that the sum should be twelve. To discover that, we must, Kant maintains, go beyond the concepts and appeal to intuition. This is more easily recognised when we take large numbers. We then clearly perceive that, turn and twist our concepts as we may, we can never, by means of mere analysis of them, and without the help of intuition, arrive at the sum that is wanted. The fundamental propositions of geometry, the so-called axioms, are similarly synthetic, *e.g.* that the straight line between two points is the shortest. The concept 'straight' only defines direction; it says nothing as to quantity.

As an instance of a synthetic *a priori* judgment in physical science Kant cites the principle: the quantity of matter remains constant throughout all changes. In the conception of matter we do not conceive its permanency, but only its presence in the space which it fills. The opposite of the principle is thoroughly conceivable.

Metaphysics is *meant* to contain *a priori* knowledge. For it seeks to determine that of which we can have no experience, as *e.g.* that the world must have a first beginning. And if, as will be proved, our *a priori* concepts have no content, which through analysis might yield such judgments, these judgments also must be synthetic.

Here, then, we find the essential problem of pure reason. Expressed in a single formula, it runs: How are synthetic *a priori* judgments possible? To ask this question is to enquire, first, how pure mathematics is possible; secondly, how pure natural science is possible; and thirdly, how metaphysics is possible. That philosophy has hitherto remained in so vacillating a state of ignorance and contradiction is entirely due to the neglect of this problem of *a priori* synthesis. "Its solution is the question of life and death to metaphysics." Hume came nearest to realising the problem, but he discovered it in too narrow a form to appreciate its full significance and its revolutionary consequences.

"Greater firmness will be required if we are not to be deterred by inward difficulties and outward opposition from endeavouring, through application of a method entirely different from any hitherto employed, to further the growth and fruitfulness of a science indispensable to human reason—a science whose every branch may be cut away but whose root cannot be destroyed." [1]

These statements are decidedly ambiguous, owing to Kant's failure to distinguish in any uniform and definite manner between immanent and transcendent metaphysics.[2] The term metaphysics is used to cover both. Sometimes it signifies the one, sometimes the other; while in still other passages its meaning is neutral. But if we draw the distinction, Kant's answer is that a genuine and valid immanent metaphysics is for the first time rendered possible by his *Critique*; its positive content is expounded in the *Analytic*. Transcendent metaphysics, on the other hand, is criticised in the *Dialectic*; it is never possible. The existing speculative sciences transgress the limits of experience and yield only a pretence of knowledge. This determination of the limits of our possible *a priori* knowledge is the second great achievement of the *Critique*. Thus the *Critique* serves a twofold purpose. It establishes a new *a priori* system of metaphysics, and also determines on principles equally *a priori* the ultimate limits beyond which metaphysics can never advance. The two results, positive and negative, are inseparable and complementary. Neither should be emphasised to the neglect of the other.

COMMENT ON THE ARGUMENT OF KANT'S
INTRODUCTION

This *Introduction*, though a document of great historical importance as being the first definite formulation of the generating problem of Kant's new philosophy, is extremely unsatisfactory as a statement of Critical teaching. The argument is developed in terms of distinctions which are borrowed from the traditional logic, and which are not in accordance with the transcendental principles that Kant is professing to establish. This is, indeed, a criticism which may be passed upon the *Critique* as a whole. Though Kant was conscious of opening a new era in the history of philosophy, and compares his task with that of Thales, Copernicus, Bacon and Galileo, it may still be said that he never fully appreciated the greatness of his own achievement. He invariably assumes that the revolutionary consequences of his teaching will not extend to the sphere of pure logic. They concern, as he believed, only our metaphysical theories

---

[1] B 24.   [2] Cf. above, pp. xliv-xlv, 22; below, pp. 52-3, 55-6, 66 ff.

regarding the nature of reality and the determining conditions of our human experience. As formal logic prescribes the axiomatic principles according to which all thinking must proceed, its validity is not affected by the other philosophical disciplines, and is superior to the considerations that determine their truth or falsity. Its distinctions may be securely relied upon in the pioneer labours of Critical investigation. This was, of course, a very natural assumption for Kant to make; and many present-day thinkers will maintain that it is entirely justified. Should that be our attitude, we may approve of Kant's general method of procedure, but shall be compelled to dissent from much in his argument and from many of his chief conclusions. If, on the other hand, we regard formal logic as in any degree adequate only as a theory of the thought processes involved in the formation and application of the generic or class concept,[1] we shall be prepared to find that the equating of this highly specialised logic with logic in general has resulted in the adoption of distinctions which may be fairly adequate for the purposes in view of which they have been formulated, but which must break down when tested over a wider field. So far from condemning Kant for departing in his later teaching from these hard and fast distinctions, we shall welcome every sign of his increasing independence.

Kant was not, of course, so blind to the real bearing of his principles as to fail to recognise that they have logical implications.[2] He speaks of the new metaphysics which he has created as being a transcendental logic. It is very clear, however, that even while so doing he does not regard it as in any way alternative to the older logic, but as moving upon a different plane, and as yielding results which in no way conflict with anything that formal logic may teach. Indeed Kant ascribes to the traditional logic an almost sacrosanct validity. Both the general framework of the *Critique* and the arrangement of the minor subdivisions are derived from it. It is supposed to afford an adequate account of discursive thinking, and such supplement as it may receive is regarded as simply an extension of its carefully delimited field. There are two logics, that of discursive or analytic reasoning, and that of synthetic interpretation. The one is formal; the other is transcendental. The one was created by Aristotle, complete at a stroke; Kant professes to have formulated the other in an equally complete and final manner.

---

[1] Needless to say, this "Aristotelian" logic, in the traditional form in which alone Kant was acquainted with it, diverges very widely from Aristotle's actual teaching.　　　　[2] Cf. above, pp. xxxvi-ix; below, pp. 36, 181, 184-6.

This latter claim, which is expressed in the most un-qualified terms in the *Prefaces* to the first and second editions, is somewhat startling to a modern reader, and would seem to imply the adoption of an ultra-rationalistic attitude, closely akin to that of Wolff.

"In this work I have made completeness my chief aim, and I venture to assert that there is not a single metaphysical problem which has not been solved, or for the solution of which the key at least has not been supplied.   Reason is, indeed, so perfect a unity that if its principle were insufficient for the solution of even a single one of all the questions to which it itself gives birth, we should be justified in forthwith rejecting it as incompetent to answer, with perfect certainty, any one of the other questions."[1]   "Metaphysics has this singular advantage, such as falls to the lot of no other science which deals with objects (for *logic* is concerned only with the form of thought in general), that should it, through this *Critique*, be set upon the secure path of science, it is capable of acquiring exhaustive knowledge of its entire field.   It can finish its work and bequeath it to posterity as a capital that can never be added to.   For metaphysics has to deal only with principles, and with the limits of their employ-ment as determined by these principles themselves.   Since it is a fundamental science, it is under obligation to achieve this complete-ness.   We must be able to say of it: *nil actum reputans, si quid superesset agendum.*"[2]

These sanguine expectations—by no means supported by the after-history of Kant's system—are not really due to Kant's immodest over-estimate of the importance of his work. They would rather seem to be traceable, on the one hand to his continuing acceptance of rationalistic assumptions proper only to the philosophy which he is displacing, and on the other to his failure to appreciate the full extent of the revolu-tionary consequences which his teaching was destined to produce in the then existing philosophical disciplines.   Kant, like all the greatest reformers, left his work in the making. Both his results and his methods call for modification and extension in the light of the insight which they have them-selves rendered possible.   Indeed, Kant was himself constantly occupied in criticising and correcting his own acquired views ; and this is nowhere more evident than in the contrast between the teaching of this *Introduction* and that of the central portions of the *Analytic*.   But even the later ex-pressions of his maturer views reveal the persisting conflict. They betray the need for further reconstruction, even in the very act of disavowing it.   Not an additional logic, but the

---

[1] A vii.   [2] B xxiii-iv.

demonstration of the imperative need for a complete revisal of the whole body of logical science, is the first, and in many respects the chief, outcome of his Critical enquiries.

The broader bearings of the situation may perhaps be indicated as follows. If our account of Kant's awakening from his dogmatic slumber[1] be correct, it consisted in his recognition that self-evidence will not suffice to guarantee any general principle. The fundamental principles of our experience are synthetic. That is to say, their opposite is in all cases conceivable. Combining this conclusion with his previous conviction that they can never be proved by induction from observed facts, he was faced with the task of establishing rationalism upon a new and altogether novel basis. If neither empirical facts nor intuitive self-evidence may be appealed to, in what manner can proof proceed? And how can we make even a beginning of demonstration, if our very principles have themselves to be established? Principles are never self-evident, and yet principles are indispensable. Such was Kant's unwavering conviction as regards the fundamental postulates alike of knowledge and of conduct.

This is only another way of stating that Kant is the real founder of the *Coherence* theory of truth.[2] He never himself employs the term Coherence, and he constantly adopts positions which are more in harmony with a *Correspondence* view of the nature and conditions of knowledge. But all that is most vital in his teaching, and has proved really fruitful in its after-history, would seem to be in line with the positions which have since been more explicitly developed by such writers as Lotze, Sigwart, Green, Bradley, Bosanquet, Jones and Dewey, and which in their tenets all derive from Hegel's restatement of Kant's logical doctrines. From this point of view principles and facts mutually establish one another, the former proving themselves by their capacity to account for the relevant phenomena, and the latter distinguishing themselves from irrelevant accompaniments by their conformity to the principles which make insight possible. In other words, all proof conforms in general type to the hypothetical method of the natural sciences. Kant's so-called transcendental method, the method by which he establishes the validity of the categories, is itself, as we have already observed,[3] of this character. Secondly, the distinction between the empirical and the *a priori* must not be taken (as Kant himself takes it in his earlier, and occasionally even in his later utterances) as marking a distinction between two

[1] Above, pp. xxv-vii, 26; below, p. 593 ff.   [2] Cf. above, p. xxxvi ff
[3] Cf. above, pp. xxxvii-viii; below, pp. 238-42.

kinds of knowledge. They are elements inseparably involved in all knowledge. And lastly, the contrast between analysis and synthesis becomes a difference not of kind but of degree. Nothing can exist or be conceived save as fitted into a system which gives it meaning and decides·as to its truth. In the degree to which it can be studied in relative independence of the supporting system analysis will suffice ; in the degree to which it refers us to this system it calls for synthetic interpretation. But ultimately the needs of adequate understanding must constrain us to the employment of both methods of enquiry. Nothing can be known save in terms of the wider whole to which it belongs.

There is, however, one important respect in which Kant diverges in very radical fashion from the position of Hegel. The final whole to which all things must be referred is represented to us only through an " Idea," for which no corresponding reality can ever be found. The system which decides what is to be regarded as *empirically* real is the mechanical system of natural science. We have no sufficient theoretical criterion of absolute reality.

These somewhat general considerations may be made more definite if we now endeavour to determine in what specific respects the distinctions employed in the *Introduction* fail to harmonise with the central doctrines of the *Analytic*.

In the first place, Kant states his problem in reference only to the attributive judgment. The other types of relational judgment are entirely ignored. For even when he cites judgments of other relational types, such as the propositions of arithmetic and geometry, or that which gives expression to the causal axiom, he interprets them on the lines of the traditional theory of the categorical proposition. As we shall find,[1] it is with the relational categories, and consequently with the various types of relational judgment to which they give rise, that the *Critique* is alone directly concerned. Even the attributive judgment is found on examination to be of this nature. What it expresses is not the inclusion of an attribute within a given group of attributes, but the organisation of a complex manifold in terms of the dual category of substance and attribute.

Secondly, this exclusively attributive interpretation of the judgment leads Kant to draw, in his *Introduction*, a hard and fast distinction between the analytic and the synthetic proposition—a distinction which, when stated in such extreme fashion, obscures the real implications of the argument of the *Analytic*. For Kant here propounds[2] as an exhaustive

---

[1] Cf. below, pp. 176 ff., 181, 191, 257.   [2] A 6=B 10.

division the two alternatives: (*a*) inclusion of the predicate concept within the subject concept, and (*b*) the falling of the predicate concept entirely outside it. He adds, indeed, that in the latter case the two concepts may still be in some way connected with one another; but this is a concession of which he takes no account in his subsequent argument. He leaves unconsidered the third possibility, that every judgment is both analytic and synthetic. If concepts are not independent entities,[1] as Kant, in agreement with Leibniz, still continues to maintain, but can function only as members of an articulated system, concepts will be distinguishable from one another, and yet will none the less involve one another. In so far as the distinguishable elements in a judgment are directly related, the judgment may *seem* purely analytic; in so far as they are related only in an indirect manner through a number of intermediaries, they may *seem* to be purely synthetic. But in every case there is an internal articulation which is describable as synthesis, and an underlying unity that in subordinating all differences realises more adequately than any mere identity the demand for connection between subject and predicate. In other words, all judgments will, on this view, be of the relational type. Even the attributive judgment, as above noted, is no mere assertion of identity. It is always expressed in terms of the dual category of substance and attribute, connecting by a *relation* contents that as contents may be extremely diverse.

This would seem to be the view to which Kant's Critical teaching, when consistently developed, is bound to lead. For in insisting that the synthetic character of a judgment need not render it invalid, and that all the fundamental principles and most of the derivative judgments of the positive sciences are of this nature, Kant is really maintaining that the justification of a judgment is always to be looked for beyond its own boundaries in some implied context of coherent experience. But though the value of his argument lies in clear-sighted recognition of the synthetic factor in all genuine knowledge, its cogency is greatly obscured by his continued acceptance of the possibility of judgments that are purely analytic. Thus there is little difficulty in detecting the synthetic character of the proposition : all bodies are heavy. Yet the

---

[1] Leibniz's interpretation of the judgment seems to result in an atomism which is the conceptual counterpart of his metaphysical monadism (cf. Adamson, *Development of Modern Philosophy*, i. p. 77 ff. ; and my *Studies in the Cartesian Philosophy*, p. 160 ff. ; also below, p. 603). Each concept is regarded as having exclusive jurisdiction, so to speak, over a content wholly internal to itself. The various concepts are like sovereign states with no mediating tribunals capable of prescribing to them their mutual dealings. Cf. below, pp. 394-400, 418 ff.

reader has first been required to admit the analytic character of the proposition : all bodies are extended. The two propositions are really identical in logical character. Neither can be recognised as true save in terms of a comprehensive theory of physical existence. If matter must exist in a state of distribution in order that its parts may acquire through mutual attraction the property of weight, the size of a body, or even its possessing any extension whatsoever, may similarly depend upon specific conditions such as may conceivably not be universally realised. We find the same difficulty when we are called upon to decide whether the judgment $7 + 5 = 12$ is analytic or purely synthetic. Kant speaks as if the concepts of 7, 5, and 12 were independent entities, each with its own quite separate connotation. But obviously they can only be formed in the light of the various connected concepts which go to constitute our system of numeration. The proposition has meaning only when interpreted in the light of this conceptual system. It is not, indeed, a self-evident identical proposition ; but neither is the connection asserted so entirely synthetic that intuition will alone account for its possibility. That, however, brings us to the third main defect in Kant's argument.

When Kant states [1] that in synthetic judgments we require, besides the concept of the subject, something else on which the understanding can rely in knowing that a predicate, not contained in the concept, nevertheless belongs to it, he entitles this something x. In the case of empirical judgments, this x is brute experience. Such judgments, Kant implies, are *merely* empirical. No element of necessity is involved, not even in an indirect manner ; in reference to empirical judgments there is no problem of *a priori synthesis*. Now in formulating the issue in this way, Kant is obscuring the essential purpose of his whole enquiry. He may, without essential detriment to his central position, still continue to preserve a hard-and-fast distinction between analytic and synthetic judgments. In so doing he is only failing to perceive the ultimate consequences of his final results. But in viewing empirical judgments as lacking in every element of necessity, he is destroying the very ground upon which he professes to base the *a priori* validity of general principles. All judgments involve relational factors of an *a priori* character. The appeal to experience is the appeal to an implied system of nature. Only when fitted into the context yielded by such a system can an empirical proposition have meaning, and only in the light of such a presupposed system

[1] A 9 = B 13.

can its truth be determined. It can be true at all, only if it can be regarded as necessarily holding, under the same conditions, for all minds constituted like our own. Assertion of a contingent relation—as in the proposition: this horse is white—is not equivalent to contingency of assertion. Colour is a variable quality of the genus horse, but in the individual horse is necessarily determined in some particular mode. If a horse is naturally white, it is necessarily white. Though, therefore, in the above proposition, necessity receives no explicit verbal expression, it is none the less implied.

In other words, the distinction between the empirical and the *a priori* is not, as Kant inconsistently assumes in this *Introduction*, a distinction between two kinds of synthesis or judgment, but between two elements inseparably involved in every judgment. Experience is transcendentally conditioned. Judgment is in all cases the expression of a relation which implies an organised system of supporting propositions; and for the articulation of this system *a priori* factors are indispensably necessary.

But the most flagrant example of Kant's failure to live up to his own Critical principles is to be found in his doctrine of pure intuition. It represents a position which he adopted in the pre-Critical period. It is prefigured in *Ueber die Deutlichkeit der Grundsätze* (1764),[1] and in *Von dem ersten Grunde des Unterschiedes der Gegenden im Raume* (1768),[2] and is definitely expounded in the *Dissertation* (1770).[3] That Kant continued to hold this doctrine, and that he himself regarded it as an integral part of his system, does not, of course, suffice to render it genuinely Critical. As a matter of fact, it is really as completely inconsistent with his Critical standpoint as is the view of the empirical proposition which we have just been considering. An appeal to our fingers or to points[4] is as little capable, in and by itself, of justifying any *a priori* judgment as are the sense-contents of grounding an empirical judgment. Even when Kant is allowed the benefit of his own more careful statements,[5] and is taken as asserting that arithmetical propositions are based on a pure *a priori* intuition which can find only approximate expression in sensuous terms, his statements run counter to the main tendencies of his Critical teaching, as well as to the recognised methods of the mathematical sciences. Intuition may, as Poincaré and others have maintained, be an indispensable element in all mathematical concepts; it cannot afford *proof*

[1] *Erste Betrachtung*, §§ 2, 3; *dritte Betrachtung*, § 1.
[2] Cf. below, p. 162.   [3] § 12, 15 C.   [4] Cf. B 15-16.
[5] Cf. below, p. 128 ff., on Kant's views regarding arithmetical science.

of any general theorem. The conceptual system which directs our methods of decimal counting is what gives meaning to the judgment $7 + 5 = 12$; it is also what determines that judgment as true. The appeal to intuition in numerical judgments must be regarded only as a means of imaginatively realising in a concrete form the abstract relations of some such governing system, or else as a means of detecting relations not previously known. The last thing in the world which such a method can yield is universal demonstration. This is equally evident in regard to geometrical propositions. That a straight line is the shortest distance between two points, cannot be proved by any mere appeal to intuition. The judgment will hold if it can be assumed that space is Euclidean in character; and to justify that assumption it must be shown that Euclidean concepts are adequate to the interpretation of our intuitional data. Should space possess a curvature, the above proposition might cease to be universally valid. Space is not a simple, unanalysable datum. Though intuitionally apprehended, it demands for its precise determination the whole body of geometrical science.[1]

The comparative simplicity of Kant's intuitional theory of mathematical science, supported as it is by the seemingly fundamental distinction between abstract concepts of reflective thinking and the construction of concepts[2] in geometry and arithmetic, has made it intelligible even to those to whom the very complicated argument of the *Analytic* makes no appeal. It would also seem to be inseparably bound up with what from the popular point of view is the most striking of all Kant's theoretical doctrines, namely, his view that space and time are given subjective forms, and that the assertion of their independent reality must result in those contradictions to which Kant has given the title antinomy. For these reasons his intuitional theory of mathematical science has received attention out of all proportion to its importance. Its pre-Critical character has been more or less overlooked, and instead of being interpreted in the light of Critical principles, it has been allowed to obscure the sounder teaching of the *Analytic*. In this matter Schopenhauer is a chief culprit. He not only takes the views of mathematical science expounded in the *Introduction* and *Aesthetic* as being in line with Kant's main teaching, but expounds them in an even more unqualified fashion than does Kant himself.

---

[1] Cf. below, p. 117 ff., on Kant and modern geometry, and p. 128 ff., on Kant's views regarding arithmetical science.
[2] Cf. below, pp. 131-3, 338-9, 418 ff.

There are thus four main defects in the argument of this *Introduction*, regarded as representative of Critical teaching. (1) Its problems are formulated exclusively in terms of the attributive judgment; the other forms of relational judgment are ignored. (2) It maintains that judgments are either merely analytic or completely synthetic. (3) It proceeds in terms of a further division of judgments into those that are purely empirical and those that are *a priori*. (4) It seems to assert that the justification for mathematical judgments is intuitional. All these four positions are in some degree retained throughout the *Critique*, but not in the unqualified manner of this *Introduction*. In the *Analytic*, judgment in all its possible forms is shown to be a synthetic combination of a given manifold in terms of relational categories. This leads to a fourfold conclusion. In the first place, judgment must be regarded as essentially relational. Secondly, the *a priori* and the empirical must not be taken as two separate kinds of knowledge, but as two elements involved in all knowledge. Thirdly, analysis and synthesis must not be viewed as co-ordinate processes; synthesis is the more fundamental; it conditions all analysis. And lastly, it must be recognised that nothing is merely given; intuitional experience, whether sensuous or *a priori*, is conditioned by processes of conceptual interpretation. Though the consequences which follow from these conclusions, if fully developed, would carry us far beyond any point which Kant himself reached in the progressive maturing of his views, the next immediate steps would still be on the strict lines of the Critical principles, and would involve the sacrifice only of such pre-Critical doctrines as that of the intuitive character of mathematical proof. Such correction of Kant's earlier positions is the necessary complement of his own final discovery that sense-intuition is incapable of grounding even the so-called empirical judgment.

The *Introduction* to the first edition bears all the signs of having been written previous to the central portions of the *Analytic*.[1] That it was not, however, written prior to the *Aesthetic* seems probable. The opening sections of the *Aesthetic* represent what is virtually an independent introduction which takes no account of the preceding argument, and which redefines terms and distinctions that have already

---

[1] That certain parts of the *Introduction* were written at different dates is shown below, pp. 71-2. That other parts may be of similarly composite origin is always possible. There is, however, no sufficient evidence to establish this conclusion. Adickes' attempt to do so (*K.* pp. 35-7 *n.*) is not convincing.

been dwelt upon. The extensive additions which Kant made in recasting the *Introduction* for the second edition are in many respects a great improvement. In the first edition Kant had not, except when speaking of the possibility of constructing the concepts of mathematical science, referred to the synthetic character of mathematical judgments. This is now dwelt upon in adequate detail. Kant's reason for not making the revision more radical was doubtless his unwillingness to undertake the still more extensive alterations which this would have involved. Had he expanded the opening statement of the second edition *Introduction*, that even our empirical knowledge is a compound of the sensuous and the *a priori*, an entirely new *Introduction* would have become necessary. The additions made are therefore only such as will not markedly conflict with the main tenor of the argument of the first edition.

How are Synthetic *a priori* Judgments possible?

Treatment of detailed points will be simplified if we now consider in systematic fashion the many difficulties that present themselves in connection with Kant's mode of formulating his central problem : *How are synthetic* a priori *judgments possible ?* This formula is less definite and precise than would at first sight appear. The central phrase 'synthetic *a priori*' is sufficiently exact (the meaning to be attached to the *a priori* has already been considered[1]), but ambiguities of the most various kinds lurk in the seemingly innocent and simple terms with which the formula begins and ends :

A. 'How' has two very different meanings :

(*a*) *How* possible = *in what manner* possible = *wie*.
(*b*) *How* possible = *in how far* possible, *i.e. whether* possible = *ob*.

In connection with these two meanings of the term 'how,' we shall have to consider the distinction between the synthetic method employed in the *Critique* and the analytic method employed in the *Prolegomena*.

B. 'Possible' has a still wider range of application. Vaihinger[2] distinguishes within it no less than three pairs of alternative meanings :

(*a*) Psychological and logical possibility.
(*b*) Possibility of explanation and possibility of existence.
(*c*) Real and ideal possibility.

[1] Cf. above, pp. xxxiii ff., 1-2, 26 ff.   [2] i. pp. 317 and 450 ff.

A. Kant personally believed that the possibility of valid *a priori* synthetic judgment is proved by the existing sciences of mathematics and physics. And that being so, there were for Kant two very different methods which could be employed in accounting for their possibility, the synthetic or progressive, and the analytic or regressive. The synthetic method would start from given, ordinary experience (in its simplest form, as consciousness of time), to discover its conditions, and from them to prove the validity of knowledge that is *a priori*. The analytic method would start " from the sought as if it were given," that is, from the existence of *a priori* synthetic judgments, and, assuming them as valid, would determine the conditions under which alone such validity can be possible. The precise formulation of these two methods, the determination of their interrelations, of their value and comparative scope, is a matter of great importance, and must therefore be considered at some length.

The synthetic method may easily be confounded with the analytic method. For in the process of its argument it makes use of analysis. By analysing ordinary experience in the form in which it is given, it determines (in the *Aesthetic* and in the *Analytic of Concepts*) the fundamental elements of which knowledge is composed, and the generating conditions from which it results. From these the validity of the *a priori* principles that underlie mathematics and physics can (in the *Analytic of Principles*) be directly deduced. The fundamental differentiating feature, therefore, of the so-called synthetic method is not its synthetic procedure, since in great part, in the solution of the most difficult portion of its task, it employs an analytic method, but only its attitude towards the one question of the validity of *a priori* synthetic knowledge. It does not postulate this validity as a premiss, but proves it as a consequence of conditions which are independently established. By a preliminary regress upon the conditions of our *de facto* consciousness it acquires data from which it is enabled to advance by a synthetic, progressive or deductive procedure to the establishment of the validity of synthetic *a priori* judgments. The analytic method, on the other hand, makes no attempt to prove the validity of *a priori* knowledge. It seeks only to discover the conditions under which such knowledge, if granted to exist, can possess validity, and in the light of which its paradoxical and apparently contradictory features can be viewed as complementary to one another. The conditions, thus revealed, will render the validity of knowledge conceivable, will account for it once it has been assumed ; but they do not prove it.

The validity is a premiss; the whole argument rests upon the assumption of its truth. The conditions are only postulated *as conditions*; and their reality becomes uncertain, if the validity, which presupposes them, is itself called in question. Immediately we attempt to reverse the procedure, and to prove validity from these conditions, our argument must necessarily adopt the synthetic form; and that, as has been indicated, involves the prior application of a very different and much more thorough process of analysis. The distinction between the two methods may therefore be stated as follows. In the synthetic method the grounds which are employed to explain *a priori* knowledge are such as also at the same time suffice to prove its validity. In the analytic method they are grounds of explanation, but not of proof. They are themselves proved only in so far as the assumption of validity is previously granted.

The analytic procedure which is involved in the complete synthetic method ought, however, for the sake of clearness, to be classed as a separate, third, method. And as such I shall henceforth regard it. It establishes by an independent line of argument the existence of *a priori* factors, and also their objective validity as conditions necessary to the very possibility of experience. So viewed, it is the most important and the most fundamental of the three methods. The argument which it embodies constitutes the very heart of the *Critique*. It is, indeed, Kant's new transcendental method; and in the future, in order to avoid confusion with the analytic method of the *Prolegomena*, I shall refer to it always by this title. It is because the transcendental method is an integral part of the complete, synthetic method, but cannot be consistently made a part of the analytic method, that the synthetic method alone serves as an adequate expression of the Kantian standpoint. This new transcendental method is proof by reference to the possibility of experience. Experience is given as psychological fact. The conditions which can alone account for it, as psychological fact, also suffice to prove its objective validity; but at the same time they limit that validity to the phenomenal realm.

We have next to enquire to what extent these methods are consistently employed in the *Critique*. This is a problem over which there has been much controversy, but which seems to have been answered in a quite final manner by Vaihinger. It is universally recognised that the *Critique* professes to follow the synthetic method, and that the *Prolegomena*, for the sake of a simpler and more popular form of exposition, adopts the analytic method. How far

these two works live up to their professions, especially the
Critique in its two editions, is the only point really in question.
Vaihinger found two diametrically opposed views dividing
the field.   Paulsen, Riehl, and Windelband maintain the view
that Kant starts from the fact that mathematics, pure natural
science, and metaphysics contain synthetic *a priori* judgments
claiming to be valid.   Kant's problem is to test these claims;
and his answer is that they are valid in mathematics and pure
natural science, but not in metaphysics.   Paulsen, and those
who follow him, further contend that in the first edition
this method is in the main consistently held to, but that
in the second edition, owing to the occasional employment
(especially in the *Introduction*) of the analytic method of the
Prolegomena, the argument is perverted and confused: Kant
assumes what he ought first to have proved.   Fischer, on
the other hand, and in a kindred manner also B. Erdmann,
maintain that Kant never actually doubted the validity of
synthetic *a priori* judgments; starting from their validity,
in order to explain it, Kant discovers the conditions upon
which it rests, and in so doing is able to show that these
conditions are not of such a character as to justify the
professed judgments of metaphysics.

Vaihinger[1] combines portions of both views, while completely accepting neither.   Hume's profound influence upon
the development and formulation of Kant's Critical problem
can hardly be exaggerated, but it ought not to prevent us
from realising that this problem, *in its first form*, was quite independently discovered.   As the letter of 1772 to Herz clearly
shows,[2] Kant was brought to the problem, how an idea in us
can relate to an object, by the inner development of his own
views, through reflection upon the view of thought which he
had developed in the *Dissertation* of 1770.   The conformity
between thought and things is in that letter presented, not as
a sceptical objection, but as an actual fact calling for explanation.   He does not ask whether there is such conformity, but
only how it should be possible.   Even after the further
complication, that thought is synthetic as well as *a priori*,
came into view through the influence of Hume, the problem
still continued to present itself to Kant in this non-sceptical
light.   And this largely determines the wording of his exposition, even in passages in which the demands of the synthetic
method are being quite amply fulfilled.   Kant, as it would
seem, never himself doubted the validity of the mathematical
sciences.   But since their validity is not beyond possible
impeachment, and since metaphysical knowledge, which is

[1] i. p. 412 ff. ; cf. p. 388 ff.   [2] Cf. below, pp. 219-20.

decidedly questionable, would appear to be of somewhat similar type, Kant was constrained to recognise that, from the point of view of strict proof, such assumption of validity is not really legitimate. Though, therefore, the analytic method would have resolved Kant's own original difficulty, only the synthetic method is fully adequate to the situation.

Kant accordingly sets himself to prove that whether or not we are ready (as he himself is) to recognise the validity of scientific judgments, the correctness of this assumption can be firmly established. And being thus able to prove its correctness, he for that very reason does not hesitate to employ it in his introductory statement. The problem, he says, is that of 'understanding' how synthetic *a priori* judgments can be valid. A 'difficulty,' a 'mystery,' a 'secret,' lies concealed in them. How can a predicate be ascribed to a subject term which does not contain it? And even more strangely (if that be possible), how can *a priori* judgments legislate for objects which are independent existences? Such judgments, even if valid beyond all disputing, would still call for explanation. This is, indeed, Kant's original and ground problem. As already indicated, no one, save only Hume, had hitherto perceived its significance. Plato, Malebranche, and Crusius may have dwelt upon it, but only to suggest explanations still stranger and more mystical than the mysterious fact itself.[1]

Paulsen is justified in maintaining that Kant, in both editions of the *Critique*, recognises the validity of mathematics and pure natural science. The fact of their validity is less explicitly dwelt upon in the first edition, but is none the less taken for granted. The sections transferred from the *Prolegomena* to the *Introduction* of the second edition make no essential change, except merely in the emphasis with which Kant's belief in the existence of valid *a priori* synthetic judgments is insisted upon. As has already been stated, only by virtue of this initial assumption is Kant in position to maintain that there is an alternative to the strict synthetic method. The *problem* from which he starts is common to both methods, and for that reason the formulation used in the *Prolegomena* can also be employed in the *Introduction* to the *Critique*. Only in their manner of *solving* the problem need they differ.[2] Kant's Critical problem first begins with this presupposition of validity, and does not exist save through it.[3] He does not first seek to discover

[1] Cf. Vaihinger, i. p. 394. Cf. above, p. 28.
[2] Cf. Vaihinger, i. pp. 415-17.
[3] Paulsen objects that if synthetic *a priori* judgments are valid without explanation, they do not need it. For two reasons the objection does not hold. (*a*) Without this explanation it would be impossible to repel the pretensions of

whether such judgments are valid, and then to explain them. He accepts them as valid, but develops a method of argument which suffices for proof as well as for explanation. The argument being directed to both points simultaneously, and establishing both with equal cogency, it may legitimately be interpreted in either way, merely as explanation, or also as proof. Kant does not profess or attempt to keep exclusively to any one line of statement. Against the dogmatists he insists upon the necessity of *explaining* the validity of *a priori* synthetic judgments, against the sceptics upon the possibility of *proving* their validity. And constantly he uses ambiguous terms, such as 'justification' (*Rechtfertigung*), 'possibility,' that may indifferently be read in either sense. But though the fundamental demand which characterises the synthetic method in its distinction from the analytic thus falls into the background, and is only occasionally insisted upon, it is none the less fulfilled. So far as regards the main argument of the *Critique* in either edition, the validity of synthetic *a priori* judgments is not required as a premiss. It is itself independently proved.

The manner in which Kant thus departs from the strict application of the synthetic method may be illustrated by an analysis of his argument in the *Aesthetic*.[1] Only in the arguments of the first edition in regard to space and time is the synthetic method employed in its ideal and rigorous form. For the most part, even in the first edition, instead of showing how the *a priori* character of pure and applied mathematics follows from conclusions independently established, he assumes both pure and applied mathematics to be given as valid, and seeks only to show how the independently established results of the *Aesthetic* enable him to explain and render comprehensible their recognised characteristics. This is not, indeed, any very essential modification of the synthetic method ; for his independently established results suffice for deducing all that they are used to explain. The validity of mathematics is not employed as a premiss. Kant's argument is, however, made less clear by the above procedure.

Further difficulty is caused by Kant's occasional employment, even in the first edition, of the analytic method. He several times cites as an argument in support of his view

---

transcendent metaphysics (cf. A 209 = B 254-5 ; A 283 = B 285). (*b*) This solution of the theoretical problem has also, as above stated, its own intrinsic interest and value. Without such explanation the validity of these judgments might be granted, but could not be understood. (Cf. *Prolegomena*, §§ 4-5 and § 12 at the end. Cf. Vaihinger, i. p. 394.)

[1] Cf. Vaihinger, ii. p. 336. The argument of the *Analytic*, which is still more complicated, will be considered later.

of space the fact that it alone will account for the existing science of geometry. That is to say, he employs geometry, viewed as valid, to *prove* the correctness of his view of space.[1] Starting from that science as given, he enquires what are the conditions which can alone render it possible. These conditions are found to coincide with those independently established. Now this is a valid argument when employed in due subordination to the main synthetic method. It offers welcome *confirmation* of the results of that method. It amounts in fact to this, that having proved (by application of the transcendental method) the mathematical sciences to be valid, everything which their validity necessarily implies must be granted. Kant's reasoning here becomes circular, but it is none the less valid on that account. This further complication of the argument is, however, dangerously apt to mislead the reader. It is in great part the cause of the above division among Kant's commentators. The method employed in the *Prolegomena* is simply this form of argument systematised and cut free from all dependence upon the transcendental method of proof.[2]

The whole matter is, however, still further complicated by the distinction, which we have already noted, between real and ideal possibility. Are the given synthetic *a priori* judgments valid? That is one question. Can the Critical philosophy discover, completely enumerate, and prove in a manner never before done, all the possible synthetic *a priori* principles? That is a very different problem, and when raised brings us to the further discussion of Kant's transcendental method. The question at issue is no longer merely whether or not certain given judgments are valid, and how, if valid, they are to be accounted for. The question is now that of discovering and of proving principles which have not been established by any of the special sciences. This shifting of the problem is concealed from Kant himself by his omission to distinguish between the undemonstrated axioms of the mathematical sciences and their derivative theorems, between the principles employed by the physicist without enquiry into their validity and the special laws based upon empirical evidence.

[1] Cf. A 46-9 = B 64-6. The corresponding sections of the *Prolegomena*, Vaihinger contends, were developed from this first edition passage, and the transcendental exposition of space in the second edition from the argument of the *Prolegomena*.

[2] The synthetic method of argument is, as we shall see later, further extended in the *Analytic* by being connected with the problem of the validity of ordinary experience. But as the mathematical sciences are proved to have the same conditions as—neither more nor less than—the consciousness of time, this also allows of a corresponding extension of the analytic method. The mathematical sciences can be substituted for the *de facto* premiss by which these conditions are proved.

As regards the mathematical axioms, the problem is fairly simple. As we shall see later, in the *Aesthetic*, they do not require a deduction in the strict transcendental sense. They really fall outside the application of the transcendental method. They require only an "exposition." But in regard to the fundamental principles of natural science we are presented with the problem of discovery as well as of proof. Unlike the axioms of the mathematician, they are frequently left unformulated. And many postulates, such as that there is a *lex continui in natura*, are current in general thought, and claim equal validity with the causal principle. Kant has thus to face the question whether in addition to those principles employed more or less explicitly by the scientist, others, such as might go to form an immanent metaphysics of nature, may not also be possible.

B. (*a*)[1] **Psychological and logical possibility.**—Both have to be recognised and accounted for. Let us consider each in order.

(1) **Psychological possibility.**—What are the *subjective* conditions of *a priori* synthetic judgments? *Through what mental faculties* are they rendered possible? Kant replies by developing what may be called a transcendental psychology. They depend upon space and time as forms of sensibility, upon the *a priori* concepts of understanding, and upon the synthetic activities by which the imagination schematises these concepts and reduces the given manifold to the unity of apperception. This transcendental psychology is the necessary complement of the more purely epistemological analysis.[2] But on this point Kant's utterances are extremely misleading. His Critical enquiry has, he declares, nothing in common with psychology. In the *Preface* to the first edition we find the following passage: " This enquiry . . . [into] the pure understanding itself, its possibility and the cognitive faculties upon which it rests . . ., although of great importance for my chief purpose, does not form an essential part of it."[3] The question, he adds, "how is the faculty of thought itself possible? . . . is as it were a search for the cause of a given effect, and therefore is of the nature of an hypothesis [or ' mere opinion '], though, as I shall show elsewhere, this is not really so." The concluding words of this passage very fairly express Kant's hesitating and inconsistent procedure. Though he has so explicitly eliminated from the central enquiry of

[1] Cf. above, p. 43.
[2] What follows should be read along with p. 235 ff. below, in which this distinction between the "subjective" and "objective" deductions is discussed in greater detail.
[3] A x-xi.

the *Critique* all psychological determination of the mental powers, statements as to their constitution are none the less implied, and are involved in his epistemological justification alike of *a priori* knowledge and of ordinary experience. If we bear in mind that Kant is here attempting to outline the possible causes of given effects, and that his conclusions are therefore necessarily of a more hypothetical character than those obtained by logical analysis, we shall be prepared to allow him considerable liberty in their formulation. But in certain respects his statements are precise and definite —the view, for instance, of sensations as non-spatial, of time as a form of inner sense, of the productive imagination as pre-conditioning our consciousness, of spontaneity as radically distinct from receptivity, of the pure forms of thought as not acquired through sense, etc. No interpretation which ignores or under-estimates this psychological or subjective aspect of his teaching can be admitted as adequate.[1]

(2) **Logical or epistemological possibility.**—How can synthetic *a priori* judgments be *valid*? This question itself involves a twofold problem. How, despite their synthetic character, can they possess truth, *i.e.* how can we pass from their subject terms to their predicates? And secondly, how, in view of their origin in our human reason, can they be objectively valid, *i.e.* legislate for the independently real? How can we pass beyond the subject-predicate relation to real things? This latter is the Critical problem in the form in which it appears in Kant's letter of 1772 to Herz.[2] The former is the problem of synthesis which was later discovered.

(*b*) (1) **Possibility of explanation and (2) possibility of existence.**—(1) How can synthetic *a priori* judgments be *accounted for*? How, despite their seemingly inconsistent and apparently paradoxical aspects, can their validity (their validity as well as their actuality being taken for granted) be rendered *comprehensible*? (2) The validity of such judgments has been called in question by the empiricists, and is likewise inexplicable even from the dogmatic standpoint of the rationalists. How, then, can these judgments be *possible at all*? These two meanings of the term 'possible' connect with the ambiguity, above noted, in the term 'how.' The former problem can be solved by an analytic method; the latter demands the application of the more radical method of synthetic reconstruction.

(*c*) **Real and ideal possibility.**[3]—We have to distinguish between the possible validity of those propositions which the mathematical and physical sciences profess to have established

---

[1] This is a criticism to which Cohen, Caird, and Riehl lay themselves open.
[2] Cf. below, pp. 219-20.
[3] Cf. above, pp. 49-50.

and the possible validity of those principles such as that of causality, which are postulated by the sciences, but which the sciences do not attempt to prove, and which in certain cases they do not even formulate. The former constitute an actually existent body of scientific knowledge, demonstrated in accordance with the demands of scientific method. The latter are employed by the scientist, but are not investigated by him. The science into which they can be fitted has still to be created; and though some of the principles composing it may be known, others remain to be discovered. All of them demand such proof and demonstration as they have never yet received.[1] This new and ideal science is the scientific metaphysics which Kant professes to inaugurate by means of the *Critique*. In reference to the special sciences, possibility means the conditions of the actually given. In reference to the new and ideal metaphysics, possibility signifies the conditions of the realisation of that which is sought. In view of this distinction, the formula—How are synthetic *a priori* judgments possible?—will thus acquire two very different meanings. (1) How are the existing *a priori* synthetic judgments to be accounted for? (2) How may all the really fundamental judgments of that type be exhaustively discovered and proved? Even in regard to immanent metaphysics Kant interprets the formula in both ways. This is due to his frequent confusion of immanent metaphysics with the principles of natural science. Its propositions are then regarded as given, and only their general validity calls for proof. It is, however, in the problem of ideal possibility that the essential problem of the *Critique* lies; and that is a further reason why it cannot be adequately dealt with, save by means of the synthetic method.

Experience.—Throughout the *Introduction* the term *experience*[2] has (even at times in one and the same sentence) two quite distinct meanings, (1) as product of sense and understanding acting co-operatively, and (2) as the raw material (the impressions) of sense. Considerable confusion is thereby caused.

Understanding and reason[3] are here, as often elsewhere in the *Critique*, used as equivalent terms. Throughout the entire two first sections of the *Introduction* to the second edition the term reason does not occur even once. As first mentioned,[4] it is taken as the source of metaphysical judgments.

---

[1] Cf. Vaihinger, i. p. 405. The existing sciences can, as Vaihinger says, be treated *en bloc*, whereas each of the principles of the new philosophy must be separately established.

[2] A 1.   [3] A 1-2.   [4] B 6=A 2.

General (a priori) truths have an inner necessity and must be clear and certain by themselves.[1]—These statements are not in accordance with Kant's new Critical teaching.[2] They have remained uncorrected from a previous way of thinking. This must be one reason for the recasting of this paragraph in the second edition.

Even with (unter) our experiences there is mingled knowledge which must be of a priori origin.[3]—Kant is here distinguishing the *immanent a priori*, such as that involved in any causal judgment, from the *transcendent a priori* dwelt upon in the next paragraph. The latter is expressed through metaphysical judgments, such as ' God exists,' ' the soul is immortal.'

Original concepts and judgments derived from them.[4]—Cf. B 5-6.

Pure.—In the title of the section the term *pure*[5] (*rein*) is, as the subsequent argument shows, taken as exactly equivalent to *a priori*. As Vaihinger notes, the adjective *apriorisch* had not yet been invented. The opposite of pure is here empirical (*empirisch*).[6]

All our knowledge begins with experience.[7]—This is a stronger statement than any in the corresponding paragraphs of the first edition. Had Kant proceeded to develop its consequences, he would have had to recast the entire *Introduction*, setting the problem of empirical knowledge alongside that of the *a priori*.[8] As it is, he is forced[9] to subdivide the absolutely *a priori* into the pure and the mixed.[10]

By objects which affect (rühren) our senses. The raw material of sensuous impressions.[11]—These incidental statements call for discussion. Cf. below, pp. 80-8, 120-1, 274 ff.

A knowledge of objects which we call experience.[12]—Kant does not keep to this definition. The term experience is still used in its other and narrower sense, as in the very next paragraph, when Kant states that knowledge does not, perhaps, arise solely from experience (= sense impressions).

In respect of time.[13]—This statement, taken as an account of Kant's teaching in the *Critique*, is subject to two reservations. In the *Aesthetic*[14] Kant sometimes claims a temporal antecedence for the *a priori*. And secondly, the *a priori* is not for Kant merely logical. It also possesses a dynamical priority.[15]

Even experience itself is a compound.[16]—The "even" seems to refer to the distinction drawn in A 2 between the immanent and the transcendent *a priori*.[17]

[1] A 2.   [2] Cf. above, pp. xxxv, 36 ff.; below, pp. 565-7.   [3] A 2.
[4] A 2.   [5] B 1.   [6] Cf. below, p. 55.   [7] B 1.
[8] Cf. below, p. 54.   [9] B 2-3.   [10] Cf. below, p. 55.   [11] B 1.
[12] B 1.   [13] B 1.   [14] Cf. below, p. 88 ff.   [15] Cf. below, p. 237 ff
[16] B 1.   [17] Cf. below, pp. 55-6.

It is therefore a question whether there exists such knowledge independent of experience.[1]—This question was not raised in the first edition.[2] The alternative methods, analytic and synthetic, are discussed above, p. 44 ff.

Such knowledge is called a priori and is distinguished from empirical knowledge.[3]—Throughout the *Introduction*, in both editions equally, Kant fails to state the problems of the *Critique* in a sufficiently comprehensive manner. He speaks as if the *Critique* dealt only with the absolutely *a priori*, in its two forms, as immanent scientific knowledge and as transcendent speculation. It also deals with the equally important and still more fundamental problem of accounting for the possibility of *experience*.[4] Our empirical knowledge involves an *a priori* element, and may not therefore be opposed to *a priori* knowledge in the manner of the passage before us.

This term a priori is not yet definite enough.[5]—It is frequently employed in a merely relative sense. Thus we can say of a person who undermines the foundations of his house that he might have known *a priori* that it would collapse, that is, that he need not wait for the experience of its actual fall. But still he could not know this entirely *a priori*; he had first to learn from experience that bodies are heavy, and will fall when their supports are taken away. But as dealt with in the *Critique* the term *a priori* is used in an absolute sense, to signify that knowledge which is independent, not of this or that experience only, but of all impressions of the senses. Thus far Kant's position is comparatively clear; but he proceeds to distinguish two forms within the absolutely *a priori*, namely, mixed and pure. The absolutely *a priori* is mixed when it contains an empirical element, pure when it does not. ("Pure" is no longer taken in the meaning which it has in the title of the section.[6] It signifies not the *a priori* as such, but only one subdivision of it.) Thus after defining absolutely *a priori* knowledge as independent of all experience, Kant takes it in one of its forms as involving empirical elements. The example which he gives of an absolutely *a priori* judgment, which yet is not pure, is the principle: every change has its cause. "Change" is an empirical concept, but the synthetic relation asserted is absolutely *a priori*. In the next section[7] this same proposition is cited as a *pure* judgment *a priori*— "pure" being again used in its more general meaning as synonymous with *a priori*. This confusion results from Kant's exclusive preoccupation with the *a priori*, and consequent

[1] B 2.   [2] Cf. above, p. 27 *n*.   [3] B 2.
[4] Cf. above, pp. 39 ff., 53; below, pp. 57-8, 222 ff., 241, 286-9.
[5] B 2-3.   [6] Cf. above, p. 53.   [7] A 9-10=B 13.

failure to give due recognition to the correlative problem of the empirical judgment. The omitted factor retaliates by thus forcing its way into Kant's otherwise clean-cut divisions. Also, it is not true that the relative *a priori* falls outside the sphere of the Critical enquiry. Such judgment expresses necessity or objectivity, and for that reason demands a transcendental justification no less urgently than the absolutely *a priori*. The finding of such justification is, indeed, the central problem of the *Analytic*.[1]

The subdivisions of the *a priori* may be tabulated thus :

A priori knowledge
- Relative, *e.g.* every unsupported house must fall.
- Absolute
  - Mixed, *e.g.* every change has its cause.
  - Pure, *e.g.* a straight line is the shortest distance between two points.

The term *pure* (*rein*) thus acquires a second meaning distinct from that defined above.[2] It is no longer employed as identical with *a priori*, but as a subdivision of it, meaning *unmixed*. Its opposite is no longer the empirical, but the impure or mixed. Owing, however, to the fact that "pure" (in its first meaning) is identical with the *a priori*, it shares in all the different connotations of the latter, and accordingly is also employed to denote that which is *not relative*. But "pure" has yet another meaning peculiar to itself. The phrase "independent of experience" has in reference to "pure" an ambiguity from which it does not suffer in its connection with "*a priori*" (since mathematical knowledge, whether pure or applied, is always regarded by Kant as *a priori*). It may signify either independence as regards *content and validity*, or independence as regards *scope*. The latter meaning is narrower than the former. By the former meaning it denotes that which originates, and can possess truth, independently of experience. By the latter it signifies that which is not only independent of sense but also applies to the non-sensuous. In this latter meaning pure knowledge therefore signifies transcendent knowledge. Its opposite is the immanent. The various meanings of "pure" (four in number) may be tabulated as follows :

(a) (1) *A priori* : independent of experience as regards origin and validity. (Its opposite = empirical.)
- (2) Absolutely independent of experience. (Its opposite = relative.)
- (3) Unmixed with experience. (Its opposite = impure or mixed.)

---

[1] Cf. above, p. 39 ff., and below, pp. 286-9. [2] P. 53; cf. also pp. 1-2.

(b) (4) Independent of experience as regards scope = transcendent. (Its opposite = immanent.)

All these varied meanings contribute to the ambiguity of the title of the *Critique*. Kant himself employs the title in all of the following senses :

1. Critique of absolutely pure *a priori* knowledge, determination of its sources, conditions, scope and limits.

2. Critique of all *a priori* knowledge, relative as well as absolute, in so far as it depends upon *a priori* principles, determination, etc.

3. Critique of all knowledge, whether *a priori* or empirical, determination, etc.

4. Critique of transcendent knowledge, its sources and limits.

Further meanings could also be enumerated but can be formulated by the reader for himself in the light of the ambiguities just noted.[1] The special context in each case can alone decide how the title is to be understood. If a really adequate definition of the purpose and scope of the *Critique* is sought by the reader, he must construct it for himself. The following may perhaps serve. *The* Critique *is an enquiry into the sources, conditions, scope and limits of our knowledge, both* a priori *and empirical, resulting in the construction of a new system of immanent metaphysics; in the light of the conclusions thus reached, it also yields an analysis and explanation of the transcendental illusion to which transcendent metaphysics, both as a natural disposition and as a professed science, is due.*

Kant further complicates matters by offering a second division of the absolutely *a priori*,[2] viz. into the original and the derivative. Also, by implication, he classes relative *a priori* judgments among the propositions to be reckoned with by the *Critique*; and yet in B 4 he speaks of the proposition, all bodies are heavy, as merely empirical.[3]

A criterion.[4]—Necessity and universality are valid criteria of the *a priori* (= the non-empirical). This follows from Kant's view[5] of the empirical as synonymous with the contingent (*zufällig*). Experience gives only the actual ; the *a priori* alone yields that which cannot be otherwise.

" Necessity and strict universality are thus safe criteria of *a priori* knowledge, and are inseparable from one another. But since in the employment of these criteria the empirical limitation of judgments

---

[1] Cf. also above, pp. 2-3.   [2] B 3.
[3] Cf. *Metaphysische Anfangsgründe*, Hauptstück ii. Lehrs. 8, Zus. 2, in which elasticity and gravity are spoken of as the only universal properties of matter which can be apprehended *a priori*.
[4] B 3-4.   [5] Cf. above, p. 27 ff.

is sometimes more easily shown than their contingency, or since, as frequently happens, their unlimited universality can be more convincingly proved than their necessity, it is advisable to use the two criteria separately, each being by itself infallible." [1]

Now Kant is here, of course, assuming the main point to be established, namely, that experience is incapable of accounting for such universality and necessity as are required for our knowledge, both ordinary and scientific. We have already considered this assumption, [2] and have also anticipated misunderstanding by noting the important qualifications to which, from Kant's new Critical standpoint, the terms 'necessity' and 'universality' become subject. [3] The very specific meaning in which Kant employs the term *a priori* must likewise be borne in mind. Though negatively the *a priori* is independent of experience, positively it originates in our human reason. The necessity and universality which differentiate the *a priori* distinguish it only from the humanly accidental. The *a priori* has no absolute validity. From a metaphysical standpoint, it is itself contingent. As already stated, [4] all truth is for Kant merely *de facto*. The necessary is not that which cannot be conceived to be otherwise, nor is it the unconditioned. Our reason legislates only for the world of appearance. But as yet Kant gives no hint of this revolutionary reinterpretation of the rationalist criteria. One of the chief unfortunate consequences of the employment in this *Introduction* of the analytic method of the *Prolegomena* is that it tends to mislead the reader by seeming to commit Kant to a logical *a priori* of the Leibnizian type.

To show that, if experience is to be possible, [pure a priori propositions] are indispensable, and so to prove their existence a priori. [5]—At first sight Kant would seem to be here referring to the alternative synthetic method of procedure, *i.e.* to the *transcendental* proof of the *a priori*. The next sentence shows, however, that neither in intention nor in fact is that really so. He argues only that *a priori* principles, such as the principle of causality, are necessary in order to give "certainty" to our experience; such a principle must be postulated if inductive inference is to be valid. Experience could have no [scientific] certainty, "if all rules according to which it proceeds were themselves in turn empirical, and therefore contingent. They could hardly be regarded as first principles." There is no attempt here to prove that empirical knowledge *as such* necessarily involves the *a priori*. Also the method of argument, though

[1] B 4. [2] Cf. above, pp. xxxiii-iv, 27, 599 ff.
[3] Cf. above, pp. xxxv-vi, 30; below, pp. 185-6, 257-9.
[4] *Loc. cit.* [5] B 5.

it seeks to establish the *necessity* of the *a priori*, is not transcendental or Critical in character. It is merely a repetition of the kind of argument which both Hume and Leibniz had already directed against the sensationalist position.[1] Very strangely, considering that these sentences have been added in the second edition, and therefore subsequent to the writing of the objective deduction, Kant gives no indication of the deeper problem to which he finally penetrated. The explanation is, probably, that to do so would have involved the recasting of the entire *Introduction*. Even on the briefest reference, the hard-and-fast distinction between the *a priori* and the empirical, as two distinct and separate classes of judgment, would have been undermined, and the reader would have been made to feel the insufficiency of the analysis upon which it is based.[2] The existence of the deeper view is betrayed only through careless employment of the familiar phrase " possibility of experience." For, as here used, it is not really meant. " Certainty of experience "—a very different matter—is the meaning that alone will properly fit the context.

Reason and understanding.[3]—They are here distinguished, having been hitherto, in A 1-2, employed as synonymous. The former carries us beyond the field of all possible experience; the latter is limited to the world of sense. Thus both *Reason* and *understanding* are here used in their narrowest meaning.

These inevitable problems of pure Reason itself are God, freedom, and immortality. The science which, with all its methods, is in its final intention directed solely to the solution of these problems, is called metaphysics.[4]—These sentences are characteristic of the second edition with its increased emphasis upon the positive results of the *Critique* on the one hand, and with its attitude of increased favour towards transcendent metaphysics on the other. The one change would seem to be occasioned by the nature of the criticisms passed upon the first edition, as, for instance, by Moses Mendelssohn who describes Kant as " the all-destroyer" (*der alles zermalmende*). The other is due to Kant's preoccupation with the problems of ethics and of teleology. The above statements are repeated with even greater emphasis in B 395 *n*.[5] The definition here given of metaphysics is not strictly kept to by Kant. As above noted,[6] Kant really distinguishes within it two forms, immanent and transcendent. In so doing, however, he still[7] regards transcendent metaphysics as the more important.

---

[1] Cf. above, pp. xxx, 599 ff.　　[3] Cf. above, pp. 39, 54.
[2] A 2=B 6.　　[4] B 7.
[5] Cf. *Kritik der Urtheilskraft*, § 91, *W.* v. p. 473. *Fortschritte, Werke* (Hartenstein), viii. pp. 572-3.　　[6] Cf. above, pp. 22, 49-50, 52.
[7] Cf. *Prolegomena*, § 40; *Fortschritte*, pp. 577-8.

Immanent metaphysics is chiefly of value as contributing to the solution of the "inevitable problems of pure Reason."

A 3-4 = B 7-8.—The reasons, here cited by Kant, for the failure of philosophical thinking to recognise the difference between immanent and transcendent judgments are : (1) the misunderstood character, and consequent misleading influence, of *a priori* mathematical judgments ; (2) the fact that once we are beyond the sensible sphere, experience can never contradict us ; (3) natural delight in the apparent enlargement of our knowledge ; (4) the ease with which logical contradictions can be avoided ; (5) neglect of the distinction between analytic and synthetic *a priori* judgments. Vaihinger points out[1] that in the *Fortschritte*[2] Kant adds a sixth reason—confusion of the concepts of understanding with the Ideas of Reason. Upon the first of the above reasons the best comment is that of the *Methodology*.[3] But the reader must likewise bear in mind that in B xvi Kant develops his new philosophical method on the analogy of the mathematical method. The latter is, he claims, *mutatis mutandis*, the true method of *legitimate* speculation, *i.e.* of immanent metaphysics. The one essential difference (as noted by Kant[4]), which has been overlooked by the dogmatists, is that philosophy gains its knowledge from concepts, mathematics from the construction of concepts.

Remain investigations only.[5]—Cf. *Prolegomena*, § 35.

The analysis of our concepts of objects.[6]—Vaihinger's interpretation, that the concepts here referred to are those which we "form *a priori* of things,"[7] seems correct.[8] The rationalists sought to deduce the whole body of rational psychology from the *a priori* conception of the soul as a simple substance, and of rational theology from the *a priori* conception of God as the all-perfect Being.

Analytic and synthetic judgments.[9]—"All analytic judgments depend wholly on the law of contradiction, and are in their nature *a priori* cognitions, whether the concepts that supply them with matter be empirical or not. For the predicate of an affirmative analytic judgment is already contained in the concept of the subject, of which it cannot be denied without contradiction. In the same way its opposite is necessarily denied of the subject in an analytic, but negative, judgment by the same law of contradiction. . . . For this very reason all analytic judgments are *a priori* even when the concepts are empirical, as, for example, gold is a yellow metal ; for to know this I require no experience beyond my concept of gold as a

---

[1] i. p. 238. [2] P. 579.
[3] A 712 ff. = B 740 ff. ; cf. also *Fortschritte*, p. 522.
[4] A 4 = B 8 ; cf. below, p. 563 ff. [5] A 4 = B 8. [6] A 5 = B 9.
[7] Cf. B 18. [8] Cf. above, p. 29. [9] A 6 ff. = B 10 ff.

yellow metal: it is, in fact, the very concept, and I need only analyse it, without looking beyond it elsewhere. . . . [Synthetic judgments, *a posteriori* and *a priori*] agree in this, that they cannot possibly spring solely from the principle of analysis, the law of contradiction They require a quite different principle. From whatever they may be deduced, the deduction must, it is true, always be in accordance with the principle of contradiction. For that principle must never be violated. But at the same time everything cannot be deduced from it." [1]

In A 594 = B 622 analytic judgments are also spoken of as identical; but in the *Fortschritte* [2] this use of terms is criticised:

"Judgments are analytic if their predicate only represents clearly (*explicite*) what was thought obscurely (*implicite*) in the concept of the subject, *e.g.* all bodies are extended. Were we to call such judgments identical only confusion would result. For identical judgments contribute nothing to the clearness of the concept, and that must be the purpose of all judging. Identical judgments are therefore empty, *e.g.* all bodies are bodily (or to use another term material) beings. Analytic judgments do, indeed, ground themselves upon identity and can be resolved into it; but they are not identical. For they demand analysis and serve for the explanation of the concept. In identical judgments, on the other hand, *idem* is defined *per idem*, and nothing at all is explained."

Vaihinger [3] cites the following contrasted examples of analytic and synthetic judgments:

Analytic.—(*a*) Substance is that which exists only as subject in which qualities inhere. [4] (*b*) Every effect has a cause. [5] (*c*) Everything conditioned presupposes a condition.

Synthetic.—(*a*) Substance is permanent. (*b*) Every event has a cause. [5] (*c*) Everything conditioned presupposes an unconditioned.

B 11-12.—The first half of this paragraph is transcribed practically word for word from the *Prolegomena.* [6] The second half is a close restatement of an omitted paragraph of the first edition. The chief addition lies in the concluding statement, that "experience is itself a synthetic connection of intuitions." This is in keeping with statements made in the deduction of the categories in the second edition, [7] and in the paragraph inserted in the proof of the second analogy in the second edition. [8] The *x* has strangely been omitted in the second

---

[1] *Prolegomena*, § 2, *b*, *c*; Eng. trans. pp. 15-16. On the connection of mathematical reasoning with the principle of contradiction, cf. below, pp. 64-5.
[2] P. 582; cf. *Logik*, § 37. [3] ii. p. 257.
[4] *Prolegomena*, § 4. [5] Cf. B 290. [6] § 2, *c*.
[7] B 161. [8] B 218.

edition in reference to empirical judgments, though retained in reference to synthetic *a priori* judgments.

The proposition : everything which happens has its cause.[1]— As we have already observed,[2] Hume influenced Kant at two distinct periods in his philosophical development—in 1756-1763, and again at some time (not quite definitely datable) after February 1772. The first influence concerned the character of concrete causal judgments; the second related to the causal axiom. Though there are few distinctions which are more important for understanding the *Critique* than that of the difference between these two questions, it has nowhere been properly emphasised by Kant, and in several of the references to Hume, which occur in the *Critique* and in the *Prolegomena*, the two problems are confounded in a most unfortunate manner. The passages in the *Introduction*[3] are clear and unambiguous; the influence exercised by Hume subsequent to February 1772 is quite adequately stated. The causal axiom claims to be *a priori*, and is, as Hume asserts, likewise synthetic. Consequently there are only two alternatives, each decisive and far-reaching. Either valid *a priori* synthesis must, contrary to all previous philosophical belief, be possible, or "everything which we call metaphysics must turn out to be a mere delusion of reason." The solution of this problem is "a question of life and death to metaphysics." To this appreciation of Hume, Kant adds criticism. Hume did not sufficiently universalise his problem. Had he done so, he would have recognised that pure mathematics involves *a priori* synthesis no less necessarily than do the metaphysical disciplines. From denying the possibility of mathematical science "his good sense would probably have saved him." Hume's problem, thus viewed, finds its final and complete expression in the formula: How are synthetic *a priori* judgments possible?

In A 760 = B 788 the account differs in two respects: first, it discusses the metaphysical validity of the causal axiom as well as its intrinsic possibility as a judgment; and secondly, reference is made to the conception of causality as well as to the axiom. The implied criticism of Hume is correspondingly modified. Otherwise, it entirely harmonises with the passages in the *Introduction*.

"Hume dwelt especially upon the principle of causality, and quite rightly observed that its truth, and even the objective validity of the concept of efficient cause in general, is based on no insight,

---

[1] A 9 = B 13.

[2] Cf. above, pp. xxv ff., 26 ; below, p. 593 ff. ; cf. Vaihinger, i. p. 340 ff.

[3] A 9 = B 13, B 11, B 19.

i.e. on no *a priori* knowledge, and that its authority cannot therefore be ascribed to its necessity, but merely to its general utility in the course of experience and to a certain subjective necessity which it thereby acquires, and which he entitles custom.   From the incapacity of our reason to make use of this principle in any manner that transcends experience he inferred the nullity of all pretensions of reason to advance beyond the empirical."

Now so far, in these references to Hume, Kant has had in view only the problems of mathematical and physical science and of metaphysics.   The problems involved in the possibility of empirical knowledge are left entirely aside. His account of Hume's position and of his relation to Hume suffers change immediately these latter problems are raised. And unfortunately it is a change for the worse.   The various problems treated by Hume are then confounded together, and the issues are somewhat blurred.   Let us take the chief passages in which this occurs.   In A 764 = B 792 ff. Kant gives the following account of Hume's argument.   Hume, recognising the impossibility of predicting an effect by analysis of the concept of the cause, or of discovering a cause from the concept of the effect, viewed all concrete causal judgments as merely contingent, and therefrom inferred the contingency of the causal axiom.   In so doing Hume, Kant argues, confuses the legitimate and purely *a priori* inference from a given event to *some* antecedent with the very different inference, possible only through special experience, to a *specific* cause.   Now this is an entire misrepresentation of Hume's real achievement, and may perhaps be explained, at least in part, as being due to the fact that Kant was acquainted with Hume's *Treatise* only through the indirect medium of Beattie's quotations.   Hume committed no such blunder.   He clearly recognised the distinction between the problem of the validity of the causal axiom and the problem of the validity of concrete causal judgments.   He does not argue from the contingency of concrete causal laws to the contingency of the universal principle, but shows, as Kant himself recognises,[1] that the principle is neither self-evident nor demonstrable *a priori*. And as necessity cannot be revealed by experience, neither is the principle derivable from that source.   Consequently, Hume concludes, it cannot be regarded as objectively valid. It must be due to a subjective instinct or natural belief. (The two problems are similarly confounded by Kant in A 217 = B 264.)

In the *Introduction* to the *Prolegomena* there is no such

[1] In A 9 = B 13, B 11, B 19.

confusion of the two problems, but matters are made even worse by the omission of all reference to Hume's analysis of the causal axiom. Only Hume's treatment of the concept of causality is dwelt upon. This is the more unfortunate, and has proved the more misleading, in that it is here that Kant makes his most explicit acknowledgment of his indebtedness to Hume. In §§ 27 ff. of the *Prolegomena* both problems reappear, but are again confounded. The section is preceded by sentences in which the problem of experience is emphasised; and in keeping with these prefatory remarks, Kant represents " Hume's *crux metaphysicorum* " as concerning only the concept of causality (viewed as a synthetic, and professedly *a priori*, connection between concrete existences). Yet in § 30 the causal axiom is also referred to, and together they are taken as constituting " Hume's problem."

Now if we bear in mind that Hume awakened Kant to both problems—how *a priori* knowledge is possible, and how experience is possible—this confusion can easily be understood. Kant had already in the early 'sixties studied Hume with profound admiration and respect.[1] In the period subsequent to 1772 this admiration had only deepened; and constantly, as we may believe, Kant had returned with fresh relish to Hume's masterly analyses of causality and of inductive inference. It is not, therefore, surprising that as the years passed, and as the other elements in Hume's teaching revealed to him, through the inner growth of his own views, their full worth and significance, he should allow the contribution that had more specifically awakened him to fall into the background, and should, in vague fashion, ascribe to Hume's teaching as a whole the specific influence which was really due to one particular part. By 1783, the date of the *Prolegomena*, Kant's first enthusiasm over the discovery of the fundamental problem of *a priori* synthesis had somewhat abated, and the problem of experience had more or less taken its place. This would seem to be the reason why in the *Prolegomena* he thus deals with both aspects of Hume's problem, and why in so doing he gives a subordinate place to Hume's treatment of the causal axiom. But though the misunderstanding may be thus accounted for, it must none the less be deplored. For the reader is seriously misled, and much that is central to the Critical philosophy is rendered obscure. The influence which Kant in the *Prolegomena* thus ascribes to

---

[1] Cf. Borowski's *Darstellung des Lebens und Charakters Im. Kants* (Hoffmann's edition, 1902), p. 252. The German translation of Hume's *Enquiry concerning the Human Understanding* appeared in 1755, and Kant probably made his first acquaintance with Hume through it. Cf. above, p. xxviii; below, p. 156.

Hume was not that which really awakened him from his dogmatic slumber, but is in part that which he had assimilated at least as early as 1763, and in part that which acted upon him with renewed force when he was struggling (probably between 1778 and 1780) with the problems involved in the deduction of the categories. It was Hume's treatment of the causal axiom, and that alone, which, at some time subsequent to February 1772, was the really effective influence in producing the Copernican change.[1]

Purely a priori and out of mere concepts.[2]—Vaihinger's comment seems correct: Kant means only that neither actual experience nor pure intuition can be resorted to. This does not contradict the complementary assertion,[3] that the principle, everything which happens has its cause, can be known *a priori*, not immediately from the concepts involved in it, but only indirectly[4] through the relation of these concepts to possible experience. "Possible experience," even though it stands for "something purely contingent," is itself a concept. Vaihinger[5] quotes Apelt upon this "mysterious" type of judgment.

"Metaphysics is synthetic knowledge from mere concepts, not like mathematics from their construction in intuition, and yet these synthetic propositions cannot be known from bare concepts, *i.e.* not analytically. The necessity of the connection in those propositions is to be apprehended through thought alone, and yet is not to rest upon the form of thought, the principle of contradiction. The conception of a kind of knowledge which arises from bare concepts, and yet is synthetic, eludes our grasp. The problem is: How can one concept be necessarily connected with another, without also at the same time being contained in it?"

The paragraphs in B 14 to B 17 are almost verbal transcripts from *Prolegomena*, § 2 c, 2 ff.

Mathematical judgments are one and all (insgesammt) synthetic.[6]—This assertion is carelessly made, and does not represent Kant's real view. In B 16 he himself recognises the existence of analytic mathematical judgments, but unduly minimises their number and importance.

All mathematical conclusions proceed according to the principle of contradiction.[7]—To the objection made by Paulsen that Kant, in admitting that mathematical judgments can be deduced from others by means of the principle of contra-

---

[1] Cf. below, *Appendix B*, p. 593 ff.
[3] A 733 = B 761.
[5] i. p. 291.
[7] B 14. Cf. above, pp. 59-60.

[2] A 9 = B 13.
[4] A 737 = B 764.
[6] B 14.

diction, ought consistently to have recognised as synthetic only axioms and principles, Vaihinger replies as follows :[1]

"The proposition—the angles of a triangle are together equal to two right angles—Kant regards as synthetic. It is indeed deduced from the axiom of parallels (with the aid of auxiliary lines), and to that extent is understood in accordance with the principle of contradiction. . . . The angles in the triangle constitute a special case of the angles in the parallel lines which are intersected by other lines. The principle of contradiction thus serves as vehicle in the deduction, because once the identity of A and A' is recognised, the predicate *b*, which belongs to A, must also be ascribed to A'. But the proposition is not for that reason itself analytic in the Kantian sense. In the analytic proposition the predicate is derived from the analysis of the subject concept. But that does not happen in this case. The synthetic proposition can never be derived *in and by itself* from the principle of contradiction ; . . . but only with the aid of that principle *from other propositions*. Besides, in this deduction intuition must always be resorted to ; and that makes an essential difference. Without it the identity of A and A' cannot become known."

Pure mathematics.[2]—"Pure," as thus currently used, is opposed only to applied, not to empirical. Kant here arbitrarily reads the latter opposition into it. Under this guise he begs the point in dispute.

$7 + 5 = 12$.[3]—Though $7 + 5 = 12$ expresses an identity or equality, it is an equality of the *objects* or *magnitudes*, $7 + 5$ and 12, not of the concepts through which we think them.[4] Analysis of the concepts can never reveal this equality. Only by constructing the concepts in intuition can it be recognised by the mind. This example has been already cited in the first edition.[5] It is further elaborated in the *Prolegomena*, § 2 *c*, and is here transcribed. Kant's mode of stating his position is somewhat uncertain. He alternates between " the representation of 7 and 5," " the representation of the combination of 7 and 5,"[6] and "the concepts 7 and 5."[7] His view would seem to be that there are *three* concepts involved. For the concept of 7 we must substitute the intuition of 7 points, for the concept of 5 the intuition of 5 points, and for the concept of their sum the intuitive operation of addition.

Call in the assistance of intuition, for instance our five fingers.[8] —This statement, repeated from the *Prolegomena*,[9] does not represent Kant's real position. The views which he has expressed upon the nature of arithmetical science are of the

---

[1] i. p. 294.   [2] B 15.   [3] B 15. Cf. above, pp. 39-41.
[4] Cf. Vaihinger, i. p. 296.   [5] A 164.   [6] A 164.
[7] In *Prolegomena* and in second edition.   [8] B 15.   [9] § 2 c.

most contradictory character,[1] but to one point he definitely commits himself, namely, that, like geometrical science, it rests, not (as here asserted) upon empirical, but upon pure intuition.[2] Except indirectly, by the reference to larger numbers, Kant here ignores his own important distinction between image and schema.[3] The above statement would also make arithmetic dependent upon space.

Segner: Anfangsgründe der Arithmetik,[4] translated from the Latin, second edition, Halle, 1773.

Natural science (physica) contains synthetic a priori judgments.[5]—There is here a complication to which Vaihinger[6] has been the first to draw attention. In the *Prolegomena*[7] Kant emphasises the distinction between physics and pure or universal science of nature.[8] The latter treats only the *a priori* form of nature (*i.e.* its necessary conformity to law), and is therefore a propaedeutic to physics which involves further empirical factors. For two reasons, however, this universal natural science falls short of its ideal. First, it contains empirical elements, such as the concepts of motion, impenetrability, inertia, etc. Secondly, it refers only to the objects of external sense, and not, as we should expect in a universal science, to natural existences without exception, *i.e.* to the objects of psychology as well as of physics.[9] But among its principles there are, Kant adds, a few which are purely *a priori* and possess the universality required : *e.g.* such propositions as that *substance is permanent*, and that *every event has a cause*. Now these are the examples which ought to have been cited in the passage before us. Those actually given fall entirely outside the scope of the *Critique*. They are treated only in the *Metaphysische Anfangsgründe*. They belong to the relatively, not to the absolutely, pure science of nature. The source of the confusion Vaihinger again traces to Kant's failure to hold fast to the important distinction between immanent and transcendent metaphysics.[10] His so-called pure or universal natural science (nature, as above noted, signifying for Kant " all that is ") is really *immanent metaphysics*, and the propositions in regard to substance and causality ought therefore to be classed as metaphysical. This, indeed, is how they are viewed in the earlier sections of the *Prolegomena*. The distinction later drawn in § 15 is ignored. Pure natural science is identified with mathematical physics,

[1] Cf. below, p. 128 ff.
[2] Cf. A 713=B 741.
[3] A 140=B 179. Cf. below, p. 337 ff.
[4] B 15.
[5] B 17.
[6] i. p. 304 ff.
[7] § 15.
[8] This latter Kant developed in his *Metaphysische Anfangsgründe* (1786).
[9] Cf. A 840=B 869. "Nature" means, in the Kantian terminology, "all that is."
[10] Cf. above, pp. xliv-v, 19, 22, 33, 52-3, 55-6.

and the propositions which in § 15 are spoken of as belonging to pure universal natural science are now regarded as metaphysical. "Genuinely metaphysical judgments are one and all synthetic. . . . For instance, the proposition—everything which in things is substance is permanent—is a synthetic, and properly metaphysical judgment."[1] In § 5 the principle of causality is also cited as an example of a synthetic *a priori* judgment in metaphysics. But Kant still omits to draw a distinction between immanent and transcendent metaphysics; and as a consequence his classification of synthetic *a priori* judgments remains thoroughly confused. They are taken as belonging to three spheres, mathematics, physics (in the relative sense), and metaphysics. The implication is that this threefold distinction corresponds to the threefold division of the *Doctrine of Elements* into *Aesthetic*, *Analytic*, and *Dialectic*. Yet, as a matter of fact, the propositions of mathematical physics, in so far as they are examples of applied mathematics, are dealt with in the *Aesthetic*, and in so far as they involve concepts of motion and the like fall entirely outside the scope of the *Critique*, while the *Analytic* deals with those *metaphysical* judgments (such as the principle of causality) which are of immanent employment.[2]

As the new paragraphs in the *Introduction* to the second edition are transferred without essential modification from the *Prolegomena*, they are open to the same criticism. To harmonise B 17 with the real teaching of the *Critique*, it must be entirely recast. Instead of "natural science" (*physica*) we must read "pure universal natural science [= immanent metaphysics]," and for the examples given we must substitute those principles of substance and causality which are dealt with in the *Analytic*. The next paragraph deals with metaphysics in its transcendent form, and accordingly states the problem peculiar to the *Dialectic*.

Metaphysics.[3]—This paragraph deals *explicitly* only with transcendent judgments, but as the terms used are ambiguous, it is possible that those of immanent metaphysics are also referred to. The paragraph is not taken from the *Prolegomena*. The corresponding passage[4] in the *Prolegomena* deals only with the judgments of immanent metaphysics.

---

[1] § 4.
[2] The propositions of pure natural science are not separately treated in § 4 of the *Prolegomena*, though the subsequent argument implies that this has been done. Vaihinger's inference (i. p. 310) that a paragraph, present in Kant's manuscript, has been dropped out in the process of printing the fourth section (the section which contains the paragraphs transposed from the end of § 2) seems unavoidable. The missing paragraph was very probably that which is here given in B 17.
[3] B 18. [4] In § 4 (at end of paragraphs transposed from § 2).

The real problem of pure reason is contained in the question: How are synthetic a priori judgments possible?[1]—Cf. above, pp. 26 ff., 33 ff., 43 ff.

David Hume.[2]—Cf. above, pp. 61 ff.

A theoretical knowledge.[3]—*i.e.* Kant explicitly leaves aside the further problem, whether such judgments may not also be possible in the practical (moral) and other spheres.

How is pure natural science possible?[4]—The note which Kant appends shows that he is here taking natural science in the relative sense.[5] The same irrelevant instances are again cited.

As these sciences really exist.[6]—Cf. above, p. 44 ff.

The poor progress which metaphysics has hitherto made.[7]—Cf. *Preface* to the second edition; *Prolegomena*, § 4, and A 175 ff.

How is metaphysics as a science possible?[8]—We may now consider how this and the three preceding questions are related to one another and to the various divisions of the *Critique*.[9] The four subordinate questions within the main problem—How are synthetic *a priori* judgments possible?—are here stated by Kant as:

1. How is pure mathematics possible?
2. How is pure natural science possible?
3. How is metaphysics as natural disposition possible?
4. How is metaphysics as science possible?

There is little difficulty as regards 1 and 2. The first is dealt with in the *Aesthetic*, and the second[10] in the *Analytic*, though, owing to the complexity of the problems, the *Aesthetic* and *Analytic* are wider than either query, and cannot be completely separated. Applied mathematics is dealt with in the *Analytic* as well as in the *Aesthetic*, and in both the determination of the limits of scientific knowledge is no less important than the task of accounting for its positive acquisitions. The third and fourth questions raise all manner of difficulties. Notwithstanding the identical mode of formulation, they do not run on all fours with the two preceding. The first two are taken as referring to actually existing and valid sciences. It is the ground of their *objective validity* that is sought. But what is investigated in the third question falsely lays claim to the title of science; we can enquire only as to the ground of its *subjective* possibility. In the fourth question, the problem takes still another form. Kant now seeks to determine *whether* a new, not yet existing, science of metaphysics is possible, and

---

[1] B 19.   [2] B 19.   [3] B 20.   [4] B 20.
[5] Cf. B 17.   [6] B 20.   [7] B 21.   [8] B 22.
[9] Vaihinger's analysis (i. p. 371 ff.) is invaluable. I follow it throughout.
[10] When corrected as above, pp. 51-2, 66-7.

in what manner it can be validly constructed.   The manifoldness of the problems is thus concealed by the fixity of the
common formula.[1]   Now with what divisions of the *Critique*
are the two last questions connected?   It has been suggested[2]
that the third question is dealt with in the *Dialectic* and the
fourth in the *Methodology*, the four questions thus corresponding to the four main divisions of the *Critique*.   But this
view is untenable, especially in its view of the fourth question.
The division of the *Critique* is by dichotomy into *doctrine of
elements* and *doctrine of methods*, the former including the
Aesthetic and *Logic*, and the *Logic* being again divided into
Analytic and *Dialectic*.   Its problems stand in an equally
complex subordination; they cannot be isolated from one
another, and set merely side by side.   Secondly, it has been
maintained[3] that the third question is dealt with in the introduction to the *Dialectic* (in its doctrine of Ideas), and the
fourth in the *Dialectic* proper.   This view is fairly satisfactory
as regards the third question, but would involve the conclusion
that the fourth question refers only to transcendent metaphysics, and that it therefore receives a negative answer.   But
that is not Kant's view of metaphysics *as a science*.   The
Critique is intended to issue in a new and genuine body of
metaphysical teaching.

The key to the whole problem of the four questions is not
to be found in the *Critique*.   This section is transcribed from
§§ 4-5 of the *Prolegomena*, and is consequently influenced by
the general arrangement of the latter work.   This fourfold
division was indeed devised for the purposes of the argument of
the *Prolegomena*, which is developed on the analytic method,
and for that reason it cannot be reconciled with the very
different structure of the *Critique*.   Yet even the *Prolegomena*
suffers from confusion, due[4] to Kant's failure to distinguish
between universal and relative natural science on the one
hand, and between immanent and transcendent metaphysics
on the other.   The four questions do not coincide with those
of the *Critique*.   Instead of the third—how is metaphysics as
natural disposition possible?—we find: *how is metaphysics in
general possible?*   In §§ 4, 5, Kant's argument is clear and
straightforward.   Pure mathematical science and mathematical
physics are actually existing sciences.   The synthetic *a priori*
judgments which they contain must be recognised as valid.
Metaphysics makes similar claims.   But, as is sufficiently

[1] Cf. above, p. 38 ff.
[2] By J. Erdmann (cited by Vaihinger, i. p. 371).
[3] By B. Erdmann, *Kriticismus*, p. 183.
[4] As above noted, pp. 66-7.

proved by the absence of agreement among philosophers, its professions are without ground. It transgresses the limits of possible experience, and contains only pretended knowledge. This false transcendent metaphysics is refuted in the *Dialectic*. Kant was, however, equally convinced that an *immanent* metaphysics is possible, and that its grounds and justification had been successfully given in the *Analytic*. His problem as formulated in the *Prolegomena* is accordingly threefold: (1) how are the existing rational sciences, mathe-matical and physical, possible? (2) *in the light of the insight acquired by this investigation*, what is the origin and explana-tion of the existing pretended sciences of transcendent metaphysics? and (3) in what manner can we establish a positive metaphysics that will harmonise with reason's true vocation? So far all is clear and definite. But the un-resolved difficulty, as to the relation in which natural science and immanent metaphysics stand to one another, brings confusion in its train. As already noted,[1] in § 15 natural science is displaced by immanent metaphysics (though not under that name); and as a result the fourth question reduces to the second, and the above threefold problem has to be completely restated. The *Prolegomena* has, however, already been divided into four parts; and in the last division Kant still continues to treat the fourth question as distinct from that which has been dealt with in the second division, though, as his answer shows, they are essentially the same. The answer given is that metaphysics as a science is possible only in and through the *Critique*, and that though the whole *Critique* is required for this purpose, the *content* of the new science is embodied in the *Analytic*.

In the second edition of the *Critique* the confusion between natural science and immanent metaphysics still persists, and a new source of ambiguity is added through the reformulation of the third question. It is now limited to the problem of the *subjective* origin of metaphysics as a natural disposition. The fourth question has therefore to be widened, so as to include transcendent as well as immanent, the old as well as the new, metaphysics. But save for this one alteration the entire section is inspired by considerations foreign to the *Critique*; this section, like B 17, must be recast before it will harmonise with the subsequent argument.

Every kind of knowledge is called pure, etc.[2]—These sentences are omitted in the second edition. They have been rendered unnecessary by the further and more adequate definition of "pure" given in B 3 ff.

---

[1] Above, p. 66.   [2] A 11.

Reason is the faculty which supplies the principles of knowledge a priori.[1]—This statement should, as Vaihinger points out, be interpreted in the light of A 299 = B 355.

" Reason, like understanding, can be employed in a merely formal, *i.e.* logical manner, wherein it abstracts from all content of knowledge. But it is also capable of a real use,[2] since it contains within itself the source of certain concepts and principles, which it does not borrow either from the senses or from the understanding."

Reason is taken in the first of the above meanings. Reason in its real use, when extended so as to include pure sensibility and understanding,[3] is the pure reason referred to in the next sentence of the *Critique*. *A priori* is here used to signify the relatively *a priori* ; in the next sentence it denotes the absolutely *a priori*.

An Organon of pure reason.[4]—What follows, from this point to the middle of the next section, is a good example of Kant's patchwork method of piecing together old manuscript in the composition of the *Critique*. There seems to be no way of explaining its bewildering contradictions save by accepting Vaihinger's[5] conclusion that it consists of three separate accounts, written at different times, and representing different phases in the development of Kant's views.

I. The first account, beginning with the above words and ending with "already a considerable gain" (*schon sehr viel gewonnen ist*), is evidently the oldest. It reveals the influence of the *Dissertation*. It distinguishes :

    1. **Critique** of pure reason (= *Propaedeutic*)
    2. **Organon** of pure reason.
    3. **System** of pure reason.

    1. **Critique** is a critical examination (*Beurtheilung*) of pure reason, its sources and limits. The implication (obscured by the direct relating of *Critique* to *System*) is that it prepares the way for the *Organon*.

    2. **Organon** comprehends all the principles by which pure knowledge can be acquired and actually established.

    3. **System** is the complete application of such an *Organon*.

This classification is, as Paulsen[6] was the first to remark, an adaptation of the *Dissertation* standpoint.

II. The second account begins : " I entitle all knowledge transcendental," but is broken by the third account—from "Such a *Critique*" to the end of the paragraph—which has

---

[1] A 11 = B 24.
[2] Cf. *Dissertation*, § 23 : *usus logicus—usus realis.*   [3] Cf. above, p. 2.
[4] A 11 = B 24.   [5] i. p. 459 ff.
[6] *Entwickelungsgeschichte der Kantischen Erkenntnistheorie*, p. 113.

been inserted into the middle of it. It is then continued in the next section. It distinguishes:

1. **Critique** of pure reason.
2. **Transcendental philosophy.**

1. **Critique** contains the principles of all *a priori synthetical* knowledge, tracing an architectonic plan which guarantees the completeness and certainty of all the parts.

2. **Transcendental philosophy** contains their complete analytic development, and is therefore the system of such knowledge.

III. The third account ("Such a *Critique*" to end of paragraph) in its main divisions follows the first account: 1. *Critique*, 2. *Organon* or *Canon*, 3. *System*. But they are now defined in a different manner. *Critique* is a propaedeutic for the *Organon*. But *Organon*, which signifies the totality of the principles through which pure knowledge is attained and extended,[1] may not be possible. In that case the *Critique* is a preparation only for a *Canon*, *i.e.* the totality of the principles of the *proper* employment of reason.[2] The *Organon* or *Canon*, in turn, will render possible a *System* of the philosophy of pure reason, the former yielding a system in extension of *a priori* knowledge, the latter a system which defines the limits of *a priori* knowledge.

It is impossible to reduce these divergencies to a single consistent view. They illustrate the varying sense in which Kant uses the term "metaphysics." In the first account, even though that account is based on a distinction drawn in the *Dissertation*, the *system* of metaphysics is immanent, in the second it is also transcendent; in the third it is neutral.[3]

Propaedeutic.[4]—That the *Critique* is only propaedeutic to a *System* of pure reason was later denied by Kant in the following emphatic terms:

"I must here observe that I cannot understand the attempt to ascribe to me the view that I have sought to supply only a Propaedeutic to transcendental philosophy, not the System of this philosophy. Such a view could never have entered my thoughts, for I have myself praised the systematic completeness (*das vollendete Ganze*) of the pure philosophy in the *Critique of Pure Reason* as the best mark of its truth."[5]

---

[1] Cf. A 795 = B 823. Cf. below, pp. 170, 174.   [2] Cf. A 796 = B 824.
[3] Cf. Vaihinger, i. pp. 461-2 for the very varied meanings in which Kant "capriciously" employs the terms *Organon, Canon, Doctrine*, and *Discipline*.
[4] A 11 = B 25.
[5] *Erklärung in Beziehung auf Fichte's Wissenschaftslehre* (1799), *Werke* (Hartenstein), viii. p. 600.

Kant thus finally, after much vacillation in his use of the terms, came to the conclusion that *Critique, Transcendental Philosophy*, and *System* all coincide. Meantime he has forgotten his own previous and conflicting utterances on this point.

As regards speculation negative only.[1]—"Speculation" here signifies the theoretical, as opposed to the practical.[2] The qualifying phrase is in line with other passages of the second edition, in which it is emphasised that the conclusions of the *Critique* are positive in their practical (moral) bearing.[3]

Transcendental — transcendent.[4]—Kant was the first to distinguish between these two terms. In the scholastic period, in which they first appear, they were exactly synonymous, the term transcendent being the more usual. The verb, to transcend, appears in Augustine in its widest metaphysical sense. "Transcende et te ipsum." "Cuncta corpora transcenderunt [Platonici] quaerentes Deum ; omnem animam mutabilesque omnes spiritus transcenderunt quaerentes summum Deum."[5] The first employment of the term in a more specific or technical sense occurs in a treatise, *De natura generis*, falsely ascribed to Thomas Aquinas. In this treatise *ens, res, aliquid, unum, bonum, verum* are entitled *transcendentia*. To understand the meaning in which the word is here used, we have, it would seem, to take account of the influence exercised upon Aquinas by a work entitled *De causis*[6]—a translation from Proclus. It contained reference to the Neo-Platonic distinction between the Aristotelian categories, which the Neo-Platonists regarded as being derivative, and the more universal concepts, *ens, unum, verum, bonum*. To these latter concepts Aquinas gave a theological application. *Ens* pertains to essence, *unum* to the person of the Father, *verum* to the person of the Son, *bonum* to the person of the Holy Ghost. In the *De natura generis* the number of these supreme concepts is increased to six by the addition of *res* and *aliquid*, and as just stated the title *transcendentia* is also now applied for the first time. In this meaning the term transcendent and its synonym transcendental are of frequent occurrence in Scholastic writings. The *transcendentia* or *transcendentalia* are those concepts which so transcend the categories as to be themselves predicable of the categories. They are the "*termini vel proprietates rebus omnibus cuiusque generis convenientes*." Thus Duns Scotus speaks of *ens* as the

---

[1] B 25. [2] Cf. A xv. [3] Cf. B xxiv. [4] A 11 = B 25.
[5] *De vera religione*, 72 ; *De civitate Dei*, viii. 6. Cited by Eisler, *Wörterbuch*, p. 1521.
[6] Professor A. E. Taylor informs me that Prantl (*Geschichte der Logik im Abendlande*, iii. pp. 114, 244-5) is in error in describing this work as of Arabian origin.

highest of the "*transcendental*" concepts. The term also occurs in a more or less similar sense in the writings of Campanella, Giordano Bruno, Francis Bacon, and Spinoza. The last named gives a psychological explanation of the "termini *Transcendentales* . . . ut Ens, Res, Aliquid" as standing for ideas that are in the highest degree confused owing to the multiplicity of the images which have neutralised one another in the process of their generation.[1] Berkeley also speaks of the "transcendental maxims" which lie outside the field of mathematical enquiry, but which influence all the particular sciences.[2] Evidently the term has become generalised beyond its stricter scholastic meaning. Lambert employs transcendent in an even looser sense to signify concepts which represent what is common to both the corporeal and the intellectual world.[3] We may, indeed, assert that in Kant's time the terms transcendent and transcendental, while still remaining synonymous, and though used on the lines of their original Scholastic connotation, had lost all definiteness of meaning and all usefulness of application. Kant took advantage of this situation to distinguish sharply between them, and to impose upon each a meaning suitable to his new Critical teaching.

"Transcendental" is primarily employed by Kant as a name for a certain kind of knowledge. Transcendental knowledge is knowledge not of objects, but of the nature and conditions of our *a priori* cognition of them. In other words, *a priori* knowledge must not be asserted, simply because it is *a priori*, to be transcendental; this title applies only to such knowledge as constitutes a *theory* or *science* of the *a priori*.[4] Transcendental knowledge and transcendental philosophy must therefore be taken as coinciding; and as thus coincident, they signify the science of the possibility, nature, and limits of *a priori* knowledge. The term similarly applies to the subdivisions of the *Critique*. The *Aesthetic* is transcendental in that it establishes the *a priori* character of the forms of sensibility; the *Analytic* in that it determines the *a priori* principles of understanding, and the part which they play in the constitution of knowledge; the *Dialectic* in that it defines and limits the *a priori* Ideas of Reason, to the

---

[1] *Ethica* (Vloten and Land), ii. prop. xl. schol. 1.

[2] *Principles of Human Knowledge*, cxviii. The above citations are from Eisler, *loc. cit.* pp. 1524-5. I have also myself come upon the term in Swift's *Gulliver's Travels* (Dent, 1897, p. 166): "And as to 'ideas, entities, abstractions, and transcendentals,' I could never drive the least conception into their heads."

[3] *Organon*, i. 484, cited by Eucken in *Geschichte der philosophischer Termino-logie*, p. 205.

[4] A 11 = B 25, A 56 = B 80.

perverting power of which all false metaphysics is due. That this is the primary and fundamental meaning common to the various uses of the term is constantly overlooked by Max Müller. Thus in A 15 = B 30 he translates *transcendentale Sinnenlehre* "doctrine of transcendental sense" instead of as "transcendental doctrine of sense." In transforming *transcendentale Elementarlehre* into "elements of transcendentalism" he avoids the above error, but only by inventing a word which has no place in Kant's own terminology.

But later in the *Critique* Kant employs the term transcendental in a second sense, namely, to denote the *a priori* factors in knowledge. All representations which are *a priori* and yet are applicable to objects are transcendental. The term is then defined through its distinction from the empirical on the one hand, and from the transcendent on the other. An intuition or conception is transcendental when it originates in pure reason, and yet at the same time goes to constitute an *a priori* knowledge of objects. The contrast between the transcendental and the transcendent, as similarly determined upon by Kant, is equally fundamental, but is of quite different character. That is transcendent which lies entirely beyond experience ; whereas the transcendental signifies those *a priori* elements which underlie experience as its necessary conditions. The transcendent is always unknowable. The transcendental is that which by conditioning experience renders all knowledge, whether *a priori* or empirical, possible. The direct opposite of the transcendent is the immanent, which as such includes both the transcendental and the empirical. Thus while Kant employs the term transcendental in a very special sense which he has himself arbitrarily determined, he returns to the original etymological meaning of the term transcendent. It gains a specifically Critical meaning only through being used to expound the doctrine that all knowledge is limited to sense - experience. The attempt to find some similar etymological justification for Kant's use of the term transcendental has led Schopenhauer and Kuno Fischer to assert that Kant entitles his philosophy transcendental because it transcends both the dogmatism and the scepticism of all previous systems ![1] Another attempt has been made by Stirling[2] and Watson,[3] who assert, at least by implication, that the transcendental is a species of the transcendent, in that while the latter transcends the scope of experience, the former transcends its sense-content. Kant himself, however,

---

[1] Cited by Vaihinger, i. p. 468.
[2] Cf. *Text-Book to Kant*, p. 13.
[3] Cf. *Kant Explained*, p. 89.

nowhere attempts to justify his use of the term by any such argument.

A third meaning of the term transcendental arises through its extension from the *a priori* intuitions and concepts to the processes and faculties to which they are supposed to be due. Thus Kant speaks of the transcendental syntheses of apprehension, reproduction, and recognition, and of the transcendental faculties of imagination and understanding. In this sense the transcendental becomes a title for the conditions which render experience possible. And inasmuch as processes and faculties can hardly be entitled *a priori*, Kant has in this third application of the term departed still further from his first definition of it.[1]

The distinction between the transcendental and the transcendent may be illustrated by reference to the Ideas of reason. Regarded as regulative only, *i.e.* merely as ideals which inspire the understanding in the pursuit of knowledge, they are transcendental. Interpreted as constitutive, *i.e.* as representing absolute realities, they are transcendent. Yet, despite the fundamental character of this distinction, so careless is Kant in the use of his technical terms that he also employs transcendental as exactly equivalent in meaning to transcendent. This is of constant occurrence, but only two instances need here be cited. In the important phrase "transcendental ideality of space and time" the term transcendental is used in place of the term transcendent. For what Kant is asserting is that judged from a *transcendent* point of view, *i.e.* from the point of view of the thing in itself, space is only subjectively real.[2] The phrase is indeed easily capable of the orthodox interpretation, but, as the context clearly shows, that is not the way in which it is actually being used by Kant. Another equally surprising example is to be found in the title "transcendental dialectic." Though it is defined in A 63-4 = B 88 in correct fashion, in A 297 = B 354 and A 308-9 = B 365-6 it is interpreted as treating of the illusion involved in transcendent judgments, and so virtually as meaning *transcendent* dialectic.[3]

Not a Critique of books and systems.[4]—Kant here inserts a statement from the omitted *Preface* to the first edition.[5] He now adds that the *Critique* will supply a criterion for the valuation of all other systems.

---

[1] Cf. below, p. 238.   [2] Cf. below, pp. 116-17, 302.

[3] Adickes has taken the liberty in his edition of the *Critique* of substituting in A 297 = B 354 transcendental for transcendent. The Berlin edition very rightly retains the original reading.

[4] B 27.   [5] A vi.

A 13 = B 27.—Kant's reason for omitting the title of Section II in the second edition was no doubt its inconsistency with the assertion of its opening sentence, viz. that the *Critique* is *not* transcendental philosophy, but only a preparation for it. Instead of it, Kant has introduced the more appropriate heading placed over the preceding paragraph.

The highest principles of morals do not belong to transcendental philosophy.[1]—Cf. A 801 = B 829. The alteration made in this passage in the second edition[2] indicates a transition towards the opposite view which Kant developed in the *Critique of Practical Reason*.[3]

The division of this science.[4]—Kant in this paragraph alternates in the most bewildering fashion between the *Critique* and *Transcendental Philosophy*. In this first sentence the *Critique* seems to be referred to. Later it is *Transcendental Philosophy* that is spoken of.

Doctrine of Elements and Doctrine of Methods.[5]—Cf. A 707 ff. = B 735 ff., and below, pp. 438, 563.

Two stems, sensibility and understanding, which may perhaps spring from a common root.[6]—Kant sometimes seems to suggest[7] that imagination is this common root. It belongs both to sensibility and to understanding, and is passive as well as spontaneous. But when so viewed, imagination is virtually regarded as an unknown supersensuous power, "concealed in the depths of the soul."[8] The supersensuous is the point of union of our disparate human faculties, as well as of nature and freedom, mechanism and teleology.

The transcendntal doctrine of sense would necessarily constitute the first part of the Science of Elements.[9]—"Necessarily constitute the first part" translates *zum ersten Theile gehören müssen*. This Vaihinger explains as an archaic mode of expression, equivalent to *ausmachen*. The point is important because, if translated quite literally, it might seem to conflict with the division actually followed, and to support the alternative division given in the *Critique of Practical Reason*. The first *Critique* is divided thus:

---

[1] A 14-15=B 28. Cf. below, p. 570 n.
[2] This alteration is not given in Max Müller's translation.
[3] Cf. the corresponding alteration made in the second edition at end of note to A 21=B 35.   [4] A 15=B 29.
[5] *Loc. cit.*   [6] *Loc. cit.* Cf. A 835=B 863.
[7] Cf. A 124, B 151-2, and below, pp. 225, 265.
[8] Cf. A 141=B 180-1. Cf. *Critique of Judgment*, § 57 : "Thus here [in the *Critique of Aesthetic Judgment*], as also in the *Critique of Practical Reason*, the antinomies force us against our will to look beyond the sensible and to seek in the supersensible the point of union for all our *a priori* faculties ; because no other expedient is left to make our Reason harmonious with itself." Cf. also below, p. 473 ff., in comment on A 649=B 677.   [9] A 16=B 30.

I. Doctrine of Elements.
  1. Aesthetic.
  2. Logic.
      (*a*) Analytic.
      (*b*) Dialectic.
II. Doctrine of Methods.

In the *Critique of Practical Reason*[1] a much more satis-factory division is suggested :

I. Doctrine of Elements.
  1. Analytic.
      (*a*) Aesthetic (Sense).
      (*b*) Logic (Understanding).
  2. Dialectic.
II. Doctrine of Methods.

The first division rests on somewhat irrelevant distinctions derived from the traditional logic ; the other is more directly inspired by the distinctions which naturally belong to Kant's own philosophical system.

[1] *Introduction* (*W.* v. p. 16). Cf. below, p. 438.

THE TRANSCENDENTAL DOCTRINE OF ELEMENTS

PART I

THE TRANSCENDENTAL AESTHETIC

THE *Aesthetic* opens with a series of definitions. Intuition (*Anschauung*) is knowledge (*Erkenntnis*) which is in immediate relation to objects (*sich auf Gegenstände unmittelbar bezieht*). Each term in this definition calls for comment. *Anschauung* etymologically applies only to visual sensation. Kant extends it to cover sensations of all the senses. The current term was *Empfindung*. Kant's reason for introducing the term intuition in place of sensation was evidently the fact that the latter could not be made to cover space and time. We can speak of pure intuitions, but not of pure sensations. *Knowledge* is used in a very wide sense, not strictly consistent with A 50-1 = B 74-5.[1] The phrase *sich bezieht* is quite indefinite and ambiguous. Its meaning will depend upon the interpretation of its context. *Object* is used in its widest and most indefinite meaning. It may be taken as signifying content (*Inhalt*, a term which does not occur in this passage, but which Kant elsewhere employs[2]). That, at least, is the meaning which best fits the context. For when Kant adds that intuition relates itself to objects *immediately*, it becomes clear that he has in mind its distinction from conception (*Begriff*) which as expressing the universal is related to objects only indirectly, representing some one or more attributes of the *given* objects. Ultimately the whole content of conception must be given.[3] The phrase "relates itself to objects" may, therefore, be paraphrased "has some content, such as red or cold, as its immediate object." Through the content of intuition the whole material of thought is supplied.

---

[1] Cf. also above, p. 25.   [2] Cf. A 51 = B 75.
[3] That thought finds in intuition its sole possible content is, of course, a conclusion first established in the *Analytic*. Kant is here defining his terms in the light of his later results. Cf. *W.* xi. pp. 311, 314-15, 338, 347-8.

Intuition in itself is blind, but not empty. " Thoughts without content are empty ; intuitions without concepts are blind."[1]

But the phrase "is in relation to objects" has also for Kant a second meaning, implied in the above, but supplementary to it. As he states in the very next sentence, intuition can have an object, meaning thereby a content, only in so far as that content is *given*. The material of thought must be supplied ; it cannot be invented.[2] The only mode, however, in which it can be supplied, at least to the human mind, is through the affecting of the mind by "the object." This is an excellent instance of Kant's careless mode of expressing himself. In the first part of the sentence object means *object of intuition*. In the latter part it signifies the *cause of intuition*. And on Kant's view the two cannot coincide. The object which affects the mind is independently real ; the immediate object of the intuition is a sense-content, which Kant, following the universally accepted view of his time, regards as purely subjective. The term object is thus used in two quite distinct meanings within one and the same sentence.

Kant's definition of intuition, when stated quite explicitly, and cleared of all ambiguity, is therefore as follows. *Intuition is the immediate apprehension of a content which as given is due to the action of an independently real object upon the mind.* This definition is obviously not meant to be a description of intuition as it presents itself to introspection, but to be a reflective statement of its indispensable conditions. Also it has in view only empirical intuitions. It does not cover the pure intuitions space and time.[3] Though space and time are given, and though each possesses an intrinsic content, these contents are not due to the action of objects upon the sensibility.

"An intuition is such a representation as immediately depends upon the presence of the object. Hence it seems impossible *originally* to intuit *a priori* because intuition would in that event take place without either a former or a present object to refer to, and by consequence could not be intuition."[4]

This interpretation is borne out by Kant's answer to Beck when the latter objected that only through subsumption under the categories can a representation become objective. Kant replies in a marginal note, the meaning of which, though difficult to decipher, admits of a fairly definite interpretation.

---

[1] A 51 = B 75.   [2] Cf. *Prolegomena*, § 12, Remark ii. at the beginning.
[3] Cf. below, p. 88 ff. ; B 146-7.   [4] *Prolegomena*, § 8 (Eng. trans. p. 33)

"The determining of a concept through intuition so as to yield knowledge of the object falls within the province of the faculty of judgment, but not the relation of the intuition to an object in general [*i.e.* the view of it as having a content which is given and which is therefore due to some object], for that is merely the logical use of the representation, whereby it is thought as falling within the province of knowledge. On the other hand, if this single representation is related only to the subject, the use is aesthetic (feeling), and the representation cannot be an act of knowledge."[1]

Mind (*Gemüt*) is a neutral term without metaphysical implications.[2] It is practically equivalent to the term which is substituted for it in the next paragraph, power of representation (*Vorstellungsfähigkeit*). **Representation** (*Vorstellung*) Kant employs in the widest possible meaning. It covers any and every cognitive state. The definition here given of **sensibility**—"the capacity (receptivity) to obtain representations through the mode in which we are affected by objects" —is taken directly over from the *Dissertation*.[3] In this definition, as in that of intuition, Kant, without argument or question, postulates the existence of independently existing objects. The existence of given sensations presupposes the existence of things in themselves. Sensibility is spoken of as the source both of objects and of intuitions. This is legitimate since object and intuition mutually imply one another; the latter is the apprehension of the former. By "objects" is obviously meant what in the third paragraph is called the matter of appearances, *i.e.* sensations in their objective aspect, as qualities or contents. The term "object" is similarly employed in the last line of this first paragraph.

Understanding (*Verstand*) is defined only in its logical or discursive employment. Kant wisely defers all reference to its more fundamental synthetic activities. *In us* (*bei uns*) is an indirect reference to the possibility of intellectual (non-sensuous) intuition which is further developed in other parts of the *Aesthetic*.[4] Sensuous intuition is due to affection by an object. In intellectual intuition the mind must produce the object in the act of apprehending it.[5]

Kant's definition of intuition applies, as already noted, only to empirical intuition. He proceeds[6] to define the relation in which **sensation** (*Empfindung*) stands to empirical intuition. What he here says amounts to the assertion that through sensation intuition acquires its object, *i.e.* that *sensa-*

---

[1] Quoted by Vaihinger, ii. p. 4.
[2] Cf. *Ueber das Organ der Seele* (1796) and *Anthropologie*, § 22.
[3] § 3.   [4] A 27 = B 43, A 34 = B 51, A 42 = B 59, A 51 = B 75.
[5] Cf. B 72.   [6] In the second paragraph, A 20 = B 34.

tion is the content of intuition. And that being so, it is also through sensation that empirical intuition acquires its relation to the object (= thing in itself) which causes it. (That would seem to be the meaning of the ambiguous second sentence; but it still remains uncertain whether the opposition intended is to pure or to intellectual intuition.) If this interpretation of the paragraph be correct, sensation is counted as belonging exclusively to the content side of subjective apprehension. But Kant views sensation in an even more definite manner than he here indicates. Though sensation is given, it likewise involves a reaction of the mind.

"Whatever is sensuous in knowledge depends upon the subject's peculiar nature, in so far as it is capable of this or that modification upon the presence of the object."[1]

Thus for Kant sensation is a modification or state of the subject, produced by affection through an object. The affection produces a modification or state of the subject, and this subjective modification is the sensation.

"Sensation is a perception [*Perception*] which relates itself solely to the subject as the modification of its state."[2]

This view of sensation, as subjective, was universally held in Kant's day. He accepts it without argument or question. That it could possibly be challenged never seems to have occurred to him. He is equally convinced that it establishes the existence of an actually present object.

"Sensation argues the presence of something, but depends as to its quality upon the nature of the subject."[3] "Sensation presupposes the actual presence of the object."[4]

Kant's view of sensation, as developed in the *Aesthetic*,[5] thus involves three points: (1) It must be counted as belonging to the content side of mental apprehension. (2) Though a quality or content, it is purely subjective, depending upon the nature of our sensibility. (3) It is due to the action of some object upon the sensibility.

Kant distinguishes between **sensation** (*Empfindung*) and **feeling** (*Gefühl*).[6] It had been usual to employ them as synonyms.

---

[1] *Dissertation*, § 4. [3] A 320 = B 376.
[2] *Dissertation*, § 4. [4] A 50 = B 74.
[5] This view, as I shall endeavour to show, is only semi-Critical, and is profoundly modified by the more revolutionary conclusions to which Kant finally worked his way. Cf. below, p. 274 ff.
[6] In this he was anticipated by Tetens, *Philosophische Versuche über die menschliche Natur*, Bd. i. (1777), *Versuch* X. v. Cf. below, p. 294.

"We understand by the word sensation an objective representation of the senses; and in order to preclude the danger of being misunderstood, we shall denote that which must always remain merely subjective and can constitute absolutely no representation of an object by the ordinary (*sonst üblichen*) term feeling."[1]

Appearance (*Erscheinung*) is here defined as the undetermined object of an intuition. By undetermined object is meant, as we have seen, the object in so far as it consists of the given sense contents. When these contents are interpreted through the categories they become *phenomena*.

"Appearances so far as they are thought as objects according to the unity of the categories are called phenomena."[2]

But this distinction between appearance and phenomenon is not held to by Kant. He more usually speaks of the categorised objects as appearances. The term phenomenon is of comparatively rare occurrence in the *Critique*. This has been concealed from English readers, as both Meiklejohn and Max Müller almost invariably translate *Erscheinung* phenomenon. The statement that appearance is the *object* of an empirical intuition raises a very fundamental and difficult question, namely, as to the relation in which representation stands to the represented.[3] Frequently Kant's argument implies this distinction, yet constantly he speaks and argues as if it were non-existent. We have to recognise two tendencies in Kant, subjectivist and phenomenalist.[4] When the former tendency is in the ascendent, he regards all appearances, all phenomena, all empirical objects, as representations, modifications of the sensibility, merely subjective. When, on the other hand, his thinking is dominated by the latter tendency, appearances gain an existence independent of the individual mind. They are known through subjective representations, but must not be directly equated with them. They have a genuine objectivity. To this distinction, and its consequences, we shall have frequent occasion to return.

The phenomenalist standpoint is dominant in these first two paragraphs of the *Aesthetic*, and it finds still more pro-

[1] *Critique of Judgment*, § 3 (Eng. trans. p. 49). Kant was the first to adopt the threefold division of mental powers—"the faculty of knowledge, the feeling of pleasure and pain, and the faculty of desire." This threefold division is first given in his *Ueber Philosophie überhaupt* (Hartenstein, vi. p. 379), which was written some time between 1780 and 1790, being originally designed as an Introduction to the *Critique of Judgment*.

[2] A 248 (occurs in a lengthy section omitted in B).

[3] This distinction between intuition and appearance practically coincides with that above noted between intuition and its object.

[4] For statement of the precise meaning in which these terms are here employed, cf. above, pp. xlv-vii; below, pp. 270 ff., 312 ff.

nounced expression in the opening of the third paragraph. "That in the appearances which *corresponds* (*correspondirt*) to sensation, I call its matter." This sentence, through the use of the term corresponds, clearly implies a distinction between sensation and the real object apprehended in and through it. That, in turn, involves a threefold distinction, between sensation as subjective content (= appearance in the strict sense), the real enduring object in space (= phenomenon, the categorised object, appearance in its wider and more usual sense), and the thing in itself.[1]   Yet in the immediately following sentence Kant says that "the matter of all appearance is given *a posteriori*." By "matter of appearance" Kant must there mean sensations, for they alone are given *a posteriori*.[2] On this view the phenomena or empirical objects reduce to, and consist of, sensations. The intermediate term of the above threefold distinction is eliminated. The matter of appearance does not correspond to, but itself *is*, sensation. Thus in these successive sentences the two conflicting tendencies of Kant's teaching find verbal expression. They intervene even in the preliminary definition of his terms. This fundamental conflict cannot, however, be profitably discussed at this stage.

The **manifold of appearance** (*das Mannichfaltige der Erscheinung*). The meaning to be assigned to this phrase must depend upon the settlement of the above question.[3] But in this passage it allows only of a subjectivist interpretation, whereby sensations *are* appearance. The given sensations as such constitute a manifold ; as objects in space they are already ordered. Kant's more usual phrase is "the manifold of intuition." His adoption of the term "manifold" (the *varia* of the *Dissertation*) expresses his conviction that synthesis is indispensable for all knowledge, and also his correlative view that nothing absolutely simple can be apprehended in sense-experience. By the manifold Kant does not mean, however, as some of his commentators would seem to imply, the chaotic or disordered. The emphasis is on manifoldness or plurality, as calling for reduction to unity and system. The unity has to be *found* in it, not introduced into it forcibly from the outside. The manifold has to be *interpreted*, even though the principles of interpretation may originate independently of it. Though, for instance, the

---

[1] This would harmonise with the view developed in A 166 (in its formulation of the principle of the *Anticipations*), A 374 ff., B 274 ff., A 723 = B 751.

[2] Cf. A 50 = B 74: "We may name sensation the matter of sensuous knowledge." Similarly in A 42 = B 59; *Prolegomena*, § 11 ; *Fortschritte*, (Hartenstein, viii. p. 527).

[3] Cf. below, p. 274 ff.

manifold as given is not in space and time, the specific space and time relations assigned by us are determined for us by the inherent nature of the manifold itself.[1]

The form of appearance is defined—if the definition given in the first edition be translated literally—as " that which causes (*dasjenige, welches macht dass*) the manifold of appearance to be intuited as ordered in certain relations." This phrase is employed by Kant in other connections, and, as Vaihinger points out,[2] need not necessarily indicate activity. " Sensation is that in our knowledge which causes it to be called *a posteriori* knowledge."[3] In the second edition Kant altered the text from " *geordnet angeschaut wird* " to " *geordnet werden kann*." The reason probably was that the first edition's wording might seem to imply that the form is (as the *Dissertation* taught) capable in and by itself of ordering the manifold. Throughout the second edition Kant makes more prominent the part which understanding plays in the apprehension of space.[4]

This distinction between matter and form is central in Kant's system.[5] As he himself says :

"These are two conceptions which underlie all other reflection, so inseparably are they bound up with all employment of the understanding. The one [matter] signifies the determinable in general, the other [form] its determination."[6]

On the side of matter falls the manifold, given, empirical, contingent material of sense ; on the side of form fall the unifying, *a priori*, synthetic, relational instruments of sensibility and thought. For Kant these latter are no mere abstractions, capable of being *distinguished* by the mind ; they differ from the matter of experience in nature, in function, and in origin. Upon this dualistic mode of conceiving the two factors depends the strength as well as the weakness of his position. To its perverting influence most of the unsatisfactory features of his doctrine of space and time can be directly traced. But to it is also due his appreciation of the new Critical problems, with their revolutionary consequences, as developed in the *Analytic*.

Kant proceeds to argue : (*a*) that the distinction is between two elements of fundamentally different nature and origin. The matter is given *a posteriori* in sensation ; the form, as distinct from all sensation, must lie ready *a priori* in the mind. (*b*) Kant also argues that form, because of its separate origin, is

---

[1] Cf. below, pp. 366-7, 370-2, 377.   [2] ii. p. 59.   [3] A 42=B 60
[4] Cf. *Reflexionen*, ii. note to 469 ; also note to 357.
[5] Cf. above, p. xxxiii ff.   [6] A 266=B 322.

capable of being contemplated apart from all sensation.   The above statements rest upon the unexpressed assumption that sensations have no spatial attributes of any kind.[1]   In themselves they have only intensive, not extensive, magnitude.[2] Kant assumes this without question, and without the least attempt at proof.[3]   The assumption appears in Kant's writings as early as 1768 as a self-evident principle ;[4] and throughout the *Critique* is treated as a premiss for argument, never as a statement calling for proof.   The only kind of supporting argument which is even indirectly suggested by Kant is that space cannot by itself act upon the senses.[5]   This would seem to be his meaning when he declares[6] that it is no object, but only an *ens imaginarium*.   "Space is no object of the senses."[7] Such argument, however, presupposes that space can be conceived apart from objects.   It is no proof that an extended object may not yield extended sensations.   Kant completely ignores the possibility that formal relations may be given in and with the sensations.   If our sensibility, in consequence of the action of objects upon it, is able to generate qualitative

---

[1] In discussing *a* and *b* we may for the present identify form with space. The problem has special complications in reference to time.

[2] Cf. B 207.

[3] Herbart's doctrine of space, Lotze's local sign theory, also the empiricist theories of the Mills and Bain, all rest upon this same assumption.   It was first effectively called in question by William James.   Cf. Bergson: *Les Données immédiates*, pp. 70-71, Eng. trans. pp. 92-3 : "The solution given by Kant does not seem to have been seriously disputed since his time : indeed, it has forced itself, sometimes without their knowledge, on the majority of those who have approached the problem anew, whether nativists or empiricists.   Psychologists agree in assigning a Kantian origin to the nativistic explanation of Johann Müller ; but Lotze's hypothesis of local signs, Bain's theory, and the more comprehensive explanation suggested by Wundt, may seem at first sight quite independent of the *Transcendental Aesthetic*.   The authors of these theories seem indeed to have put aside the problem of the nature of space, in order to investigate simply by what process our sensations come to be situated in space and to be set, so to speak, alongside one another : but this very question shows that they regard sensations as inextensive, and make a radical distinction, just as Kant did, between the matter of representation and its form.   The conclusion to be drawn from the theories of Lotze and Bain, and from Wundt's attempt to reconcile them, is that the sensations by means of which we come to form the notion of space are themselves unextended and simply qualitative : extensity is supposed to result from their synthesis, as water from the combination of two gases.   The empirical or genetic explanations have thus taken up the problem of space at the very point where Kant left it : Kant separated space from its contents : the empiricists ask how these contents, which are taken out of space by our thought, manage to get back again."   Bergson proceeds to argue that the analogy of chemical combination is quite inapplicable, and that some "unique act very like what Kant calls an *a priori* form" must still be appealed to.   With the Kantian standpoint in this matter Bergson does not, of course, agree.   He is merely pointing out what the consequences must be of this initial assumption of inextensive sensations.

[4] Cf. *Von dem ersten Grunde des Unterschiedes der Gegenden im Raume*, in its penultimate paragraph.

[5] Cf. *Dissertation*, last sentence of § 4, quoted below, p. 87.

[6] A 291 = B 347 ; A 429 = B 457.   [7] *Reflexionen*, ii. 334.

sensations, why, as Vaihinger very pertinently enquires,[1] should it be denied the power of also producing, in consequence of these same causes, impressions of quantitative formal nature? Sensations, on Kant's view, are the product of mind much more than of objects. Why, then, may not space itself be sensational?[2] From the point of view of empirical science there is no such radical difference between cause and effect in the latter case as exists in the former. As Herbert Spencer has remarked,[3] Kant makes the enormous assumption

" . . . that no differences among our sensations are determined by any differences in the *non-ego* (for to say that they are so determined is to say that the form under which the *non-ego* exists produces an effect upon the *ego*); and as it similarly follows that the order of coexistence and sequence among these sensations is not determined by any order in the *non-ego*; we are compelled to conclude that all these differences and changes in the *ego* are self-determined."

Kant's argument in the *Dissertation* is exactly of this nature.

"Objects do not strike the senses by their form. In order, therefore, that the various impressions from the object acting on the sense may coalesce into some whole of representation, there is required an inner principle of the mind through which in accordance with stable and innate laws that manifold may take on some form."[4]

In the paragraph before us Kant may, at first sight, seem to offer an argument. He is really only restating his premiss. "That wherein alone sensations can be arranged (*sich ordnen*[5]) and placed in a certain form cannot itself again be sensation." Now, of course, if the term sensation is to be limited to the sense qualities, *i.e.* to content or matter, conceived as existing apart from all formal relations, the formal elements cannot possibly be sensational. The legitimacy of

---

[1] ii. p. 73.

[2] Cf. Stout: *Manual of Psychology* (3rd edition), pp. 465-6. "We find that the definite apprehension of an order of coexistence, as such, arises and develops only in connection with that peculiar aspect of sense-experience which we have called *extensity*, and more especially the extensity of sight and touch. Two sounds or a sound and a smell may be presented as coexistent in the sense of being simultaneous; but taken by themselves apart from association with experiences of touch and sight, they are not apprehended as spatially juxtaposed or separated by a perceived spatial interval or as having perceived spatial direction and distance relatively to each other. Such relations can only be perceived or imagined, except perhaps in a very rudimentary way, when the external object is determined for us as an extensive whole by the extensity of the same presentation through which we apprehend it."

[3] *Principles of Psychology*, § 399, cited by Vaihinger.   [4] § 4.

[5] *Sich ordnen* has here, in line with common German usage, the force of a passive verb.

that limitation is, however, the question at issue. It cannot be thus decided by an arbitrary verbal distinction.

"Were the contention that the relations of sensations are not themselves sensed correct, the inference to the pure apriority of the form of our perception would be inevitable. For sensation is the sole form of interaction between consciousness and reality. . . . But that contention is false. The relations of sensations, their determined coexistence and sequence, impress consciousness, just as do the sensations. We feel this impression in the compulsion which the determinateness of the empirical manifolds lays upon the perceiving consciousness. The mere affection of consciousness by these relations does not, indeed, by itself suffice for their apprehension; but neither does it suffice for the apprehension of the sensation itself. Thus there is in these respects no difference between the matter and the form of appearance."[1]

In this way, then, by means of his definition of sensation, Kant surreptitiously introduces his fundamental assumption. That assumption reappears as the conclusion that since the form of appearance cannot be sensation, it does not arise through the action of the object, and consequently must be *a priori*. Though the paragraph seems to offer an argument in support of the apriority of space and time, it is found on examination merely to unfold a position adopted without the slightest attempt at proof.[2]

The form of appearance must lie ready in the mind.[3]— Comment upon this, in order to be adequate, had best take the form of a systematic discussion of Kant's views, here and elsewhere, of space as an *a priori* form of intuition. As already stated, the definition which Kant gives of intuition—as knowledge which stands in immediate relation to objects—applies only to empirical intuition. Though by the term object Kant, in so far as he is definite, means content, that content is such as can arise only through the action of some independent object upon the sensibility. In other words, the content apprehended must be sensuous. Now such a view of intuition obviously does not apply to pure intuition. As the concluding line of the paragraph before us states, pure intuition "can be contemplated in separation from all sensation;" and as the next paragraph adds, it exists in the mind "without any actual object of the senses." Yet Kant does not mean to imply that it is without content of any kind. "This pure

---

[1] Riehl : *Kriticismus* (1876–1879) ii. *Erster Theil*, p. 164. As already noted, Kant tacitly admits this in regard to time relations of coexistence and sequence. He continues, however, to deny it in regard to space relations.
[2] Cf. below, pp. 101-2, 105.   [3] A 20=B 34.

form of sensibility may also itself be called pure intuition."[1]
"It can be known before all actual perception, and for that
reason is called pure intuition."[2]   Though, therefore, pure
intuition has an intrinsic content, and is the immediate
apprehension of that content, it stands in no relation to any
actual independent object.   The content as well as the form
is *a priori*.   That, however, raises wider questions, and these
we must now discuss.

Here, as in most of his fundamental positions, Kant enter-
tains divergent and mutually contradictory doctrines.   Only
in his later utterances does he in any degree commit himself
to one consistent view.   The position to which he finally
inclines must not, however, be allowed to dominate the interpretation of his earlier statements.   The *Aesthetic* calls
for its own separate exegesis, quite as if it formed by itself
an independent work.   Its problems are discussed from a
standpoint more or less peculiar to itself.   The commentator
has the twofold task of stating its argumentation both in
its conflict with, and in its relation to, the other parts of the
Critique.

One essential difference between Kant's earlier and later
treatments of space is that in his earlier utterances it is
viewed almost exclusively as a psychological *a priori.*   The
logical aspect of the problem first receives anything like
adequate recognition in the *Analytic.*   If we keep this important fact in mind, two distinct and contradictory views
of the psychological nature of space intuition can be traced
throughout the *Aesthetic.*   On one view, it antedates experience as an actual, completed, conscious intuition.   On
the other view, it precedes experience only as a potential disposition.   We rule ourselves out from understanding Kant's
most explicit utterances if we refuse to recognise the
existence of both views.   Kant's commentators have too
frequently shut their eyes to the first view, and have then
blamed Kant for using misleading expressions.   It is always
safer to take Kant quite literally.   He nearly always means
exactly what he says at the time when he says it.   Frequently
he holds views which run completely counter to present-day
psychology, and on several occasions he flatly contradicts
what he has with equal emphasis maintained in other con-
texts.   The aspects of Kant's problems are so complex and
various, and he is so preoccupied in doing complete justice

[1] A 20 = B 34.
[2] A 42 = B 60.   Cf. *Dissertation*, § 12 : ["Space and time, the objects of pure
mathematics,] are not only formal principles of all intuition, but themselves
original intuitions."

to each in turn, that the question of the mutual consistency of his results is much less considered than is ideally desirable.

The two views can be more explicitly formulated. The first view alone is straightforward and unambiguous. Space lies ready (*liegt bereit*) in the mind, *i.e.* it does not arise. Prior even to sense-experience it exists as a *conscious* intuition. For this reason it can be contemplated apart from all sensation. It still remains when all sense content is thought away, and yet is not a mere form. In independence of the sensuous manifold it possesses a pure manifold of its own. The ground thesis of the second view—that space, prior to sense-experience, exists only as a permanent endowment of the mind—is likewise unambiguous. But in its development Kant throws consistency to the winds. The possible ways in which, on the second view, consciousness of space may be gained, can be tabulated as follows :

(*a*) By reflection upon the activity of the mind in the construction of experience, yielding the intuition of a pure manifold ; or (*b*) by reflection upon the space-endowed products of experience.[1] The latter mode of reflection may reveal :

(α) A pure manifold distinct from the manifold of sense ; or

(β) Space as a form of the sensuous manifold.

There are thus three different ways (*a*, α, β) in which the second view can be developed: (*a*) represents the view of the *Dissertation* (1770), of the reply to Eberhard (1790), and of those parts of the first edition's deduction of the categories which are of very early origin ; (α) represents the final standpoint of the *Analytic* ; (β), the prevailing view of the present day, is nowhere accepted by Kant.[2]

Kant's utterances in the *Aesthetic* are all of them coloured by the first main view. We can best approach them by way of the contrasted teaching of the *Dissertation* of 1770. The teaching there formulated practically coincides, as above stated, with (*a*) of the second main view. Space, he maintains, is neither innate nor acquired from sense-experience.

"Certainly both conceptions [of time and of space] are undoubtedly acquired, not indeed by abstraction from our sensations of objects (for sensation gives the matter, not the form of human

---

[1] A 196 = B 241 ; A 293 = B 349.

[2] That is to say, in his published writings. It finds expression in one, and only one, of the *Reflexionen* (ii. 410: "Both space and time are nothing but combinations of sensuous impressions ").

cognition), but from the mind's own action in co-ordinating its sensations in accordance with unchanging laws. Each represents, as it were, an immutable type, and so can be known intuitively. Sensations excite this act of mind but do not contribute to the intuition. There is here nothing innate except this law of the mind according to which it conjoins in a certain manner the sensations derived from the presence of some object."[1]

How this view is to be reconciled with the contention, no less explicitly maintained,[2] that space is not only a form of intuition but itself a pure intuition, Kant does not make clear. Reflection upon an activity of the mind may yield the representation of space as a form ; it is difficult to comprehend how it should also yield an *a priori* content.

Kant nowhere in the *Critique* directly discusses the question whether the representation of space is innate or acquired. Such suggestions as occur refer (with the solitary exceptions of A 196 = B 241 and B 166 ff.)[3] only to the categories,[4] or as in the *Prolegomena*[5] to the Ideas of reason. But in 1790 Kant in his reply to Eberhard[6] again formulates the view of the *Dissertation*. The *Critique* allows, he there says, of no innate representations. All, without exception, are acquired. But of certain representations there is an original acquisition (*ursprüngliche Erwerbung*). Their ground (*Grund*) is inborn. In the case of space this ground is the mind's peculiar capacity for acquiring sensations in accordance with its subjective constitution.[7]

"This first formal ground is alone inborn, not the space representation itself. For it always requires impressions to determine the faculty of knowledge to the representation of an object (which in every case is its own action). Thus arises the formal intuition, which we name space, as an originally acquired representation (the form of outer objects in general), the ground of which (as mere receptivity) is likewise inborn, and the acquisition of which long antedates the determinate *conception* of things which are in accordance with this form."[8]

That last remark is confusing. Kant cannot mean that the representation of space is acquired prior to sense-experience, but only that since the mind gains it by reflection upon its own activity, it is among the first things to be

---

[1] § 15, Coroll. at the end.　　　　　[2] Cf. § 12, quoted above, p. 89 n. 2.
[3] There also Kant teaches that the representation of space is gained from the space-endowed objects of experience.
[4] Cf. B 1.　　　　　　　　　　　[5] § 43.
[6] *Ueber eine Entdeckung nach der alle neue Kritik der reinen Kritik durch eine ältere entbehrlich gemacht werden soll.*
[7] *Op. cit. W.* viii. pp. 221-2.　　　　[8] *Loc. cit.* p. 222.

apprehended—an extremely questionable assertion, could the premisses be granted. If "the determinate conception of things" comes late, still later must come the determinate conception of anything so abstract as pure space. The above passage thus repeats without essential modification the teaching of the *Dissertation*, and is open to the same objections. This teaching coincides with that of Leibniz in his *Nouveaux Essais*; and in formulating it in the *Dissertation* Kant was very probably influenced by Leibniz. Though it is an improvement upon the more extreme forms of the Cartesian doctrine of innate ideas, it does not go sufficiently far.

Now while Kant thus in 1770 and in 1790 so emphatically teaches that the representation of space is not innate, he none the less, in the intermediate period represented by the *Aesthetic*, would seem to maintain the reactionary view. Space is no mere potential disposition. As a conscious representation it lies ready in the mind. What, then, were the causes which constrained Kant to go back upon his own better views and to adopt so retrograde a position? The answer must be conjectural, but may perhaps be found in the other main point in which the teaching of the *Aesthetic* is distinguished from that of the *Dissertation*. Throughout the *Critique* Kant insists that space is a form of *receptivity*. It is *given* to the mind. It has nothing to do with spontaneity or understanding, and therefore cannot be acquired by reflection upon any activity of the mind. But neither can it, as *a priori*, be acquired from without. Consequently it cannot be acquired at all. But if given, and yet not acquired, it must as a representation lie ready in the mind from the very birth of consciousness. Constrained by such reasoning, Kant views it as given in all its completeness just as truly as is a sensation of colour or sound. This conclusion may not be satisfactory. Kant's candid recognition of it is, however, greatly preferable to the blurring of the issue by most of his commentators.

Kant came, no doubt, to the more consistent position of the *Aesthetic* chiefly through further reflection upon the arguments of the *Dissertation*,[1] and especially by recognition of the fact that though reflection upon an activity of the mind may be regarded as yielding a form of intuition, it can hardly be capable of yielding a pure manifold which can be substituted for, and take the place of, the manifold of sense. There are for Kant only two ways of escape from this unhappy quandary: (a) Either he must return to the *Dissertation* position, and admit that the mind is active in the construction of space.

[1] Especially those which he had offered in support of the contention that pure mathematical science is intuitive, not merely conceptual.

This he does in the 1790 reply to Eberhard, but only by misrepresenting his own teaching in the *Critique*. In order consistently to maintain that space is acquired by reflection upon an activity of the mind, he would have to recast the entire *Aesthetic*, as well as much of the *Analytic*, and to do so in ways which cannot genuinely harmonise with the main tendencies of his teaching.[1] (*b*) No such obstacle lay in the way of an alternative modification of his position. Kant might very easily have given up the contention that space is a pure intuition. If he had been willing to recognise that the sole possible manifold of intuition is sensuous, he could then have maintained that though space is innate as a potential form of receptivity, it is acquired only through reflection upon the space-endowed products of sensibility. So obvious are the advantages of this position, so completely does it harmonise with the facts of experience and with the teaching of modern psychology, and so obscure are the various passages in which Kant touches on this central issue, that many of his most competent commentators are prepared to regard it as being the actual teaching of the *Critique*. The evidence[2] seems to me, however, to refute this interpretation of Kant's position. The traditional, Cartesian, semi-mystical worship of mathematical truth, as altogether independent of the contingencies of sense-experience, and as a body of knowledge absolutely distinct in origin from the merely empirical sciences, influences Kant's thinking even at the very moment when he is maintaining, in opposition to the Cartesians, that its subject matter is a merely subjective intuition. Kant, as it would seem, still maintains that there is a pure manifold of intuition distinct from the manifold of sense; and so by the inevitable logic of his thought is constrained to view space as innate in conscious form. This is not, of course, a conclusion which he could permanently stand by, but its elimination would have involved a more radical revision of his whole view of pure intuition and of mathematical science than he was willing to undertake. Though in the *Analytic* he has come to recognise[3] that it is acquired by reflection upon *objects*, to the end he would seem to persist in the difficult contention that such reflection yields a pure manifold distinct from the manifold of sense.[4] His belief that mathematical

[1] Cf. below, p. 291 ff., on Kant's reasons for developing his doctrine of inner sense.

[2] As no one passage can be regarded as quite decisively proving Kant's belief in a pure manifold of intuition, the question can only be decided by a collation of all the relevant statements in the light of the general tendencies of Kant's thinking.

[3] This at least would seem to be implied in the wording of his later positions; it is not explicitly avowed.   [4] Cf. A 76-7 = B 102.

science is based upon pure intuition prevented him from recognising that though space may be a pure form of intuition, it can never by itself constitute a complete intuition. Its sole possible *content* is the manifold of sense.   But even apart from the fact that our apprehension of space is always empirically conditioned, Kant's view of mathematical propositions as grounded in intuition is, as already observed, not itself tenable.   For though intuitions may perhaps be the ultimate subject matter of geometry, concepts are its sole possible instruments.   Intuitions yield scientific insight in exact proportion to our powers of restating their complex content in the terms of abstract thought.   Until the evidence which they supply has been thus intellectually tested and defined, they cannot be accepted as justifying even the simplest proposition.[1]

The complicated ambiguities of Kant's treatment of space may be illustrated and further clarified by discussion of another difficulty.   Is space a *totum analyticum* or a *totum syntheticum*?   Does the whole precondition the parts, or does it arise through combination of the parts?   Or to ask another but connected question, do we intuit infinitude, or is it conceptually apprehended only as the presupposition of our limited intuitions?   To these questions diametrically opposite answers can be cited from the *Critique*.   As we have above noted, Kant teaches in the *Aesthetic* that space is given as a whole, and that the parts arise only by limitation of it.   But in A 162 = B 203 we find him also teaching that a magnitude is to be entitled extensive

". . . when the representation of the parts makes possible, and therefore necessarily precedes, the representation of the whole.   I cannot represent to myself a line, however small, without drawing it in thought, *i.e.* generating from a point all its parts one after another, and thus for the first time recording this intuition."[2]

He adds in the second edition[3] that extensive magnitude cannot be apprehended save through a "synthesis of the manifold," a "combination of the homogeneous."

The note which Kant appends to B 136 is a very strange combination of both views.   It first of all reaffirms the doctrine of the *Aesthetic* that space and time are not concepts, but intuitions within which as in a unity a multitude of representations are contained ; and then proceeds to argue that space

---

[1] Cf. above, pp. xlii, 38-42; below, pp. 118-20, 128-34.
[2] The last statement may be more freely translated : "Only in this way can I get the intuition before me in visible form."   Cf. below, pp. 135-6, 347-8, 359.
[3] B 202-3.

and time, as thus *composite*, must presuppose an antecedent synthesis. In A 505 = B 533 we find a similar attempt to combine both assertions.

"The parts of a given appearance are first given through and in the regress of *decomposing synthesis* (*decomponirenden Synthesis*)."

The clash of conflicting tenets which Kant is striving to reconcile could hardly find more fitting expression than in this assertion of an *analytic synthesis*. The same conflict appears, though in a less violent form, in A 438 = B 466.

"Space should properly be called not *compositum* but *totum*, since its parts are possible only in the whole, not the whole through the parts. It might, indeed, be said to be a *compositum* that is *ideale*, but not *reale*. That, however, is a mere subtlety."[1]

The arguments by which Kant proves space to be an *a priori* intuition rest upon the view that *space is given as infinite*, and that *its parts arise through limitation of this prior-existent whole*. But a principle absolutely fundamental to the entire *Critique* is the counter principle, that all analysis rests upon and presupposes a previously exercised synthesis. *Synthesis or totality as such can never be given.* Only in so far as a whole is synthetically constructed can it be apprehended by the mind. *Representation of the parts precedes and renders possible representation of the whole.*

The solution of the dilemma arising out of these diverse views demands the drawing of two distinctions. First, between a synthesised totality and a principle of synthesis; the former may involve a prior synthesis; the latter does not depend upon synthesis, but expresses the predetermined nature of some special form of synthesis. Secondly, it demands a distinction between the *a priori* manifolds of space and time and the empirical manifold which is apprehended in and through them. This, as we have already noted, is a distinction difficult to take quite seriously, and is entirely unsupported by psychological evidence. But it would seem to be insisted upon by Kant, and to have been a determining factor in the formulation of several of his main doctrines.

In terms of the first distinction we are compelled to recognise that the view of space which underlies the *Aesthetic* is out of harmony with the teaching of the *Analytic*. In the *Aesthetic* Kant interprets space not merely as a form of intuition but also as a formal intuition, which is given com-

[1] Cf. *Reflexionen*, ii. 393, 409, 465, 630, 649.

plete in its totality, and which is capable of being apprehended independently of its empirical contents, and even prior to them. That would seem to be the view of space which is presupposed in Kant's explanation of pure mathematical science. The passages from the *Analytic*, quoted above, are, however, its express recantation. Space, as the intuition of a manifold, is a *totum syntheticum*, not a *totum analyticum*. It is constructed, not given. The divergence of views between the *Aesthetic* and the *Analytic* springs out of the difficulty of meeting at once the logical demands of a world which Kant conceives objectively, and the psychological demands which arise when this same world is conceived as subjectively conditioned. In principle, the whole precedes the parts; in the process of being brought into existence as an intuition, the parts precede the whole. The principle which determines our apprehension of any space, however small or however large, is that it exists in and through universal space. This is the principle which underlies both the synthetic construction of space and also its apprehension once it is constructed. In principle, therefore, *i.e.* in the order of logical thought, the whole precedes the parts.[1] The process, however, which this principle governs and directs, cannot start with space as a whole, but must advance to it through synthesis of smaller parts.

But Kant does not himself recognise any conflict between this teaching and the doctrine of the *Aesthetic*. He seems to himself merely to be making more definite a position which he has consistently held all along; and this was possible owing to his retention and more efficient formulation of the second of the two distinctions mentioned above, viz. that between the manifold of sense and the manifold of intuition. This distinction enables him to graft the new view upon the old, and so in the very act of insisting upon the indispensableness of the conceptual syntheses of understanding, none the less to maintain his view of geometry as an intuitive science.[2]

"Space and time contain a manifold of pure *a priori* intuition, but at the same time are conditions of the receptivity of our mind —conditions under which alone it can receive representations of

---

[1] This, indeed, is Kant's reason for describing space as an Idea of reason. Cf. below, pp. 97-8.

[2] Geometry is for Kant the fundamental and chief mathematical science (cf. A 39 = B 56 and *Dissertation*, § 15 c). In this respect he is a disciple of Newton, not a follower of Leibniz. His neglect to take adequate account of arithmetic and algebra is due to this cause. Just as in speaking of the manifold of sense he almost invariably has sight alone in view, so in speaking of mathematical science he usually refers only to geometry and the kindred discipline of pure mechanics.

objects, and which therefore must also affect the concept of them. But if this manifold is to be known, the spontaneity of our thinking requires that it be gone through in a certain way, taken up, and connected. This action I name synthesis. . . . Such a synthesis is pure, if the manifold is not empirical, but is given *a priori*, as is that of space and of time." [1]

Thus Kant recognises that space, as apprehended by us, is constructed, not given, and so by implication that the infinitude of space is a principle of apprehension, not a given intuition. But he also holds to the view that it contains a pure, and presumably infinite, manifold, given as such.[2] In what this pure manifold consists, and how the description of it as a manifold, demanding synthesis for its apprehension, is to be reconciled with its continuity, Kant nowhere even attempts to explain. Nor does he show what the simple elements are from which the synthesis of apprehension and reproduction in pure intuition might start. The unity and multiplicity of space are, indeed, as he himself recognises,[3] inseparably involved in one another ; and recognition of this fact must render it extremely difficult to assign them to separate faculties. For the same reason it is impossible to distinguish temporally, as Kant so frequently does, the processes of synthesis and of analysis, making the former in all cases precede the latter in time. The very nature of space and time, and, as he came to recognise, the very nature of all Ideas of reason, in so far as they involve the notion of the unconditioned, conflict with such a view.

Even when Kant is dealing with space as a principle of synthesis, he speaks with no very certain voice. In the *Analytic* it is ascribed to the co-operation of sensibility and understanding. In the *Dialectic* it is, by implication, ascribed to Reason ; and in the *Metaphysical First Principles* it is explicitly so ascribed.

"Absolute space cannot be object of experience ; for space without matter is no object of perception, and yet it is a necessary conception of Reason, and therefore nothing but a mere Idea." [4] "Absolute space is not necessary as a conception of an actual object, but as an Idea which can serve as rule. . . ." [5]

Kant's teaching in the *Critique of Judgment* is a further development of this position.

"The mind listens to the voice of Reason which, for every given

[1] A 76-7 = B 102. Cf. B 160-1 *n*.
[2] Cf. above, pp. 90, 92 ff. ; below, pp. 171, 226-9, 267-70, 337.
[3] Cf. B 160. [4] *Metaphysical First Principles, W.* iv. p. 559, cf. p. 481.
[5] *Op. cit.* p. 560.

magnitude—even for those that can never be entirely apprehended, although (in sensible representation) they are judged as entirely given—requires totality. . . . It does not even except the infinite (space and past time) from this requirement; on the contrary, it renders it unavoidable to think the infinite (in the judgment of common reason) as *entirely given* (in its totality).   But the infinite is absolutely (not merely comparatively) great.   Compared with it everything else (of the same kind of magnitudes) is small.   But what is most important is that the mere ability to think it as *a whole* indicates a faculty of mind which surpasses every standard of sense. . . . The *bare capability of thinking* the given infinite without contradiction requires in the human mind a faculty itself supersensible.   For it is only by means of this faculty and its Idea of a noumenon . . . that the infinite of the world of sense, in the pure intellectual estimation of magnitude, can be *completely* comprehended *under* one concept. . . . Nature is, therefore, sublime in those of its phenomena, whose intuition brings with it the Idea of its infinity. . . . For just as imagination and *understanding*, in judging of the beautiful, generate a subjective purposiveness of the mental powers by means of their harmony, so imagination and *Reason* do so by means of their conflict."[1]

Kant has here departed very far indeed from the position of the *Aesthetic*.[2]

[1] *Critique of Judgment*, §§ 26-7, Eng. trans. pp. 115-16 and 121.
[2] Cf. below, pp. 102 *n*., 165-6, 390-1.

THE TRANSCENDENTAL AESTHETIC

SECTION I

SPACE

METAPHYSICAL EXPOSITION OF THE CONCEPTION OF SPACE[1]

Space: First Argument.—"Space is not an empirical concept (*Begriff*) which has been abstracted from outer experiences. For in order that certain sensations be related to something outside me (*i.e.* to something in another region of space from that in which I find myself), and similarly in order that I may be able to represent them as outside [and *alongside*][2] one another, and accordingly as not only [qualitatively] different but as in different places, the representation of space must be presupposed (*muss schon zum Grunde liegen*). The representation of space cannot, therefore, be empirically obtained at second-hand from the relations of outer appearance. This outer experience is itself possible at all only through that representation."[3]

The first sentence states the thesis of the argument: *space is not an empirical concept abstracted from outer experiences*. The use of the term *Begriff* in the title of the section, and also in this sentence, is an instance of the looseness with which Kant employs his terms. It is here synonymous with the term representation (*Vorstellung*), which covers intuitions as well as general or discursive concepts. Consequently, the contradiction is only verbal, not real, when Kant proceeds to prove that the concept of space is an intuition, not a concept. But this double employment of the term is none the less misleading. When Kant employs it in a strict sense, it signifies solely the general class concept.[4] All true concepts are for Kant of that single type. He has not re-defined the term concept in any

---

[1] The title of this section, and the points raised in the opening paragraph, are commented upon below. Cf. pp. 110, 114-15, 134 ff. I pass at once to the first space argument.

[2] Added in second edition.

[3] This argument is an almost verbal repetition of the first argument on space in the *Dissertation*, § 15.

[4] Cf. below, pp. 106-7, 126, 132-3, 177-84, 338-9.

manner which would render it applicable to the relational categories. For unfortunately, and very strangely, he never seems to have raised the question whether categories are not also concepts. The application to the forms of understanding of the separate title categories seems to have contented him. Much that is obscure and even contradictory in his teaching might have been prevented had he recognised that the term concept is a generic title which includes, as its sub-species, both general notions and relational categories.

Kant's limitation of the term concept to the merely generic,[1] and his consequent equating of the categorical proposition with the assertion of the substance-attribute relation,[2] would seem in large part to be traceable to his desire to preserve for himself, in the pioneer labours of his Critical enquiries, the guiding clues of the distinctions drawn in the traditional logic. Kant insists on holding to them, at least in outward appearance, at whatever sacrifice of strict consistency. Critical doctrine is made to conform to the exigencies of an artificial framework, with which its own tenets are only in very imperfect harmony. Appreciation of the ramifying influence, and, as regards the detail of exposition, of the far-reaching consequences, of this desire to conform to the time-honoured rubrics, is indeed an indispensable preliminary to any adequate estimate whether of the strength or of the defects of the Critical doctrines. As a separate and ever-present influence in the determining of Kant's teaching, this factor may conveniently and compendiously be entitled Kant's logical *architectonic.*[3] We shall have frequent occasion to observe its effects.[4]

The second sentence gives expression to the fact through which Kant proves his thesis. Certain sensations, those of the special senses as distinguished from the organic sensations,[5] are related to something which stands in a different region of space from the embodied self, and consequently are apprehended as differing from one another not only in quality but also in spatial position. As is proved later in the *Analytic,* thought plays an indispensable part in constituting this reference of sensations to objects. Kant here, however, makes no mention of this further complication. He postulates, as he may legitimately do at this stage, the fact that our sensations are

---

[1] Cf. above, p. 37 ff. ; below, p. 178 ff.

[2] That is particularly obvious in Kant's formulation of his problem in the *Introduction.* For that is the assumption which underlies his mode of distinguishing between analytic and synthetic judgments. Cf. above, p. 37.

[3] Cf. above, p. xxii.   [4] Cf. especially, pp. 184, 332-6, 419, 474, 479.

[5] I here use the more modern terms. Kant, in *Anthropologie,* § 14, distinguishes between them as *Organenempfindungen* and *Vitalempfindungen.*

thus objectively interpreted, and limits his enquiry to the spatial factor. Now the argument, as Vaihinger justly points out,[1] hinges upon the assumption which Kant has already embodied[2] in his definition of the "form" of sense, viz. that sensations are non-spatial, purely qualitative. Though this is an assumption of which Kant nowhere attempts to give proof, it serves none the less as an unquestioned premiss from which he draws all-important conclusions. This first argument on space derives its force entirely from it.

The proof that the representation of space is non-empirical may therefore be explicitly stated as follows. As sensations are non-spatial and differ only qualitatively, the representation of space must have been added to them. And not being supplied by the given sensations, it must, as the only alternative, have been contributed by the mind. The representation of space, so far from being derived from external experience, is what first renders it possible. As a subjective form that lies ready in the mind, it precedes experience and co-operates in generating it. This proof of the apriority of space is thus proof of the priority of the *representation* of space to every empirical perception.

In thus interpreting Kant's argument as proving more than the thesis of the first sentence claims, we are certainly reading into the proof more than Kant has himself given full expression to. But, as is clearly shown by the argument of the next section, we are only stating what Kant actually takes the argument as having proved, namely, that the representation of space is not only non-empirical but is likewise of subjective origin and precedes experience in temporal fashion.

The point of view which underlies and inspires the argument can be defined even more precisely. Kant's conclusion may be interpreted in either of two ways. The form of space may precede experience only as a potentiality. Existing as a power of co-ordination,[3] it will come to consciousness only indirectly through the addition which it makes to the given sensations. Though subjective in origin, it will be revealed to the mind only in and through experience. This view may indeed be reconciled with the terms of the proof. But a strictly literal interpretation of its actual wording is more in keeping with what, as we shall find, is

---

[1] ii. p. 165.   [2] Cf. above, pp. 85-8.

[3] Cf. *Dissertation*, § 15 D : "Space is not anything objective and real. It is neither substance, nor accident, nor relation, but is subjective and ideal, proceeding by a fixed law from the nature of the mind, and being, as it were, a schema for co-ordinating, in the manner which it prescribes, all external sensations whatsoever." And § 15, corollary at end : "Action of the mind co-ordinating its sensations in accordance with abiding laws."

the general trend of the *Aesthetic* as a whole. We are then confronted by a very different and extremely paradoxical view, which may well seem too naive to be accepted by the modern reader, but which we seem forced,[1] none the less, to regard as the view actually presented in the text before us. Kant here asserts, in the most explicit manner, that the mind, in order to construe sensations in spatial terms, must already be in possession of a *representation* of space, and that it is in the light of this representation that it apprehends sensations. The conscious representation of space precedes in time external experience. Such, then, would seem to be Kant's first argument on space. It seeks to establish a negative conclusion, viz. that space is not derived from experience. But, in so doing, it also yields a positive psychological explanation of its origin.

Those commentators[2] who refuse to recognise that Kant's problem is in any degree psychological, or that Kant himself so regards it, and who consequently seek to interpret the *Aesthetic* from the point of view of certain portions of the *Analytic*, give a very different statement of this first argument. They state it in purely logical terms.[3] Its problem, they claim, is not that of determining the origin of our representation of space, but only its logical relation to our specific sense-experiences. The notion of space in general precedes, as an indispensable logical presupposition, all particular specification of the space relation. Consciousness of space as a whole is not constructed from consciousness of partial spaces; on the contrary, the latter is only possible in and through the former.

Such an argument does of course represent a valuable truth; and it alone harmonises with much in Kant's maturer teaching;[4] but we must not therefore conclude that it is also the teaching of the *Aesthetic*. The *Critique* contains too great a variety of tendencies, too rich a complexity of issues, to allow of such simplification. It loses more than it gains by such rigorous pruning of the luxuriant secondary tendencies of its exposition and thought. And above all, this procedure involves the adoption by the commentator of impossible responsibilities, those of deciding what is essential and valuable in Kant's thought and what is irrelevant. The value

---

[1] Especially in view of the third and fourth arguments on space, and of Kant's teaching in the transcendental exposition.

[2] *E.g.* Cohen, Riehl, Caird, Watson.

[3] Cf. Watson, *The Philosophy of Kant explained*, p. 83: "Kant, therefore, concludes from the logical priority of space that it is *a priori*."

[4] Upon it Kant bases the assertion that space is an Idea of reason; cf. above, pp. 96-8, and below, pp. 165-6, 390-1.

and suggestiveness of Kant's philosophy largely consist in his
sincere appreciation of conflicting tendencies, and in his
persistent attempt to reduce them to unity with the least
possible sacrifice.   But in any case the logical interpretation
misrepresents this particular argument.   Kant is not here distinguishing between space in general and its specific modifications.   He is maintaining that no space relation can be revealed
in sensation.   It is not only that the apprehension of any
limited space presupposes the representation of space as a
whole.   Both partial and infinite space are of mental origin ;
sensation, as such, is non-spatial, purely subjective.   And
lastly, the fact that Kant means to assert that space is not
only logically presupposed but is subjectively generated, is
sufficiently borne out by his frequent employment elsewhere
in the *Aesthetic* of such phrases as "the subjective condition
of sensibility," "lying ready in our minds," and "necessarily
preceding [as the form of the subject's receptivity] all intuitions
of objects."

Second Argument.—Having proved by the first argument
that the representation of space is not of empirical origin,
Kant in the second argument proceeds to establish the positive conclusion that it is *a priori*.[1]   The proof, when all its
assumptions are rendered explicit, runs as follows.   *Thesis :*
Space is a necessary representation, and consequently is
a priori.   *Proof :* It is impossible to imagine the absence of
space, though it is possible to imagine it as existing without
objects to fill it.   A representation which it is impossible for
the mind to be without is a necessary representation.   But
necessity is one of the two criteria of the *a priori*.   The proof
of the necessary character of space is therefore also a proof
of its being *a priori*.

The argument, more freely stated, is that what is empirically given from without can be thought away, and that
since space cannot be thus eliminated, it must be grounded
in our subjective organisation, *i.e.* must be psychologically *a
priori*.   The argument, as stated by Kant, emphasises the
apriority, not the subjectivity, of space, but none the less
the asserted apriority is psychological, not logical in character.
For the criterion employed is not the impossibility of thinking
otherwise, but our incapacity to represent this specific element
as absent.   The ground upon which the whole argument is
made to rest is the merely brute fact (asserted by Kant) of
our incapacity to think except in terms of space.

The argument is, however, complicated by the drawing
of a further consequence, which follows as a corollary from

[1] This second argument is not in the *Dissertation*.

the main conclusion.   From the subjective necessity of space
follows its objective necessity.   Space being necessary *a
priori*, objects can only be apprehended in and through it.
Consequently it is not dependent upon the objects apprehended, but itself underlies outer appearances as the condition
of their possibility.   This corollary is closely akin to the first
argument on space, and differs from it only in orientation.
The first argument has a psychological purpose.   It maintains
that the representation of space precedes external experience,
causally conditioning it.   The corollary has a more objective
aim.   It concludes that space is a necessary constituent of
the external experience thus generated.   The one proves
that space is a necessary *subjective antecedent* ; the other that
it is a necessary *objective ingredient*.[1]

To consider the proof in detail.   The exact words which
Kant employs in stating the *nervus probandi* of the argument
are that we can never *represent* (*eine Vorstellung davon machen*)
space as non-existent, though we can very well *think* (*denken*)
it as being empty of objects.   The terms *Vorstellung* and
denken are vague and misleading.   Kant himself recognises
that it is possible to conceive that there are beings who intuit
objects in some other manner than in space.   He cannot
therefore mean that we are unable to *think* or *conceive* space
as non-existent.   He must mean that we cannot in imagination intuit it as absent.   It is the necessary form of all our
intuitions, and therefore also of imagination, which is intuitive
in character.   Our consciousness is dependent upon given
intuitions for its whole content, and to that extent space is
a form with which the mind can never by any possibility
dispense.   Pure thought enables it to realise this *de facto*
limitation, but not to break free from it.   Even in admitting
the possibility of other beings who are not thus constituted,
the mind still recognises its own ineluctable limitations.

Kant offers no proof of his assertion that space can be
intuited in image as empty of all sensible content ; and as a
matter of fact the assertion is false.   Doubtless the use of
the vague term *Vorstellung* is in great part responsible for
Kant's mistaken position.   So long as imagination and
thought are not clearly distinguished, the assertion is correspondingly indefinite.   Pure space may possibly be *conceived*,
but it can also be conceived as altogether non-existent.   If,
on the other hand, our imaginative power is alone in question,

---

[1] Cf. Vaihinger, ii. pp. 196-7.   The corresponding argument on time, in the
form in which it is given in the second edition, is, as we shall find, seriously misleading.   It has caused Herbart and others to misinterpret the connection in which
this corollary stands to the main thesis.   Herbart's interpretation is considered
below, p. 124.

the asserted fact must be categorically denied.   With the elimination of all sensible content space itself ceases to be a possible image.   Kant's proof thus rests upon a misstatement of fact.

In a second respect Kant's proof is open to criticism.   He takes the impossibility of imagining space as absent as proof that it originates from within.   The argument is valid only if no other psychological explanation can be given of this necessity, as for instance through indissoluble association or through its being an invariable element in the given sensations. Kant's ignoring of these possibilities is due to his unquestioning belief that sensations are non-spatial, purely qualitative. That is a presupposition whose truth is necessary to the cogency of the argument.

Third Argument.—This argument, which was omitted in the second edition, will be considered in its connection with the transcendental exposition into which it was then merged.

Fourth (in second edition, Third) Argument.—The next two arguments seek to show that space is not a discursive or general concept but an intuition.   The first proof falls into two parts.   (*a*) We can represent only a single space.   For though we speak of many spaces, we mean only parts of one and the same single space.   Space must therefore be an intuition.   For only intuition is thus directly related to a single individual.   A concept always refers indirectly, *per notas communes*, to a plurality of individuals.   (*b*) The parts of space cannot precede the one all-comprehensive space. They can be thought only in and through it.   They arise through limitation of it.   Now the parts (*i.e.* the attributes) which compose a concept precede it in thought.   Through combination of them the concept is formed.   Space cannot, therefore, be a concept.   Consequently it must, as the only remaining alternative, be an intuition.   Only in an intuition does the whole precede the parts.   In a concept the parts always precede the whole.   Intuition stands for multiplicity in unity, conception for unity in multiplicity.

The first part of the argument refers to the extension, the second part to the intension of the space representation.   In both aspects it appears as intuitional.[1]

Kant, in repeating his thesis as a conclusion from the above grounds, confuses the reader by an addition which is not strictly relevant to the argument, viz. by the statement that this intuition must be non-empirical and *a priori*. This is simply a recapitulation of what has been established in the preceding proofs.   It is not, as might at first sight

[1] Cf. Vaihinger, ii. p. 220.

appear, part of the conclusion established by the argument under consideration. The reader is the more apt to be misled owing to the fact that very obviously arguments for the non-empirical and for the *a priori* character of space *can* be derived from proof (*b*). That space is non-empirical would follow from the fact that representation of space as a whole is necessary for the apprehension of any part of it. Empirical intuition can only yield the apprehension of a limited space. The apprehension of the comprehensive space within which it falls must therefore be non-empirical.

" As we intuitively apprehend (*anschauend erkennen*) not only the space of the object which affects our senses, but the whole space, space cannot arise out of the actual affection of the senses, but must precede it in time (*vor ihr vorhergehen*)." [1]

But in spite of its forcibleness this argument is nowhere presented in the *Critique*.

Similarly, in so far as particular spaces can be conceived only in and through space as a whole, and in so far as the former are limitations of the one antecedent space, the intuition which underlies all external perception must be *a priori*. This is in essentials a stronger and more cogent mode of formulating the second argument on space. But again, and very strangely, it is nowhere employed by Kant in this form.

The concluding sentence, ambiguously introduced by the words *so werden auch*, is tacked on to the preceding argument. Interpreted in the light of § 15 C of the *Dissertation*,[2] and of the corresponding fourth [3] argument [4] on time, it may be taken as offering further proof that space is an intuition. The concepts of line and triangle, however attentively contemplated, will never reveal the proposition that in every triangle two sides taken together are greater than the third. An *a priori* intuition will alone account for such apodictic knowledge. This concluding sentence thus really belongs to the transcendental exposition; and as such ought, like the third argument, to have been omitted in the second edition.

Kant's proof rests on the assumption that there are only two kinds of representation, intuitions and concepts, and also in equal degree upon the further assumption that all concepts

---

[1] *Reflexionen*, ii. 403.

[2] " That in space there are no more than three dimensions, that between two points there can be but one straight line, that in a plane surface from a given point with a given straight line a circle is describable, cannot be inferred from any universal notion of space, but can only be discerned in space as in the concrete." Cf. also *Prolegomena*, § 12.

[3] In the second edition, the third.

[4] For a different view cf. Vaihinger, ii. p. 233.

are of one and the same type.[1] Intuition is, for Kant, the apprehension of an individual.   Conception is always the representation of a class or genus. Intuition is immediately related to the individual. Conception is reflective or discursive; it apprehends a plurality of objects indirectly through the representation of those marks which are common to them all.[2] Intuition and conception having been defined in this manner, the proof that space is single or individual, and that in it the whole precedes the parts, is proof conclusive that it is an intuition, not a conception.   Owing, however, to the narrowness of the field assigned to conception, the realm occupied by intuition is proportionately wide, and the conclusion is not as definite and as important as might at first sight appear. By itself, it amounts merely to the statement, which no one need challenge, that space is not a generic class concept. Incidentally certain unique characteristics of space are, indeed, forcibly illustrated; but the implied conclusion that space on account of these characteristics must belong to receptivity, not to understanding, does not by any means follow. It has not, for instance, been proved that space and time are radically distinct from the categories, *i.e.* from the relational forms of understanding.

In 1770, while Kant still held to the metaphysical validity of the pure forms of thought, the many difficulties which result from the ascription of independent reality to space and time were, doubtless, a sufficient reason for regarding the latter as subjective and sensuous. But upon adoption of the Critical standpoint such argument is no longer valid. If all our forms of thought may be subjective, the existence of antinomies has no real bearing upon the question whether space and time do or do not have a different constitution and a different mental origin from the categories. The antinomies, that is to say, may perhaps suffice to prove that space and time are subjective; they certainly do not establish their sensuous character.

But though persistence of the older, un-Critical opposition between the intellectual and the sensuous was partly responsible for Kant's readiness to regard as radical the very obvious differences between a category such as that of substance and attribute and the visual or tactual extendedness with which objects are endowed, it can hardly be viewed as the really decisive influence. That would rather seem to be traceable to Kant's conviction that mathematical knowledge is unique both in fruitfulness and in certainty, and to his further belief that it owes this distinction to the *content* character of

---

[1] Cf. above, pp. 99-100; below, pp. 126, 180-1, 184, 338-9.
[2] Cf. below, p. 180.

the *a priori* forms upon which it rests. For though the categories of the physical sciences are likewise *a priori*, they are exclusively *relational*,[1] and serve only to organise a material that is empirically given. To account for the superiority of mathematical knowledge Kant accordingly felt constrained to regard space and time as not merely *forms* in terms of which we interpret the matter of sense, but as also themselves intuited *objects*, and as therefore possessing a character altogether different from anything which can be ascribed to the pure understanding. The opposition between forms of sense and categories of the understanding, in the strict Kantian mode of envisaging that opposition, is thus inseparably bound up with Kant's doctrine of space and time as being not only forms of intuition, but as also in their purity and independence themselves intuitions. *Even the sensuous subject matter of pure mathematics*—so Kant would seem to contend—*is* a priori *in nature*. If this latter view be questioned —and to the modern reader it is indeed a stone of stumbling —much of the teaching of the *Aesthetic* will have to be modified or at least restated.

Fifth (in second edition, Fourth) Argument.—This argument is quite differently stated in the two editions of the *Critique*, though the purpose of the argument is again in both cases to prove that space is an intuition, not a general concept. In the first edition this is proved by reference to the fact that space is given as an infinite magnitude. This characteristic of our space representation cannot be accounted for so long as it is regarded as a concept. A general conception of space which would abstract out those properties and relations which are common to all spaces, to a foot as well as to an ell, could not possibly determine anything in regard to magnitude. For since spaces differ in magnitude, any one magnitude cannot be a common quality. Space is, however, given us as determined in magnitude, namely, as being of infinite magnitude; and if a general conception of space relations cannot determine magnitude, still less can it determine infinite magnitude. Such infinity must be derived from limitlessness in the progression of intuition. Our conceptual representations of infinite magnitude must be derivative products, acquired from this intuitive source.

In the argument of the second edition the thesis is again established by reference to the infinity of space. But in all other respects the argument differs from that of the first edition. A general conception, which abstracts out common

---

[1] Cf. above, p. xxxvi; below, pp. 176 ff., 191, 195-6, 257, 290-1, 404 ff., 413.

qualities from a plurality of particulars, contains an infinite number of possible different representations *under* it; but it cannot be thought as containing an infinite number of representations *in* it. Space must, however, be thought in this latter manner, for it contains an infinite number of coexisting parts.[1] Since, then, space cannot be a concept, it must be an intuition.

The definiteness of this conclusion is somewhat obscured by the further characterisation of the intuition of space as *a priori*, and by the statement that it is the *original (ursprüngliche)* representation which is of this intuitive nature. The first addition must here, again, just as in the fourth argument, be regarded as merely a recapitulation of what has already been established, not a conclusion from the present argument. The introduction of the word 'original' seems to be part of Kant's reply to the objections which had already been made to his admission in the first edition that there is a conception as well as an intuition of space. It is the *original given intuition* of space which renders such reflective conception possible.

The chief difficulty of these proofs arises out of the assertion which they seem to involve that space is given as actually infinite. There are apparently, on this point, two views in Kant, which were retained up to the very last, and which are closely connected with his two representations of space, on the one hand as a *formal intuition* given in its purity and in its completeness, and on the other hand as the *form of intuition*, which exists only so far as it is constructed, and which is dependent for its content upon given matter.

Third Argument, and Transcendental Exposition of Space.— The distinction between the metaphysical and the transcendental expositions, introduced in the second edition of the *Critique*,[2] is one which Kant seems to have first made clear to himself in the process of writing the *Prolegomena*.[3] It is a genuine improvement, marking an important distinction. It separates out two comparatively independent lines of argument. The terms in which the distinction is stated are not, however, felicitous. Kant's reason for adopting the title metaphysical is indicated in the *Prolegomena*:[4]

"As concerns the sources of metaphysical cognition, its very concept implies that they cannot be empirical. . . . For it must not

---

[1] This statement occurs in a parenthesis; it has already been dwelt upon in the fourth (third) argument.
[2] It has led Kant to substitute *erörtern* for *betrachten* in A 23 = B 38.
[3] Cf. Vaihinger, ii. p. 151.
[4] § 1 (Eng. trans. p. 13). Cf. above, p. 64.

be physical but metaphysical knowledge, *i.e.* knowledge lying beyond experience. . . . It is therefore *a priori* knowledge, coming from pure understanding and pure Reason."

The metaphysical exposition, it would therefore seem, is so entitled because it professes to prove that space is *a priori*, not empirical, and to do so by analysis of its concept.[1] Now by Kant's own definition of the term transcendental, as the theory of the *a priori*, this exposition might equally well have been named the transcendental exposition. In any case it is an essential and chief part of the *Transcendental Aesthetic.* Such division of the *Transcendental Aesthetic* into a metaphysical and a transcendental part involves a twofold use, wider and narrower, of one and the same term. Only as descriptive of the whole *Aesthetic* is transcendental employed in the sense defined.

Exposition (*Erörterung*, Lat. *expositio*) is Kant's substitute for the more ordinary term definition. Definition is the term which we should naturally have expected; but as Kant holds that no *given* concept, whether *a priori* or empirical, can be defined in the strict sense,[2] he substitutes the term exposition, using it to signify such definition of the nature of space as is possible to us. To complete the parallelism Kant speaks of the transcendental enquiry as also an exposition. It is, however, in no sense a definition. Kant's terms here, as so often elsewhere are employed in a more or less arbitrary and extremely inexact manner.

The distinction between the two expositions is taken by Kant as follows. The metaphysical exposition determines the nature of the concept of space, and shows it to be a given *a priori* intuition. The transcendental exposition shows how space, when viewed in this manner, renders comprehensible the possibility of synthetic *a priori* knowledge.

The omission of the third argument on space from the second edition, and its incorporation into the new transcendental exposition, is certainly an improvement. In its location in the first edition, it breaks in upon the continuity of Kant's argument without in any way contributing to the further definition of the concept of space. Also, in emphasising that

---

[1] This is, no doubt, one reason why Kant employs, in reference to space, the unfortunate and confusing term concept (*Begriff*) in place of the wider term representation (*Vorstellung*). Cf. B 37, and above, p. 64.

[2] Cf. A 729 = B 757 : "In place of the term *definition* I should prefer to employ the term exposition. For that is a more guarded expression, the claims of which the critic may allow as being in a certain degree valid even though he entertain doubts as to the completeness of the analysis." Cf. *Logic*, §§ 99 ff., 105. Cf. also *Untersuchung über die Deutlichkeit der Grundsätze, W.* ii. pp. 183-4: "Augustine has said, 'I know well what time is, but if any one asks me, I cannot tell.'"

mathematical knowledge depends upon the *construction* of concepts,[1] Kant presupposes that space is intuitional; and that has not yet been established.

The argument follows the strict, rigorous, synthetic method. From the already demonstrated *a priori* character of space, Kant deduces the apodictic certainty of all geometrical principles. But though the paragraph thus expounds a consequence that follows from the *a priori* character of space, not an argument in support of it, something in the nature of an argument is none the less implied. The fact that this view of the representation of space alone renders mathematical science possible can be taken as confirming this interpretation of its nature. Such an argument, though circular, is none the less cogent. Consideration of Kant's further statements, that were space known in a merely empirical manner we could not be sure that in all cases only one straight line is possible between two points, or that space will always be found to have three dimensions, must meantime be deferred.[2]

In the new transcendental exposition Kant adopts the analytic method of the *Prolegomena*, and accordingly presents his argument in independence of the results already established. He starts from the assumption of the admitted validity of geometry, as being a body of synthetic *a priori* knowledge. Yet this, as we have already noted, does not invalidate the argument; in both the first and the last paragraphs it is implied that the *a priori* and intuitive characteristics of space have already been proved. From the synthetic character of geometrical propositions Kant argues[3] that space must be an intuition. Through pure concepts no synthetic knowledge is possible. Then from the apodictic character of geometry he infers that space exists in us as pure and *a priori*;[4] no experience can ever reveal necessity. But geometry also exists as an applied science; and to account for our power of anticipating experience, we must view space as existing only in the perceiving subject as the form of its sensibility. If it precedes objects as the necessary subjective condition of their apprehension, we can to that extent predetermine the conditions of their existence.

In the concluding paragraph Kant says that this is the only explanation which can be given of the possibility of geometry. He does not distinguish between pure and applied

---

[1] For explanation of the phrase "construction of concepts" cf. below, pp. 132-3.
[2] Cf. below, p. 117 ff.
[3] Cf. conclusion of fourth argument on space.
[4] *A priori* is here employed in its ambiguous double sense, as *a priori* in so far as it precedes experience (as a *representation*), and in so far as it is valid independently of experience (as a *proposition*). Cf. Vaihinger, ii. p. 268.

geometry, though the proof which he has given of each differs in a fundamental respect.   Pure geometry presupposes only that space is an *a priori* intuition ; applied geometry demands that space be conceived as the *a priori* form of external sense. Only in reference to applied geometry does the Critical problem arise :—viz. how we can form synthetic judgments *a priori* which yet are valid of objects ; or, in other words, how judgments based upon a subjective form can be objectively valid.   But any attempt, at this point, to define the nature and possibility of applied geometry must anticipate a result which is first established in *Conclusion b*.[1]   Though, therefore, the substitution of this transcendental exposition for the third space argument is a decided improvement, Kant, in extending it so as to cover applied as well as pure mathematics, over- looks the real sequence of his argument in the first edition. The employment of the analytic method, breaking in, as it does, upon the synthetic development of Kant's original argument, is a further irregularity.[2]

It may be noted that in the third paragraph Kant takes the fact that geometry can be applied to objects as proof of the subjectivity of space.[3]   He refuses to recognise the possibility that space may be subjective as a form of re- ceptivity, and yet also be a mode in which things in them- selves exist.   This, as regards its conclusion, though not as regards its argument, is therefore an anticipation of *Conclusion a*.   In the last paragraph Kant is probably referring to the views both of Leibniz and of Berkeley.

CONCLUSIONS FROM THE ABOVE CONCEPTS[4]

Conclusion a.—*Thesis :* Space is not a property of things in themselves,[5] nor a relation of them to one another.   *Proof :* The properties of things in themselves can never be intuited prior to their existence, *i.e. a priori*.   Space, as already proved, is intuited in this manner.   In other words, the apriority of space is by itself sufficient proof of its subjectivity.

[1] Cf. below, p. 114 ff.
[2] Cf. below, pp. 115-16.
[3] Cf. *Lose Blätter*, i. p. 18 : "This is a proof (*Beweis*) that space is a sub- jective condition.   For its propositions are synthetic and through them objects can be known *a priori*.   This would be impossible if space were not a subjective condition of the representation of these objects."   Cf. *Reflexionen*, ii. p. 396, in which this *direct* proof of the ideality of space is distinguished from the *indirect* proof by means of the antinomies.
[4] By "concepts" Kant seems to mean the five arguments, though as a matter of fact other conclusions and presuppositions are taken into account, and quite new points are raised.
[5] This, according to Vaihinger (ii. p. 287), is the first occurrence of the phrase *Dinge an sich* in Kant's writings.

This argument has been the subject of a prolonged controversy between Trendelenburg and Kuno Fischer.[1] Trendelenburg was able to prove his main point, namely, that the above argument is quite inconclusive. Kant recognises only two alternatives, either space as objective is known *a posteriori*, or being an *a priori* representation it is subjective in origin. There exists a third alternative, namely, that though our intuition of space is subjective in origin, space is itself an inherent property of things in themselves. The central thesis of the rationalist philosophy of the Enlightenment was, indeed, that the independently real can be known by *a priori* thinking. Even granting the validity of Kant's later conclusion, first drawn in the next paragraph, that space is the subjective form of all external intuition, that would only prove that it does not belong to *appearances*, prior to our apprehension of them ; nothing is thereby proved in regard to the character of things in themselves. We anticipate by *a priori* reasoning only the nature of appearances, never the constitution of things in themselves. Therefore space, even though *a priori*, may belong to the independently real. The above argument cannot prove the given thesis.

Vaihinger contends[2] that the reason why Kant does not even attempt to argue in support of the principle, that the *a priori* must be purely subjective, is that he accepts it as self-evident. This explanation does not, however, seem satisfactory. But Vaihinger supplies the data for modification of his own assertion. It was, it would seem, the existence of the antinomies which first and chiefly led Kant to assert the subjectivity of space and time.[3] For as he then believed that a satisfactory solution of the antinomies is possible only on the assumption of the subjectivity of space and time, he regarded their subjectivity as being conclusively established, and accordingly failed to examine with sufficient care the validity of his additional proof from their apriority. This would seem to be confirmed by the fact that when later,[4] in reply to criticisms of the arguments of the first edition, he so far modified his position as to offer reasons in support of the above general principle, even then he nowhere discussed the principle in reference to the forms of sense. All his discussions concern only the possible independent reality of the forms of thought.[5] To the very last Kant would seem to have regarded the above argument

---

[1] Cf. Vaihinger's analysis of this discussion, ii. pp. 290-313.
[2] ii. pp. 289-90.   [3] Cf. below, pp. 415 ff., 515 ff., 558 ff.   [4] In B 166 ff.
[5] This is likewise true of the references in the letter to Herz, 21st Feb. 1772. Cf. below, pp. 219-20.

as an independent, and by itself a sufficient, proof of the subjectivity of space.

The refutation of Trendelenburg's argument which is offered by Caird[1] is inconclusive. Caird assumes the chief point at issue, first by ignoring the possibility that space may be known *a priori* in reference to appearances and yet at the same time be transcendently real; and secondly by ignoring the fact that to deny spatial properties to things in themselves is as great a violation of Critical principles as to assert them. One point, however, in Caird's reply to Trendelenburg calls for special consideration, viz. Caird's contention that Kant did actually take account of the third alternative, rejecting it as involving the "absurd" hypothesis of a pre-established harmony.[2] Undoubtedly Kant did so. But the contention has no relevancy to the point before us. The doctrine of pre-established harmony is a metaphysical theory which presupposes the possibility of gaining knowledge of things in themselves. For that reason alone Kant was bound to reject it. A metaphysical proof of the validity of metaphysical judgments is, from the Critical point of view, a contradiction in terms. As the validity of *all* speculations is in doubt, a proof which is speculative cannot meet our difficulties. And also, as Kant himself further points out, the pre-established harmony, even if granted, can afford no solution of the Critical problem how *a priori* judgments can be passed upon the independently real. The judgments, thus guaranteed, could only possess *de facto* validity; we could never be assured of their necessity.[3] It is chiefly in these two inabilities that Kant locates the "absurdity" of a theory of pre-established harmony. The refutation of that theory does not, therefore, amount to a disproof of the possibility which we are here considering.

Conclusion b.—The next paragraph maintains two theses: (*a*) that space is the form of all outer intuition; (*b*) that this fact explains what is otherwise entirely inexplicable and paradoxical, namely, that we can make *a priori* judgments which yet apply to the objects experienced. The first thesis, that the pure intuition of space is only conceivable as the form of appearances of outer sense, is propounded in the opening sentence without argument and even without citation of grounds. The statement thus suddenly made is not anticipated

---

[1] *The Critical Philosophy of Kant*, i. pp. 306-9.

[2] Cf. letter to Herz, *W.* x. p. 126. It is, Kant there says, the most absurd explanation which can be offered of the origin and validity of our knowledge, involving an illegitimate *circulus in probando*, and also throwing open the door to the wildest speculations. Cf. above, p. 28; below, pp. 141-2, 290, 590.

[3] Cf. B 167-8.

save by the opening sentences of the section on space.[1] It is an essentially new doctrine. Hitherto Kant has spoken of space only as an *a priori* intuition. The further assertion that as such it must necessarily be conceived as the form of outer sense (*i.e.* not only as a formal intuition but also as a form of intuition), calls for the most definite and explicit proof. None, however, is given. It is really a conclusion from points all too briefly cited by Kant in the general *Introduction*, namely, from his distinction between the matter and the form of sense. The assertions there made, in a somewhat casual manner, are here, without notification to the reader, employed as premisses to ground the above assertion. His thesis is not, therefore, as by its face value it would seem to profess to be, an inference from the points established in the preceding expositions. It interprets these conclusions in the light of points considered in the *Introduction*; and thereby arrives at a new and all-important interpretation of the nature of the *a priori* intuition of space.

The second thesis employs the first to explain how prior to all experience we can determine the relations of objects. Since (*a*) space is merely the form of outer sense, and (*b*) accordingly exists in the mind prior to all empirical intuition, all appearances must exist in space, and we can predetermine them from the pure intuition of space that is given to us *a priori*. Space, when thus viewed as the *a priori* form of outer sense, renders comprehensible the validity of applied mathematics.

As we have already noted,[2] Kant in the second edition obscures the sequence of his argument by offering in the new transcendental exposition a justification of applied as well as of pure geometry. In so doing he anticipates the conclusion which is first drawn in this later paragraph. This would have been avoided had Kant given two separate transcendental expositions. First, an exposition of pure mathematics, placed immediately after the metaphysical exposition; for pure mathematics is exclusively based upon the results of the metaphysical exposition. And secondly, an exposition of applied mathematics, introduced after *Conclusion b*. The explanation of applied geometry is really the more essential and central of the two, as it alone involves the truly Critical problem, how judgments formed *a priori* can yet apply to objects. *Conclusion b* constitutes, as Vaihinger rightly insists,[3] the very heart of the *Aesthetic*. The arrangement of Kant's argument diverts the reader's attention from where it ought properly to centre.

[1] That is, in the first edition. Cf. above, p. 85 ff.; and below, p. 116.
[2] Above, pp. 111-12.   [3] ii. p. 335.

The use which Kant makes of the *Prolegomena* in his statement of the new transcendental exposition is one cause of the confusion.   The exposition is a brief summary of the corresponding *Prolegomena*[1] sections.   In introducing this summary into the *Critique* Kant overlooked the fact that in referring to applied mathematics he is anticipating a point first established in *Conclusion b*.   The real cause, however, of the trouble is common to both editions, namely Kant's failure clearly to appreciate the fundamental distinction between the view that space is an *a priori* intuition and the view that it is the *a priori* form of all external intuition, *i.e.* of outer sense. He does not seem to have fully realised how very different are those two views.   In consequence of this he fails to distinguish between the transcendental expositions of pure and applied geometry.[2]

Third paragraph.—Kant proceeds to develop the subjectivist conclusions which follow from *a* and *b*.

"We may say that space contains all things which can appear to us externally, but not all things in themselves, whether intuited or not, nor again all things intuited by any and every subject."[3]

This sentence makes two assertions: (*a*) space does not belong to things in and by themselves; (*b*) space is not a necessary form of intuition for all subjects whatsoever.

The grounds for the former assertion are not here considered, and that is doubtless the reason why the *oder nicht* is excised in Kant's private copy of the *Critique*.   As we have seen, Kant does not anywhere in the *Aesthetic* even attempt to offer argument in support of this assertion.   In defence of (*a*) Kant propounds for the first time the view of sensibility as a limitation.   Space is a limiting condition to which human intuition is subject.   Whether the intuitions of other thinking beings are subject to the same limitation, we have no means of deciding.   But for all human beings, Kant implies, the same conditions must hold universally.[4]

In the phrase "transcendental ideality of space"[5] Kant, it may be noted, takes the term ideality as signifying subjectivity, and the term transcendental as equivalent to transcendent.   He is stating that judged from a *transcendent* point of view, *i.e.* from the point of view of the thing in itself, space has a merely subjective or "empirical" reality.   This is an

---

[1] §§ 6-11.
[2] This identification of the two is especially clear in A 39 = B 56.
[3] A 27 = B 43.
[4] Cf. above, p. xxxv ; below, pp. 117-20, 142, 185-6, 241-2, 257, 290-1.
[5] A 28 = B 44, cf. A 35 = B 52.

instance of Kant's careless use of the term transcendental. Space is empirically real, but taken *transcendently*, is merely ideal.[1]

KANT'S ATTITUDE TO THE PROBLEMS OF MODERN GEOMETRY

This is an appropriate point at which to consider the consistency of Kant's teaching with modern developments in geometry. Kant's attitude has very frequently been misrepresented. As he here states, he is willing to recognise that the forms of intuition possessed by other races of finite beings may not coincide with those of the human species. But in so doing he does not mean to assert the possibility of other *spatial* forms, *i.e.* of spaces that are non-Euclidean. In his pre-Critical period Kant had indeed attempted to deduce the three-dimensional character of space as a consequence of the law of gravitation; and recognising that that law is in itself arbitrary, he concluded that God might, by establishing different relations of gravitation, have given rise to spaces of different properties and dimensions.

"A science of all these possible kinds of space would undoubtedly be the highest enterprise which a finite understanding could undertake in the field of geometry."[2]

But from the time of Kant's adoption, in 1770, of the Critical view of space as being the universal form of our outer sense, he seems to have definitely rejected all such possibilities. Space, to be space at all, must be Euclidean; the uniformity of space is a presupposition of the *a priori* certainty of geometrical science.[3] One of the criticisms which in the *Dissertation*[4] he passes upon the empirical view of mathematical

---

[1] Cf. Vaihinger, i. pp. 351-4; and above, p. 76; below, p. 302. Cf. Caird, *The Critical Philosophy*, i. pp. 298-9, 301; and Watson, *Kant Explained*, p. 91.

[2] *Gedanken von der wahren Schätzung der lebendigen Kräfte* (1747), § 10.

[3] This important and far-reaching assertion we cannot at this point discuss. Kant's reasoning is really circular in the bad sense. Kant may legitimately argue from the *a priori* character of space to the apodictic character of *pure* mathematical science; but when he proceeds similarly to infer the apodictic character of *applied* mathematics, he is constrained to make the further assumption that space is a fixed and absolutely uniform mode in which alone members of the human species can intuit objects. That, as we point out below (p. 120), is an assumption which Kant does not really succeed in proving. In any case the requirements of the strict synthetic method preclude him from arguing, as he does both in the *Dissertation* (§ 15) and in the third space argument of the first edition, that the *a priori* certitude of applied mathematics affords proof of the necessary uniformity of all space.

[4] § 15 D.

science is that it would leave open the possibility that "a space may some time be discovered endowed with other fundamental properties, or even perhaps that we may happen upon a two-sided rectilinear figure." This is the argument which reappears in the third argument on space in the first edition of the *Critique*.[1] The same examples are employed with a somewhat different wording.

"It would not even be necessary that there should be only one straight line between two points, though experience invariably shows this to be so. What is derived from experience has only comparative universality, namely, that which is obtained through induction. We should therefore only be able to say that, so far as hitherto observed, no space has been found which has more than three dimensions."

But that Kant should have failed to recognise the possibility of other spaces does not by itself point to any serious defect in his position. There is no essential difficulty in reconciling the recognition of such spaces with his fundamental teaching. He admits that other races of finite beings may perhaps intuit through *non-spatial* forms of sensibility; he might quite well have recognised that those other forms of intuition, though not Euclidean, are still spatial. It is in another and more vital respect that Kant's teaching lies open to criticism. Kant is convinced that space is given to us in intuition as being definitely and irrevocably Euclidean in character. Both our intuition and our thinking, when we reflect upon space, are, he implies, bound down to, and limited by, the conditions of Euclidean space. And it is in this positive assumption, and not merely in his ignoring of the possibility of other spaces, that he comes into conflict with the teaching of modern geometry. For in making the above assumption Kant is asserting that we definitely know physical space to be three-dimensional, and that by no elaboration of concepts can we so remodel it in thought that the axiom of parallels will cease to hold. Euclidean space, Kant implies, is *given* to us as an unyielding form that rigidly resists all attempts at conceptual reconstruction. Being quite independent of thought and being given as complete, it has no inchoate plasticity of which thought might take advantage. The modern geometer is not, however, prepared to admit that *intuitional* space has any definiteness or preciseness of nature apart from the concepts through which it is apprehended; and he therefore allows, as at least possible, that upon clarification of our concepts space may be discovered to be radically different from what it at first sight appears to be. In any

[1] Cf. above, p. 111.

case, the perfecting of the concepts must have some effect upon their object. But even—as the modern geometer further maintains—should our space be definitely proved, upon analytic and empirical investigation, to be Euclidean in character, other possibilities will still remain open for speculative thought. For though the nature of our intuitional data may constrain us to interpret them through one set of concepts rather than through another, the competing sets of alternative concepts will represent genuine possibilities beyond what the actual is found to embody.

Thus the defect of Kant's teaching, in regard to space, as judged in the light of the later teaching of geometrical science, is closely bound up with his untenable isolation of the *a priori* of sensibility from the *a priori* of understanding.[1] Space, being thus viewed as independent of thought, has to be regarded as limiting and restricting thought by the unalterable nature of its initial presentation. And unfortunately this is a position which Kant continued to hold, despite his increasing recognition of the part which concepts must play in the various mathematical sciences. In the deduction of the first edition we find him stating that synthesis of apprehension is necessary to all representation of space and time.[2] He further recognises that all arithmetical processes are syntheses *according to concepts*.[3] And in the *Prolegomena*[4] there occurs the following significant passage.

" Do these laws of nature lie in space, and does the understanding learn them by merely endeavouring to find out the fruitful meaning that lies in space ; or do they inhere in the understanding and in the way in which it determines space according to the conditions of the synthetical unity towards which its concepts are all directed ? Space is something so uniform and as to all particular properties so indeterminate, that we should certainly not seek a store of laws of nature in it. That which determines space to the form of a circle or to the figures of a cone or a sphere, is, on the contrary, the understanding, so far as it contains the ground of the unity of these constructions. The mere universal form of intuition, called space, must therefore be the substratum of all intuitions determinable to particular objects, and in it, of course, the condition of the possibility and of the variety of these intuitions lies. But the unity of the objects is solely determined by the understanding, and indeed in accordance with conditions which are proper to the nature of the understanding . . ."

Obviously Kant is being driven by the spontaneous development of his own thinking towards a position much more

---

[1] Cf. above, pp. 40-2, 93-4 ; below, pp. 131-3, 338-9, 418 ff.   [2] A 99-100.
[3] A 78 = B 104. Cf. A 159 = B 198, B 147.
[4] § 38, Eng. trans. p. 81.

consistent with present-day teaching, and completely at variance with the hard and fast severance between sensibility and understanding which he had formulated in the *Dissertation* and has retained in the *Aesthetic*. In the above *Prolegomena* passage a plasticity is being allowed to space, sufficient to permit of essential modification in the conceptual processes through which it is articulated. But, as I have just stated, that did not lead Kant to disavow the conclusions which he had drawn from his previous teaching.

This defect in Kant's doctrine of space, as expounded in the *Aesthetic*, indicates a further imperfection in his argument. He asserts that the form of space cannot vary from one human being to another, and that for this reason the judgments which express it are universally valid. Now, in so far as Kant's initial datum is consciousness of time,[1] he is entirely justified in assuming that everything which can be shown to be a necessary condition of such consciousness must be uniform for all human minds. But as his argument is not that consciousness of *Euclidean* space is necessary to consciousness of time, but only that consciousness of the *permanent* in space is a required condition, he has not succeeded in showing the necessary uniformity of the human mind as regards the specific mode in which it intuits space. The permanent might still be apprehended as permanent, and therefore as yielding a possible basis for consciousness of sequence, even if it were apprehended in some four-dimensional form.

Fourth Paragraph.—The next paragraph raises one of the central problems of the *Critique*, namely, the question as to the kind of reality possessed by appearances. Are they subjective, like taste or colour? Or have they a reality at least relatively independent of the individual percipient? In other words, is Kant's position subjectivism or phenomenalism? Kant here alternates between these positions. This fourth paragraph is coloured by his phenomenalism, whereas in the immediately following fifth paragraph his subjectivism gains the upper hand. The taste of wine, he states in the fourth paragraph, is purely subjective, because dependent upon the particular constitution of the gustatory organ on which the wine acts. Similarly, colours are not properties of the objects which cause them.

"They are only modifications of the sense of sight which is affected in a certain manner by the light. . . . They are connected

---

[1] Cf. p. 241 ff.

with the appearances only as effects accidentally added by the particular constitution of the sense organs." [1]

Space, on the other hand, is a necessary constituent of the outer objects.   In contrast to the subjective sensations of taste and colour, it possesses objectivity.   This mode of distinguishing between space and the matter of sense implies that extended objects are not mere ideas, but are sufficiently independent to be capable of acting upon the sense organs, and of thereby generating the sensations of the secondary qualities.

Kant, it must be observed, refers only to taste and colour. He says nothing in regard to weight, impenetrability, and the like.   These are revealed through sensation, and therefore on his view ought to be in exactly the same position as taste or colour.   But if so, the relative independence of the extended object can hardly be maintained.   Kant's distinction between space and the sense qualities cannot, indeed, be made to coincide with the Cartesian distinction between primary and secondary qualities.

A second difference, from Kant's point of view, between space and the sense qualities is that the former can be represented *a priori*, in complete separation from everything empirical, whereas the latter can only be known *a posteriori*. This, as we have seen, is a very questionable assertion.   The further statement that all determinations of space can be represented in the same *a priori* fashion is even more questionable.   At most the difference is only between a homogeneous subjective form yielded by outer sense and the endlessly varied and consequently unpredictable contents revealed by the special senses.   The contention that the former can be known apart from the latter implies the existence of a pure manifold additional to the manifold of sense.

Fifth Paragraph.—In the next paragraph Kant emphasises the distinction between the empirical and the transcendental meanings of the term appearance.   A rose, viewed *empirically*, as a thing with an intrinsic independent nature, may appear of different colour to different observers.

"The *transcendental* conception of appearances in space, on the other hand, is a Critical reminder that nothing intuited in space is a thing in itself, that space is not a form inhering in things in themselves . . . and that what we call outer objects are nothing but mere representations of our sensibility, the form of which is space."

In other words, the distinction drawn in the preceding paragraph between colour as a subjective effect and space as

[1] A 28-9.   Cf. B 1; *Prolegomena*, § 13, Remark II. at the end : "Cinnabar excites the sensation of red in me."   Cf. above, pp. 80-8 ; below, pp. 146 ff., 274 ff.

an objective existence is no longer maintained. Kant, when thus developing his position on subjectivist lines, allows no kind of independent existence to anything in the known world. Objects as known are mere Ideas (*blosse Vorstellungen unserer Sinnlichkeit*), the sole correlate of which is the unknowable thing in itself. But even in this paragraph both tendencies find expression. "Colour, taste, etc., must not rightly be regarded as properties of things, but only as changes, in the subject." This implies a threefold distinction between subjective sensations, empirical objects in space, and the thing in itself. The material world, investigated by science, is recognised as possessing a relatively independent mode of existence.

Substituted Fourth Paragraph of second edition.—In preparing the second edition Kant himself evidently felt the awkwardness of this abrupt juxtaposition of the two very different points of view; and he accordingly adopts a non-commital attitude, substituting a logical distinction for the ontological. Space yields synthetic judgments *a priori*; the sense qualities do not. Only in the concluding sentence does there emerge any definite phenomenalist implication. The sense qualities, "as they are mere sensations and not intuitions, in themselves reveal no object, least of all [an object] *a priori*." [1] The assertion that the secondary qualities have no *ideality* implies a new and stricter use of the term ideal than we find anywhere in the first edition—a use which runs counter to Kant's own constant employment of the term. On this interpretation it is made to signify what though subjective is also *a priori*. Here, as in many of the alterations of the second edition, Kant is influenced by the desire to emphasise the points which distinguish his idealism from that of Berkeley.

---

[1] Kant continues the discussion of this general problem in A 45 ff. = B 62 ff.

THE TRANSCENDENTAL AESTHETIC

SECTION II

TIME

METAPHYSICAL EXPOSITION OF THE CONCEPTION OF TIME

Time : First Argument.—This argument is in all respects the same as the first argument on space. The thesis is that the representation[1] of time is not of empirical origin. The proof is based on the fact that this representation must be previously given in order that the perception of coexistence or succession be possible. It also runs on all fours with the first argument in the *Dissertation.*

"*The idea of time does not originate in, but is presupposed by the senses.* When a number of things act upon the senses, it is only by means of the idea of time that they can be represented whether as simultaneous or as successive. Nor does succession generate the conception of time; but stimulates us to form it. Thus the notion of time, even if acquired through experience, is very badly defined as being a series of actual things existing one *after* another. For I can understand what the word *after* signifies only if I already know what time means. For those things are *after* one another which exist at *different* times, as those are *simultaneous* which exist at one and the same time."[2]

Second Argument.—Kant again applies to time the argument already employed by him in dealing with space. The thesis is that time is given *a priori.* Proof is found in the fact that it cannot be thought away, *i.e.* in the fact of its subjective necessity. From this subjective necessity follows its objective necessity, so far as all appearances are concerned. In the second edition Kant added a phrase—"as the general condition of their possibility"—which is seriously misleading. The concluding sentence is thereby made to

---

[1] Kant himself again uses the confusing term conception.
[2] § 14, 1.

read as if Kant were arguing from the objective necessity of time, *i.e.* from its necessity as a constituent in the appearances apprehended, to its apriority. It is indeed possible that Kant himself regarded this objective necessity of time as contributing to the proof of its apriority. But no such argument can be accepted. Time may be necessary to appearances, *once appearances are granted.* This does not, however, prove that it must therefore precede them *a priori.* This alteration in the second edition is an excellent, though unfortunate, example of Kant's invincible carelessness in the exposition of his thought. It has contributed to a misreading by Herbart and others of this and of the corresponding argument on space.

"Let us not talk of an absolute space as the presupposition of all our constructed figures. Possibility is nothing but thought, and it arises only when it is thought. Space is nothing but possibility, for it contains nothing save images of the existent; and absolute space is nothing save the abstracted general possibility of such constructions, abstracted from it after completion of the construction. The necessity of the representation of space ought never to have played any rôle in philosophy. To think away space is to think away the *possibility* of that which has been previously posited as *actual.* Obviously that is impossible, and the opposite is necessary."[1]

Were Kant really arguing here and in the second argument on space solely from the *objective* necessity of time and space, this criticism would be unanswerable. But even taking the argument in its first edition form, as an argument from the *psychological* necessity of time, it lies open to the same objection as the argument on space. It rests upon a false statement of fact. We cannot retain time in the absence of all appearances of outer and inner sense. With the removal of the given manifold, time itself must vanish.

Fourth Argument.[2]—This argument differs only slightly, and mainly through omissions,[3] from the fourth[4] of the arguments in regard to space; but a few minor points call for notice. (*a*) In the first sentence, instead of intuition, which alone is under consideration in its contrast to conception, Kant employs the phrase "pure form of intuition." (*b*) In the third sentence Kant uses the quite untenable phrase "given through a single object (*Gegenstand*)." Time is not given

---

[1] Herbart, *Werke,* ii. 30. Quoted by Vaihinger, ii. p. 198.

[2] The third argument on time will be considered below in its connection with the transcendental exposition.

[3] The chief omission goes, as we shall see, to form the concluding argument on time.

[4] In the second edition, the third.

from without, nor is it due to an object. (*c*) The concluding sentences properly belong to the transcendental exposition. They are here introduced, not in the ambiguous manner of the fourth[1] argument on space, but explicitly as a further argument in proof of the intuitive character of time. The synthetic proposition which Kant cites is taken neither from the science of motion nor from arithmetic. It expresses the nature of time itself, and for that reason is immediately contained in the intuition of time.

Fifth Argument.—This argument differs fundamentally from the corresponding argument on space, whether of the first or of the second edition, and must therefore be independently analysed. The thesis is again that time is an intuition. Proof is derived from the fact that time is a representation in which the parts arise only through limitation, and in which therefore, the whole must precede the parts. The original (*ursprüngliche*) time-representation, *i.e.* the fundamental representation through limitation of which the parts arise as secondary products, must be an intuition.

To this argument Kant makes two explanatory additions. (*a*) As particular times arise through limitation of one single time, time must in its original intuition be given as infinite, *i.e.* as unlimited. The infinitude of time is not, therefore, as might seem to be implied by the prominence given to it, and by analogy with the final arguments of both the first and the second edition, a part of the proof that it is an intuition, but only a consequence of the feature by which its intuitive character is independently established. The unwary reader, having in mind the corresponding argument on space, is almost inevitably misled. All reference to infinitude could, so far as this argument is concerned, have been omitted. The mode in which the argument opens seems indeed to indicate that Kant was not himself altogether clear as to the cross-relations between the arguments on space and time respectively. The real parallel to this argument is to be found in the second part of the fourth[1] argument on space. That part was omitted by Kant in his fourth argument on time, and is here developed into a separate argument. This is, of course, a further cause of confusion to the reader, who is not prepared for such arbitrary rearrangement. Indeed it is not surprising to find that when Kant became the reader of his own work, in preparing it for the second edition, he was himself misled by the intricate perversity of his exposition. In re-reading the argument he seems to have forgotten that it represents the second part of the fourth[1] argument

---

[1] In the second edition, the third.

on space. Interpreting it in the light of the fifth [1] argument on space which he had been recasting for the second edition, it seemed to him possible, by a slight alteration, to bring this argument on time into line with that new proof.[2] This unfortunately results in the perverting of the entire paragraph. The argument demands an opposition between intuition in which the whole precedes the parts, and conception in which the parts precede the whole. In order to bring the opposition into line with the new argument on space, according to which a conception contains an infinite number of parts, not in it, but only under it, Kant substitutes for the previous parenthesis the statement that "concepts contain only partial representations," meaning, apparently, that their constituent elements are merely abstracted attributes, not real concrete parts, or in other words, not strictly parts at all, but only partial representations. But this does not at all agree with the context. The point at issue is thereby obscured.

(b) The main argument rests upon and presupposes a very definite view as to the manner in which alone, according to Kant, concepts are formed. Only if this view be granted as true of all concepts without exception is the argument cogent. This doctrine[3] of the concept is accordingly stated by Kant in the words of the parenthesis. The partial representations, i.e. the different properties which go to constitute the object or content conceived, precede the representation of the whole. "The aggregation of co-ordinate attributes (Merkmale) constitutes the totality of the concept."[4] Upon the use which Kant thus makes of the traditional doctrine of the concept, and upon its lack of consistency with his recognition of relational categories, we have already dwelt.[5]

Third Argument and the Transcendental Exposition.—The third argument ought to have been omitted in the second edition, and its substance incorporated in the new transcendental exposition, as was done with the corresponding argument concerning space. The excuse which Kant offers for not making the change, namely, his desire for brevity, is not valid. By insertion in the new section the whole matter could have been stated just as briefly as before.

The purpose of the transcendental exposition has been already defined. It is to show how time, when viewed in the manner required by the results of the metaphysical deduction,

---

[1] In the second edition, the fourth.
[2] Cf. Vaihinger, ii. pp. 380-1.
[3] Cf. second part of fourth (third) argument on space.
[4] Kant's *Logik*, *Einleitung*, § 8, Eng. trans. p. 49.
[5] Cf. above, pp. 99-100.

as an *a priori* intuition, renders synthetic *a priori* judgments possible.

This exposition, as it appears in the third argument of the first edition, grounds the apodictic character of two axioms in regard to time[1] on the proved apriority of the representation of time, and then by implication finds in these axioms a fresh proof of the apriority of time.

The new transcendental exposition extends the above by two further statements : (*a*) that only through the intuition of time can any conception of change, and therewith of motion (as change of place), be formed ; and (*b*) that it is because the intuition of time is an *a priori* intuition that the synthetic *a priori* propositions of the "general doctrine of motion" are possible. To take each in turn. (*a*) Save by reference to time the conception of motion is self-contradictory. It involves the ascription to one and the same thing of contradictory predicates, *e.g.* that an object both is and is not in a certain place. From this fact, that time makes possible what is not possible in pure conception, Kant, in his earlier rationalistic period, had derived a proof of the subjectivity of time.[2] (*b*) In 1786 in the *Metaphysical First Principles of Natural Science* Kant had developed the fundamental principles of the general science of motion. He takes the opportunity of the second edition (1787) of the *Critique* to assign this place to them in his general system. The implication is that the doctrine of motion stands to time in the relation in which geometry stands to space. Kant is probably here replying, as Vaihinger has suggested,[3] to an objection made by Garve to the first edition, that no science, corresponding to geometry, is based on the intuition of time. For two reasons, however, the analogy between mechanics and geometry breaks down. In the first place, the conception of motion is empirical ; and in the second place, it presupposes space as well as time.[4]

Kant elsewhere explicitly disavows this view that the science of motion is based on time. He had already done so in the preceding year (1786) in the *Metaphysical First*

---

[1] These axioms are : (1) time has only one dimension ; (2) different times are not simultaneous but successive. In the fourth argument the *synthetic* character of these axioms is taken as further evidence of the intuitive nature of time. This passage also is really part of the transcendental exposition. That exposition has to account for the synthetic character of the axioms as well as for their apodictic character ; and as a matter of fact the intuitive and consequent synthetic character of the *a priori* knowledge which arises from time is much more emphasised in the transcendental exposition than its apodictic nature.

[2] Cf. *Reflexionen*, ii. 374 ff.　　　　[3] Vaihinger, ii. p. 387.

[4] Cf. A 41 = B 58 : "Motion which combines both [space and time] presupposes something empirical."

Principles. He there points out[1] that as time has only one dimension, mathematics is not applicable to the phenomena of inner sense. At most we can determine in regard to them (in addition, of course, to the two axioms already cited) only the law that all these changes are continuous. Also in Kant's *Ueber Philosophie überhaupt* (written some time between 1780 and 1790, and very probably in or about the year 1789) we find the following utterance:

"The general doctrine of time, unlike the pure doctrine of space (geometry), does not yield sufficient material for a whole science."[2]

Why, then, should Kant in 1787 have so inconsistently departed from his own teaching? This is a question to which I can find no answer. Apparently without reason, and contrary to his more abiding judgment, he here repeats the suggestion which he had casually thrown out in the *Dissertation*[3] of 1770:

"Pure mathematics treats of space in geometry and of time in pure mechanics."

But in the *Dissertation* the point is only touched upon in passing. The context permits of the interpretation that while geometry deals with space, mechanics deals with time in addition to space.

KANT'S VIEWS REGARDING THE NATURE OF ARITHMETICAL SCIENCE

In the *Dissertation*, and again in the chapter on *Schematism* in the *Critique* itself, still another view is suggested, namely, that the science of arithmetic is also concerned with the intuition of time. The passage just quoted from the *Dissertation* proceeds as follows:

"Pure mathematics treats of space in geometry and of time in pure mechanics. To these has to be added a certain concept which is in itself intellectual, but which demands for its concrete actualisation (*actuatio*) the auxiliary notions of time and space (in the successive addition and in the juxtaposition of a plurality). This is the concept of number which is dealt with in *Arithmetic*."[4]

This view of arithmetic is to be found in both editions of the *Critique*. Arithmetic depends upon the synthetic activity

---

[1] *W.* iv. p. 471.
[2] *Ueber Philosophie überhaupt* (Hartenstein, vi. p. 395).
[3] § 12.   [4] *Loc. cit.*

of the understanding; the conceptual element is absolutely essential.

"Our counting (as is easily seen in the case of large numbers) is a synthesis according to concepts, because it is executed according to a common ground of unity, as, for instance, the decade (*Dekadik*)."[1] "The pure image . . . of all objects of the senses in general is time. But the pure *schema* of quantity, in so far as it is a concept of the understanding, is *number*, a representation which combines the successive addition of one to one (homogeneous). Thus number is nothing but the unity of the synthesis of the manifold of a homogeneous intuition in general,—an unity due to the fact that I generate time itself in the apprehension of the intuition."[2]

This is also the teaching of the *Methodology*.[3] Now it may be observed that in none of these passages is arithmetic declared to be the *science of time*, or even to be based on the intuition of time. In 1783, however, in the *Prolegomena*, Kant expresses himself in much more ambiguous terms, for his words imply that there is a parallelism between geometry and arithmetic.

"Geometry is based upon the pure intuition of space. Arithmetic produces its concepts of number through successive addition of units in time, and pure mechanics especially can produce its concepts of motion only by means of the representation of time."[4]

The passage is by no means explicit, the "especially" (*vornehmlich*) seems to indicate a feeling on Kant's part that the description which he is giving of arithmetic is not really satisfactory. Unfortunately this casual statement, though never repeated by Kant in any of his other writings, was developed by Schulze in his *Erläuterungen*.

"Since geometry has space and arithmetic has counting as its object (and counting can only take place by means of time), it is evident in what manner geometry and arithmetic, that is to say pure mathematics, is possible."[5]

---

[1] A 78 = B 104.
[2] A 142-3 = B 182. It should be observed that in Kant's view schemata "exist nowhere but in thought" (A 141 = B 180). It may also be noted that time is taken as conditioning the schemata of *all* the categories.
[3] A 717 ff. = B 745 ff.   [4] § 10.
[5] *Erläuterungen über des Herrn Professor Kant Critik der reinen Vernunft* (Königsberg, 1784), p. 24. Johann Schulze (or Schultz) was professor of mathematics in Königsberg. He was also *Hofprediger*, and is frequently referred to as Pastor Schulze. Kant has eulogised him (*W*. x. p. 128) as "the best philosophical head that I am acquainted with in our part of the world." In preparing the *Erläuterungen*, which is a paraphrase or simplified statement of the argument of the *Critique*, with appended comment, Schulze had the advantage of Kant's advice in all difficulties. Kant also read his manuscript, and suggested a few modifications (*op. cit.* pp. 329, 343).

Largely, as it would seem,[1] through Schulze, whose *Erläuterungen* did much to spread Kant's teaching, this view came to be the current understanding of Kant's position The nature of arithmetic, as thus popularly interpreted, is expounded by Schopenhauer in the following terms :

"In time every moment is conditioned by the preceding. The ground of existence, as law of the sequence, is thus simple, because time has only one dimension, and no manifoldness of relations can be possible in it. Every moment is conditioned by the preceding; only through the latter can we attain to the former; only because the latter was, and has elapsed, does the former now exist. All counting rests upon this nexus of the parts of time ; its words merely serve to mark the single steps of the succession. This is true of the whole of arithmetic, which throughout teaches nothing but the methodical abbreviations of counting. Every number presupposes the preceding numbers as grounds of its existence ; I can only reach them through all the preceding, and only by means of this insight into the ground of its existence do I know that, where ten are, there are also eight, six, four."[2]

Schulze was at once challenged to show that this was really Kant's teaching, and the passage which he cited was Kant's definition of the schema of number, above quoted.[3] It is therefore advisable that we should briefly discuss the many difficulties which this passage involves. What does Kant mean by asserting that in the apprehension of number we generate time ? Does he merely mean that time is required for the process of counting ? Counting is a process through which numerical relations are discovered ; and it undoubtedly occupies time. But so do all processes of apprehension, in the study of geometry no less than of arithmetic. That this is not Kant's meaning, and that it is not even what Schulze, notwithstanding his seemingly explicit mode of statement, intends to assert, is clearly shown by a letter written by Kant to Schulze in November 1788. Schulze, it appears, had spoken of this very matter.

"*Time, as you justly remark, has no influence upon the properties of numbers* (as pure determinations of quantity), such as it may have upon the nature of those changes (of quantity) which are possible only in connection with a specific property of inner sense and its form (time). *The science of number, notwithstanding the succession which every construction of quantity demands, is a pure intellectual synthesis which we represent to ourselves in thought.* But so far as *quanta* are to be numerically determined, they must be given to us

[1] Cf. Vaihinger, ii. pp. 388-9.
[2] *Werke* (Frauenstädt's ed., 1873), i. p. 133.
[3] P. 129.

in such a way that we can apprehend their intuition in successive order, and such that their *apprehension* can be subject to time. . . ."[1]

No more definite statement could be desired of the fact that though in arithmetical science as in other fields of study our processes of apprehension are subject to time, the quantitative relations determined by the science are independent of time and are intellectually apprehended.

But if the above psychological interpretation of Kant's teaching is untenable, how is his position to be defined? We must bear in mind the doctrine which Kant had already developed in his pre-Critical period, that mathematical differs from philosophical knowledge in that its concepts can have concrete individual form.[2] In the *Critique* this difference is expressed in the statement that the mathematical sciences alone are able to *construct* their concepts. And as they are *pure* mathematical sciences, this construction is supposed to take place by means of the *a priori* manifold of space and of time. Now though Kant had a fairly definite notion of what he meant by the construction of geometrical figures in space, his various utterances seem to show that in regard to the nature of arithmetical and algebraic construction he had never really attempted to arrive at any precision of view. To judge by the passage already quoted[3] from the *Dissertation*, Kant regarded space as no less necessary than time to the construction or intuition of number. "[The intellectual concept of number] demands for its concrete actualisation the auxiliary notions of time *and space* (in the successive addition and in the *juxtaposition of a plurality*)." A similar view appears in the *Critique* in A 140 = B 179 and in B 15. In conformity, however, with the general requirements of his doctrine of *Schematism*, Kant defines the schema of number in exclusive reference to time; and, as we have noted, it is to this definition that Schulze appeals in support of his view of arithmetic as the science of counting and therefore of time. It at least shows that Kant perceived *some* form of connection to exist between arithmetic and time. But in this matter Kant's position was probably simply a corollary from his general view of the nature of mathematical science, and in particular of his view of geometry, the "exemplar"[4] of all the others. Mathematical science, as such, is based on intuition;[5] therefore arithmetic, which is one of its departments,

---

[1] *W.* x. p. 530. Italics not in Kant.
[2] *Untersuchung über die Deutlichkeit der Grundsätze: Erste Betrachtung*, §§ 2, 3; *dritte Betrachtung*, § 1; *Dissertation*, §§ 12, 15 C.
[3] P. 128. [4] *Dissertation*, § 15 C.
[5] Cf. above, pp. 40-2, 118-20; below, pp. 338-9.

must be so likewise.   No attempt, however, is made to define the ·nature of the intuitions in which it has its source. Sympathetically interpreted, his statements may be taken as suggesting that arithmetic is the study of *series* which find concrete expression in the order of sequent times.   The following estimate, given by Cassirer,[1] does ample justice both to the true and to the false elements in Kant's doctrine.

"[Even discounting Kant's insistence upon the conceptual character of arithmetical science, and] allowing that he derives arithmetical concepts and propositions from the *pure intuition of time*, this teaching, to whatever objections it may lie open, has certainly not the merely *psychological* meaning which the majority of its critics have ascribed to it.   If it contained only the trivial thought, that the empirical act of counting requires time, it would be completely refuted by the familiar objection which B. Beneke has formulated: 'The fact that time elapses in the process of counting can prove nothing; for what is there over which time does not flow?' It is easily seen that Kant is only concerned with the 'transcendental' determination of the concept of time, according to which it appears as the type of an ordered sequence.   William [Rowan] Hamilton, who adopts Kant's doctrine, has defined algebra as 'science of pure time or *order in progression*.' That the whole content of arithmetical concepts can really be obtained from the fundamental concept of *order* in unbroken development, is completely confirmed by Russell's exposition.   As against the Kantian theory it must, of course, be emphasised, that it is not the *concrete* form of time intuition which constitutes the *ground* of the concept of number, but that on the contrary the pure logical concepts of sequence and of order are already implicitly contained and embodied in that concrete form."

Much of the unsatisfactoriness of Kant's argument is traceable to his mode of conceiving the "construction"[2] of mathematical concepts.   All concepts, he seems to hold, even those of geometry and arithmetic, are abstract class concepts —the concept of triangle representing the properties common to all triangles, and the concept of seven the properties common to all groups that are seven.   Mathematical concepts differ, however, from other concepts in that they are capable of *a priori* construction, that is, of having their objects represented in pure intuition.   Now this is an extremely unfortunate mode of statement.   It implies that mathematical concepts have a dual mode of existence, first as abstracted, and secondly as constructed.   Such a position is not tenable.   The concept of seven, in its primary form, is not abstracted from a variety of particular groups of

---

[1] *Kant und die moderne Mathematik* in *Kant-Studien*, xii. (1907) p. 34 *n.*
[2] Cf. A 713 ff. = B 741 ff. ; A 4 = B 8; B 15-16; A 24; A 47-8 = B 64-5.

seven; it is already involved in the apprehension of each of them as being seven. Nor is it a concept that is itself constructed. It may perhaps be described as being the representation of something constructed; but that something is not itself. It represents the process or method generative of the complex for which it stands. Thus Kant's distinction between the intuitive nature of mathematical knowledge and the merely discursive character of conceptual knowledge is at once inspired by the very important distinction between the product of construction and the product of abstraction, and yet at the same time is also obscured by the quite inadequate manner in which that latter distinction has been formulated. Kant has again adhered to the older logic even in the very act of revising its conclusions; and in so doing he has sacrificed the Critical doctrines of the *Analytic* to the pre-Critical teaching of the *Dissertation* and *Aesthetic*. *Mathematical concepts are of the same general type as the categories; their primary function is not to clarify intuitions, but to make them possible.* They are derivable from intuition only in so far as they have contributed to its constitution. If intuition contains factors additional to the concepts through which it is interpreted, these factors must remain outside the realm of mathematical science, until such time as conceptual analysis has proved itself capable of further extension.

I may now summarise this general discussion. Though Kant in the first edition of the *Critique* had spoken of the mathematical sciences as based upon the intuition of space and time, he had not, despite his constant tendency to conceive space and time as parallel forms of existence, based any separate mathematical discipline upon time. His definition of number, in the chapter on *Schematism*, had recognised the essentially conceptual character of arithmetic, and had connected it with time only in a quite indirect manner. A passage in the *Prolegomena* is the one place in all Kant's writings in which he would seem to assert, though in brief and quite indefinite terms, that arithmetic is related to time as geometry is related to space. No such view of arithmetic is to be found in the second edition of the *Critique*. In the transcendental exposition of time, added in the second edition, only pure mechanics is mentioned. This would seem to indicate that Kant had made the above statement carelessly, without due thought, and that on further reflection he found himself unable to stand by it. The omission is the more significant in that Kant refers to arithmetic in the passages added in the second edition *Introduction*. The teaching of these passages, apart from the asserted necessity of appealing to fingers or points,[1] harmonises with the view so briefly outlined in the *Analytic*. Arithmetic is a conceptual science; though it finds in ordered sequence its intuitional material, it cannot be adequately defined as being the science of time.

CONCLUSIONS FROM THE PRECEDING CONCEPTS[2]

These *Conclusions* do not run parallel with the corresponding *Conclusions* in regard to space. In the first paragraph there are two differences. (*a*) Kant takes account of a view not considered under space, viz. that time is a self-existing substance. He rejects it on a ground which is difficult to reconcile with his recognition of a manifold of intuition as well as a manifold of sense, namely that it would then be something real without being a real object. In A 39 = B 57 and B 70 Kant describes space and time, so conceived, as *unendliche Undinge*. (*b*) Kant introduces into his first *Conclusion* the argument[3] that only by conceiving time as the form of inner intuition can we justify *a priori* synthetic judgments in regard to objects.

Second Paragraph (Conclusion b).—This latter statement is repeated at the opening of the second *Conclusion*. The emphasis is no longer, however, upon the term "form" but upon the term "inner"; and Kant proceeds to make assertions which by no means follow from the five arguments, and which must be counted amongst the most difficult and controversial tenets of the whole *Critique*. (*a*) Time is not a determination of outer appearances. For it belongs neither to their shape nor to their position—and prudently at this point the property of motion is smuggled out of view under cover of an etc. *Time does not determine the relation of appearances to one another, but only* the relation of representations *in our inner state*.[4] It is the form only of the intuition of ourselves and of our inner state.[5] Obviously these are assertions which Kant cannot possibly hold to in this unqualified form. In the very next paragraph they are modified and restated. (*b*) As this inner intuition supplies no shape (*Gestalt*), we seek to make good this deficiency by means of analogies. We represent the time-sequence through a line

---

[1] Cf. below, pp. 337-8.
[2] Cf. above, pp. 112 *n*. 4.
[3] The content of the second *Conclusion* in regard to space.
[4] This expresses the matter a little more clearly than Kant himself does. The term representation is ambiguous. It is frequently used to cover the appearances as well as their representation.
[5] Cf. *Dissertation*, § 15 Coroll. : "Space properly concerns the intuition of the *object* ; time the *state*, especially the *representative* state."

progressing to infinity in which the manifold constitutes a series of only one dimension. From the properties of this line, with the one exception that its parts are simultaneous whereas those of time are always successive, we conclude to all the properties of time.

The wording of the passage seems to imply that such symbolisation of time through space is helpful but not indispensably necessary for its apprehension. That it is indispensably necessary is, however, the view to which Kant finally settled down.[1] But he has not yet come to clearness on this point. The passage has all the signs of having been written prior to the *Analytic*. Though Kant seems to have held consistently to the view that time has, in or by itself, only one dimension,[2] the difficulties involved drove him to recognise that this is true only of time as the order of our representations. It is not true of the objective time apprehended in and through our representations. When later Kant came to hold that consciousness of time is conditioned by consciousness of space, he apparently also adopted the view that, by reference to space, time indirectly acquires simultaneity as an additional mode. The objective spatial world is in time, but in a time which shows simultaneity as well as succession. In the *Dissertation*[3] Kant had criticised Leibniz and his followers for neglecting simultaneity, "the most important consequence of time."

"Though time has only one dimension, yet the *ubiquity* of time (to employ Newton's term), through which all things sensuously thinkable are *at some time*, adds another dimension to the quantity of actual things, in so far as they hang, as it were, upon the same point of time. For if we represent time by a straight line extended to infinity, and simultaneous things at any point of time by lines successively erected [perpendicular to the first line], the surface thus generated will represent the *phenomenal world* both as to substance and as to accidents."

Similarly in A 182 = B 226 of the *Critique* Kant states that simultaneity is not a mode of time,[4] since none of the parts of time can be simultaneous, and yet also teaches in A 177 = B 219 that, as the order of *appearances*, time possesses in addition to succession the two modes, duration and simultaneity. The significance of this distinction between time as the order of our inner states, and time as the order of objective appearances, we shall consider immediately.

A connected question is as to whether or not Kant teaches the possibility of simultaneous apprehension. In the *Aesthetic*

---

[1] Cf. below, pp. 309 ff., 347-8, 359.   [2] Cf. *Reflexionem*, ii. 365 ff.
[3] § 14, 5 and note to 5.   [4] The opposite is, however, asserted in B 67.

and *Dialectic* he certainly does so. Space is given as containing coexisting parts, and[1] can be intuited as such without successive synthesis of its parts. In the *Analytic*, on the other hand, the opposite would seem to be implied.[2] The apprehension of a manifold can only be obtained through the successive addition or generation of its parts.

(*c*) Lastly, Kant argues that the fact that all the relations of time can be expressed in an outer intuition is proof that the representation of time is itself intuition. But surely if, as Kant later taught, time can be apprehended at all only in and through space, that, taken alone, would rather be a reason for denying it to be itself intuition. In any case it is difficult to follow Kant in his contention that the intuition of time is similar in general character to that of space.[3]

Third Paragraph (Conclusion c).—Kant now reopens the question as to the relation in which time stands to outer appearances. As already noted, he has argued in the beginning of the previous paragraph that it cannot be a determination of outer appearances, but only of representations in our inner state. External appearances, however, as Kant recognises, can be known only in and through representations. To that extent they belong to inner sense, and consequently (such is Kant's argument) are themselves subject to time. Time, as the immediate condition of our representations, is also the mediate condition of appearances. Therefore, Kant concludes, "all *appearances*, *i.e.* all *objects* of the senses, are in time, and necessarily stand in time-relations."

Now quite obviously this argument is invalid if the distinction between representations and their objects is a real and genuine one. For if so, it does not at all follow that because our *representations* of objects are in time that the objects themselves are in time. In other words, the argument is valid only from the standpoint of extreme subjectivism, according to which objects are, in Kant's own phraseology, *blosse Vorstellungen*. But the argument is employed to establish a realist conclusion, that outer objects, as objects, stand in time-relations to one another. In contradiction of the previous paragraph he is now maintaining that time is a determination of outer appearances, and that it reveals itself in the motion of bodies as well as in the flux of our inner states.

[1] Cf. A 427-8 *n*. = B 456 *n*.

[2] A 99. Cf. A 162 = B 203: "I cannot represent to myself a line, however small, without drawing it in thought, *i.e.* generating from a point all its parts one after another." Cf. pp. 94, 347-8.

[3] Cf. *Lose Blätter*, i. 54: "Without space time itself would not be represented as quantity (*Grösse*), and in general this conception would have no object." Cf. *Dissertation*, § 14. 5.

The distinction between representations and their objects also makes it possible for Kant both to assert and to deny that simultaneity is a mode of time. "No two years can be co-existent. Time has only one dimension. But existence (*das Dasein*), measured through time, has two dimensions, succession and simultaneity." There are, for Kant, two orders of time, sub-jective and objective. Recognition of the latter (emphasised and developed in the *Analytic*)[1] is, however, irreconcilable with his contention that time is merely the form of inner sense.

We have here one of the many objections to which Kant's doctrine of time lies open. It is the most vulnerable tenet in his whole system. A mere list of the points which Kant leaves unsettled suffices to show how greatly he was troubled in his own mind by the problems to which it gives rise. (1) The nature of the *a priori* knowledge which time yields. Kant ascribes to this source sometimes only the two axioms in regard to time, sometimes pure mechanics, and sometimes also arithmetic. (2) Whether time only allows of, or whether it demands, representation through space. Sometimes Kant makes the one assertion, sometimes the other. (3) Whether it is possible to apprehend the coexistent without successive synthesis of its parts. This possibility is asserted in the *Aesthetic* and *Dialectic*, denied in the *Analytic*. (4) Whether simultaneity is a mode of time. (5) Whether, and in what manner, appearances of outer sense are in time. Kant's answer to 4 and to 5 varies according as he identifies or distinguishes representations and empirical objects.

The manifold difficulties to which a theory of time thus lies open are probably the reason why Kant, in the *Critique*, reverses the order in which he had treated time and space in the *Dissertation*.[2] But the placing of space before time is none the less unfortunate. It greatly tends to conceal from the reader the central position which Kant has assigned to time in the *Analytic*. Consciousness of time is the fundamental fact, taken as bare fact, by reference to which Kant gains his transcendental proof of the categories and principles of under-standing.[3] In the *Analytic* space, by comparison, falls very much into the background. A further reason for the reversal may have been Kant's Newtonian view of geometry as the mathematical science *par excellence*.[4] In view of his formu-lation of the Critical problem as that of accounting for synthetic *a priori* judgments, he would then naturally be led to throw more emphasis on space.

[1] Cf. below, p. 365 ff. [2] In the *Dissertation* time is treated before space.
[3] Cf. above, pp. xxxiv, 120; below, pp. 241-2, 365, 367-70, 390-1.
[4] Cf. *Dissertation*, § 15 C.

To sum up our main conclusions. Kant's view of time as a form merely of inner sense, and as having only one dimension, connects with his subjectivism. His view of it as inhering in objects, and as having duration and simultaneity as two of its modes, is bound up with his phenomenalism. Further discussion of these difficulties must therefore be deferred until we are in a position to raise the more fundamental problem as to the nature of the distinction between a representation and its object.[1] Motion is not an inner state. Yet it involves time as directly as does the flow of our feelings and ideas. Kant's assertion that "time can no more be intuited externally than space can be intuited as something in us,"[2] if taken quite literally, would involve both the subjectivist assertion that motion of bodies is non-existent, and also the phenomenalist contention that an extended object is altogether distinct from a representation.

The *fourth* and *fifth paragraphs* call for no detailed analysis.[3] Time is empirically real, transcendentally ideal— these terms having exactly the same meaning and scope as in reference to space.[4] The fourth sentence in the fifth paragraph is curiously inaccurate. As it stands, it would imply that time is given through the senses.   In the concluding sentences Kant briefly summarises and applies the points raised in these fourth and fifth paragraphs.

ELUCIDATION

First and Second Paragraphs.—Kant here replies to a criticism which, as he tells us in his letter of 1772 to Herz, was first made by Pastor Schulze and by Lambert.[5] In that letter the objection and Kant's reply are stated as follows.

"In accordance with the testimony of inner sense, changes are something real. But they are only possible on the assumption of time. Time is, therefore, something real which belongs to the determinations of things in themselves. Why, said I to myself, do we not argue in a parallel manner: 'Bodies are real, in accordance with the outer senses. But bodies are possible only under the condition of space. Space is, therefore, something objective and real which inheres in the things themselves.' The cause [of this differential treatment of space and of time] is the observation that in respect to outer things we cannot infer from the reality of representations the reality of their objects, whereas in inner sense the thought or the existing of the thought and of myself are one

---

[1] Cf. below, pp. 272 ff., 294-5, 308 ff., 365 ff.   [2] A 23 = B 37.
[3] They correspond to the third paragraph dealing with space. Cf. above, p. 116.   [4] Cf. above, pp. 116-17.
[5] Cf. *W*. x. p. 102. Mendelssohn had also protested ; cf. *op. cit.* x. p. 110.

and the same. Herein lies the key to the difficulty. Undoubtedly I must think my own state under the form of time, and the form of the inner sensibility consequently gives me the appearance of changes. Now I do not deny that changes are something real any more than I deny that bodies are something real, but I thereby mean only that something real corresponds to the appearance. I may not even say the inner appearance undergoes change (*verändere sich*), for how could I observe this change unless it appeared to my inner sense? *To the objection that this leads to the conclusion that all things in the world objectively and in themselves are unchangeable, I would reply that they are neither changeable nor unchangeable.* As Baumgarten states in § 18 of his *Metaphysica*, the absolutely impossible is hypothetically neither possible nor impossible, since it cannot be mentally entertained under any condition whatsoever; so in similar manner *the things of the world are objectively or in themselves neither in one and the same state nor in different states at different times, for thus understood* [*viz. as things in themselves*] *they are not represented in time at all.*"[1]

Thus Kant's contention, both in this letter and in the passage before us, is that even our inner states would not reveal change if they could be apprehended by us or by some other being apart from the subjective form of our inner sense. We may not say that our inner states undergo change, or that they succeed one another, but only that to us they necessarily appear as so doing.[2] Time is no more than subjectively real.[3] As Körner writes to Schiller: "Without time man would indeed *exist* but not *appear*. Not his reality but only his appearance is dependent upon the condition of time." "Man *is* not, but only *appears*, when he undergoes change."[4] The objects of inner sense stand in exactly the same position as those of outer sense. Both are appearances, and neither can be identified with the absolutely real. As Kant argues later in the *Critique*,[5] inner processes are not known with any greater certainty or immediacy than are outer objects; the reality of time as subjective proves its unreality in relation to things in themselves. The statement that the constitution of

---

[1] *W.* x. pp. 128-9. Italics not in Kant. Kant is entirely justified in protesting against the view that in denying things in themselves to be in time he is asserting that they remain eternally the same with themselves. To make a dancer preserve one and the same posture is not to take him out of time, but to bring home to him the reality of time in an extremely unpleasant manner. Duration is one of the modes of time.

[2] This is Kant's reply to Mendelssohn's objection (December 1770, *W.* x. p. 110): "Succession is at least a necessary condition of the representations of finite spirits. Now the finite spirits are not only subjects but also objects of representations, both for God and for our fellow-men. The succession must therefore be regarded as something objective."

[3] Cf. A 277 = B 333: "It is not given to us to observe even our own mind with any intuition but that of our inner sense."

[4] Quoted by Vaihinger, ii. p. 406.

[5] In the fourth *Paralogism*, A 366, and in the *Refutation of Idealism*, B 274.

things in themselves is " problematic " is an exceptional mode
of expression for Kant.   Usually—as indeed throughout the
whole context of this passage [1]—he asserts that though things
in themselves are unknowable, we can with absolute certainty
maintain that they are neither in space nor in time.   Upon
this point we have already dwelt in discussing Trendelenburg's controversy with Fischer.[2]

Third Paragraph.—The third and fourth paragraphs of this
section ought to have had a separate heading.   They summarise the total argument of the *Aesthetic* in regard to space
as well as time, distinguish its tenets from those of Newton
and of Leibniz, and draw a general conclusion.   The summary
follows the strict synthetic method.   The opening sentences
illustrate Kant's failure to distinguish between the problems
of pure and of applied mathematics, and also show how
completely he tends to conceive mathematics as typified by
geometry.   The criticism of alternative views traverses the
ground of the famous controversy between Leibniz and
Clarke.   Their *Streitschriften* were, as we have good circumstantial grounds for believing,[3] a chief influence in the
development of Kant's own views.   Kant, who originally
held the Leibnizian position, was by 1768[4] more or less con-
verted to the Newtonian teaching, and in the *Dissertation*
of 1770 developed his subjectivist standpoint with the conscious intention of retaining the advantages while remedying
the defects of both alternatives.[5]   For convenience we may
limit the discussion to space.   (*a*) The view propounded by
Newton, and defended by Clarke, is that space has an
existence in and by itself, independent alike of the mind
which apprehends it and of the objects with which it is filled.
(*b*) The view held by Leibniz is that space is an empirical
concept abstracted from our confused sense-experience of
the relations of real things.[6]

The criticism of (*a*) is twofold.   First, it involves belief

---

[1] Cf. A 42 = B 59.   [2] Above, pp. 113-14.   [3] Cf. Vaihinger, ii. p. 114.
[4] The date of Kant's *Von dem ersten Grunde des Unterschiedes der Gegenden
im Raume.*
[5] Cf. below, p. 161 ff.
[6] Cf. *Dissertation*, § 15 D : " Those who defend the reality of space conceive
it either as an absolute and immense *receptacle* of possible things—a view which
appeals not only to the English [thinkers] but to most geometricians—or they
contend that it is *nothing but a relation* holding between existing things, which
must vanish when the things are removed, and which is thinkable only in actual
things.   This latter is the teaching of Leibniz and of most of our countrymen."
That the account of Leibniz's teaching given in the paragraphs under consideration
is not altogether accurate, need hardly be pointed out.   Kant, following his
usual method in the discussion of opposing systems, is stating what he regards
as being the logical consequences of certain of Leibniz's tenets, rather than his
avowed positions.

in an eternal and infinite *Unding*. Secondly, it leads to metaphysical difficulties, especially in regard to the existence of God. If space is absolutely real, how is it to be reconciled with the omnipresence of God? Newton's view of space as the *sensorium Dei* can hardly be regarded as satisfactory.

The objection to (*b*) is that it cannot account for the apodictic certainty of geometry, nor guarantee its application to experience. The concept of space, when regarded as of sensuous origin, is something that may distort (and according to the Leibnizian teaching does actually distort) what it professes to represent, and is something from which restrictions that hold in the natural world have been omitted.[1] As empirical, it cannot serve as basis for the universal and neces-sary judgments of mathematical science.[2]

The first view has, however, the advantage of keeping the sphere of appearances open for mathematical science. As space is infinite and all-comprehensive, its laws hold universally. The second view has the advantage of not subjecting reality to space conditions. These advantages are retained, while the objections are removed, by the teaching of the *Aesthetic*.

---

[1] Cf. A 275-6 = B 331-2: "Leibniz conceived space as a certain order in the community of substances, and time as the dynamical sequence of their states. But that which both seem to possess as proper to themselves, in independence of things, he ascribed to the confused character of their concepts, asserting this confusion to be the reason why what is a mere form of dynamical relations has come to be regarded as a special intuition, self-subsistent and antecedent to the things themselves. Thus space and time were [for Leibniz] the intelligible form of the connection of things (substances and their states) in themselves." Cf. also *Prolegomena*, § 13, *Anm.* i.

[2] Kant has stated that both views conflict with "the principles of experience." But his criticisms are not altogether on that line. The statement strictly applies only to his criticism of the Leibnizian view. Cf. *Dissertation*, § 15 D: "That first inane invention of reason, assuming as it does the existence of true infinite relations in the absence of all interrelated entities, belongs to the realm of fable. But those who adopt the other view fall into a much worse error. For whereas the former place an obstacle in the way only of certain rational concepts, *i.e.* concepts that concern noumena, and which also in themselves are extremely obscure bearing upon questions as to the spiritual world, omnipresence, etc., the latter set themselves in direct antagonism to the phenomena themselves and to geometry, the most faithful interpreter of all phenomena. For—not to dwell upon the obvious circle in which they necessarily become involved in defining space—they cast geometry down from its position at the highest point of certitude, and throw it back into the class of those sciences the principles of which are empirical. For if all modifications of space are derived only through experience from external relations, geometrical axioms can have only comparative universality, like that acquired through induction, in other words, such as extends only as far as observation has gone. They cannot lay claim to any necessity save that of being in accordance with the established laws of nature, nor to any precision except of the artificial sort, resting upon assumptions. And as happens in matters empirical, the possibility is not excluded that a space endowed with other original modifications, and perhaps even a rectilineal figure enclosed by two lines, may sometime be discovered." Cf. above, p. 114; below, p. 290.

Kant further criticises the former view in A 46 ff. = B 64 ff. There is no possibility of accounting for the *a priori* synthetic judgments of geometry save by assuming that space is the pure form of outer intuition.   For though the Newtonian view will justify the assertion that the laws of space hold universally, it cannot explain how we come to know them *a priori*.   And assuming, as Kant constantly does, that space cannot be both an *a priori* form of intuition and also independently real, he concludes that it is the former only.

In B 71 Kant also restates the metaphysical difficulties to which the Newtonian view lies open.   In natural theology we deal with an existence which can never be the object of sensuous intuition, and which has to be freed from all conditions of space and time.   This is impossible if space is so absolutely real that it would remain though all created things were annihilated.

Fourth Paragraph.—Space and time are the only two forms of sensibility; all other concepts belonging to the senses, such as motion and change, are empirical.[1]   As Kant has himself stated, no reason can be given why space and time are the sole forms of our possible intuition :

"Other forms of intuition than space and time, . . . even if they were possible, we cannot render in any way conceivable and comprehensible to ourselves, and even assuming that we could do so, they still would not belong to experience, the only kind of knowledge in which objects are given to us."[2]

The further statement,[3] frequently repeated in the *Critique*, that time itself does not change, but only what is in time,[4] indicates the extent to which Kant has been influenced by the Newtonian receptacle view.   As Bergson very justly points out, time, thus viewed as a homogeneous medium, is really being conceived on the analogy of space.   "It is merely the phantom of space obsessing the reflective consciousness."[5]

---

[1] In B 155 *n.* Kant distinguishes between motion of an object in space, and motion as generation of a geometrical figure.   The former alone involves experience ; the latter is a pure act of the productive imagination, and belongs not only to geometry but also to transcendental philosophy.   This note, as Erdmann has pointed out (*Kriticismus*, pp. 115, 168), was introduced by Kant into the second edition as a reply to a criticism of Schütz.   The distinction as thus drawn is only tenable on the assumption of a pure manifold distinct from the manifold of sense.

[2] A 230 = B 283.   Cf. above, pp. 57, 118 ; below, pp. 185-6, 257.
[3] A 41 = B 58.   [4] Cf. below, pp. 359-60.
[5] *Les Données Immédiates*, p. 75.

GENERAL OBSERVATIONS ON THE
TRANSCENDENTAL AESTHETIC

I. First Paragraph.—" To avoid all misapprehension " Kant proceeds to state "as clearly as possible" his view of sensuous knowledge. With this end in view he sets himself to enforce two main points: (*a*) that as space and time are only forms of sensibility, everything apprehended is only appearance; (*b*) that this is not a mere hypothesis but is completely certain. Kant expounds (*a*) indirectly through criticism of the opposing views of Leibniz and of Locke. But before doing so he makes in the next paragraph a twofold statement of his own conclusions.

Second Paragraph.—This paragraph states (*a*) that through intuition we can represent only appearances, not things in themselves, and (*b*) that the appearances thus known exist only in us. Both assertions have implications, the discussion of which must be deferred to the *Analytic*. The mention of the "relations of things by themselves" may, as Vaihinger suggests,[1] be a survival from the time when (as in the *Dissertation*[2]) Kant sought to reduce spatial to dynamical relations. The assertion that things in themselves are completely unknown to us goes beyond what the *Aesthetic* can establish and what Kant here requires to prove. His present thesis is only that no knowledge of things in themselves can be acquired either through the forms of space and time or through sensation; space and time are determined solely by our pure sensibility, and sensations by our empirical sensibility. Failure to recognise this is, in Kant's view, one of the chief defects of the Leibnizian system.

Third and Fourth Paragraphs. Criticism of the Leibniz-Wolff Interpretation of Sensibility and of Appearance.—Leibniz vitiates both conceptions. Sensibility does not differ from thought in clearness but in content. It is a difference of kind.[3] They originate in different sources, and neither can by any transformation be reduced to the other.

"Even if an appearance could become completely transparent to us, such knowledge would remain *toto coelo* different from knowledge of the object in itself."[4] "Through observation and analysis of appearances we penetrate to the secrets of nature, and no one can say how far this may in time extend. . . . [But however far we advance, we

---

[1] ii. p. 446.   [2] §§ 4 and 27.
[3] Cf. *Ueber eine Entdeckung*, etc. : *W*. viii. p. 220.
[4] A 44 = B 61.

shall never be able by means of] so ill-adapted an instrument of investigation [as our sensibility] to find anything except still other
appearances, the non-sensuous cause of which we yet long to
discover." [1]

We should still know only in terms of the two inalienable
forms of our sensibility.[2] The dualism of thought and sense
can never be transcended by the human mind. By no extension of its sphere or perfecting of its insight can sensuous
knowledge be transformed into a conceptual apprehension of
purely intelligible entities.

Leibniz's conception of appearances as things in themselves confusedly apprehended is equally false, and for the
same reasons.[3] Appearance and reality are related as distinct
existences, each of which has its own intrinsic character and
content. Through the former there can be no hope of pene-
trating to the latter. Appearance is subjective in matter as
well as in form. For Leibniz our knowledge of appearances
is a confused knowledge of things in themselves. Properly
viewed, it is the apprehension, whether distinct or confused,
of objects which are never things in themselves. Sense-
knowledge, such as we obtain in the science of geometry, has
often the highest degree of clearness. Conceptual apprehension is all too frequently characterised by obscurity and
indistinctness.

This criticism of Leibniz, as expounded in these two
paragraphs, is thoroughly misleading if taken as an adequate
statement of Kant's view of the relations between sense and
understanding, appearance and reality. These paragraphs
are really a restatement of a passage in the *Dissertation*.

"It will thus be seen that we express the nature of the sensuous
very inappropriately when we assert that it is the *more confusedly*
known, and the nature of the intellectual when we describe it as the *distinctly* known. For these are merely logical distinctions, and obviously
have nothing to do with the given facts which underlie all logical
comparison. The sensuous may be absolutely distinct, and the
intellectual extremely confused. That is shown on the one hand in
geometry, the prototype of sensuous knowledge, and on the other in
metaphysics, the instrument of all intellectual enquiry. Every one
knows how zealously metaphysics has striven to dispel the mists of
confusion which cloud the minds of men at large and yet has not

---

[1] A 277 = B 334. Cf. A 278-9 = B 335-6.
[2] When Kant says that the distinction is not logical (that of relative clearness
and obscurity) but transcendental, the latter term is taken as practically equivalent
to epistemological. It does not mean 'relating to the *a priori*,' but relating to
transcendental philosophy, just as logical here means relating to logic. Cf.
Vaihinger, ii. p. 452.   [3] Cf. A 270 ff. = B 326 ff.

always attained the happy results of the former science. Nevertheless each of these kinds of knowledge preserves the mark of the stock from which it has sprung. The former, however distinct, is on account of its origin entitled sensuous, while the latter, however confused, remains intellectual—as *e.g.* the *moral* concepts, which are known not by way of experience, but through the pure intellect itself. I fear, however, that the illustrious Wolff by this distinction between the sensuous and the intellectual, which for him is merely logical, has checked, perhaps wholly (to the great detriment of philosophy), that noblest enterprise of antiquity, the investigation of *the nature of phenomena and noumena,* turning men's minds from such enquiries to what are very frequently only logical subtleties." [1]

The paragraphs before us give expression only to what is common to the *Dissertation* and to the *Critique,* and do so entirely from the standpoint of the *Dissertation.* Thus the illustration of the conception of "right" implies that things in themselves can be known through the understanding. The conception, as Kant says, represents "a moral property which belongs to actions in and by themselves." Similarly, in distinguishing the sensuous from "the intellectual," he says that through the former we do not apprehend things in themselves, thus implying that things in themselves can be known through the pure intellect. The view developed in the *Analytic,* alike of sensibility and of appearance, is radically different. Sensibility and understanding *may* have a common source; and both are indispensably necessary for the apprehension of appearance. Neither can function save in co-operation with the other. Appearance does not differ from reality solely through its sensuous content and form, but also in the intellectual order or dispensation to which it is subject. But in the very act of thus deepening the gulf between appearance and reality by counting even understanding as contributing to the knowledge only of the former, he was brought back to a position that has kinship with the Leibnizian view of their interrelation. Since understanding is just as essential as sensibility to the apprehension of appearances, and since understanding differs from sensibility in the universality of its range, it enables us to view appearances in their relation to ultimate reality, and so to apprehend them as being, however subjective or phenomenal, ways in which the thing in itself presents itself to us. Such a view is, however, on Kant's principles, quite consistent with the further contention, that appearance does not differ from reality in a merely logical manner. Factors that are peculiar to the realm of appearance have intervened to transform the real;

[1] §7 (I read *autem* for *autor*). Cf. below, p. 187.

and in consequence even completed knowledge of the phenomenal—if such can be conceived as possible—would not be
equivalent to knowledge of things in themselves.

Fifth Paragraph. Criticism of Locke's View of Appearance.—
This paragraph discusses Locke's doctrine [1] that the secondary
qualities are subjective, and that in the primary qualities we
possess true knowledge of things in themselves. The distinction is drawn upon empirical grounds, namely, that while certain
qualities are uniform for more than one sense, and belong to
objects under all conditions, others are peculiar to the different
senses, and arise only through the accidental relation of objects
to the special senses.[2] This distinction is, Kant says, entirely
justified from the physical standpoint.[3] A rainbow is an
appearance of which the raindrops constitute the true empirical
reality. But Locke and his followers interpret this distinction
wrongly. They ignore the more fundamental transcendental
(*i.e.* metaphysical) distinction between empirical reality and
the thing in itself. From the transcendental standpoint the
raindrops are themselves merely appearance. Even their
round shape, and the very space in which they fall, are only
modifications of our sensuous intuition. The 'transcendental
object'[4] remains unknown to us.

When Kant thus declares that the distinction between
primary and secondary qualities is justified (*richtig*) from the
physical standpoint, he is again [5] speaking from a phenomenalist point of view. And it may be noted that in developing
his transcendental distinction he does not describe the
raindrops as mere representations. His phrase is much more
indefinite. Their primary qualities are "modifications or
fundamental forms (*Grundlagen*) of our sensuous intuition."

Kant does not here criticise the view of sensibility which
underlies Locke's view of appearance. But he does so in
A 271 = B 327, completing the parallel and contrast between
Leibniz and Locke.

"Leibniz *intellectualised* appearances, just as Locke, according to
his system of noogony (if I may be allowed these expressions), *sensual-
ised* all concepts of the understanding, *i.e.* interpreted them as simply
empirical or abstracted concepts of reflection. Instead of interpreting understanding and sensibility as two quite different sources of
representations, which yet can supply objectively valid judgments of

---

[1] Cf. *Prolegomena*, § 13, Remark II.
[2] Cf. above, pp. 120-1.   [3] Cf. A 257 = B 313.
[4] A 46 = B 63. This is the first occurrence in the *Critique* of the phrase
transcendental object. Transcendental is employed as synonymous with transcendent. Cf. below, p. 204 ff.
[5] Cf. above, pp. 120-2.

things only in *conjunction* with each other, each of these great men holds only to one of the two, viewing it as in immediate relation to things in themselves. The other faculty is regarded as serving only to confuse or to order the representations which this selected faculty yields."[1]

Proof that the above View of Space and Time is not a mere Hypothesis, but completely certain.[2]—The proof, which as here recapitulated and developed follows the analytic method, has already been considered in connection with A 39 = B 56. It proceeds upon the assumption that space cannot be both an *a priori* form of intuition and also independently real. The argument as a whole lacks clearness owing to Kant's failure to distinguish between the problems of pure and applied geometry, between pure intuition and form of intuition. This is especially obvious in the very unfortunate and misleading second application of the triangle illustration.[3] Kant's tendency to conceive mathematical science almost exclusively in terms of geometry is likewise illustrated.

"There is in regard to both [space and time] a large number of *a priori* apodictic and synthetic propositions. This is especially true of space, which for this reason will be our chief illustration in this enquiry."[4]

II. Paragraphs added in the Second Edition.[5]—Kant proceeds to offer further proof of the ideality of the appearances (*a*) of outer and (*b*) of inner sense. Such proof he finds in the fact that these appearances consist solely of relations. (*a*) Outer appearances reduce without remainder to relations of position in intuition (*i.e.* of extension), of change of position (motion), and to the laws which express in merely relational terms the motive forces by which such change is determined. What it is that is thus present in space, or what the dynamic agencies may be to which the motion is due, is never revealed. But a real existent (*Sache an sich*) can never be known through mere relations. Outer sense consequently reveals through its representations only the relation of an object to the subject, not the intrinsic inner nature of the object in itself (*Object an sich*). Kant's avoidance of the term *Ding an sich* may be noted.[6]

---

[1] A 271 = B 327.
[2] A 46-9 = B 63-6.
[3] A 48 = B 65-6. Vaihinger (ii. pp. 470-2) gives what appears to be a sufficient explanation of what Kant had in mind in its employment.
[4] A 46 = B 64. Cf. *Dissertation*, § 15 C.
[5] B 66-73.
[6] *a* does not contain anything not to be found elsewhere in the first edition. It is a restatement of A 265 ff. = B 321 ff., A 274 = B 330, A 277 ff. = B 333 ff., A 283-5 = B 339-41.

(*b*) The same holds true of inner sense, not only because the representations of outer sense constitute its proper (*eigentlichen*) material, but also because time, in which these are set, contains only relations of succession, coexistence, and duration. This time (which as consisting only of relations can be nothing but a form[1]) is itself, in turn, a mere relation. It is only the manner in which through its own activity the mind is affected by itself. But in order to be affected by itself it must have receptivity, in other words, sensibility. Time, consequently, must be regarded as the form of this inner sense.

That everything represented in time, like that which is represented in space, consists solely of relations, Kant does not, however, attempt to prove. He is satisfied with repeating the conclusion reached in the first edition of the *Aesthetic*, that, as time is the object of a sense, it must of necessity be appearance. This, like everything which Kant wrote upon inner sense, is profoundly unsatisfactory. The obscurities of his argument are not to be excused on the ground that "the difficulty, how a subject can have an internal intuition of itself, is common to every theory." For no great thinker,[2] except Locke, has attempted to interpret inner consciousness on the analogy of the senses. Discussion of the doctrine must meantime be deferred.[3]

III. B 69.—Kant here formulates the important distinction between appearance (*Erscheinung*) and illusion (*Schein*). The main text is clear so far as it goes; but the appended note is thoroughly confused. Together they contain no less than three distinct and conflicting views of illusion.[4] According to the main text, *Schein* signifies a representation, such as may occur in a dream, to which nothing real corresponds. *Erscheinung*, on the other hand, is always the appearance of a *given* object; but since the qualities of that object depend solely on our mode of intuition, we have to distinguish the object as appearance from the object as thing in itself.

"[Every appearance] has two sides, the one by which the object is viewed in and by itself, . . . the other by which the form of the intuition of the object is taken into account. . . ."[5]

Obviously, when illusion is defined in the above manner,

[1] An assertion, it may be noted, which conflicts with Kant's view of it as a pure manifold.

[2] Kant was probably influenced by Tetens. Cp. below, p. 294.

[3] Cf. below, p. 291 ff. *b* together with B 152-8 is a more explicit statement of the doctrine of inner sense than Kant had given in the first edition.

[4] Vaihinger (ii. p. 486 ff.), who has done more than any other commentator to clear up the ambiguities of this passage, distinguishes only two views.

[5] A 38 = B 55.

the assertion that objects in space are mere appearances cannot be taken as meaning that they are illusory.

But this view of illusion is peculiar to the passage before us and to A 38 = B 55. It occurs nowhere else, either in the *Critique* or in the *Prolegomena*; and it is not, as Kant has himself admitted,[1] really relevant to the purposes of the *Critique*. The issues are more adequately faced in the appended note, which, however, at the same time, shows very clearly that Kant has not yet properly disentangled their various strands. The above definition of appearance is too wide. It covers illusory sense perception as well as appearance proper. The further qualification must be added, that the predicates of appearance are constant and are inseparable from its representation. Thus the space predicates can be asserted of any external object. Redness and scent can be ascribed to the rose. All of these are genuine appearances. If, on the other hand, the two handles, as observed by Galileo, are attributed to Saturn, roundness to a distant square tower, bentness to a straight stick inserted in water, the result is mere illusion. The predicates, in such cases, do not stand the test of further observation or of the employment of other senses. Only in a certain position of its rings, relatively to the observer, does Saturn *seem* (*scheint*) to have two handles. The distant tower only *seems* to be round. The stick only *seems* to be bent. But the rose *is* extended and *is* red. Obviously Kant is no longer viewing *Schein* as equivalent to a merely mental image. It now receives a second meaning. It is illusion in the modern, psychological sense. It signifies an abnormal perception of an actually present object. The distinction between appearance and illusion is now reduced to a merely relative difference in constancy and universality of appearance. Saturn necessarily appears to Galileo as possessing two handles. A square tower viewed from the distance cannot appear to the human eye otherwise than round. A stick inserted in water must appear bent. If, however, Saturn be viewed under more favourable conditions, if the distance from the tower be diminished, if the stick be removed from the water, the empirical object will appear in a manner more in harmony with the possible or actual experiences of touch. The distinction is practical, rather than theoretical, in its justification. It says only that certain sets of conditions may be expected to remain uniform;

---

[1] Cf. *Prolegomena*, *W*. iv. p. 376 *n*., Eng. trans. p. 149: "The reviewer often fights his own shadow. When I oppose the truth of experience to dreaming, he never suspects that I am only concerned with the *somnium objective sumtum* of Wolff's philosophy, which is merely formal, and has nothing to do with the distinction of dreaming and waking, which indeed has no place in any transcendental philosophy."

those, for instance, physical, physiological, and psychical, which cause a rose to appear red. Other sets of conditions, such as those which cause the stick to appear bent, are exceptional, and for that reason the bentness may be discounted as illusion. Among the relatively constant are the space and time properties of bodies. To employ the terms of the main text, it is not only by illusion that bodies seem to exist outside me ; they actually are there.

So long as we keep to the sphere of ordinary experience, and require no greater exactitude than practical life demands, this distinction is, of course, both important and valid. But Kant, by his references to Saturn, raises considerations which, if faced, must complicate the problem and place it upon an entirely different plane. If, in view of scientific requirements, the conditions of observation are more rigorously formulated, and if by artificial instruments of scientific precision we modify the perceptions of our human senses, what before was ranked as appearance becomes illusion ; and no limit can be set to the transformations which even our most normal human experiences may thus be made to undergo. Even the most constant perceptions then yield to variation. The most that can be asserted is that throughout all change in the conditions of observation objects still continue to possess, in however new and revolutionary a fashion, some kind of space and time predicates. The application of this more rigorous scientific standard of appearance thus leads to a fourfold distinction between ultimate reality, scientific appearances, the appearances of ordinary consciousness, and the illusions of ordinary consciousness. The appearances of practical life are the illusions of science, and the appearances of science would similarly be illusions to any being who through 'intuitive understanding' could apprehend things in themselves.

But if the distinction between appearance and illusion is thus merely relative to the varying nature of the conditions under which observation takes place, it can afford no sufficient answer to the criticisms which Kant is here professing to meet. Kant has in view those critics (such as Lambert, Mendelssohn, and Garve) who had objected that if bodies in space are representations existing, as he so often asserts, only "within us," their appearing to exist "outside us" is a complete illusion. These critics have, indeed, found a vulnerable point in Kant's teaching. The only way in which he can effectively meet it is by frank recognition and development of the phenomenalism with which his subjectivism comes into so frequent conflict.[1] That certain perceptions are

[1] Cf. below, p. 270 ff.

more constant than others does not prove that all alike may not be classed as illusory. The criticism concerns only the reality of extended objects. From Kant's own extreme sub-jectivist position they *are* illusions of the most thoroughgoing kind. If, as Kant so frequently maintains, objects are repre-sentations and exist only "within us," their existence "outside us" must be denied. The criticism can be met only if Kant is prepared consistently to formulate and defend his own alternative teaching, that sensations arise through the action of external objects upon the sense-organs, and that the world of physical science has consequently a reality not reducible to mere representations in the individual mind.

It may be objected that Kant has in the main text cited one essential difference between his position and that which is being ascribed to him. Extended objects, though mere representations, are yet due to, and conditioned by, things in themselves. They are illusory only in regard to their pro-perties, not in regard to their existence. But this distinction is not really relevant. The criticism, as just stated, is directed only against Kant's view of space. The fact that the spatial world is a grounded and necessary illusion is not strictly relevant to the matter in dispute. Kant has, indeed, else-where, himself admitted the justice of the criticism. In A 780 = B 808 he cites as a possible hypothesis, entirely in harmony with his main results, though not in any degree established by them, the view

"that this life is an appearance only, that is, a sensuous representa-tion of purely spiritual life, and that the whole sensible world is a mere image (*ein blosses Bild*) which hovers before our present mode of knowledge, and like a dream has in itself no objective reality."

Kant's reply is thus really only verbal. He claims that illusion, if constant, has earned the right to be called appear-ance. He accepts the criticism, but restates it in his own terms. The underlying phenomenalism which colours the position in his own thoughts, and for which he has not been able to find any quite satisfactory formulation, is the sole possible justification, if any such exists, for his contention that the criticism does not apply. Such phenomenalism crops out in the sentence, already partially quoted:

"If I assert that the quality of space and time, according to which, as a condition of their existence, I posit both external objects and my own soul, lies in my mode of intuition and not in these objects in themselves, I am not saying that only by illusion do bodies seem to exist outside me or my soul to be given in my self-consciousness."[1]

But, so far, I have simplified Kant's argument by leaving out of account a third and entirely different view of illusion which is likewise formulated in the appended note. In the middle of the second sentence, and in the last sentence, illusion is defined as the attribution to the thing in itself of what belongs to it only in its relation to the senses. Illusion lies not in the object apprehended, but only in the *judgment* which we pass upon it. It is due, not to sense, but to understanding.[2] Viewing illusion in this way, Kant is enabled to maintain that his critics are guilty of "an unpardonable and almost intentional misconception,"[3] since this is the very fallacy which he himself has been most concerned to attack. As he has constantly insisted, appearance is appearance just because it can never be a revelation of the thing in itself.

Now the introduction of this third view reduces the argument of the appended note to complete confusion. Its first occurrence as a parenthesis in a sentence which is stating an opposed view would seem to indicate that the note has been carelessly recast. Originally containing only a statement of the second view, Kant has connected therewith the view which he had already formulated in the first edition and in the *Prolegomena*. But the two views cannot be combined. By the former definition, illusion is necessitated but abnormal perception ; according to the latter, it is a preventable error of our conscious judgment. The opposite of illusion is in the one case *appearance*, in the other *truth*. The retention of the reference to Saturn, in the statement of the third view at the end of the note, is further evidence of hasty recasting. While the rose and the extended objects are there treated as also things in themselves, Saturn is taken only in its phenomenal existence. In view of the general confusion, it is a minor inconsistency that Kant should here maintain, in direct opposition to A 28-9, that secondary qualities can be attributed to the empirical object.

This passage from the second edition is a development of *Prolegomena*, § 13, iii. Kant there employs the term appearance in a quite indefinite manner. For the most part he seems to mean by it any and every sense-experience, whether normal or abnormal, and even to include under it dream images.

---

[1] B 69. For explanation of the references to time and self-consciousness, cf. below, pp. 308, 323.
[2] This view of illusion likewise appears in A 293 = B 349, A 377-8, A 396, and *Prolegomena*, § 13, III., at the beginning.
[3] *Prolegomena, loc. cit.*

But it is also employed in the second of the above meanings, as signifying those sense-perceptions which harmonise with general experience.   Illusion is throughout employed in the third of the above meanings.   Kant's illustration, that of the apparently retrograde movements of the planets, necessitates a distinction between apparent and real motion in space, and consequently leads to the fruitful distinction noted above. Kant gives, however, no sign that he is conscious of the complicated problems involved.

In the interval between the *Prolegomena* (1783) and the second edition of the *Critique* (1787) Mendelssohn had published (1785) his *Morgenstunden*.   In its introduction, entitled *Vorerkenntniss von Wahrheit, Schein und Irrthum*,[1] he very carefully distinguishes between illusion (*Sinnenschein*) and error of judgment (*Irrthum*).   This introduction Kant had read.   In a letter to Schütz[2] he cites it by title, and praises it as "acute, original, and of exemplary clearness." It is therefore the more inexcusable that he should again in the second edition of the *Critique* have confused these two so radically different meanings of the term *Schein*.   Mendelssohn, however, drew no distinction between *Schein* and *Erscheinung*. They were then used as practically synonymous,[3] though of course *Schein* was the stronger term.   Kant seems to have been the first to distinguish them sharply and to attempt to define the one in opposition to the other.   But the very fact that *Erscheinung* and *Schein* were currently employed as equivalent terms, and that the distinction, though one of his own drawing, had been mentioned only in the most cursory manner in the first edition of the *Critique*,[4] removes all justification for his retort upon his critics of "unpardonable misconception."   His anger was really due, not to the objection in itself, but to the implied comparison of his position to that of Berkeley.   Such comparison never failed to arouse Kant's wrath.   For however much this accusation might be justified by his own frequent lapses into subjectivism of the most extreme type, even its partial truth was more than he was willing to admit.   Berkeley represents in his eyes, not merely a subjectivist interpretation of the outer world, but the almost diametrical opposite of everything for which he himself stood.   Discussion of Kant's relation to Berkeley had best, however, be introduced through consideration of

---

[1] Cf. in the 1863 edition, Bd. ii. 267 ff.   The examples of illusion employed by Mendelssohn are reflection in a mirror and the rainbow.

[2] *W.* x. p. 405.

[3] *Schein* is so used by Kant himself (*W.* x. p. 105) in a letter to Lambert in 1770.

[4] A 38.

the passage immediately following in which Kant refers to Berkeley by name.

III. (Second Part) B 70.—Kant urges that his doctrine of the ideality of space and time, so far from reducing objects to mere illusion, is the sole means of defending their genuine reality. If space and time had an independent existence, they would have to be regarded as more real than the bodies which occupy them. For on this view space and time would continue to exist even if all their contents were removed ; they would be antecedent necessary conditions of all other existences. But space and time thus interpreted are impossible conceptions.[1] The reality of bodies is thereby made to depend upon *Undinge*. If this were the sole alternative, "the good Bishop Berkeley [could] not be blamed for degrading bodies to mere illusion." We should, Kant maintains, have to proceed still further, denying even our own existence. For had Berkeley taken account of time as well as of space, a similar argument, consistently developed in regard to time, would have constrained him to reduce the self to the level of mere illusion. Belief in the reality of things in themselves, whether spiritual or material, is defensible only if space and time be viewed as subjective. In other words, Berkeley's idealism is an inevitable consequence of a realist view of space. But it is also its *reductio ad absurdum*.

["Berkeley in his dogmatic idealism] maintains that space, with all the things of which it is the inseparable condition, is something impossible in itself, and he therefore regards the things in space as merely imaginary entities (*Einbildungen*). Dogmatic idealism is inevitable if space be interpreted as a property which belongs to things in themselves. For, when so regarded, space, and everything to which it serves as condition, is a non-entity (*Unding*). The ground upon which this idealism rests we have removed in the *Transcendental Aesthetic*."[2]

The term *Schein* is not employed throughout this passage in either of the two meanings of the appended note, but in that of the main text. It signifies a representation, to which no existence corresponds.

[1] Cf. above, A 39=B 57. This is, however, merely asserted by implication ; it is not proved. As already noted, Kant does not really show that space and time, viewed as absolute realities, are "inconsistent with the principles of experience." Nor does Kant here supply sufficient grounds for his description of space and time as *Undinge*. Kant, it must be observed, does not regard the conception of the actual infinite as in itself self-contradictory. Cf. below, p. 486.

[2] B 275.

KANT'S RELATION TO BERKELEY

By idealism[1] Kant means any and every system which maintains that the sensible world does not exist in the form in which it presents itself to us. The position is typified in Kant's mind by the Eleatics, by Plato, and by Descartes, all of whom are rationalists. With the denial of reality to sense-appearances they combine a belief in the possibility of rationally comprehending its supersensible basis. Failing to appreciate the true nature of the sensible, they misunderstand the character of geometrical science, and falsely ascribe to pure understanding a power of intellectual intuition. Kant's criticisms of Berkeley show very clearly that it is this more general position which he has chiefly in view. To Berkeley Kant objects that only in sense-experience is there truth, that it is sensibility, not understanding, which possesses the power of *a priori* intuition, and that through pure understanding, acting .in independence of sensibility, no knowledge of any kind can be acquired. In other words, Kant classes Berkeley with the rationalists. And, as we have already seen, he even goes the length of regarding Berkeley's position as the *reductio ad absurdum* of the realist view of space. Kant does, indeed, recognise[2] that Berkeley differs from the other idealists, in holding an empirical view of space, and consequently of geometry, but this does not prevent Kant from maintaining that Berkeley's thinking is influenced by certain fundamental implications of the realist position. Berkeley's insight—such would seem to be Kant's line of argument—is perverted by the very view which he is attacking. Berkeley appreciates only what is false in the Cartesian view of space; he is blind to the important element of truth which it contains. Empiricist though he be, he has no wider conception of the function and powers of sensibility than have the realists from whom he separates himself off; and in order to comprehend those existences to which alone he is willing to allow true reality, he has therefore, like the rationalists, to fall back upon pure reason.[3]

[1] Cf. below, p. 298 ff., on Kant's *Refutations of Idealism.* This is also the meaning in which Kant employs the term in his pre-Critical writings. Cf. *Dilucidatio* (1755), prop. xii. *usus*; *Träume eines Geistersehers* (1766), ii. 2, *W.* ii. p. 364. These citations are given by Janitsch (*Kant's Urtheile über Berkeley*, 1879, p. 20), who also points out that the term is already used in this sense by Bülffinger as early as 1725, *Dilucidationes philos.* This is also the meaning in which the term is employed in B xxxiv. Cf. A 28 = B 44.

[2] *Prolegomena*; *Anhang. W.* iv. pp. 374-5.

[3] In his *Kleine Aufsätze* (3. *Refutation of Problematic Idealism*, Hartenstein, v. p. 502) Kant would seem very inconsistently to accuse Berkeley of maintaining

That Kant's criticism of Berkeley should be extremely external is not, therefore, surprising. He is interested in Berkeley's positive teaching only in so far as it enables him to illustrate the evil tendencies of a mistaken idealism, which starts from a false view of the functions of sensibility and of understanding, and of the nature of space and time. The key to the true idealism lies, he claims, in the Critical problem, how *a priori* synthetic judgments can be possible. This is the fundamental problem of metaphysics, and until it has been formulated and answered no advance can be made.

"My so-called (Critical) idealism is thus quite peculiar in that it overthrows ordinary idealism, and that through it alone *a priori* cognition, even that of geometry, attains objective reality, a thing which even the keenest realist could not assert till I had proved the ideality of space and time."[1]

In order to make Kant's account of Berkeley's teaching really comprehensible, we seem compelled to assume that he had never himself actually read any of Berkeley's own writings. Kant's acquaintance with the English language was most imperfect, and we have no evidence that he had ever read a single English book.[2] When he quotes Pope and Addison, he does so from German translations.[3] Subsequent to 1781 he could, indeed, have had access to Berkeley's *Dialogues between Hylas and Philonous*[4] in a German translation ; but in view of the account which he continues to give of Berkeley's teaching, it does not seem likely[5] that he had availed himself of this opportunity. As to what the indirect sources of Kant's knowledge of Berkeley may have been, we cannot decide with any certainty, but amongst them must undoubtedly be reckoned Hume's statements in regard to Berkeley in the *Enquiry*,[6] and very probably also the references to Berkeley in Beattie's *Nature of Truth*.[7] From

---

a solipsistic position. "Berkeley denies the existence of all things save that of the being who asserts them." This is probably, however, merely a careless formulation of the statement that thinking beings alone exist. Cf. *Prolegomena*, § 13, Anm. ii.

[1] *Prolegomena*, W. iv. p. 375 ; Eng. trans. p. 148.

[2] Borowski (*Darstellung des Lebens und Charakters Immanuel Kant*, in Hoffman's ed. 1902, p. 248 ff.) gives a list of English writers with whom Kant was acquainted. They were, according to Janitsch (*loc. cit.* p. 35), accessible in translation. Cf. above, pp. xxviii *n.* 3, 63 *n.* 1.

[3] Cf. *W.* i. pp. 318, 322. When Kant cites Hume in the *Prolegomena* (Introduction), the reference is to the German translation.

[4] This was the first of Berkeley's writings to appear in German. The translation was published in Leipzig in 1781.

[5] Cf. below, pp. 307-8. The opposite view has, however, been defended by Vaihinger : *Philos. Monatshefte*, 1883, p. 501 ff.

[6] *Enquiry Concerning the Human Understanding* (sec. xii. at the end of pt. 1. and of pt. ii.).   [7] Sixth edition, pp. 132, 214, 243 ff.

the former Kant would learn of Berkeley's empirical view of space and also of the sceptical tendencies of his idealist teaching. From it he might also very naturally infer that Berkeley denies all reality to objects. By Beattie Kant would be confirmed in this latter view, and also in his contention that Berkeley is unable to supply a criterion for distinguishing between reality and dreams. Kant may also have received some impressions regarding Berkeley from Hamann.

To take Kant's criticisms of Berkeley more in detail. In the first edition of the *Critique*[1] Kant passes two criticisms, without, however, mentioning Berkeley by name: first, that he overlooks the problem of time, and, like Descartes, ascribes complete reality to the objects of inner sense. This is the cause of a second error, namely, that he views the objects of outer sense as mere illusion (*blosser Schein*). Proceeding, Kant argues that inner and outer sense are really in the same position. Though they yield only appearances, these appearances are conditioned by things in themselves. Through this relation to things in themselves they are distinguished from all merely subjective images. Berkeley is again referred to in the fourth *Paralogism*.[2] His idealism is distinguished from that of Descartes. The one is dogmatic; the other is sceptical. The one denies the existence of matter; the other only doubts whether it is possible to prove it. Berkeley claims, indeed, that there are contradictions in the very conception of matter; and Kant remarks that this is an objection which he will have to deal with in the section on the *Antinomies*. But this promise Kant does not fulfil; and doubtless for the reason that, however unwilling he may be to make the admission, on this point his own teaching, especially in the *Dialectic*, frequently coincides with that of Berkeley. So little, indeed, is Kant concerned in the first edition to defend his position against the accusation of subjectivism, that in this same section he praises the sceptical idealist as a "benefactor of human reason."

"He compels us, even in the smallest advances of ordinary experience, to keep on the watch, lest we consider as a well-earned possession what we perhaps obtain only in an illegitimate manner. We are now in a position to appreciate the value of the objections of the idealist. They drive us by main force, unless we mean to contradict ourselves in our commonest assertions, to view all our perceptions, whether we call them inner or outer, as a consciousness only of what is dependent on our sensibility. They also compel us to regard the outer objects of these perceptions not as things in

---

[1] A 38.   [2] A 377.

themselves, but only as representations, of which, as of every other representation, we can become immediately conscious, and which are entitled outer because they depend on what we call 'outer sense' whose intuition is space. Space itself, however, is nothing but an inner mode of representation in which certain perceptions are connected with one another." [1]

These criticisms are restated in A 491-2 = B 519-20, with the further addition that in denying the existence of extended beings "the empirical idealist" removes the possibility of distinguishing between reality and dreams. This is a new criticism. Kant is no longer referring to the denial of unknowable things in themselves. He is now maintaining that only the Critical standpoint can supply an immanent criterion whereby real experiences may be distinguished from merely subjective happenings. This point is further insisted upon in the *Prolegomena*, [2] but is nowhere developed with any direct reference to Berkeley's own personal teaching. Kant assumes as established that any such criterion must rest upon the *a priori*; and in this connection Berkeley is conveniently made to figure as a thoroughgoing empiricist.

The *Critique*, on its publication, was at once attacked, especially in the Garve-Feder review, as presenting an idealism similar to that of Berkeley. As Erdmann has shown, the original plan of the *Prolegomena* was largely modified in order to afford opportunity for reply to this "unpardonable and almost intentional misconception." [8]   Kant's references to Berkeley, direct and indirect, now for the first time manifest a polemical tone, exaggerating in every possible way the difference between their points of view. Only the transcendental philosophy can establish the possibility of *a priori* knowledge, and so it alone can afford a criterion for distinguishing between realities and dreams. It alone will account for the possibility of geometrical science ; Berkeley's idealism would render the claims of that science wholly illusory. The Critical idealism transcends experience only so far as is required to discover the conditions which make empirical cognition possible ; Berkeley's idealism is 'visionary' and 'mystical.' [4] Even sceptical idealism now comes in for severe handling. It may be called "dreaming idealism" ; it makes things out of

---

[1] A 377-8. Though Kant here distinguishes between perceptions and their "outer objects," the latter are none the less identified with mental representations.
[2] Cf. below, p. 305 ff.
[3] *Prolegomena*, § 13, *Remark* III. ; and *Anhang* (*W*. iv. p. 374).
[4] Kant's description of Berkeley's idealism as visionary and mystical is doubtless partly due to the old-time association of idealism in Kant's mind with the spiritualistic teaching of Swedenborg (*W*. ii. p. 372). This association of ideas was further reinforced owing to his having classed Berkeley along with Plato.

mere representations, and like idealism in its dogmatic form it virtually denies the existence of the only true reality, that of things in themselves. Sceptical idealism misinterprets space by making it empirical, dogmatic idealism by regarding it as an attribute of the real. Both entirely ignore the problem of time. For these reasons they underestimate the powers of sensibility (to which space and time belong as *a priori* forms), and exaggerate those of pure understanding.

"The position of all genuine idealists from the Eleatics to Berkeley is contained in this formula: 'All cognition through the senses and experience is nothing but mere illusion, and only in the ideas of pure understanding and Reason is there truth.' The fundamental principle ruling all my idealism, on the contrary, is this: 'All cognition of things solely from pure understanding or pure Reason is nothing but mere illusion and only in experience is there truth.'"[1]

This is an extremely inadequate statement of the Critical standpoint, but it excellently illustrates Kant's perverse interpretation of Berkeley's teaching.

To these criticisms Kant gives less heated but none the less explicit expression in the second edition of the *Critique*. He is now much more careful to avoid subjectivist modes of statement. His phenomenalist tendencies are reinforced, and come to clearer expression of all that they involve. The fourth *Paralogism* with its sympathetic treatment of empirical idealism is omitted, and in addition to the above passage Kant inserts a new section, entitled *Refutation of Idealism*, in which he states his position in a much more adequate manner.

IV. B 71.—Kant continues the argument of A 39.[2] If space and time condition all existence, they will condition even divine existence, and so must render God's omniscience, which as such must be intuitive, not discursive, difficult of conception. Upon this point Kant is more explicit in the *Dissertation*.[3]

"*Whatever is, is somewhere and sometime,* is a spurious axiom. . . . By this spurious principle all beings, even though they be known intellectually, are restricted in their existence by conditions of space and time. Philosophers therefore discuss every form of idle question regarding the locations in the corporeal universe of substances that are immaterial—and of which for that very reason there can be no sensuous intuition nor any possible spatial representation—or regard-

---

[1] *Prolegomena, Anhang, W.* iv. p. 374; Eng. trans. p. 147.
[2] Cf. above, pp. 140-1.
[3] § 27. In translating Kant's somewhat difficult Latin I have found helpful the English translation of the *Dissertation* by W. J. Eckoff (New York, 1894).

ing the seat of the soul, and the like. And since the sensuous mixes with the intellectual about as badly as square with round, it frequently happens that the one disputant appears as holding a sieve into which the other milks the he-goat. The presence of immaterial things in the corporeal world is virtual, not local, although it may conveniently be spoken of as local. Space contains the conditions of possible interaction only when it is between material bodies. What, however, in immaterial substances constitutes the external relations of force between them or between them and bodies, obviously eludes the human intellect. . . . But when men reach the conception of a highest and extra-mundane Being, words cannot describe the extent to which they are deluded by these shades that flit before the mind. They picture God as present in a place: they entangle Him in the world where He is supposed to fill all space at once. They hope to make up for the [spatial] limitation they thus impose by thinking of God's place *per eminentiam, i.e.* as infinite. But to be present in different places at the same time is absolutely impossible, since different places are mutually external to one another, and consequently what is in several places is outside itself, and is therefore present to itself outside itself —which is a contradiction in terms. As to time, men have got into an inextricable maze by releasing it from the laws that govern sense knowledge, and what is more, transporting it beyond the confines of the world to the Being that dwells there, as a condition of His very existence. They thus torment their souls with absurd questions, for instance, why God did not fashion the world many ages earlier. They persuade themselves that it is easily possible to conceive how God may discern present things, *i.e.* what is actual in the time in which He is. But they consider that it is difficult to comprehend how He should foresee the things about to be, *i.e.* the actual in the time in which He is not yet. They proceed as if the existence of the Necessary Being descended successively through all the moments of a supposed time, and as though having already exhausted part of His duration, He foresaw the eternal life that still lies before Him together with the events which [will] occur simultaneously [with that future life of His]. All these speculations vanish like smoke when the notion of time has been rightly discerned."

The references in B 71-2 to the intuitive understanding are among the many signs of Kant's increased preoccupation, during the preparation of the second edition, with the problems which it raises. Such understanding is not sensuous, but intellectual; it is not derivative, but original; the object itself is created in the act of intuition. Or, as Kant's position may perhaps be more adequately expressed, all of God's activities are creative, and are inseparable from the non-sensuous intuition whereby both they and their products are apprehended by Him. Kant's reason for again raising this point may be Mendelssohn's theological defence of the reality of space in his *Morgenstunden*.[1] Mendelssohn has there argued that just as knowledge of independent reality is confirmed by the agreement of different senses, and is rendered the more certain in proportion to the number of senses which support the belief, so the validity of our spatial perceptions is confirmed in proportion as men are found to agree in this type of experience with one another, with the animals, and with angelic beings. Such inductive inference will culminate in the proof that even the Supreme Being apprehends things in this same spatial manner.[2] Kant's reply is that however general the intuition of space may be among finite beings, it is sensuous and derivative, and therefore must not be predicated of a Divine Being. For obvious reasons Kant has not felt called upon to point out the inadequacy of this inductive method to the solution of Critical problems. In A 42 Kant, arguing that our forms of intuition are subjective, claims that they do not necessarily belong to all beings, though they must belong to all men.[3] He is quite consistent in now maintaining[4] that their characteristics, as sensuous and derivative, do not necessarily preclude their being the common possession of all finite beings.

THE PARADOX OF INCONGRUOUS COUNTERPARTS

The purpose, as already noted, of the above sections II. to IV., as added in the second edition, is to afford 'confirmation' of the ideality of space and time. That being so, it is noticeable that Kant has omitted all reference to an argument embodied, for this same purpose, in § 13 of the *Prolegomena*. The matter is of sufficient importance to call for detailed consideration.[5]

As the argument of the *Prolegomena* is somewhat complicated, it is advisable to approach it in the light of its history in Kant's earlier writings. It was to his teacher Martin Knutzen that Kant owed his first introduction to Newton's cosmology; and from Knutzen he inherited the problem of reconciling Newton's mechanical view of nature and absolute view of space with the orthodox Leibnizian tenets. In his first published work[6] Kant seeks to prove

---

[1] Besides the internal evidence of the passage before us, we also have Kant's own mention of Mendelssohn in this connection in notes (to A 43 and A 66) in his private copy of the first edition of the *Critique*. Cf. Erdmann's *Nachträge su Kant's Kritik*, xx. and xxxii. ; and above, p. 11.

[2] Cf. *Morgenstunden*, Bd. ii. of *Gesammelte Schriften* (1863), pp. 246, 288.

[3] Cf. above, p. 116.　　　　[4] B 72.

[5] Upon this subject cf. Vaihinger's exhaustive discussion in ii. p. 518 ff.

[6] *Gedanken von der wahren Schätzung der lebendigen Kräfte* (1747).

that the very existence of space is due to gravitational force, and that its three-dimensional character is a consequence of the specific manner in which gravity acts. Substances, he teaches, are unextended. Space results from the connection and order established between them by the balancing of their attractive and repulsive forces. And as the law of gravity is merely contingent, other modes of interaction, and therefore other forms of space, with more than three dimensions, must be recognised as possible.

"A science of all these possible kinds of space would undoubtedly be the highest enterprise which a finite understanding could undertake in the field of geometry."[1]

In the long interval between 1747 and 1768 Kant continued to hold to some such compromise, retaining Leibniz's view that space is derivative and relative, and rejecting Newton's view that it is prior to, and pre-conditions, all the bodies that exist in it. But in that latter year he published a pamphlet[2] in which, following in the steps of the mathematician, Euler,[3] he drew attention to certain facts which would seem quite conclusively to favour the Newtonian as against the Leibnizian interpretation of space. The three dimensions of space are primarily distinguishable by us only through the relation in which they stand to our body. By relation to the plane that is at right angles to our body we distinguish 'above' and 'below'; and similarly through the other two planes we determine what is 'right' and 'left,' 'in front' and 'behind.' Through these distinctions we are enabled to define differences which cannot be expressed in any other manner. All species of hops—so Kant maintains—wind themselves around their supports from left to right, whereas all species of beans take the opposite direction. All snail shells, with some three exceptions, turn, in descending from their apex downwards, from left to right. This determinate direction of movement, natural to each species, like the difference in spatial configuration between a right and a left hand, or between a right hand and its reflection in a mirror, involves in all cases a reference of the given object to the wider space within which it falls, and ultimately to space as a whole. Only so can its determinate character be distinguished from its opposite counterpart. For as Kant points out, though the right and the left hand are *counterparts*, that is to say, objects which have a common

---

[1] *Op. cit.* § 10. Cf. above, p. 117 ff.
[2] *Von dem ersten Grunde des Unterschiedes der Gegenden im Raume.*
[3] Euler, *Réflexions sur l'espace et le temps* (1748). Vaihinger (ii. p. 530) points out that Kant may also have been here influenced by certain passages in the controversy between Leibniz and Clarke.

definition so long as the arrangement of the parts of each is determined in respect to its central line of reference, they are none the less inwardly *incongruent*, since the one can never be made to occupy the space of the other. As he adds in the *Prolegomena*, the glove of one hand cannot be used for the other hand. This inner incongruence compels us to distinguish them as different, and this difference is only determinable by location of each in a single absolute space that constrains everything within it to conform to the conditions which it prescribes. In three-dimensional space everything must have a right and a left side, and must therefore exhibit such inner differences as those just noted. Spatial determinations are not, as Leibniz teaches, subsequent to, and dependent upon, the relations of bodies to one another; it is the former that determine the latter.

" . . . the reason why that which in the outline of a body exclusively concerns its relation to pure space can be apprehended by us only through comparison with other bodies, is that absolute space is not an object of any outer sensation, but a fundamental conception which makes all such sensations possible."[1]

Kant enforces his point by arguing that if the first portion of creation were a human hand, it would have to be either a right or a left hand. Also, a different act of creation would be demanded according as it was the one or the other. But if the hand alone existed, and there were no pre-existing space, there would be no inward difference in the relations of its parts, and nothing outside it to differentiate it. It would therefore be entirely indeterminate in nature, *i.e.* would suit either side of the body, which is impossible.

This adoption of the Newtonian view of space in 1768 was an important step forward in the development of Kant's teaching, but could not, in view of the many metaphysical difficulties to which it leads, be permanently retained; and in the immediately following year—a year which, as he tells us,[2] "gave great light"—he achieved the final synthesis which enabled him to combine all that he felt to be essential in the opposing views. Though space is an absolute and pre-conditioning source of differences which are not conceptually resolvable, it is a merely subjective form of our sensibility.

Now it is significant that when Kant expounds this view in the *Dissertation* of 1770, the argument from incongruous counterparts is no longer employed to establish the absolute

---

[1] *Loc. cit.*, at the end.
[2] In the Dorpater manuscript, quoted by Erdmann in his edition of the *Prolegomena*, p. xcvii *n*.

and pre-conditioning character of space, but only to prove that it is a pure non-conceptual intuition.

"Which things in a given space lie towards one side, and which lie towards the other, cannot by any intellectual penetration be discursively described or reduced to intellectual marks. For in solids that are completely similar and equal, but incongruent, such as the right and the left hand (conceived solely in terms of their extension), or spherical triangles from two opposite hemispheres, there is a diversity which renders impossible the coincidence of their spatial boundaries. This holds true, even though they can be substituted for one another in all those respects which can be expressed in marks that are capable of being made intelligible to the mind through speech. It is therefore evident that the diversity, that is, the incongruity, can only be apprehended by some species of pure intuition." [1]

There is no mention of this argument in the first edition of the *Critique*, and when it reappears in the *Prolegomena* it is interpreted in the light of an additional premiss, and is made to yield a very different conclusion from that drawn in the *Dissertation*, and a *directly opposite conclusion* from that drawn in 1768. Instead of being employed to establish either the intuitive character of space or its absolute existence, it is cited as evidence in proof of its subjectivity. As in 1768, it is spoken of as strange and paradoxical, and many of the previous illustrations are used. The paradox consists in the fact that bodies and spherical figures, conceptually considered, can be absolutely identical, and yet for intuition remain diverse. This paradox, Kant now maintains [2] in opposition to his 1768 argument, proves that such bodies and the space within which they fall are not independent existences. For were they things in themselves, they would be adequately cognisable through the pure understanding, and could not therefore conflict with its demands. Being conceptually identical, they would necessarily be congruent in every respect. But if space is merely the form of sensibility, the fact that in space the part is only possible through the whole will apply to everything in it, and so will generate a fundamental difference between conception and intuition. [3] Things in themselves are, as such, unconditioned, and cannot, therefore, be dependent upon anything beyond themselves. The objects of intuition, in order to be possible, must be merely ideal.

[1] § 15 C.
[2] So also in the *Metaphysical First Principles of Natural Science* (1786), *Erstes Hauptstück, Erklärung 2, Anmerkung 3.*
[3] Cf. above, p. 105.

Now the new premiss which differentiates this argument from that of 1768, and which brings Kant to so opposite a conclusion, is one which is entirely out of harmony with the teaching of the *Critique*. In this section of the *Prolegomena* Kant has unconsciously reverted to the dogmatic standpoint of the *Dissertation*, and is interpreting understanding in the illegitimate manner which he so explicitly denounces in the section on *Amphiboly*.

"'The mistake . . . lies in employing the understanding contrary to its vocation transcendentally [*i.e.* transcendently] and in making objects, *i.e.* possible intuitions, conform to concepts, not concepts to possible intuitions, on which alone their objective validity rests."[1]

The question why no mention of this argument is made in the second edition of the *Critique* is therefore answered. Kant had meantime, in the interval between 1783 and 1787,[2] become aware of the inconsistency of the position. So far from being a paradox, this assumed conflict rests upon a false view of the function of the understanding.[3] The relevant facts may serve to confirm the view of space as an intuition in which the whole precedes the parts;[4] but they can afford no evidence either of its absoluteness or of its ideality. In 1768 they seem to Kant to prove its absoluteness, only because the other alternative has not yet occurred to him. In 1783 they seem to him to prove its ideality, only because he has not yet completely succeeded in emancipating his thinking from the dogmatic rationalism of the *Dissertation*.

As already noted,[5] Kant's reason for here asserting that space is intuitive in nature, namely, that in it the parts are conditioned by the whole, is also his reason for elsewhere describing it as an Idea of Reason. The further implication of the argument of the *Prolegomena*, that in the noumenal sphere the whole is made possible only by its unconditioned parts, raises questions the discussion of which must be deferred. The problem recurs in the *Dialectic* in connection with Kant's definition of the Idea of the unconditioned. In the Ideas of Reason Kant comes to recognise the existence of concepts which do not conform to the reflective type analysed by the traditional logic, and to perceive that these Ideas can yield

---

[1] A 289=B 345.
[2] More exactly between the writing of the *Metaphysical First Principles* (in which as above noted the argument of the *Prolegomena* is endorsed) and 1787.
[3] Cf. A 260 ff. = B 316 ff. on the *Amphiboly of Reflective Concepts*.
[4] The *Dissertation* cites the argument only with this purpose in view. And yet it is only from the *Dissertation* standpoint that the wider argument of the *Prolegomena* can be legitimately propounded.
[5] Above, pp. 96-8, 102 *n.* 4; below, pp. 390-1.

a deeper insight than any possible to the discursive under-standing. The above rationalistic assumption must not, therefore, pass unchallenged. It may be that in the noumenal sphere all partial realities are conditioned by an unconditioned whole.

Concluding Paragraph.[1]—The wording of this paragraph is in keeping with the increased emphasis which in the *Intro-duction* to the second edition is given to the problem, how *a priori* synthetic judgments are possible. Kant character-istically fails to distinguish between the problems of pure and applied mathematics, with resulting inconsecutiveness in his argumentation.

[1] B 73.

THE TRANSCENDENTAL DOCTRINE OF ELEMENTS

PART II

THE TRANSCENDENTAL LOGIC

INTRODUCTION

I. Concerning Logic in General.—This *Introduction*,[1] which falls into four divisions, is extremely diffuse, and contributes little that is of more than merely architectonic value. It is a repetition of the last section of the general *Introduction*, and of the introductory paragraphs of the *Aesthetic*, but takes no account of the definitions given in either of those two places. It does not, therefore, seem likely that it could have been written in immediate sequence upon the *Aesthetic*. It is probably later than the main body of the *Analytic*.[2] In any case it is externally tacked on to it; as Adickes has noted,[3] it is completely ignored in the opening section of the *Analytic*.[4]

In treating of intuition in the first sentence, Kant seems to have in view only empirical intuition.[5] Yet he at once proceeds to state that intuition may be pure as well as empirical.[6] Also, in asserting that "pure intuition contains only the form under which something is intuited," Kant would seem to be adopting the view that it does not yield its own manifold, a conclusion which he does not, however, himself draw.

In defining sensibility,[7] Kant again ignores pure intuition. Sensuous intuition, it is stated, is the mode in which we are affected by objects.[8] Understanding, in turn, is defined only

---

[1] A 50 = B 74.   [2] Cf. below, p. 176 *n*. 1.
[3] K. p. 99 *n*.   [4] A 64 = B 89.
[5] The definition of intuition given in A 19 = B 33 also applies only to empirical intuition.
[6] For discussion of Kant's view of sensation as the matter of sensuous intuition, cf. above, p. 80 ff.
[7] Second paragraph, A 51 = B 75.
[8] Object (*Gegenstand*) is here used in the strict sense and no longer as merely equivalent to content (*Inhalt*).

in its opposition to sensibility, in the ordinary meaning of that term. Understanding is the faculty which yields thought of the object to which sense-affection is due. It is "the power of thinking the object of sensuous intuition"; and acts, it is implied, in and through pure concepts which it supplies out of itself.

"Without sensibility objects would not be given to us [*i.e.* the impressions, in themselves merely subjective contents, through which alone independent objects can be revealed to us, would be wanting]; without understanding they would not be thought by us [*i.e.* they would be apprehended only in the form in which they are given, viz. as subjective modes of our sensibility]."

Kant has not yet developed the thesis which the central argument of the *Analytic* is directed to prove, namely, that save through the combination of intuition and conception no consciousness whatsoever is possible. In these paragraphs he still implies that though concepts without intuition are empty they are not meaningless, and that though intuitions without concepts are blind they are not empty.[1] Their union is necessary for genuine knowledge, but not for the existence of consciousness as such.

"It is just as necessary to make our concepts sensuous, *i.e.* to add to them their object in intuition, as to make our intuitions intelligible, *i.e.* to bring them under concepts."

Kant's final Critical teaching is very different from this. Concepts are not first given in their purity, nor is "their object" added in intuition. Only through concepts is apprehension of an object possible, and only in and through such apprehension do concepts come to consciousness. Nor are intuitions "made intelligible" by being "brought under concepts." Only as thus conceptually interpreted can they exist for consciousness. The co-operation of concept and intuition is necessary for consciousness in any and every form, even the simplest and most indefinite. Consciousness of the subjective is possible only in and through consciousness of the objective, and *vice versa*. The dualistic separation of sensibility from understanding persists, however, even in Kant's later utterances; and, as above stated,[2] to this sharp opposition are due both the strength and the weakness of Kant's teaching. Intuition and conception must, he here insists, be carefully distinguished. *Aesthetic* is the "science of the rules of sensibility in general." *Logic* is the "science of the rules of understanding in general."

---

[1] Cf. above, p. 79 ff.   [2] P. 85.

Kant's classification of the various kinds of logic[1] may be exhibited as follows :

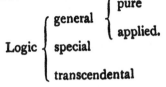

Adickes[2] criticises Kant's classification as defective, owing to the omission of the intermediate concept 'ordinary.' Adickes therefore gives the following table :

Logic

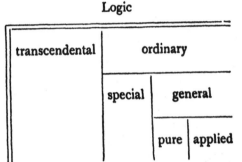

General logic is a logic of elements, *i.e.* of the absolutely necessary laws of thought, in abstraction from all differences in the objects dealt with, *i.e.* from all content, whether empirical or transcendental. It is a canon of the understanding in its general discursive or analytic employment. When it is pure, it takes no account of the empirical psychological conditions under which the understanding has to act. When it is developed as an applied logic, it proceeds to formulate rules for the employment of understanding under these subjective conditions. It is then neither canon, nor organon, but simply a catharticon of the ordinary understanding. Special logic is the organon of this or that science, *i.e.* of the rules governing correct thinking in regard to a certain class of objects. Only pure general logic is a pure doctrine of reason. It alone is absolutely independent of sensibility, of everything empirical, and therefore of psychology. Such pure logic is a body of demonstrative teaching, completely *a priori*. It stands to applied logic in the same relation as pure to applied ethics.

"Some logicians, indeed, affirm that logic presupposes *psychological* principles. But it is just as inappropriate to bring principles

---

[1] Third paragraph, A 52 = B 77.   [2] K. p. 100.

of this kind into logic as to derive the science of morals from life. If we were to take the principles from psychology, that is, from observations on our understanding, we should merely see *how* thought takes place, and *how* it is affected by the manifold subjective hindrances and conditions; so that this would lead only to the knowledge of *contingent* laws. But in logic the question is not of *contingent*, but of *necessary* laws; not how we do think, but how we ought to think. The rules of logic, then, must not be derived from the *contingent*, but from the *necessary* use of the understanding which without any psychology a man finds in himself. In logic we do not want to know how the understanding is and thinks, and how it has hitherto proceeded in thinking, but how it ought to proceed in thinking. Its business is to teach us the correct use of reason, that is, the use which is consistent with itself." [1]

By a canon Kant means a system of *a priori* principles for the correct employment of a certain faculty of knowledge. [2] By an organon Kant means instruction as to how knowledge may be extended, how new knowledge may be acquired. A canon formulates positive principles through the application of which a faculty can be directed and disciplined. A canon is therefore a discipline based on positive principles of correct use. The term discipline is, however, reserved by Kant [3] to signify a purely negative teaching, which seeks only to prevent error and to check the tendency to deviate from rules. When a faculty has no correct use (as, for instance, pure speculative reason), it is subject only to a discipline, not to a canon. A discipline is thus "a separate, negative code," "a system of caution and self-examination." It is further distinguished from a canon by its taking account of other than purely *a priori* conditions. It is related to a pure canon much as applied is related to general logic. As a canon supplies principles for the *directing* of a faculty, its distinction from an organon obviously cannot be made hard and fast. But here as elsewhere Kant, though rigorous and almost pedantic in the drawing of distinctions, is correspondingly careless in their application. He describes special logic as the organon of this or that science. [4] We should expect from the definition given in the preceding sentence that it would rather be viewed as a canon. In A 46 = B 63 Kant speaks of the *Aesthetic* as an organon.

11. **Concerning Transcendental Logic.**—It is with the distinction between general and transcendental logic that Kant is chiefly concerned. It is a distinction which he has himself

---

[1] Kant's *Logik: Einleitung*, i. (Abbott's trans. p. 4).
[2] Cf. A 796 = B 824; A 130 = B 169; also above, pp. 71-2.   [3] A 709 = B 737.
[4] *Logik: Einleitung*, i. (Eng. trans. p. 3).

invented, and which is of fundamental importance for the purposes of the *Critique*. Transcendental logic is the new science which he seeks to expound in this second main division of the *Doctrine of Elements*. The distinction, from which all the differences between the two sciences follow, is that while general logic abstracts from all differences in the objects known, transcendental logic abstracts only from empirical content. On the supposition, not yet proved by Kant, but asserted in anticipation, that there exist pure *a priori* concepts which are valid of objects, there will exist a science distinct in nature and different in purpose from general logic. The two logics will agree in being *a priori*, but otherwise they will differ in all essential respects.

The reference in A 55 = B 79 to the forms of intuition is somewhat ambiguous. Kant might be taken as meaning that in transcendental logic abstraction is made not only from everything empirical but also from all intuition. That is not, however, Kant's real view, or at least not his final view. In sections A 76-7 = B 102, A 130-1 = B 170, and A 135-6 = B 174-5, which are probably all of later origin, he states his position in the clearest terms. Transcendental logic, he there declares, differs from general logic in that it is not called upon to abstract from the pure *a priori* manifolds of intuition.[1] This involves, it may be noted, the recognition, so much more pronounced in the later developments of Kant's Critical teaching, of space and time as not merely forms for the apprehension of sensuous manifolds but as themselves presenting to the mind independent manifolds of *a priori* nature.

As the term *transcendental* indicates, the new logic will have as its central problems the origin, scope, conditions and possibility of valid *a priori* knowledge of objects. None of these problems are treated in general logic, which deals only with the understanding itself. The question which it raises is, as Kant says in his *Logic*,[2] *How can the understanding know itself?* The question dealt with by transcendental logic we may formulate in a corresponding way : *How can the understanding possess pure a priori knowledge of objects?* It is a canon of pure understanding in so far as that faculty is capable of synthetic, objective knowledge *a priori*.[3] General logic involves, it is true. the idea of reference to objects,[4] but the possibility of such reference is not itself investigated. In general logic the understanding deals only with itself. It assumes indeed that all objects must conform to its laws, but this assumption plays no part in the science itself.

---

[1] Cf. below, p. 194.   [2] *Einleitung*, i. (Eng. trans. p. 4).
[3] Cf. A 796 = B 824.   [4] *Logik : Einleitung*, i. (Eng. trans. p. 5).

A further point, not here dwelt upon by Kant, calls for notice, namely, that the activities of understanding dealt with by general logic are its merely discursive activities,—those of discrimination and comparison; whereas those dealt with by transcendental logic are the originative activities through which it produces *a priori* concepts from within itself, and through which it attains, independently of experience, to an *a priori* determination of objects. Otherwise stated, general logic deals only with analytic thinking, transcendental logic with the synthetic activities that are involved in the generation of the complex contents which form the subject matter of the analytic procedure.

III. **Concerning the Division of General Logic into Analytic and Dialectic.**[1]—The following passage from Kant's *Logic*[2] forms an excellent and sufficient comment upon the first four paragraphs of this section:

"An important perfection of knowledge, nay, the essential and inseparable condition of all its perfection, is truth. Truth is said to consist in the agreement of knowledge with the object. According to this merely verbal definition, then, my knowledge, in order to be true, must agree with the object. Now I can only compare the object with my knowledge by this means, namely, *by having knowledge of it*. My knowledge, then, is to be verified by itself, which is far from being sufficient for truth. For as the object is external to me, I can only judge whether my knowledge of the object agrees with my knowledge of the object. Such a circle in explanation was called by the ancients Diallelos. And, indeed, the logicians were accused of this fallacy by the sceptics, who remarked that this account of truth was as if a man before a judicial tribunal should make a statement, and appeal in support of it to a witness whom no one knows, but who defends his own credibility by saying that the man who had called him as a witness is an honourable man. The charge was certainly well-founded. The solution of the problem referred to is, however, absolutely impossible for any man.

"The question is in fact this: whether and how far there is a certain, universal, and practically applicable criterion of truth. For this is the meaning of the question, What is truth? . . .

"A *universal material* criterion of truth is not possible; the phrase is indeed self-contradictory. For being *universal* it would necessarily abstract from all distinction of objects, and yet being a material criterion, it must be concerned with just this distinction in order to be able to determine whether a cognition agrees with the very object to which it refers, and not merely with some object or other, by which nothing would be said. But *material* truth must consist in this agreement of a cognition with the definite object to which it refers. For a cognition which is true in reference to one object

---

[1] A 57 = B 81.   [2] *Einleitung*, vii. (Eng. trans. p. 40 ff.).

may be false in reference to other objects. It is therefore absurd to demand a universal material criterion of truth, which is at once to abstract and not to abstract from all distinction of objects.

"But if we ask for a universal *formal* criterion of truth, it is very easy to decide that there may be such a criterion. For formal truth consists simply in the agreement of the cognition with itself when we abstract from all objects whatever, and from every distinction of objects. And hence the universal formal criteria of truth are nothing but universal logical marks of agreement of cognitions with themselves, or, what is the same thing, with the general laws of the understanding and the Reason. These formal universal criteria are certainly not sufficient for objective truth, but yet they are to be viewed as its *conditio sine qua non.* For before the question, whether the cognition agrees with the object, must come the question, whether it agrees with itself (as to form). And this is the business of logic."[1]

The remaining paragraphs[2] of Section III. may similarly be compared with the following passage from an earlier section of Kant's *Logic*:[3]

"Analytic discovers, by means of analysis, all the activities of reason which we exercise in thought. It is therefore an analytic of the form of understanding and of Reason, and is justly called the logic of truth, since it contains the necessary rules of all (formal) truth, without which truth our knowledge is untrue in itself, even apart from its objects. It is therefore nothing more than a canon for deciding on the formal correctness of our knowledge.

"Should we desire to use this merely theoretical and general doctrine as a practical art, that is, as an organon, it would become a *dialectic,* i.e. a *logic of semblance* (*ars sophistica disputatoria*), arising out of an abuse of the analytic, inasmuch as by the mere logical form there is contrived the semblance of true knowledge, the characters of which must, on the contrary, be derived from agreement with objects, and therefore from the *content.*

"In former times dialectic was studied with great diligence. This art presented false principles in the semblance of truth, and sought, in accordance with these, to maintain things in semblance. Amongst the Greeks the dialecticians were advocates and rhetoricians who could lead the populace wherever they chose, because the populace lets itself be deluded with semblance. Dialectic was therefore at that time the art of semblance. In logic, also, it was for a long time treated under the name of the *art of disputation,* and during that period all logic and philosophy was the cultivation by certain chatterboxes of the art of semblance. But nothing can be more unworthy of a philosopher than the cultivation of such an art. Dialectic in this form, therefore, must be altogether suppressed, and instead of it there

---

[1] Kant might have added that transcendental logic defines further conditions, those of possible experience, and that by implication it refers us to coherence as the ultimate test even of material truth.

[2] A 60-2 = B 84-6.   [3] *Einleitung,* ii. (Eng. trans. pp. 6-7).

must be introduced into logic a critical examination of this semblance.

"We should then have two parts of logic: the *analytic*, which will treat of the formal criteria of truth, and the *dialectic*, which will contain the marks and rules by which we can know that something does not agree with the formal criteria of truth, although it seems to agree with them. Dialectic in this form would have its use as a *cathartic* of the understanding."

Dialectic is thus interpreted in a merely negative sense. It is, Kant says, a catharticon. So far from being an organon, it is not even a canon. It is merely a discipline.[1] By this manner of defining dialectic Kant causes some confusion. It does not do justice to the scope and purpose of that section of the *Critique* to which it gives its name.[2]

IV. **Concerning the Division of Transcendental Logic into Transcendental Analytic and Dialectic.**—The term object[3] is used throughout this section in two quite distinct senses. In the second and third sentences it is employed in its wider meaning as equivalent to content or matter. In the fourth sentence it is used in the narrower and stricter sense, more proper to the term, namely, as meaning 'thing.' Again, in the fifth sentence content (*Inhalt*) would seem to be identified with object in the narrower sense, while in the sixth sentence matter (*Materie*, a synonym for content) appears to be identified with object in the wider sense. *Transcendental Dialectic*, in accordance with the above account of its logical correlate, is defined in a manner which does justice only to the negative side of its teaching. Its function is viewed as merely that of protecting the pure understanding against sophistical illusions.[4]

THE TRANSCENDENTAL LOGIC

DIVISION I

THE TRANSCENDENTAL ANALYTIC

The chief point of this section[5] lies in its insistence that, as the *Analytic* is concerned only with the pure understanding, the *a priori* concepts with which it deals must form a unity or system. Understanding is viewed as a separate faculty,

---

[1] Cf. above, pp. 71-2, 170; below, pp. 438, 563.   [2] Cf. below, p. 425 ff.
[3] Kant employs *Gegenstand* and *Object* as synonymous terms.
[4] Cf. below, p. 426.   [5] A 64 = B 89.

and virtually hypostatised. As a separate faculty, it must, it is implied, be an independent unity, self-containing and complete. Its concepts are determined in number, constitution, and interrelation, by its inherent character. They originate independently of all differences in the material which they are employed to organise.

BOOK I

THE ANALYTIC OF CONCEPTS

Introductory Paragraph.—Kant's view of the understanding as a separate faculty is in evidence again in this paragraph.[1] The *Analytic* is a "dissection of the faculty of the understanding." A *priori* concepts are to be sought nowhere but in the understanding itself, as their birthplace. There "they lie ready till at last, on the occasion of experience, they become developed." But such statements fail to do justice to Kant's real teaching. They would seem to reveal the persisting influence of the pre-Critical standpoint of the *Dissertation*.

CHAPTER I

THE CLUE TO THE DISCOVERY OF ALL PURE CONCEPTS
OF THE UNDERSTANDING

That the understanding is "an absolute unity" is repeated. From this assertion, thus dogmatically made, without even an attempt at argument, Kant deduces the important conclusion that the pure concepts, originating from such a source, "must be connected with each other according to *one* concept or idea (*Begriff oder Idee*)." And he adds the equally unproved assertion :

"But such a connection supplies a rule by which we are enabled to assign its proper place to each pure concept of the understanding and by which we can determine in an *a priori* manner their systematic completeness. Otherwise we should be dependent in these matters on our own discretionary judgment or merely on chance."

---

[1] A 65 = B 90.

In the next section he sets himself to discover from an examination of analytic thinking what this rule or principle actually is, and in so doing he for the first time discloses, in any degree at all adequate, the real nature of the position which he is seeking to develop. He connects the required principle with the nature of the act of judging, considered as a function of unity.

Section I. The Logical Use of the Understanding.—This section,[1] viewed as introductory to the metaphysical deduction of the categories, is extremely unsatisfactory. It directs attention to the wrong points, and conceals rather than defines Kant's real position. Its argumentation is also contorted and confused, and only by the most patient analysis can it be straightened out. The commentator has presented to him a twofold task from which there is no escape. He must render the argument consistent by such modification as will harmonise it with Kant's later and more deliberate positions, and he must explain why Kant has presented it in this misleading manner.

The title of the section would seem to imply that only the discursive activities of understanding are to be dealt with. That is, indeed, in the main true. Confusion results, however, from the clashing of this avowed intention with the ultimate purpose in view of which the argument is propounded. Kant is seeking to prove that we can derive from the more accessible procedure of the discursive understanding a clue sufficient for determining those pre-logical activities which have to be postulated in terms of his new Copernican hypothesis. But though that is the real intention of this section, it has, unfortunately, not been explicitly recognised, and can be divined by the reader only after he has mastered the later portions of the *Analytic*. Kant's argument has also the further defect that no sufficient statement is given either of the nature of the discursive concept or of its relation to judgment. These lacunae we must fill out as best we can from his utterances elsewhere. I shall first state Kant's view of the distinction between discursive and synthetic thinking, and then examine his treatment of the nature of the concept and of its relation to judgment.

As already noted,[2] the distinction between transcendental and general logic marks for Kant all-important differences in the use of the understanding. In the one employment

---

[1] The opening statement, A 67 = B 92, that hitherto understanding has been defined only negatively, is not correct, and would seem to prove that this section was written prior to the introduction to the *Analytic*, cf. above, p. 167.

[2] See above, pp. 170-1.

the understanding, by creative synthetic activities, generates from the given manifold the complex objects of sense-experience.   In so doing it interprets and organises the manifold through concepts which originate *from within itself*. By the other it discriminates and compares, and thereby derives *from the content of sense-experience* the generic concepts of the traditional logic.   Now Kant would seem to argue in this section that if the difference in the origin of the concepts in those two cases be left out of account, and if we attend only to the quite general character of their respective activities, they will be found to agree in one fundamental feature, namely, that they express functions of unity.   Each is based on the spontaneity of thought—on the spontaneity of synthetic interpretation on the one hand, of discrimination and comparison on the other.   This feature common to the two types of activity can be further defined as being the unity of the act whereby a multiplicity is comprehended under a single representation.   In the judgment "every metal is a body" the variety of metals is reduced to unity through the concept body.   In an analogous manner the synthetic understanding organises a manifold of intuition through some such form of unity as that of substance and attribute.   That is the category which underlies the above proposition, and which renders possible the specific unity of the total judgment. To quote the sentence with which in a later section Kant introduces his table of categories :

"The same understanding, through the same operations by which in concepts, by means of analytic unity, it has produced the logical form of a judgment, introduces, by means of the synthetic unity of the manifold in intuition in general, a transcendental element into its representations. . . ."[1]

Now Kant's exposition is extremely misleading.   As his later utterances show, his real argument is by no means that which is here given.   We shall have occasion to observe that Kant is unable to prove, and does not ultimately profess to prove, that it is "the *same* understanding," and still less that it is "the *same* operations," which are exercised in discursive and in creative thinking.   But this is a criticism which it would be premature to introduce at this stage.   We must proceed to it by way of preliminary analysis of the above exposition.   Kant's argument does not rest upon any such analogy as that just drawn, between the concepts formed by consciously comparing contents and the concepts which originate from within the understanding itself.   Both, it is

[1] A 79=B 105.   'Element' translates the misleading term 'Inhalt.'

true, are functions of unity, but otherwise there is, according to Kant's own teaching, not the least resemblance between them.   A generic or abstract concept expresses common qualities found in each of a number of complex contents.   It is itself a content.   A category, on the other hand, is always a function of unity whereby contents are interpreted.   It is not a content, but a form for the organisation of content.[1] It can gain expression only in the total act of judging, not in any one element such as the discursive concept.   But though the analogy drawn by Kant thus breaks down, his argument is continued in a new and very different form.   It is no longer made to rest on any supposed resemblance between discursive and creative thinking, regarded as co-ordinate and independent activities.   It now consists in the proof that the former presupposes and is conditioned by the latter.   Through study of the understanding in its more accessible discursive procedure, we may hope to discover the synthetic forms according to which it has proceeded in its pre-logical activities. When we determine the various forms of analytic judgment, the categories which are involved in synthetic thinking reveal themselves to consciousness.

Thus in spite of Kant's insistence upon the conceptual predicate, and upon the unity to which it gives expression, immediately he proceeds to the deduction of the categories, the emphasis is shifted to the unity which underlies the judgment as a whole.   What constitutes such propositions as "all bodies are divisible," "every metal is a body," a unique and separate type of judgment is not the character of the predicate, but the category of substance and attribute whereby the predicate is related to the subject.   To that category they owe their specific form ; and it is a function of unity for which the discursive understanding can never account.   As Kant states in the *Prolegomena*, if genuine judgments, that is, judgments that are "objectively valid," are analysed,

". . . it will be found that they never consist of mere intuitions connected only (as is commonly believed) by comparison in a judgment. They would be impossible were not a pure concept of the under-

---

[1] Kant's definition of transcendental logic as differing from general logic in that it does not abstract from *a priori* content must not be taken as implying that the categories of understanding are contents, though of *a priori* nature.   As we shall find, though that is Kant's view of the forms of sense, it is by no means his view of the categories.   They are, he repeatedly insists, merely functions, and are quite indeterminate in meaning save in so far as a content is yielded to them by sense.   In A 76-7 = B 102, in distinguishing between the two logics, Kant is careful to make clear that the *a priori content* of transcendental logic consists exclusively of the *a priori* manifolds of sense.

standing superadded to the concepts abstracted from intuition. The abstract concepts are subsumed under a pure concept, and in this manner only can they be connected in an objectively valid judgment." [1]

Thus the analogy between discursive and *a priori* concepts is no sooner drawn than it is set aside as irrelevant. Though generic concepts rest upon functions of unity, and though (as we shall see immediately) they exist only as factors in the total act of judging, there is otherwise not the least resemblance between them and the categories. [2] The clue to the categories is not to be found in the inherent characteristics of analytic thinking, or of its specific products (namely, concepts), but solely in what, after all abstraction, it must still retain from the products which synthetic thinking creates. Each type of analytic judgment will be found on examination to involve some specific function whereby the conceptual factors are related to, and unified with, the other elements in the judgment. This function of unity is in each case an *a priori* category of the understanding. That is the thesis which underlies the concluding sentence of this section.

"The functions of the understanding [*i.e.* the *a priori* concepts of understanding] can be discovered in their completeness, if it is possible to state exhaustively the functions of unity [*i.e.* the forms of relation] in judgments."

The adoption of such a position involves, it may be noted, the giving up of the assertion, which is so emphatically made in the passage above quoted, that it is *by the same activities* that the understanding discursively forms abstract concepts and creatively organises the manifold of sense. That is in no respect true. There is no real identity—there is not even analogy—between the processes of comparison and abstraction on the one hand and those of synthetic interpretation on the other. The former are merely reflective : the latter are genuinely creative. Discursive activities are conscious processes, and are under our control : the synthetic processes, are non-conscious ; only their finished products appear within the conscious field. This, however, is to anticipate a conclusion which was among the last to be realised by Kant himself, namely that there is no proof that these two types of activity are ascribable to one and the same source. The synthetic activities—as he himself finally came to hold—are due to a faculty of imagination.

---

[1] § 20, Eng. trans. p. 58.
[2] The view of the two as co-ordinate reappears in the *Prolegomena* (§ 20) in a section the general tendency of which runs directly counter to any such standpoint.

"Synthesis in general . . . is the mere result of the power of imagination, a blind but indispensable function of the soul, without which we should have no knowledge whatsoever, but of which we are scarcely ever conscious."[1]

This sentence occurs in a passage which is undoubtedly a later interpolation.[2] The "scarcely ever" (*selten nur einmal*) indicates Kant's lingering reluctance to recognise this fundamental fact, destructive of so much in his earlier views, even though it completes and reinforces his chief ultimate conclusions. With this admission Kant also gives up his sole remaining ground for the contention that there must be a complete parallelism between discursive and creative thinking. If they arise from such different sources, we have no right to assume, without specific proof, that they must coincide in the forms of their activity. This is a point to which we shall return in discussing Kant's formulation of the principle which is supposed to guarantee the completeness of the table of categories.

This unavowed change in point of view is the main cause of confusion in this section. Its other defects are chiefly those of omission. Kant fails to develop in sufficient detail his view of the nature of the discursive concept, or to make sufficiently clear the grounds for his assertion that conception as an activity of the understanding is identical with judgment. To take the former point first. Kant's mode of viewing the discursive concept finds expression in the following passage in the *Introduction* to his *Logic*:[3]

"Human knowledge is on the side of the understanding *discursive*; that is, it takes place by means of ideas which make what is common to many things the ground of knowledge: and hence by means of attributes as such. We therefore cognise things only by means of attributes. An attribute is that in a thing which constitutes part of our cognition of it; or, what is the same, a partial conception so far as it is considered as a ground of cognition of the whole conception. *All our concepts, therefore, are attributes, and all thought is nothing but conception by means of attributes.*"

The limitations of Kant's view of the concept could hardly find more definite expression. The only type of judgment which receives recognition is the categorical, interpreted in the traditional manner.[4]

"To compare something as a mark with a thing, is called 'to judge.' The thing itself is the subject, the mark [or attribute] is the predi-

---

[1] A 78 = B 103.
[2] *Einleitung*, viii., Eng. trans. p. 48.
[3] Cf. below, pp. 196, 204, 226.
[4] Cf. above, pp. 37-8.

cate. The comparison is expressed by the word 'is,' . . . which when used without qualification indicates that the predicate is a mark [or attribute] of the subject, but when combined with the sign of negation states that the predicate is a mark opposed to the subject." [1]

Kant's view of analytic thinking is entirely dominated by the substance-attribute teaching of the traditional logic. A concept must, in its connotation, be an abstracted attribute, and in its denotation represent a class. Relational thinking, and the concepts of relation, are ignored. Thus, in the *Aesthetic*, as we have already noted,[2] Kant maintains that since space and time are not generic class concepts they must be intuitions. This argument, honestly employed by Kant, shows how completely unconscious he was of the revolutionary consequences of his new standpoint. Even in the very act of insisting upon the relational character of the categories, he still continues to speak of the concept as if it must necessarily conform to the generic type. In this, as in so many other respects, transcendental logic is not, as he would profess, supplementary to general logic ; it is its tacit recantation. Modern logic, as developed by Lotze, Sigwart, Bradley, and Bosanquet, is, in large part, the recasting of general logic in terms of the results reached by Kant's transcendental enquiries. Meantime, sufficient has been said to indicate the strangely limited character of Kant's doctrine of the logical concept.

But on one fundamental point Kant breaks entirely free from the traditional logic. The following passage occurs in the above-quoted pamphlet on *The Mistaken Subtlety of the Four Syllogistic Figures* :

"It is clear that in the ordinary treatment of logic there is a serious error in that distinct and complete concepts are treated before judgments and ratiocinations, although the former are only possible by means of the latter." "I say, then, first, that a *distinct* concept is possible only by means of a *judgment*, a *complete* concept only by means of a *ratiocination*. In fact, in order that a concept should be distinct, I must clearly recognise something as an attribute of a thing, and this is a judgment. In order to have a distinct concept of body, I clearly represent to myself impenetrability as an attribute of it. Now this representation is nothing but the thought, 'a body is impenetrable.' Here it is to be observed that this judgment is not the distinct concept itself, but is the act by which it is realised ; for the idea of the thing which arises after this act is distinct. It is easy to show that a complete concept is only possible by means of a ratiocination : for this it is sufficient to refer to the first section

---

[1] *The Mistaken Subtlety of the Four Syllogistic Figures* (1762). *W.* ii. p. 47, Eng. trans. p. 79.   [2] Cf. above, pp. 99-100, 106-7.

of this essay. We might say, therefore, that a distinct concept is one which is made clear by a judgment, and a complete concept one which is made distinct by a ratiocination. If the completeness is of the first degree, the ratiocination is simple; if of the second or third degree, it is only possible by means of a chain of reasoning which the understanding abridges in the manner of a sorites. . . . Secondly, as it is quite evident that the completeness of a concept and its distinctness do not require different faculties of the mind (since the same capacity which recognises something immediately as an attribute in a thing is also employed to recognise in this attribute another attribute, and thus to conceive the thing by means of a remote attribute), so also it is evident that understanding and reason, that is, the power of cognising distinctly and the power of forming ratiocinations, are not different faculties. Both consist in the power of judging, but when we judge mediately we reason." [1]

In the section before us this same standpoint is maintained, but is expressed in a much less satisfactory manner. Concepts are no longer spoken of as complete judgments. In the above passages Kant always speaks of the concept as the subject of the proposition; it is now treated only as a predicate.[2] This difference is significant. The concept as subject can represent the judgment as a whole (or at least it does so from the traditional standpoint to which Kant holds); the concept as predicate is merely one element, even though it be a unifying element, in the total act of judging. This falling away from his own maturer standpoint would seem to be due to Kant's lack of clearness as to the nature of the analogy which he is here drawing between analytic and synthetic thinking. It is connected with his mistaken, and merely temporary, comparison of *a priori* with discursive concepts. His position in 1762 alone harmonises with his essential teaching. Now, as then, he is prepared to view judgment as the sole ultimate activity of the understanding, and therefore to define understanding as the faculty of judging.

But the new Critical standpoint compels Kant to reinterpret this definition in a manner which involves a still more radical transformation of the traditional doctrine. The categories constitute a unique type of concept, and condition the processes of discursive thought. They are embodied in the complex contents from which analytic thinking starts; and however far the processes of discursive comparison and abstraction be carried, one or other of these categories must still persist, determining the form which the analytic judgment is to take. The categorical judgment can formulate itself

[1] *W.* ii. pp. 58-9, Eng. trans. pp. 92-3.
[2] Cf. *Reflexionen*, ii. 599.

only by means of the *a priori* concept of subject and attribute, the hypothetical only by means of the pure concept of ground and consequence, and so with the others. And there are in consequence just as many categories as there are forms of the analytic judgment. This is how the principle of the metaphysical deduction must be interpreted when the later and deeper results of the transcendental deduction are properly taken into account. In deducing the forms of the understanding from the modes of discursive judgment Kant is virtually maintaining that analytic judgment involves the same problems as does judgment of the synthetic type. But, in reality, the categories can be derived from the forms of discursive judgment only because they are the conditions in and through which it becomes possible.

But though Kant, both here and in the central portions of the *Analytic*, seems to be on the very brink of this conclusion, it is never explicitly drawn. As we shall see,[1] it would have involved the further admission that there is no absolute guarantee of the completeness of the table of categories, and no satisfactory method of determining their interrelations. To the very last general logic is isolated from transcendental logic. The Critical enquiry is formulated as if it concerned only such judgments as are explicitly synthetic. The principle of the metaphysical deduction is not, therefore, stated by Kant himself in the above manner; and we have still to decide the difficult question as to what the principle employed by Kant in the deduction actually is.

Kant makes a twofold demand upon the principle. It must enable us to discover the categories, and it must also in so doing enable us to view them as together forming a systematic whole, and so as having their completeness guaranteed by other than merely empirical considerations. The principle is stated sometimes in a broader and sometimes in a more specific form; for on this point also Kant speaks with no very certain voice.[2] The broader formulation of the principle is that all acts of understanding are judgments, and that therefore the possible ultimate *a priori* forms of understanding are identical with the possible ultimate forms of the judgment.[3] The more specific and correct formulation is that to every form of analytic judgment there corresponds a pure concept of understanding. The first statement of the principle is obviously inadequate. It merely reformulates the

---

[1] Below, pp. 185-6.
[2] The same indefiniteness of statement is discernible in Caird's (i. p. 322 ff.) and Watson's (*Kant Explained*, pp. 121-2) discussions of the principle supposed to be involved.
[3] Cf. A 80 = B 106.

problem as being a problem not of conception but of judgment. If a principle is required to guarantee the completeness of our list of *a priori* concepts, it will equally be required to guarantee the completeness of our list of judgments.   Even if the above principle be more explicitly formulated, as in the *Prolegomena*,[1] where judging is defined as the act of understanding which comprises all its other acts, it will not enable us to guarantee the completeness of any list of the forms of judgment or to determine their systematic interrelation.   We are therefore thrown back upon the second view.   This, however, only brings us face to face with the further question, what principle guarantees the completeness of the table of analytic judgments.   And to that query Kant has absolutely no answer.   The reader's questionings break vainly upon his invincible belief in the adequacy and finality of the classification yielded by the traditional logic.

The *fons et origo* of all the confusions and obscurities of this section are thus traceable to Kant's attitude towards formal logic.   He might criticise it for ignoring the interdependence of conception, judgment, and reasoning; he might reject the second, third, and fourth syllogistic figures; and he might even admit that its classification of the forms of judgment is not as explicit as might be desired ; but however many provisos he made and defects he acknowledged, they were to him merely minor matters, and he accepted its teaching as complete and final.   This unwavering faith in the fundamental distinctions of the traditional logic was indeed, as we shall have constant occasion to observe, an ever present influence in determining alike the general framework and much of the detail of Kant's Critical teaching.   The defects of the traditional logic were very clearly indicated in his own transcendental logic.   He showed that synthetic thinking is fundamental ; that by its distinctions the forms and activities of analytic thought are predetermined; that judgment in its various forms can be understood only by a regress upon the synthetic concepts to which these forms are due; that notions are not merely of the generic type, but that there are also categories of relation.   None the less, to the very last, Kant persisted in regarding general logic as a separate discipline, and as quite adequate in its current form.   He continued to ignore the fact that the analytic judgment, no less than the synthetic judgment, demands a transcendental justification.

The resulting situation is strangely perverse.   In the very act of revolutionising the traditional logic, Kant relies upon its prestige and upon the assumed finality of its results to

[1] § 39.

make good the shortcomings of the logic which is to displace it. By Kant's own admission transcendental logic is incapable of guaranteeing that completeness upon which, throughout the whole *Critique*, so great an emphasis is laid. General logic is allowed an independent status, sufficient to justify its authority being appealed to; and the principle which is supposed to guarantee the completeness of the table of categories is so formulated as to contain no suggestion of the dependence of discursive upon synthetic thinking. Formal logic, Kant would seem to hold, can supply a criterion for the classification of the ultimate forms of judgment just because its task is relatively simple, and is independent of all epistemological views as to the nature, scope, and conditions of the thought process. Since formal logic is a completed and perfectly *a priori* science, which has stood the test of 2000 years, and remains practically unchanged to the present day, its results can be accepted as final, and can be employed without question in all further enquiries. Analytic thinking is scientifically treated in general logic; the *Critique* is concerned only with the possibility and conditions of synthetic judgment. The table of analytic judgments therefore supplies a complete and absolutely guaranteed list of the possible categories of the understanding. But the perverseness of this whole procedure is shown by the manner in which, as we shall find, Kant recasts, extends, or alters, to suit his own purposes, the actual teaching of the traditional logic.

As noted above,[1] the asserted parallelism of analytic and synthetic judgment rests upon the further assumption that discursive thinking and synthetic interpretation are the outcome of one and the same faculty of understanding. It is implied, in accordance with the attitude of the pre-Critical *Dissertation*, that understanding, viewed as the faculty to which all thought processes are due, has certain laws in accordance with which it necessarily acts in all its operations, and that these must therefore be discoverable from analytic no less than from synthetic thinking. The mingling of truth and falsity in this assumption has already been indicated. Such truth as it contains is due to the fact that analytic thinking is not co-ordinate with, but is dependent upon, and determined by, the forms of synthetic thinking. Its falsity consists in its ignoring of what thus gives it partial truth. The results of the transcendental deduction call for a complete recasting of the entire argument of the metaphysical deduction. And when this is done, there is no longer any ground for the contention that the number of the categories is determinable

[1] P. 176 ff.

on *a priori* grounds. On Kant's own fundamental doctrine of the synthetic, and therefore merely *de facto*, character of all *a priori* principles, the necessity of the categories is only demonstrable by reference to the contingent fact of actual experience. The possible conceptual forms are relative to actual and ultimate differences in the contingent sensuous material; and being thus relative, they cannot possibly be systematised on purely *a priori* grounds. This Kant has himself admitted in a passage added in the second edition,[1] though apparently without full consciousness of the important consequences which must follow.

"This peculiarity of our understanding that it can produce *a priori* unity of apperception solely by means of the categories, and only by such and so many, is as little capable of further explanation as why we have just these and no other functions of judgment, or why space and time are the only forms of our possible intuition."

STAGES IN THE DEVELOPMENT OF KANT'S METAPHYSICAL DEDUCTION

The character of the metaphysical deduction will be placed in a clearer light if we briefly trace the stages, so far as they can be reconstructed, through which it passed in Kant's mind. We may start from the *Dissertation* of 1770. Kant there modifies his earlier Wolffian standpoint, developing it, probably under the direct influence of the recently published *Nouveaux Essais*, on more genuinely Leibnizian lines.

"The use of the intellect . . . is twofold. By the one use concepts, both of things and of relations, are themselves *given*. This is the *real use*. By the other use concepts, whencesoever given, are merely *subordinated* to each other, the lower to the higher (the common attributes), and compared with one another according to the principle of contradiction. This is called the *logical use*. . . . Empirical concepts, therefore, do not become intellectual in the *real sense* by reduction to greater universality, and do not pass beyond the type of sensuous cognition. However high the abstraction be carried, they must always remain sensuous. But in dealing with things *strictly intellectual*, in regard to which the *use of the intellect* is *real*, intellectual concepts (of objects as well as of relations), are given by the very nature of the intellect. They are not abstracted from any use of the senses, and do not contain any form of sensuous knowledge as such. We must here note the extreme ambiguity of the word *abstract*. . . . An intellectual concept *abstracts* from everything sensuous; it is not *abstracted* from things sensuous. It would perhaps

---

[1] B 145-6. Cf. above, pp. xxxv-vi, xliv, 57, 142; below, pp. 257, 291.

be more correctly named *abstracting* than *abstract*. It is therefore preferable to call the intellectual concepts *pure ideas*, and those which are given only empirically *abstract ideas*."[1]   "I fear, however, that Wolff, by this distinction between the sensuous and the intellectual, which for him is merely logical, has checked, perhaps wholly (to the great detriment of philosophy), that noblest enterprise of antiquity, the investigation of *the nature of phenomena and noumena*, turning men's minds from such enquiries to what are very frequently only logical subtleties.   Philosophy, in so far as it contains the *first principles* of the use of the *pure intellect*, is *metaphysics*. . . . As empirical principles are not to be found in metaphysics, the concepts to be met with in it are not to be sought in the senses but in the very nature of the pure intellect.   They are not *connate* concepts, but are *abstracted* from laws inherent in the mind (*legibus menti insitis*), and are therefore *acquired*.   Such are the concepts of possibility, existence, necessity, substance, cause, etc. with their opposites or correlates.   They never enter as parts into any sensuous representation, and therefore cannot in any fashion be abstracted from such representations."[2]

The *etcetera*, with which in that last passage Kant concludes his list of pure intellectual concepts, indicates a problem that must very soon have made itself felt.   That it did so, appears from his letter to Herz (February 21, 1772).   He there informs his correspondent, that, in developing his *Transcendentalphilosophie* (the first occurrence of that title in Kant's writings), he has

". . . sought to reduce all concepts of completely pure reason to a fixed number of categories [this term also appearing for the first time], not in the manner of Aristotle, who in his ten predicaments merely set them side by side in a sort of order, just as he might happen upon them, but as they distribute themselves of themselves according to *some few principles* of the understanding."[3]

Though in this same letter Kant professes to have solved his problems, and to be in a position to publish his *Critique of Pure Reason* (this title is already employed) "within some three months," the phrase "some few principles" clearly shows that he has not yet developed the teaching embodied in the metaphysical deduction.   For its keynote is insistence upon the necessity of a *single* principle, sufficient to reduce them not merely to classes but to system.   The difficulty of discovering such a principle must have been one of the causes which delayed completion of the *Critique*.   The only data at our disposal for reconstructing the various stages through which Kant's views may have passed in the period between

---

[1] §§ 5-6.   [2] §§ 7-8.   Cf. above, pp. 144-5.
[3] *W*. x. p. 126.   Italics not in Kant.

February 1772 and 1781 are the *Reflexionen*, but they are sufficiently ample to allow of our doing so with considerable definiteness.[1]

In the *Dissertation* Kant had traced the concepts of space and time, no less than the concepts of understanding, to mental activities.

"Both concepts [space and time] are undoubtedly acquired. They are not, however, abstracted from the sensing of objects (for sensation gives the matter, not the form of human cognition). As immutable types they are intuitively apprehended from the activity whereby the mind co-ordinates its sensuous data in accordance with perpetual laws."[2]

Now the *Dissertation* is quite vague as to how the "mind" (*animus*), active in accordance with laws generative of the intuitions space and time, differs from "understanding" (*intellectus*), active in accordance with laws generative of pure concepts. Kant's reasons, apart from the intuitive character of space and time, for contrasting the former with the latter, as the sensuous with the intellectual, were the existence of the antinomies and his belief that through pure concepts the absolutely real can be known. When, however, that belief was questioned by him, and he had come to regard the categories as no less subjective than the intuitional forms, the antinomies ceased to afford any ground for thus distinguishing between them. The intuitional nature of space and time, while certainly peculiar to them, is in itself no proof that they belong to the sensuous side of the mind.[3]

A difficulty which immediately faced Kant, from the new Critical standpoint, was that of distinguishing between space and time, on the one hand, and the categories on the other. This is borne out by the *Reflexionen* and by the following passage in the *Prolegomena*.[4]

"Only after long reflection, expended in the investigation of the pure non-empirical elements of human knowledge, did I at last succeed in distinguishing and separating with certainty the pure elementary concepts of sensibility (space and time) from those of the understanding."

The first stage in the development of the metaphysical

---

[1] The relevant *Reflexionen* have been carefully discussed by Adickes (*Kant's Systematik*, p. 21 ff.). In what follows I have made extensive use of his results, though not always arriving at quite the same conclusions.

[2] § 15, Coroll.

[3] In his later writings Kant recognises that the representations of space and time involve an Idea of Reason. Cf. above, pp. 97-8; below, pp. 390-1.

[4] § 39.

deduction would seem to have consisted in the attempt to view the categories as acquired by reflection upon the activities of the understanding in "comparing, combining, or separating";[1] and among the *notiones rationales, notiones intellectus puri*, thus gained, the idea of space is specially noted. The following list is also given :

"The concepts of existence (reality), possibility, necessity, ground, unity and plurality, parts, all, none, composite and simple, space, time, change, motion, substance and accident, power and action, and everything that belongs to ontology proper."[2]

In *Reflexionen*, ii. 507 and 509, the fundamental feature of such rational concepts is found in their *relational* character. They all agree in being concepts of form.[3]

Quite early, however, Kant seems to have developed the view, which has created so many more difficulties than it resolves, that space and time are given to consciousness through outer and inner sense. Though still frequently spoken of as concepts, they are definitely referred to the receptive, non-spontaneous, side of the mind. This is at once a return to the *Dissertation* standpoint, and a decided modification of its teaching. It holds to the point of view of the *Dissertation* in so far as it regards them as sensuous, and departs from it in tracing them to receptivity.[4]

The passage quoted from the letter of 1772 to Herz may perhaps be connected with the stage revealed in the *Reflexionen* already cited. "Comparing, combining, and separating" may be the "some few principles of the understanding" there referred to. That, however, is doubtful, for the next stage in the development likewise resulted in a threefold division. This second stage finds varied expression in *Reflexionen*, ii. 483, 522, 528, 556-63. These, in so far as they agree, distinguish three classes of categories—of thesis, of analysis, and of synthesis. The first covers the categories of quality and modality, the second those of quantity, the third those of relation.

Reflexionen, ii. 528 is as follows :

[Thesis =] "The metaphysical concepts are, first, absolute: possibility and existence ; secondly, relative:
        (*a*) Unity and plurality: *omnitudo* and *particularitas*.
[Analysis =] (*b*) Limits: the first, the last: *infinitum, finitum.*
        [Anticipates the later category of limitation.]

---

[1] *Reflexionen*, ii. 513, cf. 502, 525-7.   [2] *Op. cit.* ii. 513.
[3] Cf. *op. cit.* ii. 537.   [4] Cf. above, p. 90 ff.

[Synthesis =]
(c) Connection: co-ordination: whole and part [anticipates the later category of reciprocity], simple and compound; subordination:
(1) Subject and predicate.
(2) Ground and consequence.

This, and the connected *Reflexionen* enumerated above, are of interest as proving that Kant's table of categories was in all essentials complete before the idea had occurred to him of further systematising it or of guaranteeing its completeness by reference to the logical classification of the forms of judgment. They also justify us in the belief that when Kant set himself to discover such a unifying principle the above list of categories and the existing logical classifications must have mutually influenced one another, each undergoing such modification as seemed necessary to render the parallelism complete. This, as we shall find, is what actually happened. The logical table, for instance, induced Kant to distinguish the categories of quality from those of modality, while numerous changes were made in the logical table itself in order that it might yield the categories required.

But the most important alteration, the introduction of the threefold division of each sub-heading, is not thus explicable, as exclusively due to one or other of the two factors. The adoption of this threefold arrangement in place of the dichotomous divisions of the logical classification and of the haphazard enumerations of Kant's own previous lists, seems to be due to the twofold circumstance that he had already distinguished three categories of synthesis or relation (always the most important for Kant), and that this sufficiently harmonised with the logical distinction between categorical, hypothetical, and disjunctive judgments. He then sought to modify the logical divisions by addition in each case of a third, and finding that this helped him to obtain the categories required, the threefold division became for him (as it remained for Hegel) an almost mystical dogma of transcendental philosophy.[1] In so far as it involved recognition that the hard and fast opposites of the traditional logic (such as the universal and the particular, the affirmative and the negative) are really aspects inseparably involved in every judgment and in all existence, it constituted an advance in the direction both of a deeper rationalism and of a more genuine empiricism. But in so far as it was due to the desire

[1] Only in one passage, *Rechtslehre*, i., Anhang 3, 2, cited by Adickes, *op. cit.* p. 13, does Kant so far depart from his own orthodoxy as to speak of the possibility of an *a priori* tetrachotomy. But he never wavers in the view that the completeness of a division cannot be guaranteed on empirical grounds.

to guarantee completeness on *a priori* grounds, and so was inspired by a persistent overestimate of our *a priori* powers, it has been decidedly harmful. Much of the useless "architectonic" of the *Critique* is due to this scholastic prejudice.

This fundamental alteration in the table of logical judgments is introduced with the naive assertion that "varieties of thought in judgments," unimportant in general logic, "may be of importance in the field of its pure *a priori* knowledge." In the *Critique of Judgment*[1] we find the following passage :

"It has been made a difficulty that my divisions in pure philosophy have almost always been threefold. But this lies in the nature of the case. If an *a priori* division is to be made, it must be either analytic, according to the principle of contradiction, and then it is always twofold (*quodlibet ens est aut A aut non A*); or else synthetic. And if in this latter case it is derived from *a priori* concepts (not as in mathematics from the *a priori* intuition corresponding to the concept) the division must necessarily be a trichotomy. For according to what is requisite for synthetic unity in general, there must be (1) a condition, (2) a conditioned, and (3) the concept which arises from the union of these two."

The last stage, as expressed in the *Critique*, was, as we have already noted, merely an application of his earlier position that all thinking is judging. This appreciation of the inseparable connection of the categories with the act of judging is sound in principle, and is pregnant with many of the most valuable results of the Critical teaching. But these fruitful consequences follow only upon the lines developed in the *transcendental* deduction. They are bound up with Kant's fundamental Copernican discovery that the categories are forms of *synthesis*, and accordingly express *functions* or *relations*. The categories can no longer be viewed, in the manner of the *Dissertation*,[2] as yielding concepts of *objects*. The view of the concept which we find in the *Dissertation* is, indeed, applied in the *Critique* to space and time—they are taken as in themselves intuitions, not as merely *forms* of intuition— but the categories are recognised as being of an altogether relational character. Though *a priori*, they are not, in and by themselves, complete objects of consciousness, and accordingly can reveal no object. They are *functions*, not *contents*. That, however, is to anticipate. We must first discharge, as briefly as possible, the ungrateful task of dwelling further upon the laboured, arbitrary, and self-contradictory character

---

[1] Introduction, § 9 *n.* Eng. trans. p. 41.
[2] §§ 4-6, 9.

of the detailed working out of the metaphysical deduction. The deduction is given in Sections II. and III.

Section II. The Logical Function of the Understanding in Judgment.[1]—Kant's introductory statement may here be noted. If, he says, we leave out of consideration the content of any judgment, and attend only to the mere form, we "find" that the function of thought in a judgment "can" be brought under four heads, each with three subdivisions. But Kant himself, in this same section, recognises in the frankest and most explicit manner, that the necessary distinctions are only to be obtained by taking account of the matter as well as of the form of judgments. And even after this contradiction is discounted, the term "find" may be allowed as legitimate only if the word "can" is correspondingly emphasised. The distinctions were not derived from any existing logic. They were reached only by the freest possible handling of the classifications currently employed. Examination of the table of judgments, and comparison of it with the table of categories, supply conclusive evidence that the former has been rearranged, in highly artificial fashion, so as to yield a more or less predetermined list of required categories.

1. **Quantity.**—Kant here frankly departs from the classification of judgments followed in formal logic; and the reason which he gives for so doing is in direct contradiction to his demand that only the form of judgment must be taken into account. The "quantity of knowledge" here referred to is determinable, not from the form, but only from the content of the judgment. Also, the statement that the singular judgment stands to the universal as unity to infinity (*Unendlichkeit*) is decidedly open to question. The universal is itself a form of unity, as Kant virtually admits in deriving, as he does, the category of unity from the universal judgment.

2. **Quality.**—Kant makes a similar modification in the logical treatment of quality, by distinguishing between affirmative and infinite judgments. The proposition, A is not-B, is to be viewed as neither affirmative nor negative. As the *content* of the predicate includes the infinite number of things that are not-B, the judgment is infinite. Kant, in a very artificial and somewhat arbitrary manner, contrives to define it as limitative in character, and so as sharing simultaneously in the nature both of affirmation and of negation. The way is thus prepared for the "discovery" of the category of limitation.

3. **Relation.** — Wolff, Baumgarten, Meier, Baumeister,

[1] A 70-6 = B 95-101.

Reimarus, and Lambert, with very minor differences, agree in the following division :[1]

$$
\text{Judgments}
\begin{cases}
\text{Simple} = \text{Categorical.} \\
\text{Complex}
\begin{cases}
\text{Copulative (\textit{i.e.} categorical with more} \\
\quad \text{than one subject or more than one} \\
\quad \text{predicate).} \\
\text{Hypothetical.} \\
\text{Disjunctive.}
\end{cases}
\end{cases}
$$

Kant omits the copulative judgment, and by ignoring the distinction between simple and complex judgments (which in Reimarus, and also less definitely in Wolff, is connected with the distinction between conditional and unconditional judgments) contrives to bring the remaining three types of judgment under the new heading of "relation." They had never before been thus co-ordinated, and had never before been subsumed under this particular title. It is by no means clear why such distinctions as those between simple and complex, conditioned and unconditioned, should be ignored, and why the copulative judgment should not be recognised as well as the hypothetical. Kant's criterion of importance and unimportance in the distinctions employed by the logicians of his day was wholly personal to himself; and, though hard to define, was certainly not dictated by any logic that is traceable to Aristotelian sources. His exposition is throughout controlled by foreknowledge of the particular categories which he desires to "discover."

4. **Modality.**—Neither Wolff nor Reimarus gives any account of modality.[2] Baumgarten classifies judgments as pure or modal (existing in *four* forms, necessity, contingency, possibility, impossibility). Baumeister and Thomasius also recognise four forms of modality. Meier distinguishes between pure judgment (*judicium purum*) and impure judgment (*judicium modale, modificatum, complexum qua copula*), but does not classify the forms of modality. Lambert alone[3] classifies judgments as "possible, actual (*wirklich*), necessary, and their opposite." But when Kant adopts this threefold division, the inclusion of actuality renders the general title "modality" inapplicable in its traditional sense. The expression of actuality in the assertoric judgment involves no adverbial modification of the predicate. Also, in its "affirmative" and "categorical" forms it has already been made to yield two other categories.

---

[1] Cf. Adickes, *Kant's Systematik*, p. 36 ff.
[2] Cf. Adickes, *op. cit.* p. 89 ff.
[3] *Organon*, § 137. Cited by Adickes.

Kant speaks of the problematic, the assertoric, and the apodictic forms of judgment as representing the stages through which knowledge passes in the process of its development.

"These three functions of modality are so many momenta of thought in general."

This statement has been eulogised by Caird,[1] as being an anticipation of the Hegelian dialectic. As a matter of fact, Kant's remark is irrelevant and misleading. The advance from consciousness of the problematic, through determination of it as actual to its explanation as necessary, represents only a psychological order in the mind of the individual. Logically, knowledge of the possible rests on and implies prior knowledge of the actual and of the necessities that constitute the actual.[2]

Section III.[3] The Categories or Pure Concepts of the Understanding.—The first three pages of this section, beginning "General logic abstracts," and concluding with the word "rest on the understanding," would seem to be a later interpolation. Embodying, as they do, some of the fundamental ideas of the transcendental deduction, they express Kant's final method of distinguishing between general and transcendental logic. But they are none the less out of harmony with the other sections of the metaphysical deduction. They are of the nature of an after-thought, even though that after-thought represents a more mature and adequate standpoint. In A 55-7, where Kant defines the distinction between general and transcendental logic, the latter is formulated in entire independence of all reference to pure intuition.[4] Kant, indeed, argues[5] that just as there are both pure and empirical intuitions, so there are both pure and empirical concepts. But there is no indication that he has yet realised the close interdependence of the two types of *a priori* elements. Even when he proceeds in A 62 to remark that the empirical employment of pure concepts is conditioned by the fact that objects are given in intuition, no special reference is made to "the manifold of pure *a priori* intuition." Now, however, Kant emphasises, as the fundamental characteristic of transcendental logic, its possession of a pure manifold through reference to which its pure concepts gain meaning. Thus not only does transcendental logic not abstract from the pure *a priori* concepts, it likewise possesses an *a priori* material.[6] It is in this twofold manner that it is now regarded as differing from formal logic.

The accounts given of the metaphysical deduction by

---

[1] i. p. 343 ff.   [2] Cf. below, p. 391 ff.   [3] A 76-79 = B 102 5.
[4] Cf. above, p. 171.   [5] A 55.   [6] Cf. also B 160.

Cohen,[1] Caird,[2] Riehl,[3] and Watson[4] are vitiated by failure to remark that this latter standpoint is a late development, and is out of keeping with the rest of the deduction. Riehl's exposition has, however, the merit of comparative consistency. He explicitly recognises the important consequence which at once follows from acceptance of this later view, namely, that it is by their implying space and time that the categories differ from the notions which determine the forms of judgment; in other words, that *the categories are actualised only as schemata.* The category of substance, for instance, differs from the merely logical notion of a propositional subject, in being the concept of that which is *always* a subject, and *never* a predicate; and such a conception has specific meaning for us only as the *permanent in time.* Logical subjects and predicates, quantitative relations apart, are interchangeable. The relation between them is the analytic relation of identity. The concept of subject, on the other hand, transcendentally viewed, that is, as a *category*, is the apprehension of what is *permanent*, in synthetic distinction from, and relation to, its changing attributes. In other words, the transcendental distinction between *substance* and *accidents* is substituted for that of *subject* and *predicate.* Similarly the logical relation of *ground* and *consequence*, conceived as expressive of logical identity, gives way to the synthetic temporal relation of *cause* and *effect*. And so with all the other pure forms. As categories, they are schemata. Kant has *virtually* recognised this by the names which he gives to the categories of relation. But the proper recognition of the necessary interdependence of the intuitional and conceptual forms came too late to prevent him from distinguishing between categories and schemata, and so from creating for himself the artificial difficulties of the section on schematism.

In A 82 Kant states that he intentionally omits definitions of the categories. He had good reason for so doing. The attempt would have landed him in manifold difficulties, since his views were not yet sufficiently ripe to allow of his perceiving the way of escape. In A 241 (omitted in second edition) Kant makes, however, the directly counter statement that definition of the categories is not possible, giving as his reason that, in isolation from the conditions of sensibility, they are merely logical functions, " without the slightest indication as to how they can possess meaning and objective validity."[5]

[1] *Kant's Theorie der Erfahrung*, 2nd ed. p. 257 ff.
[2] *The Critical Philosophy of Kant*, i. p. 327 ff.
[3] *Philosophischer Kriticismus*, 2nd ed. i. p. 484 ff.
[4] *Kant explained*, p. 124 ff.   [5] Cf. below, p. 198.

It cannot be too often repeated that the *Critique* is not a unitary work, but the patchwork record of twelve years of continuous development. Certain portions of the transcendental deduction, of which A 76-9 is one, represent the latest of all the many stages; and their teaching, when accepted, calls for a radical recasting of the metaphysical deduction. The bringing of the entire *Critique* into line with its maturest parts would have been an Herculean task; and it was one to which Kant, then fifty-seven years of age, was very rightly unwilling to sacrifice the time urgently needed for the writing of his other *Critiques*. The passage before us is one of the many interpolations by which Kant endeavoured to give an external unity to what, on close study, is found to be the plain record of successive and conflicting views. Meantime, in dealing with this passage, we are concerned only to note that if this later mode of defining transcendental logic be accepted, far-reaching modifications in Kant's Critical teaching have to be made. The other points developed in A 76-9 we discuss below [1] in their proper connection.

The same Function, etc.[2]—This passage has already been sufficiently commented upon.[3] Kant here expresses in quite inadequate fashion the standpoint of the transcendental deduction. The implication is that analytic and synthetic thinking are co-ordinate, one and the same faculty exercising, on these two levels, the same operations. The true Critical teaching is that synthetic thinking is alone fundamental, and that only by a regress upon it can judgments be adequately accounted for. This passage, like the preceding, may be of later origin than the main sections of the metaphysical deduction.

Term "Categories"[4] **borrowed from Aristotle.**—Cf. below, p. 198.

Table of Categories. Quantity.—Kant derives the category of unity from the universal,[5] and that of totality (*Allheit*)[6] from the singular. These derivations are extremely artificial. In *Reflexionen*, ii. 563, Kant takes the more natural line of identifying totality with the universal, and unity with the singular. Probably[7] the reason of Kant's change of view is the necessity of obtaining totality by combining unity with multiplicity. That can only be done if universality is thus equated with unity. Watson's explanation,[8] that Kant has reversed the order of the categories, seems to be erroneous.

Quality.—Cf. above, p. 192.

Relation.—The correlation of the categorical judgment

[1] P. 226.   [2] A 79=B 105.   [3] Cf. above, p. 177 ff.
[4] A 79-80.   [5] Cf. above, p. 192.   [6] Cf. B 111.
[7] Cf. Adickes, *Systematik*, pp. 42-3.   [8] *Kant Explained*, p. 128.

with the conception of substance and attribute is only possible [1] owing to Kant's neglect of the relational judgment and to the dominance in his logical teaching of the Aristotelian substance-attribute view of predication. The correlation is also open to question in that the relation of subject and predicate terms in a logical judgment is a reversible one. It is a long step from the merely grammatical subject to the conception of that which is always a subject and never a predicate.

Kant's identification of the category of community or reciprocity with the disjunctive judgment, though at first sight the most arbitrary of all, is not more so than many of the others. Its essential correctness has been insisted upon in recent logic by Sigwart, Bradley, and Bosanquet. In Kant's own personal view [2] co-ordination in the form of co-existence is only possible through reciprocal interaction. The relation of whole and part (the parts in their relations of reciprocal exclusion exhausting and constituting a genuine whole) thus becomes, in its application to actual existences, that of reciprocal causation. The reverse likewise holds; interaction is only possible between existences which together constitute a unity. [3] Kant returns to this point in *Note* 3, added in the second edition. [4] The objection which Kant there considers has been very pointedly stated by Schopenhauer.

"What real analogy is there between the problematical determination of a concept by disjunctive predicates and the thought of reciprocity? The two are indeed absolutely opposed, for in the disjunctive judgment the actual affirmation of one of the two alternative propositions is also necessarily the negation of the other; if, on the other hand, we think of two things in the relation of reciprocity, the affirmation of one is also necessarily the affirmation of the other, and *vice versa*." [5]

The answer to this criticism is on the lines suggested by Kant. The various judgments which constitute a disjunction do not, *when viewed as parts of the disjunction*, merely negate one another; they mutually presuppose one another in the total complex. Schopenhauer also fails to observe that in locating the part of a real whole in one part of space, we exclude it from all the others. [6]

Modality.—The existence of separate categories of modality

1 Cf. above, p. 37.   2 Cf. *Dissertation*, §§ 16 to 28, and below, p. 381 ff.
3 Cf. *Reflexionen*. ii. 795.   4 B 111-13.
5 *World as Will and Idea*, *Werke* (Frauenstädt), ii. p. 544; Eng. trans. ii. p. 61.
6 Cf. Stadler, *Grundsätze der reinen Erkenntnisstheorie* (1876), p. 122. Cf. also below, pp. 387-9.

seems highly doubtful. The concepts of the possible and of the probable may be viewed as derivative; the notion of existence does not seem to differ from that of reality; and necessity seems in ultimate analysis to reduce to the concept of ground and consequence. These are points which will be discussed later.[1]

Aristotle's ten categories[2] are enumerated by Kant in *Reflexionen*, ii. 522,[3] as: (1) *substantia, accidens*, (2) *qualitas*, (3) *quantitas*, (4) *relatio*, (5) *actio*, (6) *passio*, (7) *quando*, (8) *ubi*, (9) *situs*, (10) *habitus*; and the five post-predicaments as: *oppositum, prius, simul, motus, habere*. Eliminating *quando, ubi, situs, prius*, and *simul* as being modes of sensibility; *actio* and *passio* as being complex and derivative; and also omitting *habitus* (condition) and *habere*, as being too general and indefinite in meaning to constitute separate categories; we are then left with *substantia, qualitas, quantitas, relatio*, and *oppositum*. The most serious defect in this reduced list, from the Kantian point of view, is its omission of causality. It is, however, a curious coincidence that when substance is taken as a form of *relatio*, and *oppositum* as a form of quality, we are left with the three groups, quality, quantity, relation. Only modality is lacking to complete Kant's own fourfold grouping. None the less, as the study of Kant's *Reflexionen* sufficiently proves,[4] it was by an entirely different route that Kant travelled to his metaphysical deduction. Watson does not seem to have any ground for his contention[5] that the above modified list of Aristotle's categories "gave Kant his starting-point." It was there indeed, as the reference to Aristotle in his letter of 1772 to Herz shows, that he first looked for assistance, only, however, to be disappointed in his expectations.

Derivative concepts.[6]—Cf. above, pp. 66, 71-2.

I reserve this task for another occasion.[7]—Cf. A 204 = B 249; A 13; above, p. 66 ff., and below, pp. 379-80.

Definitions of categories omitted.[8]—Cf. above, pp. 195-6, and A 241 there cited; also below, pp. 339-42, 404-5.

Note 1.[9]—On this distinction between mathematical and dynamical categories cf. below, pp. 345-7, 510-11.

Note 2.[10]—This remark is inserted to meet a criticism which had been made by Johann Schulze,[11] and to which Kant in February 1784 had replied in terms almost identical with those of the present passage.

---

[1] Cf. below, p. 391 ff.   [2] A 81.   [3] Cf. *Prolegomena*, § 39.
[4] Cf. above, p. 186 ff.   [5] *Kant Explained*, p. 120
[6] A 81.   [7] A 82.   [8] A 82.
[9] B 110.   [10] B 110-11.   [11] Cf. below, pp. 199-200

"The third category certainly springs from the connection of the first and second, not, indeed, from their mere combination, but from a connection the possibility of which constitutes a concept that is a special category. For this reason the third category may not be applicable in instances in which the other two apply: *e.g. one* year, *many* years of future time, are real concepts, but the *totality* of future years, that is, the collective unity of a future eternity, conceived as entire (so to say, as completed), is something that cannot be thought. But even in those cases in which the third category is applicable, it always contains something more than the first and the second taken separately and together, namely the *derivation* of the second from the first, a process which is not always practicable. Necessity, for example, is nothing else than existence, *in so far as* it can be inferred from possibility. Community is the reciprocal *causality* of *substances* in respect of their determinations. But that determinations of one substance can be produced by another substance, is something that we may not simply assume; it is one of those connections without which there could be no reciprocal relation of things in space, and therefore no outer experience. In a word, I find that just as the conclusion of a syllogism indicates, in addition to the operations of understanding and judgment in the premisses, *a special operation peculiar to reason* . . ., so also the third category is a special, and in part original, concept. For instance, the concepts, *quantum, compositum, totum*, come under the categories unity, plurality, totality, but a *quantum* thought as *compositum* would not yield the concept of totality unless the concept of the *quantum* is thought as determinable through the *composition*, and in certain *quanta*, such as infinite space, that cannot be done."[1]

Kant's assertion that in certain cases the third category is not applicable is misleading. His proof of the validity of the category of reciprocity in the third *Analogy* really consists in showing that it is necessary to the apprehension of spatial co-existence;[2] and if, as Kant maintains, consciousness of space is necessary to consciousness of time, it is thereby proved to be involved in each and every act of consciousness. It is presupposed in the apprehension even of substantial existence and of causal sequence. His proof that it is a unique category, distinct from the mere combination of the categories of substance and causality, does not, therefore, assume what his words in the above letter would seem to imply, that it is only occasionally employed. The same remark holds in regard to totality; it is presupposed even in the apprehension of a single year. Kant's references, both here and in other parts of the *Critique*,[3] to totality in its bearing upon the conception of infinitude, reveal considerable

---

[1] *W.* x. p. 344-5.   [2] Cf. below, p. 382 ff.
[3] Cf. below, pp. 433-4, 451, 480, 529, 559-60.

lack of clearness as to the relation in which it stands to the Idea of the unconditioned. Sometimes, as in this letter, he would seem to be identifying them; elsewhere this confusion is avoided. In B 111 totality is defined as multiplicity regarded as unity, and in A 142-3 = B 182 its schema is defined as number. (The identification of totality with number has led Kant to say in B 111 that number is not applicable in the representation of the infinite, a much more questionable assertion than that of the letter above quoted.) The statement that necessity is existence in so far as it can be inferred from possibility, or that it is existence given through possibility, is similarly misleading. Kant's true position is that all three are necessary to the conception of any one of the three.

Thus Kant's reply to Schulze, alike in his letter and in *Note* 2, fails to indicate with any real adequacy the true bearing of Critical teaching in this matter; and consequently fails to reveal the full force of his position. Only in terms of totality can unity and plurality be apprehended; only through the reciprocal relations which determine co-existence can we acquire consciousness of either permanence or sequence; only in terms of necessity can either existence or possibility be defined. The third category is not derived from a prior knowledge of the subordinate categories. It represents in each case a higher complex within which alone the simpler relations defined by the simpler concepts can exist or have meaning.

B 113-16, § 12.—This section, of no intrinsic importance, is an example of Kant's loving devotion to this "architectonic." His reasoning is extremely artificial, especially in its attempt to connect "unity, truth, and perfection" with the three categories of quantity. The *Reflexionen* show how greatly Kant was preoccupied with these three concepts, seeking either to base a table of categories upon them (B. Erdmann's interpretation), or to reduce them to categories (Adickes' interpretation). For some time Kant himself ranked with those who[1] "incautiously made these criteria of thought to be properties of the things in themselves." In *Reflexionen*, ii. 903,[2] we find the following statement: "Unity (connection, agreement), truth (quality), completeness (quantity)." In ii. 916[3] Kant makes trial to connect them, as conceptions of possibility, with the categories of relation. In ii. 911 and 912 the later view, that they are logical in character and function, appears, but leads to their being set in relation to the three faculties of understanding, judgment, and reason. This is

---

[1] B 114.   [2] Cf. 904-5.   [3] Cf. 907-10.

conjectured by B. Erdmann to have been Kant's view at the time of the first edition.   ii. 915, 919, 920 present the view expounded in the section before us.[1]   Erdmann[2] remarks that in this section Kant " is settling accounts with certain thoughts which in the 'seventies had yielded suggestions for the transformation of ontology into the transcendental analytic."

[1] Cf. B. Erdmann, *Mittheilungen* in *Phil. Monatshefte*, 1884, p. 80, and Adickes, *Systematik*, pp. 55-9.

[2] *Reflexionen*, ii. p. 252 *n.*

CHAPTER II

DEDUCTION OF THE PURE CONCEPTS OF THE UNDERSTANDING

First edition Subjective and Objective Deductions.—In dealing with the transcendental deduction, as given in the first edition, we can make use of the masterly and convincing analysis which Vaihinger [1] (building upon Adickes' previous results, but developing an independent and quite original interpretation) has given of its inconsecutive and strangely bewildering argumentation. Vaihinger's analysis is an excellent example of detective genius in the field of scholarship. From internal evidence, circumstantially supported by the *Reflexionen* and *Lose Blätter*, he is able to prove that the deduction is composed of manuscripts, externally pieced together, and representing no less than four distinct stages in the slow and gradual development of Kant's views. Like geological deposits, they remain to record the processes by which the final result has come to be. Though they do not in their present setting represent the correct chronological order, that may be determined once the proper clues to their disentanglement have been duly discovered. That discovery is itself, however, no easy task ; for the unexpected, while lending colour and incident to the commentator's enterprise, baffles his natural expectations at every turn. The first stage is one in which Kant *dispenses* with the categories, and in which, when they are referred to, they are taken as applying *to things in themselves*. The last stage, worked out, as there is ground for believing, in the haste and excitement of the final revision, is not represented in the *Prolegomena* or in the second edition of the *Critique*, the author retracing his steps and resuming the standpoint of the stage which preceded it. The fortunate accident of Kant's having jotted down upon the back of a dated paper the record of

[1] "Die transcendentale Deduktion der Kategorien" in the *Gedenkschrift für Rudolf Haym*. Published separately in 1902

his passing thought (one of the few *Lose Blätter* that are thus datable) is the culminating incident in this philosophical drama. It felicitously serves as a keystone in the body of evidence supported by general reasoning.

Before becoming acquainted with Vaihinger's analysis I had observed Kant's ascription to empirical concepts of the functions elsewhere allotted to the categories, but had been hopelessly puzzled as to how such teaching could be fitted into his general system. Vaihinger's view of it as a pre-Critical survival would seem to be the only possible satisfactory solution. For the view which I have taken of Kant's doctrine of the transcendental object as also pre-Critical, and for its employment as a clue to the dating of passages, I am myself alone responsible.

The order of my exposition will be as follows : [1]

I. Enumeration, in chronological order, of the four stages which compose the deduction of the first edition, and citation of the passages which represent each separate stage.

II. Detailed analysis, again in chronological order, of each successive stage, with exposition of the views which it embodies.

III. Examination of the evidence yielded by the *Reflexionen* and *Lose Blätter* in support of the above analysis.

IV. Connected statement and discussion of the total argument of the deduction.

I. Enumeration of the Four Stages

(1) FIRST STAGE: THAT OF THE TRANSCENDENTAL OBJECT, WITHOUT CO-OPERATION OF THE CATEGORIES.— This stage is represented by [2]: (*a*) II. 3 (from beginning of the third paragraph to end of 3) = A 104-10; (*b*) I. § 13 (the entire section) = A 84-92 (retained in second edition as B 116-24). *a* discusses the problem of the reference of sensations to an object, *b* that of the objective validity of the categories. *b* is therefore transitional to the second stage.

(2) SECOND STAGE: THAT OF THE CATEGORIES, WITHOUT CO-OPERATION OF THE PRODUCTIVE IMAGINATION.— This stage is represented by: (*a*) I. [§ 14] (with the exception of its concluding paragraph) = A 92-4 (retained in second edition as B 124-7); (*b*) II. (the first four paragraphs) = A 95-7; (*c*) II. 4 (the entire section) = A 110-14.

---

[1] Readers who are not immediately interested in the analysis of the text or in the history of Kant's earlier semi-Critical views may omit pp. 203-34, with exception of pp. 204-19, on Kant's doctrine of the transcendental object, which should be read.

[2] The reader is recommended to mark off the passages in a copy of the *Critique*.

(3) THIRD STAGE: THAT OF THE PRODUCTIVE IMAGINA-
TION, WITHOUT MENTION OF THE THREEFOLD TRANSCEND-
ENTAL SYNTHESIS.—This stage is represented by (a) III.β
(from beginning of seventh paragraph to end of twelfth)
= A 119-23; (b) III.α (from beginning of third paragraph
to end of sixth) = A 116-19; (c) I. § 14 (Concluding paragraph)
= A 94-5; (d) III.δ (from beginning of sixteenth paragraph
to end of section preceding summary) = A 126-8; (e)
S(ummary) (in conclusion to III.) = A 128-30; (f) III.γ
(from beginning of thirteenth paragraph to end of fifteenth)
= A 123-6; (g) I(ntroduction) (from beginning of section to
end of second paragraph) = A 115-16; (h) § 10 T(ransitional
to the fourth stage) = A 76-9 (retained as B 102-4).

(4) FOURTH STAGE: THAT OF THE THREEFOLD TRAN-
SCENDENTAL SYNTHESIS.—This stage is represented by: (a)
II. 1-3 (from opening of 1 to end of second paragraph in 3)
= A 98-104; (b) II. (the two paragraphs immediately pre-
ceding a) = A 97-8.

II. Detailed Analysis of the Four Stages

First Stage.—A 104-10; A 84-92 (B 116-24).

A 104-10; II. § 3.—This is the one passage in the *Critique*
in which Kant explicitly defines his doctrine of the " transcendental object"; and careful examination of the text shows
that by it he means the *thing in itself*, conceived as being the
object of our representations. Such teaching is, of course,
thoroughly un-Critical; and as I shall try to show, this was
very early realised by Kant himself. The passages in which
the phrase "transcendental object" occurs are, like the section
before us, in every instance of early origin. It is significant
that the transcendental object is not again referred to in the
deduction of the first edition.[1] Though it reappears in the
chapter on phenomena and noumena, it does so in a passage
which Kant excised in the second edition. The paragraphs
which he then substituted make no mention of it. The doctrine
is of frequent occurrence in the *Dialectic*, and combines with
other independent evidence to show that the larger part of
the *Dialectic* is of early origin. That the doctrine of the
transcendental object is thus a pre-Critical or semi-Critical
survival has, so far as I am aware, not hitherto been observed
by any writer upon Kant. It has invariably been interpreted
in the light of the sections in which it does not occur, and,
as thus toned down and tempered to something altogether

---

[1] Its first occurrence in the *Critique* is in the *Aesthetic* A 46 = B 63. It
there signifies the thing in itself

different from what it really stands for, has been taken as an essential and characteristic tenet of the Critical philosophy. It was in the course of an attempt to interpret Kant's entire argument in the light of his doctrine of the transcendental object that I first came to detect its absence from all his later utterances. But it is important to recognise that the difficulties which would result from its retention are quite insuperable, and would by themselves, even in the absence of all external evidence of Kant's rejection of it, compel us to regard it as a survival of pre-Critical thinking. As Vaihinger does not seem to have detected the un-Critical character of this doctrine, it is the more significant that he should, on other grounds, have felt constrained to regard the passage in which it is expounded as embodying the earliest stage in the development of the deduction. He would seem to continue in the orthodox view so far as to hold that though the doctrine of the transcendental object is here stated in pre-Critical terms, it was permanently retained by Kant in altered form.

The doctrine of the transcendental object, as here expounded, is as follows :

"Appearances are themselves nothing but sensuous representations which must not be taken as capable of existing in themselves (*an sich*) with exactly the same character (*in ebenderselben Art*) outside our power of representation." [1]

These sense-representations are our only possible representations, and when we speak of an object corresponding to them, we must be conceiving an object in general, equal to x.

"They have their object, but an object which can never be intuited by us, and which may therefore be named the non-empirical, *i.e.* transcendental object $= x$." [2]

This object is conceived as being that which prevents our representations from occurring at haphazard, necessitating their order in such manner that, manifold and varied as they may be, they can yet be self-consistent in their several groupings, and so possess that unity which is essential to the concept of an object.

"The pure concept of this transcendental object, which in fact throughout all our knowledge is always one and the same, is that which can alone confer upon all our empirical concepts relation in general to an object, *i.e.* objective reality." [3]

---

[1] A 104.   [2] A 109.   [3] A 109.

What renders this doctrine impossible of permanent retention was that it allowed of no objective existence mediate between the merely subjective and the thing in itself. On such teaching there is no room for the empirical object; and immediately upon the recognition of that latter phenomenal form of existence in space, Kant was constrained to recognise that it is in the empirical object, not in the thing in itself, that the contents of our representations are grounded and unified. Any other view must involve the application of the categories, especially those of substance and causality, to the thing in itself. The entire empirical world has still to be conceived as grounded in the non-empirical, but that is a very different contention from the thesis that the thing in itself is the object and the sole object of our representations. The doctrine of the transcendental object has thus a twofold defect: it advocates an extreme subjectivism, and yet at the same time applies the categories to the thing in itself.

But the latter consequence is one which could not, at the stage represented by this section, be appreciated by Kant. For, as we shall find, he is endeavouring to solve the problem of the reference of sense-representation to an object without assumption of *a priori* categories. It is in *empirical* concepts, conditioned only by a transcendental apperception, that he professes to discover the grounds and conditions of this objective reference. Let us follow Kant's argument in detail. The section opens[1] with what may be a reference to the *Aesthetic*, and proceeds to deal with the first of the two problems cited in the 1772 letter to Herz[2]—how *sense*-representations stand related to their object. The exact terms in which this question was there formulated should be noted.

"I propounded to myself this question: on what ground rests the relation of that in us which we name representation (*Vorstellung*) to the object. If the representation contains only the mode in which the subject is affected by the object, it is easily understood how it should accord (*gemäss sei*) with that object as an effect with its cause, and how [therefore] this determination of our mind should be able to *represent* something, *i.e.* have an object. The passive or sensuous representations have thus a comprehensible (*begreifliche*) relation to objects, and the principles, which are borrowed from the nature of our soul, have a comprehensible validity for all things in so far as they are to be objects of the senses."[3]

Thus in 1772 there was here no real problem for Kant. The assumed fact, that our representations are generated in

---

[1] A 104.   [2] Cf. above, p. 28; below, pp. 219-20.   [3] *W.* x. pp. 124-5.

us by the action of independent existences, is taken as sufficient explanation of their being referred to objects.

The section of the *Critique* under consideration shows that Kant had come to realise the inadequacy of this explanation quite early, indeed prior to his solution of the second and further question which in that same letter is spoken of as "the key to the whole secret" of metaphysics. On what grounds, he now asks, is a subjective idea, *even though it be a sense impression*, capable of yielding consciousness of an object? In the letter to Herz the use of the term representation (*Vorstellung*) undoubtedly helped to conceal this problem. It is now emphasised that appearances are nothing but sense representations, and must never be regarded as objects capable of existing in themselves, with exactly the same character, outside our power of representation. Now also Kant employs, in place of the phrase "in accord with," the much more definite term "corresponding to." He points out that when we speak of an object *corresponding* to our knowledge, we imply that it is distinct from that knowledge. Consciousness of such an object must therefore be acquired from some other source than the given impressions. In other words, Kant is now prepared to withdraw his statement that "the passive or sensuous representations have an [easily] comprehensible relation to objects." In and by themselves they are purely subjective, and can involve no such concept. The latter is a thought (*Gedanke*), a concept (*Begriff*), additional to, and distinct from, the given impressions. Its possibility, as regards both origin[1] and validity, must be "deduced."

There then results this first and very peculiar form of the transcendental deduction. That part of it which persists in the successive stages rests upon an explicitly developed distinction between empirical and transcendental apperception. Kant teaches, in agreement with Hume, though, as we may believe, independently of his direct influence, that there is no single empirical state of the self which is constant throughout experience.[2]

"The consciousness of the self, according to the determinations of our state in inner perception, is merely empirical, and always in process of change. . . . That which has to be represented as of necessity numerically identical cannot be thought as such through empirical data. There must be a condition which precedes all experience, and renders experience itself possible, if a transcendental pre-supposition of this kind is to be rendered valid. . . . This pure,

---

[1] Cf. below, pp. 209-10.
[2] Hume's view of the self is not developed in the *Enquiry*, and is not mentioned by Beattie.

original, unchangeable consciousness I shall name transcendental apperception." [1]

Kant would seem to have first developed this view in a quite crude form. The consciousness of the self, he seems to have held, consists in its awareness of its own unceasing activities. As consciousness of *activity*, it is entirely distinct in nature and in origin from all apprehension of sense impressions.[2] This teaching is a natural extension of the doctrine of the *Dissertation*,[3] that such pure notions as those of possibility, existence, necessity, substance, cause, are "acquired by attending to the actions of the mind on the occasion of experience." Kant would very naturally hold that consciousness of the identity and unity of the self is obtained in a similar manner. Such, indeed, is the teaching of the section before us.

"No knowledge can take place in us . . . without that unity of consciousness which precedes all data of intuitions, and in relation to which all representation of objects is alone possible." [4] "It is precisely this transcendental apperception that constructs out of (*macht aus*) all possible appearances, which are capable of coexisting in one experience, a connection of all these representations according to laws. For this unity of consciousness would be impossible if the mind could not become conscious, in the knowledge of the manifold, of the identity of the function whereby it combines it synthetically in one knowledge. Thus the mind's original and necessary consciousness of the identity of itself is at the same time a consciousness of an equally necessary unity of the synthesis of all appearances according to concepts, *i.e.* according to rules. . . . For the mind could not possibly think the identity of itself in the manifold of its representations, and indeed *a priori*, if it did not have before its eyes the identity of its action. . . ." [5]

That is to say, the self is the sole source of all unity. As a pure and original unity it precedes experience; to its synthetic activities all conceptual unity is due; and by reflection upon the constancy of these activities it comes to consciousness of its own identity.

" . . . even the purest objective unity, namely that of the *a priori* concepts (space and time), is possible only through relation

---

[1] A 107.

[2] Cf. *Reflexionen*, ii. 952 (belonging, as Erdmann notes, to the earliest Critical period): "Appearances are representations whereby we are affected. The representation of our free self-activity (*Selbsttätigkeit*) does not involve affection, and accordingly is not appearance, but apperception." Cf. below, p. 296.

[3] § 8. Cf. above, pp. l-ii; below, pp. 243, 260-3, 272-3, 327-8, 473-7, 515.

[4] A 107. It is significant that Kant in A 107 uses, in reference to apperception, the very unusual phrase, "*unwandelbares Bewusstsein*."

[5] A 108.

of the intuitions to [transcendental apperception]. The numerical unity of this apperception is therefore the *a priori* condition of all concepts, just as the manifoldness of space and of time is of the intuitions of sensibility."[1]

To this consciousness of the abiding unity of the self Kant also traces the notion of the transcendental object. The latter, he would seem to argue, is formed by analogy from the former.

"This object is nothing else than the subjective representation (of the subject) itself, but made general, for I am the original of all objects."[2] "The mind, through its original and underived thinking, is itself the pattern (*Urbild*) of such a synthesis."[3] "I would not represent anything as outside me, and so make [subjective] appearances into objective experience if the representations were not related to something which is parallel to my ego, and so in that way referred by me to another subject."[4]

These quotations from the *Lose Blätter* would seem to contain the key to Kant's extremely enigmatic statement in A 105, that "the unity which the object makes necessary can be nothing else than the formal unity of consciousness in its synthesis of the manifold of its representations," and again in A 109, that "this relation [of representations to an object] is nothing else than the necessary unity of consciousness."[5] But this does not complete the sum-total of the functions which Kant is at this stage prepared to assign to apperception. It mediates our consciousness of the transcendental object in still another manner, namely, by rendering possible the formation of the *empirical* concepts which unify and direct its synthetic activities. This is, indeed, the feature in which this form of the deduction diverges most radically from all later positions. Space and time are, it would seem, regarded as being the sole *a priori* concepts.[6] The instruments through which the unity of apperception acts, and through which the thought of an object becomes possible, are *empirical* concepts. Such general concepts as "body" or "triangle" serve as rules constraining the synthetic processes of apprehension and

[1] A 107.
[2] Reicke, *Lose Blätter*, p. 19. The bearing and date of this passage is discussed below, p. 233.
[3] *Op. cit.* p. 20.
[4] *Op. cit.* p. 22 (written on a letter dated May 20, 1775).
[5] This last statement cannot possibly be taken literally. In view of the manner in which the transcendental object is spoken of elsewhere in this section, and also in the *Dialectic*, we must regard it as standing for an independent existence, and the relation of representations to it as being, therefore, something else than simply the unity of consciousness.
[6] It may be observed that when Kant in A 107, quoted above, refers to "*a priori* concepts," he adds in explanation, and within brackets, "space and time."

reproduction to take place in such unitary fashion as is required for unitary consciousness. The notion of objectivity is specified in terms of the necessities which these empirical concepts thus impose.

"We think a triangle as object in so far as we are conscious of the combination of three straight lines according to a rule by which such an intuition can at all times be generated. This unity of rule determines the whole manifold and limits it to conditions which make the unity of apperception possible; and the concept of this unity [of rule] is the representation of the object. . . . All knowledge demands a concept, . . . and a concept is always, as regards its form, something general, something that serves as a rule. Thus the concept of body serves as a rule to our knowledge of outer appearances, in accordance with the unity of the manifold which is thought through it. . . . The concept of body necessitates . . . the representation of extension, and therewith of impenetrability, shape, etc." [1]

Such is the manner in which Kant accounts for our concept of the transcendental object. It consists of two main elements: first, the notion of an unknown x, to which representations may be referred; and secondly, the consciousness of this x as exercising compulsion upon the order of our thinking. The former notion is framed on the pattern of the transcendental subject; it is conceived as another but unknown subject. The consciousness of it as a source of external necessity is mediated by the empirical concepts which transcendental apperception also makes possible. And from this explanation of the *origin* of the concept of the transcendental object Kant derives the proof of its *validity*.[2] It is indispensable for the realisation by the unitary self of a unitary consciousness.

"This relation [of representations to an object] is nothing else than the necessary unity of consciousness, and therefore also of the synthesis of the manifold, by a common (*gemeinschaftlich*) functioning of the mind, which unites it in one representation." [3]

Through instruments empirical in origin, and subjectively necessary, the notion of an objective necessity is rendered possible to the mind.

It is not surprising that Kant did not permanently hold to this view of the empirical concept. The objections are obvious. Such a view of the function of general concepts renders unintelligible their own first formation. For as they

---

[1] A 105-6.
[2] The actual nature of Kant's teaching as to the origin and constitution of the notion of the transcendental object is largely masked by the fact that he places this proof of its validity so prominently in the foreground. The general nature of this proof is, of course, identical with that of his later positions.
[3] A 109.

are empirical, they can only be acquired by conscious processes that do not involve them. That is to say, consciousness of objects follows upon a prior consciousness in and through which concepts, such as that of body, are discovered and formed. Yet, as the argument claims, general concepts are the indispensable conditions of unitary consciousness. How through a consciousness that is not yet unified can general concepts be formed? Also it is difficult to see how empirical concepts can be viewed as directly conditioned by, and as immediately due to, anything so general as pure apperception. These objections Kant must have come very quickly to recognise. This was the first part of his teaching to be modified. In the immediately succeeding stage,[1] so far as the stages can be reconstructed from the survivals in the *Critique*, the empirical concepts are displaced once and for all by the *a priori* categories.

The only sentences which can be regarded as possibly conflicting with the above interpretation are those two (in the second last and in the last paragraphs) in which the phrase "rules *a priori*" occurs. Even granting (what is at least questionable as regards the first) that the words are meant to be taken together, it does not follow that Kant is here speaking of categories. For contrary to his usual teaching he speaks of the concept of body as a source of necessity. If so, it may well, with equal looseness, be spoken of as *a priori*. That is indeed done, by implication, in the second and third paragraphs, where he speaks of a rule (referring to "body and triangle") as making the synthesis of reproduction "*a priori* necessary." Such assertions are completely, inconsistent with Kant's Critical teaching, but so is the entire section.

The setting in which the passage before us occurs has its own special interest.[2] When Kant, as it would seem, on the very eve of the publication of the *Critique*, developed the doctrine of a threefold synthesis culminating in a "synthesis of recognition in the concept," he must have bethought himself of this earlier position, and have completed his subjective deduction by incorporation, probably with occasional alterations of phrasing, of the older manuscript. This procedure has bewildered even the most discerning among Kant's readers; but now, thanks to Vaihinger's convincing analysis, it may be welcomed as of illuminating interest in the historical study of Kant's development.

I may here draw attention to the two important respects

[1] As in the *Lose Blätter*. Cf. below, p. 233.
[2] Cf. below, pp. 227, 233-4, 268-9.

in which the positions revealed in this section continued to influence Kant's later teaching : namely, in the emphasis laid upon the transcendental unity of apperception, and in the view of objectivity as involving the thought of the thing in itself.

The excessive emphasis which in this first stage is laid upon the transcendental unity of apperception persists throughout the later forms of the deduction, and, as I shall try to show, does so to the detriment of the argument. Though its functions are considerably diminished, they are still exaggerated ; this is perhaps in part due to its having been in this early stage regarded as in and by itself the sole ultimate ground of unitary experience. There were, however, two other influences at work. Kant continued to employ the terminology of his earlier view, and in his less watchful moments was betrayed thereby into conflict with his considered teaching. But even more important was the influence of his personal convictions. He was irrevocably committed in his own private thinking to a belief in the spiritual and abiding character of the self ; and this belief frequently colours, in illegitimate ways, the expression of his views. This is especially evident in some of the alterations[1] of the second edition, written as they were at a time when he was chiefly preoccupied with moral problems.

As regards the other factor, the view adopted in regard to the nature of objectivity, there is ample evidence that even after the empirical concepts had been displaced by the categories Kant still continued for some time (possibly for several years in the earlier and middle 'seventies) to hold to his doctrine of the transcendental object. Passages which expound it in this later form occur in the *Note on Amphiboly* and throughout the *Dialectic*.[2] That this may not be taken for his final teaching is equally certain. The entire first layer of the deduction of the first edition, all the relevant passages in the chapter on phenomena and noumena, and some of those in the *Dialectic*, were omitted in the second edition ; and nowhere, either in the other portions of the deduction of the first edition, or in the deduction of the second edition, or in any passages added elsewhere in the second edition, is such teaching to be found.

A brief statement of Kant's doctrine of the transcendental object *in its later form* seems advisable at this point ; it is required in order to complete and to confirm the interpreta-

---

[1] Cf. below, pp. 322-8 ; also pp. 260-3.
[2] As above noted (p. 204 *n.*) it also occurs in the *Aesthetic* (A 46 = B 63), as signifying the thing in itself.

tion which I have given of the earlier exposition. At the same time I shall endeavour to show that the sections in which the doctrine occurs, though later than the first layer of the deduction of the first edition, are all of comparatively early origin, and that they reveal not the least trace of Kant's more mature, phenomenalist view of the empirical world in space.

We may begin with the passages in the chapter on phenomena and noumena. The meaning in which the term transcendental is employed is there made sufficiently clear.

"The transcendental employment of a concept in any principle consists in its being referred to things *in general and in themselves.*" [1]

That is to say, the term transcendental, as used in the phrase transcendental object, is not employed in any sense which would oppose it to the transcendent. In so far as the thought of the thing in itself is a necessary ingredient in the concept of objectivity, it is a condition of apperception, and therefore of possible experience; in other words, *the thought of a transcendent object is one of the transcendental conditions of our experience.* As Kant is constantly interchanging the terms transcendent and transcendental, such an explanation of the phrase is perhaps superfluous; but if any is called for, the above would seem to suffice. As we shall have occasion to observe,[2] other factors besides the *a priori* must be reckoned among the conditions of experience; and to both types of conditions Kant applies the epithet transcendental.

In the chapter on phenomena and noumena Kant enquires at considerable length whether the categories (meaning, of course, the pure forms of understanding, not their schematised correlates) allow of transcendental (*i.e.* transcendent) employment. The passages in which this discussion occurs [3] would seem, however, to be highly composite; many paragraphs, or portions of paragraphs, are of much later date than others. We may therefore limit our attention to those in which the phrase transcendental object is actually employed, *i.e.* to those which appear only in the first edition.

"All our representations are referred by the understanding to some object; and since appearances are merely representations, the understanding refers them to a *something* as the object of sensuous intuition. But this something, thus conceived (*in so fern*), is only the transcendental object; and by that is meant a something $= x$, of which we know, and with the present constitution of our understanding can know, nothing whatsoever, but which, as a correlate of the unity of apperception, can serve only for the unity

---

[1] A 238 = B 298.   [2] Cf. below, p. 238.   [3] A 238 ff. = B 298 ff.

of the manifold in sensuous intuition. By means of this unity the understanding combines the manifold into the concept of an object. This transcendental object cannot be separated from the sense data, for nothing then remains over through which it might be thought. Consequently it is not in itself an object of knowledge, but only the representation of appearances under the concept of an object in general which is determinable through the manifold of those appearances. Precisely for this reason also the categories do not represent a special object given to the understanding alone, but only serve to specify the transcendental object (the concept of something in general) through that which is given in sensibility, in order thereby to know appearances empirically under concepts of objects."[1] "The object to which I relate appearance in general is the transcendental object, *i.e.* the completely indeterminate thought of *something* in general. This cannot be entitled the *noumenon* [*i.e.* the thing in itself more specifically determined as being the object of a purely intelligible intuition];[2] for I know nothing of what it is in itself, and have no concept of it save as the object of a sensuous intuition in general, and so as being one and the same for all appearances."[3]

Otherwise stated, Kant's teaching is as follows. The thought of the thing in itself remains altogether indeterminate; it does not *specify* its object, and therefore yields no knowledge of it; none the less it is a necessary ingredient in the concept of objectivity as such. The object as specified in terms of sense is *mere representation*; the object as genuinely objective can only be thought. The correlate of the unity of apperception is the thought of the thing in itself. This is what Kant is really asserting, though in a hesitating manner which would seem to indicate that he is himself already more or less conscious of its unsatisfactory and un-Critical character.

The phrase transcendental object occurs once in the second *Analogy*[4] and twice in the *Note on Amphiboly*.[5] The passage in the second *Analogy* may very well, in view of the kind of subjectivism which it expounds, be of early date of writing. By transcendental object Kant there quite obviously means the thing in itself. From the first reference in the *Note on Amphiboly* no definite conclusions can be drawn. The argument is too closely bound up with his criticism of Leibniz to allow of his own independent standpoint being properly developed. There is, however, nothing in it which compels us to regard it as of late origin; and quite evidently Kant here means by the transcendental object the thing in itself. The phrase *substantia phaenomenon* is not, as might at first sight seem, equivalent to the empirical object of Kant's

---

[1] A 250-1.   [2] Cf. below, p. 407 ff.   [3] A 253.
[4] A 191 = B 236.   [5] A 277-8 = B 333-4; A 288 = B 344.

phenomenalist teaching. It is an adaptation of Leibnizian phraseology.[1] The second reference in the *Note on Amphiboly* occurs in a passage which may perhaps be of later origin;[2] but the transcendental object is there mentioned only in order to afford opportunity for the statements that it cannot be thought through any of the categories, that we are completely ignorant whether it is within or without us, and whether if sensibility were removed it would vanish or remain, and that it can therefore serve only as a limiting concept. We here observe it in the very process of being eliminated. As we shall find, Kant's teaching is ill-expressed in the sections on *Amphiboly*; so much so that they could not be recast without seriously disturbing the balance of his architectonic. They were therefore allowed to remain unaltered in the second edition.

We may now pass to the *Dialectic*. The subjectivist doctrine of the transcendental object is there expressed in a much more uncompromising manner. Let us first consider the references to the transcendental object in the *Paralogisms* and in the subsequent *Reflection*. The phrase transcendental object occurs twice in the second *Paralogism*, once in the third, twice in the fourth, and three times in the *Reflection*;[3] and in all these cases there is not the least uncertainty as to its denotation. It is taken as equivalent to the thing in itself, and is expounded as a necessary ingredient in the consciousness of our subjective representations as noumenally grounded.

"What matter may be as a thing in itself (transcendental object) is completely unknown to us, though, owing to its being represented as something external, its permanence as appearance can indeed be observed."[4]   "We can indeed admit that something, which may be (in the transcendental[5] sense) 'outside us,' is the cause of our outer intuitions, but this is not the object of which we are thinking in the representations of matter and of corporeal things, for these are merely appearances, *i.e.* mere kinds of representation which are never to be met with save in us, and whose actuality depends on immediate consciousness just as does the consciousness of my own thoughts. The transcendental object is equally unknown in respect to inner and to outer intuition."[6]

---

[1] Cf. *mundus phaenomenon* in A 272 = B 328.

[2] It is so dated by Adickes (K. p. 272 *n.*), owing to a single reference to schemata in A 286 = B 342.

[3] A 358 and A 361 (cf. A 355); A 366; A 372 and A 379-80; A 390-1, A 393, and A 394.

[4] A 366.

[5] "Transcendental" here means "transcendent." Cf. A 379.

[6] A 372; so also in A 613-14 = B 641-2.

Here Kant at one and the same time distinguishes between, and confounds together, representation and its empirical object. What is alone clear is that by the transcendental object he means simply the thing in itself viewed as the cause of our sensations.   In A 358 it is used in a wider sense as also comprehending the noumenal conditions which underlie the conscious subject.

". . . this something which underlies the outer appearances and which so affects our sense that it obtains the representations of space, matter, shape, etc., this something viewed as noumenon (or better as transcendental object) might also at the same time be the subject that does our thinking. . . ."

Similarly in A 379-80:

"Though the I, as represented through inner sense in time, and objects in space outside me, are specifically quite distinct appearances, they are not for that reason thought as being different things. Neither the transcendental object which underlies outer appearances, nor that which underlies inner intuition, is in itself either matter or a thinking being, but is a ground (to us unknown) of the appearances which supply to us the empirical concepts of the former as well as of the latter kind."

The references in the *Reflection on the Paralogisms* are of the same general character and are equally definite.[1]   A 390-1 has special interest in that it explicitly states that to appearances, taken as Kant invariably takes them throughout the *Paralogisms* in the first edition as mere subjective representations, the category of causality, and therefore by implication the category of substance, is inapplicable.

"No one could dream of asserting that that which he has once come to recognise as mere representation is an outer cause."

We may now turn to the passages in the chapter on the *Antinomies*.

"The non-sensuous cause of our representations is completely unknown to us, and therefore we cannot intuit it as object. . . . We may, however, entitle the purely intelligible cause of appearances in general the transcendental object. . . . To this transcendental object we can ascribe the whole extent and connection of our possible perceptions. . . ."[2]

Appearances can be regarded as real only to the extent to which they are actually experienced.   Otherwise they exist only in some unknown noumenal form of which we can

---

[1] The passage in A 393 is given below, p. 464.
[2] A 494 = B 522.   Cf. A 492 = B 521: "The true self (*das eigentliche Selbst*) as it exists in itself, *i.e.* the transcendental subject."

acquire no definite concept, and which is therefore really nothing to us. This, Kant declares, is true even of that immemorial past of which we are ourselves the product.

" . . . all the events which have taken place in the immense periods that have preceded my own existence mean really nothing but the possibility of extending the chain of experience from the present perception back to the conditions which determine it in time." [1]

In other words, we may not claim that such events, empirically conceived, have ever actually existed in any such empirical form. A similar interpretation is given to the assertion of the present reality of what has never been actually experienced.

" Moreover, in outcome it is a matter of indifference whether I say that in the empirical progress in space I can meet with stars a hundred times farther removed than the outermost now perceptible to me, or whether I say that they are perhaps to be met with in cosmical space even though no human being has ever perceived or ever will perceive them. For though they might be given as things in themselves, without relation to possible experience, they are still nothing for me, and therefore are not objects, save in so far as they are contained in the series of the empirical regress." [2] " The cause of the empirical conditions of this process, that which determines what members I shall meet with and how far by means of such members I can carry out the regress, is transcendental and is therefore necessarily unknown to me." [3]

Such is the form in which Kant's pre-Critical doctrine of the transcendental object survives in the *Critique*.[4] It contains no trace of the teaching of the objective deduction of the first and second edition or of the teaching of the refutation of idealism in the second edition. It closely resembles Mill's doctrine of the permanent possibilities of sensation, and is almost equally subjectivist in character. As already noted,[5] it also lies open to the further objection that it involves an illegitimate application of the categories to things in themselves. As Kant started from the naïve and natural assumption that reference of representations to objects must be their reference to things in themselves, he also took over the current Cartesian view that it is by an inference in terms of the category of causality that we advance from a representation to its cause. The thing in itself is regarded as the sole true substance and as the real cause of everything which happens in the natural world. Appearances,

[1] A 495 = B 523.　　　[2] A 496 = B 524.　　　[3] *Loc. cit.*
[4] Cf. also A 538 = B 566; A 540 = B 568; A 557 = B 585; A 564 = B 592; A 565-6 = B 593-4; A 613 = B 641-2.　　　[5] Above, p. 206.

being representations merely, are wholly transitory and completely inefficacious. *Not only, therefore, are the categories regarded as valid of things in themselves, they are also declared to have no possible application to phenomena.* Sense appearances do not, on this view, constitute the mechanical world of the natural sciences; they have a purely subjective, more or less epi-phenomenal, existence in the mind of each separate observer. It was very gradually, in the process of developing his own Critical teaching, that Kant came to realise the very different position to which he was thereby committed. The categories, including that of causality, are pre-empted for the *empirical* object which is now regarded as immediately apprehended; and the function of mediating the reference of phenomena to things in themselves now falls to the Ideas of Reason. The distinction between appearance and reality is no longer that between representations and their noumenal causes, but between the limited and relative character of the entire world in space and time and the unconditioned demanded by Reason. But these are questions whose discussion must meantime be deferred.[1]

I may now briefly summarise the evidence in favour of the view that the doctrine of the transcendental object is a pre-Critical or semi-Critical survival and must not be taken as forming part of Kant's final and considered position. (1) Of the six sections in which the phrase transcendental object occurs, three[2] were omitted in the second edition, and in the passages which were substituted for them it receives no mention. There are various reasons which can be suggested in explanation of the retention of the other three[3] in the second edition. The *Note on Amphiboly* was too unsatisfactory as a whole to encourage Kant to improve upon it in detail. The other two are outside the limit at which Kant thought good to terminate all attempts to improve, whether in major or in minor matters, the text of the first edition.[4] To have recast the *Antinomies* as he had recast the *Paralogisms*

---

[1] Cf. above, pp. liii-v; below, pp. 280, 331, 373-4, 390-1, 414-17, 429-31, 558-61.

[2] Viz. the first layer of the deduction of the first edition, the relevant sections in the chapter on phenomena and noumena (A 250 ff.), and the *Paralogisms* with the subsequent *Reflection*.

[3] Viz. the *Note on Amphiboly*, the chapter on the *Antinomies*, and the chapter on the *Ideal*.

[4] To the statement that the alterations in the second edition cease at the close of the chapter on the *Paralogisms*, there is only one single exception, namely, the very brief note appended to A 491 = B 519. This exception, however, supports our general thesis. It is of polemical origin, referring to the nature of the distinction between transcendental and subjective idealism, and was demanded by the new *Refutation of Idealism* which in the second edition he had attached to the *Postulates*.

would have involved alterations much too extensive. Also, there were no outside polemical influences—or at least none acting quite directly—such as undoubtedly reinforced his other reasons for revising the *Paralogisms*. (2) Secondly, the transcendental object is not mentioned in the later layers of the deduction of the first edition, nor in the deduction of the second edition, nor in any passage or note added in the second edition. That Kant should thus suddenly cease to employ a phrase to which he had accustomed himself is the more significant in view of his conservative preference for the adapting of familiar terminology to new uses. It can only be explained as due to his recognition of the completely untenable character of the teaching to which it had given expression. As the object of knowledge is always empirical, it can never legitimately be called transcendental. (3) Thirdly, the general teaching of the passages in which the phrase transcendental object occurs is by itself sufficient proof of their early origin. They reveal not the least trace of the deepened insight of his final standpoints. As we know, it was certain difficulties involved in the working out of the objective deduction that delayed the publication of the *Critique* for so many years; and the sections which deal with these difficulties contain Kant's maturest teaching. In them he seems to withdraw definitely from the positions to which he had unwarily committed himself by his un-Critical doctrine of the transcendental object. I now pass to the second section constitutive of the first stage.

A 84-92 = B 116-24, I. § 13.—Just as in II. § 3 Kant deals solely with the first of the two questions formulated in the letter of 1772 to Herz—the reference of *sense*-representations to an object,—so in I. § 13 he raises only the second—that of the objective validity of *intellectual* representations (now spoken of as pure concepts of understanding, or pure *a priori* concepts, and only in one sentence as categories). And just as in the former section he carries the problem a step further, yet without attaining to the true Critical position, so in this latter he still assumes that it is the application of these pure concepts to real independent objects, *i.e.* to *things in themselves*, which calls for justification. We must again consider the exact terms in which this problem is formulated in the letter to Herz.[1]

"Similarly, if that in us which is called a representation, were active in relation to the object, that is to say, if the object itself were produced by the representation (as on the view that the ideas

---

[1] It follows immediately upon the passage quoted above, p. 206.

in the Divine Mind are the archetypes of things), the conformity of representations with objects might be understood. We can thus render comprehensible at least the possibility of two kinds of intelligence—of an *intellectus archetypus*, on whose intuition the things themselves are grounded, and of an *intellectus ectypus* which derives the data of its logical procedure from the sensuous intuition of things. But our understanding (leaving moral ends out of account) is not the cause of the object through its representations, nor is the object the cause of its intellectual representations (*in sensu reali*). Hence, the pure concepts of the understanding cannot be abstracted from the data of the senses, nor do they express our capacity for receiving representations through the senses. But, whilst they have their sources in the nature of the soul, they originate there neither as the result of the action of the object upon it, nor as themselves producing the object. In the *Dissertation* I was content to explain the nature of these intellectual representations in a merely negative manner, viz. as not being modifications of the soul produced by the object. But I silently passed over the further question, how such representations, which refer to an object and yet are not the result of an affection due to that object, can be possible. I had maintained that the sense representations represent things as they appear, the intellectual representations things as they are. But how then are these things given to us, if not by the manner in which they affect us? And if such intellectual representations are due to our own inner activity, whence comes the agreement which they are supposed to have with objects, which yet are not their products? How comes it that the axioms of pure reason about these objects agree with the latter, when this agreement has not been in any way assisted by experience? In mathematics such procedure is legitimate, because its objects only *are* quantities for us, and can only be represented as quantities, in so far as we can generate their representation by repeating a unit a number of times. Hence the concepts of quantity can be self-producing, and their principles can therefore be determined *a priori*. But when we ask how the understanding can form to itself completely *a priori* concepts of things in their *qualitative* determination, with which these things must of necessity agree, or formulate in regard to their possibility principles which are independent of experience, but with which experience must exactly conform,—we raise a question, that of the origin of the agreement of our faculty of understanding with the things in themselves, over which obscurity still hangs."[1]

The section before us represents the same general standpoint as that given in the above letter. Here, too, it is the validity of the *a priori* concepts in reference to *things in themselves* that is under consideration. The implication of Kant's argument is that the categories, being neither determinable nor discoverable by means of experience, will only apply

[1] *W.* x. pp. 125-6.

to appearances if they determine, or rather reveal, the actual non-experienced nature of things in themselves. These pure concepts, it is implied, owing to their combined *a priori* and intellectual characteristics, make this inherent claim. Either they are altogether empty and illusory, or such unlimited validity must be granted to them. Kant, that is to say, still holds, as in the *Dissertation*, that sense-representations reveal things as they *appear*, intellectual representations things as they *are*.

"We have either to surrender completely all claims to judgments of pure reason, in the most esteemed of all fields, that which extends beyond the limits of all possible experience, or we must bring this Critical investigation to perfection."[1]

The pure concepts, unlike space, "apply to objects generally, apart from the conditions of sensibility."[2] But here also, as in the letter to Herz, the strange and problematic character of such knowledge is clearly recognised.

Kant's discussion of the concept of causality in A 90 may seem to conflict with the above contention—that it is its applicability to things in themselves which Kant is considering. But this difficulty vanishes if we bear in mind that here, as in the *Dissertation*, there is no such distinction as we find in Kant's later more genuinely phenomenalist position, between the objects causing our sensations and *things in themselves*.[3] The purely intelligible object, supposed to remain after elimination of the empirical and *a priori* sensory factors, *is* the thing in itself. The objects apprehended through sense are real, only not in their sensuous form.

There are two connected facts which together may perhaps be taken as evidence that I. § 13 is later than II. 3 *b*. Intellectual concepts are reinstated alongside the *a priori* concepts of space and time. Kant has evidently in the meantime given up the attempt to construe the former as empirical in origin. That that attempt was earlier in time would seem to be proved by the further fact, that the *a priori* concepts are here viewed as performing the same kind of function as that ascribed in II.3 *b* to concepts that are empirical. They are conditions of the "synthetic unity of thought."[3] This view of the function of concepts is certainly fundamental and important, and Kant permanently retained it from his previous abortive method of 'deduction.' But it was a long step from the discovery of the distinction between empirical and *a priori* concepts to its fruitful application. That involved appreciation

[1] A 89 = B 121.   I adopt B. Erdmann's reading of *auf* for *als*.
[2] A 88 = B 120.   [3] A 90.

of the further fact that the two problems, separately stated in the letter to Herz and separately dealt with in II. 3 *b* and in I. § 13—the problem of the relation of *sense*-representations, and the problem of the relation of *intellectual* representations, to an object,—are indeed one and the same, soluble from one and the same standpoint, by one and the same method of deduction, namely, by reference to the possibility of experience. Only in and through relation to an object can sense-representations be apprehended ; and only as conditions of such sense-experience are the categories objectively valid. Relation to an object is constituted by the categories, and is necessary in reference to sense-representations, because only thereby is consciousness of any kind possible at all.

That this truly Critical position had not been attained when I. § 13 was written,[1] is shown not only by its concentration on the single problem of the validity of *a priori* concepts, but also by its repeated assertion that representations can be consciously apprehended independently of all relation to the faculty of understanding. The directly counter assertion appears, however, in the sections (I. § 14, II.: first four paragraphs) which immediately follow in the text of the *Critique*—indicating that in the period represented by these latter the revolutionary discovery, the truly Copernican hypothesis, had at last been achieved. They constitute the second stage, and to it we may now proceed.

Second Stage.—A 92-4 = B 124-7 ; A 95-7 ; A 110-14.

A 92-4, I. § 14 (with the exception of the concluding classification of mental powers).—This section makes a fresh start ; it stands in no necessary relation to any preceding section. The problem is still formulated, in its opening sentences, in terms reminiscent of the letter to Herz ; but otherwise the standpoint is entirely new, and save for the wording of a single sentence (A 93: " if not intuited, yet "), is genuinely Critical. The phrase " possibility of experience " now appears, and is at once assigned the central rôle. The words " if not intuited, yet " in A 93 may possibly have been inserted later in order to tone down the flagrant contradiction with the preceding paragraphs. In any case, even this qualification is explicitly retracted in A 94.

A 95-7.—The same standpoint appears in the first three paragraphs of Section II. The categories are "the *a priori*

---

[1] As we have already found (above, p. 27 *n.* 1), it had not been attained at the time when the *Introduction* to the first edition was written.

conditions on which the possibility of experience depends."[1]
By the categories alone "can an object be thought."[2] The
further important point that only in their empirical employment do the categories have use and meaning is excellently
developed.

"An *a priori* concept not referring to experience would be the
logical form only of a concept, but not the concept itself by which
something is thought."[3]

A 110-14, II. 4.—In this section also the argument starts
afresh, indicating (if such evidence were required) that, like
I. § 14, it must have been written independently of its present
context. But the argument is now advanced one step further.
The categories are recognised as simultaneously conditioning
both unity of consciousness and objectivity.

"There is but one experience . . . as there is but one space and
one time. . . ." "The *a priori* conditions of a possible experience
are at the same time conditions of the possibility of objects of
experience"[4] ". . . the necessity of these categories rests on the
relation which our whole sensibility, and with it also all possible
appearances, have to the original unity of apperception. . . ."[5]

Now also it is *emphasised* that save in and through *a priori*
concepts no representations can exist for consciousness.

"They would then belong to no experience, would be without
an object, a blind play of representations, less even than a dream."[6]
They "would be to us the same as nothing."[7]

The wording is still not altogether unambiguous, but the
main point is made sufficiently clear.

These paragraphs are the earliest in which traces of a
genuine phenomenalism can be detected.   The transcendental
object, one and the same for all our knowledge, is not referred
to.   'Objects' (in the plural) is the term which is used
wherever the context permits.   The empirical object is thus
made to intervene between the thing in itself and the subjective representations.   But the distinction between empirical
objects and subjective representations on the one hand, and
between empirical objects and things in themselves on the
other, is not yet drawn in any really clear and definite manner.
A similar phenomenalist tendency crops out in Kant's
distinction[8] between objective affinity and subjective
association.

[1] A 95-96.   [2] A 97.   [3] A 95 ; cf. A 96.
[4] A 111.   [5] *Loc. cit.*   [6] A 112.
[7] A 111.   [8] A 112-14.

"The ground of the possibility of the association of the manifold, so far as it lies in the object, is named the affinity of the manifold."

None the less Kant's subjectivism finds one of its most decided expressions in A 114.

Third Stage.—A 119-23 = III. β; A 116-19 = III. α; A 94-5 = I. § 14 C(oncluding paragraph); A 126-8 = III. δ; A 128-30 = S(ummary); A 123-6 = III. γ; A 115-16 = III. I(ntroduction); A 76-9 (B 102-4) = § 10 T(ransition to fourth stage).

A 119-23, III. β (from the beginning of the seventh paragraph to the end of the twelfth). The doctrine of objective affinity already developed in the above sections is now made to rest upon a new faculty, the productive imagination. As Vaihinger remarks, the wording of this section would seem to indicate that it is Kant's first attempt at formulating that new doctrine. He has not as yet got over his own surprise at the revolutionary nature of the conclusions to which he feels himself driven by the exigencies of Critical teaching. He finds that it is deepening into consequences which may lead very far from the current psychology and from his own previous views regarding the nature and conditions of the knowing process and of personality. As evidence that this section was not written continuously with II. 4,[1] we have the further fact that though the doctrine of objective affinity is dwelt upon, it is described afresh, with no reference to the preceding account. Also, the empirical processes of apprehension and reproduction, already mentioned in A 104-10, are now ascribed to the empirical imagination which is carefully distinguished from the productive.

III. α repeats "from above" the argument given in III. β "from below." It insists upon the close connection between the categories (first introduced in II. 4[1]) with the productive imagination of III. β.

Vaihinger places III. δ next in order, on account of the connection of its argument with III. α.[2] But it dwells only upon the chief outcome of the total argument, viz. that the orderliness of nature is due to understanding. That productive imagination is not mentioned, is taken by Vaihinger to signify Kant's recognition that it can be postulated only hypothetically, and that as doctrine it is not absolutely essential to the strict deduction.

[1] A 110-14.
[2] I. § 14 C Vaihinger regards as intermediate in date, but it is a comparatively unimportant paragraph, and may for the present be left out of account. Cf. below, pp. 225-6.

S summarises the entire argument, and in it "pure imagination" receives mention.

Within this third stage III. γ is subsequent to the above four sections. For it carries the doctrine of productive imagination one step further. In III. β, III. α, and S, productive imagination has been treated merely as an auxiliary function of pure understanding.

"The unity of apperception in relation to the synthesis of imagination is the *understanding*; and the same unity with reference to the transcendental synthesis of the imagination is the *pure understanding*." [1]

It is now treated as a separate and distinct faculty. So far from being a function of understanding, its synthesis "by itself, though carried out *a priori*, is always sensuous." [2] It is

"one of the fundamental faculties of the human soul. . . . The two extreme ends, sensibility and understanding, must be brought into connection with each other by means of this transcendental function of imagination." [3]

In this section there also appears a new element which would seem to connect it with the next following stage, namely, the addition to the series, apprehension, association, and reproduction, of the further process, recognition. As here introduced it is extremely ambiguous in character. It is counted as being empirical, and yet as containing *a priori* concepts. This decidedly hybrid process would seem to represent Kant's first formulation of the even more ambiguous process, which corresponds to it in the fourth stage.

In III. I recognition is again mentioned, but this time in a form still more akin to its treatment in the fourth stage. It is not recognition through categories, but, as a form in apperception, is the

"empirical consciousness of the identity of the reproductive representations with the appearances by which they were given." [4]

In all other respects, however, the above six sections agree (along with I. § 14 C) in holding to a threefold division of mental powers : sensibility, imagination, and apperception. This third stage is thereby marked off sufficiently clearly from the second stage in which pure imagination is wanting, and from the fourth stage in which it is dissolved into a threefold *a priori* synthesis.

In both I. § 14 C and in III. I the classification which underlies the third stage is explicitly formulated. Their

---

[1] A 118-19. [2] A 124. [3] *Loc. cit.* [4] A 115.

statements harmoniously combine to yield the following tabular statement:

1. The *synopsis* of the manifold—*a priori* through sense, *i.e.* in pure intuition.

2. The synthesis of this manifold—through pure transcendental imagination.

3. The unity of this synthesis — through pure original transcendental apperception.

At this point Vaihinger adds to the above section the earlier passage § 10 T.[1] It is even more definitely than III. γ and III. I transitional to the fourth stage. It must be classed within the third stage, as it holds to the above threefold classification. But it modifies that classification in two respects. First, in that it does not employ the term *synopsis*, but only speaks of pure intuition as required to yield us a manifold. The term synopsis, as used by Kant, is, however, decidedly misleading.[2] His invariable teaching is that all connection is due to synthesis. By synopsis, therefore, which he certainly does not employ as synonymous with synthesis, can be meant only apprehension of external side-by-sideness. It never signifies anything except apprehension of the lowest possible order. Kant's omission of the term, therefore, tends to clearness of statement. Secondly, the classification is also modified by the substitution of understanding for the unity of apperception. Apperception is, however, so obscurely treated in all of the above sections, that this cannot be regarded as a vital alteration. What is new in this section, and seems to connect it in a curious and interesting manner with sections in the fourth stage, is its doctrine of

"a manifold of *a priori* sensibility." "Space and time contain a manifold of pure *a priori* intuition."[3]

That is, in this connection, an entirely new doctrine. In all the previous sections of the deduction (previous in the assumed order of original writing) the manifold supplied through intuition is taken as being empirical, and as consisting of sensations. Kant here also adds that the manifold, "whether given empirically or *a priori*,"[4] must be synthesised before it can be known.

"The spontaneity of our thought requires that this manifold [of pure *a priori* intuition] should be run through in a certain manner, taken up, and connected, in order that a knowledge may be formed out of it. This action I call synthesis."

---

[1] A 76-9 = B 102-4. Not yet commented upon.
[2] Cf. Vaihinger, *loc. cit.* p. 63.   [3] A 77 = B 102. Cf. above, pp. 96-7.   [4] *Loc. cit.*

Fourth Stage.—A 98-104; A 97-8.—As already noted, there are in Kant two persistent but conflicting interpretations of the nature of the synthetic processes exercised by imagination and understanding, the subjectivist and the phenomenalist.[1] Now, on the former view, imagination is simply understanding *at work*.   In other words, imagination is merely the active synthesising side of a faculty whose complementary aspect appears in the logical unity of the concept.   From this point of view the transcendental and the empirical factors may be taken as forming a single series.   The transcendental and the empirical processes will vary together, some form of transcendental activity corresponding to every fundamental form of empirical activity and *vice versa*.   Such an inference only follows *if* the subjectivist standpoint be accepted to the exclusion of the phenomenalist point of view.   But since Kant constantly alternates between them, and never quite definitely formulates them in their distinction and opposition ; since, in fact, they were rather of the nature of obscurely felt tendencies than of formulated standpoints, it is quite intelligible that an inference derived from the one should be drawn even at the very time when the other is being more explicitly developed. This, it would seem, is what actually happened.   When we come to consider the evidence derivable from the *Reflexionen* and *Lose Blätter*, we shall find support for the view that after January 1780, on the very eve of the publication of the *Critique*, while the revolutionary, phenomenalist consequences of the Critical hypothesis were becoming clearer to him, he unguardedly allowed the above inference to lead him to recast his previous views in a decidedly subjectivist manner.   The view that transcendental imagination has a special and unique activity altogether different in type from any of its empirical processes, namely, the " productive," is now allowed to drop ; and in place of it Kant develops the view that transcendental functions run exactly parallel with the empirical processes of apprehension, reproduction, and recognition. Accordingly, in place of the classification presented in the third stage, we find a new and radically different one introduced into the text, without the least indication that Kant's standpoint has meantime changed.   It is given in A 97 :

A. **Synopsis** of the manifold through sense.
B. **Synthesis**.
      1. Synthesis of apprehension of representations in [inner] intuition.

[1] For explanation of the exact meaning in which these terms are employed and for discussion of the complicated issues involved, cf. below, p. 270 ff.

> 2. Synthesis of reproduction of representations in imagination. ·
> 3. Synthesis of recognition of representations in the concept.

And Kant adds in explanation that "these point to three subjective sources of knowledge which make the understanding itself possible, and which in so doing make all experience possible, in so far as it is an empirical product of the understanding." What, now, are these three subjective sources of knowledge? They certainly are not those classified in the table of the third stage. *A* roughly coincides with its first member; consequently *B* 1 is left without proper correlate. *B* 2 is altogether different from the previous synthesis of imagination, for in the earlier table transcendental imagination is regarded as being solely productive, *never* reproductive.[1] It is now asserted to be reproductive—a contradiction of one of his own most emphatic contentions, which can only be accounted for by some such explanation as we are here stating. Nothing is lacking as regards explicitness in the statement of this new position. ". . . the *reproductive* synthesis of imagination belongs to the transcendental acts of the soul, and, in reference to it [viz. to the reproductive synthesis], we will call this power too the transcendental power of the imagination."[2] Lastly, even B 3 does not coincide with the pure apperception of the other table. B 3 is more akin to the recognition which in the third stage is declared to be always empirical. In any case, it is recognition *in the concept*; and though that may ultimately involve and condition transcendental apperception, it remains, in the manner in which it is here developed by Kant, something very different. But this is a point to which we shall return. There is an added complication, running through this entire stage, which first requires to be disentangled. The transcendental syntheses are declared to condition the pure representations of space and time no less than those of sense-experience.

"This synthesis of apprehension also must be executed *a priori*, *i.e.* in reference to representations which are not empirical. For without it we could not have the *a priori* representations either of space or of time, since these can be generated only through the synthesis of the manifold which sensibility presents in its original receptivity. Thus we have a pure synthesis of apprehension"[3] ". . . if I draw a line in thought or desire to think of the time from one noon to another, or merely represent to myself a certain number, I must, firstly, apprehend these manifold representations one after

---

[1] Cf. A 118.   [2] A 102.   [3] A 99-100.

the other. But if the preceding representations (the first parts of the line, the antecedent parts of time or the units serially represented) were always to drop out of my thought, and were not reproduced when I advance to those that follow, no complete representation, and none of all the aforementioned thoughts, not even the purest and first basal representations of space and time, could ever arise."[1]

This, as Vaihinger remarks, is a point of sufficient importance to justify separate treatment. But it is introduced quite incidentally by Kant, and obscures quite as much as it clarifies the main argument.

It is convenient to start with the second synthesis. Kant's argument is much clearer in regard to it than in regard to the other two. He distinguishes between empirical and transcendental reproduction. Reproduction in ordinary experience, in accordance with the laws of association, is merely empirical. The *de facto* conformity of appearances to rules is what renders such empirical reproduction possible ;

". . . otherwise our faculty of empirical imagination would never find any opportunity of action suited to its capacities, and would remain hidden within the mind as a dead, and to us unknown power."[2]

Kant proceeds to argue, consistently with his doctrine of objective affinity, that empirical reproduction is itself transcendentally conditioned. The form, however, in which this argument is developed is peculiar to the section before us, and is entirely new.

"If we can show that even our purest *a priori* intuitions yield no knowledge, save in so far as they contain such connection of the manifold as will make possible a thoroughgoing synthesis of reproduction, this synthesis of the imagination must be grounded, prior to all experience, on *a priori* principles; and since experience necessarily presupposes that appearances can be reproduced, we shall have to assume a pure transcendental synthesis of the imagination as conditioning even the possibility of all experience."[3]

In the concluding paragraph Kant makes clear that he regards this *transcendental* activity as being exercised in a twofold manner: in relation to the *empirically* given manifold as well as in relation to the *a priori* given manifold. How this transcendental activity is to be distinguished from the empirical is not further explained. I discuss this point below.[4]

The argument of the section on the synthesis of *apprehension*, to which we may now turn back, suffers from serious

---

[1] A 102.   [2] A 100.   [3] A 101. Cf. below, p. 255.   Pp. 238, 263 ff.

ambiguity. It is not clear whether a distinction, analogous to that between empirical and transcendental reproduction, is being made in reference to apprehension. The actual wording of its two last paragraphs would lead to that conclusion. That, however, is a view which would seem to be excluded by the wider context. Kant is dealing with the synthesis of apprehension in *inner* intuition, *i.e.* in time. By the fundamental principles of his teaching such intuition must always be transcendental. Empirical apprehension can only concern the data of the special senses. The process of apprehension referred to in the middle paragraph must therefore itself be transcendental.

But it is in dealing with the synthesis of *recognition* that the argument is most obscure. It is idle attempting to discover any possible distinction between an empirical and a transcendental process of recognition. For the transcendental process here appears as being the consciousness that what we are thinking now is the same as what we thought a moment before; and it is illustrated not by reference to the pure intuitions of space and time, but only by the process of counting. It may be argued that empirical recognition is mediated by transcendental factors—by pure concepts and by apperception. But unless we are to take transcendental recognition as synonymous with transcendental apperception, which Kant's actual teaching does not seem to justify us in doing, such considerations will not enable us to distinguish two forms of recognition. Apart, however, from this difficulty, there is the further one that the concepts in and through which the recognition is executed are here described as being empirical. The only key that will solve the mystery of this extraordinary section, hopelessly inexplicable when viewed as a single continuous whole, is, it would seem, the theory of Vaihinger, namely,[1] that from the third paragraph onwards (already dealt with as forming the first stage of the deduction) Kant is making use of manuscript which represents the *earliest* form in which his explanation of the consciousness of objects was developed, with the strange result that this section is a combination of the latest and of the earliest forms of the deduction. While seeking to make out a parallelism between the empirical, conscious activities of imagination and understanding on the one hand, and its transcendental functions on the other, he must have bethought himself of the earlier attempt to explain consciousness of objects through empirical concepts conditioned by transcendental apperception, and so have attempted to expound the third form of synthesis by

[1] Cf. above, p. 211.

means of it. As thus extended it involves a distinction between transcendental and empirical apperception, and upon that the discussion, so far as it concerns anything akin to recognition, altogether turns. But there is not the least further mention of recognition itself. As transcendental, it cannot be taken as the equivalent of empirical apperception; and as a synthesis through concepts, can hardly coincide with pure apperception. The title of the section, "the synthesis of recognition in the concept," is thus no real indication of the astonishing fare prepared for the reader. The doctrine of a threefold synthesis seems to have occurred to Kant on the very eve of the publication of the *Critique*. The passage expounding it may well have been hurriedly composed, and when unforeseen difficulties accumulated, especially in regard to recognition as a transcendental process, Kant must have resolved simply to close the matter by inserting the older manuscript.

III. Evidence yielded by the "Reflexionen" and "Lose Blätter" in support of the above analysis

The evidence, derived by Vaihinger from the *Reflexionen* and *Lose Blätter*, briefly outlined, is as follows.[1] (1) In the *Reflexionen zur Anthropologie* relevant passages are few in number, and represent a standpoint very close to that of the 1770 *Dissertation*. Imagination is treated only as an empirical faculty.[2] Recognition, which is only once mentioned,[3] is also viewed as merely empirical. The understanding is spoken of as the faculty through which objects are thought.[4] The categories are not mentioned, and it is stated that the understanding yields only ideas of reflection. "All knowledge of things is derived, as regards its matter, from sensation—the understanding gives only ideas of reflection."[5] So far, these *Reflexionen* would seem to coincide, more or less, with the first stage of the deduction. They contain, however, no reference to *transcendental* apperception; and are therefore regarded by Vaihinger as representing a still earlier standpoint.

(2) In the *Reflexionen zur Kritik der reinen Vernunft* there is a very large and valuable body of relevant passages. No. 925 must be of the same date as the letter of 1772 to Herz; it formulates its problem in practically identical terms.[6] Nos. 946-52 and 955 may belong to the period of the first stage. For though the doctrine of the transcendental object as the

---

[1] For Vaihinger's own statement of it, cf. *op. cit.* pp. 79-98.
[2] Nos. 64-5, 117, 140-5.   [3] No. 146.   [4] Nos. 41, 81.
[5] No. 104.   [6] Cf. Nos. 964-5.

opposite counterpart of the transcendental subject is not mentioned, the spiritualist view of the self is prominent. In No. 946 it is asserted that the representation of an object is " made by us through freedom."

" Free actions are already given *a priori*, namely our own."[1] " To pass universal objective judgments, and to do so apodictically, reason must be free from subjective grounds of determination. For were it so determined the judgment would be merely accidental, namely in accordance with its subjective cause. Thus reason is conscious *a priori* of its freedom in objectively necessary judgments in so far as it apprehends them as exclusively grounded through their relation to the object."[2] " Transcendental freedom is the necessary hypothesis of all rules, and therefore of all employment of the understanding."[3] " Appearances are representations whereby we are affected. The representation of our free self-activity does not involve affection, and accordingly is not appearance, but apperception."[4]

It is significant that the categories receive no mention. Almost all the other *Reflexionen* would seem to have originated in the period of the second stage of the deduction ; but they still betray a strong spiritualist bias.

" Impressions are not yet representations, for they must be related to something else which is an action. Now the reaction of the mind is an action which relates to the impression, and which if taken alone[5] may in its special forms receive the title categories."[6] " We can know the connection of things in the world only if we produce it through a universal action, and so out of a principle of inner power (*aus einem Prinzip der inneren Potestas*) : substance, ground, combination."[7]

These *Reflexionen* recognise only the categories of relation,[8] and must therefore be prior to the twelvefold classification. There is not the least trace of the characteristic doctrines of the third and fourth stages of the deduction, viz. of the transcendental function of the imagination or of a threefold transcendental synthesis. The nature of apprehension is also most obscure. It is frequently equated with apperception.

(3) The *Lose Blätter aus Kants Nachlass* (Heft I.) contains fragments which also belong to the second stage of the deduction, but which would seem to be of somewhat earlier

---

[1] No. 947.   [2] No. 948.   [3] No. 949.   [4] No. 952.
[5] This is Erdmann's reading. Vaihinger substitutes *allgemein* for *allein*, but without reason given.
[6] No. 935. The translation is literal. Kant in the last sentence changes from singular to plural.
[7] No. 952.
[8] Cf. also Nos. 957, 961. The latter shows how Kant already connected the categories of relation with the logical functions of judgment.

date than the above *Reflexionen*.[1] They have interesting points
of contact with the first stage.   Thus though the phrase
transcendental object does not occur in them, the object of
knowledge is equated with *x*, and is regarded in the manner
of the first stage as the opposite counterpart of the unity of
the self.[2] These fragments belong, however, to the second
stage in virtue of their recognition of the *a priori* categories
of relation.   There is also here, as in the *Reflexionen*, great
lack of clearness regarding the nature of apprehension ;
and there is still no mention of the transcendental faculty
of imagination.   Fragment 8 is definitely datable.   It
covers the free spaces of a letter of invitation dated May 20,
1775.[3] Fragment B 12[4] belongs to a different period from the
above.   This is sufficiently evident from its contents ; but
fortunately the paper upon which it is written—an official
document in the handwriting of the Rector of the Philosophical
Faculty of Königsberg—enables us to decide the exact year of
its origin.   It is dated January 20, 1780. The fragment must
therefore be subsequent to that date.   Now in it transcendental
imagination appears as a third faculty alongside sensibility and
understanding, and a distinction is definitely drawn between
its empirical and its transcendental employment. The former
conditions the synthesis of apprehension ; the latter conditions
the synthetic unity of apperception.   It further distinguishes
between reproductive and productive imagination, and ascribes
the former exclusively to the empirical imagination.   In all
these respects it stands in complete agreement with the
teaching of the third stage of the deduction.   The fact that
this fragment is subsequent to January 1780 would seem to
prove that even at that late date Kant was struggling with
his deduction.[5]   But the most interesting of all Vaihinger's
conclusions has still to be mentioned.   He points out that at
the time when this fragment was composed Kant had not yet
developed the doctrine characteristic of the fourth stage,
namely, of a threefold transcendental synthesis.   Moreover,
as he observes, the statement which it explicitly contains, that
reproductive imagination is always empirical, is inconsistent
with any such doctrine.   The teaching of the fourth stage
must consequently be ascribed to an even later date.[6]

[1] Reicke, Nos. 7, 8, 10-18 (pp. 16-26, 29-49).
[2] The chief relevant passages have been quoted above, p. 209.
[3] The letter is given in *W.* x. p. 173.   [4] Reicke, pp. 113-16.
[5] According to Adickes the *Critique* was "brought to completion" in the first
half of 1780 ; in Vaihinger's view, on the other hand, Kant was occupied with
it from April to September.   Cf. above, p. xx.
[6] In two respects, however, fragment B 12 anticipates the teaching of the fourth
stage : (*a*) in suggesting (p. 114) the necessity of a pure synthesis of pure intuition,
and (*b*) in equating (p. 115) synthesis of apprehension with synthesis of imagination.

(4) The *Lose Blätter* (Heft II.), though almost exclusively devoted to moral and legal questions, contain in E 67[1] a relevant passage which Reicke regards as belonging to the 'eighties, but which Adickes and Vaihinger agree in dating "shortly before 1781." On Vaihinger's view it is a preliminary study for the passages of the fourth stage of the deduction. But such exact dating is not essential to Vaihinger's argument. It is undoubtedly quite late, and contains the following sentence:

"All representations, whatever their origin, are yet ultimately as representations modifications of inner sense, and their unity must be viewed from this point of view. A spontaneity of synthesis corresponds to their receptivity: either of apprehension as sensations or of reproduction as images (*Einbildungen*) or of recognition as concepts."

This is the doctrine from which the deduction of the first edition *starts*; it was, it would seem, *the last to be developed*.[2] That we find no trace of it in the *Prolegomena*, and that it is not only eliminated from the second edition, but is expressly disavowed,[3] would seem to indicate that it had been hastily adopted on the very eve of publication, and that upon reflection Kant had felt constrained definitively to discard it. The threefold synthesis can be verified on the empirical level, but there is no evidence that there exist corresponding transcendental activities.

IV. Connected Statement and Discussion of Kant's Subjective and Objective Deductions in the First Edition

Such are the varying and conflicting forms in which Kant has presented his deduction of the categories. We may now apply our results to obtain a connected statement of the essentials of his argument. The following exposition, which endeavours to emphasise its main broad features, to distinguish its various steps, and to disentangle its complex and conflicting tendencies, will, I trust, yield to the reader such steady orientation as is necessary in so bewildering a labyrinth.

---

[1] Pp. 231-3.   [2] Cf. below, pp. 268-9.

[3] In B 160 Kant states that the synthesis of apprehension is only empirical; and in B 152 we find the following emphatic sentence: "In so far as the faculty of imagination is spontaneously active I sometimes also name it [*i.e.* in addition to entitling it transcendental and figurative] *productive*, and thereby distinguish it from the *reproductive* imagination whose synthesis is subject only to empirical laws, *i.e.* those of association, and which therefore contributes nothing in explanation of the possibility of *a priori* knowledge. Hence it belongs, not to transcendental philosophy, but to psychology." Cf. the directly counter statement in A 102: "The reproductive synthesis of the faculty of imagination must be counted among the transcendental actions of the mind."

In the meantime I shall take account only of the deductions of the first edition,[1] and from them shall strive to construct the ideal statement to which they severally approximate. Any single relatively consistent and complete deduction that is thus to serve as a standard exposition must, like the root-languages of philology, be typical or archetypal, representing the argument at which Kant aimed; it cannot be one of the alternative expositions which he himself gives. Such reconstruction of an argument which Kant has failed to express in a final and genuinely adequate form must, of course, lie open to all the dangers of arbitrary and personal interpretation. It is an extremely adventurous undertaking, and will have to be carefully guarded by constant reference to Kant's *ipsissima verba*. Proof of its historical validity will consist in its capacity to render intelligible Kant's own departures from it, and in its power of explaining the reasons of his so doing. Its expository value will be in proportion to the assistance which it may afford to the reader in deciphering the actual texts.

Our first task is to make clear the nature of the distinction which Kant draws between the "subjective" and the "objective" deductions. This is a distinction of great importance, and raises issues of a fundamental character. In regard to it students of Kant take widely different views. For it brings to a definite issue many of the chief controversies regarding Critical teaching. Kant has made some very definite statements in regard to it; and one of the opposing schools of interpretation finds its chief and strongest arguments in the words which he employs. But for reasons which will appear in due course, adherence to the letter of the *Critique* would in this case involve the commentator in great difficulties. We have no option except to adopt the invidious position of maintaining that we may now, after the interval of a hundred years and the labours of so many devoted students, profess to understand Kant better than he understood himself. For such procedure we may indeed cite his own authority.

"Not infrequently, upon comparing the thoughts which an author has expressed in regard to his subject, whether in ordinary conversation or in writing, we find that we can understand him better than he understood himself. As he has not sufficiently determined his concept, he has sometimes spoken, or even thought, in opposition to his own intention."[2]

Let us, then, consider first the distinction between the two types of deduction in the form in which it is drawn by Kant.

---

[1] Though, as we shall find, the deduction of the second edition is in certain respects more mature, it is in other respects less complete.   [2] A 314 = B 370.

In the *Preface* to the first edition,[1] Kant states that his transcendental deduction of the categories has two sides, and assigns to them the titles subjective and objective.

"This enquiry, which is somewhat deeply grounded, has two sides. The one refers to the objects of pure understanding, and is intended to expound and render intelligible the objective validity of its *a priori* concepts. It is therefore essential to my purposes. The other seeks to investigate the pure understanding itself, its possibility and the cognitive faculties upon which it rests. Although this latter exposition is of great importance for my chief purpose, it does not form an essential part of it. For the chief question is always simply this,—what and how much can the understanding and Reason know apart from all experience? not—how is the faculty of thought itself possible? The latter is as it were a search for the cause of a given effect; and therefore is of the nature of an hypothesis (though, as I shall show elsewhere, this is not really so); and I would appear to be taking the liberty simply of expressing an opinion, in which case the reader would be free to express a different opinion.[2] For this reason I must forestall the reader's criticism by pointing out that the objective deduction, with which I am here chiefly concerned, retains its full force even if my subjective deduction should fail to produce that complete conviction for which I hope. . . ."

The subjective deduction seeks to determine the subjective conditions which are required to render knowledge possible, or to use less ambiguous terms the generative processes to whose agency human knowledge is due. It is consequently psychological in character. The objective deduction, on the other hand, is so named because it deals not with psychological processes but with questions of objective validity. It enquires how concepts which are *a priori*, and which as *a priori* must be taken to originate in pure reason, can yet be valid of objects. In other words, the objective deduction is logical, or, to use a post-Kantian term, epistemological in character.

It is indeed true, as Kant here insists, that the subjective deduction does not concern itself in any quite direct fashion with the Critical problem—how *a priori* ideas can relate to objects. "Although of great importance for my chief purpose, it does not form an essential part of it." This, no doubt, is one reason why Kant omitted it when he revised the *Critique* for the second edition.[3] None the less it is, as

[1] A x-xi. Cf. above, pp. 50-1.
[2] Cf. below, pp. 543 ff., 576-7.
[3] Whether it was the chief reason is decidedly open to question. The un-Critical character of its teaching as regards the function of empirical concepts and of the transcendental object, and the unsatisfactoriness of its doctrine of a three-

he recognises, important ; and what exactly this importance amounts to, and whether it is really true that it has such minor importance as to be rightly describable as unessential, is what we have to decide.

Though empirical psychology, in so far as it investigates the temporal development of our experience, is, as Kant very justly claims, entirely distinct in aim and method from the Critical enquiry, the same cannot be said of a psychology which, for convenience, and on the lines of Kant's own employment of terms, may be named transcendental.[1] For it will deal, not with the temporal development of the concrete and varied aspects of consciousness, but with the more fundamental question of the generative conditions indispensably necessary to consciousness as such, *i.e.* to consciousness in each and every one of its possible embodiments. In the definition above given of the objective deduction, I have intentionally indicated Kant's unquestioning conviction that the *a priori* originates independently of the objects to which it is applied. This independent origin is only describable in mental or psychological terms. The *a priori* originates from within ; it is due to the specific conditions upon which human thinking rests. Now this interpretation of the *a priori* renders the teaching contained in the subjective deduction much more essential than Kant is himself willing to recognise. The conclusions arrived at may be highly schematic in conception, and extremely conjectural in detail ; they are none the less required to supplement the results of the more purely logical analysis. For though in the second edition the sections devoted to the subjective deduction are suppressed, their teaching, and the distinctions which they draw between the different mental processes, continue to be employed in the exposition of the objective deduction, and indeed are presupposed throughout the *Critique* as a whole. They are indispensably necessary in order to render really definite many of the contentions which the objective deduction itself contains. To eliminate the subjective deduction is not to cut away these presuppositions, but only to leave them in the obscure region of the undefined. They will still continue to influence our mode of formulating and of solving the Critical problem, but will do so as untested and vaguely outlined assumptions, acting as unconscious influences rather than as

---

fold synthesis, would of themselves account for the omission. The passage in the chapter on phenomena and noumena (A 250 ff.) in which the doctrine of the transcendental object is again developed was likewise omitted in the second edition.

[1] Cf. below, pp. 238, 263 ff.

established principles. For these reasons the omission of the subjective deduction is to be deplored. The explicit statement of the implied psychological conditions is preferable to their employment without prior definition and analysis. The deduction of the second edition rests throughout upon the initial and indispensable assumption, that though connection or synthesis can never be given, it is yet the generative source of all consciousness of order and relation. Factors which are transcendental in the strict or logical meaning of the term rest upon processes that are transcendental in a psychological sense.

This last phrase, 'transcendental in a psychological sense,' calls for a word of justification. The synthetic processes generative of experience are not, of course, transcendental in the strict sense. For they are not *a priori* in the manner of the categories. None the less they are discoverable by the same transcendental method, namely, as being, like the categories, indispensably necessary to the possibility of experience. They differ from the categories in that they are not immanent in experience, constituent of it, and cannot therefore be known in their intrinsic nature. As they fall outside the field of consciousness, they can only be hypothetically postulated. None the less, formal categories and generative processes, definable elements and problematic postulates, alike agree in being conditions *sine qua non* of experience. And further, in terms of Kant's presupposed psychology, the latter are the source to which the former are due. There would thus seem to be sufficient justification for extending the term transcendental to cover both; and in so doing we are following the path which Kant himself willingly travelled. For such would seem to have been his unexpressed reasons for ascribing, as he does, the synthetic generative processes to what he himself names transcendental faculties.

This disposes of Kant's chief reason for refusing to recognise the subjective deduction as a genuine part of the Critical enquiry, namely, the contention upon which he lays such emphasis in the prefaces both of the first and of the second edition,[1] that in transcendental philosophy nothing hypothetical, nothing in any degree dependent upon general reasoning from contingent fact, can have any place. That contention proves untenable even within the domain of his purely logical analyses. The very essence of his transcendental method consists in the establishment of *a priori* elements through proof of their connection with factual

[1] Cf. also in *Methodology*, below, p. 543 ff.

experience. Kant is here revealing how greatly his mind is still biased by the Leibnizian rationalism from which he is breaking away. His *a priori* cannot establish itself save in virtue of hypothetical reasoning.[1] His transcendental method, rightly understood, does not differ in essential nature from the hypothetical method of the natural sciences; it does so only in the nature of its starting-point, and in the character of the analyses which that starting-point prescribes. And if hypothetical reasoning may be allowed in the establishment of the logical *a priori*, there is no sufficient reason why it may not also be employed for the determination of dynamical factors. The sole question is as to whether the hypotheses conform to the logical requirements and so raise themselves to a different level from mere opinion and conjecture.[2] As Kant himself says,[3] though his conclusions in the subjective deduction may seem to be hypothetical in the illegitimate sense, they are not really so. From the experience in view of which they are postulated they receive at once the proof of their actuality and the material for their specification.

We may now return to the question of the nature of the two deductions. The complex character of their interrelations may be outlined as follows :

1. Though the subjective deduction is in its later stages coextensive with its objective counterpart, in its earlier stages it moves wholly on what may be called the empirical level. The data which it analyses and the conditions which it postulates are both alike empirical. The objective deduction, on the other hand, deals from start to finish with the *a priori*.

2. The later stages of the subjective deduction are based upon the results of the objective deduction. The existence and validity of *a priori* factors having been demonstrated by transcendental, *i.e.* logical, analysis, the subjective deduction can be extended from the lower to the higher level, and can proceed to establish for the *a priori* elements what in its earlier stages it has determined for empirical consciousness, namely, the nature of the generative processes which require to be postulated as their ground and origin. When the two deductions are properly distinguished the objective deduction has, therefore, to be placed midway between the initial and the final stages of the subjective deduction.

3. The two deductions concentrate upon different aspects of experience. In the subjective deduction experience is

---

[1] Cf. above, pp. xxxvi, xxxvii-viii, 36 ; below, pp. 241-3.
[2] Cf. below, p. 543 ff.　　　　　　　[3] A xi.

chiefly viewed as a *temporal process* in which the given falls apart into successive events, which, in and by themselves, are incapable of constituting a unified consciousness. The fundamental characteristic of human experience, from this point of view, is that it is *serial* in character. Though it is an apprehension of time, it is itself also a process in time. In the objective deduction, on the other hand, the time element is much less prominent. Awareness of *objects* is the subject-matter to which analysis is chiefly devoted. This difference very naturally follows from the character of the two deductions. The subjective enquiry is mainly interested in the conditions generative of experience, and finds its natural point of departure in the problem by what processes a unified experience is constructed out of a succession of distinct happenings. The objective deduction presents the logical problem of validity in its most striking form, in our awareness of objects; the objective is contrasted with the subjective as being that which is universally and necessarily the same for all observers. Ultimately each of the two deductions must yield an analysis of both types of consciousness—awareness of time and awareness of objects; *a priori* factors are involved in the former no less than in the latter, and both are conditioned by generative processes. Unfortunately the manner in which this is done in the *Critique* causes very serious misunderstanding. The problem of the psychological conditions generative of consciousness of objects is raised[1] before the logical analysis of the objective deduction has established the data necessary for its profitable discussion. The corresponding defect in the objective deduction is of a directly opposite character, but is even more unfortunate in its effects. The results obtained from the analysis of our awareness of objects are not, within the limits of the objective deduction, applied in further analysis of our consciousness of time. That is first done, and even then by implication rather than by explicit argument, in the *Analytic of Principles*. This has the twofold evil consequence, that the relations holding between the two deductions are very greatly obscured, and that the reader is not properly prepared for the important use to which the results of the objective deduction are put in the *Analytic of Principles*. For it is there assumed—a quite legitimate inference from the objective deduction, but one whose legitimacy Kant has nowhere dwelt upon and explained—that to be conscious of time we must be conscious of it as existing in two distinct orders, subjective and objective. To

[1] A 100-1.

be conscious of time we must be conscious of objects, and to be conscious of objects we must be able to distinguish between the order of our ideas and the order of the changes (if any) in that which is known by their means.

Thus the two deductions, properly viewed in their full scope, play into one another's hands. The objective deduction is necessary to complete the analysis of time-consciousness given in the subjective deduction, and the extension of the analysis of object - consciousness to the explanation of time-consciousness is necessary in order to make quite definite and clear the full significance of the conclusions to which the objective enquiry has led.[1]

One last point remains for consideration. Experience is a highly ambiguous term, and to fulfil the rôle assigned to it by Kant's transcendental method—that of establishing the reality of the conditions of its own possibility—its actuality must lie beyond the sphere of all possible controversy. It must be itself a datum, calling indeed for explanation, but not itself making claims that are in any degree subject to possible challenge. Now if we abstract from all those particularising factors which are irrelevant in this connection, we are left with only three forms of experience—experience of self, experience of objects, and experience of time. The two former are open to question. They may be illusory, as Humé has argued. And as their validity, or rather actuality, calls for establishment, they cannot fulfil the demands which the transcendental method exacts from the experience whose possibility is to yield proof of its discoverable conditions. Consciousness of time, on the other hand, is a fact whose actuality, however problematic in its conditions, and however mysterious in its intrinsic nature, cannot, even by the most metaphysical of subtleties, be in any manner or degree challenged. It is an unquestioned possession of the human mind. Whether time itself is real we may not be metaphysically certain, but that, whatever be its reality or unreality, we are conscious of it in the form of change, is beyond all manner of doubt. Consciousness of time is the *factual* experience, as conditions of whose possibility the *a priori* factors are transcendentally proved. In so far as they can be

---

[1] Kant's failure either to distinguish or to connect the two deductions in any really clear and consistent manner is a defect which is accentuated rather than diminished in the second edition. Though the sections devoted to the subjective enquiry are omitted, and the argument of the objective deduction is so recast as to increase the emphasis laid upon its more strictly logical aspects, the teaching of the subjective deduction is retained and influences the argument at every point. For the new deduction, no less than that of the first edition, rests throughout upon the initial assumption that though connection or synthesis can never be given, it is yet the generative source of all consciousness of order and relation.

shown to be its indispensable conditions, its mere existence proves their reality. And such in effect is the ultimate character of Kant's proof of the objective validity of the categories. They are proved in that it is shown that only in and through them is consciousness of time possible.

The argument gains immeasurably in clearness when this is recognised; [1] and the deduction of the first edition of the *Critique*, in spite of its contorted character, remains in my view superior to that of the second edition owing to this more explicit recognition of the temporal aspect of consciousness and to employment of it as the initial starting-point. Analysis at once reveals that though consciousness of time is undeniably actual, it is conditioned in complex ways, and that among the conditions indispensably necessary to its possibility are both consciousness of self and consciousness of an objective order of existence. Starting from the undeniable we are thus brought to the problematic; but owing to the factual character of the starting-point we can substantiate what would otherwise remain open to question.

As this method of formulating Kant's argument gives greater prominence to the temporal factor than Kant himself does in his statement of the deductions, the reader may very rightly demand further evidence that I am not, by this procedure, setting the deductions in a false or arbitrary perspective. Any statement of Kant's position in other than his own *ipsissima verba* is necessarily, in large part, a matter of interpretation, and proof of its correctness must ultimately consist in the success with which it can be applied in unravelling the manifold strands that compose his tortuous and many-sided argument; but the following special considerations may be cited in advance. Those parts of the *Critique*, such as the chief paragraphs of the subjective deduction and the chapter on *Schematism*, which are demonstrably late in date of writing, agree in assigning greater prominence to the temporal aspect of experience. This is also true of those numerous passages added in the second edition which deal with inner sense. All of these show an increasing appreciation of the central rôle which time must play in the Critical enquiries. Secondly, proof of the validity of *specific* categories is given, as we shall find,[2] not in the objective deduction of the *Analytic of Concepts*, but only in the *Analytic of Principles*. What Kant gives in the former is only the quite general demonstration that forms of unity, such as are involved in all judgment, are demanded

---

[1] It appears most clearly in Kant's proof of the category of causality in the second *Analogy*. Cf. below, p. 364 ff.

[2] Cf. below, pp. 252-3, 258, 287, 333, 343.

for the possibility of experience. Now when proof of the specific categories does come, in the *Analytic of Principles*, it is manifestly based on the analysis of time-experience. In the three *Analogies*, for example, Kant's demonstration of the objective validity of the categories of relation consists in the proof that they are necessary conditions of the possibility of our time-consciousness. That is to say, the transcendental method of proof, when developed in full detail, in reference to some specific category, agrees with the formulation which I have given of the subjective and objective deductions. In the third place, Kant started from a spiritualist standpoint, akin to that of Leibniz,[1] and only very gradually broke away from the many illegitimate assumptions which it involves. But this original starting-point reveals its persisting influence in the excessive emphasis which Kant continued to lay upon the unity of apperception. He frequently speaks[2] as if it were an ultimate self-justifying principle, by reference to which the validity of all presupposed conditions can be established. But that, as I have already argued, is a legitimate method of procedure only if it has previously been established that self-consciousness is involved in all consciousness, that is, involved even in consciousness of sequence and duration. And as just stated, the deductions of specific categories, given in the *Analytic of Principles*, fulfil these requirements of complete proof. They start from the time-consciousness, not from apperception.

I shall now summarise these introductory discussions in a brief tabulated outline of the main steps in the argument of the two deductions, and shall add a concluding note upon their interconnection.

Subjective Deduction.—1. Consciousness of time is an experience whose actuality cannot be questioned; by its actuality it will therefore establish the reality of everything that can be proved to be its indispensable condition.

2. Among the conditions indispensably necessary to all consciousness of time are synthetic processes whereby the contents of consciousness, occurring in successive moments, are combined and unified. These processes are processes of apprehension, reproduction, and recognition.

3. Recognition, in turn, is conditioned by self-consciousness.

4. As no consciousness is possible without self-consciousness, the synthetic processes must have completed themselves before consciousness of any kind is possible, and consequently are not verifiable by introspection but only by hypothetical construction.

---

[1] Cf. above, p. 208 ff.

[2] Cf. above, pp. l-lii, 207-12; below, pp. 260-3, 272-3, 327-8, 473-7, 515.

[1, 2, 3, and 4 are steps which can be stated independently of the argument of the objective deduction.]

5. Self-consciousness presupposes consciousness of objects, and consciousness of objects presupposes the synthetic activities of productive imagination whereby the matter of sense is organised in accordance with the categories. These productive activities also are verifiable only by conjectural inference, and only upon their completion can consciousness of any kind make its appearance.

6. Consciousness of self and consciousness of objects thus alike rest upon a complexity of non-phenomenal conditions. For anything that critical analysis can prove to the contrary, consciousness and personality may not be ultimates. They may be resultants due to realities fundamentally different from themselves.

[5 is a conclusion obtained only by means of the argument of the objective deduction. 6 is a further conclusion, first explicitly drawn by Kant in the *Dialectic*.]

Objective Deduction.—1. The starting-point coincides with that of the subjective deduction. Consciousness of time is an experience by whose actuality we can establish the reality of its indispensable conditions.

2. Among the conditions necessary to all consciousness of time is self-consciousness.

3. Self-consciousness, in turn, is itself conditioned by consciousness of objects.

4. Consciousness of objects is possible only if the categories have validity within the sphere of sense-experience.

5. Conclusion.—The empirical validity of the categories, and consequently the empirical validity of our consciousness alike of the self and of objects, must be granted as a *conditio sine qua non* of our consciousness of time. They are the indispensable conditions of that fundamental experience.

As above stated,[1] the preliminary stages of the subjective deduction prepare the way for the argument of the objective deduction, while the results obtained by the latter render possible the concluding steps of the former. That is to say, the objective deduction has to be intercalated midway between the opening and the concluding stages of the subjective deduction. It may also be observed that whereas the objective deduction embodies the main positive teaching of the *Analytic*, in that it establishes the possibility of natural science and of a metaphysics of experience, the subjective deduction is more directly concerned with the subject-matter of the *Dialectic*, reinforcing, as it does, the more negative

[1] P. 239.

consequences which follow from the teaching of the objective deduction—the impossibility of transcendent speculation. It stands in peculiarly close connection with the teaching of the section on the *Paralogisms*. We may now proceed to a detailed statement of the argument of the two deductions.

THE SUBJECTIVE DEDUCTION IN ITS INITIAL EMPIRICAL STAGES

In the opening of the subjective deduction Kant is careful to give due prominence to the temporal aspect of our human experience.

" . . . all the contents of our knowledge are ultimately subject to the formal condition of inner sense, that is, to time, as that wherein they must all be ordered, connected, and brought into relation to one another. This is a general remark which the reader must bear in mind as being a fundamental presupposition of my entire argument." [1]

Consciousness of time is thus the starting-point of the deduction. Analysis reveals it as highly complex ; and the purpose of the deduction is to discover, and, as far as may be possible, to define its various conditions. The argument can best be expounded by reference to a single concrete example —say, our experience of a series of contents, *a, b, c, d, e, f*, as in succession to one another and as together making up the total six. In order that such an experience may be possible the successive members of the series must be held together simultaneously before the mind. Obviously, if the earlier members dropped out of consciousness before the mind reached *f*, *f* could not be apprehended as having followed upon them. There must be a synthesis of apprehension of the successive items.

Such a synthesis of apprehension is, however, only possible through reproduction of the earlier experiences. If when the mind has passed from *a* to *f*, *f* is apprehended as having followed upon *a, b, c, d, e*, such consciousness is only possible in so far as these earlier contents are reproduced in image. Synthesis of apprehension is conditioned by synthesis of reproduction in imagination.

" But if the preceding representations (the first parts of [a] line, the earlier moments of time or the units represented in sequent order) were always to drop out of my thought, and were not reproduced when I advance to those that follow, no complete representation, and none of all the aforementioned thoughts, not even the purest and first basal representations of space and time, could ever arise." [2]

---

[1] A 99.   [2] A 102.

In order, however, that the reproduced images may fulfil their function, they must be recognised as standing for or representing contents which the self has just experienced.

"Without the consciousness that what we are thinking is the same as what we thought a moment before, all reproduction in the series of representations would be in vain."[1]

Each reproduced image would in its present state be a new experience, and would not help in the least towards gaining consciousness of order or number in the succession of our experiences. Recognition is, therefore, a third form of synthesis, indispensably necessary to consciousness of time. But further, the recognition is recognition of a succession as forming a unity or whole, and that unity is always conceptual.

"The word concept (*Begriff*) might of itself have suggested this remark. For it is this unitary consciousness which unites into a single representation a manifold that has been successively intuited and then subsequently reproduced."[2] "If in counting I forgot that the units . . . have been added to one another in succession, I should never recognise what the sum-total is that is being produced through the successive addition of unit to unit; and so would remain ignorant of the number. For the concept of this number is nothing but the consciousness of this unity of synthesis."[3]

The synthesis of recognition is thus a synthesis which takes place in and through empirical concepts. In the instance which we have chosen, the empirical concept is that of the number six.

The analysis, however, is not yet complete. Just as reproduction conditions apprehension and both rest on recognition, so in turn recognition presupposes a still further condition, namely, self-consciousness. For it is obvious, once the fact is pointed out, that the recognition of reproduced images as standing for past experiences can only be possible in so far as there is an abiding self which is conscious of its identity throughout the succession. Such an act of recognition is, indeed, merely one particular form or concrete instance of self-consciousness. The unity of the empirical concept in and through which recognition takes place finds its indispensable correlate in the unity of an empirical self. Thus an analysis of our consciousness, even though conducted wholly on the empirical level, that is, without the least reference to the *a priori*, leads by simple and cogent argument to the

---

[1] A 103.   [2] *Loc. cit.*   [3] *Loc. cit.*

conclusion that it is conditioned by complex synthetic processes, and that these syntheses in turn presuppose a unity which finds twofold expression for itself, objectively through a concept and subjectively in self-consciousness.

So far I have stated the argument solely in reference to serial consciousness. Kant renders his argument needlessly complex and diminishes its force by at once extending it so as to cover the connected problem, how we become aware of objects. This occurs in the section on the synthesis of reproduction. An analysis of our consciousness of objects, as distinct from consciousness of the immediately successive, forces us to postulate further empirical conditions. Since the reproductive imagination, to whose agency the apprehension of complex unitary existences is psychologically due, acts through the machinery of association, it presupposes constancy in the apprehended manifold.

"If cinnabar were sometimes red, sometimes black, sometimes light, sometimes heavy, if a man changed sometimes into this and sometimes into that animal form, if the country on the longest day were sometimes covered with fruits, sometimes with ice and snow, my empirical imagination would never even have occasion when representing red colour to bring to mind heavy cinnabar. . . ."[1]

This passage may be compared with the one which occurs in the section on the synthesis of recognition. Our representations, in order to constitute knowledge, must have the unity of some concept; the manifold cannot be apprehended save in so far as this is possible.

"All knowledge demands a concept, though that concept may be quite imperfect or obscure. But a concept is always, as regards its form, something general which serves as a rule. The concept of body, for instance, as the unity of the manifold which is thought through it, serves as a rule to our knowledge of outer appearances. . . . It necessitates in the perception of something outside us the representation of extension, and therewith the representations of impenetrability, form, etc."[2]

So far the deduction still moves on the empirical level. When Kant, however, proceeds to insist[3] that this empirical postulate itself rests upon a transcendental condition, the argument is thrown into complete confusion, and the reader is bewildered by the sudden anticipation of one of the most difficult and subtle conclusions of the objective deduction. The same confusion is also caused throughout these sections as a whole by Kant's description of the various syntheses as

[1] A 100-1.   [2] A 106.   [3] A 101.

being transcendental.[1]   They cannot properly be so described.
The concepts referred to as unifying the syntheses, and the
self-consciousness which is proved to condition the syntheses,
are all empirical.   They present themselves in concrete form,
and presuppose characteristics due to the special contingent
nature of the given manifold; as Kant states in so many
words in the second edition.

"Whether I can become *empirically* conscious of the manifold
as simultaneous or as successive depends on circumstances or
empirical conditions.   The empirical unity of consciousness, through
association of representations, therefore itself relates to an appearance, and is wholly contingent."[2]

The argument in these preliminary stages of the subjective
deduction, in so far as it is employed to yield proof that all
consciousness involves the unity of concepts and the unity of
self-consciousness, is independent of any reference to the
categories, and consequently to transcendental conditions.
In accordance with the plan of exposition above stated, we
may now pass to the objective deduction.

OBJECTIVE DEDUCTION AS GIVEN IN THE FIRST EDITION

The transition from the preliminary stages of the subjective
deduction to the objective deduction may be made by further
analysis either of the objective unity of empirical concepts or
of the subjective unity of empirical self-consciousness.   It is
the former line which the argument of the first edition follows.
Kant is asking what is meant by an object corresponding
to our representations,[3] and answers by his objective deduction.   He substitutes the empirical for the transcendental
object,[4] and in so doing propounds one of the central and
most revolutionary tenets of the Critical philosophy.   Existence takes a threefold, not a merely dual form.   Besides
representations and things in themselves, there exist the
objects of our representations—the extended world of ordinary

---

[1] Such statements are in direct conflict with his own repeated assertions in
other passages that reproduction and recognition are always merely empirical.
Cf. above, pp. 227-31, and below, pp. 264, 268-9.

[2] B 139-40.

[3] In the first edition the subjective and objective deductions shade into one
another; and this question is raised in the section on synthesis of recognition
(A 104), where, as above noted (p. 204 ff.), Kant's argument is largely pre-Critical,
empirical concepts exercising the functions which Kant later ascribed to the
categories.   But as we have already considered the resulting doctrine of the
transcendental object both in its earlier and in its subsequent form, we may at
once pass to the more mature teaching of the other sections.

[4] Cf. above, p. 204 ff.

experience and of science.   Such a threefold distinction is
prefigured in the Leibnizian metaphysics, and is more or less
native to every philosophy that is genuinely speculative.
Kant himself claims Plato as his philosophical progenitor.
The originality is not in the bare thesis, but in the fruitful,
tenacious, and consistent manner in which it is developed
through detailed analysis of our actual experience.

In its first stages the argument largely coincides with the
argument of the paragraphs which deal with the transcendental
object.   When we examine the objective, we find that the
primary characteristic distinguishing it from the subjective is
that it lays a compulsion upon our minds, constraining us to
think about it in a certain way.   By an object is meant something which will not allow us to think at haphazard.   Cinnabar
is an object which constrains us to think it as heavy and red.
An object is thus the external source of a necessity to which
our thinking has to conform.   The two arguments first begin
to diverge when Kant sets himself to demonstrate that our
consciousness of this external necessity is made possible by
categories which originate from within.

For this conclusion Kant prepares the way by an analysis
of the second main characteristic constitutive of an object, viz.
its unity.   This unity is of a twofold nature, involving either
the category of substance and attribute or the category of
cause and effect.   The two categories are ultimately inseparable, but lead us to conceive the object in two distinct modes.
When we interpret an object through the *a priori* concept of
substance and attribute, we assert that all the contents of our
perceptions of it are capable of being regarded as qualities of
one and the same identical substance.   No one of its qualities
can be incongruent with any other, and all of them together,
in their unity, must be expressive of its substantial nature.

The causal interpretation of the object is, however, the
more important, and is that which is chiefly emphasised by
Kant.   It is, indeed, simply a further and more adequate
mode of expressing the substantial unity of the object.   All
the qualities must be causally bound up with one another in
such a way that the nature of each is determined by the
nature of all the others, and that if any one quality be
changed all the others must undergo corresponding alterations.
Viewed in this manner, in terms of the category of causality,
an object signifies a necessitated combination of interconnected
qualities or effects.   But since no such form of *necessita-
tion* can be revealed in the manifold of sense, our *consciousness* of compulsion cannot originate from without, and must
be due to those *a priori* forms which, though having their

source within, control and direct our interpretation of the given. Though the objective compulsion is not itself due to the mind, our *consciousness* of it has this mental *a priori* source. The concept of an object consists in the thought of a manifold so determined in its specific order and groupings as to be interpretable in terms of the categories of substance and causality.

But the problem of the deduction proper is not yet raised. On the one hand, Kant has defined what the concept of the objective must be taken as involving, and on the other, has pointed out that since the given as given is an unconnected manifold, any categories through which it may be interpreted must be of independent origin; but it still remains to be proved that the above is a valid as well as a possible mode of construing the given appearances. The categories, as *a priori* concepts, originate from within. By what right may we assert that they not only relate to an object, but even constitute the very concept of it? Are appearances legitimately interpretable in any such manner? It was, we may believe, in the process of answering this question that Kant came to realise that the objects of our representations must no longer be regarded as things in themselves. For, as he finds, a solution is possible only on the further assumption that the mind is legislating merely for the world of sense-experience, and is making no assertion in regard to the absolutely and independently real. Kant's method of proof is the transcendental, *i.e.* he seeks to demonstrate that this interpretation of the given is indispensably necessary as being a *sine qua non* of its possible apprehension. This is achieved by means of the conclusion already established through the preliminary steps of the subjective deduction, namely, that all consciousness involves self-consciousness. Kant's proof of the objective validity of the categories consists in showing that only by means of the interpretation of appearances as *empirically* objective is self-consciousness possible at all.

The self-consciousness of the subjective deduction, in the preliminary form above stated, is, however, itself empirical. Kant, developing on more strictly Critical lines the argument which had accompanied his earlier doctrine of the transcendental object, now proceeds to maintain in what is at once the most fruitful and the most misleading of his tenets, that the ultimate ground of the possibility of consciousness and therefore also of empirical self-consciousness is the transcendental unity of apperception. Such apperception, to use Kant's ambiguous phraseology, precedes experience as its *a priori* condition.   The interpretation of given appearances through *a priori* categories is a necessity of consciousness because it is a condition of self-consciousness; and it is a condition of self-consciousness because it alone will account for the transcendental apperception upon which all empirical self-consciousness ultimately depends.

One chief reason why Kant's deduction is found so baffling and illusive is that it rests upon an interpretation of the unity of apperception which is very definitely drawn, but to which Kant himself gives only the briefest and most condensed expression.   I shall therefore take the liberty of restating it in more explicit terms.   The true or transcendental self has no content of its own through which it can gain knowledge of itself.   It is mere identity, I am I.   In other words, self-consciousness is a mere *form* through which contents that never themselves constitute the self are yet apprehended as being objects to the self.   Thus though the self in being conscious of time or duration must be conscious of itself as *identical* throughout the succession of its experiences, this identity can never be discovered in those experiences; it can only be thought as a condition of them.   The continuity of memory, for instance, is not a possible substitute for transcendental apperception.   As the subjective deduction demonstrates, self-consciousness conditions memory, and cannot therefore be reduced to or be generated by it.[1] When, however, such considerations are allowed their due weight, the necessity of postulating a transcendental unity becomes only the more evident.   Though it can never itself be found among appearances, it is an interpretation which we are none the less compelled to give to appearances.

To summarise before proceeding.   We have obtained two important conclusions: first, that all consciousness involves self-consciousness; and secondly, that self-consciousness is a form in terms of which contents that do not constitute the self are apprehended as existing for the self.   The first leads up to the second, and the second is equivalent to the assertion that there can be no such thing as a pure self-consciousness, *i.e.* a consciousness in which the self is aware of itself and of nothing but itself.   Self-consciousness, to be

---

[1] Memory is only one particular mode in which recognition presents itself in our experience; Kant's purpose is to show that it is not more fundamental, nor more truly constitutive of apperception, than is recognition in any of its other manifestations.   Indeed the central contention of the objective deduction is that it is through consciousness of *objects, i.e.* through consciousness of *objective* meanings, that self-consciousness comes to be actualised at all.   Only in contrast with, and through relation to, an objective system is consciousness of inner experience, past or present, and therefore self-consciousness in its contingent empirical forms, possible to the mind.   Cf. above, pp. li-ii; below, pp. 260-3.

possible at all, must at the same time be a consciousness of something that is not-self. Only one further step is now required for the completion of the deduction, namely, proof that this not-self, consciousness of which is necessary to the possibility of self-consciousness, must consist in empirical objects apprehended in terms of the categories. For proof Kant again appeals to the indispensableness of apperception. As no intuitions can enter consciousness which are not capable of being related to the self, they must be so related to one another that, notwithstanding their variety and diversity, the self can still be conscious of itself as identical throughout them all. In other words, no intuition can be related to the self that is incapable of being combined together with all the other intuitions to form a unitary consciousness. I may here quote from the text of the second edition : [1]

" . . . only in so far as I can grasp the manifold of the representations in one consciousness, do I call them one and all mine. For otherwise I should have as many-coloured and diverse a self as I have representations of which I am conscious to myself."

Or as it is stated in the first edition : [2]

"We are *a priori* aware of the complete identity of the self in respect of all representations which belong to our knowledge . . . as a necessary condition of the possibility of all representations."

These are the considerations which lead Kant to entitle the unity of apperception *transcendental*. He so names it for the reason that, though it is not itself *a priori* in the manner of the categories, we are yet enabled by its means to demonstrate that the unity which is necessary for possible experience can be securely counted upon in the manifold of all possible representations, and because (as he believed) it also enables us to prove that the forms of such unity are the categories of the understanding.

To the argument supporting this last conclusion Kant does not give the attention which its importance would seem to deserve. He points out that as the given is an unconnected manifold, its unity can be obtained only by synthesis, and that such synthesis must conform to the conditions prescribed by the unity of apperception. That these conditions coincide with the categories he does not, however, attempt to prove. He apparently believes that this has been already established in the metaphysical deduction.[3] The forms of unity demanded by apperception, he feels justified in assuming,

---

[1] B 134.   [2] A 116.   [3] Cf. above, p. 242 ; below, pp. 258, 332-3.

are the categories. They may be regarded as expressing the minimum of unity necessary to the possibility of self-consciousness. If sensations cannot be interpreted as the diverse attributes of unitary substances, if events cannot be viewed as arising out of one another, if the entire world in space cannot be conceived as a system of existences reciprocally interdependent, all unity must vanish from experience, and apperception will be utterly impossible.[1]

The successive steps of the total argument of the deduction, as given in the first edition, are therefore as follows : Consciousness of time involves empirical self-consciousness ; empirical self-consciousness is conditioned by a transcendental self-consciousness ; and such transcendental self-consciousness is itself, in turn, conditioned by consciousness of objects. The argument thus completed becomes the proof of mutual interdependence. Self-consciousness and consciousness of objects, as polar opposites, mutually condition one another. Only through consciousness of both simultaneously can consciousness of either be attained. Only in and through reference to an object can an idea be related to a self, and so be accompanied by that self-consciousness which conditions recognition, and through recognition all the varying forms in which our consciousness can occur. From the point of view, however, of a Critical enquiry apperception is the more important of the two forms of consciousness. For though each is the *causa existendi* of the other, self-consciousness has the unique distinction of being the *causa cognoscendi* of the objective and *a priori* validity of the forms of understanding.

"The synthetic proposition, that all the variety of empirical consciousness must be combined in a single self-consciousness, is the absolutely first and synthetic principle of our thought in general."[2]

We may at this point consider Kant's doctrine of "objective affinity." It excellently enforces the main thesis which he is professing to establish, namely, that the conditions of *unitary* consciousness are the conditions of *all* consciousness. The language, however, in which the doctrine is expounded is extremely obscure and difficult ; and before commenting upon Kant's own methods of statement, it seems advisable to paraphrase the argument in a somewhat free manner, and also to defer consideration of the transcendental psychology which Kant has employed in its exposition.[3] Association can subsist only between ideas, both of which have

---

[1] Cf. A 111.   [2] A 117 *n.*
[3] This transcendental psychology is considered below (p. 263 ff.), in its connection with the later stages of the subjective deduction. Cf. above, p. 238.

occurred within the same conscious field. Now the fundamental characteristic of consciousness, the very condition of
its existing at all, is its unity ; and until this has been
recognised, there can be no understanding of the associative
connection which arises under the conditions which consciousness supplies. To attempt to explain the unity of
consciousness through the mechanism of association is to
explain an agency in terms of certain of its own effects. It is
to explain the fundamental in terms of the derivative, the
conditions in terms of what they have themselves made
possible. Kant's argument is therefore as follows. Ideas do
not become associated merely by co-existing. They must
occur together in a unitary consciousness ; and among the
conditions necessary to the possibility of association are
therefore the conditions of the possibility of experience.
Association is transcendentally grounded. So far from
accounting for the unity of consciousness, it presupposes the
latter as determining the conditions under which alone it can
come into play.

"... how, I ask, is association itself possible ? ... On my
principles the thorough-going affinity of appearances is easily
explicable. All possible appearances belong as representations
to the totality of a possible self-consciousness. But as this self-
consciousness is a transcendental representation, numerical identity
is inseparable from it and is *a priori* certain. For nothing can
come to our knowledge save in terms of this original apperception.
Now, since this identity must necessarily enter into the synthesis of
all the manifold of appearances, so far as the synthesis is to yield
empirical knowledge, the appearances are subject to *a priori* conditions, with which the synthesis of their apprehension must be in
complete accordance. ... Thus all appearances stand in a thoroughgoing connection according to necessary laws, and therefore in a
transcendental affinity of which the empirical is a mere consequence."[1]

In other words, representations must exist in consciousness before they can become associated ; and they can exist
in consciousness only if they are consciously apprehended.
But in order to be consciously apprehended, they must
conform to the transcendental conditions upon which all
consciousness rests ; and in being thus apprehended they are
set in thoroughgoing unity to one another and to the self.
They are apprehended as belonging to an objective order or
unity which is the correlate of the unity of self-consciousness.
This is what Kant entitles their objective affinity ; it is what

---

[1] A 113-14.

conditions and makes possible their associative or empirical connection.

This main point is very definitely stated in A 101.

"If we can show that even our purest *a priori* intuitions yield no knowledge, save in so far as they contain such a connection of the manifold as will make possible a thoroughgoing synthesis of reproduction, this synthesis of the imagination" [which acts through the machinery of association] "must be grounded, prior to all experience, on *a priori* principles, and since experience necessarily presupposes that appearances can be reproduced, we shall have to assume a pure transcendental synthesis of the imagination" [*i.e.* such synthesis as is involved in the unity of consciousness] "as conditioning even the possibility of all experience."[1]

In A 121-2 Kant expresses his position in a more ambiguous manner. He may seem to the reader merely to be arguing that a certain minimum of regularity is necessary in order that representations may be associated, and experience may be possible.[2] But the general tenor of the passage as a whole, and especially its concluding sentences, enforce the stronger, more consistent, thesis.

"[The] subjective and empirical ground of reproduction according to rules is named the association of representations. If this unity of association did not also have an objective ground, which makes it impossible that appearances should be apprehended by the imagination except under the condition of a possible synthetic unity of this apprehension, it would be entirely accidental that appearances should fit into a connected whole of human knowledge. For even though we had the power of associating perceptions, it would remain entirely undetermined and accidental whether they would themselves be associable; and should they not be associable, there might exist a multitude of perceptions, and indeed an entire sensibility, in which much empirical consciousness would arise in my mind, but in a state of separation, and without belonging to one consciousness of myself. That, however, is impossible. For only in so far as I ascribe all perceptions to one consciousness (original apperception), can I say in all perceptions that I am conscious of them. There must therefore be an objective ground (that is, one that can be recognised *a priori*, antecedently to all empirical laws of the imagination) upon which may rest the possibility, nay the necessity, of a law that extends to all appearances. . . ."

Kant is not merely asserting that the associableness of ideas, and the regularity of connection which that implies, must be postulated as a condition of experience. That would be a mere begging of the issue; the correctness of the

---

[1] Cf. above, p. 229.　　　　[2] Cf. A 100-1.

postulate would not be independently proved.   Kant is really maintaining the much more important thesis, that the unity of experience, *i.e.* of consciousness, is what makes association possible at all.   And since consciousness must be unitary in order to exist, there cannot be any empirical consciousness in which the conditions of association, and therefore of reproduction, are not to be found.

A further misunderstanding is apt to be caused by Kant's statement that associative affinity rests upon objective affinity. This seems to imply, in the same manner as the passage which we have just considered, that instead of proving that appearances are subject to law and order, he is merely postulating that an abiding ground of such regularity must exist in the noumenal conditions of the sense manifold.   But he himself again supplies the needful correction.

"This [objective ground of all association of appearances] can nowhere be found, except in the principle of the unity of apperception in respect of all forms of knowledge which can belong to me. In accordance with this principle all appearances must so enter the mind, or be so apprehended, that they fit together to constitute the unity of apperception.   This would be impossible without synthetic unity in their connection, and that unity is therefore also objectively necessary.   The objective unity of all empirical consciousness in one consciousness, that of original apperception, is therefore the necessary condition of all (even of all *possible*) perception ; and the affinity of all appearances, near or remote, is a necessary consequence of a synthesis in imagination which is grounded *a priori* on rules." [1]

The fundamental characteristic of consciousness is the unified form in which alone it can exist; only when this unity is recognised as indispensably necessary, and therefore as invariably present whenever consciousness exists at all, can the inter-relations of the contents of consciousness be properly defined.

If this main contention of the Critical teaching be accepted, Hume's associationist standpoint is no longer tenable. Association cannot be taken to be an ultimate and inexplicable property of our mental states.   Nor is it a property which can be regarded as belonging to presentations viewed as so many independent existences.   It is conditioned by the unity of consciousness, and therefore rests upon the "transcendental" conditions which Critical analysis reveals. Since the unity of consciousness conditions association, it cannot be explained as the outcome and product of the mechanism of association.

[1] A 122-3.

In restating the objective deduction in the second edition, Kant has omitted all reference to this doctrine of objective affinity. His reasons for this omission were probably twofold. In the first place, it has been expounded in terms of a transcendental psychology, which, as we shall find, is conjectural in character. And secondly, the phrase "objective affinity" is, as I have already pointed out, decidedly misleading. It seems to imply that Kant is postulating, without independent proof, that noumenal conditions must be such as to supply an orderly manifold of sense data. But though the doctrine of objective affinity is eliminated, its place is to some extent taken [1] by the proof that all apprehension is an act of judgment and therefore involves factors which cannot be reduced to, or explained in terms of, association.

There are a number of points in the deduction of the first edition which call for further explanatory and critical comment. The first of these concerns the somewhat misleading character of the term *a priori* as applied to the categories. It carries with it rationalistic associations to which the Critical standpoint, properly understood, yields no support. The categories are for Kant of merely *de facto* nature. They have no intrinsic validity. They are proved only as being the indispensable conditions of what is before the mind as brute fact, namely, conscious experience. By the *a priori* is meant merely those *relational* factors which are required to supplement the given manifold in order to constitute our actual consciousness. And, as Kant is careful to point out, the experience, as conditions of which their validity is thus established, is of a highly specific character, resting upon synthesis of a manifold given in space and time. That is to say, their indispensableness is proved only for a consciousness which in these fundamental respects is constituted like our own.[2] And secondly, the validity of the *a priori* categories, even in our human thinking, is established only in reference to that empirical world which is constructed out of the given manifold in terms of the intuitive forms, space and time. Their validity is a merely phenomenal validity. They are valid of appearances, but not of things in themselves. The *a priori* is thus doubly *de facto*: first as a condition of brute fact, namely, the actuality of our human consciousness; and

---

[1] Cf. B 140-3; B 151-2; B 164-5; and below, p. 286.

[2] Here again the second edition text is more explicit than the first: "This peculiarity of our understanding, that it can produce *a priori* unity of apperception solely by means of the categories, and only by such and so many, is as little capable of further explanation as why we have just these and no other functions of judgment, or why space and time are the sole forms of our possible intuition." --B 145-6. Cf. above, pp. xxxiii-vi, xliv, 57, 142, 186; below, pp. 291, 411.

secondly, as conditioning a consciousness whose knowledge is limited to appearances. It is a relative, not an absolute *a priori*. Acceptance of it does not, therefore, commit us to rationalism in the ordinary meaning of that term. Its credentials are conferred upon it by what is mere fact ; it does not represent an order superior to the actual and legislative for it. In other words, it is Critical, not Leibnizian in character. No transcendent metaphysics can be based upon it. In formulating this doctrine of the *a priori* as yielding objective insight and yet as limited in the sphere of its application, the *Critique of Pure Reason* marks an epoch in the history of scepticism, no less than in the development of Idealist teaching.

There is one important link in the deduction, as above given, which is hardly calculated to support the conclusions that depend upon it. Kant, as we have already noted,[1] asserts that the categories express the minimum of unity necessary for the possibility of apperception. A contention so essential to the argument calls for the most careful scrutiny and a meticulous exactitude of proof. As a matter of fact, such proof is not to be found in any part of the deductions, whether of the first or of the second editions. It is attempted only in the later sections on the *Principles of Understanding*, and even there it is developed, in any really satisfactory fashion, only in regard to the categories of causality and reciprocity.[2] This proof, however, as there given, is an argument which in originality, subtlety and force goes far to atone for all shortcomings. It completes the objective deduction by developing in masterly fashion (in spite of the diffuse and ill-arranged character of the text) the central contention for which the deduction stands. But in the transcendental deduction itself, we find only such an argument—if it may be called an argument—as follows from the identification of apperception with understanding.

"The unity of apperception, in relation to the synthesis of imagination, is the understanding. . . . In understanding there are pure *a priori* forms of knowledge which contain the necessary unity of pure synthesis of imagination in respect of all possible appearances. But these are the categories, *i.e.* pure concepts of understanding."[3]

The point is again merely assumed in A 125-6. So also in A 126 :

"Although through experience we learn many laws, these are only special determinations of still higher laws, of which the highest,

---

[1] Cf. above, pp. 252-3.
[2] The second *Analogy* embodies the argument which is implied in, and necessary to, the establishment of the assertions dogmatically made in A 111-12.
[3] A 119.

under which all others stand, originate *a priori* in the understanding itself. . . ."[1]

Again in A 129 it is argued that as we prescribe *a priori* rules to which all experience must conform, those rules cannot be derived from experience, but must precede and condition it, and can do so only as originating from ourselves (*aus uns selbst*).

"[They] precede all knowledge of objects as [their] intellectual form, and constitute a formal *a priori* knowledge of all objects in so far as they are thought (categories)."

But this is only to repeat that such forms of unity as are necessary to self-consciousness must be realised in all synthesis. It is no sufficient proof that those forms of relation coincide with the categories. As we shall find in considering the deduction of the second edition, Kant to some extent came to recognise the existence of this gap in his argument and sought to supply the missing steps. But his method of so doing still ultimately consists in an appeal to the results of the metaphysical deduction, and therefore rests upon his untenable belief in the adequacy of formal logic. It fails to obviate the objection in any satisfactory manner.

As regards the negative aspect of the conclusion reached— that the validity of the categories is established only for appearances—Kant maintains that this is a necessary corollary of their validity being *a priori*. That things in themselves must conform to the conditions demanded by the nature of our self-consciousness is altogether impossible of proof. Even granting, what is indeed quite possible, that things in themselves embody the pure forms of understanding, we still cannot have any ground for maintaining that they must do so of necessity and will be found to do so universally. For even if we could directly experience things in themselves, and apprehend them as conforming to the categories, such conformity would still be known only as contingent. But when it is recognised that nature consists for us of nothing but appearances, existing only in the mode in which they are experienced, and therefore as necessarily conforming to the conditions under which experience is alone possible, the paradoxical aspect of the apriority ascribed to the categories at once vanishes. Proof of their *a priori* validity presupposes the phenomenal character of the objects to which they apply. They can be proved to be universal and necessarily valid of objects only in so far as it can be shown that they have

---

[1] Cf. A 128. On this whole question cf. above, p. 242; below, pp. 287-8.

antecedently conditioned and constituted them. The sole sufficient reason for asserting them to be universally valid throughout experience is that they are indispensably necessary for rendering it possible.[1] The transcendental method of proof, *i.e.* proof by reference to the very possibility of experience, is for this reason, as Kant so justly emphasises, the sole type of argument capable of fulfilling the demands which have to be met. It presupposes, and itself enforces, the truth of the fundamental Critical distinction between appearances and things in themselves.

Kant entitles the unity of apperception *original* (*ursprünglich*);[2] and we may now consider how far and in what sense this title is applicable.[3] *From the point of view of method* there is the same justification for employing the term 'original' as for entitling the unity of apperception transcendental.[4] Self-consciousness is more fundamental or original than consciousness of objects, in so far as[5] it is only from the subjective standpoint which it represents that the objective deduction can demonstrate the necessity of synthesis, and the empirical validity of the pure forms of understanding. It is as a condition of the possibility of self-consciousness that the objective employment of the categories is proved to be legitimate. *In the development of the deduction* self-consciousness is, therefore, more original than consciousness of objects. Kant's employment of the term is, however, extremely misleading. For it would seem to imply that the self has been proved to be original or ultimate in an ontological sense, as if it preceded experience, and through its antecedent reality rendered objective experience possible of achievement. Such a view is undoubtedly reinforced by Kant's transformation of apperception into a faculty—*das Radicalvermögen aller unsrer Erkenntniss*[6]—and his consequent identification of it with the understanding.[7] It then seems as if he were maintaining that the transcendental ego is ultimate and is independent of all conditions, and that to its synthetic activities the various forms of objective consciousness are due.[8]

This unfortunate phraseology is directly traceable to the spiritualistic or Leibnizian character of Kant's earlier standpoint. In the *Dissertation* the self is viewed as an ultimate

---

[1] Cf. A 113, 125-9.   [2] A 107, 111.

[3] The explanation given in the second edition (B 132) is artificial, and does not reveal Kant's real reasons. It is also obscure owing to its employment of dynamical terms to denote the relation of apperception to self-consciousness.

[4] Cf. above, pp. 251-3.   [5] Cf. A 112, 113, 128.

[6] A 114.   [7] A 94, 115, 118. Cf. also end of note to B 134.

[8] Cf. above, pp. lii, 207-12, 243; below, pp. 327-8, 473-7, 515.

and unconditioned existence, antecedent to experience and creatively generative of it. We have already noted that a somewhat similar view is presented in the *Critique* in those paragraphs which Vaihinger identifies as embodying the earliest stage in the development of the argument of the deduction. The self is there described as coming to consciousness of its permanence through reflection upon the constancy of its own synthetic activities. Our consciousness of a transcendental object, and even the possibility of the empirical concepts through which such consciousness is, in these paragraphs, supposed to be mediated, are traced to this same source. To the last this initial excess of emphasis upon the unity of apperception remained characteristic of Kant's Critical teaching; and though in the later statements of his theory, its powers and prerogatives were very greatly diminished, it still continued to play a somewhat exaggerated rôle. The early spiritualistic views were embodied in a terminology which he continued to employ; and unless the altered meaning of his terms is recognised and allowed for, misunderstanding is bound to result. The terms, having been forged under the influence of the older views, are but ill adapted to the newer teaching which they are employed to formulate.

There was also a second influence at work. When Kant was constrained in the light of his new and unexpected results, to recognise his older views as lacking in theoretical justification, he still held to them in his own personal thinking. For there is ample evidence that they continued to represent his *Privatmeinungen*.[1]

Only, therefore, when these misleading influences, verbal, expository, and personal, are discounted, do the results of the deduction appear in their true proportions. Kant's Critical philosophy does not profess to prove that it is self-consciousness, or apperception, or a transcendental ego, or anything describable in kindred terms, which ultimately renders experience possible. The most that we can legitimately postulate, as noumenally conditioning experience, are "syntheses" (themselves, in their generative character, not definable)[2] in accordance with the categories. For only upon the completion of such syntheses do consciousness of self and consciousness of objects come to exist. Consciousness of objects does, indeed, according to the argument of the deduction, involve consciousness of self; self-consciousness is the form of all consciousness. But, by the same argument, it is equally true

---

[1] This is shown, not only by Kant's ethical writings, but also by his less formal utterances, especially in his *Lectures on Metaphysics* and on *Religion*, in his *Reflexionen*, and in his *Lose Blätter*.   [2] Cf. below, pp. 277-8.

that only in and through consciousness of objects is any self-consciousness possible at all. Consciousness of self and consciousness of objects *mutually* condition one another. Only through consciousness of both simultaneously can consciousness of either be attained. Self-consciousness is not demonstrably in itself any more ultimate or original than is consciousness of objects. Both alike are forms of experience which are conditioned in complex ways. Upon the question as to whether or not there is any such thing as abiding personality, the transcendental deduction casts no direct light. Indeed consciousness of self, as the more inclusive and complex form of awareness, may perhaps be regarded as pointing to a greater variety of contributory and generative conditions.

Unfortunately Kant, for the reasons just stated, has not sufficiently emphasised this more negative, or rather noncommittal, aspect of the results of the deduction. But when later in the chapter on the *Paralogisms* he is brought face to face with the issue, and has occasion to pronounce upon the question, he speaks with no uncertain voice. In the theoretical sphere there is, he declares, no sufficient proof of the spirituality, or unitary and ultimate character, of the self. Like everything else the unity of apperception must be noumenally conditioned, but it cannot be shown that in itself, *as self-consciousness 'or apperception*, it represents any noumenal reality. It may be a resultant, resting upon, and due to, a complexity of generative conditions ; and these conditions may be fundamentally different in character from itself. They may, for all that we can prove to the contrary, be of a non-conscious and non-personal nature. There is nothing in our cognitive experience, and no result of the Critical analysis of it, which is inconsistent with such a possibility.[1] Those commentators, such as Cohen, Caird, and Watson, who more or less follow Hegel in his criticism of Kant's procedure, give an interpretation of the transcendental deduction which makes it inconsistent with the sceptical conclusions which the *Critique* as a whole is made by its author to support. Unbiassed study of the *Analytic*, even if taken by itself in independence of the *Dialectic*, does not favour such a view. The argument of the transcendental deduction itself justifies no more than Kant is willing to allow in his discussion of the nature of the self in the section on the *Paralogisms*. It may, indeed, as Caird has so forcibly shown in his massive work upon the Critical philosophy, be developed upon Hegelian lines, but only through a process of essential reconstruction which

[1] Cf. above, pp. l-lii ; below, pp. 277 ff., 461-2, 473-7.

departs very far from many of Kant's most cherished tenets, and which does so in a manner that radically conflicts with the spirit which dominates the *Critique* as a whole.

THE LATER STAGES OF THE SUBJECTIVE DEDUCTION

The reader will have noted that several of the factors in Kant's exposition have so far been entirely ignored. The time has now come for reckoning with them. They constitute, in my view, the later stages of the subjective deduction. That is to say, they refer to the transcendental generative powers which Kant, *on the strength of the results obtained in the more objective enquiry*, feels justified in postulating. Separate consideration of them tends to clearness of statement. Kant's constant alternation between the logical and the dynamical standpoints is one of the many causes of the obscurity in his argument. In this connection we shall also find opportunity to discuss the fundamental conflict, to which I have already had occasion to refer, between the subjectivist and the phenomenalist modes of developing the Critical standpoint.

The conclusions arrived at in the objective deduction compelled Kant to revise his previous psychological views. Hitherto he had held to the Leibnizian theory that *a priori* concepts are obtained by reflection upon the mind's native and fundamental modes of action. In the *Dissertation* he carefully distinguishes between the *logical* and the *real* employment of the understanding. Through the former empirical concepts are derived from concrete experience. Through the latter pure concepts are creatively generated. Logical and real thinking agree, however, Kant there argues, in being activities of the *conscious* mind. Both can be apprehended and adequately determined through the revealing power of reflective consciousness. Such a standpoint is no longer tenable for Kant. Now that he has shown that the consciousness of self and the consciousness of objects mutually condition one another, and that until both are attained neither is possible, he can no longer regard the mind as even possibly conscious of the activities whereby experience is brought about. The activities generative of consciousness have to be recognised as themselves falling outside it. Not even in its penumbra, through some vague form of apprehension, can they be detected. Only the finished products of such activities, not the activities themselves, can be presented to consciousness ; and only by general reasoning, inferential of agencies that lie outside the conscious field, can we hope to determine them.

Now Kant appears to have been unwilling to regard the 'understanding' as ever unconscious of its activities. Why he was unwilling, it does not seem possible to explain ; at most his rationalist leanings and Wolffian training may be cited as contributing causes. To the end he continued to speak of the understanding as the faculty whereby the *a priori* is brought to consciousness. In order to develop the distinctions demanded by the new Critical attitude, he had therefore to introduce a new faculty, capable of taking over the activities which have to be recognised as non-conscious. For this purpose he selected the imagination, giving to it the special title, *productive* imagination. The empirical reproductive processes hitherto alone recognised by psychologists are not, he declares, exhaustive of the nature of the imagination. It is also capable of *transcendental* activity, and upon this the "objective affinity" of appearances and the resulting possibility of their empirical apprehension is made to rest. The productive imagination is also viewed as rendering possible the understanding, that is, the conscious apprehension of the *a priori* as an element embedded in objective experience. Such apprehension is possible because in the pre-conscious elaboration of the given manifold the productive imagination has conformed to those *a priori* principles which the understanding demands for the possibility of its own exercise in conscious apprehension. Productive imagination acts in the manner required to yield experiences which are capable of relation to the unity of self-consciousness, *i.e.* of being found to conform to the unity of the categories. Why it should act in this manner cannot be explained ; but it is none the less, on Critical principles, a legitimate assumption, since only in so far as it does so can experience, which *de facto* exists, be possible in any form. As a condition *sine qua non* of actual and possible experience, the existence of such a faculty is, Kant argues, a legitimate inference from the results of the transcendental deduction.

Though Kant's insistence upon the conscious character of understanding compels him to distinguish between it and the imagination, he has also to recognise their kinship. If imagination can never act save in conformity with the *a priori* forms of understanding, some reason must exist for their harmony. This twofold necessity of at once distinguishing and connecting them is the cause of the hesitating and extremely variable account which in both editions of the *Critique* is given of their relation. In several passages the understanding is spoken of as simply imagination which has attained to consciousness of its activities.[1] Elsewhere he explicitly states that they are distinct and separate. From this second point of view Kant regards imagination as mediating between sense and understanding, and, though reducible to neither, akin to both.

Only on one point is Kant clear and definite, namely, that it is to productive imagination that the *generation* of unified experience is primarily due. In it something of the fruitful and inexhaustible character of noumenal reality is traceable. Doubtless one chief reason for his choice of the title imagination is the creative character which in popular thought has always been regarded as its essential feature. As Kant, speaking of schematism, which is a process executed by the imagination, states in A 141: "This schematism . . . is an *art (Kunst)* concealed in the depths of the human soul."[2] This description may perhaps be interpreted in the light of Kant's account of the creative character of artistic genius in the *Critique of Judgment*, for there also imagination figures as the truly originative or creative faculty of the human spirit. To its noumenal character we may also trace its capacity of combining those factors of sense and understanding which in the realm of appearance remain persistently opposed.[3] Imagination differs from the understanding chiefly in that it is at once more comprehensive and also more truly creative. It supplements the functional forms with a sensuous content, and applies them dynamically in the generation of experience.

The schemata, which the productive imagination is supposed to construct, are those generalised forms of temporal and spatial existence in which alone the unity of experience necessary to apperception can be realised. They are

"pure (without admixture of anything empirical), and yet are in one aspect intellectual and in another sensuous."[4]

Or as Kant describes the process in the chapter before us:[5]

"We name the synthesis of the manifold in imagination transcendental, if without distinction of intuitions it is directed exclusively to the *a priori* combination of the manifold; and the unity of this synthesis is entitled transcendental, if it is represented as *a priori* necessary in relation to the original unity of apperception.

---

[1] In note to B 162 they are indeed identified.
[2] Kant's vacillating attitude appears in the added phrase "of whose activity we are *hardly ever* conscious." Cf. A 78: it is a "blind" power.
[3] Cf. above, p. 225; below, p. 337.
[4] A 138 = B 177.   [5] A 118.

As this unity of apperception conditions the possibility of all knowledge, the transcendental unity of the synthesis of imagination is the pure form of all possible knowledge. Hence, through it all objects of possible experience must be represented *a priori*."

The schemata, thus transcendentally generated, are represented by Kant as limiting and controlling the empirical processes of apprehension, reproduction, and recognition. As no experience is attainable save in terms of the schemata, they enable us to determine, on *a priori* grounds, the degree of constancy and regularity that can be securely counted upon in all experience. This is Kant's psychological explanation of what he has entitled "objective affinity." [1] The empirical ground of reproduction is the association of ideas; its transcendental ground is an objective affinity which is "a necessary consequence of a synthesis in imagination, grounded *a priori* on rules." [2]

"[The] subjective and empirical ground of reproduction according to rules is named the association of representations. If this unity of association did not also have an objective ground, which makes it impossible that appearances should be apprehended by the imagination except under the condition of a possible synthetic unity of this apprehension, it would be entirely accidental that appearances should fit into a connected whole of human knowledge. . . . There might exist a multitude of perceptions, and indeed an entire sensibility, in which much empirical consciousness would arise in my mind, but in a state of separation, and without belonging to one consciousness of myself. That, however, is impossible." [As the subjective and objective deductions have demonstrated, where there is no self-consciousness there is no consciousness of any kind.] "There must therefore be an objective ground (that is, one that can be determined *a priori*, antecedently to all empirical laws of the imagination) upon which may rest the possibility, nay, the necessity of a law that extends to all appearances—the law, namely, that all appearances must be regarded as data of the senses which are associable in themselves and subject to general rules of universal connection in their reproduction. This objective ground of all association of appearances I entitle their *affinity*. . . . The objective unity of all empirical consciousness in one consciousness, that of original apperception, is the necessary condition of all possible perception; and the affinity of all appearances, near or remote, is a necessary consequence of a synthesis in imagination which is grounded *a priori* on rules." [3]

This part of Kant's teaching is apt to seem more obscure than it is. For the reader is not unnaturally disinclined to

---

[1] Cf. above, p. 253 ff.   [2] A 123.   [3] A 121-3.

accept it in the very literal sense in which it is stated. That Kant means, however, exactly what he says, appears from the further consequence which he himself not only recognises as necessary, but insists upon as valid. The doctrine of objective affinity culminates in the conclusion[1] that it is " we ourselves who introduce into the appearances that order and regularity which we name nature." The "we ourselves" refers to the mind in the transcendental activities of the productive imagination. The conscious processes of apprehension, reproduction, and recognition necessarily conform to schemata, non-consciously generated, which express the combined *a priori* conditions of intuition and understanding required for unitary consciousness.

Many points in this strange doctrine call for consideration. It rests, in the first place, upon the assumption of a hard and fast distinction, very difficult of acceptance, between transcendental and empirical activities of the mind. Secondly, Kant's assertion, that the empirical manifolds can be relied upon to supply a satisfactory content for the schemata, calls for more adequate justification than he himself adduces. It is upon independent reality that the fixity of empirical co-existences and sequences depends. Is not Kant practically assuming a pre-established harmony in asserting that as the mind creates the *form* of nature it can legislate *a priori* for all possible experience?

As regards the first assumption Kant would seem to have been influenced by the ambiguities of the term transcendental. It means, as we have already noted,[2] either the science of the *a priori*, or the *a priori* itself, or the conditions which render experience possible. Even the two latter meanings by no means coincide. The conditions of the possibility of experience are not in all cases *a priori*. The manifold of outer sense is as indispensable a precondition of experience as are the forms of understanding, and yet is not *a priori* in any valid sense of that term. It does not, therefore, follow that because the activities of productive imagination "transcendentally" condition experience, they must themselves be *a priori*, and must, as Kant also maintains,[3] deal with a pure *a priori* manifold. Further, the separation between transcendental and empirical activities of the mind must defeat the very purpose for which the productive imagination is postulated, namely, in order to account for the generation of a complex consciousness in which no one element can temporally precede any of the others. If the productive imagination generates only schemata, it will not

---

[1] A 125-6.   [2] Above, pp. 74 ff., 238, 252.   [3] Cf. above, pp. 96-7.

account for that complex experience in which consciousness of self and consciousness of objects are indissolubly united. The introduction of the productive imagination seems at first sight to promise recognition of the dynamical aspect of our temporally sequent experience, and of that aspect in which as appearance it refers us beyond itself to non-experienced conditions. As employed, however, in the doctrines of schematism and of objective affinity, the imagination exhibits a formalism hardly less extreme than that of the understanding whose shortcomings it is supposed to make good.

In his second assumption Kant, as so often in the *Critique*, is allowing his old-time rationalistic leanings to influence him in underestimating the large part which the purely empirical must always occupy in human experience, and in exaggerating the scope of the inferences which can be drawn from the presence of the formal, relational factors. But this is a point which we are not yet in a position to discuss.[1]

Fortunately, if Vaihinger's theory be accepted,[2] section A 98-104 enables us to follow the movement of Kant's mind in the interval between the formulating of the doctrine of productive imagination and the publication of the *Critique*. He himself would seem to have recognised the unsatisfactoriness of dividing up the total conditions of experience into transcendental activities that issue in schemata, and supplementary empirical processes which transform them into concrete, specific consciousness. The alternative theory which he proceeds to propound is at first sight much more satisfactory. It consists in duplicating each of the various empirical processes with a transcendental faculty. There are, he now declares, three transcendental powers—a transcendental faculty of apprehension, a transcendental faculty of reproduction (=imagination), and a transcendental faculty of recognition. Thus Kant's previous view that transcendental imagination has a special and unique activity, namely, the productive, altogether different in type from any of its empirical processes, is now allowed to drop; in place of it Kant develops the view that the transcendental functions run exactly parallel with the empirical processes.[3] But though such a position may at first seem more promising than that which it displaces, it soon reveals its unsatisfactoriness. The two types of mental activity, transcendental and empirical, no longer, indeed, fall apart; but the difficulty now arises of distinguishing in apprehension, reproduction, and recognition

---

[1] Cf. below, pp. 367, 371-2.
[2] Cf. above, pp. 211, 227, 233-4.
[3] In direct contradiction of his previous view of transcendental imagination as purely productive, it is now stated that it is reproductive. Cf. A 102.

any genuinely transcendental aspect.[1] Apprehension, reproduction, and recognition are so essentially conscious processes that to view them as also transcendental does not seem helpful. They contain elements that are transcendental in the logical sense, but cannot be shown to presuppose in any analogous fashion mental powers that are transcendental in the dynamical sense. This is especially evident in regard to recognition, which is described as being "the *consciousness* that what we are thinking is the same as what we thought a moment before." In dealing with apprehension and reproduction the only real difference which Kant is able to suggest, as existing between their transcendental and their empirical activities, is that the former synthesise the pure *a priori* manifolds of space and time, and the latter the contingent manifold of sense. But even this unsatisfactory distinction he does not attempt to apply in the case of recognition. Nor can we hold that by the transcendental synthesis of recognition Kant means transcendental apperception. That is, of course, the suggestion which at once occurs to the reader. But however possible it might be to inject such a meaning into kindred passages elsewhere, it cannot be made to fit the context of this particular section.

Vaihinger's theory seems to be the only thread which will guide us through this labyrinth. Kant, on the eve of the publication of the *Critique*, recognising the unsatisfactoriness of his hard and fast separation of transcendental from empirical processes, adopted the view that some form of transcendental activity corresponds to every fundamental form of empirical activity and *vice versa*. Hastily developing this theory, he incorporated it into the *Critique* alongside his older doctrine. It does not, however, reappear in the *Prolegomena*, and its teaching is explicitly withdrawn in the second edition of the *Critique*. Its plausibility had entrapped him into its temporary adoption, but the defects which it very soon revealed speedily led him to reject it.

One feature of great significance calls for special notice. The breakdown of this doctrine of a threefold transcendental synthesis did not, as might naturally have been expected from what is stated in the prefaces to the *Critique* regarding the unessential and seemingly conjectural character of the subjective deduction, lead Kant to despair of developing a transcendental psychology. Though in the second edition he cuts away the sections containing the earlier stages of the subjective deduction,[2] and in recasting the other sections

[1] Cf. above, pp. 225 ff., 264.
[2] It must be remembered that this was also rendered necessary by the archaic character of their teaching in regard to the transcendental object and the function of empirical concepts.

gives greater prominence to the more purely logical analyses, the older doctrine of productive imagination is reinstated in full force,[1] and is again developed in [2] connection with the doctrine of pure *a priori* manifolds. Evidently, therefore, Kant was not disheartened by the various difficulties which lie in the path of a transcendental psychology, and it seems reasonable to conclude that there were powerful reasons inclining him to its retention. I shall now attempt, to the best of my powers, to explain—the task is a delicate and difficult one—what we may believe these reasons to have been.[3]

THE DISTINCTION BETWEEN PHENOMENALISM AND SUBJECTIVISM

A wider set of considerations than we have yet taken into account must be borne in mind if certain broader and really vital implications of Kant's enquiry are to be properly viewed. The self has a twofold aspect. It is at once animal in its conditions and potentially universal in its powers of appre-hension. Though man's natural existence is that of an animal organism, he can have consciousness of the spatial world out of which his organism has arisen, and of the wider periods within which his transitory existence falls. Ultimately such consciousness would seem to connect man cognitively with reality as a whole. Now it is to this universal or absolutist aspect of our consciousness, to its transcendence of the embodied and separate self, that Kant is seeking to do justice in his transcendental deductions, especially in his doctrine of the transcendental unity of apperception. For he views that apperception as conditioned by, and the correlate of, the consciousness of objectivity. It involves the conscious-ness of a single cosmical time and of a single cosmical space within which all events fall and within which they form a whole of causally interdependent existences. That is why he names it the *objective* unity of apperception. It is that aspect in which the self correlates with a wider reality, and through which it stands in fundamental contrast to the subjective states and to the conditions of its individual, animal existence. The transcendental self, so far from being identical with the empirical self, would seem to be of directly opposite nature. The one would seem to point beyond

---

[1] Cf. B 151-2. There is no mention, however, of objective affinity.
[2] B 160-1. Cf. above, pp. 226-9.
[3] In what follows I make use of an article, entitled "The Problem of Know-ledge," which I have contributed to the *Journal of Philosophy, Psychology, and Scientific Methods* (1912), vol. ix. pp. 113-28.

the realm of appearance, the other to be in its existence strictly natural. The fact that they are inextricably bound up with one another, and co-operate in rendering experience possible, only makes the more indispensable the duty of recognising their differing characters. Even should they prove to be inseparable aspects of sense-experience, without metaphysical implications, that would not obviate the necessity of clearly distinguishing them. The distinction remains, whatever explanation may be adopted of its speculative or other significance.

Now obviously in so fundamental an enquiry, dealing as it does with the most complicated and difficult problem in the entire field of metaphysics, no brief and compendious answer can cover all the various considerations which are relevant and determining. The problem of the deduction being what it is, the section dealing with it can hardly fail to be the most difficult portion of the whole *Critique*. The conclusions at which it arrives rest not merely upon the argument which it contains but also upon the results more or less independently reached in the other sections. The doctrine of the empirical object as appearance requires for its development the various discussions contained in the *Aesthetic*, in the sections on *Inner Sense* and on the *Refutation of Idealism*, in the chapters on *Phenomena and Noumena* and on the *Antinomies*. The metaphysical consequences and implications of Kant's teaching in regard to the transcendental unity of apperception are first revealed in the chapter on the *Paralogisms*. The view taken of productive imagination is expanded in the section on *Schematism*. In a word, the whole antecedent teaching of the *Critique* is focussed, and the entire subsequent development of the Critical doctrine is anticipated, in this brief chapter.

But there are, of course, additional causes of the difficulty and obscurity of the argument. One such cause has already been noted, namely, that the *Critique* is not a unitary work, developed from a previously thought-out standpoint, but in large part consists of manuscripts of very various dates, artificially pieced together by the addition of connecting links. In no part of the *Critique* is this so obvious as in the *Analytic of Concepts*. Until this is recognised all attempts to interpret the text in any impersonal fashion are doomed to failure. For this reason I have prefaced our discussion by a statement of Vaihinger's analysis. No one who can accept it is any longer in danger of underestimating this particular cause of the obscurity of Kant's deduction.

But the chief reason is one to which I have thus far made

only passing reference, and to which we may now give the attention which its importance demands, namely, the tentative and experimental character of Kant's own final solutions. The arguments of the deduction are only intelligible if viewed as an expression of the conflicting tendencies to which Kant's thought remained subject. He sought to allow due weight to each of the divergent aspects of the experience which he was analysing, and in so doing proceeded, as it would seem, simultaneously along the parallel lines of what appeared to be the possible, alternative methods of explanation. And to the end these opposing tendencies continued side by side, to the confusion of those readers who seek for a single unified teaching, but to the great illumination of those who are looking to Kant, not for clear-cut or final solutions, but for helpful analysis and for partial disentanglement of the complicated issues which go to constitute these baffling problems.

The two chief tendencies which thus conflicted in Kant's mind may be named the subjectivist and the phenomenalist respectively. This conflict remained, so to speak, underground, influencing the argument at every point, but seldom itself becoming the subject of direct discussion. As we shall find, it caused Kant to develop a twofold view of inner sense, of causality, of the object of knowledge, and of the unity of apperception. One of the few sections in the *Critique* where it seems on the point of emerging into clear consciousness is the section, added in the second edition, on the *Refutation of Idealism*. But this section owes its origin to polemical causes. It represents a position peculiar to the maturer portions of the *Analytic*; the rest of the *Critique* is not rewritten so as to harmonise with it, or to develop the consequences which consistent holding to it must involve.[1]

I shall use the term *subjectivism* (and its equivalent *subjective idealism*) in the wide sense[2] which makes it applicable to the teaching of Descartes and Locke, of Leibniz and Wolff, no less than to that of Berkeley and Hume. A common element in all these philosophies is the belief that subjective or mental states, "ideas" in the Lockean sense, are the objects of consciousness, and further are the sole possible objects of which it can have any direct or immediate awareness. Knowledge is viewed as a process entirely internal to the individual mind, and as carrying us further only in virtue of some additional supervening process, inferential, conjectural, or instinctive. This subjectivism also tends to combine with a view of consciousness as an ultimate self-revealing property

---

[1] Cf. below, Appendix C.

[2] The same wide sense in which Kant employs "empirical idealism."

of a purely individual existence.[1]   For Descartes consciousness is the very essence, both of the mind and of the self.   It is indeed asserted to be exhaustive of the nature of both.   Though the self is described as possessing a faculty of will as well as a power of thinking, all its activities are taken as being disclosed to the mind through the revealing power of its fundamental attribute.   The individual mind is thus viewed as an existence in which everything takes place in the open light of an all-pervasive consciousness.   Leibniz, it is true, taught the existence of subconscious perceptions, and so far may seem to have anticipated Kant's recognition of non-conscious processes; but as formulated by Leibniz that doctrine has the defect which frequently vitiates its modern counterpart, namely that it represents the subconscious as analogous in nature to the conscious, and as differing from it only in the accidental features of intensity and clearness, or through temporary lack of control over the machinery of reproductive association.   The subconscious, as thus represented, merely enlarges the private content of the individual mind; it in no respect transcends it.

The genuinely Critical view of the generative conditions of experience is radically different from this Leibnizian doctrine of *petites perceptions*.   It connects rather with Leibniz's mode of conceiving the origin of *a priori* concepts. But even that teaching it restates in such fashion as to free it from subjectivist implications.   Leibniz's contention that the mind is conscious of its fundamental activities, and that it is by reflection upon them that it gains all ultimate *a priori* concepts, is no longer tenable in view of the conclusions established in the objective deduction.   Mental processes, in so far as they are generative of experience, must fall outside the field of consciousness, and as activities dynamically creative cannot be of the nature of ideas or contents. They are not subconscious ideas but non-conscious processes. They are not the submerged content of experience, but its conditioning grounds.   Their most significant characteristic has still, however, to be mentioned.   They must no longer be interpreted in subjectivist terms, as originating in the separate existence of an individual self.   In conditioning experience they generate the only self for which experience can vouch, and consequently, in the absence of full and independent proof, must not be conceived as individually circum-

---

[1] Cf. above, pp. xliii-v, 208; below, pp. 295-6, 298 ff.   Malebranche, Hume, and Spinoza are the only pre-Kantian thinkers of whose position the last statement is not strictly descriptive, but even they failed to escape its entangling influence.

scribed. The problem of knowledge, properly conceived, is no longer how consciousness, individually conditioned, can lead us beyond its own bounds, but what a consciousness, which is at once consciousness of objects and also conscious-ness of a self, must imply for its possibility. Kant thus obtains what is an almost invariable concomitant of scientific and philosophical advance, namely a more correct and scientific formulation of the problem to be solved. The older formula-tion assumes the truth of the subjectivist standpoint; the Critical problem, when thus stated, is at least free from pre-conceptions of that particular brand. Assumptions which hitherto had been quite unconsciously held, or else, if reflected upon, had been regarded as axiomatic and self-evident, are now brought within the field of investigation. Kant thereby achieves a veritable revolution; and with it many of the most far-reaching consequences of the Critical teaching are closely bound up.

This new standpoint, in contrast to *subjective* idealism, may be named *Critical*, or to employ the term which Kant himself applies both to his transcendental deduc-tion and to the unity of apperception, *objective* idealism. But as the distinction between appearance and reality is no less fundamental to the Critical attitude, we shall perhaps be less likely to be misunderstood, or to seem to be identifying Kant's standpoint with the very different teaching of Hegel, if by preference we employ the title *phenomenalism*.

In the transcendental deduction Kant, as above noted, is seeking to do justice to the universal or absolutist aspect of our consciousness, to its transcendence of the embodied and separate self. The unity of apperception is entitled *objective*, because it is regarded as the counterpart of a single cosmical time and of a single cosmical space within which all events fall. Its objects are not mental states peculiar to itself, nor even ideal contents numerically distinct from those in other minds. It looks out upon a common world of genuinely independent existence. In developing this position Kant is constrained to revise and indeed completely to recast his previous views both as to the nature of the synthetic processes, through which experience is constructed, and of the given manifold, upon which they are supposed to act. From the subjectivist point of view the synthetic activities consist of the various cognitive processes of the individual mind, and the given manifold consists of the sensations aroused by material bodies acting upon the special senses. From the objective or phenomenalist standpoint the synthetic processes are of a noumenal character, and the given manifold is similarly viewed as being due to noumenal agencies acting, not upon the sense-organs, which as appearances are themselves noumenally conditioned, but upon what may be called "outer sense." These distinctions may first be made clear.

Sensations, Kant holds, have a twofold origin, noumenal and mechanical. They are due in the first place to the action of things in themselves upon the noumenal conditions of the self, and also in the second place to the action of material bodies upon the sense-organs and brain. To take the latter first. Light reflected from objects, and acting on the retina, gives rise to sensations of colour. For such causal interrelations there exists, Kant teaches, the same kind of empirical evidence as for the causal interaction of material bodies.[1] Our sensational experiences are as truly events in time as are mechanical happenings in space. In this way, however, we can account only for the existence of our sensations and for the order in which they make their appearance in or to consciousness, not for our awareness of them. To state the point by means of an illustration. The impinging of one billiard ball upon another accounts causally for the motion which then appears in the second ball. But no one would dream of asserting that by itself it accounts for our consciousness of that second motion. We may contend that in an exactly similar manner, to the same extent, no more and no less, the action of an object upon the brain accounts only for the occurrence of a visual sensation as an event in the empirical time sequence. A sensation just as little as a motion can carry its own consciousness with it. To regard that as ever possible is ultimately to endow events in time with the capacity of apprehending objects in space. In dealing with causal connections in space and time we do not require to discuss the problem of knowledge proper, namely, how it is possible to have or acquire knowledge, whether of a motion in space or of a sensation in time. When we raise that further question we have to adopt a very different standpoint, and to take into account a much greater complexity of conditions.

[1] Cf. A 28-9 ; also *Lectures on Metaphysics* (Pölitz's edition, 1821), p. 188 ff. In Kant's *Opus Postumum*, his *Transition from the Metaphysical First Principles of Natural Science to Physics*, it is asserted in at least twenty-six distinct passages that sensations are due to the action of "the moving forces of matter" upon the sense-organs. Cf. below, p. 283 n. 2. In his *Ueber das Organ der Seele* (1796) (Hartenstein, vi. p. 457 ff.), Kant agrees with Sömmerring in holding that the soul has virtual, *i.e.* dynamical, though not local, presence in the fluid contained in the cavities of the brain. Cf. below, Appendix C.

Kant applies this point of view no less rigorously to feelings, emotions, and desires than to the sensations of the special senses. All of them, he teaches, are 'animal'[1] in character. They are one and all conditioned by, and explicable only in terms of, the particular constitution of the animal organism. They one and all belong to the realm of appearance.[2]

The term 'sensation' may also, however, be applied in a wider sense to signify the material of knowledge in so far as it is noumenally conditioned. Thus viewed, sensations are due, not to the action of physical stimuli upon the bodily organs, but to the affection by things in themselves of those factors in the noumenal conditions of the self which correspond to "sensibility." Kant is culpably careless in failing to distinguish those two very different meanings of the phrase 'given manifold.' The language which he employs is thoroughly ambiguous. Just as he frequently speaks as if the synthetic processes were conscious activities exerted by the self, so also he frequently uses language which implies that the manifold upon which these processes act is identical with the sensations of the special senses. But the sensations of the bodily senses, even if reducible to it, can at most form only part of it. The synthetic processes, interpreting the manifold in accordance with the fixed forms, space, time, and the categories, generate the spatial world within which objects are apprehended as causally interacting and as giving rise through their action upon the sense-organs to the various special sensations as events in time. Sensations, as mechanically caused, are thus on the same plane as other appearances. They depend upon the same generating conditions as the motions which produce them. As minor incidents within a more comprehensive totality they cannot possibly represent the material out of which the whole has been constructed. To explain the phenomenal world as constructed out of the sensations of the special senses is virtually to equate it with a small selection of its constituent parts. Such professed explanation also commits the further absurdity of attempting to account for the origin of the phenomenal world by means of events which can exist only under the conditions which it itself supplies. The manifold of the special senses and the primary manifold are radically distinct. The former is due to material bodies acting upon the material sense-organs. The latter is the product of noumenal agencies acting upon "outer sense," *i.e.* upon those noumenal conditions of the self

---

[1] Cf. *Critique of Practical Reason*, Bk. i. ch. i. § iii.
[2] Cf. below, pp. 279 ff., 293-6, 312 ff., 321, 361 *n.* 3, 384-5, 464-5, 476.

which constitute our "sensibility"; it is much more comprehensive than the former; it must contain the material for all modes of objective existence, including many that are usually regarded as purely mental.[1]

To turn, now, to the other aspect of experience. What are the factors which condition its form? What must we postulate in order to account for the existence of consciousness and for the unitary form in which alone it can appear? Kant's answer is again ambiguous. He fails sufficiently to insist upon distinctions which yet are absolutely vital to any genuine understanding of the new and revolutionary positions towards which he is feeling his way. The synthetic processes which in the subjective and objective deductions are proved to condition all experience may be interpreted either as conscious or as non-conscious activities, and may be ascribed either to the agency of the individual self or to noumenal conditions which fall outside the realm of possible definition. Now, though Kant's own expositions remain thoroughly ambiguous, the results of the Critical enquiry would seem— at least so long as the fundamental distinction between matter and form is held to and the temporally sequent aspect of experience is kept in view—to be decisive in favour of the latter alternative in each case. The synthetic processes must take place and complete themselves before any consciousness can exist at all. And as they thus precondition consciousness, they cannot themselves be known to be conscious; and not being known to be conscious, it is not even certain that they may legitimately be described as mental. We have, indeed, to conceive them on the analogy of our mental processes, but that may only be because of the limitation of our knowledge to the data of experience. Further, we have no right to conceive them as the activities of a noumenal self. We know the self only as conscious, and the synthetic processes, being the generating conditions of consciousness, are also the generating conditions of the only self for which our experience can vouch. Kant, viewing as he does the temporal aspect of human experience as fundamental, would seem to be justified in naming these processes "synthetic." For consciousness in its very nature would seem to involve the carrying over of content from one time to other times, and the construction of a more comprehensive total consciousness from the elements thus combined. Kant is here analysing in its simplest and most fundamental form that aspect of consciousness which William James has

[1] Cf. below, pp. 279-80, and pp. 293-4, on inner sense.

described in the *Principles of Psychology*,[1] and which we may entitle the telescoping of earlier mental states into the successive experiences that include them. They telescope in a manner which can never befall the successive events in a causal series, and which is not explicable by any scheme of relations derivable from the physical sphere.

Obviously, what Kant does is to apply to the interpretation of the noumenal conditions of our conscious experience a distinction derived by analogy from conscious experience itself—the distinction, namely, between our mental processes and the sensuous material with which they deal. The application of such a distinction may be inevitable in any attempt to explain human experience; but it can very easily, unless carefully guarded, prove a source of serious misunderstanding. Just as the synthetic processes which generate consciousness are not known to be themselves conscious, so also the manifold cannot be identified with the sensations of the bodily senses. These last are events in time, and are effects not of noumenal but of mechanical causes.

Kant's conclusion when developed on consistent Critical lines, and therefore in phenomenalist terms, is twofold: positive, to the effect that consciousness, for all that our analysis can prove to the contrary, may be merely a resultant, derivative from and dependent upon a complexity of conditions; and negative, to the effect that though these conditions may by analogy be described as consisting of synthetic processes acting upon a given material, they are in their real nature unknowable by us. Even their bare possibility we cannot profess to comprehend. We postulate them only because given experience is demonstrably not self-explanatory and would seem to refer us for explanation to some such antecedent generative grounds.

Kant, as we have already emphasised, obscures his position by the way in which he frequently speaks of the transcendental unity of apperception as the supreme condition of our experience. At times he even speaks as if it were the source of the synthetic processes. That cannot, however, be

---

[1] i. p. 339: "Each pulse of cognitive consciousness, each Thought, dies away and is replaced by another. . . . Each later Thought, knowing and including thus the Thoughts which went before, is the final receptacle—and appropriating them is the final owner—of all that they contain and own. Each Thought is thus born an owner, and dies owned, transmitting whatever it realized as its Self to its own later proprietor. As Kant says [cf. below, pp. 461-2], it is as if elastic balls were to have not only motion but knowledge of it, and a first ball were to transmit both its motion and its consciousness to a second, which took both up into *its* consciousness and passed them to a third, until the last ball held all that the other balls had held, and realized it as its own."

regarded as his real teaching. Self-consciousness (and the unity of apperception, in so far as it finds expression through self-consciousness) rests upon the same complexity of conditions as does outer experience, and therefore may be merely a product or resultant. It is, as he insists in the *Paralogisms*, the emptiest of all our concepts, and can afford no sufficient ground for asserting the self to be an abiding personality. We cannot by theoretical analysis of the facts of experience or of the nature of self-consciousness prove anything whatsoever in regard to the ultimate nature of the self.

Now Kant is here giving a new, and quite revolutionary, interpretation of the distinction between the subjective and the objective. The objective is for the Cartesians the independently real ;[1] the subjective is that which has an altogether different kind of existence in what is entitled the field of consciousness. Kant, on the other hand, from his phenomenalist standpoint, views existences as objective when they are determined by purely physical causes, and as subjective when they also depend upon physiological and psychological conditions. On this latter view the difference between the two is no longer a difference of kind ; it becomes a difference merely of degree. Objective existences, owing to the simplicity and recurrent character of their conditions, are uniform. Subjective existences, resting upon conditions which are too complex to be frequently recurrent, are by contrast extremely variable. But both types of existence are objective in the sense that they are objects, and immediate objects, for consciousness. Subjective states do not run parallel with the objective system of natural existences, nor are they additional to it. For they do not constitute our consciousness of nature ; they are themselves part of the natural order which consciousness reveals. That they contrast with physical existences in being unextended and incapable of location in space is what Kant would seem by implication to assert, but he challenges Descartes' right to infer from this particular difference a complete diversity in their whole nature. Sensations, feelings, emotions, and desires, so far as they are experienced by us, constitute the empirical self which is an objective existence, integrally connected with the material environment, in terms of which alone it can be understood. In other words, the distinction between the subjective and the objective is now made to fall within the system of natural

---

[1] I here use "objective" in its modern meaning: I am not concerned with the special meaning which Descartes himself attached to the terms *objective* and *formaliter*.

law.   The subjective is not opposite in nature to the objective, but is a subspecies within it.

The revolutionary character of this reformulation of Cartesian distinctions may perhaps be expressed by saying that what Kant is really doing is to substitute the distinction between appearance and reality for the Cartesian dualism of the mental and the material.   The psychical is a title for a certain class of known existences, *i.e.* of appearances; and they form together with the physical a single system.   But underlying this entire system, conditioning both physical and psychical phenomena, is the realm of noumenal existence; and when the question of the possibility of knowledge, that is, of the experiencing of such a comprehensive natural system, is raised, it is to this noumenal sphere that we are referred.   Everything experienced, even a sensation or desire, is an event; but the experiencing of it is an act of awareness, and calls for an explanation of an altogether different kind.

Thus Kant completely restates the problem of knowledge. The problem is not how, starting from the subjective, the individual can come to knowledge of the independently real; but how, if a common world is alone immediately apprehended, the inner private life of the self-conscious being can be possible, and how such inner experience is to be interpreted.   How does it come about that though sensations, feelings, etc., are events no less mechanically conditioned than motions in space, and constitute with the latter a single system conformed to natural law, they yet differ from all other classes of natural events in that they can be experienced only by a single consciousness. To this question Kant replies in terms of his fundamental distinction between appearance and reality.   Though everything of which we are conscious may legitimately be studied in terms of the natural system to which it belongs, consciousness itself cannot be so regarded.   In attempting to define it we are carried beyond the phenomenal to its noumenal conditions.   In other words, it constitutes a problem, the complete data of which are not at our disposal.   This is by itself a sufficient reason for our incapacity to explain why the states of each empirical self can never be apprehended save by a single consciousness, or otherwise stated, why each consciousness is limited, as regards sensations and feelings, exclusively to those which arise in connection with some one animal organism.   It at least precludes us from dogmatically asserting that this is due to their being subjective in the dualistic and Cartesian sense of that term—namely, as constituting, or being states of, the knowing self.

A diagram may serve, though very crudely, to illustrate Kant's phenomenalist interpretation of the cognitive situation.

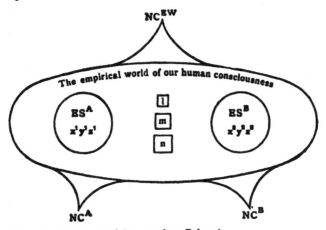

ES^A = Empirical self of the conscious Being A.
ES^B = Empirical self of the conscious Being B.
NC^A = Noumenal conditions of the conscious Being A.
NC^B = Noumenal conditions of the conscious Being B.
l, m, n = Objects in space.
x^1, y^1, z^1 = Sensations caused by objects l, m, n acting on the sense-organs of the empirical self A.
x^2, y^2, z^2 = Sensations caused by l, m, n acting on the sense-organs of the empirical self B.
NC^{EW} = Noumenal conditions of the empirical world.

Everything in this empirical world is equally open to the consciousness of both A and B, save only certain psychical events which are conditioned by physiological and psychological factors. x^1, y^1, z^1 can be apprehended only by A; x^2, y^2, z^2 can be apprehended only by B. Otherwise A and B experience one and the same world; the body of B is perceived by A in the same manner in which he perceives his own body. This is true *a fortiori* of all other material existences. Further, these material existences are known with the same immediacy as the subjective states. As regards the relation in which NC^A, NC^B, and NC^{EW} stand to one another, no assertions can be made, save, as above indicated,[1] such conjectural statements as may precariously be derived through argument by analogy from distinctions that fall within our human experience.[2]

Kant's phenomenalism thus involves an objectivist view of

[1] Pp. 277-8.
[2] On this whole matter cf. above, p. xlv; below, pp. 312-21 on Kant's *Refutation of Idealism*; pp. 373-4 on the *Second Analogy*; pp. 407 ff., 414 ff. on *Phenomena and Noumena*; p. 461 ff. on the *Paralogisms*; p. 546; and below, Appendix C. Cf. also A 277-8 = B 334.

individual selves and of their interrelations. They fall within the single common world of space. Within this phenomenal world they stand in external, mechanical relations to one another. They are apprehended as embodied, with known contents, sensations, feelings, and desires, composing their inner experience. There is, from this point of view, no problem of knowledge. On this plane we have to deal only with events known, not with any process of apprehension. Even the components of the empirical self, the subject-matter of empirical psychology, are not processes of apprehension, but apprehended existences. It is only when we make a regress beyond the phenomenal as such to the conditions which render it possible, that the problem of knowledge arises at all. And with this regress we are brought to the real crux of the whole question — the reconciliation of this phenomenalism with the conditions of our self-consciousness. For we have then to take into account the fundamental fact that each self is not only an animal existence within the phenomenal world, but also in its powers of apprehension coequal with it. The self known is external to the objects known; the self that knows is conscious of itself as comprehending within the field of its consciousness the wider universe in infinite space.

Such considerations would, at first sight, seem to force us to modify our phenomenalist standpoint in the direction of subjectivism. For in what other manner can we hope to unite the two aspects of the self, the known conditions of its finite existence and the consciousness through which it correlates with the universe as a whole? In the one aspect it is a part of appearance; in the other it connects with that which makes appearance possible at all.

Quite frequently it is the subjectivist solution which Kant seems to adopt. Objects known are "mere representations," "states of the identical self." Everything outside the individual mind is real; appearances are purely individual in origin. But such a position is inconsistent with the deeper implications of Kant's Critical teaching, and would involve the entire ignoring of the many suggestions which point to a fundamentally different and much more adequate standpoint. The individual is himself known only as appearance, and cannot, therefore, be the medium in and through which appearances exist. Though appearances exist only in and through consciousness, they are not due to any causes which can legitimately be described as individual. From this standpoint Kant would seem to distinguish between the grounds and conditions of phenomenal existence and the special determining causes of individual consciousness. Transcendental conditions generate consciousness of the relatively permanent and objective world in space and time ; empirical conditions within this space and time world determine the sensuous modes through which special portions of this infinite and uniform world appear diversely to different minds.

This, however, is a point of view which is only suggested, and, as we have already observed,[1] the form in which it is outlined suggests many objections and difficulties. Consciousness of the objective world in space and time does not exist complete with one portion of it more specifically determined in terms of actual sense-perceptions. Rather the consciousness of the single world in space and time is gradually developed through and out of sense experience of limited portions of it. We have still to consider the various sections in the *Analytic of Principles* (especially the section added in the second edition on the *Refutation of Idealism*) and in the *Dialectic*, in which Kant further develops this standpoint. But even after doing so, we shall be forced to recognise that Kant leaves undiscussed many of the most obvious objections to which his phenomenalism lies open. To the very last he fails to state in any really adequate manner how from the phenomenalist standpoint he would regard the world described in mechanical terms by science as being related to the world of ordinary sense - experience,[2] or how different individual consciousnesses are related to one another. The new form, however, in which these old-time problems here emerge is the best possible proof of the revolutionary character of Kant's Critical enquiries. For

---

[1] P. 267 ff.

[2] Though Kant's *Opus Postumum*, parts of which have been published by R. Reicke in the *Altpreussische Monatsschrift* (1882-4), under the title *Transition from the Metaphysical First Principles of Natural Science to Physics*, exists only in the form of preliminary studies and detached notes, and though in its later sections it bears in some degree the marks of weakening powers, it enables us to appreciate the extent to which Kant had come to be preoccupied with the problem as to how the world of physical science stands related, on the one hand to the sensible world of ordinary consciousness, and on the other to the world of things in themselves. As above noted (p. 275 *n.*), Kant asserts in at least twenty-six distinct passages that sensations are due to the action of "the moving forces of matter" upon the sense-organs. What is especially significant is the adoption and frequent occurrence (*op. cit.* (1882), pp. 236, 287, 289, 290, 292, 294, 295-6, 300, 308, 429, 436, 439) of the phrase "*Erscheinung von der Erscheinung.*" Kant attaches to this phrase very varying meanings, according as he has metaphysical or physical existence in view, and according as he is considering the material or the formal aspect of experience. In a few passages the phrase "*Erscheinung vom ersten Range*" (*op. cit.* p. 436) (*i.e.* appearance as such) quite definitely denotes the objective world as determined by physical science. "*Erscheinung vom zweiten Range*" (*i.e.* appearance of the appearance) is then taken as meaning the sensations, the secondary sense-qualities, generated in the empirical self through the action of physical bodies on the sense-organs. Cf. below, Appendix C.

these problems are no longer formulated in terms of the individualistic presuppositions which govern the thinking of all Kant's predecessors, even that of Hume. The concealed presuppositions are now called in question, and are made the subject of explicit discussion. But further comment must meantime be deferred.[1]

TRANSCENDENTAL DEDUCTION OF THE CATEGORIES, IN THE SECOND EDITION

The argument of the second edition transcendental deduction can be reduced to the following eight points :

(1)[2] It opens with the statement of a fundamental assumption which Kant does not dream of questioning and of which he nowhere attempts to offer proof. The representation of combination is the one kind of representation which can never be given through sense. It is not so given even in the pure forms of space and time yielded by outer and inner sense.[3] It is due to an act of spontaneity, which as such must be performed by the understanding. As it is one and the same for every kind of combination, it may be called by the general name of synthesis. And as all combination, without exception, is due to this source, its dissolution, that is, analysis, which seems to be its opposite, always presupposes it.

(2)[4] Besides the manifold and its synthesis a further factor is involved in the conception of combination, namely, *the representation of the unity* of the manifold. The combination which is necessary to and constitutes knowledge is *representation* of the synthetical unity of the manifold. This is a factor additional to synthesis and to the manifold synthesised. For such representation cannot arise out of any antecedent consciousness of synthesis. On the contrary, it is only through supervention upon the unitary synthesis that the conception of the combination becomes possible. In other words, the representation of unity conditions *consciousness* of synthesis, and therefore cannot be the outcome or product of it. This is an application, or rather generalisation, of a position which in the first edition is developed only in reference to the empirical process of recognition. Recognition preconditions consciousness, and therefore cannot be subsequent upon it.

(3)[5] The unity thus represented is not, however, that

---

[1] Cf. below, pp. 312-21, 373-4, 414 ff., 425 ff., 558 ff.,.and Appendix C.
[2] B 129. [3] B 161 *n.* [4] B 130-1. [5] B 131.

which is expressed through the category of unity. The consciousness of unity which is involved in the conception of synthesis is that of apperception or transcendental self-consciousness. This is the highest and most universal form of unity, for it is a presupposition of the unity of all possible concepts, whether analytic or synthetic, in the various forms of judgment.

(4)[1] A manifold though given is not for that reason also represented. It must be possible for the 'I think' to accompany it and all my other representations:

" . . . for otherwise something would be represented in me which could not be thought at all; and that is equivalent to saying that the representation would be impossible or at least would be nothing to me."[2]

But to ascribe a manifold as my representations to the identical self is to comprehend them, as synthetically connected, in one apperception.[3] Only what can be combined in one consciousness can be related to the 'I think.' The analytic unity of self-consciousness presupposes the synthetic unity of the manifold.

(5)[4] The unity of apperception is analytic or self-identical. It expresses itself through the proposition, *I am I*. But being thus pure identity without content of its own, it cannot be conscious of itself in and by itself. Its unity and constancy can have meaning only through contrast to the variety and changeableness of its specific experiences; and yet, at the same time, it is also true that such manifoldness will destroy all possibility of unity unless it be reconcileable with it. The variety can contribute to the conditioning of apperception only in so far as it is capable of being combined into a single consciousness. Through synthetic unifying of the manifold the self comes to consciousness both of itself and of the manifold.

(6)[5] The transcendental original unity of apperception is an objective, not a merely subjective, unity. Its conditions are also the conditions in and through which we acquire consciousness of objects. An object is that in the conception of which the manifold of given intuitions is combined. (This point, though central to the argument, is more adequately developed in the first than in the second edition.) Such combination requires unity of consciousness. Thus the same unity which conditions apperception likewise conditions the relation of representations to an object. The unity of pure

[1] B 131-4.   [2] B 131.   [3] Cf. B 138.
[4] B 135.   [5] B 136-40.

apperception may therefore be described as an *objective* unity for two reasons: first, because it can apprehend its own analytical unity only through discovery of unity in the given, and secondly, for the reason that such synthetical unifying of the manifold is also the process whereby representations acquire reference to objects.

(7)[1] Kant reinforces this conclusion, and shows its further significance, by analysis of the act of judgment. The logical definition of judgment, as the representation of a relation between two concepts, has many defects. These, however, are all traceable to its initial failure to explain, or even to recognise, the nature of the assertion which judgment as such claims to make. Judgment asserts relations of a quite unique kind, altogether different from those which exist between ideas connected through association. If, for instance, on seeing a body the sensations of weight due to the attempt to raise it are suggested by association, there is nothing but subjective sequence; but if we form the judgment that the body is heavy, the two representations are then connected together *in the object*. This is what is intended by the copula 'is.' It is a relational term through which the objective unity of given representations is distinguished from the subjective. It indicates that the representations stand in objective relation under the pure unity of apperception, and not merely in subjective relation owing to the play of association in the individual mind. "Judgment is nothing but the mode of bringing cognitions to the objective unity of apperception," *i.e.* of giving to them a validity which holds independently of the subjective processes through which it is apprehended. Objective relations are not, of course, all necessary or universal; and a judgment may, therefore, assert a relation which is empirical and contingent. None the less the fundamental distinction between it and any mere relation of association still persists. The empirical relation is still in the judgment asserted to be objective. The subject and the predicate are asserted, in the particular case or cases to which the judgment refers, to be connected in the object and not merely in the mind of the subject. Or otherwise stated, though subject and predicate are not themselves declared to be necessarily and universally related to one another, their contingent relation has to be viewed as objectively, and therefore necessarily, grounded. Judgment always presupposes the existence of necessary relations even when it is not concerned to assert them. Judgment is the organ of objective knowledge, and is therefore

[1] B 140-2.

bound up, indirectly when not directly, with the universality and necessity which are the sole criteria of knowledge. The judgment expressive of contingency is still judgment, and is therefore no less necessary in its conditions, and no less objective in its validity, than is a universal judgment of the scientific type. To use Kant's own terminology, judgment acquires objective validity through participation in the necessary unity of apperception. In so doing it is made to embody those principles of the objective determination of all representations through which alone cognition is possible.

(8)[1] As judgment is nothing but the mode of bringing cognitions to the objective unity of apperception, it follows that the categories, which in the metaphysical deduction have been proved to be the possible functions in judging, are the conditions in and through which such pure apperception becomes possible. Apperception conditions experience, and the unity which both demand for their possibility is that of the categories.

Before passing to the remaining sections of the deduction,[2] which are supplementary rather than essential, I may add comment upon the above points. Only (7) and (8) call for special consideration. They represent a form of argument which has no counterpart in the first edition. As we noted,[3] the first edition argument is defective owing to its failure to demonstrate that the categories constitute the unity which is necessary to knowledge. By introducing in the second edition this analysis of judgment, and by showing the inseparable connection between pure apperception, objective consciousness and judgment, this defect is in some degree removed. As the categories correspond to the possible functions of judgment, their objective validity is thereby established. By this means also the connection which in Kant's view exists between the metaphysical and the transcendental deductions receives for the first time proper recognition. The categories which in the former deduction are discovered and systematised through *logical* analysis of the *form* of judgment, are in the latter deduction, through *transcendental* analysis of the *function* of judgment, shown to be just those forms of relation which are necessary to the possibility of knowledge. It must, however, be noted that the transcendental argument is brought to completion only through assumption of the adequacy of the metaphysical deduction. No independent attempt is made to show that the particular categories obtained in the metaphysical deduction are those which are required, that there are no others, or that all the twelve are indispensable.

(7) is a development of an argument which first appears in the *Prolegomena*. The statement of it there given is, however, extremely confused, owing to the distinction which Kant most unfortunately introduces[1] between judgments of experience and judgments of perception. That distinction is entirely worthless and can only serve to mislead the reader. It cuts at the very root of Kant's Critical teaching. Judgments of perception involve, Kant says, no category of the understanding, but only what he is pleased to call the "logical connection of perceptions in a thinking subject." What that may be he nowhere explains, save by adding[2] that in it perceptions are "compared and conjoined in a consciousness of my state" (also spoken of by Kant as "empirical consciousness"), and not "in consciousness in general."

"All our judgments are at first mere judgments of perception; they hold good merely for us (that is, for the individual subject), and we do not till afterwards give them a new reference, namely, to an object. . . . To illustrate the matter: that the room is warm, sugar sweet, and wormwood bitter—these are merely subjectively valid judgments. I do not at all demand that I myself should at all times, or that every other person should, find the facts to be what I now assert; they only express a reference of two sensations to the same subject, to myself, and that only in my present state of perception. Consequently they are not intended to be valid of the object. Such judgments I have named those of perception. Judgments of experience are of quite a different nature. What experience teaches me under certain circumstances, it must teach me always and teach everybody, and its validity is not limited to the subject or to its state at a particular time."[3]

The illegitimacy and the thoroughly misleading character of this distinction hardly require to be pointed out. Obviously Kant is here confusing assertion of contingency and contingency of assertion.[4] A judgment of contingency, in order to be valid, must itself be necessary. Even a momentary state of the self is referable to an object in judgment only if that object is causally, and therefore necessarily, concerned in its production.[5]

The distinction is repeated in § 22 as follows:

"Thinking is the combining of representations in one consciousness. This combination is either merely relative to the subject, and is contingent and subjective, or is absolute, and is necessary or

---

[1] *Prolegomena*, § 18.　　　　　　　　　[2] *Op. cit.* § 20.

[3] *Op. cit.* §§ 18-19; Eng. trans. pp. 54-5.

[4] Cf. above, pp. 39-40, 286-7.　　　　　[5] Cf. below, p. 370.

objective. The combination of representations in one consciousness is judgment. Thinking, therefore, is the same as judging, or the relating of representations to judgments in general. Judgments, therefore, are either merely subjective, or they are objective. They are subjective when representations are related to a consciousness in one subject only, and are combined in it alone. They are objective when they are united in a consciousness in general, that is, necessarily."[1]

To accept this distinction is to throw the entire argument into confusion. This Kant seems to have himself recognised in the interval between the *Prolegomena* and the second edition of the *Critique*. For in the section before us there is no trace of it. The opposition is no longer between subjective and objective judgment, but only between association of ideas and judgment which as such is always objective. The distinction drawn in the *Prolegomena* is only, indeed, a more definite formulation of the distinction which runs through the first edition of the *Critique* between the indeterminate and the determinate object of consciousness. The more definite formulation of it seems, however, to have had the happy effect of enabling Kant to realise the illegitimacy of any such distinction.

We may now proceed to consider the remaining sections.[2] In section 21[3] Kant makes a very surprising statement. The above argument, which he summarises in a sentence, yields, he declares, "the *beginning* of a deduction of the pure concepts of understanding." This can hardly be taken as representing Kant's real estimate of the significance of the preceding argument, and would seem to be due to a temporary preoccupation with the problems that centre in the doctrine of schematism. So far, Kant adds in explanation, no account has been taken of the particular manner in which the manifold of empirical intuition is supplied to us.[4] The necessary supplement, consisting of a very brief outline statement of the doctrine of schematism, is given in section 26.[5] It differs from the teaching of the special chapter devoted to schematism in emphasising space equally with time. The doctrine of pure *a priori* manifolds is incidentally asserted.[6] Section 26 concludes by consideration of the question why appearances must conform to the *a priori* categories. It is no more surprising, Kant claims, than that

---

[1] *Op. cit.* § 22. Cf. below, p. 311 *n.* 4.   [2] §§ 21-7.   [3] B 143.
[4] This leads on in the second paragraph of § 21 to further statements, already commented upon above, pp. 186, 257-8. Cf. also § 23.
[5] Cf. also § 24.   [6] Cf. above, pp. 90 ff., 171, 226-9, 267-70; below, p. 337.

they should agree with the *a priori* forms of intuition. The categories and the intuitional forms are relative to the same subject to which the appearances are relative; and the appearances "as mere representations are subject to no law of connection save that which the combining faculty prescribes."

The summary of the deduction given in section 27 discusses the three possible theories regarding the origin of pure concepts, viz. those of *generatio aequivoca* (out of experience), *epigenesis*, and *preformation*. The first is disproved by the deduction. The second is the doctrine of the deduction and fulfils all the requirements of demonstration. The proof that the categories are at once independent of experience and yet also universally valid for all experience is of the strongest possible kind, namely, that they make experience itself possible. The third theory, that the categories, while subjective and self-discovered, originate in faculties which are implanted in us by our Creator and which are so formed as to yield concepts in harmony with the laws of nature, lies open to two main objections. In the first place, this is an hypothesis capable of accounting equally well for any kind of *a priori* whatsoever; the predetermined powers of judgment can be multiplied without limit. But a second objection is decisive, namely, that on such a theory the categories would lack the particular kind of necessity which is required. They would express only the necessities imposed upon our thinking by the constitution of our minds, and would not justify any assertion of necessary connection *in the object*. Kant might also have added,[1] that this hypothesis is metaphysical, and therefore offers in explanation of the *empirical* validity of *a priori* concepts a theory which rests upon and involves their *unconditioned* employment. That is a criticism which is reinforced by the teaching of the *Dialectic*.

To return now to the omitted sections 22 to 25. Section 22 makes no fresh contribution to the argument of the first edition. Its teaching in regard to pure intuition and mathematical knowledge has already been commented upon. In section 23 Kant dwells upon an interesting consequence of the argument of the deduction. The categories have a wider scope than the pure forms of sense. Since the argument of the deduction has shown that judgment is the indispensable instrument both for reducing a manifold to the unity of apperception and also for conferring upon representations a relation to an object, it follows that the categories which are simply the possible functions of unity in judgment are valid for any and

[1] Cf. above, pp. 28, 47, 114, 141-2.

every consciousness that is sensuously conditioned and whose knowledge is therefore acquired through synthesis of a given manifold. Though such consciousness may not intuit in terms of space and time, it must none the less apprehend objects in terms of the categories. The categories thus extend to *objects of sensuous intuition in general.* They are not, however, valid of objects as such, that is, of things in themselves. As empty relational forms they have *meaning* only in reference to a given matter; and as instruments for the reduction of variety to the unity of apperception their *validity* has been proved only for conscious and sensuous experience. Even if the possibility of a non-sensuous intuitive understanding, capable of apprehending things in themselves, be granted, we have no sufficient ground for asserting that the forms which such understanding will employ must coincide with the categories.[1] These are points which will come up for discussion in connection with Kant's more detailed argument in the chapter on the distinction between phenomena and noumena.[2]

The heading to section 24 is decidedly misleading. The phrase "objects of the senses in general" might be synonymous with "objects of intuition in general" of the preceding section. To interpret it, however, by the contents of the section, it means "objects of *our* senses." This section ought, therefore, to form part of section 26, which in its opening sentences supplies its proper introduction. (It may also be noted that the opening sentences of section 24 are a needless repetition of section 23. This would seem to show that it was not written in immediate continuation of it.) The first three paragraphs of section 24 expound the same doctrine of schematism as that outlined in section 26, save that time alone is referred to. The remaining paragraphs of section 24 deal with the connected doctrine of inner sense. Section 25 deals with certain consequences which follow from that doctrine of inner sense.[3]

THE DOCTRINE OF INNER SENSE

We have still to consider a doctrine of great importance in Kant's thinking, that of inner sense. The significance of this doctrine is almost inversely proportionate to the scantiness and obscurity of the passages in which it is expounded and developed. Much of the indefiniteness and illusiveness of the current interpretations of Kant would seem

[1] Cf. § 21, second paragraph.
[2] Cf. above, pp. 160, 186, 257, and below, pp. 325-6, 330-1, 390-1, 404 ff.
[3] Cf. below, pp. 324, 329

to be directly traceable to the commentator's failure to appreciate the position which it occupies in Kant's system. Several of Kant's chief results are given as deductions from it, while it itself, in turn, is largely inspired by the need for a secure basis upon which these positions may be made to rest. The relation of the doctrine to its consequences is thus twofold. Kant formulates it in order to safeguard or rather to justify certain conclusions ; and yet these conclusions have themselves in part been arrived at owing to his readiness to accept such a doctrine, and to what would seem to have been his almost instinctive feeling of its kinship (notwithstanding the very crude form in which alone he was able to formulate it) with Critical teaching. It was probably one of the earliest of the many new tenets which Kant adopted in the years immediately subsequent to the publication of the inaugural *Dissertation*, but it first received adequate statement in the second edition of the *Critique*. Kant took advantage of the second edition to reply to certain criticisms to which his view of time had given rise, and in so doing was compelled to formulate the doctrine of inner sense in a much more explicit manner. Hitherto he had assumed its truth, but had not, as it would seem, sufficiently reflected upon the various connected conclusions to which he was thereby committed. This is one of the many instances which show how what is most fundamental in Kant's thinking is frequently that of which he was himself least definitely aware. Like other thinkers, he was most apt to discuss what he himself was inclined to question and feel doubt over. The sources of his insight as well as the causes of his failure often lay beyond the purview of his explicitly developed tenets; and only under the stimulus of criticism was he constrained and enabled to bring them within the circle of reasoned conviction. We may venture the prophecy that if Kant had been able to devote several years more to the maturing of the problems which in the face of so many difficulties he had brought thus far, the doctrine of inner sense, or rather the doctrines to which it gives expression, would have been placed in the forefront of his teaching, and their systematic interconnection, both in the way of ground and of consequence, with all his chief tenets would have been traced and securely established.

This would have involved, however, two very important changes. In the first place, Kant would have had to recognise the unsatisfactory character of the supposed analogy between inner and outer sense. As already remarked,[1] no great thinker, except Locke, has attempted to interpret inner consciousness

---

[1] Above, p. 148.

on the analogy of the senses; and the obscurities of Kant's argument are not, therefore, to be excused on the ground that "the difficulty, how a subject can have an internal intuition of itself, is common to every theory." Secondly, Kant would have had to define the relation in which he conceived this part of his teaching to stand to his theory of consciousness. But both these changes could have been made without requiring that he should give up the doctrines which are mainly responsible for his theory of inner sense, namely, that there can be no awareness of awareness, but only of existences which are objective, and that there is consequently no consciousness of the generative, synthetic processes[1] which constitute consciousness on its subjective side. It is largely in virtue of these conclusions that Kant's phenomenalism differs from the subjective idealism of his predecessors. If we ignore or reject them, merely because of the obviously unsatisfactory manner in which alone Kant has been able to formulate them, we rule ourselves out from understanding the intention and purpose of much that is most characteristic of Critical teaching.

The doctrine of inner sense, as expounded by Locke, suffers from an ambiguity which seems almost inseparable from it, namely, the confusion between inner sense, on the one hand as a *sense* in some degree analogous in nature to what may be called outer sense, and on the other as consisting in self-conscious reflection. This same confusion is traceable throughout the *Critique*, and is, as we shall find, in large part responsible for Kant's failure to recognise, independently of outside criticism, the central and indispensable part which this doctrine is called upon to play in his system.

The doctrine is stated by Kant as follows. Just as outer sense is affected by noumenal agencies, and so yields a manifold arranged in terms of a form peculiar to it, namely, space, so inner sense is affected by the mind itself and its inner state.[2] The manifold thereby caused is arranged in terms of a form peculiar to inner sense, namely, time. The content thus arranged falls into two main divisions. On the one hand we have feelings, desires, volitions, that is, states of the mind in the strict sense, subjective non-spatial existences. On the other hand we have sensations, perceptions, images, concepts, in a word, representations (*Vorstellungen*) of every possible type. These latter all refer to the external world in space, and yet, according to Kant, speaking from the limited point of view of a critique of *knowledge*, form the proper

---

[1] Cf. above, pp. xliii-v, l-ii, 238, 261-2, 263 ff.; below, pp. 295 ff., 322 ff.   [2] Cf. B 67-8; A 33 = B 49.

content of inner sense. ". . . the representations of the outer senses constitute the actual material with which we occupy our minds,"[1] "the whole material of knowledge even for our inner sense."[2] (These statements, it may be observed, are first made in the second edition.) As Kant explains himself in B 67-8, he would seem to mean that the mind in the process of "setting" representations of outer sense in space affects itself, and is therefore constrained to arrange the given representations likewise in time. No new content, additional to that of outer sense, is thereby generated, but what previously as object of outer sense existed merely in space is now also subjected to conditions of time. The representations of outer sense are all by their very nature likewise representations of inner sense. To outer sense is due both their content and their spatial form ; to inner sense they owe only the additional form of time ; their content remains unaffected in the process of being taken over by a second sense. This yields such explanation as is possible of Kant's assertion in A 33 that "time can never be a determination of outer appearances." He may be taken as meaning that time is never a determination of outer sense *as such*, but only of its contents as always likewise subject to the form of inner sense.[3]

This is how Kant formulates his position from the extreme subjectivist point of view which omits to draw any distinction between representation and its object, between inner states of the self and appearances in space. All representations, he says,[4] all appearances without exception, are states of inner sense, modifications of the mind. Some exist only in time, some exist both in space and in time ; but all alike are modes of the identical self, mere representations (*blosse Vorstellungen*). Though appearances may exist outside one another in space, space itself exists only as representation, merely "in us."

Now without seeking to deny that this is a view which we find in the second edition of the *Critique* as well as in the first,[5] and that even in passages which are obviously quite late in date of writing Kant frequently speaks in terms which conform to it, we must be no less insistent in maintaining that

[1] B 67.   [2] B xxxix *n.*

[3] Kant very probably arrived at this view of inner sense under the influence of Tetens who teaches a similar doctrine in his *Philosophische Versuche über die menschliche Natur und ihre Entwickelung.* Cf. Bd. i.; *Versuch* i. 7, 8. The first volume of Tetens' work was published in 1777 (re-issued by the *Kantgesellschaft* in 1913), and had been carefully read by Kant prior to the final preparation of the *Critique.* Cf. B. Erdmann, *Kriticismus*, p. 51.

[4] Cf. A 128-9.

[5] As just noted, it is in the second edition that the above view of the content of inner sense is first definitely formulated.

an alternative view more and more comes to the front in proportion as Kant gains mastery over the conflicting tendencies that go to constitute his new Critical teaching. From the very first he uses language which implies that *some* kind of distinction must be drawn between representations and objects represented, between subjective cognitive states in the proper sense of the term and existences in space.

"Time can never be a determination of outer appearances. It belongs neither to form nor position, etc. On the other hand it determines the relation of representations in our inner state."[1]

Similarly in those very sentences in which he asserts all appearances to be *blosse Vorstellungen*, a distinction is none the less implied.

"Time is the formal *a priori* condition of all appearances in general. Space, as the pure form of all outer intuition, is as *a priori* condition limited exclusively (*bloss*) to outer appearances. On the other hand as all representations, *whether they have outer things as their object or not*, still in themselves belong, as determinations of the mind, to the inner state, and this inner state is subject to the formal condition of inner intuition, that is of time, time is an *a priori* condition of all appearance whatever. It is, indeed, the immediate condition of the inner appearance (of our souls), and thereby mediately likewise of outer appearances."[2]

As the words which I have italicised show, Kant, even in the very sentence in which he asserts outer representations to be inner states, none the less recognises that appearances in space are not representations in the same meaning of that term as are subjective states. They are the *objects* of representation, not representation itself. The latter alone is correctly describable as a state of the mind. The former may be conditioned by representation, and may therefore be describable as appearances, but are not for that reason to be equated with representation. But before the grounds and nature of this distinction can be formulated in the proper Critical terms, we must consider the reasons which induced Kant to commit himself to this obscure and difficult doctrine of inner sense. As I shall try to show, it is no mere excrescence upon his system ; on the contrary, it is inseparably bound up with all his main tenets.

One of the chief influences which constrained Kant to develop this doctrine is the conclusion, so essential to his position, that knowledge must always involve an intuitional

[1] A 33 = B 49-50.   [2] A 34 = B 50.

manifold in addition to *a priori* forms and concepts. That being so, he was bound to deny to the mind all power of gaining knowledge by mere reflection. If our mental activities and states lay open to direct inspection, we should have to recognise in the mind a non-sensuous intuitional power. Through self-consciousness or reflection we should acquire knowledge independently of sense. Such apprehension, though limited to the mind's own operations and states, would none the less be *knowledge,* and yet would not conform to the conditions which, as the transcendental deduction has shown, are involved in all knowledge. In Kant's view the belief that we possess self-consciousness of this type, a power of reflection thus conceived, is wholly illusory. To assume any such faculty would be to endow the mind with occult or mystical powers, and would throw us back upon the Leibnizian rationalism, which traces to such reflection our consciousness of the categories, and which rears upon this foundation the entire body of metaphysical science.[1]

The complementary *negative* conclusion of the transcendental deduction is a no less fundamental and constraining influence in compelling Kant to develop a doctrine of inner sense. If all knowledge is knowledge of appearances, or if, as he states his position in the *Analytic of Principles,*[2] our knowledge can extend no further than sense experience and inference from such experience, either knowledge of our inner states must be mediated, like our knowledge of outer objects, by sensation, or we can have no knowledge of them whatsoever. On Critical principles, consistently applied, there can be no middle course between acceptance of an indirect empirical knowledge of the mind and assertion of its unknowableness. Mental activities may perhaps be thought in terms of the pure forms of understanding, but in that case their conception will remain as purely problematic and as indeterminate as the conception of the thing in itself. It is impossible for Kant to admit *immediate* consciousness of the mind's real activities and states, and at the same time to deny that we can have knowledge of things in themselves. The *Aesthetic,* in proving that everything in space and time is appearance, implicitly assumes the impossibility of direct self-conscious reflection; and the transcendental deduction in showing that all knowledge involves as correlative factors both sense and thought, has reinforced this conclusion, and

---

[1] Cf. above, pp. 208-9, 251-2, 260-4; below, 311 *n.* 4. It may be observed that Caird (i. pp. 625-7) interprets inner sense as equivalent to inner *reflection.* This is one of the respects in which Caird's Hegelian standpoint has led him to misrepresent even Kant's most central doctrines.

[2] Cf. below, pp. 399-400, and A 277-8 = B 333-4.

calls for its more explicit recognition, in reference to the more inward aspect of experience.

As we have already noted,[1] Kant's doctrine of inner sense was probably adopted in the early 'seventies, and though it is not itself definitely formulated in the first edition, the chief consequence that follows from it is clearly recognised. Thus in the *Aesthetic* Kant draws the conclusion that, as time is the form of inner sense, everything apprehended in time, and consequently all inner states and activities, can be known only as appearances. The mind (meaning thereby the ultimate conditioning grounds of consciousness) is as indirectly known as is any other mode of noumenal existence. In the *Analytic*, whenever he is called upon to express himself upon this and kindred points, he continues to hold to this position; and in the section on the *Paralogisms* all the main consequences that follow from its acceptance are drawn in the most explicit and unambiguous manner. It is argued that as the inner world, the feelings, volitions and representations of which we are conscious, is a world constructed out of a given manifold yielded by inner sense, and is therefore known only as the appearance of a deeper reality which we have no power of apprehending, it possesses no superiority either of certainty or of immediacy over the outer world of objects in space. We have immediate consciousness of both alike, but in both cases this immediate consciousness rests upon the transcendental synthetic processes whereby such consciousness is conditioned and generated. The transcendental activities fall outside the field of empirical consciousness and therefore of knowledge.

Thus Kant would seem to be maintaining that the radical error committed by the subjective idealists, and with which all the main defects of their teaching are inseparably bound up, lies in their ascription to the mind of a power of direct self-conscious reflection, and consequently in their confusion of the transcendental activities which condition consciousness with the inner states and processes which such consciousness reveals. This has led them to ascribe priority and independence to our inner states, and to regard outer objects as known only by an inference from them. The Critical teaching insists on the distinction between appearance and reality, applies it to the inner life, and so restores to our consciousness of the outer world the certainty and immediacy of which subjective idealism would profess to deprive it. Such are the important conclusions at which Kant arrives in his various "refutations of idealism"; and it will be advisable to consider

[1] Above, p. 292.

these refutations in full detail before attempting to complete our statement of his doctrine of inner sense.

KANT'S REFUTATIONS OF IDEALISM

Kant has in a number of different passages attempted to define his Critical standpoint in its distinction from the positions of Descartes and Berkeley. Consideration of these will enable us to follow Kant in his gradual recognition of the manifold consequences to which he is committed by his substitution of inner sense for direct self-conscious intuition or reflection, or rather of the various congenial tenets which it gives him the right consistently to defend and maintain. In Kant's Critical writings we find no less than seven different statements of his refutation of idealism: (I.) in the fourth *Paralogism* of the first edition of the *Critique*; (II.) in section 13 (*Anm.* ii. and iii.) of the *Prolegomena*; (III.) in section 49 of the *Prolegomena*; (IV.) in the second appendix to the *Prolegomena*; (V.) in sections added in the second edition at the conclusion of the *Aesthetic* (B 69 ff.); (VI.) in the "refutation of idealism" (B 274-8), in the supplementary section at the end of the section on the *Postulates* (B 291-4), and in the note to the new preface (B xxxix-xl); (VII.) in the "refutation of problematic idealism" given in the *Seven Small Papers* which originated in Kant's conversations with Kiesewetter. Consideration of these in the above order will reveal Kant's gradual and somewhat vacillating recognition of the new and revolutionary position which alone genuinely harmonises with Critical principles. But first we must briefly consider the various meanings which Kant at different periods assigned to the term idealism. Even in the *Critique* itself it is employed in a great variety of diverse connotations.

In the pre-Critical writings[1] the term idealism is usually employed in what was its currently accepted meaning, namely, as signifying any philosophy which denied the existence of an independent world corresponding to our subjective representations. But even as thus used the term is ambiguous.[2] It may signify either denial of a *corporeal* world independent of our representations or denial of an immaterial world "corresponding to" the represented material world, *i.e.* the denial of *Dinge an sich*. For there are traceable in Leibniz's writings two very different views as to the reality of the material world. Sometimes the monads are viewed as purely intelligible substances without materiality of any kind. The

---

[1] Cf. above, p. 155.
[2] Cf. Vaihinger in *Strassburger Abhandlungen sur Philosophie* (1884), p. 106 ff.

kingdom of the extended is set into the representing subjects; only the immaterial world of unextended purely spiritual monads remains as independently real. At other times the monads, though in themselves immaterial, are viewed as constituting through their coexistence an independent material world and a materially occupied space. Every monad has a spatial sphere of activity. The material world is an objective existence due to external relations between the monads, not a merely subjective existence internal to each of them. This alternation of standpoints enabled Leibniz's successors to deny that they were idealists; and as the more daring and speculative aspects of Leibniz's teaching were slurred over in the process of its popularisation, it was the second, less consistent view, which gained the upper hand. Wolff, especially in his later writings, denounces idealism; and in the current manuals, sections in refutation of idealism became part of the recognised philosophical teaching. Idealism still, however, continued to be used ambiguously, as signifying indifferently either denial of material bodies or denial of things in themselves. This is the dual meaning which the term presents in Kant's pre-Critical writings. In his *Dilucidatio* (1755)[1] he refutes idealism by means of the principle that a substance cannot undergo changes unless it is a substance independent of other substances. Obviously this argument can at most prove the existence of an independent world, not that it is spatial or material. And as Vaihinger adds, it does not even rule out the possibility that changes find their source in a Divine Being. In the *Dreams of a Visionseer* (1766)[2] Swedenborg is described as an idealist, but without further specification of the exact sense in which the term is employed. In the inaugural *Dissertation* (1770)[3] idealism is again rejected, on the ground that sense-affection points to the presence of an intelligible object or *noumenon*.

In Kant's class lectures on metaphysics,[4] which fall, in part at least, between 1770 and 1781, the term idealism is employed in a very different sense, which anticipates its use in the *Appendix* to the *Prolegomena*.[5] The teaching of the *Dissertation*, that things in themselves are knowable, is now described as dogmatic, Platonic, mystical (*schwärmerischer*) idealism. He still rejects the idealism of Berkeley, and still entitles it simply idealism, without limiting or descriptive predicates. But now also he employs the phrase " problematic

---

[1] Section III., Prop. *XII Usus.*
[2] Theil II. Hauptstück II. *W.* ii. p. 364.
[3] § 11.
[4] Pölitz's edition (1821), pp. 100-2.
[5] *W.* iv. p. 373 ff.

idealism " as descriptive of his own new position.   This is, of course, contrary to his invariable usage elsewhere, but is interesting as showing that about this time his repugnance to the term idealism begins to give way, and that he is willing to recognise that the relation of the Critical teaching to idealism is not one of simple opposition.   He now begins to regard idealism as a factor, though a radically transformed factor, in his own philosophy.

Study of the *Critique* reinforces this conclusion.   In the *Aesthetic* Kant teaches the " transcendental ideality " of space and time; and in the *Dialectic* (in the fourth *Paralogism*) describes his position as idealism, though with the qualifying predicate transcendental.[1]   But though this involves an extension of the previous connotation of the term idealism, and might therefore have been expected to increase the existing confusion, it has the fortunate effect of constraining Kant to recognise and discriminate the various meanings in which it may be employed.   This is done somewhat clumsily, as if it were a kind of afterthought.   In the introductory syllogism of the fourth *Paralogism* Descartes' position and his own are referred to simply as idealism and dualism respectively.   The various possible sub-species of idealism as presented in the two editions of the *Critique* and in the *Prolegomena* may be tabulated as follows :

The distinction between problematic idealism and idealism of the more strictly sceptical type is not clearly drawn by Kant.[2]   Very strangely Kant in this connection never mentions Hume : the reference in B xxxix *n.* is probably not to Hume but to Jacobi.   Transcendental idealism is taken as involving an empirical realism and dualism, and is set in opposition to transcendental realism which is represented as involving empirical idealism.   In B xxxix *n.* Kant speaks of " psychological idealism," meaning, as it would seem, material or non-Critical idealism.

---

[1] It may be noted that in the *Aesthetic* (A 38 = B 55) Kant employs the term idealism, without descriptive epithet, in the same manner as in his pre-Critical writings, as signifying a position that must be rejected.

[2] Cf. below, p. 301 ff.

In the second appendix to the *Prolegomena* Kant draws a further distinction, in line with that already noted in his lectures on metaphysics. Tabulated it is as follows:

Idealism
- Mystical, in the sense of belief in and reliance on a supposed human power of intellectual intuition. It is described as idealism in the strict (*eigentlich*) sense—the position of the Eleatics, of Plato and Berkeley.
- Formal or Critical—Kant's own position.

This latter classification can cause nothing but confusion. The objections that have to be made against it from Kant's own critical standpoint are stated below.[1]

Let us now consider, in the order of their presentation, the various refutations of idealism which Kant has given in his Critical writings.

I. Refutation of Idealism as given in First Edition of "Critique"

(A 366-80). — This refutation is mainly directed against Descartes, who is mentioned by name in A 367. Kant, as Vaihinger suggests, was very probably led to recognise Descartes' position as a species of idealism in the course of a re-study of Descartes before writing the section on the *Paralogisms*. As already pointed out, this involves the use of the term idealism in a much wider sense than that which was usually given to it in Kant's own day. In the development of his argument Kant also wavers between two very different definitions of this idealism, as being denial of *immediate* certainty and as denial of all certainty of the existence of material bodies.[2] The second interpretation, which would make it apply to Hume rather than to Descartes, is strengthened in the minds of his readers by his further distinction[3] between dogmatic and sceptical idealism, and the identification of the idealism under consideration with the latter. The title problematic which Kant in the second edition[4] applies to Descartes' position suffers from this same ambiguity. As a matter of fact, Kant's refutation applies equally well to either position. The teaching of Berkeley, which coincides with dogmatic idealism as here defined by Kant, namely, as consisting in the contention that the conception of matter is inherently contradictory, is not dwelt upon, and the appended promise of refutation is not fulfilled.

Descartes' position is stated as follows: only our own existence and inner states are immediately apprehended by us; all perceptions are modifications of inner sense; and

---

[1] Pp. 307-8.   [2] Cf. A 368-9 and 372.
[3] A 377: a passage which bears signs of being a later interpolation.
[4] B 274.

the existence of external objects can therefore be asserted only by an inference from the inner perceptions viewed as effects.   In criticism, Kant points out that since an effect may result from more than one cause, this inference to a quite determinate cause, viz. objects as bodies in space, is doubtfully legitimate.   The cause of our inner states may lie within and not without us, and even if external, need not consist in spatial objects.   Further, leaving aside the question of a possible alternative to the assumption of independent material bodies, the assertion of the existence of such objects would, on Descartes' view, be merely conjectural.   It could never have certainty in any degree equivalent to that possessed by the experiences of inner sense.

"By an idealist, therefore, we must not understand one who denies the existence of outer objects of the senses, but only one who does not admit that their existence is known through immediate perception, and who therefore concludes that we can never, by way of any possible experience, be completely certain of their reality."[1]

No sooner is the term idealist thus clearly defined than Kant, in keeping with the confused character of the entire section, proceeds to the assertion (a) that there are idealists of another type, namely, transcendental idealists,[2] and (b) that the non-transcendental idealists sometimes also adopt a dogmatic position, not merely questioning the immediacy of our knowledge of matter, but asserting it to be inherently contradictory.   All this points to the composite origin of the contents of this section.

Transcendental idealism is opposed to empirical idealism. It maintains that phenomena are representations merely, not things in themselves.   Space and time are the sensuous forms of our intuitions.   Empirical idealism, on the other hand, goes together with transcendental realism.   It maintains that space and time are given as real in themselves, in independence of our sensibility.   (Transcendental here, as in the phrase "transcendental ideality,"[3] is exactly equivalent to transcendent.)   But such a contention is inconsistent with the other main tenet of empirical idealism.   For if our inner representations have to be taken as entirely distinct from their objects, they cannot yield assurance *even of the existence* of these objects.   To the transcendental idealist no such difficulty is presented.   His position naturally combines with empirical realism, or, as it may also be entitled, empirical dualism. Material bodies in space, being merely subjective representations, are immediately apprehended. The existence of matter can be established "without our requiring to issue out beyond our bare self-consciousness or to assume anything more than the certainty of the representations in us, *i.e.* of the *cogito ergo sum*." [1] Though the objects thus apprehended are outside one another in space, space itself exists only in us.

"Outer objects (bodies) are mere appearances, and are therefore nothing but a species of my representations, the objects of which are something only through these representations. Apart from them they are nothing. Thus outer things exist as well as I myself, and both, indeed, upon the immediate witness of my self-consciousness. . . ." [2]

The only difference is that the representation of the self belongs only to inner, while extended bodies also belong to outer sense. There is thus a dualism, but one which falls entirely within the field of consciousness, and which is therefore empirical, not transcendental. There is indeed a transcendental object which "in the transcendental sense may be outside us," [3] but it is unknown and is not in question. It ought not to be confused with our representations of matter and corporeal things.

From this point [4] the argument becomes disjointed and repeats itself, and there is much to be said in support of the contention of Adickes that the remainder of the section is made up of a number of separate interpolations. [5] First, Kant applies the conclusion established in the *Postulates of Empirical Thought*, viz. that reality is revealed only in sensation. As sensation is an element in all outer perception, perception affords immediate certainty of real existence, Kant next enters [6] upon a eulogy of sceptical idealism as "a benefactor of human reason." It brings home to us the utter impossibility of proving the existence of matter on the assumption that spatial objects are things in themselves, and so constrains us to justify the assertions which we are at every moment making. And such justification is, Kant here claims, only possible if we recognise that outer objects as mere representations are immediately known. In the next paragraph we find a sentence which, together with the above eulogistic estimate of the merits of idealism, shows how very

---

[1] A 370.   [2] *Loc. cit.*   [3] A 372.
[4] A 373 : *Weil indessen*, etc.
[5] Adickes regards them as *later* additions. To judge by their content (cf. above, pp. 204 ff., 215-16, on Kant's doctrine of the transcendental object), they are more probably of quite early origin.
[6] A 377-8.

far Kant, at the time of writing, was from feeling the need of differentiating his position from that of subjectivism. The sentence is this :

"We cannot be sentient of what is outside ourselves, but only of what is in ourselves, and the whole of our self-consciousness therefore yields nothing save merely our own determinations."

It is probable, indeed, that the paragraph in which this occurs is of very early origin, prior to the development of the main body of the *Analytic* ; for in the same paragraph we also find the assertion, utterly at variance with the teaching of the *Analytic* and with that of the first and third *Paralogisms*, that "the thinking ego" is known phenomenally as *substance*.[1] We seem justified in concluding that the various manuscripts which have gone to form this section on the fourth *Paralogism* were written at an early date within the Critical period.

We may note, in passing, two sentences in which, as in that quoted above, a distinction between representations and their objects is recognised in wording if not in fact.

"All outer perception furnishes immediate proof of something actual in space, or rather is the actual itself.　To this extent empirical realism is beyond question, *i.e.* there corresponds to our outer perceptions something actual in space."[2]

Again in A 377 the assertion occurs that "our outer senses, as regards the data from which experience can arise, have their actual corresponding objects in space." Certainly these statements, when taken together with the other passages in this section, form a sufficiently strange combination of assertion and denial.　Either there is a distinction between representation and its object or there is not ; if the former, then objects in space are not merely representations ; if the latter, then the "correspondence" is merely that of a thing with itself.[3]

This refutation of idealism will not itself stand criticism. For two separate reasons it entirely fails to attain its professed end.　In the first place, it refutes the position of Descartes only by virtually accepting the still more extreme

---

[1] Adickes argues that this paragraph is subsequent to the main body of the *Analytic*, but that is in keeping with the tendency which he seems to show of dating passages, which cannot belong to the "Brief Outline," later rather than earlier.

[2] A 375.

[3] The remaining passages in the fourth *Paralogism*, together with the corresponding passages in B 274 ff., in Kant's note to B xxxix, and in B 291-3, are separately dealt with below, pp. 308 ff., 322 ff., 462-3.

position of Berkeley. Outer objects, Kant argues, are immediately known because they are ideas merely. There is no need for inference, because there is no transcendence of the domain of our inner consciousness. In other words, Kant refutes the problematic idealism of Descartes by means of the more subjective idealism of Berkeley. The "dogmatic" idealism of Berkeley in the form in which Kant here defines it,[1] namely, as consisting in the assertion that the notion of an independent spatial object involves inherent contradictions, is part of his own position. For this reason he was bound to fail in his promise[2] to refute such dogmatic idealism. Fortunately he never even attempts to do so. In the second place, Kant ignores the fact that he has himself adopted an "idealist" view of inner experience. Inner experience is not for him, as it was for Descartes, the immediate apprehension of genuine reality. As it is only appearance, the incorporation of outer experience within it, so far from establishing the reality of the objects of outer sense, must rather prove the direct contrary. No more is really established than Descartes himself invariably assumes, namely, the actual existence of mental representations of a corporeal world in space. Descartes' further assertion that the world of things in themselves can be inferred to be material and spatial, Kant, of course, refuses to accept. On this latter point Kant is in essential agreement with Berkeley.

It is by no means surprising that Kant's first critics,[3] puzzled and bewildered by the obscurer and more difficult portions of the *Critique*, should have based their interpretation of Kant's general position largely upon the above passages; and that in combining the extreme subjective idealism which Kant there advocates with his doctrine that the inner life of ever-changing experiences is itself merely ideal, should have come to the conclusion that Kant's position is an extension of that of Berkeley. Pistorius objected that in making outer appearances relative to an inner consciousness which is itself appearance, Kant is reducing everything to mere illusion. Hamann came to the somewhat similar conclusion, that Kant, notwithstanding his very different methods of argument, is "a Prussian Hume," in substantial agreement with his Scotch predecessor.

II. **"Prolegomena," Section 13, Notes II. and III.**—In the *Prolegomena* Kant replies to the criticism which the first edition of the *Critique* had called forth, that his position is an

---

[1] A 377.   [2] *Loc. cit.*   [3] *E.g.* Garve.

extension of the idealism of Descartes, and even more thoroughgoing than that of Berkeley. Idealism he redefines in a much narrower sense, which makes it applicable only to Berkeley

". . . as consisting in the assertion that there are none but thinking beings, and that all other things which we suppose ourselves to perceive in intuition are nothing but representations in the thinking beings, to which no object external to them corresponds in fact."[1]

In reply Kant affirms his unwavering belief in the reality of *Dinge an sich*

". . . which though quite unknown to us as to what they are in themselves, we yet know by the representations which their influence on our sensibility procures us. . . . Can this be termed idealism? It is the very contrary."[2]

Kant adds that his position is akin to that of Locke, differing only in his assertion of the subjectivity of the primary as well as of the secondary qualities.

"I should be glad to know what my assertions ought to have been in order to avoid all idealism. I suppose I ought to have said, not only that the representation of space is perfectly conformable to the relation which our sensibility has to objects (for that I have said), but also that it is completely similar to them—an assertion in which I can find as little meaning as if I said that the sensation of red has a similarity to the property of cinnabar which excites this sensation in me."[3]

Kant is here very evidently using the term idealism in the narrowest possible meaning, as representing only the position of Berkeley, and as excluding that of Descartes and Leibniz. Such employment of the term is at variance with his own previous usage. Though idealism here corresponds to the " dogmatic idealism " of A 377, it is now made to concern the assertion or denial of things in themselves, not as previously the problem of the reality of material objects and of space. Kant is also ignoring the fact, which he more than once points out in the *Critique*, that his philosophy cannot prove that the cause of our sensations is without and not within us. His use of " body "[4] as a name for the thing in itself is likewise without justification. This passage is mainly polemical ; it is hardly more helpful than the criticism to which it was designed to reply.

In Section 13, Note iii., Kant meets the still more

[1] § 13, *W.* iv. pp. 288-9 : Eng. trans. p. 42. [2] *Loc. cit.*
[3] *Op. cit.* pp. 289-90 : Eng. trans. pp. 43-4. [4] In Note II.

extreme criticism (made by Pistorius), that his system turns all the things of the world into mere illusion (*Schein*). He distinguishes transcendental idealism from "the mystical and visionary idealism of Berkeley" on the one hand, and on the other from the Cartesian idealism which would convert mere representations into things in themselves. To obviate the ambiguities of the term transcendental, he declares that his own idealism may perhaps more fitly be entitled Critical. This distinction between mystical and Critical idealism connects with the contents of the second part of the Appendix, treated below.

III. "**Prolegomena**," **Section 49.**—This is simply a repetition of the argument of the fourth *Paralogism*. The Cartesian idealism, now (as in B 274) named material idealism, is alone referred to. The Cartesian idealism does nothing, Kant says, but distinguish external experience from dreaming. There is here again the same confusing use of the term "corresponds."

"That something actual without us not only corresponds but must correspond to our external perceptions can likewise be proved. . . ."[1]

IV. "**Prolegomena**," **Second Part of the Appendix.**—Kant here returns to the distinction, drawn in Section 13, Note iii., between what he now calls "idealism proper (*eigentlicher*),"[2] *i.e.* visionary or mystical idealism, and his own.

"The position of all genuine idealists from the Eleatics to Bishop Berkeley is contained in this formula: 'All cognition through the senses and experience is nothing but mere illusion, and only in the ideas of pure understanding and Reason is there truth. The fundamental principle ruling all my idealism, on the contrary, is this: 'All cognition of things solely from pure understanding or pure Reason is nothing but mere illusion and only in experience is there truth.'"[3]

This mode of defining idealism can, in this connection, cause nothing but confusion. Its inapplicability to Berkeley would seem to prove that Kant had no first-hand knowledge of Berkeley's writings.[4] As Kant's Note to the Appendix to the *Prolegomena*[5] shows, he also had Plato in mind. But the definition given of "the fundamental principle" of his own idealism is almost equally misleading. It omits the all-essential point, that for Kant experience itself yields truth only by conforming to *a priori* concepts. As it is, he proceeds

[1] § 49, *W.* iv. 336: Eng. trans. p. 99.   [3] *Anhang*, *W.* iv. p. 375 *n.*
[2] *W.* iv. p. 374: Eng. trans. p. 147.   [4] Cf. above, p. 155 ff.
[5] *W.* iv. p. 375.

to criticise Berkeley for failure to supply a sufficient criterion of distinction between truth and illusion. Such criterion, he insists, is necessarily *a priori*. The Critical idealism differs from that of Berkeley in maintaining that space and time, though sensuous, are *a priori*, and that in combination with the pure concepts of understanding they

". . . prescribe *a priori* its law to all possible experience : the law which at the same time yields the sure criterion for distinguishing within experience truth from illusion. My so-called idealism—which properly speaking is Critical idealism—is thus quite peculiar in that it overthrows ordinary idealism, and that through it all *a priori* cognition, even that of geometry, now attains objective reality, a thing which even the keenest realist could not assert till I had proved the ideality of space and time."[1]

V. **Sections added in Second Edition at the Conclusion of the Aesthetic.** (B 69 ff.)—Kant here again replies to the criticism of Pistorius that all existence has been reduced to the level of illusion (*Schein*). His defence is twofold : first, that in naming objects appearances he means to indicate that they are independently grounded, or, as he states it, are "something actually given." If we *mis*interpret them, the result is indeed illusion, but the fault then lies with ourselves and not with the appearances as presented. Secondly, he argues that the doctrine of the ideality of space and time is the only secure safeguard against scepticism. For otherwise the contradictions which result from regarding space and time as independently real will likewise hold of their contents, and everything, including even our own existence, will be rendered illusory. "The good Berkeley [observing these contradictions] cannot, indeed, be blamed for reducing bodies to mere illusion." This last sentence may perhaps be taken as supporting the view that notwithstanding the increased popularity of Berkeley in Germany and the appearance of new translations in these very years, Kant has not been sufficiently interested to acquire first-hand knowledge of Berkeley's writings.[2] The epithet employed, if meant to be depreciatory, is characteristic of the attitude which Kant invariably adopts in speaking of Berkeley.

VI. **"Refutation of Idealism" in Second Edition of the "Critique."** (B 274-9, supplemented by note to B xxxix.).— The refutation opens by equating idealism with material idealism (so named in contradistinction to his own "formal or rather Critical" teaching). Within material idealism Kant

---

[1] *W.* iv. p. 375 : Eng. trans. p. 147-8.   [2] Cf. above, p. 156.

distinguishes between the problematic idealism of Descartes, and the dogmatic idealism of Berkeley. The latter has, he says, been overthrown in the *Aesthetic*. The former alone is dealt with in this refutation. This is the first occurrence in the *Critique* of the expression "problematic idealism": it is nowhere employed in the first edition.[1] Problematic idealism consists in the assertion that we are incapable of having experience of any existence save our own; only our inner states are immediately apprehended; all other existences are determined by inference from them. The refutation consists in the proof that we have experience, and not mere imagination of outer objects. This is proved by showing that inner experience, unquestioned by Descartes, is possible only on the assumption of outer experience, and that this latter is as immediate and direct as is the former.

Thesis.—The empirically determined consciousness of my own existence proves the existence of objects in space outside me.[2]

Proof.—I am conscious of my own existence as determined in time. Time determination presupposes the perception of something permanent. But nothing permanent is intuitable in the empirical self. On the cognitive side (*i.e.* omitting feelings, etc., which in this connection are irrelevant), it consists solely of representations; and these demand a permanent, distinct from ourselves, in relation to which their changes, and so my own existence in the time wherein they change, may be determined.[3] Thus perception of this permanent is only possible through a thing outside, and not through the mere representation of a thing outside. And the same must hold true of the determination of my existence in time, since this also depends upon the apprehension of the permanent. That is to say, the consciousness of my existence is at the same time an immediate awareness of the existence of other things outside me.

In the note to the *Preface* to the second edition [4] occurs the following emphatic statement.

"Representation of something permanent in existence is not the same as permanent representation. For though the representation [of the permanent] may be very changing and variable like all our other representations, not excepting those of matter, it yet refers to

---

[1] As already noted above, p. 299, it is employed by Kant in his lectures on Metaphysics.

[2] Kant's phrase "in space outside me" is on Kant's principles really pleonastic. Cf. *Prolegomena*, § 49; Eng. trans. p. 101: "the notion 'outside me' only signifies existence in space." Cf. A 373.

[3] Cf. text as altered by note to B xxxix.   [4] B xxxix.

something permanent. This latter must therefore be an external thing distinct from all my representations, and its existence must be included in the determination of my own existence, constituting with it but a single experience such as would not take place even internally if it were not also at the same time, in part, external. How this should be possible we are as little capable of explaining further as we are of accounting for our being able to think the abiding in time, the coexistence of which with the variable generates the conception of change."

The argument of this note varies from that of B 274 ff. only in its use of an ambiguous expression which is perhaps capable of being taken as referring to things in themselves, but which does not seem to have that meaning. "I am just as certainly conscious that there are things outside me which relate to my sense. . . ."

In B 277-8 Kant refers to the empirical fact that determination of time can be made only by relation to outer happenings in space, such as the motion of the sun. This is a point which is further developed in another passage which Kant added in the second edition.

". . . in order to understand the possibility of things in conformity with the categories, and so to demonstrate the objective reality of the latter, we need not merely intuitions, but intuitions that are in all cases outer intuitions. When, for instance, we take the pure concepts of *relation*, we find firstly that in order to obtain something *permanent* in intuition corresponding to the concept of substance, and so to demonstrate the objective reality of this concept, we require an intuition in space (of matter). For space alone is determined as permanent, while time, and therefore everything that is in inner sense, is in constant flux. Secondly, in order to exhibit *change* as the intuition corresponding to the concept of *causality*, we must take as our example motion, *i.e.* change in space. Only in this way can we obtain the intuition of changes, the possibility of which can never be comprehended through any pure understanding. For change is combination of contradictorily opposed determinations in the existence of one and the same thing. Now how it is possible that from a given state of a thing an opposite state should follow, not only cannot be conceived by any reason without an example, but is actually incomprehensible to reason without intuition. The intuition required is the intuition of the movement of a point in space. The presence of the point in different spaces (as a sequence of opposite determinations) is what first yields to us an intuition of change. For in order that we may afterwards make inner changes likewise thinkable, we must represent time (the form of inner sense) figuratively as a line, and the inner change through the drawing of this line (motion), and so in this manner by means of outer intuition make comprehensible the successive existence of ourselves in different states. The reason of this is that all change, if it is indeed to be perceived as change, presupposes something permanent in intuition, and that in inner sense no permanent intuition is to be met with. Lastly, the possibility of the category of *community* cannot be comprehended through mere reason alone. Its objective reality is not to be understood without intuition and indeed outer intuition in space."[1]

In this passage Kant is modifying the teaching of the first edition in two very essential respects. In the first place, he is now asserting that consciousness of both space and motion is necessary to consciousness of time;[2] and in the second place, he is maintaining that the *categories* can acquire meaning only by reference to outer appearances. Had Kant made all the necessary alterations which these new positions involve, he would, as we shall find,[3] have had entirely to recast the chapters on *Schematism* and on the *Principles of Understanding*. Kant was not, however, prepared to make such extensive alterations, and these chapters are therefore left practically unmodified. This is one of the many important points in which the reader is compelled to reinterpret passages of earlier date in the light of Kant's later utterances. There is also a further difficulty. Does Kant, in maintaining that the categories can *acquire* significance only in reference to outer perception, also mean to assert that their subsequent employment is limited to the mechanical world of the material sciences? This is a point in regard to which Kant makes no quite direct statement; but indirectly he would seem to indicate that that was not his intention.[4] He frequently speaks of the states of inner sense as mechanically conditioned. Sensations,[5] feelings, and desires,[6] are, he would seem to

---

[1] B 291-2. The remaining points in B 274 ff. as well as in B xxxix *n*. are separately dealt with below, p. 322 ff.

[2] The nearest approach to such teaching in the first edition is in A 33 = B 50. Cf. above, pp. 135-8.

[3] Cf. below, pp. 333, 341, 360, 384-5.

[4] Adamson (*Development of Modern Philosophy*, i. pp. 241 ff.) takes the opposite view as to what is Kant's intended teaching, but remarks upon its inconsistency with Kant's own fundamental principles. "Now, in truth, Kant grievously endangers his own doctrine by insisting on the absence of *a priori* elements from our apprehension of the mental life; for it follows from that, if taken rigorously, that according to Kant sense and understanding are not so much sources which unite in producing knowledge, as, severally, sources of distinct kinds of apprehension. If we admit at all, in respect to inner sense, that there is some kind of apprehension without the work of understanding, then it has been acknowledged that sense is *per se* adequate to furnish a kind of apprehension." As pointed out above (p. 296), by the same line of reasoning Kant is disabled from viewing inner consciousness as merely reflective. In other words it can neither be more immediate nor less sensuous than outer perception. Cf. below, pp. 361, *n*. 3, 384-5.

[5] Above, pp. xlvi, 275-82; below, pp. 313-14, 384-5.

[6] Above, pp. 276, 279-80; below, pp. 312, 384-5.

assert, integral parts of the unitary system of phenomenal existence. Such a view is not, indeed, easily reconcilable with his equating of the principle of substance with the principle of the conservation of matter.[1] There are here two conflicting positions which Kant has failed to reconcile: the traditional dualistic attitude of Cartesian physics and the quite opposite implications of his Critical phenomenalism. When the former is being held to, Kant has to maintain that psychology can never become a science;[2] but his Critical teaching consistently developed seems rather to support the view that psychology, despite special difficulties peculiar to its subject matter, can be developed on lines strictly analogous to those of the material sciences.

We may now return to Kant's main argument. This new refutation of idealism in the second edition differs from that given in the fourth *Paralogism* of the first edition, not only in method of argument but also in the nature of the conclusion which it seeks to establish. Indeed it proves the *direct opposite* of what is asserted in the first edition. The earlier proof sought to show that, as regards immediacy of apprehension and subjectivity of existence, outer appearances stand on the same level as do our inner experiences. The proof of the second edition, on the other hand, argues that though outer appearances are immediately apprehended they must be existences distinct from the subjective states through which the mind represents them. The two arguments agree, indeed, in establishing immediacy, but as that which is taken as immediately known is in the one case a subjective state and in the other an independent existence, the immediacy calls in the two cases for entirely different methods of proof. The first method consisted in viewing outer experiences as a subdivision within our inner experiences. The new method views their relation as not that of including and included,

---

[1] Cf. below, p. 361.

[2] Cf. *Metaphysical First Principles of Natural Science* (1786), *W.* iv. pp. 470-1. It should be observed, however, that the reasons which Kant gives in this treatise for denying that psychology can ever become more than a merely historical or descriptive discipline are not that the objects of inner sense fall outside the realm of mechanically determined existence. Kant makes no assertion that even distantly implies any such view. His reasons are—(1) that, as time has only one dimension, the main body of mathematical science is not applicable to the phenomena of inner sense and their laws; (2) that such phenomena are capable only of a merely ideal, not of an experimental, analysis; (3) that, as the objects of inner sense do not consist of parts outside each other, their parts are not substances, and may therefore be conceived as diminishing in intensity or passing out of existence without prejudice to the principle of the permanence of substance (*op. cit.* p. 542, quoted below, p. 361, *n.* 2); (4) that inner observation is limited to the individual's own existence; (5) that the very act of introspection alters the state of the object observed.

but of conditioning and conditioned; and it is now to outer experience that the primary position is assigned. So far is outer experience from being possible only as part of inner experience, that on the contrary inner experience, consciousness of the flux of inner states, is only possible in and through experience of independent material bodies in space. A sentence from each proof will show how completely their conclusions are opposed.

"Outer objects (bodies) are mere appearances, and are therefore nothing but a species of my representations, the objects of which are something only through these representations. Apart from them they are nothing."[1]   "Perception of this permanent is possible only through a *thing* outside me, and not through the mere *representation* of a thing outside me."[2]

The one sentence asserts that outer objects are representations; the other argues that they must be existences distinct from their representations. The one inculcates a subjectivism of a very extreme type; the other results in a realism, which though ultimately phenomenalist, is none the less genuinely objective in character. This difference is paralleled by the nature of the idealisms to which the two proofs are opposed and which they profess to refute. The argument of the *Paralogism* of the first edition is itself Berkeleian, and refutes only the problematic idealism of Descartes. The argument of the second edition, though formally directed only against Descartes, constitutes a no less complete refutation of the position of Berkeley. In its realism it has kinship with the positions of Arnauld and of Reid; while, in attempting to combine this realism with due recognition of the force and validity of Hume's sceptical philosophy, it breaks through all previous classifications, formulates a profoundly original substitute for the previously existing theories, and inaugurates a new era in the theory of knowledge.

As already pointed out,[3] Kant restates the distinction between the subjective and the objective in a manner which places the problem of knowledge in an entirely new light. The subjective is not to be regarded as opposite in nature to the objective, but as a subspecies within it. It does not proceed parallel with the sequence of natural existences, but is itself part of the natural system which consciousness reveals. Sensations, in the form in which they are consciously apprehended by us, do not constitute our consciousness of nature,

---

[1] A 370.
[2] B 275.   These two sentences are cited in this connection by Vaihinger *Strassburger Abhandlungen zur Philosophie* (1884), p. 131.
[3] Above, pp. xlv-vii, 279 ff.

but are themselves events which are possible only under the conditions which the natural world itself supplies.[1] The Cartesian dualism of the subjective and the objective is thus subordinated to the Critical distinction between appearance and reality. Kant's phenomenalism is a genuine alternative to the Berkeleian teaching, and not, as Schopenhauer and so many others have sought to maintain, merely a variant upon it.

The striking contradiction between Kant's various refutations of idealism has led some of Kant's most competent critics to give a different interpretation of the argument of the second edition from that given above. These critics take the independent and permanent objects which are distinguished from our subjective representations to be things in themselves. That is to say, they interpret this refutation as based upon Kant's semi-Critical doctrine of the transcendental object (in the form in which it is employed for the solution of the *Antinomies*), and so as agreeing with the refutation given in the *Prolegomena*.[2] Kant is taken as rejecting idealism because of his belief in things in themselves. This is the view adopted by Benno Erdmann,[3] Sidgwick,[4] A. J. Balfour.[5]

As Vaihinger,[6] Caird,[7] and Adamson[8] have shown, such an interpretation is at complete variance with the actual text. This is, indeed, so obvious upon unbiassed examination that the only point which repays discussion is the question, why Benno Erdmann and those who follow him should have felt constrained to place so unnatural an interpretation upon Kant's words. The explanation seems to lie in Erdmann's convinced belief, plainly shown in all his writings upon Kant, that the *Critique* expounds a single consistent and uniform standpoint.[9] If such belief be justified, there is no alternative save to interpret Kant's refutation of idealism in the manner which Erdmann adopts. For as the subjectivism of much of Kant's teaching is beyond question, consistency can be obtained only by sacrifice of all that conflicts with it. Thus, and thus alone, can Erdmann's rendering of the refutation of the second edition be sustained; the actual wording,

---

[1] Cf. also above, pp. 275-7, and below, Appendix C.
[2] § 13, *Anmerkung II.*   [3] *Kriticismus*, p. 197 ff. Cf. below, Appendix C.
[4] *Mind* (1879), iv. p. 408 ff.; (1880), v. p. 111.
[5] *A Defence of Philosophic Doubt* (1879), p. 107 ff.; *Mind* (1878), iii. p. 481; v. p. 115; vi. p. 260.   [6] *Op. cit.* p. 128 ff.
[7] *Critical Philosophy*, i. 632 ff.; *Mind* (1879), iv. pp. 112, 560-1; v. p. 115.
[8] *The Philosophy of Kant*, p. 249 ff.
[9] The one fundamental question to which Erdmann would seem to allow that Kant gives conflicting answers is as to whether or not categories can be transcendently employed. The assumption of a uniform teaching is especially obvious in Sidgwick's comments; cf. *Mind* (1880), v. p. 113; *Lectures on the Philosophy of Kant* (1905), p. 28.

taken in and by itself, does not support it. Kant here departs from his own repeated assertion, in the second hardly less than in the first edition of the *Critique*, of the subjectivity of outer appearances. But, as Vaihinger justly contends, Kant was never greater than in this violation of self-consistency, "never more consistent than in this inconsistency." Tendencies, previously active but hitherto inarticulate, are at last liberated. If the chrysalis stage of the intense brooding of the twelve years of Critical thinking was completed in the writing of the first edition of the *Critique*, the philosophy which then emerged only attains to mature stature in those extensions of the *Critique*, scattered through it from *Preface* to *Paralogisms*, which embody this realistic theory of the independent existence of material nature. For this theory is no mere external accretion, and no mere reversal of subordinate tenets, but a ripening of germinal ideas to which, even in their more embryonic form, the earlier Critical teaching owed much of its inspiration, and which, when consciously adopted and maturely formulated, constitute such a deepening of its teaching as almost amounts to transformation. The individual self is no longer viewed as being the bearer of nature, but as its offspring and expression, and as being, like nature, interpretable in its twofold aspect, as appearance and as noumenally grounded. The bearer of appearance is not the individual subject, but those transcendental creative agencies upon which man and nature alike depend. Both man and nature transcend the forms in which they are apprehended; and nothing in experience justifies the giving of such priority to the individual mind as must be involved in any acceptance of subjectivist theory. Though man is cognisant of space and time, comprehending them within the limits of his consciousness, and though in all experience unities are involved which cannot originate within or be explained by experience, it is no less true that man is himself subject to the conditions of space and time, and that the synthetic unities which point beyond experience do not carry us to a purely individual subject. If man is not a part or product of nature, neither is nature the product of man. Kant's transcendentalism, in its maturest form, is genuinely phenomenalist in character. That is the view which has already been developed above, in the discussion of Kant's transcendental deduction. I shall strive to confirm it by comparison of the teaching of the two editions of the *Critique* in regard to the reality of outer appearances.

Schopenhauer, to whom this new development of the Critical teaching was altogether anathema, the cloven hoof of the Hegelian heresies, denounced it as a temporary and ill-judged distortion of the true Critical position, maintaining that it is incapable of combination with Kant's central teaching, and that it finds no support in the tenets, pure and unperverted, of the first edition. Kant, he holds, is here untrue to himself, and temporarily, under the stress of polemical discussion, lapses from the heights to which he had successfully made his way, and upon which he had securely established, in agreement with Plato and in extension of Berkeley, the doctrine of all genuine philosophical thinking, the doctrine of the *Welt als Vorstellung*.

We may agree with Schopenhauer in regarding those sections of the first edition of the *Critique* which were omitted in the second edition as being a permanently valuable expression of Kantian thought, and as containing much that finds no equally adequate expression in the passages which were substituted for them ; and yet may challenge his interpretation of both editions alike. If, as we have already been arguing, we must regard Kant's thinking as in large degree tentative, that is, as progressing by the experimental following out of divergent tendencies, we may justly maintain that among the most characteristic features of his teaching are the readiness with which he makes changes to meet deeper insight, and the persistency with which he strives to attain a position in which there will be least sacrifice or blurring of any helpful distinction, and fullest acknowledgment of the manifold and diverse considerations that are really essential. Recognising these features, we shall be prepared to question the legitimacy of Schopenhauer's opposition between the teaching of the two editions. We shall rather expect to find that the two editions agree in the alternating statement and retraction of conflicting positions, and that the later edition, however defective in this or that aspect as compared with the first edition, none the less expresses the maturer insight, and represents a further stage in the development of ideas that have been present from the start. It may perhaps for this very reason be more contradictory in its teaching ; it will at least yield clearer and more adequate formulation of the diverse consequences and conflicting implications of the earlier tenets. It will be richer in content, more open-eyed in its adoption of mutually contradictory positions, freer therefore from unconscious assumptions, and better fitted to supply the data necessary for judgment upon its own defects. Only those critics who are blind to the stupendous difficulties of the tasks which Kant here sets himself, and credulous of their speedy and final completion, can complain of the result.

Philosophical thinkers of the most diverse schools in Germany, France, and England, have throughout the nineteenth century received from the *Critique* much of their inspiration. The profound influence which Kant has thus exercised upon succeeding thought must surely be reckoned a greater achievement than any that could have resulted from the constructing of a system so consistent and unified, that the alternative would lie only between its acceptance and its rejection. Ultimately the value of a philosophy consists more in the richness of its content and the comprehensiveness of its dialectic, than in the logical perfection of its formal structure. The latter quality is especially unfitted to a philosophy which inaugurated a new era, and formulated the older problems in an altogether novel manner. Under such conditions fertility of suggestion and readiness to modify or even recast adopted positions, openness to fuller insight acquired through the very solutions that may at first have seemed to satisfy and close the issues, are more to be valued than the power to remove contradictions and attain consistency. This is the point of view which I shall endeavour to justify in reference to the matters now before us. In particular there are two points to be settled : first, whether and how far the argument of the second edition is prefigured in the first edition ; and secondly, whether and to what extent it harmonises with, and gives expression to, all that is most central and genuinely Critical in both editions.

In the first place we must observe that the fourth *Paralogism* occurs in a section which bears all the signs of having been independently written and incorporated later into the main text. It is certainly of earlier origin than those sections which represent the third and fourth layers of the deduction of the first edition, and very possibly was composed in the middle 'seventies. Indeed, apart from single paragraphs which may have been added in the process of adapting it to the main text, it could quite well, so far as its refutation of idealism is concerned, be of even earlier date. The question as to the consistency of the refutation of the second edition with the teaching of the first edition must therefore chiefly concern those parts of the *Analytic* which connect with the later forms of the transcendental deduction, that is to say, with the transcendental deduction itself, with the *Analogies* and *Postulates*, and with particular paragraphs that have been added in other sections. We have already noted how Kant from the very first uses terms which involve the drawing of a distinction between representations and their objects. Passages in which this distinction occurs can be cited from both the *Aesthetic* and the *Analytic*, and two such· occur in the fourth *Paralogism* itself.[1] Objects, he says, "correspond" to their representations. A variation in expression is found in such passages as the following :

". . . the objects of outer perception also actually exist (*auch wirklich sind*) in that very form in which they are intuited in space. . . ."[2]

Such language is meaningless, and could never have been chosen, if Kant had not, even in the earlier stages of his thinking, postulated a difference between the existence of an object and the existence of its representation. He must at least have distinguished between the representations and their content. That, however, he could have done without advancing to the further assertion of their independent existence. Probably he was not at all clear in his own mind, and was too preoccupied with the other complexities of his problem, to have thought out his position to a definite decision. When, however, as in the fourth *Paralogism*, he made any attempt so to do, he would seem to have felt constrained to adopt the extreme subjectivist position. Expressions to that effect are certainly very much more common than those above mentioned. This is what affords Schopenhauer such justification, certainly very strong, as he can cite for regarding subjectivism as the undoubted teaching of the first edition.

When, however, we also take account of the very different teaching which is contained in the important section on the *Postulates of Empirical Thought*, the balance of evidence is decisively altered. The counter-teaching, which is suggested by certain of the conflicting factors of the transcendental deduction and of the *Analogies*, here again receives clear and detailed expression. This is the more significant, as it is in this section that Kant sets himself formally to define what is to be understood by empirical reality. It thus contains his, so to speak, official declaration as to the mode of existence possessed by outer appearances. The passage chiefly relevant is as follows :

"If the existence of the thing is bound up with some perceptions according to the principles of their empirical connection (the Analogies), we can determine its existence antecedently to the perception of it, and consequently, to that extent, in an *a priori* manner. For as the existence of the thing is bound up with our perceptions in a possible experience, we are able in the series of possible perceptions, and under the guidance of the Analogies, to make the transition from our actual perception to the thing in

---

[1] Cf. above, pp. 303-4.   [2] A 491 = B 520.

question. Thus we discover the existence of a magnetic matter pervading all bodies from the perception of the attracted iron filings, although the constitution of our organs cuts us off from all immediate perception of that matter. For in accordance with the laws of sensibility and the connection of our perceptions in a single experience, we should, were our senses more refined, actually experience it in an immediate empirical intuition. The grossness of our senses does not in any way decide the form of possible experience in general." [1]

Now it cannot, of course, be argued that the above passage is altogether unambiguous. We can, if we feel sufficiently constrained thereto, place upon it an interpretation which would harmonise it with Kant's more usual subjectivist teaching, namely as meaning that in the progressive construction of experience, or in the ideal completion which follows upon assumption of more refined sense-organs, possible empirical realities are made to become, or are assumed to become, real, but that until the possible experiences are thus realised in fact or in ideal hypothesis, they exist outwardly only in the form of their noumenal conditions. And as a matter of fact, this is how Kant himself interprets the teaching of this section in the process of applying it in solution of the antinomies.

"Accordingly, if I represent to myself the aggregate of all objects of the senses existing in all time and all places, I do not set them, antecedently to experience, in space and time. The representation is nothing but the thought of a possible experience in its absolute completeness. Since the objects are mere representations, only in such a possible experience are they given. To say that they exist prior to all my experience, can only be taken as meaning that they will be met with, if, starting from actual perception, I advance to that part of experience to which they belong. The cause of the empirical conditions of this advance (that which determines what members I shall meet with, or how far I can meet with any such in my regress) is transcendental, and is therefore necessarily unknown to me. We are not, however, concerned with this transcendental cause, but only with the rule of progression in that experience in which objects, that is to say, appearances, are given. Moreover, in outcome it is a matter of indifference whether I say that in the empirical progress in space I can meet with stars a hundred times farther removed than the outermost now perceptible to me, or whether I say that they are perhaps to be met with in cosmical space even though no human being has ever perceived or ever will perceive them. For though they might be given as things in themselves, without relation to possible experience, they are still nothing to me, and therefore are not objects, save in so far as they are contained in the series of the empirical regress." [2]

---

[1] A 225-6 = B 273.   Cf. below, Appendix C.   [2] A 495-6 = B 523-4.

But though this is a possible interpretation of the teaching of the *Postulates*, and though further it is Kant's own interpretation in another portion of the *Critique*, it is not by any means thereby decided that this is what the section itself actually teaches. Unbiassed study of the section, in independence of the use to which it is elsewhere put, can find within it no such limitation to its assertion of the actual independent existence of non-perceived bodies. We have to remember that the doctrine and solution of the *Antinomies* was completed prior to the writing of the central portions of the *Critique*. The section treating of their *solution* seems, indeed, in certain parts to be later [1] than the other main portions of the chapter on the *Antinomies*, and must have been at least recast after completion of the *Postulates*. But the subjectivist solution is so much simpler in statement, so much more fully worked out, and indeed so much more capable of definite formulation, and also so much more at one with the teaching developed in the preceding chapter on the *Paralogisms*, that even granting the doctrine expounded in the section on the *Postulates* to be genuinely phenomenalist, it is not surprising that Kant should have been unwilling to recast his older and simpler solution of the *Antinomies*. In any case we are not concerned to argue that Kant, even after formulating the phenomenalist view, yields to it an unwavering adherence. As I have already insisted, his attitude continues to the very last to be one of alternation between two opposed standpoints.

But the most significant feature of Kant's treatment of the argument of the *Postulates* still remains for consideration. It was in immediate succession to the paragraph above quoted [2] that Kant, in the second edition, placed his "*Refutation of Idealism*" with the emphatic statement that this (not as in the first edition in connection with the *Paralogisms*) was its "correct location." It is required, he says, as a reply to an objection which the teaching of the *Postulates* must at once suggest. The argument of the second edition in proof of the independent reality of material bodies, and in disproof of subjectivism, is thus given by Kant as a necessary extension and natural supplement of the teaching of the first edition.

There is therefore reason for concluding that the same preconception which has led to such radical misinterpretation of Kant's *Refutation of Idealism* has been at work in inducing a false reading of Kant's argument in the *Postulates*, namely the belief that Kant's teaching proceeds on consistent lines, and that it must at all costs be harmonised with itself.

[1] Cf. below, p. 506.   [2] Viz. A 225·6 = B 273.

Finding subjectivism to be emphatically and unambiguously inculcated in all the main sections of the *Critique*, and the phenomenalist views, on the other hand, to be stated in a much less definite and somewhat elusive manner, commentators have impoverished the Critical teaching by suppression of many of its most subtile and progressive doctrines. Kant's experimental, tentative development of divergent tendencies is surely preferable to this artificial product of high-handed and unsympathetic emendation.

INNER SENSE AND APPERCEPTION

We are now in position to complete our treatment of inner sense. When the inner world of feelings, volitions, and representations is placed on the same empirical level as the outer world of objects in space, when the two are correlated and yet also at the same time sharply distinguished, when, further, it is maintained that objects in space exist independently of their representations, and that in this independence they are necessary for the possibility of the latter, the whole aspect of the Critical teaching undergoes a genial and welcome transformation. Instead of the forbidding doctrine that the world in space is merely my representation, we have the very different teaching that only through consciousness of an independent world in space is consciousness of the inner subjective life possible at all, and that, as each is "external" to the other, neither can be reduced to, or be absorbed within, the other. The inner representations do not produce or generate the spatial objects, do not even condition their existence, but are required only for the individual's empirical consciousness of them. Indeed the relations previously holding between them are now reversed. It is the outer world which renders the subjective representations possible. The former is prior to the latter; the latter exist in order to reveal the former. The outer world in space must, indeed, be regarded as conditioned by, and relative to, the noumenal conditions of its possibility; but these, on Kant's doctrine of outer and inner sense, are distinct from all experienced contents and from all experienced mental processes. This will at once be recognised as holding of the noumenal conditions of the given manifold. But it is equally true, Kant maintains, in regard to the noumenal conditions of our mental life. We have no immediate knowledge of the transcendental syntheses that condition all consciousness, and in our complete ignorance of their specific nature they cannot legitimately be equated with any individual or personal agent. As the empirical self is only what it is known as, namely, appearance, it cannot be the bearer of appearance. This function falls to that which underlies both inner and outer appearances equally, and which within experience gains twofold expression for itself, in the conception of the thing in itself $= x$ on the one hand, and in the correlative conception of a transcendental subject, likewise $= x$, on the other.

But with mention of the transcendental subject we are brought to a problem which in the second edition invariably accompanies Kant's discussion of inner sense. The 'I think' of apperception can find expression only in an empirical judgment, and yet, so far from being the outcome of inner sense, preconditions its possibility. What then is its relation to inner sense? Does not its recognition conflict with Kant's denial of the possibility of self-conscious reflection, of direct intuitive apprehension by the self of itself? The pure apperception, 'I think,' is equivalent, Kant declares, to the judgment 'I am,' and therefore involves the assertion of the subject's existence.[1] Does not this conflict on the one hand with the Critical doctrine that knowledge of existence is only possible in terms of sense, and on the other with the Critical limitation of the categories to the realm of appearance? How are such assertions as that the 'I think' of pure apperception refers to a non-empirical reality, and that it predicates its existence, to be reconciled with the doctrine of inner sense as above stated?

As we have already observed,[2] Kant's early doctrine of the transcendental object was developed in a more or less close parallelism with that of the transcendental unity of apperception. They were regarded as correlative opposites, the dual centres of noumenal reference for our merely subjective representations. Kant's further examination of the nature of apperception, as embodied in alterations in the second edition, was certainly, as we shall find, inspired by the criticisms which the first edition had called forth. His replies, however, are merely more explicit statements of the distinction which he had already developed in the first edition between the transcendental and the empirical self, and that distinction in turn was doubtless itself largely determined by his own independent recognition of the untenability of his early view of the transcendental object. Though it is much more difficult to differentiate between the empirical and the transcendental self than to distinguish between the empirical object and the thing in itself, both distinctions are from a

[1] B 277.   [2] Above, p. 208 ff.

genuinely Critical standpoint equally imperative, and rest upon considerations that are somewhat similar in the two cases.

One of the chief and most telling criticisms directed against the teaching of the first edition was that Kant's doctrine of a transcendental consciousness of the self's existence, *i.e.* of the existence of a noumenal being, "this I or he or it (the thing) which thinks,"[1] is inconsistent with the teaching of the *Postulates of Empirical Thought*. In that section, as also later in the section on the theological *Ideal*, Kant had declared most emphatically that existence is never discoverable in the content of any mere concept. It is revealed in perception, and in perception alone, in virtue of the element of sensation contained in the latter.

"... to know the *actuality* of things demands *perception*, and therefore sensation. ... For that the concept precedes perception, signifies the concept's mere possibility; the perception which supplies the content [*Stoff*] to the concept, is the sole characteristic [*Charakter*] of actuality."[2]

Yet Kant had also maintained that the 'I think' is equivalent to 'I am,'[3] and that in this form, as an intellectual consciousness of the self's existence, it precedes all experience. The teaching of the *Postulates* is, however, the teaching of the *Critique* as a whole, and such critics as Pistorius seemed therefore to be justified in maintaining that Kant, in reducing the experiences of inner sense to mere appearance, destroys the possibility of establishing reality in any form. Appearance, in order to be appearance, presupposes the reality not only of that which appears, but also of the mental process whereby it is apprehended. But if reality is given only in sensation, and yet all experience that involves sensation is merely appearance, there is no self by which appearance can be conditioned; and only illusion (*Schein*), not appearance (*Erscheinung*), is left. To quote Pistorius' exact words:

"[If our inner representations give not things in themselves but only their appearances] there will be nothing but illusion (*Schein*), for nothing remains to which anything can appear."[4]

Kant evidently felt the force of this criticism, for in the second edition he replies to it on no less than seven different occasions.[5] In three of these passages[6] the term *Schein* is

---

[1] A 346 = B 404.   [2] A 224-5 = B 272-3.   [3] Cf. B 277.
[4] Quoted by B. Erdmann: *Kriticismus*, p. 107.
[5] B xxxix *n.*, 67-8, 70, 157-8 with appended note, 276-8, 422 *n.*, 427-9.
[6] B 70, 157, 428.

employed, and in the note to B xxxix the term *Erdichtung* appears. This shows very conclusively that what Kant has in mind is such criticism as the above. The most explicit passage is B 428 :

"The proposition, 'I think,' or 'I exist thinking,' is an empirical proposition. Such a judgment, however, is conditioned by empirical intuition, and the object that is thought therefore underlies it as appearance. It would consequently seem that on our theory the soul is completely transformed, even in thinking [*selbst im Denken*], into appearance, and that in this way our consciousness itself, as being a mere illusion [*Schein*], must refer in fact to nothing."

Kant, in his reply, is unyielding in the contention that the 'I think,' even though it involves an empirical judgment, is itself intellectual. "This representation is a thinking, not an intuiting,"[1] or as he adds, "The 'I think' expresses the *actus* whereby I determine my existence." Existence is therefore already given thereby.[2] Kant also still maintains that the self thus revealed is not "appearance and still less illusion."

"I am conscious of myself . . ., not as I appear to myself, nor as I am in myself, but only that I am."[3] "I thereby represent myself to myself neither as I am nor as I appear to myself. I think myself only as I do any object in general from whose mode of intuition I abstract."[4]

Kant's method of meeting the criticism, while still holding to these positions, is twofold. It consists in the first place in maintaining that the 'I think,' though intellectual, can find expression only in empirical judgments—in other words, that it is in and by itself formal only, and presupposes as the occasion of its employment a given manifold of inner sense ; and secondly, by the statement that the 'existence' which is involved in the 'I think' is not the category of existence. Let us take in order each of these two points.

Kant's first method of reply itself appears in two forms, a stronger and a milder. The milder mode of statement[5] is to the effect that though the representation 'I am' already immediately involves the *thought* of the existence of the subject, it yields no knowledge of it. Knowledge would involve intuition, namely, consciousness of inner determinations in time, which in turn would itself presuppose consciousness of outer objects. As a merely intellectual representation,

---

[1] B 157.
[2] B 157 *n.* Regarding the un-Critical character of Kant's language in this passage, and of the tendencies which inspire it, cf. below, p. 329.
[3] B 157.   [4] B 429.
[5] Cf. B 277-8 and B 157.

"... this 'I' has not the least predicate of intuition which, in its character of permanence, could, somewhat after the manner of impenetrability in the empirical intuition of matter, serve as correlate of time determination in inner sense."[1]

The stronger and more definite mode of statement is that the 'I think' is an empirical proposition.[2] Though it involves as one factor the intellectual representation, 'I think,' it is none the less empirical.

"Without some empirical representation supplying the material for thought, the *actus*, 'I think,' would not take place. . . ."[3]

The empirical is indeed "only the condition of the application or employment of the pure intellectual faculty," but as such is indispensable. This is repeated in even clearer terms in B 429.

"The proposition, 'I think,' in so far as it amounts to the assertion, 'I exist thinking,' is no mere logical function but determines the subject (which is then at the same time object) in respect of existence, and cannot take place without inner sense. . . ."

This admission is the more significant in that it follows immediately upon a passage in which Kant has been arguing that thinking, taken in and by itself, is a merely logical function.

The real crux lies in the question as to the legitimacy of Kant's application of the predicate existence to the transcendental subject. Its employment in reference to the empirical self in time is part of the problem of the *Refutation of Idealism* in the second edition; and the answer there given is clear and definite. Consciousness of the empirical self as existing in time involves consciousness of outer objects in space. But as Kant recognises that a transcendental ego, not in time, is presupposed in all consciousness of the empirical self, the question whether the predicate of existence is also applicable to the transcendental self cannot be altogether avoided, and is indeed referred to in B 277. The attitude to be taken to this latter question is not, however, defined in that section.

In the first edition Kant has insisted that the categories as pure forms of the understanding, in isolation from space and time, are merely logical functions "without content." Interpreted literally, this would signify that they are devoid of meaning, and therefore are incapable of yielding the thought of any independent object or existence. As merely logical forms of relation, they presuppose a material, and that

---

[1] B 278.   [2] B 420 and B 422 *n*.   [3] B 422 *n*.

is supplied only through outer and inner sense. Such is not, however, the way in which Kant interprets his own statement. It is qualified so as to signify only that they are without *specific* or *determinate* content. They are taken as yielding the conception of object in general. Passages in plenty can be cited from the first edition[1]—passages allowed to remain in the second edition—in which Kant teaches that the pure forms of understanding, as distinct from the schematised categories, yield the conception of things in themselves. This view is, indeed, a survival from his earlier doctrine of the transcendental object.[2] In all passages added in the second edition the consequences of his argument are more rigorously drawn, and the doctrine of the transcendental object is entirely eliminated. It is now unambiguously asserted that the pure forms of understanding, the "*modes* of self-consciousness in thinking,"[3] are not intellectual concepts of *objects*. They "yield no object whatsoever." The only object is that given through sense. And since in thinking the transcendental subject we do, by Kant's own account, think an "object," he is led to the conclusion, also explicitly avowed, that the notion of existence involved in the ' I think ' is not the category of the same name.[4] So also of the categories of substance and causality.

"If I represent myself as *subject* of thoughts or as *ground* of thinking, these modes of representation do not signify the categories of substance or of cause. . . ."[5]

The notion of the self, like the notion of things in themselves, is a concept distinct from all the categories.[6]

This conclusion is reinforced by means of an argument which is employed in the section of the first edition on *Paralogisms*. Apperception is the ground of the possibility of the categories, and these latter on their side represent only the synthetic unity which that apperception demands. Self-consciousness is therefore the representation of that which is

---

[1] Cf. above, pp. 204 ff. ; below, 404 ff.   [2] Cf. above, p. 204 ff.   [3] B 407.
[4] B 422 *n.*   Though both concepts are denoted by the same term, they may not—such is the implication—be for that reason identified.
[5] B 429.   Kant does not, however, even in the second edition, hold consistently to this position. In the sentence immediately preceding that just quoted he equates the transcendental self with the notion of "object in general." " I represent myself to myself neither as I am nor as I appear to myself, but think myself only as I do any object in general from whose mode of intuition I abstract."
[6] The broader bearing of this view may be noted.   If consistently developed, it must involve the assertion that noumenal reality is apprehended in terms of the Ideas of reason, for these are the only other concepts at the disposal of the mind. Cf. above, pp. liii-v, 217-18; below, pp. 331, 390-1, 414-17, 426 ff:, 558-61.

the condition of all unity, and which yet is itself unconditioned.

" . . . it does not represent itself through the categories, but
knows the categories and through them all objects in the absolute
unity of apperception, and so through itself. Now it is, indeed, very
evident that I cannot know as an object that which I must presuppose in order to know any object. . . ."[1]

This argument recurs in B 422.

"The subject of the categories cannot by thinking the categories
acquire a conception of itself as an object of the categories. For,
in order to think them, its pure self-consciousness, which is what
was to be accounted for, must itself be presupposed."

It is extremely difficult to estimate the value and cogency
of this argument.[2] Many objections or rather qualifications
must be made before it can be either accepted or rejected. If
it be taken only as asserting that the unity of self-consciousness is not *adequately* expressible through any of the categories,
it is undoubtedly valid. If, further, the categories be identified
with the schemata, it is also true that they are not applicable
in any degree or manner. The schemata are applicable only
to natural existences in space and time. Self-consciousness
can never be reduced to a natural existence of that type.
On the other hand, if it is not self-consciousness as such, but
the self-conscious *subject*, which on Kant's view is always
noumenal—"this I or he or it (the thing) which thinks"[3]—
that is referred to, and if we distinguish between the categories
strictly so called, that is, the pure forms of understanding,
and the schemata, it is not at all evident that the self-conscious
subject may not be described as being an existence that is
always a subject and never a predicate, and as being related
to experience as a ground or condition. These indefinite
assertions leave open alternative possibilities. They do not
even decide whether the self is "I or he or it."[4] In so far
as they advance beyond the mere assertion that the self rests
upon noumenal conditions they are, indeed, incapable of proof,
but by no Critical principle can they be shown to be inapplicable. When, therefore, Kant may seem to extract a more
definite conclusion from the above argument,[5] he advances
beyond what it can be made to support.

---

[1] A 402.
[2] It is doubtful whether A 401-2 represents a genuinely Critical position.
Several of its phrases seem reminiscent of Kant's semi-Critical view of the nature
of apperception. This is especially true of the assertion that self-consciousness is
"itself unconditioned."

A 346 = B 404. Cf. below, pp. 456, 461-2.   [4] Cf. A 346.

[5] That he does not really do so is clear from the context and also from the
manner in which he restated this argument in the second edition (B 421-2).

Kant is here influenced by the results of the ethical enquiries with which in the period subsequent to 1781 he was chiefly preoccupied.   He believed himself to have proved that the self, as a self-conscious being, is a genuinely noumenal existence.   That being so, he was bound to hold that the categories, even as pure logical forms, are inadequate to express its real determinate nature.   But he confounds this position with the assertion that they are not only inadequate, but in and by themselves are likewise inapplicable.   That is not a legitimate conclusion, for even if the self is more than mere subject or mere ground, it will at least be so much. When ethical considerations are left out of account, the only proper conclusion is that the applicability of the categories to the self-conscious subject is capable neither of proof nor of disproof, but that when the distinction between appearance and reality (which as we shall find is ultimately based upon the Ideas of Reason) has been drawn, the categories can be employed to define the possible difference between self-conscious experience and its unknown noumenal conditions. Any other conclusion conflicts with the teaching of the section on the *Paralogisms*.

It is important to observe—a point ignored by such critics as Caird and Watson—that in the sections under considera-tion[1] Kant most explicitly declares self-consciousness to be merely "the *representation* of that which is the condition of all unity."   He maintains that this representation, as stand-ing for "the determining self (the thinking), is to be dis-tinguished from the self which we are seeking to determine (the subject which thinks) as knowledge from its object,"[2] or in other words, that, without special proof, unattainable on theoretical grounds, "the unity of thought" may not be taken as equivalent to the unity of the thinking subject.[3]   They may be as diverse as unity of representation and unity of object represented are frequently found to be.   We may never argue from simplicity in a representation to simplicity in its object.

But to return to the main thesis, it may be observed that these arguments, with the exception of that which we have just been considering from the nature of self-consciousness, lead to the conclusion that the categories are as little applicable to the thing in itself as to the transcendental subject.   Even the argument from the necessary and invariable presence of self-consciousness in each and every act of judgment is itself valid only from a point of view which regards self-conscious-ness in the manner of Kant's early semi-Critical view of the

[1] A 401-2; cf. below, pp. 461-2.
[2] A 402; cf. B 407   [3] Cf. B 421-2.

transcendental subject[1] as an ultimate.   But if, as is maintained in the section in which this argument occurs, viz. that
on the *Paralogisms*, self-consciousness may be complexly conditioned, and may indeed have conditions similar in nature
to those which underlie outer experience, the categories may
be just as applicable, or as inapplicable, to its noumenal
nature as to the nature of the thing in itself.   It is noticeable
that in the second edition, doubtless under the influence of
preoccupation with ethical problems, some of Kant's utterances betray a tendency to relax the rigour of his thinking,
and to bring his theoretical teaching into closer agreement
with his ethical results than the theoretical analysis in and by
itself at all justifies.   This tendency was, of course, reinforced
by the persisting influence of that view of the transcendental
subject which he had held in the middle 'seventies, and from
which he never completely emancipated either his language
or his thinking.[2]   Indeed in several of the passages added in
the second edition[3] Kant even goes so far as to adopt language
which if taken quite literally would mean that the ' I think' is
an immediate consciousness of the mind's purely intellectual
activity—a view which, as we have seen,[4] is altogether alien
to the Critical position.   It would, as he argues so forcibly
elsewhere, involve a kind of experience which does not conform to Critical requirements, and which would lie open to
the attacks of sceptics such as Hume.

In B 157-8 the difficulties of Kant's position are again
manifest.   Speaking of the representation of the self, he
declares that " I am conscious of myself . . ., not as I appear
to myself, nor as I am in myself, but only that I am."   This
may seem to imply that existence is predicable of the transcendental self.   He adds that though the determination, *i.e.*
specification in empirical form, of my existence (*mein eigenes
Dasein*) is possible only in inner sensuous intuition, it is " not
appearance and still less mere illusion."   But in the appended
note it is urged that my existence (*Dasein*) as self-active
being is represented in purely indeterminate fashion.   Only
my existence *as sensuous*, and therefore as appearance, can
be known, *i.e.* can be made determinate.

The problem is more directly and candidly faced in the
note to B 422.   That note is interesting for quite a number
of reasons.   It reveals Kant in the very act of recasting
his position, and in the process of searching around for a
mode of formulation which will enable him to hold to
a transcendental consciousness of the self's existence and

---

[1] Cf. above, pp. l-lii, 208-9, 260-3.   [2] Cf. above, *loc. cit.* ; below, Appendix C.
[3] Cf. B 157-8 and 157 *n.*, B 278, B 428-9.   [4] Above, pp. 295-6, 311 *n.* 4.

at the same time not to violate the definition of existence given in the *Postulates*, *i.e.* both to posit the transcendental self as actual and yet to deny the applicability to it of any of the categories. After stating that the 'I think' is an empirical proposition in which my existence is immediately involved, he proceeds further to describe it as expressing "an undetermined empirical intuition, *i.e.* perception," and so as showing that sensation underlies its assertion of existence. Kant does not, however, mean by these words that the existence asserted is merely that of the empirical self; for he proceeds:

"... existence is here not a category, which as such does not apply to an indeterminately-given object. ... An indeterminate perception here signifies only something real that is given, given indeed to thought in general, and so not as appearance, nor as thing in itself (*Noumenon*), but as something which actually [*in der That*] exists, and which in the proposition, I think, is denoted [*bezeichnet*] as such."

The phrases here employed are open to criticism on every side. Kant completely departs from his usual terminology when he asserts that through an "indeterminate perception" the self is given, and "given to thought in general" as "something real." The contention, that the existence asserted is not a category, is also difficult to accept.[1] It is equally sur-

---

[1] There is this difference between the category of existence and the categories of relation, namely, that it would seem to be impossible to distinguish between a determinate and an indeterminate application of it. Either we assert existence or we do not; there is no such third alternative as in the case of the categories of substance and causality. The category of substance, determinately used, signifies material existence in space and time; indeterminately applied it is the purely problematic and merely logical notion of something that is always a subject and never a predicate. The determinate category of causality is the conception of events conditioning one another in time; indeterminately employed it signifies only the quite indefinite notion of a ground or condition. Also, Kant's explicit teaching (A 597 ff. = B 625 ff.) is that the notion of existence stands in an altogether different position from other predicates. It is not an attribute constitutive of the concept of the subject to which it is applied, but is simply the positing of the content of that concept as a whole. Nor, again, is it a relational form for the articulation of content. These would seem to be the reasons why no distinction is possible between a determinate and an indeterminate application of the notion of existence, and why, therefore, Kant, in defending the possible dual employment of it, has difficulty in holding consistently to the doctrines expounded in the *Postulates*. He is, by his own explicit teaching, interdicted from declaring that the notion of existence is both a category and not a category, or, in other words, that it may vary in meaning according as empirical or noumenal reality is referred to, and that only in the former case is it definite and precise. Yet such a view would, perhaps, better harmonise with certain other lines of thought which first obtain statement in the *Dialectic*. For though it is in the *Dialectic* that Kant expounds his grounds for holding that existence and content are separate and independent, it is there also that he first begins to realise the part which the Ideas of Reason are called upon to play in the drawing of the distinction between appearance and reality.

prising to read that its reality is given " neither as appearance nor as thing [*Sache*] in itself (*Noumenon*)"; for hitherto no such alternative form of real existence has been recognised.

But to press such criticisms is to ignore the spirit for the sake of the letter. Kant here breaks free from all his habitual modes of expression for the very good and sufficient reason that he is striving to develop a position more catholic and comprehensive than any previously adopted. He is seeking to formulate a position which, without in any way justifying or encouraging the transcendent employment of the categories, will yet retain for thought the capacity of self-limitation, that is, of forming concepts which will reveal the existence of things in themselves and so will enable the mind to apprehend the radical distinction between things in themselves and things experienced. But he has not yet discovered that in so doing he is committing himself to the thesis that the distinction is mediated, not by the understanding, but by Reason, not by categories, but by Ideas.[1] As I have already indicated, this tendency is crossed by another derived from his preoccupation with moral problems, namely, the desire to defend, in a manner which his Critical teaching does not justify, the noumenal existence of the self as a *thinking* being.

---

[1] In the *Fortschritte* (*Werke* (Hartenstein), viii. p. 548 ff.) this step is quite definitely taken. Cf. below, pp. 390-1, 414-17, 426 ff., 558-61. We have, as we shall find, to recognise a second fundamental conflict in Kant's thinking, additional to that between subjectivism and phenomenalism. He alternates between what may be entitled the sceptical and the Idealist views of the function of Reason and of its relation to the understanding, or otherwise stated, between the regulative and the absolutist view of the nature of thought. But this conflict first gains explicit expression in the *Dialectic*. Cf. below, Appendix C.

THE TRANSCENDENTAL ANALYTIC

Book II

THE ANALYTIC OF PRINCIPLES

The distinction which Kant here introduces for the first time between understanding (now viewed as the faculty only of concepts) and the faculty of judgment (*Urtheilskraft*) is artificial and extremely arbitrary.[1] As we have seen,[2] his own real position involves a complete departure from the traditional distinction between conceiving, judging, and reasoning, as separate processes. All thinking without exception finds expression in judgment. Judgment is the fundamental activity of the understanding. It is "an act which contains all its other acts." Kant is bent, however, upon forcing the contents of the *Critique* into the external framework supplied by the traditional logic, viewed as an architectonic; and we have therefore no option save to take account of his exposition in the actual form which he has chosen to give to it. Since general logic develops its teaching under three separate headings, as the logic of conception, the logic of judgment, and the logic of reasoning, the *Critique* has to be made to conform to this tripartite division. The preceding book is accordingly described as dealing with concepts, and this second book as dealing with judgments or principles; while understanding and the faculty of judgment, now viewed as independent, are redefined to meet the exigencies of this new arrangement, the former as being "the faculty of rules," and the latter as being "the faculty of subsuming under rules, *i.e.* of distinguishing whether something does or does not stand under a given rule (*casus datae legis*)."

The reader need not strive to discover any deep-lying ground or justification for these definitions.[3] Architectonic,

---

[1] For Kant's use of the terms 'canon' and 'dialectic' cf. above, pp. 72, 77-8, 173-4, and below, p. 425 ff.   [2] Above, pp. 181-2.

[3] As we shall have occasion to observe below (p. 336), when Kant defines judgment as "the faculty of subsumption under rules," he is really defining it in

that 'open sesame' for so many of the secrets of the *Critique*, is the all-sufficient spell to resolve the mystery. As a matter of fact, Kant is here taking advantage of the popular meaning of the term judgment in the sense in which we speak of a man of good judgment; and in order that judgment and understanding may be distinguished he then imposes an artificial limitation upon the meaning in which the latter term is to be employed.

As formal logic abstracts from all content, it cannot, Kant maintains, supply rules for the exercise of "judgment." It is otherwise with transcendental logic, which in the pure forms of sensibility possesses a content enabling it to define in an *a priori* manner the specific cases to which concepts must be applicable. The *Analytic of Principles* is thus able to supply "a canon for the faculty of judgment, instructing it how to apply to appearances the concepts of understanding which contain the condition of *a priori* rules."[1] This will involve (1) the defining of the sensuous conditions under which the *a priori* rules may be applied—the problem of the chapter on schematism; and (2) the formulating of the rules in their sensuous, though *a priori*, concreteness—the problem of the chapter on "the system of all principles of pure understanding."

Such is Kant's own very misleading account of the purposes of these two chapters. There are other and sounder reasons why they should be introduced. In the *Analytic of Concepts*, as we have seen,[2] the transcendental deduction only succeeds in proving that *a priori* forms of unity are required for the possibility of experience. No proof is given that the various categories are just the particular forms required, and that they are one and all indispensable. This omission can be made good only by a series of proofs, directed to showing, in reference to each separate category, its validity within experience and its indispensableness for the possibility of experience. These proofs are given in the second of the two chapters. The chapter on schematism is preparatory in character; it draws attention to the importance of the temporal aspect of human experience, and defines the categories in the form in which they present themselves in an experience thus conditioned by *a priori* intuition.

---

terms of the process of reasoning, and thus violating the principle which he is professedly following in dividing the *Transcendental Logic* into the *Analytic of Concepts*, the *Analytic of Judgment*, and the *Dialectic of Reasoning*.

[1] A 132=B 171.   [2] Pp. 252-3, 258-9, 287-8.

CHAPTER I

THE SCHEMATISM OF PURE CONCEPTS OF UNDERSTANDING [1]

The more artificial aspect of Kant's argument again appears in the reason which he assigns for the existence of a problem of schematism, namely, that pure concepts, and the sensuous intuitions which have to be subsumed under them, are completely opposite in nature. No such explanation can be accepted. For if category and sensuous intuition are really heterogeneous, no subsumption is possible; and if they are not really heterogeneous, no such problem as Kant here refers to will exist. The heterogeneity which Kant here asserts is merely that difference of nature which follows from the diversity of their functions. The category is formal and determines structure; intuition yields the content which is thereby organised. Accordingly, the "third thing," which Kant postulates as required to bring category and intuition together, is not properly so describable; it is simply the two co-operating in the manner required for the possibility of experience. Kant's method of stating the problem of schematism is, however, so completely misleading, that before we can profitably proceed, the various strands in his highly artificial argument must be further disentangled. This is an ungrateful task, but has at least the compensating interest of admirably illustrating the kind of influence which Kant's logical architectonic is constantly exercising upon his statement of Critical principles.

The architectonic has in this connection two very unfortunate consequences. It leads Kant to describe schematism as a process of *subsumption*, and to speak of the transcendental schema as "a *third thing*." Neither assertion is legitimate. Schematism, properly understood, is not a process of subsumption, but, as Kant has already recognised in A 124,

---

[1] The passages that have gone to constitute this chapter are probably quite late in date of writing. This would seem to be proved by the view taken of productive imagination, and also by the fact that in the *Reflexionen* there is no mention of schematism.

of synthetic interpretation. Creative synthesis, whereby contents are apprehended in terms of functional relations, not
subsumption of particulars under universals that are homogeneous with them, is what Kant must ultimately mean by
the schematism of the pure forms of understanding. A
category, that is to say, cannot be viewed as a *predicate*
of a possible judgment, and as being applied to a subject
independently apprehended; its function is to articulate
the judgment as a whole. The category of substance and
attribute, for instance, is the *form* of the categorical judgment,
and must not be equated with any one of its single parts.

Thus the criticisms which we have already passed upon
Kant's mode of formulating the distinction between formal and
transcendental logic,[1] are no less applicable to the sections now
before us. The terminology which Kant is here employing
is borrowed from the traditional logic, and is out of harmony
with his Critical principles.

Kant's description of the schema as a third thing, additional
to category and intuition, and intermediate between them, is
also a result of his misleading mode of formulating his
problem. What Kant professes to do is to interpret the
relation of the categories to the intuitional material as
analogous to that holding between a class concept and the
particulars which can be subsumed under it. This is implied
in his use of the plate and circle illustration.[2] But as the
relation holding between categories and the material of sense
is that of form and matter, structure and content, the analogy
is thoroughly misleading. As *all* content, strictly so called,
falls on the side of the intuitional material, there is no content, *i.e.* no quality or attribute, which is common to both.
And thus it happens that the *inappropriateness* of the analogy
which Kant is seeking to enforce is ultimately the sole ground
which he is able to offer in support of his description of the
schema as "a third thing."

"Now it is clear [!] that there must be a third thing, which is
homogeneous on the one hand with the category and on the other
with the appearance, and which thus makes the application of the
one to the other possible."[3]

On the contrary, the true Critical teaching is that category
and intuition, that is to say, form and content, mutually con-

---

[1] Cf. above, p. 176 ff.
[2] Cf. A 137 = B 176. "The empirical concept of a plate is homogeneous
with the pure geometrical concept of a circle, since the roundness which is thought
in the former can be intuited in the latter."
[3] A 138 = B 177.

dition one another, and that the so-called schema is simply a name for the latter as apprehended in terms of the former.

But there is a further complication. Kant, as we have already observed,[1] defines judgment as being

". . . the faculty of subsuming under *rules*, *i.e.* of distinguishing whether something does or does not stand under a given rule (*casus datae legis*)."

Now this view of judgment really connects with the syllogism, not with the proposition.[2] As Kant states in his *Logic*, there are

". . . three essential elements in all inference: (1) a universal rule which is entitled the major premiss; (2) the proposition which subsumes a cognition under the condition of the universal rule, and which is entitled the minor premiss; and lastly, (3) the conclusion, the proposition which asserts or denies of the subsumed cognition the predicate of the rule."[3]

Regarded in this way, as the application of a *rule*, subsumption is more broadly viewed and becomes a more appropriate analogy for the relation of category to content. And obviously it is this comparison that Kant has chiefly in mind in these introductory sections. For only when the subsumption is that of a particular instance under a universal *rule*, can the necessity of a *mediating* condition be allowed.

Such, then, are the straits to which Kant is reduced in the endeavour to hold loyally to his architectonic. He has to identify the two very different kinds of subsumption which find expression in the proposition and in the syllogism respectively; and when his analogy between logical subsumption, thus loosely interpreted, and synthetic interpretation, proves inapplicable, he uses the failure of the analogy as an argument to prove the necessity of "a third thing." On his own Critical teaching, as elsewhere expounded, no such third thing need be postulated. Even the definitions which he proceeds to give of the various schemata do not really support this description of them.

But though Kant's method of introducing and expounding the argument of this chapter is thus misleading, the contents themselves are of intrinsic value, and have a threefold bearing: (*a*) on the doctrine of productive imagination; (*b*) on the relation holding between image and concept; and

---

[1] Above, p. 334.
[2] Cf. E. Curtius, *Das Schematismuskapitel in der Kritik der reinen Vernunft* (*Kantstudien*, Bd. xix. p. 348 ff.). [3] *Op. cit.* § 58.

(c) on the nature of the categories in their distinction from the pure forms of understanding.

(a) Kant gives definite and precise expression to the two chief characteristics of the productive imagination, namely, that it deals with an *a priori* manifold of pure intuition[1] and that it exercises a "hidden art in the depths of the human soul."[2] Kant's description of the schema as "a third thing," *at once intellectual and sensuous*, seems to be in large part due to the transference to it of predicates already applied to the faculty which is supposed to be its source. The distinction between the transcendental schema and the particularised image is also given as analogous to that between the pure and the empirical faculties of imagination. In A 141-2 = B 180-1, Kant speaks of the *empirical* faculty of *productive* imagination, and so is led, to the great confusion of his exposition, though also to the enrichment of his teaching, to allow of empirical as well as of transcendental schemata, and thus contrary to his own real position to recognise schemata of such empirical objects as dog or horse—a view which empirical psychology has since adopted in its doctrine of the schematic image. This passage was doubtless written at the time when he was inclining to the view that the empirical processes run parallel with the transcendental.[3] Kant's final view is that empirical imagination is always reproductive. This brings us, however, to our second main point.

(b) Kant makes a statement which serves as a valuable corrective of his looser assertions in other parts of the *Critique*.[4] Five points set after one another, thus, ... , form an image of the number five. The schema of the number five is, however, of very different nature, and must not be identified with any such image. It is

". . . rather *the representation of a method* whereby a multiplicity [in this case five] may be represented in an image in accordance with a certain concept, than this image itself. . . ."[5]

This becomes more evident in the case of large numbers, such as a thousand. The thought or schema of the number remains just as clear and definite as in the case of smaller numbers, but cannot be so adequately embodied and surveyed in a concrete image.

"This representation of a general procedure of imagination in providing its image for a concept, I name the schema to this concept."[6]

---

[1] A 138 = B 177. Cf. above, pp. 96-7.
[3] Cf. above, pp. 268-9.
[5] A 140 = B 179.
[2] A 141 = B 180.
[4] Cf. above, pp. 133-4.
[6] *Loc. cit.*

But even in the simplest cases an image can never be completely adequate to the concept. The image of a triangle, for instance, is always some particular triangle, and therefore represents only a part of the total connotation. As the schema represents a universal rule of production in accordance with a concept, it resembles the concept in its incapacity to subsist in an objective form. Images become possible only through and in accordance with schemata, but can never themselves be identified with them. Schemata, therefore, and not images—such is the implied conclusion—form the true subject-matter of the mathematical sciences. Images are always particular; schemata are always universal. Images represent existences; schemata represent methods of construction.

There are three criticisms which must be passed upon this position. In the first place, the selection of the triangle as an illustration tends to obscure the main point of Kant's argument. As there are three very different species of triangle, the concept triangle is a class concept in a degree and manner which is not to be found in the concepts, say, of the circle or of the number five. So that while Kant may seem to be chiefly insisting upon the *inadequacy*[1] of the image to represent more than a part of the connotation of the corresponding concept, his real intention is to emphasise that the schema expresses the conceptual rule whereby, even in images that cover the whole connotation, the true meaning of the image can alone be determined.

Secondly, the above definition of the schema as being "the representation of a general procedure of imagination in providing an image for a concept" is obviously bound up with Kant's view of it as "a third thing," additional to the concept, and as intermediate between it and the image.[2] But as we have already found occasion to note, in discussing Kant's doctrine of the "construction" of mathematical concepts,[3] this threefold distinction is out of harmony with his Critical principles. It results from his retention of the traditional view of the concept as in all cases a mere concept, *i.e.* an abstracted or class concept. In defining the schema Kant is defining the true nature of the concept as against the false interpretation of it in the traditional class-theory; he misrepresents the logic of his own standpoint when he interpolates

---

[1] Cf. E. Curtius, *op. cit.* p. 356.

[2] Kant's other definition of the schema as "a rule for the determination of our intuition in accordance with a certain universal concept" (A 141 = B 180) is open to similar objections. When, however, Kant states that "schemata, and not images, *underlie* our pure sensuous concepts," he seems to be inclining to the truer view that the schema *is* the concept.   [3] Above, pp. 131-3.

a third kind of representation intermediate between the concept and the image. The concept 'triangle,' *as a concept*, is (to employ Kant's own not very satisfactory terms) the representation of the method of constructing a certain type of object; and the only other mode of representing this kind of object is the image. There may, indeed, as Kant has himself suggested, be a species of image that may be entitled schematic; but if that be identified with a blurred or indeterminate or merely symbolic form of representation, it can have nothing in common with the *transcendental* or *conceptual* schema, save the name.

Thirdly, the entire discussion of the nature of the schemata of "sensuous concepts" and of their relation to the sense image, is out of order in this chapter; and however valuable in itself, bewilders the reader who very properly assumes for it a relevancy which it does not possess. The pure concepts of the understanding, whose schemata Kant is endeavouring to define, are altogether different in nature from sensuous representations, and can never be reduced in any form or degree to an image. They are wholly transcendental, representing pure syntheses unified through categories in accordance with the form of inner sense. This, however, brings us to our last main point.

(c) Kant's manner of employing the term category is a typical example of his characteristic carelessness in the use of his technical terms. Sometimes it signifies the pure forms of understanding. But more frequently it stands for what he now, for the first time, entitles schemata, namely, the pure conceptual forms as modified through relation to time. To take as examples the two chief categories of relation. The first category of relation, viewed as a form of the pure understanding, is the merely logical conception of that which is always a subject and never a predicate. The corresponding schema is the conception of that which has permanent existence in time; it is not the logical notion of *subject*, but the transcendental conception of *substance*. The pure logical conception of ground and consequence is similarly distinguished from the transcendental schema of cause and effect.

This contrast is of supreme importance in the Critical philosophy, and ought therefore to have been marked by a careful distinction of terms. Had Kant restricted the term category to denote the pure forms, and invariably employed the term schemata to signify their more concrete counterparts, many ambiguities and confusions would have been prevented. The table of categories, in its distinction from the table of logical forms, would then have been named the table of schemata, and the definitions given in this chapter would have been appended to it, as the proper supplement to the metaphysical deduction, completing it by a careful definition of each separate schema. For what Kant usually means when he speaks of the categories *are* the schemata ; and the chapter before us therefore contains their delayed definitions.[1] As Kant has constantly been insisting, and as he again so emphatically teaches in this chapter, the pure forms of understanding, taken in and by themselves, apart from the forms of intuition, have no relation to any object, and are mere logical functions without content or determinate meaning.

From this point of view the misleading influence of Kant's architectonic may again be noted. It forces him to preface his argument by introductory remarks which run entirely counter to the very point which he is chiefly concerned to illustrate and enforce, namely, the inseparability of conception and intuition in all experience and knowledge. He does, indeed, draw attention to the fact that the conditions which serve to realise the pure concepts of understanding also at the same time restrict them, but it is with their empirical employment that he is here chiefly concerned.

Caird's[2] mode of expounding Kant's doctrine of schematism may serve as an example of the misleading influence of Kant's artificial method of introducing his argument. As Caird accepts Kant's initial statements at their face value, he is led to read the entire chapter in accordance with them, and so to interpret it as being a virtual recantation of the assumptions which underlie the statement of its problem. The truer view would rather seem to be that the introduction is demanded by the exigencies of Kant's architectonic, and therefore yields no true account either of the essential purpose of the chapter or of its actual contents. Cohen not unjustly remarks that

". . . recent writers are guilty of a very strange misreading of Kant when they maintain, as if in opposition to him, a thought to which his doctrine of schematism gives profound expression, namely, that intuition and conception do not function independently, and that thought, and still more knowledge, is and must always be intuitive."[3]

Cohen fails, however, to draw attention to the cause of the misunderstanding for which Kant must certainly share the blame. Riehl,[4] while adopting a somewhat similar view to

---

[1] Cf. Riehl, *Philos. Krit.* 2nd ed. i. pp. 488, 533. Cf. above, pp. 195-6, 198; below, pp. 404-5.

[2] *Critical Philosophy*, i. bk. i. chap. v., especially pp. 437 and 440.

[3] *Theorie der Erfahrung*, second edition, p. 384.   [4] *Op. cit.* p. 532.

that here given, traces Kant's misleading mode of stating the problem to his holding a false view of the universality of the concept. Such criticism of Kant, like that passed by Caird, is in many respects justified, but the occasion upon which the admonition is made to follow would none the less seem to be ill-chosen.

It may be asked why Kant in this chapter so completely ignores space. No really satisfactory answer seems to present itself. It is true that time is the one universal form of all intuition, of outer as well as of inner experience. It is also true that, as Kant elsewhere shows, consciousness of time presupposes consciousness of space for its own possibility, and so to that extent may be regarded as including the latter form of consciousness within itself. Nevertheless Kant's concentration on the temporal aspect of experience is exceedingly arbitrary, and results in certain unfortunate consequences. Owing to the manner in which Kant envisages his problem[1] he is bound, indeed, to lay the greater emphasis upon time, but that need not have involved so exclusive a recognition of its field and function. Possibly Kant's very natural preoccupation with his new and revolutionary doctrines of inner sense and productive imagination has something to do with the matter.

Though the definitions given of the various schemata, especially of those of reality and existence, raise many difficulties, consideration of them must be deferred.[2] They can be properly discussed only in connection with the principles which Kant bases upon them. Only one further point calls for present remark. Kant does not give a schema for each of the categories. In the first two groups of pure conceptual forms, those of quantity and of quality, he gives a schema only for the third category in each case. Number is strictly not the schema of quantity as such, but of *totality*. The schema of quality is a definition only of *limitation*.[3] This departure from the demands of strict architectonic is made without comment or explanation of any kind. Kant delights to insist upon the confirmation given to his teaching by the fulfilment of architectonic requirements; he is for the most part silent when they fail to correspond. This architectonic was a hobby sufficiently serious to yield him keen pleasure in its elaboration, but was not so vital to his main purposes as to call for stronger measures when shortcomings occurred.

---

[1] Cf. above, pp. 240-3.
[2] For comment upon the definition of number, which Kant takes as being the schema of quantity, and upon the view of arithmetic which this definition may seem to imply, cf. above, p. 128 ff.　　　　　[3] Cf. above, p. 192.

In concluding this chapter Kant draws attention to the fact that the sensuous conditions which serve to realise the pure concepts also at the same time restrict their meaning. Their wider meaning is, however, of merely logical character.[1] Their function, as pure concepts, lies solely in establishing unity of representation ; they do not therefore suffice to yield knowledge of any object. Objective application "comes to them solely from sensibility." In these statements Kant expounds one of his fundamental doctrines, but in a manner which does less than justice to the independent value of pure thought. As he elsewhere teaches,[2] it is not sense that sets limits to understanding ; it is the pure forms of thought that enable the mind to appreciate the limited and merely phenomenal character of the world experienced.

[1] Cf. above, pp. 339-40, and below, pp. 357, 404 ff.
[2] Cf. above, pp. 20, 25, 290-1 ; below, pp. 407, 412, 414-17.

CHAPTER II

SYSTEM OF ALL PRINCIPLES OF PURE UNDERSTANDING

The introductory remarks to this important chapter are again dictated by Kant's architectonic, and set its actual contents in an extremely false light. Kant would seem to imply that as the *Analytic of Concepts* has determined all the various conceptual elements constitutive of experience, and has proved that they serve as predicates of possible judgments, it now remains to show in an *Analytic of Principles* what *a priori* synthetic judgments, or in other words what principles, can actually be based upon them. Though this is a quite misleading account of the relation holding between the two books of the *Analytic*, it has been accepted by many commentators.[1] For several reasons it must be rejected. The pure forms of understanding are not predicates for possible judgments. They underlie judgment as a whole, expressing the relation through which its total contents are organised. Thus in the proposition "cinnabar is heavy" the category of substance and attribute is not in any sense the predicate; it articulates the entire judgment, interpreting the experienced contents in terms of the dual relation of substance and attribute. Judgment, its nature and conditions, is the real problem of the misnamed *Analytic of Concepts*. As already indicated,[2] the two main divisions of the *Analytic* deal with one and the same problem. But while doing so, they differ in two respects. In the first place, as above noted, the *Analytic of Concepts* supplies no proof of the validity of particular categories, but only a quite general demonstration that forms of unity, such as are involved in all judgment, are demanded for the possibility of apperception. The proofs of the indispensableness of *specific* categories are first given in the *Analytic of Principles*. Secondly, in the *Analytic of Concepts* the temporal aspect of experience falls somewhat into the background, whereas in the *Analytic of Principles* it is emphasised.

---

[1] *E.g.* Riehl, *Philos. Krit.* 2nd ed. i. pp. 535-6.   [2] Above, pp. 258, 332-3.

From these two fundamental points of difference there arises a third distinguishing feature. When the categories, or rather schemata, are explicitly defined, and receive individual proof, they are found to be just those principles that are demanded for the possibility of the positive sciences. This is, from Kant's point of view, no mere coincidence. Scientific knowledge is possible only in so far as experience is grounded on *a priori* conditions ; and the conditions of *sense*-experience are also the conditions of its conceptual interpretation. But while the *Analytic of Concepts* deals almost exclusively with ordinary experience, in the *Analytic of Principles* the physical sciences receive their due share of consideration.

First and Second Sections. The Highest Principles of Analytic and Synthetic Judgments.—These two sections contain nothing not already developed earlier in the *Critique*. Though the principle of non-contradiction is a merely negative test of truth, it can serve as a universal and completely adequate criterion in the case of all judgments that are analytic of given concepts. The principle of synthetic judgments, on the other hand, is the principle whereby we are enabled to advance beyond a given concept so as to attach a predicate which does not stand to it in the relation either of identity or of contradiction. This principle is the principle of the possibility of experience. Though *a priori* synthetic judgments cannot be *logically* demonstrated as following from higher and more universal propositions,[1] they are capable of a *transcendental* proof, that is, as being conditions of sense-experience.

"The possibility of experience is what gives objective reality to all our *a priori* knowledge."[2] "Although we know *a priori* in synthetic judgments a great deal regarding space in general and the figures which productive imagination describes in it, and can obtain such judgments without actually requiring any experience ; yet even this knowledge would be nothing but a playing with a mere figment of the brain, were it not that space has to be regarded as a condition of the appearances which constitute the material for outer experience. . . ."[3]

In the first part of the last sentence, as in the page which precedes it, Kant would seem to be inculcating his doctrine of a pure *a priori* manifold, but the latter part of the statement would not be affected by the admission that space is not an independent intuition but only the form of outer sense.

Third Section. Systematic Representation of all the Synthetic Principles of Understanding.—Kant is not concerned in this

---

[1] A 148=B 188.   [2] A 156=B 195.   [3] A 157=B 196.

section with the fundamental propositions of mathematical science, since, on his view, they rest upon the evidence of intuition. He claims, however, that their objective validity depends upon two principles, which, though not themselves mathematical in the strict sense, may conveniently be so described from the transcendental standpoint—the principle of the "axioms of intuition," and the principle of the "anticipations of experience." The physicist, who takes the legitimacy of applied mathematics for granted, has no occasion to formulate these principles. That he none the less presupposes them is shown, however, by his unquestioning assumption that nature conforms to the strict requirements of pure mathematics. And since the principles involve pure concepts, the one embodying the schema of number, and the other the schema of quality, they fall outside the scope of the *Transcendental Aesthetic*, and call for a deduction similar to that of the other categories.

As already indicated, Kant's procedure is extremely arbitrary, and is due to the perverting influence of his architectonic. Proof of the validity of applied mathematics has already been given in the *Aesthetic*[1] of the first edition—a proof which is further developed in the *Prolegomena*,[2] and recast in the second edition so as to constitute a separate "transcendental exposition."[3] As Kant teaches in these passages, the objective validity of applied mathematics rests upon proof that space and time are the *a priori* forms of outer and inner sense. The new deductions of the schemata of number and quality, which he now proceeds to formulate, are quite unnecessary, and also are by no means conclusive in the manner of their proof. This, however, is more than compensated by the extremely valuable proofs of the schematised categories of relation which he gives in the section on the *Analogies of Experience*. The section on the *Postulates of Empirical Experience*, which deals with the principles of modality, also contains matter of very real importance.

The principles with which this chapter has to deal can thus be arranged according to the fourfold division of the table of categories : (1) *Axioms of Intuition*, (2) *Anticipations of Perception*, (3) *Analogies of Experience*, (4) *Postulates of Empirical Thought*. And following the distinction already drawn in the *Analytic of Concepts*,[4] Kant distinguishes between the Axioms and Anticipations on the one hand, and the Analogies and Postulates on the other. The former determine the conditions of intuition in space and time, and

[1] A 24.   [2] § 13, *Anmerkung* i.   [3] B 40-1.   [4] B 110.

may therefore be called mathematical and constitutive. They express what is necessarily involved in every intuition as such. The latter are dynamical. They are principles according to which we must think the existence of an object as determined in its relation to others. While, therefore, the first set of principles can be intuitively verified, the second set have only an indirect relation to the objects experienced. Whereas a relation of causality can never be intuited as holding between two events, but only thought into them, spatial and temporal relations are direct objects of the mind. Similarly, the relation of substance and attribute cannot be intuited; it can only be thought into what is intuited. The mathematical principles thus acquire an immediate (though, be it remembered, merely *de facto*) evidence; the *a priori* certainty, equally complete, of the dynamical principles can be verified only through the circuitous channel of transcendental proof.

The composite constitution of these sections finds striking illustration in the duplicated account of this distinction which precedes and follows the table of principles. The two accounts can hardly have been written in immediate succession to one another. The earlier in location[1] is probably the later in date. It would seem to rest upon some such uncritical distinction as that drawn in the *Prolegomena* between judgments of perception and judgments of experience.[2] The second and briefer account[3] is not open to this objection.

In A 178-80 = B 220-3 Kant develops a further point of difference between the mathematical and the dynamical principles, or rather explains what he means by his all too brief and consequently ambiguous reference in the first of the above accounts to "existence" (*Dasein*). The mathematical principles are *constitutive*; the dynamical are *regulative*. That is to say, the mathematical principles lay down the conditions for the generation or construction of appearances. The dynamical only specify rules whereby we can define the relation in which existences contingently given are connected. As existence can never be constructed *a priori*, we are limited to the determination of the interrelations between existences all of which must be given. Thus the principle of causality enables us to predict *a priori* that for every event there must exist *some* antecedent cause; but only through empirical investigation can we determine which of the particular given antecedents may be so described. That is to say, the principle defines conditions to which experience must conform, but does

[1] A 160 = B 199-200.   [2] Cf. above, pp. 288-9.   [3] A 161-2 = B 201-2.

not enable us to construct it in advance. This distinction is inspired by the contrast between mathematical and physical science, and is valuable as defining the empirically regulative function of the *a priori* dynamical principles; but its somewhat forced character[1] becomes apparent when we bear in mind Kant's previous distinction between the principles of pure mathematical science and the transcendental principles which justify their application to experience. Those latter principles concern existence as apprehended through schematised categories, and are consequently, as regards certainty and method of proof, in exactly the same position as the dynamical principles. This is sufficiently evident from his own illustration of sunlight.[2] There is as little possibility of "constructing" its intensity as of determining *a priori* the cause of an effect.

1. THE AXIOMS OF INTUITION

All appearances are in their intuition extensive magnitudes. Or as in the second edition: *All intuitions are extensive magnitudes.*

'Extensive' is here used in a very wide sense to include temporal as well as spatial magnitude. Kant bases this principle upon the schema of number, and the proof which he propounds in its support is therefore designed to show that apprehension of an object of perception, whether spatial or temporal, is only possible in so far as we bring that schema into play. But though this is the professed purpose of the argument, number is itself never even mentioned; and the reason for the omission is doubtless Kant's consciousness of the obvious objections to any such position. That aspect of the argument is therefore, no doubt without explicit intention, kept in the background. But even as thus given, the argument must have left Kant with some feeling of dissatisfaction. Loyalty to his architectonic scheme prevents such doubt and disquietude from finding further expression.

The argument, in its first-edition statement, starts from the formulation of a view of space and time directly opposed to that of the *Aesthetic*:[3]

"I entitle a magnitude extensive when the representation of the parts makes possible, and therefore necessarily precedes, the representation of the whole. I cannot represent to myself a line, however small, without drawing it in thought, *i.e.* generating from a point all its parts one after another, and thus for the first time recording this intuition."

---

[1] Cf. below, pp. 510-11.   [2] A 178-9 = B 221.   [3] Cf. above, pp. 94-5.

Similarly with even the smallest time. And as all appearances are intuited in space or time, every appearance, so far as intuited, is an extensive magnitude, that is to say, can be apprehended only through successive generation of its parts. All appearances are "aggregates, *i.e.* manifolds of antecedently given parts."

This definition of extensive magnitude involves an assumption which Kant also employs elsewhere in the *Critique*,[1] but which he nowhere attempts to establish by argument ; namely, that it is impossible to apprehend a manifold save in succession. This assumption is, of course, entirely false (at least as applied to our empirical consciousness), as has since been amply demonstrated by experimental investigation. Kant adopted it in the earlier subjectivist stage of his teaching, before he had come to recognise that consciousness of space is involved in consciousness of time. But even after he had done so, the earlier view still tended to gain the upper hand whenever the doctrines of inner sense and of productive imagination were under consideration. For in regard to the transcendental activities of productive imagination, which are essentially synthetic, Kant continued to treat time as more fundamental than space. But, as already noted,[2] a directly opposite view of the interrelations of space and time is expounded in passages added in the second edition.

The two central paragraphs are very externally connected with the main argument, and are probably later interpolations.[3] In the first of these two paragraphs Kant ascribes the synthetic activity involved in the "generation of figures" to the productive imagination, and maintains that geometry is rendered possible by this faculty. In the other paragraph Kant deals with arithmetic, but makes no reference to the productive imagination. Its argument is limited to the contention that propositions expressive of numerical relation, though synthetic, are not universal. They are not axioms, but numerical formulae. This distinction has no very obvious bearing on the present argument, and serves only to indicate Kant's recognition that no rigid parallelism can be established between geometry and arithmetic. There are, it would seem, no arithmetical axioms corresponding to the axioms of Euclid.[4]

The concluding paragraph is a restatement of the argument of the *Aesthetic* and of § 13, *Note* i. of the *Prolegomena*. Appearances are not things in themselves. They are conditioned by the pure intuitional forms, and are

---

[1] Cf. below, pp. 358-9, 367-8, 371-2, 381-2.
[2] Cf. Adickes, *K.* p. 190 *n.*
[3] Above, p. 309 ff.
[4] Cf. above, p. 127 ff

therefore subject to pure mathematics "in all its precision." Were we compelled to regard the objects of the senses as things in themselves, an applied science of geometry (again taken, in Kant's habitual manner, as typically representing the mathematical disciplines) would not be possible. The only new element in the argument is the reference to synthesis as presupposed in all apprehension.

The additional proof with which in the second edition Kant prefaces the entire argument calls for no special comment. It may, however, be noted that though in the argument of the first edition the need of synthesis in all apprehension is clearly taught, the term synthesis is not itself employed except in the central and final paragraphs. In the proof given in the second edition both the term and what it stands for are allowed due prominence.

2. THE ANTICIPATIONS OF PERCEPTION

In all appearances sensation and the real which corresponds to it in the object (realitas phaenomenon) has an intensive magnitude or degree. Or as in the second edition: *In all appearances the real, which is an object of sensation, has intensive magnitude or degree.*

We may first analyse the total section. The first paragraph[1] explains the term anticipation. The second and third paragraphs give a first proof of the principle. Paragraphs four to ten treat of continuity in space, time and change, and of the impossibility of empty space, and also afford Kant the opportunity to develop his dynamical theory of matter, and so to indicate the contribution which transcendental philosophy is able to make towards a more adequate understanding of the principles of physical science. The eleventh and twelfth paragraphs, evidently later interpolations, give a second proof of the principle which in one important respect varies from the first proof. In the second edition a third proof akin to this second proof, but carrying it a stage further, is added in the form of a new first paragraph.

Kant's reason for changing the formulation of the principle in the second edition is evidently the unsatisfactoriness of the phrase "sensation *and* the real."[2] The principle, properly interpreted, applies not, as the first edition title and also the second proof would lead us to expect, to sensation itself, but to its object, *realitas phaenomenon*. It is phenomenalist in its teaching. The emphatic term "anticipation" is adopted by

[1] That is to say, in the first edition.
[2] The phrase is followed, ungrammatically, by a verb in the third person singular.

Kant to mark that in this principle we are able in *a priori* fashion to determine something in regard to what in itself is purely empirical. Sensation as such, being the matter of experience, can never be known *a priori*. Its quality, as being a colour or a taste, depends upon factors which are for us, owing to the limitations of our knowledge, wholly contingent. None the less in one particular respect we can predetermine the object of all sensation, and so can *anticipate* experience, even in its material aspect.

The first proof is as follows. Apprehension, so far as it takes place through a sensation, occupies only a single moment; it does not involve any successive synthesis proceeding from parts to the complete representation. That which is apprehended cannot, therefore, possess extensive magnitude. But, as already stated in the chapter on *Schematism*, reality is that in appearance which corresponds to a sensation. It is *realitas phaenomenon*. The absence of it is negation = o. Now every sensation is capable of diminution; between reality in the appearance and negation there is a continuous series of many possible intermediate sensations, the difference between any two of which is always smaller than the difference between the given sensation and zero. That is to say, the real in appearance has intensive magnitude or degree. The argument is from capability of variation in the intensity of sensation to existence of degree in its object or cause. For the most part this reality is spoken of as that which is apprehended in sensation, but Kant adds that if it be

". . . viewed as cause either of sensation or of other reality in appearance, such as change, the degree of its reality . . . is then entitled a moment, as for instance the moment of gravity."

The obscurity of what in itself is a very simple and direct argument would seem to be traceable to the lack of clearness in Kant's own mind as to what is to be signified by reality. The implied distinction between sensation and its object has not been clearly formulated. Definitions have, indeed, been given of reality in the chapter on *Schematism* ;[1] but they are extremely difficult to decipher. Kant never varies from the assertion that reality is "that which corresponds to sensation in general." Our difficulty is with the additional qualifications This reality, he further declares, is

". . . that, the concept of which in itself points to an existence [*Sein* in time."[2]

---

[1] A 143 = B 182.
[2] *Loc. cit.* in the chapter on *Schematism.*

The words 'in time' would seem to show that what is referred to is reality *in the realm of appearance*, the *realitas phaenomenon* of the *Anticipations*. But immediately below we find the following sentence:

"As time is only the form of intuition, and consequently of objects as appearances, what corresponds in them to sensation is the transcendental matter of all objects *as things in themselves*, thinghood [*Sachheit*], reality."[1]

The teaching of the first sentence is phenomenalist; that of the other is subjectivist.

Now in the section on *Anticipations of Perception* the phenomenalist tendencies of Kant's thought are decidedly the more prominent. The implied distinction is threefold, between sensation as subjective state possessing intensive magnitude, spatial realities that possess both intensive and extensive magnitude, and the thing in itself. Objects as appearances are regarded as causes of sensation and as producing changes in one another.

The explanation of the phenomenalist character of this section is not far to seek. Kant's chief purpose in it, as we shall find, is to develop the dynamical theory of matter to which he had long held, and which, as he was convinced, would ultimately be substituted for the mechanistic view to which almost all physicists then adhered. We can easily understand how in this endeavour the realist tendencies of his thinking should at once come to the surface, and why he should have been constrained to develop a position more precise and less ambiguous than that expressed in the definitions of reality and degree given in the chapter on *Schematism*. With these preliminary explanations we may pass to Kant's second proof of his principle.

A link of connection between the two proofs may be found in the reason which Kant in the first proof gives for his assertion that sensation cannot possess extensive magnitude—the reason, namely, that as its apprehension takes place in a single moment, it involves no element of synthesis. In his second proof Kant modifies this contention, and maintains that we can abstract from the extensive magnitude of the appearance, and yet can recognise a synthesis as being involved.

"The real which corresponds to sensations in general, as opposed to negation = o, represents only something the very conception of which contains an existence [*ein Sein*], and signifies nothing but the synthesis in an empirical consciousness in general."[2]

---

[1] *Loc. cit.* Italics not in Kant.   [2] Cf. A 175 = B 217. Cf. above, pp. 350-1.

Kant adds that in a single moment we can represent to ourselves as involved in the bare sensation

". . . a synthesis of the uniform progression from zero to the given empirical consciousness."

These statements are far from clear; but it is hardly necessary to criticise them in detail. Since Kant is endeavouring to prove that a schema, that of reality or limitation, is involved in the apprehension of sensation, he is bound in consistency to maintain, in accordance with the teaching of his deduction of the categories, that the application of the schema demands some species of synthesis.

The third proof, added in the second edition,[1] is somewhat more explicit, and represents a further and last stage in Kant's vain endeavour to harmonise the teaching of this section with his general principles. In the empirical consciousness of sensation there is

". . . a synthesis of the different quantities involved in the generation of a sensation from its beginning in pure intuition $= 0$ to its particular required magnitude."

Or again, apprehension of magnitude is apprehension

". . . in which the empirical consciousness can in a certain time increase from zero up to its given measure."

Here, again, what Kant asserts as occurring in our awareness of sensation calls for much more rigorous demonstration. Like the argument of the second proof, it is not independently established; it is a mere corollary to the general principles of his deduction of the categories.

Thus Kant's thesis, that the apprehension of sense qualities as intensive magnitudes presupposes a synthesis according to an *a priori* schema, is both obscure in statement, and unconvincing in argument; and some of the assertions made, especially in reference to the occurrence of synthesis, would seem to be hardly less arbitrary than the connection which Kant professes to trace between logical "quality," as affirmation or negation, and the dynamical intensity of sensuous qualities. For, as already indicated,[2] logical "quality" and intensive magnitude have nothing in common save the name.

Kant next proceeds to a discussion of the general problem of continuity. The connection is somewhat forced. But if we overlook the artificial ordering of the argument and are

---

[1] B 207-8.   [2] Cf. above, pp. 192, 341.

content to regard what is given as in the nature of parenthetical comment, we find in the middle paragraph of this section an excellent statement of his view of the nature of continuity and a very clear statement of his dynamical theory of matter.

Kant develops the conception of continuity (*a*) in reference to space and time, and (*b*) in its application to the intensity of sensations and of their causes.

(*a*) Kant's own words require no comment:

"Space and time are *quanta continua* because no part of them can be given, save as enclosed between limits (points or moments), and therefore as being itself a space or a time. Space therefore consists only of spaces, time only of times. Points and moments are only limits, *i.e.* mere positions that limit space and time. But positions always presuppose the intuitions which they limit or are intended to limit; and out of mere positions, viewed as constituents capable of being given prior to space and time, neither space nor time can be constructed. Such magnitudes may also be called *flowing*, since the synthesis of productive imagination involved in their production is a progression in time, and the continuity of time is ordinarily denoted by the expression *flowing*."[1]

(*b*) When Kant proceeds to apply the principle of continuity to intensive magnitude, his conclusion rests upon a somewhat different basis. He argues that appearances must be continuous owing to the fact that they are apprehended in space and time.[2] So far as they are extended in space and enduring in time that may perhaps be true; but Kant's assertion has a wider sweep. It implies that sensations and the physical conditions of sensation, as for instance the sensation of red or the force of gravity, are capable of existing in every possible degree between zero and any given intensity. This affords the key to his method of formulating his second and third proofs of the principle of *Anticipations of Perception*, which, in the form in which he interprets it, contains this further implication of continuity. These proofs are inspired by the desire to make all apprehension, even that of simple sensation, a temporal process, and by that indirect means to establish for sensuous intensity and its objective conditions a continuity similar to that of space and time. The proof is,

[1] A 169-70 = B 211-12. For comment upon Kant's Aristotelian view of the point as a limit, cf. below, p. 489 ff.

[2] Though Kant maintains in A 171 = B 212-13 that owing to our dependence upon empirical data and our necessary ignorance of the nature of the causal relation we cannot similarly demonstrate the principle of the continuity of change, he has himself, in characteristically inconsistent fashion, given three such demonstrations. Cf. below, pp. 380-1.

however, as we have seen, inconclusive. This application of
continuity must be regarded as more in the nature of a mere
hypothesis than Kant is willing to recognise. As regards
sensations, it would seem to have been positively disproved
by the results of experimental psychology.

From his supposed proof of the continuity of all intensive
magnitudes Kant draws two further conclusions: first, that
experience can never be made to yield proof of the void in
either space or time. For if all reality can exist in innumerable degrees, and if each sense has a determinate degree of
receptivity, the complete absence of reality can never be itself
experienced. Inference to such absence is also impossible
for a second reason, namely, that one and the same extensive magnitude may be completely occupied by an infinite
number of different intensive degrees, indefinitely approximating to, and yet also indefinitely differing from, zero.
Kant is here referring to the dynamical theory of matter
which he had long held,[1] and which he expounds in opposition
to the current mechanistic view.[2] The mechanistic theory
rests, he contends, upon an assumption purely metaphysical
and therefore wholly dogmatic, that the real in space has
no internal differences, but is uniform like the empty space
in which it exists.[3] In accordance with this assumption
physicists infer that all qualitative differences in our sensations must be due to merely quantitative differences in their
material causes, and ultimately to differences in the number
and distribution of the constituent parts of material bodies.

[1] Cf. Kant's *Monadologia physica* (1756), and *New Doctrine of Motion and Rest*
(1758). Kant's final statement of this dynamical theory is given in his *Metaphysical First Principles of Natural Science* (1786).

[2] In this matter Kant regards himself as defending the Newtonian theory of an
attractive gravitational force. The mechanistic view admits only one form of action,
viz. transference of motion through impact and pressure. "From . . . Democritus
to Descartes, indeed up to our own day, the mechanistic method of explanation
. . . has, under the title of atomism or corpuscular philosophy, maintained its
authority with but slight modification; and has continued to exercise its influence upon the principles of natural science. Its essential teaching consists in the
assumption of the *absolute impenetrability* of primitive matter, in the *absolute
homogeneity* of its constitution (difference of shape being the sole remaining
difference), and in the *absolutely indestructible coherence* of matter in its fundamental corpuscles" (*Metaphysical First Principles*, *W.* vol. iv. p. 533; ii. Allgemeine Anmerkung, 4).

[3] This is additional to its other correlative assumption of the absolute void.
"The absolute void and the absolutely full are in the doctrine of nature very much
what blind chance and blind fate are in metaphysical cosmology, namely, a barrier
to the enquiring reason, which either causes its place to be taken by arbitrary
fictions, or lays it to rest on the pillow of obscure qualities" (*Metaphysical First
Principles*, *W.* vol. iv. p. 532 (I read *forschende* for *herrschende*)). "There are
only two methods of procedure . . .: the mechanistic, through combination
of the absolutely full with the absolute void, or an opposite dynamical method,
that of explaining all material differences through mere differences in the combination of the original forces of repulsion and attraction" (*loc. cit.*).

If two bodies of the same volume differ in weight or in inertia, the variation must be traced to differences in the amount of matter, or, otherwise stated, to differences in the amount of un-occupied space, in the two bodies.   To this view Kant opposes his own hypothesis—for it is in this more modest form that it is presented in these paragraphs—namely, that matter occupies space by intensity and not by mere bulk, and that it may therefore be diminished indefinitely in degree without for that reason ceasing completely to fill the same extensive area. Thus an expanded force such as heat, filling space without leaving the smallest part of it empty, may be indefinitely diminished in degree, and yet may still with these lesser degrees continue to occupy that space as completely as before. This may not, Kant admits, be the true explanation of physical differences, but it at least has the merit of freeing the under-standing from metaphysical preconceptions, and of demon-strating the possibility of an alternative to the current view. If matter has intensity as well as extensity, and so can vary in quality as well as in quantity, physical science may perhaps be fruitfully developed on dynamical lines.

3. THE ANALOGIES OF EXPERIENCE

The principle of the *Analogies* is : *Experience is possible only through the representation of a necessary connection of perceptions.*[1]

Kant introduces the three analogies with the statement of an underlying principle, which corresponds to the central thesis of the transcendental deduction.   In the second edition this general principle is reformulated, and a new proof is added. These alterations do not seem, however, to be of any special significance.   The two proofs repeat the main argument of the transcendental deduction, but with special emphasis upon the temporal aspect of experience.   The categories of relation, as schematised, yield the *Analogies*, which acquire objective validity in so far as they render experience possible.   The first proof (given in the second paragraph of the first edition) maintains that they are indispensable for apperception, and the second proof (that of the second edition) that they are indispensable for knowledge of objects.   The references to time in the second proof are too condensed to be intelligible save in the light of the more explicit arguments given in support of the three *Analogies*.

[1] In the first edition Kant formulates this principle in the light of his extremely misleading distinction between mathematical and dynamical principles (cf. above, pp. 345-7) : "All appearances, *as regards their existence*, are subject *a priori* to rules determining their relation to one another in one time."

The first paragraph in the first edition must be a later interpolation, as its assertion that simultaneity is a mode of time conflicts with the proof given of the first *Analogy*, but agrees with what must be regarded as a later interpolated passage introductory to that proof.[1] This paragraph is also peculiar in another respect. Hitherto Kant has traced the existence of the three analogies to the three categories of relation, each of which conditions a separate schema. But in this paragraph he bases their threefold form on the fact that time has three modes, duration, sequence,[2] and coexistence, and that there is therefore a threefold problem : first, what is involved in consciousness of duration ; secondly, what is involved in consciousness of succession ; and thirdly, what is involved in consciousness of coexistence. This is not, however, a satisfactory mode of stating the matter, for it might seem to imply that the three aspects of time can be separately apprehended, and that each has its own independent conditions. What Kant really proves is that all three involve one another. We can only be conscious of duration in contrast to succession, and of succession in contrast to the permanent, while both involve consciousness of coexistence. The three analogies thus treat of three aspects of the same problem, the first connecting with the category of substance, the second with that of causality, and the third with that of reciprocity.

The only point that calls for further comment[3] concerns Kant's adoption of the term *Analogy* as a title for the three principles of " relation." The term is employed in contradistinction to constitutive principle or axiom ; and Kant points out that this usage of the term must be carefully distinguished from the other or mathematical. "In philosophy analogy is not the likeness of two quantitative but of two qualitative relations." In mathematical analogy a fourth term can be discovered from three given terms ; but in an 'analogy of experience' we possess a rule that suffices only for the determination of the *relation* to a term not given, never for knowledge of this term itself. Thus if we are informed that 15 is to x as 5 is to 10, the value of x can be determined as 30. But if it be stated that a given event stands to an antecedent event as effect to cause, only the relation holding between the events can be specified, not the actual cause itself. The principle of causality thus serves only as a

[1] Cf. below, p. 358.
[2] In A 182 = B 225 the stronger term change (*Wechsel*) is employed.
[3] A 178-80 = B 221-3 (on the distinction between mathematical and dynamical principles) has been commented upon above, pp. 345-7.

regulative principle, directing us to search for the cause of an event among its antecedents.

Riehl has suggested a very different explanation of the term, namely, as signifying that the categories of relation are employed only on the analogy of the corresponding, pure logical forms.

"In so far as I know matter in terms of its empirical properties as the substance of outer experiences, I do not gain knowledge of the nature of matter but only of its relation to my thinking. In all judgments upon outer things I employ matter as the *subject*. That knowledge is therefore nothing but an *analogy* to the conceptual relation of a subject to its predicates. Matter is related to its properties and effects in the realm of appearance as the subject of a categorical judgment is related to its predicates. In so far as an antecedent is entitled the cause of an event, we do not gain knowledge of its nature but only of the analogy of the relation of cause and effect with that of antecedent and consequent in a hypothetical proposition ; the connection of the changes is analogous to the conceptual relation of ground and consequence ; the principle of the sufficient ground of changes is an *analogy of experience*."[1]

This explanation may at first sight seem to be supported by Kant's own statement in the concluding paragraph of the section before us.

"Through these principles we are justified in combining appearances only according to an analogy with the logical and general unity of concepts. . . ."[2]

This assertion is, however, incidental to Kant's explanation that the analogies are not principles of " transcendental " (*i.e.* transcendent), but only of empirical application—an explanation itself in turn occasioned by his desire to connect his present argument with the chapter on *Schematism*. This interpretation of the term analogy is probably, therefore, of the nature of an afterthought. Having adopted the term on the grounds above stated in A 179-80 = B 222, he finds in it an opportunity to reinforce his previous assertion of the restricting character of the time condition through which categories are transformed into schemata. The entire paragraph is probably, as Adickes remarks, a later interpolation. But there are further reasons why we cannot accept this passage as representing the real origin of the term analogy. It would involve adoption of the subjectivist standpoint from which Riehl, despite his otherwise realistic reading

[1] *Philos. Krit.* 2nd ed. i. p. 545. Caird adopts a similar view, i. pp. 540, 580.

[2] A 181 = B 224.

of Kant, interprets Kant's phenomenalist doctrines. For it implies that it is only in the noumenal, and not also in the phenomenal sphere, that substantial existences and genuinely dynamical activities are to be found.[1] It would also seem to imply, what is by no means Kant's invariable position, the absolute validity of the logical forms. And lastly, it would involve the priority of the logical to the real use of the categories, a violation of Critical principles of which Kant is himself occasionally guilty, but never, as it would seem, in this exaggerated form.

A. **First Analogy.**—*All appearances contain the permanent (substance) as the object itself, and the changeable as its mere determination, i.e. as a mode in which the object exists.* Or as in the second edition : *In all change of appearances substance is permanent ; its quantum in Nature neither increases nor diminishes.*

The second paragraph[2] is of composite character. Its first part (consisting of the first three sentences) and its second part give separate proofs, involving assertions directly contradictory of one another. The one asserts change and simultaneity to be modes of time ; the other denies this. They cannot, therefore, be of the same date. The first would seem to be the later; it connects with the first paragraph of the preceding section.

In the first edition the principle is defined as expressing the schema of the dual category of substance and attribute. In the second edition it is reformulated in much less satisfactory form, as being the scientific principle of the conservation (*i.e.* indestructibility) of matter. This second formulation emphasises the weaker side of the argument of the first edition, and is largely due to the perverting influence of Kant's method of distinguishing between the *Analytic of Concepts* and the *Analytic of Judgments*. It reveals Kant's growing tendency to contrast the two divisions of the *Analytic*, as dealing, the one with ordinary experience, and the other with its scientific reorganisation.[3]

The first proof in the first edition gives explicit expression to a presupposition underlying this entire section, namely, that all apprehension is necessarily successive, or in other words that it is impossible to apprehend a manifold save in succession.[4] From this assumption it follows that if such succession is not only to occur but is to be apprehended as occurring, and if we are to be able to distinguish between

---

[1] Cf. below, pp. 373-4.　　　[2] That is to say, in the first edition.
[3] Cf. above, pp. 332-3, 343-4.
[4] Cf. above, p. 348; below, pp. 367-8, 371-2, 381-2.

the successive order of all our apprehensions and the order of coexisting independent existences, a permanent must be thought into the succession, that is to say, the successive experiences must be interpreted into an objective order in terms of the category of abiding substance and changing attributes. Kant neither here nor elsewhere makes any attempt to explain how this position is to be reconciled with his doctrine that space can be intuited as well as time; and there is equal difficulty in reconciling it with the doctrine developed in his second proof (in the second, division of this same paragraph) that time itself does not change but only the appearances in it.

As above shown,[1] there are two tendencies in Kant's treatment of time, each of which carries with it its own set of connected consequences. There is the view that consciousness of time *as a whole* preconditions consciousness of any part of it. This tends to recognition of simultaneity as a mode of time and of the simultaneous as apprehended in a single non-successive act of apprehension. On the other hand, there is the counter-view that consciousness of time is only possible through the successive combination of its parts. This leads to the assertion that simultaneity is not a mode of time, and that time itself cannot be apprehended save as the result of synthesis in accordance with unifying categories. Through the categories there arises consciousness of objectivity, and so for the first time consciousness of a distinction between the subjective which exists invariably and exclusively in succession, and the objective which may exist either as successive or as permanent, and in whose existence both elements are, indeed, inseparably involved.

To turn now to Kant's second[2] proof of the principle;[3] it is as follows. All our perceptions are in time, and in time are represented as either coexistent or successive. Time itself cannot change,[4] for only as in it can change be repre-

---

[1] Cf. above, pp. 94, 135-8, 309 ff., 347-8.
[2] That is to say, in the first edition.
[3] The new proof added in the second edition calls for no special comment. In all essentials it agrees with this second proof of the first edition. It differs only in such ways as are called for by the mode of formulating the principle in the second edition.
[4] This statement, as Caird has pointed out (i. p. 541), is extremely questionable. "It may be objected that to say that 'time itself does not change' is like saying that passing away does not itself pass away. So far the endurance of time and the permanence of the changing might even seem to mean only that the moments of time never cease to pass away, and the changing never ceases to change. A perpetual flux would therefore sufficiently 'represent' all the permanence that is in time." This is not, however, in itself a vital objection to Kant's argument. For he is here stating more than his argument really requires. Events are dated in a *single* time, not in an unchanging time. Kant's statement betrays the

sented. Time, however, cannot by itself be apprehended. As such, it is the mere empty form of our perceptions. There must be found in the objects of perception some abiding substrate or substance which will represent the permanence of time in consciousness, and through relation to which coexistence and succession of events may be perceived. And since only in relation to this substrate can time relations be apprehended, it must be altogether unchangeable, and may therefore[1] be called substance. And being unchangeable it can neither increase nor diminish in quantity. Kant, without further argument, at once identifies this substance with matter.

This proof may be restated in briefer fashion.[2] The consciousness of events in time involves the dating of them in time. But that is only possible in so far as we have a representation of the time in which they are to be dated. Time, however, not being by itself experienced, must be represented in consciousness by an abiding substrate in which all change takes place, and since, as the substrate of *all* change, it will necessarily be unchangeable, it may be called substance.

The argument, in both proofs, is needlessly abstract, and as already remarked,[3] the reason of this abstractness is that Kant here, as in the chapter on *Schematism*, unduly ignores space, limiting his analysis to inner sense. He defines the schema of substance as the permanence of the real in time, *i.e.* as the representation of the real which persists while all else changes. As the second edition of the *Critique* shows,[4] Kant himself came to recognise the inadequacy of this definition, and therefore of the proof of the first *Analogy*. Consciousness is only possible through the representation of objects in *space*. Only in outer sense is a permanent given in contrast to which change may be perceived. The proof ought therefore to have proceeded in the following manner. Time can be conceived only as motion, and motion is perceivable only against a permanent background in space. Consciousness of time therefore involves consciousness of a permanent in space. He might have added that consciousness of relative time involves consciousness of change in relation to something

---

extent to which, as Bergson has very justly pointed out, Kant spatialises time, *i.e.* interprets it on the analogy of space. It is based on "the mixed idea of a measurable time, which is space in so far as it is homogeneity, and duration in so far as it is succession ; that is to say, at bottom, the contradictory idea of succession in simultaneity" (*Les Données immédiates*, p. 173, Eng. trans. p. 228).

[1] Cf. A 184 = B 227 : "the proposition, that substance is permanent, is tautological."   [2] Cf. A 188 = B 231.

[3] Above, p. 341.   [4] Cf. above, p. 309 ff.

relatively permanent, and that the scientific conception of all changes as taking place in a single absolute time involves the determining of change through relation to something absolutely permanent, this ultimate standard being found in the heavenly bodies. By the permanent is not meant the immovable, but only that which is uniform and unchanging in its motions. The uniform motions of the heavenly bodies constitute our ultimate standard of time. The degree of their uniformity is the measure of our approximation to an absolute standard. A marginal note upon this *Analogy* in Kant's private copy of the *Critique* reveals Kant's late awakened recognition of the necessity of this mode of restating the argument.

" Here the proof must be so developed as to apply only to substances as phenomena of outer sense, and must therefore be drawn from space, which with its determinations exists at all times. In space all change is motion. . . ."[1]

That the new argument of the second edition still proceeds on the same lines as the second argument of the first edition is probably due, as Erdmann remarks,[2] to Kant's unwillingness to make the extensive alterations which would have been called for in the chapter on *Schematism* as well as in the statement of this *Analogy*.

A second serious objection to Kant's treatment of the first *Analogy* follows at once from the above. Kant identifies the permanent which represents time in consciousness with matter, and seeks to prove by means of this identification the principle of the conservation of matter.[3] That principle is not really capable of transcendental proof. It is not a presupposition of possible experience, but merely a generalisation empirically grounded. Kant is here confounding a

---

[1] B. Erdmann's edition of the *Nachträge*, lxxx. p. 32. Cited by Caird, i. pp. 541-2.   [2] *Op. cit.* pp. 33-4.

[3] That Kant does not mean to imply that the category of substance has no application to the contents of inner sense is made clear by a curious argument in the *Metaphysical First Principles of Natural Science* (1786), *W.* iv. p. 542: " What in this proof essentially characterises substance, which is possible only in space and under spatial conditions, and therefore only as object of the outer senses, is that its quantity cannot be increased or diminished without substance coming into being or ceasing to be. For the quantity of an object which is possible only in space must consist of parts which are external to one another, and these, therefore, if they are real (something movable), must necessarily be substances. On the other hand, that which is viewed as object of inner sense can, *as substance*, have a quantity which does not consist of parts external to one another. Its parts are therefore not substances, and their coming into being and ceasing to be must not be regarded as creation or annihilation of a substance. Their increase or diminution is therefore possible without prejudice to the principle of the permanence of substance." (Italics not in Kant.) Cf. also *Prolegomena*, § 49, and below, pp. 367, 377 *n*. 3.

particular theory as to the manner in which the element of permanence, necessary to possible experience, is realised, with the much more general conclusion which alone can be established by transcendental methods. His argument also conflicts with his own repeated assertion that the notion of change, in so far as it is distinct from that of temporal succession or of motion in space, is empirical, and consequently falls outside the scope of transcendental enquiry. By the conservation of matter we mean the constancy of the weight of matter throughout all changes. But the only permanent which can be postulated as necessary to render our actual consciousness of time possible, consists of spatial objects sufficiently constant to act as a standard by comparison with which motions may be measured against one another. And as this first *Analogy*, properly understood, thus deals solely with spatial changes of bodies, the principle of the conservation of matter has no real connection with it.

Then thirdly, and lastly, Kant takes this first *Analogy* as showing the indispensable function performed in experience by the category of substance and attribute. Substance, he argues, corresponds to the time in which events happen, and its attributes correspond to the changing events. Just as all events are only to be conceived as happening in time, so too all changes are only to be conceived as changes in an abiding substance. These, he would seem to hold, are simply two ways of making one and the same assertion. Now Kant may perhaps be right in insisting that all change is change in, and not of, time. Unity of consciousness would seem to demand consciousness of a single time in which all events happen. But this relation of time to its events does not justify the same assertion being made of substance. Substance may be what corresponds to time in general, and may represent it in consciousness, but we cannot for that reason say that changes are also only in and not of it. To regard the changes in this way as attributes inhering in substance directly contradicts the view developed in the second *Analogy*. For the notion of substance is there treated as an implication of the principle of causality. Substance, Kant there insists, is not a bare static existence in which changes take place, but a dynamic energy which from its very nature is in perpetual necessitated change. Change is not change in, but change of, substance.

Even in the passage in which Kant identifies the notion of the permanent in change with that of substance and attribute, he shows consciousness of this difficulty. We must not, he says, separate the substance from its accidents, treating it as a separate existence. The accidents are merely the special forms of its existence. But all the same, he adds, withdrawing the words which he has just uttered, such a separation of the changing accidents from the abiding substance is "*unavoidable, owing to the conditions of the logical employment of our understanding.*"[1] Kant is here so hard pressed to account for the use of the category of substance and attribute in experience, and to explain the contradictions to which it gives rise, that the only way he sees out of the difficulty is to refer the contradictions involved in the category to the constitution of our understanding in its *logical* employment. Yet as such employment of understanding is, according to his own showing, secondary to, and dependent upon, its "real" employment, the category of substance and attribute can hardly have originated in this way.

We must, then, conclude that Kant offers no sufficient deduction or explanation of the category of substance and attribute, and as he does so nowhere else, we are driven to the further conclusion that he is unable to account for its use in experience, or at least to reconcile it in any adequate fashion with the principle of causality.

B. Second Analogy.—*Everything that happens, i.e. begins to be, presupposes something on which it follows according to a rule.* Or as in the second edition : *All changes take place in conformity with the law of the connection of cause and effect.*

This section, as Kant very rightly felt, contains one of the most important and fundamental arguments of the entire *Critique* ; and this would seem to be the reason why he has so multiplied the proofs which he gives of the *Analogy.* Within the limits of the section no less than five distinct proofs are to be found, and still another was added in the second edition. As Adickes[2] argues, it is extremely unlikely that Kant should have written five very similar proofs in immediate succession. The probability is that they are of independent origin and were later combined to constitute this section ; or, if we hold with Adickes that Kant first composed a "brief outline," we may conclude that he combined the one or more proofs, which that outline contained, with others of earlier or of later origin. The first to the fourth paragraphs of the first edition contain a first proof ; the fifth to the seventh a second proof (a repetition of the first proof but in indirect form) ; the eighth to the tenth a third proof (almost identical with the first) ; the eleventh to the thirteenth a fourth proof (different in character from all the others) ; the four-

[1] A 187 = B 230.   [2] *K.* p. 211 *n.*

teenth a fifth proof (probably the latest in time of writing ; an anticipation of the argument in the second edition).   The paragraph added in the second edition (the second paragraph in the text of the second edition) gives a sixth and last proof.

We may first state the central argument, deferring treatment of such additional points as arise in connection with Kant's varying formulations of it in his successive proofs. The second *Analogy*, though crabbedly, diffusely, and even confusedly stated, is one of the finest and most far-reaching pieces of argument in the whole *Critique*. It is of special historical importance as being Kant's answer to Hume's denial of the validity of the causal principle. Hume had maintained that we can never be conscious of anything but mere succession. Kant in reply seeks to prove that consciousness of succession is only possible through consciousness of a necessity that determines the order of the successive events.

Kant, we must bear in mind, accepts much of Hume's criticism of the category of causality. The general principle that every event must have an antecedent cause is, Kant recognises, neither intuitively certain nor demonstrable by general reasoning from more ultimate truths. It is not to be accounted for by analytic thought, but like all synthetic judgments *a priori* can only be proved by reference to the contingent fact of actual experience. Secondly, Kant makes no attempt, either in this *Analogy* or elsewhere in the *Critique*, to explain the nature and possibility of causal connection, that is, to show how one event, the cause, is able to give rise to another and different event, the effect. We can never by analysis of an effect discover any reason why it must necessarily be preceded by a cause.[1]   Thirdly, the principle of causality, as deduced by Kant and shown to be necessarily involved in all consciousness of time, is the quite general principle that every event must have *some* cause in what immediately precedes it. What in each special case the cause may be, can only be empirically discovered ; and that any selected event is really the cause can never be absolutely certain. The particular causal laws are discovered from experience, not by means of the general principle but only in accordance with it, and are therefore neither purely empirical nor wholly *a priori*. As even J. S. Mill teaches, the general principle is assumed in every inference to a causal law, and save by thus assuming the general principle the particular inference to causal connection cannot be proved. But at the same time, since the proof of causal connection depends upon

[1] Cf. A 205-7 = B 252.

satisfaction of those empirical tests which Mill formulates
in his inductive methods, such special causal laws can be
gathered only from experience.

The starting-point of Kant's analysis is our consciousness
of an *objective* order in time. This is for Kant a legitimate
starting-point since he has proved in the *Transcendental
Deduction* that only through consciousness of the objective is
consciousness of the subjective in any form possible. The
independent argument by which it is here supported is merely
a particular application of the general principle of that deduction. When we apprehend any very large object, such as a
house, though we do so by successively perceiving the different
parts of it, we never think of regarding these successive perceptions as representing anything successive in the house.
On the other hand, when we apprehend successive events in
time, such as the successive positions of a ship sailing down
stream, we do regard the succession of our experiences as
representing objective succession in what is apprehended.
Kant therefore feels justified in taking as fact, that we have
the power of distinguishing between subjective and objective
succession, *i.e.* between sequences which are determined by
the order of our attentive experience and sequences which are
given as such. It is this fact which affords Kant a precise
method of formulating the problem of the second *Analogy*,
viz. *how consciousness of objective change, as distinguished from
subjective succession, is possible?*

Schopenhauer, owing to the prominence in his system of
the principle of sufficient reason, has commented upon this
second *Analogy* in considerable detail;[1] and we may here
employ one of his chief criticisms to define more precisely the
general intention of Kant's argument. The succession in our
experiences of the parts of a house and of the positions of a
ship is, Schopenhauer maintains, in both cases of genuinely
objective character. In both instances the changes are due to
the position of two bodies relatively to one another. In the
first example one of these bodies is the body of the observer, or
rather one of his bodily organs, namely the eye, and the other
is the house, in relation to the parts of which the position of
the eye is successively altered. In the second example the
ship changes its position relatively to the stream. The motion
of the eye from roof to cellar is one event; its motion from
cellar to roof is a second event; and both are events of the
same nature as the sailing of the ship. Had we the same
power of dragging the ship upstream that we have of moving
the eye in a direction opposite to that of its first movement,

[1] *Werke* (Frauenstädt, 1873), i. p. 85 ff.

the positions of the ship could be reversed in a manner exactly analogous to our reversal of the perceptions of the house.

This criticism is a typical illustration of Schopenhauer's entire failure to comprehend the central thesis of Kant's Critical idealism.[1] The *Analytic*, so far as the main argument of its objective deduction is concerned, was to him a closed book; and as this second analogy is little else than a special application of the results of the deduction, he was equally at a loss in its interpretation. Kant was himself, of course, in large part responsible for the misunderstanding. The distinction which would seem to be implied by Kant's language between sequence that is objective and sequence that is *merely* subjective is completely inconsistent with Critical principles,[2] and is as thoroughly misleading as that other distinction which he so frequently employs between *a priori* and empirical judgments. Schopenhauer, however, regarded these distinctions as valid, and accordingly applies them in the interpretation of Kant's method of argument. If inner and outer experience are to be contrasted as two kinds of experience, there is, as Schopenhauer rightly insists, no sufficient ground for regarding changes due to movements of the eye as being subjective and those that are due to movements of a ship as being objective. That is not, however, Kant's intention in the employment of these illustrations. He uses them only to make clear the fairly obvious fact that while in certain cases the order of our perceptions is subjectively initiated, in other

---

[1] As evidence of this failure I may cite Schopenhauer's comment upon A 371 and 372 : "From these passages it is quite clear that for Kant the perception of outer things in space is antecedent to all application of the causal law, and that this law does not therefore enter into it as its element and condition : mere sensation amounts in Kant's view to perception" (*Werke*, i. p. 81). Even when, as in the passages referred to, Kant is speaking in his most subjectivist vein, he gives no justification for any such assertion. Schopenhauer, notwithstanding his sincere admiration for Kant—"I owe what is best in my own system to the impression made upon me by the works of Kant, by the sacred writings of the Hindoos, and by Plato" (*World as Will and Idea*, *Werke*, ii. p. 493, Eng. trans. ii. p. 5)—is one of the most unreliable of Kant's critics. His comments are extremely misleading, and largely for the reason that he was interested in Kant only as he could obtain from him confirmation of his own philosophical tenets. Several of these tenets he certainly derived directly from the *Critique*; but they are placed by him in so different a setting that their essential meaning is greatly altered. We have already noted (above, p. 41) Schopenhauer's exaggerated statement of Kant's intuitive theory of mathematics. Kant's subjectivism is similarly expounded in a one-sided and quite unrepresentative manner (cf. below, p. 407 *n.*). Hutchison Stirling's criticisms of Kant in his *Text Book to Kant* are vitiated by a similar failure to recognise the completely un-Critical character of the occasional passages in which Kant admits a distinction between "judgments of perception" and "judgments of experience" (cf. above, pp. 288-9). Stirling (cf. below, p. 377) has amplified his criticism of Kant in *Princeton Review* (Jan. 1879, pp. 178-210), *Fortnightly Review* (July 1872), and in *Mind* (ix., 1884, p. 531, and x., 1885, p. 45).

[2] Cf. above, pp. 240-2, 365, and below, p. 377.

cases we apprehend the subjective order of our experiences as corresponding to, and explicable only through, the objective sequence of events. In holding to this distinction Kant is not concerned to deny that even in the order which is determined by the subject's purposes or caprice objective factors are likewise involved. The fact that the foundations of a house support its roof, and will therefore determine what it is that we shall apprehend when we turn the eye upwards, does not render the order of our apprehensions any the less subjective in character. But that this order is *purely* subjective, Kant could never have asserted. His Critical principles definitely commit him to the view that even sensations and desires are integral parts of the unitary system of natural law. Kant, as we shall find, is maintaining that some such distinction between subjective and objective sequence as is illustrated in the above contrasted instances must be present from the very start of our experience—must, indeed, be constitutive of experience as such. Out of a consciousness of the purely subjective the notion of the objective can never arise.[1] Or otherwise stated, consciousness of a time order, even though subjective, must ultimately involve the application of some non-subjective standard.

"I shall be obliged . . . to derive the subjective sequence of apprehension from the objective sequence of appearances, because otherwise the former is entirely undetermined, and does not distinguish any one appearance from any other."[2]

We interpret the subjective order in terms of an objective system; consciousness of the latter is the necessary presupposition of all awareness. It is as necessary to the interpretation of what is apprehended through the rotating eyeballs as to the apprehension of a moving ship. So far from refusing to recognise that the subjective order of our experiences is objectively conditioned, Kant is prepared to advance to the further assertion that it is only apprehensible when so conceived.

In the third *Analogy* Kant proceeds to the connected

---

[1] Cf. Stout, *Manual of Psychology*, third edition, pp. 444-6: "Unless we assume from the outset that the primitive mind treats a perceived change which challenges its interest and attention, not as something self-existent in isolation, but as something conditioned by and conditioning other changes, it seems hopeless to attempt to show how this causal point of view could have arisen through any extension of knowledge in accordance with ascertained psychological laws and conditions. . . . There is good reason for denying that customary repetition is even required to furnish a first occasion or opportunity for the first emergence of the apprehension of causal relations. For, as we have already insisted, the process of learning by experience is from the first experimental. . . . Regularities are only found because they are sought. But it is in the seeking that the category of causal unity is primarily involved." Cf. below, pp. 371-2.   [2] A 193 = B 238.

problem, how we can apprehend the parts of a house as simultaneous notwithstanding the sequent relation of our perceptions of them, and what justification we have for thus interpreting the subjectively sequent experiences as representing objective coexistence.   Just as Kant in this second *Analogy* does not argue that irreversibility is by itself proof of causal relation, but only that the consciousness of such irreversibility demands the employment of the conception of causality, so in the third *Analogy* he does not attempt to reduce the consciousness of coexistence to the consciousness of reversibility, but to prove that only through the application of the conception of reciprocity can the reversibility be properly interpreted.   In each case the category conditions the empirical consciousness; the latter is an apprehension of determinate order only in so far as it presupposes the category. Though Kant's treatment of the third *Analogy* has less historical importance, and perhaps less intrinsic interest, than the proof of the second *Analogy*, it is even more significant of the kind of position which he is endeavouring to establish, and I may therefore forewarn the reader that he must not spare himself the labour of mastering its difficult, and somewhat illusive, argument.   The doctrines which it expounds at once reinforce and extend the results of the second *Analogy*, while the further difficulties which it brings to view, but which it is not itself capable of meeting, indicate that the problems of the *Analytic* call for reconsideration in the light of certain wider issues first broached in the *Dialectic*.

We may now return to Kant's main argument.   His problem, as we have found, is how consciousness of objective change, as distinguished from subjective succession, is possible. The problem, being formulated in this particular way, demands, Kant felt, careful definition of what is meant by the term 'objective,' upon which so much depends.   To apply the illustration above used, the house as apprehended is not a thing in itself but only an appearance to the mind.   What, then, do we mean by the house, as distinguished from our subjective representations of it, when that house is nothing but a complex (*Inbegriff*) of representations?[1]   The question and Kant's answer to it are stated in subjectivist fashion, in terms of his earlier doctrine of the transcendental object.   To contrast an object with the representations through which we apprehend it, is only possible if these representations stand under a rule which renders necessary their combination in some one particular way, and so distinguishes this one particular mode of representation as the only true mode from

[1] A 191 = B 236.

all others. The origin, therefore, of our distinction between the subjectively successive and the succession which is also objective must be due in the one case to the presence of a rule compelling us to combine the events in some particular successive order, and in the other to the absence of such a rule. Our apprehension of the house, for instance, may proceed in any order, from the roof downwards or *vice versa*, and as the order may always be reversed there is no compulsion upon the mind to regard the order of its apprehension as representing objective sequence. But since in our apprehension of an event B in time, the apprehension of B follows upon the apprehension of a previous event A, and we cannot reverse the order, the mind is compelled to view the order of succession, in terms of the category of causality, as necessitated, and therefore as objective. The order is a necessary order not in the sense that A must always precede B, that A is the cause of B, but that the order, if we are to apprehend it correctly, must in this particular case be conceived as necessary. The succession, that is, need not be conceived as a causal one, but in order to be conceived as objective succession it must be conceived as rendered necessary by connections that are causal.

Having, in this general fashion, shown the bearing of his previous analysis of objective experience upon the problem in hand, Kant proceeds to develop from it his proof of the special principle of causality. The schema of causality is necessary succession in time, and it is through this, its time aspect, that Kant approaches the principle. It has to do with the special case of *change*. To be conscious of change we must be conscious of an *event*, that is, of something as happening at a particular point in time. The change, in other words, requires to be dated, and as we are not conscious of time in general, it must be dated by reference to other events, and obviously in this case in relation to the preceding events, in contrast to which it is apprehended *as change*. But according to the results of our analysis of what constitutes objective experience, it can be fixed in its position in objective time only if it be conceived as related to the preceding events according to a necessary law ; and the law of necessary connection in time is the law of causality. In order, then, that something which has taken place may be apprehended as having occurred, that is, as being an objective change, it must be apprehended as necessarily following upon that which immediately precedes it in time, *i.e.* as causally necessary.

The principle of causality thus conditions consciousness of objective succession, and Hume in asserting that we are

conscious of the succession of *events*, therefore admits all that
need be assumed in order to prove the principle. The reason
why Hume failed to recognise this, is that he ignored the
distinction between consciousness of the subjective order of
our apprehensions and consciousness of the objective sequence
of events. Yet that is a distinction upon which his own
position rested. For he teaches that determination of causal
laws, sufficiently certain to serve the purposes alike of practical
life and of natural science, can be obtained through observation
of those sequences which remain constant. Such is also the
position of all empiricists. They hold that causal relation is
discovered by comparison of *given* sequences. Kant's contention is that the apprehension of change as change, and therefore ultimately the apprehension even of an arbitrarily
determined order of subjective succession,[1] presupposes, and
is only possible through, an application of the category of
causality. The primary function of the understanding does
not consist in the clarification of our representation of an event,
but in making such representation possible at all.[2] The
primary field of exercise for the understanding lies not in
the realm of reflective comparison, but in the more fundamental sphere of creative synthesis.[3] In determining the
nature of the given it predetermines the principles to which
all reflection upon the given must conform. The discursive
activities of scientific reflection are secondary to, and conditioned by, the transcendental processes which generate the
experience of ordinary consciousness. Only an experience
which conforms to the causal principle can serve as foundation either for the empirical judgments of sense experience,
or for that ever-increasing body of scientific knowledge into
which their content is progressively translated. The principle
of causality ·is applicable to everything experienced, for the
sufficient reason that experience is itself possible only in terms
of it. This conclusion finds its most emphatic and adequate
statement in the *Methodology*.

". . . through concepts of understanding pure reason establishes
secure principles, not however directly from concepts, but always
only indirectly through relation of these concepts to something
altogether contingent, namely, *possible experience*. For when such
experience (*i.e.* something as object of possible experience) is presupposed, the principles are apodictically certain, though by them-

---

[1] By an "arbitrary" order Kant does not, of course, mean an order of
succession that is not determined, but only one that is determined by subjectively
conditioned direction of attention. Cf. below, p. 377.
[2] Cf. A 199=B 244, and above, pp. 133, 288-9; below, p. 377.
[3] Cf. A 195-6=B 240-1, and above, pp. 172, 176 ff., 182-3, 263 ff., 277-8.

selves (directly) *a priori* they cannot even be recognised at all. Thus no one can acquire insight into the proposition that everything which happens has its cause, merely from the concepts involved. It is not, therefore, a dogma, although from another point of view, namely, from that of the sole field of its possible employment, *i.e.* experience, it can be proved with complete apodictic certainty. But though it needs proof, it should be entitled a *principle*, not a *theorem*, because *it has the peculiar character that it makes possible the very experience which is its own ground of proof, and in this experience must always itself be presupposed.*" [1]

Before making further comment upon Kant's central argument, it is advisable to consider the varying statements which Kant has given of it. We may take his successive proofs in the order in which they occur in the first edition.

First Proof. [2]—The argument is developed in terms of Kant's early doctrine of the transcendental object. The only points specially characteristic of the statement here given of that doctrine consist (*a*) in the emphasis with which it is asserted that representations can be experienced only in succession to one another, and that they can never stand in the relation of coexistence, [3] and (*b*) in the almost complete ignoring of the transcendental object as source or ground of the rule in terms of which the successive representations are organised. (*a*) This is a point common to the arguments of all three *Analogies*. In the first and third the problem is how, from representations merely successive, permanence and coexistence can be determined. In the second *Analogy* the problem is how from representations invariably successive a distinction can be drawn between the subjectively determined order of our apprehensions and the objective sequence of events. Or in other words: how under such conditions we can recognise an order as given, and so as prescribing the order in which it must be apprehended. Or to state the same point in still another manner: how we can distinguish between an arbitrary or reversible order and an imposed or fixed order, and so come to apprehend the subjective order of our apprehensions as in certain cases controlled by, and explicable only through, the objective sequence of events. [4]

(*b*) The reason why the transcendental object, as source of the determinate and prescribed order of the given events, falls into the background in this passage is that Kant is concerned only with the general principle or category by means of which the order is apprehended as necessary. That

---

[1] A 736-7 = B 765.   Italics of last sentence not in Kant.
[2] A 189-94 = B 234-9 : first to fourth paragraphs (first edition).
[3] Cf. above, pp. 348, 358.   [4] Cf. A 192-3 = B 238-9.

principle has a subjective origin even though the particular sequences of concrete events have by means of that concept to be conceived as inexorably determined by their noumenal conditions.[1] The principle accounts for the *comprehension* of the order as objective, and that is the only point with which Kant is here immediately concerned. That the assertion of the subjective origin of the category is not inconsistent with recognition of the imposed order of the given has already been shown above.[2] Kant's own illustration, in this section, of the ship sailing down stream shows that he was prepared to assume without question that they are compatible. His argument is, however, obscure, owing to his failure to distinguish between the two senses in which the term 'rule' may be employed. The term may signify either the universal and merely formal principle that every event must have a cause, or it may be used to denote the fixed order in which concrete events are presented to sense-perception. The latter order need not represent a series the members of which are causally connected *with one another*, but only one that is due to causal necessities. Thus the successive positions of a ship sailing down stream are not interrelated as cause and effect, and yet in order to be apprehended as objectively successive must be conceived as causally conditioned. The term 'rule' has very different meanings in the two cases. 'Rule' in the first sense is of subjective origin. It is *formal*, and can never be given. It is read into the given. 'Rule' in the second sense is given merely, and being due to noumenal conditions constitutes the *material* element in natural science, the empirical content of some particular causal law. Owing to Kant's failure explicitly to distinguish between these two very different connotations of the term, such a sentence as the following is ambiguous : "That in appearance which contains the condition of this necessary rule of apprehension is the object." Kant may mean that the prescribed order of the concrete events is due to the transcendental object ; but in that case it is not given as *necessary*. Necessity, as he constantly insists, is the one thing that can never be given. The sentence is also mis-

---

[1] Cf. Riehl, *Philosophischer Kriticismus* (second edition), i. pp. 551-2. While recognising the above main point, Riehl seems to assert that empirical sequence determines the *application* of the causal concept. It would be truer, and more in accordance with the position which Kant is endeavouring to establish, to assert that appeal to constancy of sequence enables us to determine which antecedents of any given event are causal conditions. The principle of causality is already applied when the sequent experiences are apprehended as sequent *events*. This ambiguity, however, would seem to be due only to Riehl's mode of expression. For, as he himself says (p. 551), the law of causality is a ground of experience, and cannot therefore be derived from it. Cf. above, pp. 267-8, 367.

[2] Pp. 365-71, 377.

leading through its use of the term 'appearance.' That term has no legitimate place in a passage inspired by the doctrine of the transcendental object; there can be no such middle term between subjective representations and the thing in itself. As Kant himself states,[1] appearance defined in terms of that doctrine is "nothing save a complex of representations."

There is a very essential difference in the view which Kant takes of the causal relation according as he is proceeding upon subjectivist or upon phenomenalist lines. From the one point of view appearances are representations merely, and accordingly are entirely devoid of causal efficacy. They are not causes and effects of one another. They have not the independence or self-persistence necessary for the exercise of dynamical energy or even for the reception of modifications. Being "states of the identical self," all causal relation, dynamically conceived, must lie solely in their noumenal conditions. Causality is regarded not as a necessitating process, but only as necessitated sequence. It is, as Kant has suggested in A 181 = B 224, a mere 'analogy' in terms of which we apply the logical relation of ground and consequence [2] to the interpretation of our subjective representations, and so view them as grounded not in one another but exclusively in the thing in itself. Causality in the strict sense, *i.e.* dynamical agency, can be looked for only in the noumenal sphere.

Caird, while adopting this explanation of the term 'analogy,'[3] is, as might be expected from his Hegelian standpoint, extremely indefinite and non-committal as to whether or not empirical objects can be genuine causes. Riehl, notwithstanding his professedly realistic interpretation of Kant, adopts the above subjectivist view of natural causation. So also do Benno Erdmann and Paulsen. The latter [4] speaks with no uncertain voice.

"Causality in the phenomenal world signifies for Kant, as for Hume, nothing but regularity in the sequence of phenomena. Real causal efficiency cannot of course occur here, for phenomena are ideational products. As such they can no more produce an effect than concepts can."

The corresponding phenomenalist view of the causal relation receives no quite definite formulation either in this section or elsewhere in the *Critique*, but may be gathered from the

---

[1] A 191 = B 236. Cf. above, pp. 216-18.
[2] As pointed out above, this is really a secondary meaning which Kant reads into the term analogy; it is not the true explanation of his choice of the term.
[3] *Critical Philosophy of Kant*, vol. i. pp. 540, 580.
[4] *Kant*, p. 198: trans. by Creighton and Lefevre, p. 196.

general trend of Kant's phenomenalist teaching.[1]   It is somewhat as follows.   The term 'analogy' is viewed as having a
meaning very different from that above suggested.   The
causal relation is not a mere analogy from the logical relation
of ground and consequence; it is the representation of
genuinely dynamical activities in the objects apprehended.
Those objects are not mere states of the self, subjective
representations.   They are part of an independent order
which in the form known to us is a phenomenalist transcript
of a deeper reality.   If the causal relation is the analogy of
anything distinguishable from itself, it is an analogon or
interpretation of dynamical powers exercised by things in
themselves,[2] not of the merely logical relation between
premisses and conclusion.   The objects of representation may
exercise powers which representations as such can never be
conceived as possessing.   Between the individual's subjective
states and things in themselves stands the phenomenal world
of the natural sciences.   Its function, whether as directly
experienced through sense-perception or as conceptually
reconstructed through scientific hypothesis, is to stand as the
representative in human consciousness of that noumenal realm
in which all existence is ultimately rooted.   The causal
interactions of material bodies in space are as essentially
constitutive of those bodies as are any of their quantitative
properties.   Causal relation, even in the phenomenal sphere,
must not be identified with mere conformity to law.   The
true and complete purpose of the natural sciences is not to
be found in the Berkeleian or sceptical ideal of simplification,
but in the older and sounder conception of causal explanation.
That, at least, is the view which Kant invariably defends
whenever he has occasion to discuss the principles of physical
science.

Second Proof.[3]—The argument of the first proof is here
developed in indirect fashion.   In the *absence* of any rule
prescribing necessary sequence, no distinction can be made
between subjective and objective succession.   The justification for such a rule lies therefore, not in an inductive inference
from repeated experience, but in its necessity for the possibility
of experience.   It is an expression of the synthetic unity in
which experience consists.

Third Proof.[4]—This is for the most part merely a restate-

---

[1] Cf. above, pp. 270 ff., 313-21.

[2] Kant, of course, recognises that we cannot make any such positive assertion;
to do so would be to transcend the limits imposed by Critical principles.   Cf.
below, p. 382.

[3] A 194-6 = B 239-41 : fifth to seventh paragraphs (first edition).

[4] A 196-9 = B 241-4 : eighth to tenth paragraphs (first edition).

ment of the first proof. It differs from it in making rather more explicit that the objective reference involved in the notion of the transcendental object is one that carries the mind beyond all representations to the thought of something which determines their order according to a rule. Otherwise the ambiguities of the terms employed are identical with those of the first proof. Its concluding paragraph, however, is a much clearer statement of the difficult argument of A 192-3 = B 238-9.

Fourth Proof.[1]—This proof differs from all the others. It argues from the characteristics of pure time to the properties necessary to the empirical representation of the time-series. As time cannot be experienced in and by itself, all its essential characteristics must be capable of being represented in terms of appearance. "Only in appearances can we empirically recognise continuity in the connection of times." The primary function of the understanding is to make such recognition possible, and it does so by "transferring the time order to the appearances and their existence." It is a necessary law of time that we can only advance to the succeeding through the preceding. Each moment of time is the indispensable condition of the existence of that which follows it. We can pass to the year 1915 only by way of the preceding year 1914. And since, as just noted, time is not cognisable by itself but only as the form of our perceptions, this law must be applicable to them. We can only be conscious of all times as successively conditioning one another in one single time, and that means in one single *objective* time, if we are conscious of all the phenomena perceived as conditioning one another in their order in time.

It is somewhat difficult to understand how Kant came to formulate the argument in this form. The explanation may perhaps be found in his preoccupation[2] with the doctrine of a transcendental activity of the productive imagination and with the connected doctrine of a pure *a priori* manifold. For this proof would seem to rest upon the assumption that the characteristics of time are known purely *a priori* and therefore with complete certainty, independently of sense experience. The unusual and somewhat scholastic character of the proof also appears in Kant's substitution of the principle of sufficient reason for the principle of causality. But despite the artificial character of the standpoint, the argument serves to bring prominently forward Kant's central thesis, viz. that the principle of causality is presupposed in all consciousness of

---

[1] A 199-201 = B 244-6 : eleventh to thirteenth paragraphs (first edition).
[2] Cf. above, pp. 224 ff., 264 ff. ; below, 377.

time, even of the subjectively successive. Also, by emphasising that time in and by itself can never be "an object of perception," and that the relating of appearances to "absolute time" is possible only through the determining of them in their relations to one another, it supplies the data for correction of its own starting-point.

Fifth Proof.[1]—This proof is probably later than the preceding proofs. Though its essential content coincides with that of the opening proof, its formulation would seem to be a first attempt at statement of the sixth proof, *i.e.* of the argument which Kant added in the second edition. Adickes considers this proof to be earlier in date than the first four proofs, but the reason which he assigns for so regarding it, viz. that Kant here postulates a synthesis of the imagination independent of the categories as preceding a synthesis of apprehension in terms of the categories, seems to be based upon a much too literal reading of Kant's loose mode of statement. The argument rather appears to be, as in the sixth proof, that synthesis of the imagination may be either subjective or objective; and the term "apprehension" would seem to be used as signifying that the manifold synthesised is *given* to the imagination through actual sense experience, and that as thus given it has a determinate order of its own. The argument concludes with the statement (more definite than any to be found in the preceding arguments), that the proof of the principle of causality consists in its indispens-ableness as a condition of all empirical judgments, and so of experience as such. As a ground of the possibility of experience it must be valid of all the objects of experience.

Sixth Proof.[2]—The argument of the fifth proof is here more clearly stated. All synthesis is due to "the faculty of imagination which determines inner sense in respect of the time relation." Such synthesis may, however, yield the consciousness either of subjective succession or of succession "in the object." In the latter form it presupposes the employment of a pure concept of the understanding, that of the relation of cause and effect. And the conclusion reached is again that only so is empirical knowledge possible. This mode of stating the argument is far from satisfactory. It tends to obscure Kant's central thesis, that only through consciousness of an objective order is consciousness of subjective sequence possible, and that the principle of causality is therefore a conditioning factor of all consciousness. The misleading distinction drawn in the *Prolegomena* between

---

[1] A 201-2 = B 246-7 : fourteenth paragraph (first edition).
[2] B 233-4 : second paragraph (second edition).

judgments of perception and judgments of experience also crops out in Kant's use of the phrase "mere perception."[1]

We may again return to Kant's central argument. For we have still to consider certain objections to which it may seem to lie open, and also to comment upon Kant's further explanations in the remaining paragraphs of the section.[2] Kant's imperfect statement of his position has suggested to Hutchison Stirling and others a problem which is largely artificial, namely, how the mind is enabled to recognise the proper occasions upon which to apply the category of causality. On the one hand sequence as such cannot be the criterion, since many sequences are not causal, and on the other hand the absence of sequence does not appear to debar its application, since cause and effect would frequently seem to be co-existent. This difficulty arises from failure to appreciate the central thesis upon which Kant's proof of the principle of causality ultimately rests. Kant's diffuse and varying mode of statement may conceal but never conflicts with that thesis, which consists in the contention that the category of causality is a necessary and invariable factor in all consciousness. Nothing can be apprehended save in terms of it.[3] It prescribes an interpretation which the mind has no option save to apply in the consciousness of each and every event, of the coexistent no less than of the sequent. Whether two changes are coexistent or are successive, each must be conceived as possessing an antecedent cause. The only difference is that in the case of sequent events one of them (*i.e.* the antecedent change) may, upon empirical investigation, be found to be itself the cause of the second and subsequent event, whereas with coexistent events this can never be possible. As the principle of causality is that every event must have an antecedent cause, it follows that where there is no sequence there can be no causation. But when Kant states that sequence is "the sole empirical criterion"[4] of the causal relation, he does less than justice to the position he is defending. The empirical criteria are manifold in number, and are such as John Stuart Mill has attempted to formulate in his inductive methods.

Schopenhauer has objected[5] that Kant's argument proves too much, since it would involve that all objective sequences,

---

[1] B 233-4.   [2] From A 202 = B 247 to the end.
[3] Kant's phenomenalist substitute for the Cartesian subjectivism (cf. above, pp. 270 ff., 312 ff.) enables him to develop this thesis in a consistent and thoroughgoing manner. The subjective is a subspecies within the class of what is determined by natural law; and the principle of causality is therefore applicable to subjective change in the same rigorous fashion as to the objectively sequent.
[4] A 204 = B 249.   [5] *W.* i. pp. 87-92.

such as that of night and day or of the notes in a piece of music, are themselves causal sequences. This criticism has been replied to by Stadler[1] in the following terms:

"When Schopenhauer adduces the sequence of musical notes or of day and night, as objective sequences which can be known without the causal law, we need only meet him with the question, Where in these cases is the substance that changes? So soon as he is forced to put his objection into the form required to bring it into relation to the question of the possibility of knowledge, his error becomes obvious. His instances must then be expressed thus:—The instrument passes from one state of sound into another; the earth changes from the measure of enlightenment which makes day, to that which makes night. Of such changes no one will say that they are not referred to a cause. And we may quote in this reference the appropriate saying of Kant himself, 'Days are, as it were, the children of Time, since the following day with that which it contains is the product of the previous day.'"

Night and day, in so far as they are sequent events, must be conceived in terms of causality, not in the sense that night causes day, but as being determined by causes that account not only for each separately, but also for the alternating sequence of the one upon the other. Such causes are found by the astronomer to lie in the changing positions of the earth relatively to the sun.

Schopenhauer adds a further objection of a more subtle nature, which has again been excellently stated and answered by Stadler:

"Schopenhauer points out that what we call chance is just a sequence of events which do not stand in causal connexion. 'I come out of the house and a tile falls from the roof which strikes me; in such a case there is no causal connexion between the falling of the tile and my coming out of the house, yet the succession of these two events is objectively determined in my apprehension of them.' How have we to criticise this case from the transcendental point of view? We know that successions become necessary, *i.e.* objective, for our consciousness, when we regard them as changes of a substance which are determined by a cause. But it is shown here that there are successions in which the single members are changes of different substances. If substance S changes its state A into B on account of the cause X, and substance S′ changes its state A′ into B′ on account of the cause X′, and if I call the first change V and the second V′, the question arises how the objectivity of the succession

---

[1] *Grundsätze der reinen Erkenntniss-Theorie*, p. 151. Quoted and translated by Caird, i. p. 572. Caird sums up the matter in a sentence (p. 571): "Kant is showing, not that objective succession is always causal, but that the determination of a succession of perceptions as referring to a succession of states in an object, involves the principle of causality."

V V' is related to the law of causality. Sequences such as V V' are very frequent, and our consciousness of the objectivity is certain. Do we owe this consciousness to the same rule as holds good in other cases? Certainly. The distinction is not qualitative, but rests only on the greater complication of the change in question. The sequence V V' can become objective only if I think it as a necessary connexion. It must be so determined that V can only follow V' in 'consciousness in general'; there must be a U, the introduction of which is the cause that V' follows V. To be convinced of this, I do not need actually to know U. I know that on every occasion U causes the succession V V'. Of course, this presupposes that all data of the states considered, A and A', remain identical. But whether these data are very simple or endlessly complex, whether they are likely to combine to the given result frequently or seldom, is indifferent for the objectifying of the event; it is not the perception of U, but the presupposition of it, which makes the change necessary and so objective for us."[1]

To turn now to the other difficulty which Kant himself raises in A 202-3 = B 247-8, viz. that cause and effect would frequently seem to be coexistent, and the "sole empirical criterion" to be therefore absent. It may from this point of view be maintained that the great majority of causes occur simultaneously with their effects, and that such time sequence as occurs is due solely to the fact that the cause cannot execute itself in one single instant. Kant has little difficulty in disposing of this objection. Causality concerns only the *order*, not the *lapse*, of time; and the sequence relation must remain even though there is no interval between the two events. If a leaden ball lies upon a cushion it makes a depression in it. The ball and the depression are coexistent. None the less, when viewed in their dynamical relation, the latter must be regarded as sequent upon the former. If the leaden ball is placed upon a smooth cushion a hollow is at once made, but if a hollow exists in a cushion a ball need not appear. In other words, the criteria for the determination of specific causal relations are neither the presence nor the absence of sequence, but are empirical considerations verifiable only upon special investigation.[2] The observer is called upon to disentangle the complicated web of given appearances under the guidance of the quite general and formal principle that every event is due to some antecedent cause. He must do so as best he can through the application of his acquired insight, and, when necessary, by means of the requisite experimental variation of conditions.

In the two following paragraphs (A 204-5 = B 249-51)

---

[1] *Loc. cit.*

[2] The connected question how we can determine the ball and the cushion as objectively coexistent is the problem of the third *Analogy*.

Kant raises points which he later discussed more fully in the *Metaphysical First Principles of Natural Science.*[1] As adequate explanation of the argument would be a very lengthy matter, and not of any very real importance for the understanding of the general Critical position, we may omit all treatment of it. In the sections of the *Metaphysical First Principles* just cited, the reader will find the necessary comment and explanation. Such bearing as these two paragraphs have upon Kant's view of the nature of the causal relation has been noted above.[2]

In the section on *Anticipations of Perception*[3] Kant has stated that the principle of the continuity of change involves empirical factors, and therefore falls outside the limits of transcendental philosophy. To this more correct attitude Kant, unfortunately, did not hold. In A 207-11 = B 252-6 he professes to establish the principle in *a priori* transcendental fashion as a necessary consequence of the nature of time. This proof is indeed thrice repeated with unessential variations, thereby clearly showing that these paragraphs also are of composite origin. The argument in all three cases consists in inferring from the continuity of time the continuity of all changes in time. As the parts of time are themselves times, of which no one is the smallest, so in all generation in time, the cause must in its action pass through all the degrees of quantity from zero to that of the final effect.

"Every change has a cause which evinces its causality in the whole time in which the change takes place. This cause, therefore, does not engender the change suddenly (at once or in one moment), but in a time, so that, as the time increases from its initial moment a to its completion in b, the quantity of the reality $(b-a)$ is in like manner generated through all lesser degrees which are contained between the first and the last."[4]

This argument is inconclusive. As Kant himself recognises in regard to space,[5] we may not without special proof assume that what is true of time must be true of the contents of time. If time, change, and causation can be equated, what is true of one will be true of all three. But the assumption upon which the argument thus rests has not itself been substantiated.

In the third proof[6] the argument is stated in extreme subjectivist terms which involve the further assumption that

---

[1] III. *Erklärung* 1 and 2, *Lehrsatz* 1 (especially *Anmerkung* thereto). Cf. also II. *Erklärung* 1 and 5, and the last pages of the *Allgemeine Anmerkung.*
[2] Pp. 351, 373-4. Cf. pp. 318-21.
[3] A 170-1 = B 212-13, above, p. 353, n. 2.   [4] A 208 = B 253-4.
[5] *Metaphysical First Principles, II. Lehrsatz 4, Anmerkung 2.*
[6] A 209-10 = B 255-6.

what is true of apprehension is *ipso facto* true of everything apprehended. The possibility of establishing the law of dynamical continuity follows, Kant declares, as a consequence of its being a law of our subjective apprehension.

"We anticipate only our own apprehension, the formal condition of which, inasmuch as it inheres in the mind prior to all given appearances, must certainly be capable of being known *a priori*."[1]

Kant's attitude towards the physical principle of continuity underwent considerable change. In his *New Doctrine of Motion and Rest* (1758)[2] he maintains that it cannot be proved, and that physicists may rightly refuse to recognise it even as an hypothesis. It is in the Essay on *Negative Quantity* (1763)[3] that Kant first adopts the attitude of the *Critique*, and rejects the "speculative" objections raised against the mathematical conception of the infinitely small. In the *Metaphysical First Principles of Natural Science*[4] the principle of continuity is defended and developed, but only in its application to material existence, not in its relation to the causal process.

C. **Third Analogy.**—*All substances, in so far as they are coexistent, stand in thoroughgoing communion,*[5] *i.e. in reciprocity with one another.* Or, as in the second edition : *All substances, so far as they can be perceived to coexist in space, are in thoroughgoing reciprocity.*

This section contains four separate proofs. The first three paragraphs in the text of the first edition contain the first proof. The fourth paragraph supplies a second proof, and the fifth paragraph a third. In the second edition Kant adds a fourth proof (the first paragraph of the text of the second edition).

We may lead up to these proofs by first formulating (*a*) the fundamental assumption upon which they proceed, and (*b*) the thesis which they profess to establish. (*a*) The argument involves the same initial assumption as the preceding *Analogies*, viz. that representations exist exclusively in succession, or stated in phenomenalist terms, that the objectively coexistent can be apprehended only in and through representations that are sequent to one another in time.[6] Upon this

---

[1] A 210 = B 256.　　　　　　[2] *W.* ii. p. 22.
[3] *W.* ii. p. 168.　　　　　　[4] *Loc. cit.*
[5] For lack of a more suitable English equivalent I have translated *Gemeinschaft* as "communion." As Kant points out in A 213 = B 260, the German term is itself ambiguous, signifying *commercium* (*i.e.* dynamical interaction) as well as *communio*.
[6] Cf. above, pp. 348, 358-9, 367-8, 371-2.

assumption the problem of the third *Analogy* is to explain
how from representations all of which are in succession we
can determine the objectively coexistent. (*b*) In the *Dissertation*[1] Kant had maintained that though the possibility of
dynamical communion of substances is not necessarily involved
in their mere existence, such interaction may be assumed as
a consequence of their common origin in, and dependence
upon, a Divine Being.   In the *Critique* no such metaphysical
speculations are any longer in order, and Kant recognises
that as regards things in themselves it is not possible to
decide whether dynamical interaction is, or is not, necessarily
involved in coexistence.   The problem of this third *Analogy*
concerns only appearances, which as such must be subject to
the conditions of unitary experience ; and one such condition
is that they be apprehended as belonging to a single objective
order of nature, and therefore as standing in reciprocal
relations of interaction.   *The apprehension of substances as
reciprocally determining one another is*, Kant contends, *an
indispensable condition of their being known even as coexistent.*
Such is Kant's thesis.   The proof may first be stated in what
may be called its typical or generic form.   Kant's four
successive proofs can then be related to it as to a common
standard.

'Two things, A and B, can be apprehended as coexistent
only in so far as we can experience them in either order, *i.e.*
when the order of our perceptions of them is reversible.   If
they existed in succession, this could never be possible.   The
earlier member of a time series is past when the succeeding
member is present, and what belongs to the past can never
be an object of perception.   The fact that the order in which
things can be perceived is reversible would thus seem to prove
that they do not exist successively to one another in time.[2]
That, however, is not the case.   By itself such experience
does not really suffice to yield consciousness of coexistence.
It can yield only consciousness of an alternating succession.[3]
A further factor, namely, interpretation of the reversibility of
our perceptions as due to their being conditioned by objects
which stand in the relation of reciprocal determination, must
first be postulated.   If these objects mutually determine one
another to be what they are, no one of them can be antecedent
to or subsequent upon the others ; and by their mutual
reference each will date the others as simultaneous with
itself.   In other words, the perception of the coexistence of

[1] § 17 ff. Cf. *Nachträge zu Kants Kritik*, lxxxvi, with B. Erdmann's comment, p. 35.

[2] A 211-12 = B 258.   Cf. A 211 = B 257.   [3] A 211 = B 257.

objects involves the conception of them as mutually determining one another. The principle of communion or reciprocity conditions the experience of coexistence, and is therefore valid for objects apprehended in that manner.

Kant also maintains, more by implication than by explicit statement, that as A and B need not stand in any direct relation, the apprehension of them as coexistent involves the conception of an all-embracing order of nature within which they fall and which determines them to be what they are. If any one of them, even the most minute and insignificant, were conceived as altered, corresponding simultaneous variations would have to be postulated for all the others. The unity of the phenomenal world is the counterpart of the unity of apperception. Unity of experience involves principles which prescribe a corresponding unity in the natural realm. Dynamical *communion* is the sufficient and necessary fulfilment of this demand. It carries to completion the unity demanded by the preceding *Analogies* of *substance* and *causality*. Kant sums up his position in a note to A 218 = B 265.

"The unity of the world-whole, in which all appearances have to be connected, is evidently a mere consequence of the tacitly assumed principle of the communion of all substances which are coexistent. For if they were isolated, they would not as parts constitute a whole. And if their coexistence alone did not necessitate their connection (the reciprocal action of the manifold) we could not argue from the former, which is a merely ideal relation, to the latter, which is a real relation. We have, however, in the proper context, shown that communion is really the ground of the possibility of an empirical knowledge of coexistence, and that therefore the actual inference is merely from this empirical knowledge to communion as its condition."

To turn now to Kant's successive proofs. The first[1] calls for no special comment. It coincides with the above. The second[2] proof is an incompletely stated argument, which differs from the first only in its more concrete statement of the main thesis and in its limitation of the argument to spatial existences. Dynamical community is the indispensable condition of our apprehension of any merely spatial side-by-sideness. Kant now adds that it is the dynamical continuity of the *spatial* world which enables us to apprehend the coexistence of its constituents. The important bearing of this argument we shall consider in its connection with the proof which Kant added in the second edition.

[1] A 211-13 = B 258-60 : first three paragraphs (first edition).
[2] A 213-14 = B 260-1 : fourth paragraph (first edition).

The third[1] proof is probably the earliest in date of writing. It draws a misleading distinction between subjective and objective coexistence, and seems to argue that only the latter form of coexistence need presuppose the employment of the category of reciprocity.   That runs directly counter to the central thesis of the other proofs, that only in terms of dynamical relation is coexistence at all apprehensible.   That the above distinction indicates an early date of writing would seem to be confirmed by the obscure phrase "community of apperception" which is reminiscent of the prominence given to apperception in Kant's earlier views, and by the concluding sentence in which Kant employs terms—inherence, consequence, and composition—that are also characteristic of the earlier stages of his Critical enquiries.[2]

It is significant that in the new argument[3] of the second edition the space factor, emphasised in the second proof of the first edition, is again made prominent.[4]   The principle is, indeed, reformulated in such manner as to suggest its limitation to spatial existences.   "All substances, so far as they can be perceived to coexist *in space*, are in thoroughgoing reciprocity." Now it is decidedly doubtful whether Kant means to limit the category of reciprocity to spatial existences.   As we have already noted,[5] he would seem to hold that though the category of causality can *acquire* meaning only in its application to events in space, it may in its subsequent employment be extended to the states of inner sense.   The latter are effects dynamically caused, and among their causal conditions are mechanical processes in space.   The extension of the category of reciprocity to include sensations and desires undoubtedly gives rise to much greater difficulties than those involved in the universal application of the causal principle.   On the other hand, its limitation to material bodies must render the co-ordination of mental states and mechanical processes highly doubtful, and would carry with it all the difficulties of an epiphenomenal view of psychical existences.   The truth probably is that in this matter Kant had not thought out his position in any quite definite manner; and that owing to the influence, on the one hand of the dualistic teaching of the traditional Cartesian physics, and on the other of his increasing appreciation of the part which space must play in the defini-

---

[1] A 214-15 = B 261-2 : fifth paragraph (first edition).
[2] Cf. above, pp. 189-90, 208 ff.   [3] B 257-8 : first paragraph (second edition).
[4] Cf. B 291-3, partially quoted above, pp. 310-11.   In the *Metaphysical First Principles* (*III. Lehrsatz*, 4) the principle that action and reaction are always equal is similarly limited to the outer relations of material bodies in space, and Kant adds that all change in bodies is motion.   Cf. *W.* xi. p. 234 ; and above, p. 147.
[5] Above pp. 311-12; below, pp. 473-7.

tion and proof of the principles of understanding, he limited the category of reciprocity to spatial existences, without considering how far such procedure is capable of being reconciled with his determinist view of the empirical self. His procedure is also open to a second objection, namely, that while thus reformulating the principle, he fails to remodel his proof in a sufficiently thoroughgoing fashion. The chief stress is still laid upon the temporal element; and in order to obtain a proof of the principle that will harmonise with the prominence given to the space-factor, we are thrown back upon such supplementary suggestions as we can extract from the second argument of the first edition. It is there stated that "without dynamical communion even spatial community (*communio spatii*) could never be known empirically."[1] This is an assertion which, if true, will yield a proof of the principle of reciprocity analogous to that which has been given of the principle of causality; for it will show that just as the conception of causality is involved in, and makes possible, the awareness of time, so the conception of reciprocity is involved in, and makes possible, the awareness of space.

The proof will be as follows. The parts of space have to be conceived as spatially interrelated. Space is not a collection of independent spaces; particular spaces exist only in and through the spaces which enclose them. In other words, the parts of space mutually condition one another. Each part exists only in and through its relations, direct or indirect, to all the others; the awareness of their coexistence involves the awareness of this reciprocal determination. But space cannot, any more than time, be known in and by itself;[2] and what is true of space must therefore hold of the contents, in terms of the interrelations of which space can alone be experienced. How, then, can the reciprocal determination of substances in space be apprehended by a consciousness which is subject in all its experiences to the conditions of time? As Kant has pointed out in A 211 = B 258,[3] objective coexistence is distinguished from objective sequence by reversibility of the perceptions through which it is apprehended. When A and B coexist, our perceptions can begin with A and pass to B, or start from B and proceed to A. There is also, as Kant observes in the second proof, a further condition, namely, that the transition is in each case made through a *continuous* series of changing perceptions.

[1] A 213 = B 260.
[2] The inconsistency of Kant's view of pure manifolds of time and space with the argument of the *Analytic of Principles* is too obvious to call for detailed comment.
[3] Cf. B 257.

"Only the continuous influences in all parts of space can lead
our senses from one object to another. The light, which plays
between our eye and the celestial bodies, produces a mediate communion between us and them, and thereby establishes the coexistence
of the latter. We cannot empirically change our position (perceive
such a change), unless matter in all parts of space makes the perception of our position possible to us. Only by means of its reciprocal
influence can matter establish the simultaneous existence of its parts,
and thereby, though only mediately, their coexistence with even the
most remote objects. Without communion, every perception of an
appearance in space is broken off from every other, and the chain of
empirical representations, *i.e.* experience, would have to begin entirely
anew with every new object, without the least connection with preceding representations, and without standing to them in any relation
of time."[1]

But even such reversibility of *continuous* series does not by
itself establish coexistence. For in the imagination[2] we can
represent such series, without thereby acquiring the right to
assert that they exist not as series but as simultaneous wholes.
And as Kant might also have pointed out, even in sense-perception we can experience reversible continuous series that do
not in any way justify the inference to coexistence. We may,
for instance, produce on a musical instrument a series of continuously changing sounds, and then in immediate succession
produce the same series in reverse order. An additional factor
is therefore required, namely, the interpretation of the reversibility of our perceptions as being grounded in objects which,
because spatially extended, and spatially continuous with one
another, can yield continuous series of perceptions, and which,
because of their thoroughgoing reciprocity, make possible the
reversing of these series. To summarise the argument in a
sentence: as the objectively coexistent, if it is to be known
at all, can only be known through sequent representations, the
condition of its apprehension is the possibility of interpreting
reversible continuous series as due to the reciprocal interaction
of spatially ordered substances.

This argument has a twofold bearing. Its most obvious
consequence is that all things apprehended as coexistent must
be conceived as standing in relations of reciprocal interaction;
but by implication this involves the further consequence that
the conceptual principle of reciprocity is an integral factor in
all apprehension of space. Space, though intuitive in character, has a meaning that demands this concept for its articulation. Just as consciousness of temporal sequence is only
possible in terms of causation, so consciousness of spatial

[1] A 213-14 = B 260-1.   [2] B 257.

coexistence is only possible through application of the category of reciprocity. And since, on Kant's view, awareness of space conditions awareness of time, these conclusions carry the Critical analysis of our consciousness of time a stage further. In confirmation of the more general argument of the objective deduction, reciprocity is added to the already large sum-total of the indispensable conditions of our time-consciousness; while in regard to time itself it is shown that, owing to its space-reference, coexistence may be counted among its possible modes.

I have made occasional reference to the positions adopted by Stout in his *Manual of Psychology*, and may here indicate their relation to the present argument. Stout cites four "categories" or ultimate principles of unity which "belong even to rudimentary perceptual consciousness as a condition of its further development,"[1] namely, spatial unity, temporal unity, causal unity, and the unity of different attributes as belonging to the same thing. The criticism which, from the standpoint of the *Analogies*, has to be passed upon this list,[2] is that it ignores the category of reciprocity, *i.e.* of systematic interconnection, and that it fails to recognise the close relation in which the various principles stand to one another. The temporal unity must not be isolated from causal unity, nor either of them from the spatial unity, with which the category of reciprocity is inseparably bound up. Further, Kant maintains that these principles are demanded, not merely for the *development* of perceptual consciousness, but for its very existence.

But Kant's argument suggests many difficulties which we have not yet considered, and we may again employ Schopenhauer's criticisms to define the issues involved.

"The conception of reciprocity ought to be banished from metaphysics. For I now intend, quite seriously, to prove that there is no reciprocity in the strict sense, and this conception, which people are so fond of using, just on account of the indefiniteness of the thought, is seen, if more closely considered, to be empty, false, and invalid. . . . It implies that both the states A and B are cause and that both are effect of each other; but this really amounts to saying that each of the two is the earlier and also the later; thus it is an absurdity."[3]

This criticism proceeds on the assumption that the category of reciprocity reduces to a dual application of the category of causality. If that were the case, there would, of course, be no

---

[1] Third edition, p. 438.
[2] Stout does not himself offer it as complete.
[3] *World as Will and Idea*, W. ii. pp. 544-5: Eng. trans. ii. pp. 61-3.

separate category of reciprocity,[1] and further it would, as Schopenhauer maintains, be impossible to regard A and B as being at one and the same time both cause and effect of one another. Causality determines the order of the states of substances in the time series; reciprocity must be distinct from causality if it is to be capable of defining the order of their coexistent states in space. A deduction from the dual application of the conception of causality has, therefore, no bearing upon the question of the possibility of this further category. Kant has laid himself open to this criticism by a passage which occurs in the first proof, and which shows that he was not quite clear in his own mind as to how reciprocity ought to be conceived.

"That alone can determine the position of anything else in time, which is its cause or the cause of its determinations. Every substance (inasmuch as only in its determinations can it be an effect) must therefore contain in itself the causality of certain determinations in the other substance, and at the same time the effects of the causality of that other, *i.e.* they must stand in dynamical communion (immediately or mediately), if their coexistence is to be known in any possible experience."[2]

It should be noted that in the new proof[3] in the second edition Kant is careful to employ the terms ground and influence in place of the terms cause and causality.

Secondly, Schopenhauer argues that if the two states necessarily belong to each other and exist at one and the same time, they will not be simultaneous, but will constitute only *one* state.[4] Schopenhauer is again refusing to recognise the conditions under which alone a special category of reciprocity is called for. We can speak of simultaneity only if a *multiplicity* be given; and if it be given, its nature as *simultaneous plurality* cannot be comprehended through a causal law, which, as such, applies only to sequent order.

Lastly, Schopenhauer endeavours to confirm his position by examination of the supposed instances of reciprocity.

"[In the continuous burning of a fire] the combination of oxygen with the combustible body is the cause of heat, and heat, again, is the cause of the renewed occurrence of the chemical combination. But this is nothing more than a chain of causes and effects, the links of which have alternately *the same name.* . . . We see before us only an application of the single and simple law of causality which gives the rule to the sequence of states, but never anything

---

[1] Cf. above, p. 197.
[2] B 258.
[3] A 212-13 = B 259.
[4] *Op. cit.* pp. 545-6: Eng. trans. p. 63.

which must be comprehended by means of a new and special function of the understanding." [1]

Schopenhauer is again misled by his equating of reciprocity with causal action. Combustion is quite obviously a case of sequent processes. Instead of proving that coexistence does not involve reciprocity, Schopenhauer is only showing that cause and effect may sometimes, as Kant himself observes,[2] seem to be simultaneous.[3] Action *followed by* reaction is not equivalent to what Kant means by reciprocal determination. Schopenhauer also cites the instance of a pair of scales brought to rest by equal weights.

"Here there is no effect produced, for there is no change; it is a state of rest; gravity acts, equally divided, as in every body which is supported at its centre of gravity, but it cannot show its force by any effect." [4]

This example is more in line with what Kant would seem to have in view, but is still defined in reference to the problem of causation, and not in reference to that of coexistence. Kant is not enquiring whether coexistent bodies are related as causes and effects, though, as we have already observed, his language betrays considerable lack of clearness on this very point. He is endeavouring to define the conditions under which we are enabled to recognise that bodies, external to one another in space and apprehensible only through sequent perceptions, are none the less coexistent. And the answer which he gives is that coexistence can only be determined by reference of each existence to the totality of systematic relations within which it is found, its particular spatial location being one of the factors which condition this reference. Causal explanation in the most usual meaning of that highly ambiguous phrase, namely, as explanation of an artificially isolated event by reference to antecedents similarly isolated from their context, may partially account for this event being of one kind rather than another, but will not explain why it is to be found at this particular time in this particular place. That is to say, it will not answer the question which is asked when we are enquiring as to what events are coexistent with it.

But the considerations which thus enable us to dispose of Schopenhauer's criticisms have the effect of involving us in new, and much more formidable, difficulties. Indeed they disclose the incomplete, and quite inadequate, character of

---

[1] *Op. cit.* pp. 546-7 : Eng. trans. pp. 63-5.
[2] Cf. above, p. 379.   [3] Cf. Stadler, *Grundsätze*, p. 124.
[4] *Op. cit.* p. 546 : Eng. trans. p. 63.

Kant's proof of the third *Analogy*. For must not spatial co-existence be independently known if it is to serve as one of the factors determinant of reciprocity? And yet, can the apprehension of extended bodies wait upon a prior knowledge of the system of nature to which they belong?

The mere propounding of these questions does not, how-ever, suffice to overthrow Kant's contention. For he is prepared—that is indeed the reason why the *Critique* came to be written—to answer them in a manner that had never before been suggested, save perhaps in the philosophies of Plato and Aristotle. This answer first emerges in the *Dialectic*, in the course of its treatment of the wider problem, of which the above difficulties are only special instances, how if conditioned parts can only be known in terms of an un-conditioned whole, any knowledge whatsoever can be ac-quired by us. But 'though Kant in the *Dialectic* gives due prominence to this fundamental problem, the hard and fast divisions of his architectonic—and doubtless other influences which would be difficult to define—intervene to prevent him from recognising its full implications. For the problem is viewed in the *Dialectic* as involving considerations altogether different from those dwelt upon in the *Analogies*, and as being without application to the matters of which they treat.

The situation thus created is very similar to that which is occasioned by Kant's unfortunate separation of the problems of space and time in the *Aesthetic* from the treatment of the categories in the *Analytic*. In the *Aesthetic* space and time are asserted to be intuitive, not conceptual, in nature; and yet in the *Analytic* we find Kant demonstrating that the principles of causality and reciprocity are indispensably in-volved in their apprehension. But even more misleading is the separation of the problems of the *Aesthetic* and *Analytic* from those of the *Dialectic*. Kant's primary and prevailing interest is in the metaphysics, not in the mere methodology, of experience; and it is in the *Dialectic* that the meta-physical principles which underlie and inspire all his other tenets first find adequate statement. Since the third *Analogy* defines the criterion of coexistence in entire independence of all reference to the Ideas of Reason, Kant is thereby precluded from even so much as indicating the true grounds upon which his position, if it is to be really tenable, must be made to rest. For as he ultimately came to recognise, the intuition of space not only involves the conceptual category of reciprocal determination, but likewise demands for its possibility an Idea of Reason. In space the wider whole is always prior in thought to the parts which go to constitute it. But though Kant states[1] that this characteristic of space justifies its being entitled an Idea of Reason, he nowhere takes notice of the obvious and very important bearing which this must have upon the problem, how we are to formulate the criterion of coexistence.

The general character of time is analogous to that of space, and our formulation of the criterion of causal sequence is therefore similarly affected. The system of nature is not the outcome of natural laws which are independently valid; natural laws are the expression of what this system prescribes; they are the modes in which it defines and embodies its inherent necessities.

The situation which these considerations would seem to disclose may, therefore, be stated as follows. If the empirical criteria of truth are independent of the Ideas of Reason, the *Analytic* may be adequate to their discussion, but will be unable to justify the assertion that there is a category of reciprocal or systematic connection distinct from that of causality. If, however, it should be found that these criteria are merely special applications of standards *metaphysical in character*—and that would seem to be Kant's final conclusion, —only in the light of the wider considerations first broached in the *Dialectic*, can we hope to define their nature and implications with any approach to completeness.

4. THE POSTULATES OF EMPIRICAL THOUGHT IN GENERAL

First Postulate.—*That which agrees, in intuition and in concepts, with the formal conditions of experience is possible.*

Second Postulate.—*That which is connected with the material conditions of experience (that is, with sensation) is actual.*

Third Postulate.—*That which is determined, in its connection with the actual, according to universal conditions of experience is (that is, exists as) necessary.*

In this section Kant maintains that when the Critical standpoint is accepted, possibility, actuality and necessity can only be defined in terms of the conditions which render sense-experience possible. In other words, the Critical position, that all truth, even that of *a priori* principles, is merely *de facto*, involves acceptance of the view that the actual reduces to the experienced, and that only by reference to the actual as thus given can possibility and necessity be defined. The Leibnizian view that possibility is capable of being defined

[1] Cf. above, pp. 97-8, 102 *n.*, 165-6; below, pp. 429 ff., 447 ff., 547 ff.

independently of the actual, and antecedently to all knowledge of it, must be rejected.

An analysis of the text can be profitably made only after a detailed examination of Kant's general argument; and to that task we may at once apply ourselves. The section affords further illustration of the perverting influence of Kant's architectonic, as well as of the insidious manner in which the older rationalism continued to pervert his thinking in his less watchful moments.

First Postulate.—In the opening paragraphs Kant uses (as it would seem without consciousness of so doing) the term possibility in two very different senses.[1] When the possible is distinguished from the actual and the necessary, it acquires the meaning defined in this first *Postulate*; it is "that which agrees with the *formal* conditions of experience." But it is also employed in a much narrower sense to signify that which can have "objective reality, *i.e.* transcendental truth."[2] The possibility of the objectively real rests upon fulfilment of a threefold condition: (1) that it agree with the formal conditions of experience; (2) that it stand in connection with the material of the sensuous conditions of experience; and (3) that it follow with necessity upon some preceding state in accordance with the principle of causality, and so form part of a necessitated order of nature. In other words, it must be causally necessitated in order to be empirically actual; and only the empirically actual is genuinely possible. Such is also the meaning that usually attaches to the term possible in the other sections of the *Critique*. A 'possible experience' is one that can become actual when the specific conditions, all of which must themselves be possible, are fulfilled. An experience which is not capable of being actual has no right to be described even as possible. As a term applicable to the objectively real, the possible is not wider than the actual, but coextensive with it. As Kant himself remarks, those terms refer exclusively to differences in the subjective attitude of the apprehending mind.

This ambiguity in the term 'possibility' has caused a corresponding ambiguity in Kant's employment of the term 'actuality.' It leads him to endeavour to define the actual, not in its connection with the conditions of possibility, but in distinction from them. The possible having been defined (in the first *Postulate*) solely in terms of the *formal* factors of experience, he proceeds to characterise the actual in a similarly one-sided fashion, exclusively in terms of the

---

[1] Cf. Adickes, *K.* p. 233 *n.*
[2] A 222 = B 269. Cf. A 220 = B 268.

material element of given sensation. Doubtless the element of sensation must play a prominent part in enabling us to decide what is or is not actually existent, but no definition which omits to take account of relational factors can be an adequate expression of Critical teaching. Indeed, we only require to substitute the words 'sensuously given' for 'actual' in Kant's definition of the third *Postulate* (*i.e.* of the necessary) in order to obtain a correct statement of the true Critical view of actual existence: it is "that which is determined in its connection with the sensuously given according to universal conditions of experience." For Kant the actual and the necessary, objectively viewed, coincide. Necessity is for the human mind always merely *de facto*; and nothing can be objectively actual that is not causally determined. As the empirically possible cannot, in its objective reference, be wider than the empirically necessary, one and the same definition adequately covers all three terms alike. While the distinctions between them will, of course, remain, they will be applicable, not to objects, but only to the subjective conditions of experience in so far as these may vary from one ndividual to another. Experiences capable of being actual for one individual may be merely possible for another. And what is merely actual to one observer may by others be comprehended in its necessitating connections. The terms will not denote differences in the real, but only variations in the cognitive attitude of the individual.

Thus in professing to show that the three *Postulates* are transcendental *principles*, Kant does less than justice to his own teaching. For though both here and in the opening sections of the chapter[1] he speaks of them in this manner, *i.e.* as being conditions alike of ordinary and of scientific experience, he has himself admitted in so many words the inappropriateness of such a description.

"The principles of modality are nothing more than explanations [not, it may be noted, proofs] of the concepts of possibility, actuality and necessity, in their empirical use, and are therefore at the same time restrictions of all the categories to this merely empirical use, ruling out and forbidding their transcendental [=transcendent] employment."[2]

That is to say, these so-called principles are not really principles; they merely embody explanatory statements designed to render the preceding results more definite, and especially to guard against the illegitimate meanings which the Leibnizian metaphysics had attached to certain of the terms involved.

[1] A 148 ff. = B 187 ff.   [2] A 219 = B 266.

These considerations bring us to the real source of Kant's perverse argumentation, namely, the artificial (but none the less imperious) demands of his architectonic. He is constrained to provide a set of *principles* corresponding to the categories of modality. The definitions of the modal categories have therefore to be called by that inappropriate name. But that is not the end of the matter. In order to meet the needs of his logical framework, Kant proceeds even further than he had ventured to do in the sections on the *Axioms of Intuition* and *Anticipations of Perception*. There he fell so far short as to provide only a single principle in each case. In dealing, however, with the categories of relation he has been able to define each of the three categories separately, and to derive from each a separate principle. Many of the defects in his argument are, indeed, traceable to this source. The close interrelations of the three principles are, as we have had occasion to note, seriously obscured. But still, in the main, separate treatment of each has proved feasible. Kant, encouraged, as we may believe, by this successful fulfilment of architectonic requirements, now sets himself to develop, in similar fashion, a separate principle for each modal category. But for any such enterprise the conditions are less favourable than in the case of the categories of relation. For, as just indicated, no one of the three can, on Critical principles, possess any genuine meaning save in its relation to the others. Before following out this line of criticism, we must however note some further points in Kant's argument.

In A 219 = B 266, and again in A 225 = B 272, Kant makes the statement that a concept can be complete prior to any decision as to its possibility, actuality, or necessity. This contention is capable of being interpreted in two quite independent ways, and in only one of those ways is it tenable. He may mean that the distinction between the possible, the actual, and the necessary, does not concern the objectively real, which as such is always both actual and necessary, but only the subjective attitude of the individual towards the objects of his thought and experience. From the Critical standpoint, as we have been arguing, such a contention is entirely just. But Kant would seem in the above statement to be chiefly concerned to maintain that a conception may be complete and determinate, even while we remain in doubt whether the existence for which it stands is even possible.[1] Such a view is merely a relic of the Leibnizian rationalism

---

[1] This, by Kant's own account (A 232-4 = B 285-7), is what led him to adopt the title 'postulates.' A geometrical postulate does not add anything to the concept of its object but only defines the conditions of its production.

from which he is striving to break away. All existences have their place in a systematic order of experience, and no conception of them can be either complete or determinate which fails to specify the causal context to which they belong. The process of specifying the detail of a concept is the only process whereby we can define its possibility, actuality, or necessity.[1] Were it capable of complete statement without determination of its modal character, it could never form part of a unified experience. The examples of "fictitious" concepts, which Kant cites, are either so determinate as to be demonstrably inconsistent with experience, and therefore empirically impossible, or so indeterminate as to afford no sufficient means of deciding even as to their possibility.

There is a further objection to the definition given of possibility in the first *Postulate*. After stating that the possible is what *agrees* with the formal conditions of experience, Kant proceeds, on the one hand, to argue that the forms of intuition and the categories of understanding may, in accordance with this criterion, be viewed as possible, and, on the other hand, to maintain that no other concepts can be so regarded.[2] That is to say, the possible, as thus interpreted, does not consist in something additional to, and in harmony with, the conditions of experience, but reduces without remainder to those very forms. Now Kant is not betrayed merely by inadvertence into thus narrowing the sphere of the possible ; such limitation is an almost inevitable consequence of the one-sided manner in which he has treated the concept of the possible in this first *Postulate*. He professes to be proceeding in the light of the results obtained in the transcendental deduction, and to be defining the possible in terms of the conditions which make sense - experience possible. But the deduction has shown that experience is possible only in so far as the material factors co-operate with the formal. And when this is recognised, it becomes obvious that a definition of the possible in terms of sensation,— namely, as that which is capable of being presented in sense-perception,—is equally legitimate, and is indeed required in order to correct the deficiencies of the definition which Kant has himself given. As both factors are indispensable in all possible experience, both must be reckoned with in defining the possible.

Kant's argument in the fifth paragraph is somewhat obscured by its context. He is contending that fictitious (*gedichtete*) concepts, elaborated from the contents presented in perception, cannot be determined as possible. As they

---

[1] Cf. above, pp. 38-9 ; below, pp. 398-9, 418 ff.   [2] Cf. A 220-3 = B 267-71.

involve sensuous contents, the formal elements of experience do not suffice for proof of their possibility; and since the contents are supposed to have been recombined in ways not supported by experience, an empirical criterion is equally inapplicable. Obviously Kant is here using the term 'possible' not in the meaning of the first *Postulate*, but in its narrower connotation as signifying that which is capable of objective reality. Such fictitious concepts may completely fulfil all the demands prescribed by space, time, and the categories, and yet, as he here insists, be none the less incapable of objective existence.

The argument is still further obscured by the character of the concrete examples which Kant cites. They involve modes of action or of intuition which contradict the very conditions of human experience, and so for that reason alone fall outside the realm of the empirically possible. That would not, however, seem to be Kant's meaning in employing them. Assumed powers of anticipating the future or of telepathic communication with other minds are, he says, concepts

". . . the possibility of which is altogether groundless, as they cannot be based on experience and its known laws, and without such confirmation are arbitrary combinations of thoughts, which, although indeed free from contradiction, can make no claim to objective reality and so to the possibility of an object such as we here profess to think." [1]

The mathematical examples which Kant gives in A 223 = B 271 [2] are no less misleading. The concept of a triangle can, it is implied, be determined as possible in terms of the first *Postulate*, since it harmonises with a formal condition of experience, namely, space. This is true only if it be granted that construction in space can be executed absolutely *a priori*, in independence of all sense-experience. Such is, of course, Kant's most usual view; and to that extent the argument is consistent. Mathematical concepts will from this point of view represent the only possible exception to the general statement that the formal conditions of experience constitute a criterion of possibility for no concepts save themselves. Kant's final conclusion is clearly and explicitly stated in the following terms:

"I leave aside everything the possibility of which can be derived only from its reality in experience, and have here in view only the possibility of things through *a priori* concepts; and I maintain the thesis that the possibility of such things can never be established

---

[1] A 223 = B 270.　　　　　[2] Cf. A 220 = B 268.

from such concepts taken in and by themselves, but only when they are viewed as formal and objective conditions of experience in general." [1]

We are now in a position to appreciate the reasons which have induced Adickes to regard the text as of composite origin. [2] Adickes argues that Kant's original intention was to treat the three concepts together, showing that they can be defined only in empirical terms, and that their significance is consequently limited to the world of appearance. Such is the content of the first, second, fourth (excepting the first sentence), and fifth paragraphs. No attempt is made to separate the three *Postulates*, and the term possibility is throughout employed exclusively as referring to objective reality. (In the third paragraph it is used in both senses.) The other paragraphs were, according to Adickes' theory, added later, when Kant unfortunately resolved to fulfil more exactly the requirements of his architectonic. That involved the formulation of three separate *Postulates*, with all the many evil consequences which that attempt carried in its train. He must then have interpolated the third paragraph, added the first sentence to the fourth paragraph, corrected the too extensive sweep of the older paragraphs through the introduction of the sixth paragraph, further supplemented the exposition of the first *Postulate* by the seventh paragraph, and added independent treatments of the postulates of actuality and necessity. This may seem a very complicated and hazardous hypothesis ; but careful examination of the text, with due recognition of the confused character of the argument as it stands, will probably convince the reader that Adickes is in the right.

Second Postulate. [3]—Perception is necessary to all determination of actuality. The actual is either itself given in perception or can be shown, in accordance with the *Analogies*, to stand within the unity of objective experience, in connection with what is thus given. So long as Kant expresses himself in these terms his statements are entirely valid. Nothing which cannot be shown to be bound up with the contingent material of sense-experience can be admitted as actual. He proceeds, however, to give a definition of actuality which entirely omits all reference to the *Analogies*, and which is open to the same fundamental criticism as his characterisation of possibility in the first *Postulate*. Though the earlier statements give due recognition both to the material content and to the relational forms constitutive of complete experience,

---

[1] A 223=B 270-1.   [2] *K.* p. 223 *n.*   [3] A 224=B 272.

Kant now contrasts the mere or bare (*blosser*) concept and the given perception in a manner which suggests the unfortunate distinction drawn in the *Prolegomena*, and repeated in the second edition of the *Critique*, between judgments of perception and judgments of experience.[1] Kant's reference to "the mere concept of a thing"[2] is on the same lines as the opening paragraph of the section. However complete the concept may be, it yields not the least ground for deciding as to the existence of its object.

Kant's thinking, as I have already pointed out, is here perverted by the continuing influence of the Leibnizian rationalism. He is forgetting that, on Critical principles, even the categories are meaningless except in their reference to the contingently given. If that be true of the strictly *a priori*, it must hold with even greater force of empirical concepts with sensuous content. As the sole legitimate function of concepts, whether *a priori* or empirical, is to organise and unify the material of sense, there can be no such thing as the mere or bare concept. Such a combination of words is without Critical significance. A concept as such must refer to, and embody insight into, the real. Only in proportion to its incompleteness, that is, to its indefiniteness, can it remain without specific and quite determinate location within the context of unified experience. It may, indeed, be found convenient to retain the phrase "mere concept" notwithstanding its misleading character and rationalistic origin. It must, however, be used only to mark the indefiniteness, indeterminateness, or incompleteness which prevents it from adequately revealing the denotation to which through the nature of its content it necessarily refers. Meaning and existence, connotation and denotation, are complementary the one to the other, and though not, perhaps, coextensive (if that term has itself meaning in this connection), are none the less inseparably conjoined. When Kant's utterances, as frequently happens, imply the contrary, they may be taken as revealing the strength and insidious tenacity of the influences from which he was sufficiently courageous, but not always sufficiently watchful, to break away.

The doctrine of the "mere concept" finds its natural supplement in the equally un-Critical assertion that

". . . perception [evidently employed in the less pregnant sense, as signifying 'sensation accompanied by consciousness'], which supplies the content to the concept, is *the sole characteristic of actuality*."[3]

---

[1] Cf. above, pp. 288-9.   [2] A 225 = B 272. Cf. above, pp. 394-6.
[3] A 225 = B 273. Italics not in Kant. Cf. above, p. 323.

This same position is expressed equally strongly by Kant in his *Reflexionen* (ii. 1095).

> "Possibility is thought without being given; actuality is given without being thought; necessity is given through being thought."

Such statements are entirely out of harmony with Kant's central teaching. There is no lack of passages in the *Critique* which inculcate the direct contrary. Though the element of sensation is a *sine qua non* of all experience of the actual, the formal elements are no less indispensable. In their absence the merely given would reduce to less than a dream; for even in dreams images are interpreted and are referred to some connected context. The given, merely as such, cannot enter the field of consciousness, and is therefore "for us as good as nothing." As Caird has pointed out, we find in Kant

> ". . . two apparently contradictory forms of expression—(1) that the understanding by means of its conceptions refers our preceptions to objects, and (2) that conceptions are referred to objects only indirectly through perceptions. The former mode of expression is preferred whenever Kant has to show that 'perceptions without conceptions are blind'; the latter when he has to show that 'conceptions without perceptions are empty.'"[1] "We can understand the possibility of Kant's looking at the subject in these two opposite ways, only if we remember the reciprocal presupposition of perception and conception in the judgment of knowledge, and the way in which Kant tries to explain it, now from the point of view of perception, and now from the point of view of conception. The effect of this is, no doubt, a formal contradiction which Kant himself never disentangles, but which *we* must endeavour to disentangle, if we would do justice to him."[2]

The one-sidedness of Kant's definition of actuality is certainly due to the cause suggested by Caird. The definition, notwithstanding its misleading character, serves to enforce against the older rationalism, with which Kant throughout this section is almost exclusively concerned, the central tenet through which the Critical teaching is distinguished from that of Leibniz, namely, that neither existence, possibility, nor necessity, can be established save by reference to the contingent nature of the sensuously given. Proof by reference to the possibility of experience can establish only those conditions which can be shown to be *de facto* necessary in order that consciousness of time may be accounted for. The formal conditions of experience, which in and by themselves

---

[1] *The Critical Philosophy of Kant*, i. p. 591.   [2] *Op. cit.* p. 595.

are determinable neither as actual nor as possible, are established as actual, and so as necessary, by reference to the merely given; they are necessary only in this merely relative fashion, as being indispensable to what can never itself be viewed as other than contingent.

"Our knowledge of the existence of things reaches, then, only so far as perception and its continuation according to laws of nature can extend. If we do not start from experience, or do not proceed according to laws of the empirical connection of appearances, our guessing or enquiring into the existence of anything will only be an idle pretence."[1]

Polemically, therefore, Kant's formulation of the second *Postulate* is not without its advantages, though from the inner standpoint of Critical teaching it is altogether inadequate.

For comment upon A 226 = B 273, and upon the general teaching of this *Postulate* in its important bearing upon Kant's phenomenalism, cf. above, pp. 318-19.

B 274-9.—*Refutation of Idealism*, cf. above, p. 308 ff.

Third Postulate.[2]—In the opening sentence Kant draws the distinction which was lacking in his treatment of the first *Postulate* between 'material' and 'formal' modality. (No distinction, however, is drawn between the 'formal' possibility of the first *Postulate* and logical possibility, which consists in absence of contradiction.) It is with the former alone that we have to deal. As existence cannot be determined completely *a priori*, necessity can never be known from concepts, but only by reference to the actually given, in accordance with the universal principles that condition experience. Further, since such empirical necessity does not concern the existence of substances, but only the existence of their states, viewed as dynamically caused, the criterion of empirical necessity reduces to the second *Analogy*, viz. that everything which happens is determined by an antecedent empirical cause. This criterion does not extend beyond the field of possible experience, and even within that field applies only to those existences which can be viewed as effects, *i.e.* as *events* which come into existence in time, and of which therefore the causes are of the same temporal and conditioned character. The necessity is a hypothetical necessity; given an empirical event, it can always be legitimately viewed as necessitated by an antecedent empirical cause.

Kant introduces, reinterprets, and in this altered form

---

[1] A 226 = B 273-4.　　　[2] A 226 ff. = B 279 ff.

professes to justify, four of the central principles of the Leibnizian metaphysics. *In mundo non datur casus* gives expression to the above empirical principle. *Non datur fatum* may be taken as meaning that natural (*i.e.* empirical) necessity is a conditioned and therefore comprehensible necessity, and is consequently not rightly described as blind. The other two principles, *non datur saltus*, and *non datur hiatus* connect with the principle of continuity already established in the *Anticipations of Perception* and in the second *Analogy*.

Kant's further remarks reveal an uneasy feeling that he is neglecting to assign these principles to the pigeon-holes provided in his architectonic. The reader, he states, may easily do so for himself. That may be so, but only if the reader be permitted the same high-handed methods of adjustment that are here illustrated in Kant's location of *non datur fatum* with the principles of modality.[1]

In the next paragraph (A 230 = B 282) Kant suddenly, without warning or explanation, attaches to the term possibility a meaning altogether different from any yet assigned to it. He now takes it as equivalent to the absolutely or metaphysically possible. Combining this with the meanings previously given to it by Kant we obtain the following table :—

Possibility

Logical : equivalent to absence of contradiction.

Empirical : in the wider sense, equivalent to agreement with the formal conditions of experience; in the narrower or stricter sense, involving in addition the capacity of being presented in sense-experience.

Metaphysical : equivalent to absolute possibility, a conception not of understanding but of Reason.

When this last meaning is given to the term, an entirely new set of problems arises, to the confusion of the reader who very properly continues to employ the term possibility in the empirical sense which, as Kant has been insisting, is alone legitimate. Kant has temporarily changed over to the standpoint of the metaphysical view which he has been criticising, and accordingly uses the term 'possibility' in the Leibnizian sense. Is Leibniz, he asks, justified in maintaining that the field of the possible is wider than the realm of the actual, and the latter in turn wider in extent than the necessary? In reply Kant accepts the metaphysical meaning assigned to the term 'possibility,' but restates the problem in Critical fashion. Do all things belong as appearances to the context of a single experience, or are other types of experience possible? Do

[1] A 218 = B 281.

other forms of intuition besides space and time, other forms of understanding besides the discursive through concepts, come within the range of the possible ? These are questions which fall to be answered, not by the mere understanding, the sole function of which is empirical, but by Reason, which transcends the world of appearance.

Kant introduces these questions, as he is careful to state,[1] only because they are currently believed to be within the competence of the understanding ; and he now for the first time points out that possibility, in this sense, means absolute possibility, that which is independent of all limiting conditions, a meaning ruled out by the preceding treatment of the modal categories. Like all other absolute conceptions, it belongs to Reason, and must therefore await treatment in the *Dialectic.* These admissions come, however, only after the discussion has been completed. Had Kant reversed the order of the two paragraphs which constitute this digression, and marked them off as being a digression, he would have greatly assisted the reader in following the argument.

Kant adds a refutation of the merely logical arguments by which Leibniz had professed to establish the priority and greater scope of the possible. From the proposition, everything actual is possible, we can infer by immediate inference that some possible things are actual. That, however, would seem to imply that part of the possible is not actual, and that something must be added to the possible in order to constitute the actual. But this, Kant replies, is obviously an untenable view. The something additional to the possible, not being itself possible, we should be constrained to regard as impossible. *For our understanding,*[2] the possible is that which connects with some perception in agreement with the formal conditions of experience. (Kant here gives the correct Critical definition of the possible, by combining the two first postulates.) Whether, and how far, other existences beyond the field of sense experience are possible, we have no means of deciding.

B 288-294.—This second edition section emphasises the fact that possibility cannot be determined through the categories alone, but only through the categories in their relation to intuition, and indeed to outer intuition. Possibility is throughout taken as referring to objective reality. The section is chiefly important in connection with the problems bearing on the relation of inner and outer sense and on the nature of our consciousness of time.[3]

In B 289-91 Kant criticises those rationalistic arguments

---

[1] A 232 = B 284.   [2] A 231 = B 284.   [3] Cf. above, p. 309 ff.

which rest upon the equating of necessity of thought with necessity of existence. When it is sought by mere analysis of concepts to prove that all accidental existence has a cause, the most that can be shown is that the existence of the accidental cannot be *comprehended* by us, unless the existence of a cause be assumed. But we may not argue that a condition of possible understanding is likewise a condition of possible existence.[1] What is or is not possible for thought is, without special proof, no sufficient criterion of what is or is not possible in the real. If, again, the term accidental be taken as meaning that which can exist only as a consequence of some other existence, the general principle becomes merely analytic, and must not be taken as establishing the synthetic principle of causality. The latter demands transcendental proof by reference to the possibility of contingent experience.

[1] Kant's argument in the note to B 290 is that of his early essay on *Negative Quantity*. Cf. below, pp. 527 ff., 533 ff., 536.

CHAPTER III

ON THE GROUND OF THE DISTINCTION OF ALL OBJECTS WHATEVER INTO PHENOMENA AND NOUMENA

THIS chapter, as Kant himself states,[1] can yield no new results. It will serve merely to summarise those already established in the *Analytic*, showing how they one and all converge upon a conclusion of supreme importance for understanding the nature and scope of human experience—the conclusion, that though the objective employment of the categories can be justified only within the realm of sense-experiences, they have a wider significance whereby they define a distinction between appearances and things in themselves. This is the conclusion which Kant now sets himself to illustrate and enforce in somewhat greater detail. It may be observed that the title of the chapter makes mention only of grounds for *distinguishing* between phenomena and noumena. That things in themselves really exist, Kant, as we shall find, never seriously thought of questioning.

Kant begins by recalling a main point in the preceding argument. The categories apart from the manifold of sensibility are merely logical functions without content.[2] Though *a priori*, they require to be supplemented through empirical intuition.

"Apart from this relation to possible experience they have no objective validity of any sort, but are a mere play of the imagination or the understanding with their respective representations."[3]

As evidence of the truth of this conclusion Kant now adds a further argument, namely, the impossibility of defining the categories except in terms that involve reference to the conditions of sensibility.[4] When these conditions are omitted,

[1] A 236 = B 295.
[2] Cf. above, pp. xxxv-vi, xxxviii, 185-6, 191, 195-6, 257-8, 290-1, 325 ff., 339.
[3] The mathematical illustrations which Kant proceeds to give (A 239 = B 299) are peculiarly crude and off-hand in manner of statement. Cf. *per contra* A 140 = B 179 for Kant's real view of the distinction between image, schema, and concept.
[4] Cf. above, pp. 195-6, 198, 339-42.

the categories are without relation to any object and consequently without meaning. They are no longer concepts of
possible empirical employment, but only of "things in general."
When, for instance, the permanence of existence in time, which
is the condition of the empirical application of the concept of
substance, is omitted, the category reduces merely to the
notion of something that is always a subject and never a
predicate.

"But not only am I ignorant of all conditions under which this
logical pre-eminence may belong to anything, I can neither put such
a concept to any use nor draw the least inference from it. For under
these conditions no object is determined for its employment, and
consequently we do not at all know whether it signifies anything
whatsoever."[1]

In abstraction from sense-data, the categories still remain
as concepts or *thoughts*, logically possible; but that is not
to be taken as signifying that they still continue to possess
meaning, *i.e.* reference to an object.[2] And in the absence of
ascertainable meaning they cannot, of course, be defined.

In A 244[3] Kant states his position in somewhat different
fashion. In abstraction from sense the categories have meaning, but not determinate meaning; they relate not to any
specific object, but only to things in general. In this latter
reference, however, they possess no objective validity, since
in the absence of intuition there is no means of deciding
whether or not any real existence actually corresponds to
them.

But whichever mode of statement be adopted, the same
conclusion follows.

"Accordingly, the transcendental *Analytic* has this important
result, that the most the understanding can achieve *a priori* is to
anticipate the form of a possible experience in general. And since
that which is not appearance cannot be an object of experience, the
understanding can never transcend those limits of sensibility within
which alone objects are given to us. Its principles are merely rules
for the exposition of appearances; and the proud title of an Ontology,
which presumptuously claims to supply, in systematic doctrinal form,
synthetic *a priori* knowledge of things in general (*e.g.* the principle
of causality), must therefore give place to the modest claims of a
mere Analytic of pure understanding."[4]

---

[1] A 243 = B 301.   [2] A 242 = B 302.
[3] Cf. A 248 = B 305.
[4] A 246-7 = B 303-4. A 247-8 = B 304-5 (beginning "Thought is the action,"
etc.) is merely a repetition of the preceding argument, and probably represents
a later intercalation.

A 248-9[1] opens a new line of argument which starts from the results obtained in the *Aesthetic*. The proof that space and time are subjective forms establishes the phenomenal character of everything which can be apprehended in and through them, and is meaningless except on the assumption that things in themselves exist. This assumption, Kant argues, is already involved in the very word 'appearance,' and unless it be granted, our thinking will revolve in a perpetual circle.[2] But, he proceeds, this conclusion may easily be misinterpreted. It might be taken as proving the objective reality of noumena, and as justifying us in maintaining a distinction between the sensible and the intelligible worlds, and therefore in asserting that whereas the former is the object of intuition, the latter is apprehended by the understanding in pure thought. We should then be arguing that though in experience things are known only as they appear, through pure understanding a nobler world than that of sense, "*eine Welt im Geiste gedacht*," is opened to our view.

But any such interpretation, Kant insists, runs directly counter to the teaching of the *Analytic*, and is ruled out by the conclusions to which it has led. Categories yield only "rules for the exposition of appearances," and cannot be extended beyond the field of possible experience. It is true that all our sense-representations are related by the understanding to an object that is "transcendental." But that object, in its transcendental aspect, signifies only a something $= x$. It cannot be thought apart from the sense-data which are referred to it. When we attempt to isolate it, and so to conceive it in its independent nature, nothing remains through which it can be thought.

"It is not in itself an object of knowledge, but only the representation of appearances under the concept of an object in general, viewed as determinable through the manifold of those appearances."

Kant is here again expounding his early doctrine of the transcendental object.[3] Evidently, at the time at which this passage was written, he had not yet come to realise that such teaching is not in harmony with his Critical principles. It is, as we have seen above, a combination of subjectivism and of

---

[1] Beginning "Appearances, so far as . . .," which was omitted in the second edition. It probably constitutes, as Adickes maintains (*K.* p. 254 *n.*), the original beginning of this chapter. The "as we have hitherto maintained" of its second paragraph, which obviously cannot apply to the pages which precede it in its present position, must refer to the argument of the *Analytic*.

[2] A 249, 251.

[3] Above, p. 204 ff.

dogmatic rationalism.[1]   The very point which he here chiefly stresses was bound, however, when consistently followed out, to reveal the untenableness of the doctrine of the transcendental object; and in the second edition Kant so recast this chapter on phenomena and noumena as to eliminate all passages in which the transcendental object is referred to.[2]

But to return to Kant's own argument: the reason why the mind is "not satisfied with this substrate of sensibility,"[3] and therefore proceeds to duplicate the phenomenal world by a second world of noumena, lies in the character of the agency whereby sensibility is limited.   Sensibility is limited by the understanding; and the understanding, overestimating its powers and prerogatives, proceeds to transform the notion of the transcendental object = x into the concept of a noumenon, viewed in a manner conformable to its etymological signifi-

---

[1] In large part it represents the Critical position as understood by Schopenhauer, who never succeeded in acquiring any genuine understanding of Kant's more mature teaching (cf. above, p. 366 n.). Schopenhauer is correct in maintaining that one chief ground of Kant's belief in the existence of things in themselves lies in his initial assumption that they must be postulated in order to account for the given manifold. Schopenhauer is also justified in stating that Kant, though starting from the dualistic Cartesian standpoint, so far modified it as to conclude that the origin of this manifold must be "*objective, since there is no ground for regarding it as subjective*" (*Parerga und Paralipomena*, 1851 ed., p. 74 ff.). But for two reasons this is a very incomplete, and therefore misleading, account of Kant's teaching. In the first place, Schopenhauer fails to take account of Kant's implied distinction between the sensations of the special senses and the manifold of outer sense. When Kant recognises that the sensations of the special senses are empirically conditioned, he is constrained in consistency to distinguish between them and the manifold which constitutes the matter of all experiences (cf. above, p. 275 ff.). Things in themselves, in accounting for the latter, account also, but in quite indirect fashion, for the former. Though sensations are empirically conditioned, the *entire* natural world is noumenally grounded. Secondly, Kant's subjectivism undergoes a similar transformation on its inner or mental side. The analysis of self-consciousness, which is given both in the *Deductions* and in the *Paralogisms*, indicates with sufficient clearness Kant's recognition that the form of experience is as little self-explanatory as its content, and that it must not, without such proof as, owing to the limitations of our experience, we are debarred from giving, be regarded as more ultimate in nature. The realities which constitute and condition our mental processes are not apprehended in any more direct manner than the thing in itself. When, therefore, Schopenhauer asserts in the *World as Will and Idea* (*Werke*, *Frauenstädt*, ii. p. 494, Eng. trans. ii. p. 6) that Kant proves the world to be merely phenomenal by demonstrating that it is conditioned by the intellect, he is taking part of Kant's teaching as equivalent to the whole. Schopenhauer's occasional identification of the intellect with the brain—the nearest approximation in his writings to what may be described as phenomenalism—itself suffices to show how entirely he is lacking in any firm grasp of Critical principles.

[2] As we have noted (above, p. 204 ff.), the doctrine of the transcendental object was entirely eliminated from those main sections that were rewritten or substantially altered in the second edition, namely, the chapters on the *Transcendental Deduction*, on *Phenomena and Noumena*, and on the *Paralogisms*. That it remained in the section on *Amphiboly*, in the *Second Analogy*, and in the chapter on the *Antinomies* is sufficiently explained by Kant's unwillingness to make the very extensive alterations which such further rewriting would have involved.

[3] A 251.

cance, as something apprehended by reason or pure intuition, *i.e.* as intuited in some non-sensuous fashion. For only by postulating the possibility of a non-sensuous species of intuition, can the notion of a noumenon, thus positively conceived, be saved from self-contradiction. Otherwise we should be asserting the apprehension of an object independently of appearances, and yet at the same time denying the only means through which such apprehension is possible. Statement of the postulate suffices, however, to reveal its unsupported character. We have no such power of non-sensuous, intuitive apprehension;[1] nor can we in any way prove that such a power is possible even in a Divine Being. Though, therefore, the concept of noumena is not self-contradictory, it involves more than we have the right to assert; the process whereby the empty notion of a transcendental object = x is transformed into the positive concept of a noumenon is easily comprehensible,[2] but it is none the less illegitimate. We must, Kant insists, keep strict hold of the central doctrine of Critical teaching, namely, that the categories are applicable only to the data of sense. We can still employ them as pure logical functions, yielding the notion of objects in general (of the transcendental object = x). But this does not widen the sphere of *known* existences. It only enables us to comprehend the limited and merely phenomenal character of the world experienced.

At this point[3] Kant's argument takes a strange and misleading turn. The concept of object in general (the transcendental object = x) has been proved to be involved in the apprehension of appearances as appearances, and in this capacity to be a limiting concept (*Grenzbegriff*), which, though negative in function, is indispensably involved in the constitution of human experience. Now, however, Kant proceeds to ascribe this function to *the concept of the noumenon*. That concept is, he repeats, purely problematic. Even the mere possibility of its object, presupposing as it does the possibility of an understanding capable through non-sensuous intuition of apprehending it, we have no right to assert. That the concept is not self-contradictory is the most that we can say of it. None the less, it is to this concept that Kant here ascribes the indispensable limiting function.

"The concept of a noumenon is a merely limiting concept, the function of which is to curb the pretensions of sensibility; and it is

---

[1] Not even, as Kant teaches in his doctrine of inner sense, in the inner world of apperception, cf. above, p. 295 ff.

[2] Kant claims in the *Dialectic* that this process is also unavoidable, constituting what he calls "transcendental illusion."

[3] A 254-7 = B 310-12.

therefore only of negative employment.   At the same time it is no arbitrary invention, and it is bound up with the limitation of sensibility, though it cannot affirm anything positive beyond the field of sensibility." [1]

This confusion, between the concept of a noumenon and the less definite concept of object in general, which is probably due to the combining of manuscripts of different dates, is corrected in the second edition by means of a new distinction which Kant introduces, evidently for this very purpose.   The term noumenon may, he there says, [2] be used either positively or negatively.   Taken positively, it signifies "an object of a non-sensuous intuition"; regarded negatively, it means only "a thing so far as it is not an object of our sensuous intuition." Only in its negative employment, he states, is it required as a limiting concept; and it is then, as he recognises, indistinguishable from the notion of the unknown thing in itself.

But despite this variation in mode of expression, in the main Kant holds consistently to his fundamental teaching.

"... understanding is not limited through sensibility; on the contrary, it itself limits sensibility by applying the term noumena to things in themselves (things not regarded as appearances).   But in so doing it at the same time sets limits to itself, recognising that it cannot know these noumena through any of the categories, and that it must therefore think them only under the title of an unknown something." [3]

Or as Kant adds in the concluding sentence of this chapter:

"... the problematic thought which leaves open a place for [intelligible objects], serves only, like an empty space, for the limitation of empirical principles, without itself containing or revealing any other object of knowledge beyond their sphere."

A sentence in A 258 = B 314 deserves special notice.

"... we can never know whether such a transcendental or exceptional knowledge is possible under any conditions—at least not if it is to be the same kind of knowledge as that which stands under our ordinary categories."

This sentence clearly shows that Kant was willing to recognise that the categories may be inapplicable, not merely owing to lack of data for their specification, but because of their inherent character.   They may be intrinsically inapplic-

---

[1] A 255 = B 310-11.   [2] Cf. below, p. 412 ff.
[3] A 256 = B 312.   For A 257 = B 312 on the empirical manner of distinguishing between the sensuous and the intelligible, cf. above, pp. 143 ff., 149 ff.

able, expressing only the *modi* of our self-consciousness. They may be merely the instruments of our human thinking, not forms necessary to knowledge as such.

RELEVANT PASSAGES IN THE SECTION ON AMPHIBOLY

Before passing to consideration of the extensive alterations made in this chapter in the second edition, it is advisable to take account of the two passages dealing with this problem in the first edition section on *Amphiboly*: namely, A 277-280 = B 333-6, and A 285-9 = B 342-6. The first of these passages is of great interest in other connections;[1] its chief importance in reference to the present problem lies in its concluding paragraph. Kant there declares that the representation of an object "as thing in general" is not only, in the absence of specific data, insufficient for the determination of an object, but is self-contradictory. For we must either abstract from all reference to an object, and so be left with a merely logical representation; or, in assuming an object, we must postulate a special form of intuition which we do not ourselves possess, and which therefore we cannot employ in forming our concept of the object. *Here again Kant is substituting the concept of a noumenon for the less definite concept of the thing in itself.* This is still more explicitly done in the second passage. The pure categories are, Kant declares, incapable of yielding the concept of an object. Apart from the data of sense they have no relation to any object. As purely logical functions, they are altogether lacking in content or meaning. By objects as things in themselves we must therefore, he contends, mean objects of a non-sensuous intuition.[2] Kant still, indeed, continues to maintain that the categories do not apply to them, and that we cannot, therefore, have any knowledge of them, either intuitional or conceptual.

"Even if we assume a non-sensuous form of intuition, our functions of thought would still have no meaning in reference to it."[3]

[1] Cf. above, pp. 143-4, 147, 214-15, 291 ff.

[2] Kant here (A 286 = B 342) speaks of this concept of the noumenon *as an object of non-sensuous intuition* as being "merely negative." This is apt to confuse the reader, as he usually comes to it after having read the passage introduced into the chapter on *Phenomena and Noumena* in the second edition, in which, as above noted (p. 409), Kant describes this meaning of the term as positive, in distinction from its more negative meaning as signifying a thing merely so far as it is not an object of *our* sense-intuition. Cf. below, p. 413.

[3] Kant's meaning here is not quite clear. He may mean either that the categories as such are inapplicable to things in themselves, or that, as this form of intuition is altogether different from our own, it will not help in giving meaning to the categories. What follows would seem to point to the former view.

But Kant now insists that the notion of noumena, viewed in the above manner, differs from the notion of "objects in general" (transcendental $= x$) in being a legitimate non-contradictory conception; and he also insists that though more positive in content, it is for that very reason less open to misunderstanding. Its function is not to extend our knowledge, but merely to limit it.

"For it merely says that our species of intuition does not extend to all things, but only to objects of our senses; that its objective validity is consequently limited; and that a place therefore remains open for some other species of intuition, and so for things as its objects."[1]

The concept of a noumenon, as thus employed to signify the objects of a non-sensuous intuition, is, Kant proceeds, merely problematic. As we have neither intuition nor (it may be) categories fitted for its apprehension, it represents something upon the possibility or impossibility of which we are quite unable to pronounce.

". . . as the problematic concept of an object for a quite different intuition and a quite different understanding than ours, it is itself a problem."

We may not therefore assert the existence of noumena, but we must none the less form to ourselves the concept of them. This concept is indispensably involved in the constitution of our empirical knowledge, and is demanded for its proper interpretation. Only when viewed as a self-sufficient representation of an absolute existence does it become dogmatic and therefore illegitimate. In its Critical aspects it stands for a problem which human reason is constrained by its very nature to propound.

"The concept of the noumenon is, therefore, not the concept of an object, but is a problem unavoidably bound up with the limitation of our sensibility—the problem, namely, as to whether there may not be objects entirely disengaged from our sensuous species of intuition. This is a question which can only be answered in an indeterminate manner, by saying that, as sense intuition does not extend to all things without distinction a place remains open for other different objects; and consequently that these latter must not be absolutely denied, though—since we are without a determinate concept of them (inasmuch as no category can serve that purpose)—neither can they be asserted as objects for our understanding."[2]

---

[1] A 286 = B 343.   [2] A 287-8 = B 344.

The fact that these fundamental concepts have not yet been quite definitely and precisely formulated in Kant's own mind, appears very clearly from the immediately following paragraph. For he there again introduces the concept of the transcendental object, and adds that if "we are pleased to name it noumenon for the reason that its representation is not sensuous, we are free so to do."[1] The characterisation given in this paragraph of the transcendental object deserves special notice, for in it Kant goes further in the sceptical expression of his position, though not indeed in the modification of it, than in any other passage.

"[The understanding in limiting sensibility] thinks for itself an object in itself, but only as transcendental object which is the cause of appearance and therefore not itself appearance, and which can be thought neither as quantity nor as reality nor as substance, etc. . . . We are completely ignorant whether it is to be met with in us or outside us, whether it would be at once removed with the cessation of sensibility, or whether in the absence of sensibility it would still remain."[2]

This sentence reveals Kant as at once holding unquestioningly to the existence of things in themselves, and yet at the same time as teaching that they must not be conceived in terms of the categories, not even of the categories of reality and existence.

ALTERATIONS IN SECOND EDITION

In the second edition certain paragraphs of the chapter on *Phenomena and Noumena* are omitted, and new paragraphs are inserted to take their place. Though these alterations do not give adequate expression to the Critical teaching in its maturest form, there are three important respects in which they indicate departures from the teaching of the first edition. In the first place, those paragraphs in which the doctrine of the transcendental object finds expression are entirely eliminated, and the phrase 'transcendental object' is no longer employed. This, as we have already noted, is in harmony with the changes similarly made in the second edition *Transcendental Deduction* and *Paralogisms*.[3]

---

[1] A 288 = B 345.

[2] A 288 = B 344. Kant allowed the section within which this passage occurs to remain, without the least modification, in the second edition.

[3] Benno Erdmann's explanation (*Kriticismus*, p. 194) of Kant's omission of all references to the transcendental object, namely, because of their being likely to conduce to a mistaken idealistic interpretation of his teaching, we cannot accept. As already argued (above, p. 204 ff.), they represent a view which he had quite definitely and consciously outgrown.

Secondly, Kant is even more emphatic than in the first edition, that the categories must not be employed save in reference to sense intuitions. In the first edition he still allows that their application to things in themselves is logically possible, though without objective validity. In the second edition he goes much further. Save in their empirical employment the categories "mean nothing whatsoever."[1]

"[In the absence of sensibility] their whole employment, and indeed all their meaning entirely ceases; for we have then no means of determining whether things in harmony with the categories are even possible. . . ."[2]

In the third place, Kant, as already noted, distinguishes between a negative and a positive meaning of the term noumenon. Noumenon in its negative sense is defined as being merely that which is not an object of sensuous intuition. By noumenon in the positive sense, on the other hand, is meant an object of non-sensuous intuition. Kant now claims that it is the concept of noumenon in the negative sense, as equivalent therefore simply to the thing in itself, that alone is involved, as a *Grenzbegriff*, in the "doctrine of sensibility." For its determination the categories cannot be employed; that would demand a faculty of non-sensuous intuition, which we do not possess, and would amount to the illegitimate assertion of noumena in the positive sense. The limiting concept, indispensably presupposed in human experience, is therefore the bare notion of things in themselves. And accordingly, in modification of the conclusion arrived at in the first edition, viz. that "the division of objects into phenomena and noumena . . . is not in any way admissible,"[3] Kant now adds to the term noumena the qualifying phrase "in the positive sense." In this way the assumption that things in themselves actually exist becomes quite explicit, despite Kant's greater insistence upon the impossibility of applying any of the categories to them.

But beyond thus placing in still bolder contrast the two counter assertions, on the one hand that the categories must not be taken by us as other than merely subjective thought-functions, and on the other that a limiting concept is indispensably necessary, Kant makes no attempt in these new passages to meet the difficulties involved. With the assertion that the categories as such, and therefore by implication

---

[1] B 306. Cf. above, pp. 290-1.
[2] B 308. This, it may be noted, is in keeping with the passages above quoted from the section on *Amphiboly*.
[3] A 255 = B 311.

those of reality and existence, are inapplicable to things in themselves,[1] he combines, without any apparent consciousness of conflict, the contention that things in themselves must none the less be postulated as actually existing.

The teaching of this chapter must be regarded as only semi-Critical. The fact that it is formulated in terms of the doctrine of the transcendental object, itself suffices to determine the date at which it must have been composed as comparatively early; and such changes as Kant could make in the second edition were necessarily of a minor character. More extensive alterations would have involved complete reconstruction of the entire chapter, and indeed anticipation of the central teaching of the *Dialectic*.

Kant is also hampered by the unfortunate location to which he has assigned this chapter. At this point in the development of his argument, namely, within the limits of the *Analytic*, Kant could really do no more than recapitulate the *negative* consequences which follow from the teaching of the transcendental deduction. For though these might justify him in asserting that it is understanding that limits sensibility, he was not in a position to explain that the term understanding, as thus employed, has a very wide meaning, and that within this faculty he is prepared to distinguish between understanding in the strict sense as the source of the categories, and a higher power to which he gives the title Reason, and which he regards as originating a unique concept, that of the unconditioned. Yet only when these distinctions, and the considerations in view of which they are drawn, have been duly reckoned with, can the problem before us be discussed in its full significance.

This placing of the chapter within the *Analytic*, and therefore prior to the discussions first broached in the *Dialectic*, has indeed the unfortunate consequence of concealing not only from the reader, but also, as it would seem, to some extent from Kant himself, the ultimate grounds upon which, from the genuinely Critical standpoint, the distinction between phenomena and noumena must be based. For neither in this chapter, nor in any other passage in the *Critique*, has Kant sought to indicate, in any quite explicit manner, the bearing which the important conclusions arrived at in the *Dialectic* may have in regard to it. Like so many of the most important and fruitful of his tenets, these consequences are suggested merely by implication; or rather remain to be discovered by the reader's own independent efforts, in proportion as he

---

[1] Cf. above, p. 404 ff., especially pp. 409-10; also above, p. 331.

thinks himself into the distinctions upon which, in other connections, Kant has himself insisted.   They are never actually
formulated in and by themselves.

In seeking, therefore, to decide upon what basis the distinction between appearance and reality ought to be regarded
as resting, we are attempting to determine how the argument
of this chapter would have proceeded had it been located
at the close of the *Dialectic.*   The task is by no means easy,
but the difficulties are hardly as formidable as may at first sight
appear.   The general outlines of the argument are fairly definitely prescribed by Kant's treatment of kindred questions,
and may perhaps, with reasonable correctness, be hypothetically constructed in view of the following considerations.

Just as Kant started from the natural assumption that
reference of representations to objects must be their reference
to things in themselves, so he similarly adopted the current
Cartesian view that it is by an inference, in terms of the
category of causality, that we advance from a representation
to its external ground.   It was very gradually in the process
of developing his own Critical teaching, and especially his
phenomenalist view of the empirical world in space, that he
came to realise the very different position to which he stood
committed.[1]   When the doctrine of the transcendental object
is eliminated from his teaching, and when the categories,
including that of causality, are pre-empted for the *empirical*
object, and that object is regarded as directly apprehended,
the function of mediating the reference of phenomenal nature
to a noumenal basis falls to the Ideas of Reason.   For the
distinction is no longer between representations and their
noumenal causes, but between the limited and relative character of the entire world in space and time, and the uncon-

---

[1] In order to form an adequate judgment upon Kant's justification for distinguishing between appearance and reality the reader must bear in mind (1) the
results obtained in the *Transcendental Deduction* (above, p. 270 ff.) ; (2) the discussions developed in the *Paralogisms* (below, p. 457 ff.) ; (3) the treatment of
noumenal causality, that is of freedom, in the *Third* and *Fourth Antinomies ;* (4)
the many connected issues raised in the *Ideal* (below, pp. 534-7, 541-2), and in the
Appendix to the Dialectic (below, p. 543 ff.).   Professor Dawes Hicks is justified
in maintaining in his book, *die Begriffe Phänomenon und Noumenon in ihrem Ver-
hältniss zu einander bei Kant* (Leipzig, 1897, p. 167)—a work which unfortunately
is not accessible to the English reader—that " the thing in itself is by no means
a mere excrescence or addendum of the Kantian system, but forms a thoroughly
necessary completion to the doctrine of appearances.   At every turn in Kant's
thought the doctrine of the noumenon, in one form or another, plays an essential
part."   Indeed it may be said that to state Kant's reasons for asserting the
existence of things in themselves, is to expound his philosophy as a whole.   Upon
this question there appears in Kant the same alternation of view as in regard to
his other main tenets.   On Kant's discussion of the applicability of the category
of existence to things in themselves, cf. above, p. 322 ff.   Also, on Kant's extension
of the concepts possibility and actuality to noumena, cf. above, pp. 391 ff., 401-3.

ditioned reality which Reason demands for its own satisfaction. To regard the world in space as phenomenal, because failing to satisfy our standards of genuine reality, is to adopt an entirely different attitude from any to be found in Descartes or Locke. The position may be outlined in the following manner, in anticipation of its more adequate statement in connection with the problems of the *Dialectic*.

The concept, whereby Reason limits sensibility, is not properly describable as being that of the thing in itself; it is the unique concept of the unconditioned. Our awareness of the conditioned as being conditioned presupposes, over and above the categories, an antecedent awareness of Ideal[1] standards; and to that latter more fundamental form of consciousness all our criteria of truth and reality are ultimately due. The criteria by means of which we empirically distinguish sense-appearance from sense-illusion, when rigorously applied, lead us to detect deficiencies in the empirical as such. We have then no alternative save to conceive absolute reality in terms of the rational Ideals, of which the empirical criteria are merely specialised forms.

There are thus two distinct, but none the less interdependent, elements involved in Kant's more mature teaching, phenomenalism, and what may be called the Idealist, or absolutist, interpretation of the function of Reason. Each demands the other for its own establishment. There must be a genuinely objective world, by reflection upon which we may come to consciousness of the standards which are involved in our judgments upon it; and we must possess a faculty through which our consciousness of these standards may be accounted for. The standards of judgment cannot be acquired by means of judgments which do not already presuppose them; the processes by which they are brought to clear consciousness cannot be the processes in which they originate. They must be part of the *a priori* conditions of experience and combine with space, time and the categories to render experience of the kind which we possess—self-transcending and self-limiting—actually possible.

From this point of view the distinction between appearance and reality is not a contrast between experience and the non-experienced, but a distinguishing of factors, which are essential to all experience, and through which we come to consciousness of an irresolvable conflict between the Ideals which inspire us in the acquisition of experience, and the

---

[1] 'Ideal' and 'Idealist' are printed with capitals, to mark the very special sense in which these terms are being used. As already noted (above, p. 3), the same remark applies to the term 'Reason.'

limiting conditions under which alone experience is attainable by us. In the higher field of Reason, as in the lower field of understanding, it is not through the given, but only through the given as interpreted by conditioning forms of an Ideal nature, that a meaningful reality can disclose itself to the mind. The ultimate meaning of experience lies in its significance when tested by the standards which are indispensably involved in its own possibility. That meaning is essentially metaphysical; more is implied in experience than the experienced can ever itself be found to be.[1]

Such is the central thesis of the Critical philosophy, when the teaching of the *Analytic* is supplemented by that of the *Dialectic*. Though the *Critique* is, indeed, the record of the manifold ways in which Kant diverged from this position, not a systematic exposition of its implications and consequences, the above thesis represents the goal upon which his various lines of thought tend to converge. It is the guiding motive of his devious and complex argument in the three main divisions of the *Dialectic*. On no other interpretation can the detail of his exposition be satisfactorily explained.

There are two chief reasons why Kant failed to draw the above conclusions in any quite explicit manner. One reason has already been sufficiently emphasised, namely, that the thesis, which I have just formulated, rests upon a phenomenalist view of the natural world, whereas the *Dialectic* is inspired by the earlier, subjectivist doctrine of the transcendental object. Upon the other main reason I shall have frequent occasion to insist. As we shall find, Kant was unable to arrive at any quite definitive decision as to the nature of the Ideals of Reason. He alternates between the sceptical and the absolutist view of their origin and function, and in the process of seeking a comprehensive mid-way position which would do justice to all that is valid in the opposing arguments, the further question as to the bearing of his conclusions upon the problem of the distinction between appearance and reality was driven into the background. But we are anticipating matters the discussion of which must meantime be deferred.

[1] Cf. above, pp. xli-ii, xliv, liii-v, 331.

APPENDIX

THE AMPHIBOLY OF THE CONCEPTS OF REFLECTION [1]

IN this appendix Kant gives a criticism of the Leibnizian rationalism—a criticism already partially stated in the section on the *Postulates*—and he does this in a manner which very clearly reveals the influence which that rationalism continued to exercise upon his own thinking. Thus Kant speaks of the " mere concept," [2] and in doing so evidently means to imply that it exists in its own right, with a nature determined solely by intrinsic factors of a strictly *a priori* character, in complete independence of the specific material of sense-experience. He denies, it is true, the objective validity of such concepts, and maintains that in their empirical employment they are completely transformed through the addition of new factors. None the less he allows to the concepts an intrinsic nature, and practically maintains that from the point of view of the pure concept, and therefore from the point of view of a logic based upon it, the Leibnizian rationalism is the one true system of metaphysics. For pure thought, Leibniz's system is the ultimate and only possible philosophy ; and were thought capable of determining the nature of things in themselves, we should be constrained to adopt it as metaphysically valid. This is the standpoint which underlies much of Kant's argument in the *Dialectic*. It leads him to maintain that the self must necessarily, in virtue of an unavoidable transcendental illusion, believe in its own independent substantial reality, that the mind is constrained to conceive reality as an unconditioned unity, and that the notions of God, freedom, and immortality are Ideas necessarily involved in the very constitution of human thought.

But we must not regard Kant's doctrine of the pure concept merely as a survival from a standpoint which the Critical teaching is destined to displace and supersede. For

---

[1] A 260 ff. = B 316 ff.   [2] Cf. above, pp. 38-9, 119, 131-3, 338-9, 394-400.

Kant is not led through inconsistency, or through any mere lack of thoroughness in the development of his Critical principles, to retain this rationalistic doctrine.   To understand the really operative grounds of Kant's argumentation, and so to place the contents of this section in proper focus, we must recall the fundamental antithesis, developed in my introduction,[1] between the alternative positions, which are represented for Kant by the philosophies of Hume and Leibniz.   Kant, as already observed, is profoundly convinced of the essential truth of the Leibnizian position.   He holds to the Leibnizian view of reason.   Human reason is essentially metaphysical; its ultimate function is to emancipate us from the limiting conditions of animal existence; it reveals its nature in those Ideas of the unconditioned, the discussion of which Kant reserves for the *Dialectic*.

The chief defect in Kant's criticism of Leibniz, as developed in this section, is that the deeper issues, which determine the extent of his agreement with Leibniz, are not raised or even indicated.   Consequently, his references to pure thought, and his assertion [2] that from the point of view of pure thought Leibniz is entirely justified in his teaching, bewilder the reader, who has been made to adopt a Critical standpoint, and therefore to believe that thought can function only in connection with the data of sense-experience.   Kant would seem, indeed, to have lapsed into the dogmatic standpoint of the *Dissertation*, distinguishing between a sensible and an intelligible world, and maintaining that pure thought is capable of determining the nature of the latter.   The only difference between his teaching here and in the *Dissertation* consists in the admission that all knowledge *is* limited to sense-experience, and that we are therefore unable to determine whether this intelligible world which we must *think*, and *think in the precise manner defined by Leibniz*, does or does not exist.

This section is, indeed, like the chapter on *Phenomena and Noumena*, wrongly located.   Giving, as it does, Kant's criticism of the Leibnizian ontology, it discusses problems of metaphysics; and ought therefore to have found its place in the *Dialectic*, in natural connection with the corresponding examination of the metaphysical sciences of rational psychology, cosmology, and theology.   Architectonic, that ever-present source of so many of Kant's idiosyncrasies, has again interposed its despotic mandate.   As there are only three forms of syllogism, only three main divisions can be recognised in the *Dialectic*; and the criticism of ontology, to its great

---

[1] Above, p. xxx ff., and below, p. 601 ff.   [2] Cf. A 267 = B 323.

detriment, must therefore be located, where it does not in the least belong, in the concluding section of the *Analytic*.[1]

But we must follow Kant's argument as here given. Leibniz views thought as capable of prescribing, antecedently to all experience, the fundamental conditions to which reality must conform. The possible is prior to, and independent of, the actual; and can be adequately determined by pure reason from its own inherent resources. Kant does not here question this assertion of the independence and priority of pure thought. He is content to maintain that what is valid for thought need not hold of those appearances which are the only possible objects of human knowledge, since in sense-experience conditions, unforeseen by pure thought, partly limitative and partly extensive of its concepts, intervene to modify the conclusions which from its own point of view are logically valid. Leibniz, through failure to realise the dual character of thought and sense, overlooked this all-important fact; and, in asserting that what is true for pure thought is valid of the sensuously real, fell victim to the fallacy which Kant entitles transcendental amphiboly.

Kant's clearest statement of the fallacy is in A 280 = B 336. It reduces, formally stated, to the fallacy of denying the antecedent. In accordance with the *dictum de omni et nullo*, we can validly assert that what belongs to or contradicts a universal concept, belongs to or contradicts the particulars which fall under that concept. Leibniz employs the principle in a negative and invalid form. He argues that what is *not* contained in a universal concept is also not contained in the particulars to which it applies. "The entire intellectualist system of Leibniz is reared upon this latter principle." And as Kant points out,[2] the reason why so acute and powerful a thinker succumbed to this obvious fallacy is to be found in his view of sense as merely confused thought; or, to state the same point in another way, in his interpretation of appearances as being the confused representations of things in themselves.[3] All differences between appearance and reality are, on this view, due merely to lack of clearness in our apprehension of the given. Sense, when completely clarified, reduces without remainder to pure thought; and in the concepts, which thought develops from within itself, lie the whole content alike of knowledge and of real existence. Owing to a metaphysical theory of the nature of the real, itself due to a false interpretation of the nature and function of pure thought, and ultimately traceable to an excessive

[1] Cf. Adickes' *Systematik*, pp. 60, 70, 72, and 111-12.
[2] A 270 = B 326.   [3] Cf. A 264 = B 319, and A 266 = B 322.

preoccupation with knowledge of the strictly mathematical type,[1] Leibniz failed to do justice to the fundamental characteristics of our human experience, and in especial to the actual given nature of space, time, and dynamical causality. His rationalistic metaphysics has its roots in the Cartesian philosophy,[2] and is, in Kant's view, the perfected product of philosophical thinking, when developed on dogmatic, *i.e.* non-Critical, lines. It is the opposite counterpart of the empirical or sceptical type of philosophy which in modern times found its first great supporter in Locke, and which, as Kant held, obtained its perfected expression in the philosophy of Hume. While Descartes and Leibniz intellectualise appearances, Locke and Hume regard the *a priori* concepts of understanding as merely empirical products of discursive reflection. Both commit the same fundamental error of failing to recognise that understanding and sensibility are two distinct sources of representations.[3] Both consequently strive, in equally one-sided fashion, to reduce the complexity of experience to one alone of its constituent elements. This section of the *Critique* ought to have developed the Critical teaching in its opposition to both these alternative attitudes; Kant arbitrarily limits it to criticism of the Leibnizian rationalism.

Kant's method of introducing and arranging his criticism is artificial, and need be no more than mentioned. Critical reflection upon the sources of our knowledge, which Kant, in order to distinguish it from reflection of the ordinary type, entitles *transcendental* reflection, is, he states, a duty imposed upon all who would profess to pass *a priori* judgments upon the real. It will trace the concepts employed to their corresponding faculties, intellectual and sensuous, and will reveal the independence and disparity of sensibility and understanding, and so will effectually prevent that false locating of concepts to which transcendental amphiboly is due. Such reflection, he argues, consists in referring the representations to the faculty to which they are due, and in comparing them with one another; and like ordinary comparison it will determine their relations of (1) *identity and difference*, (2) *agreement and opposition*, (3) *inner and outer*, (4) *determinable and determining* (matter and form). In this arbitrary but ingenious fashion Kant contrives to obtain the four main headings required for his criticism of the Leibnizian ontology.

(1) Under the first heading he deals with the principle

---

[1] Cf. below, pp. 563-5, 589 ff., 601 ff.
[2] I have dwelt upon this at length in my *Studies in the Cartesian Philosophy*.
[3] A 271 = B 327.

of the identity of indiscernibles. It is, Kant maintains, a typical example of the fallacy of transcendental amphiboly. Leibniz argues that if no difference is discoverable in the concept of things, there can be none in the things themselves; things which are identical in conception must be identical in all respects. But this, Kant replies, is true only so long as the concepts abstract from the sensuous conditions of existence. Thus no two cubic feet of space are alike. They are distinguishable from one another by their spatial location; and that is a difference which concerns the conditions of intuition; it is not to be discovered in the pure concept.[1] Spaces, alike for thought, are distinguishable for sense. To take another of Kant's illustrations: two drops of water, if indistinguishable in all their internal properties of quality or quantity, are conceptually identical. Through differences of location in space, irrelevant to their conception, they can none the less be intuited as numerically different. The principle of indiscernibles is not a law of nature, but only an analytic rule for the comparison of things through mere concepts.[2]

(2) A second principle of the Leibnizian metaphysics is that realities can never conflict with one another. This is supposed to follow from the fact that in pure thought the only form of opposition is logical negation. Realities, being pure affirmations, must necessarily harmonise with one another. This principle ignores the altogether different conditions of sense-existence. Space, time, and the resulting possibility of dynamical causality supply the conditions for real opposition. Two existences, though equally real and positive, may annul one another. Two forces acting upon a body may neutralise one another. From the above logical principle Leibniz's successors[3] profess to obtain the far-reaching metaphysical conclusions, that all realities agree with one another, that evil is merely negative, consisting exclusively in limitation of existence, and that God, without detriment to the unity of his being, can be constituted of all possible realities.

(3) Viewing space and time, which condition external relation, as merely confused forms of apprehension, Leibniz further concluded that the reality of substance is purely internal. And ruling out position, shape, contact and motion, all of which involve external relations, he felt justified in endowing the monads with the sole remaining form of known existence, namely consciousness. The assertion that the monads are incapable of external relation leads to the further

[1] The un-Critical character of Kant's doctrine of the pure concept has already been noted (above, pp. 418-19), and need not be further discussed.
[2] A 272 = B 328.   [3] A 273 = B 329.

conclusion that they are incapable of interaction, and stand in systematic relation to one another, solely in virtue of a pre-established harmony.

(4) From the point of view of pure thought matter must precede form. The universal must precede the particular which is a specification of it.[1] Unlimited reality is taken as being the matter of all possibility, and its limitation or form as being due to negation. Substances must antecedently exist in order that external relations may have something upon which to ground themselves. Space and time must be interpreted as confused apprehensions of purely intellectual orders, space representing a certain order in the reciprocal (pre-established) correspondence of substances, and time the dynamical sequence of their states. On the other hand, from the standpoint of sense and its intuitional forms the reverse holds. The world of appearance is conditioned by the forms of space and time; the objectively possible coincides with the actual; and the *substantia phaenomenon* has no independent essence, but reduces without remainder to external relations. For pure thought this world of given appearance is an utterly paradoxical form of existence; it is the direct opposite of everything that genuine reality ought to be. In this strange conclusion the problems of the *Dialectic*, in one of their most suggestive forms, at once loom up before us. As stated above, this entire discussion is an anticipation of questions which cannot be adequately treated within the limits of the *Analytic*.

The text of this section is highly composite. The entire content of the *Appendix* is twice reintroduced and restated at full length in the accompanying *Note*. These successive expositions of one and the same argument were doubtless independently written, and then later pieced together in this external fashion. A 277-8 = B 333-4, on the nature of the *substantia phaenomenon*, would by its references to the transcendental object seem to be of early origin.[2] It has already been commented upon.[3] A 285-9 = B 342-6, on the other hand, which supplements the chapter on *Phenomena and Noumena*,[4] would seem to be of late origin. It is so dated by Adickes,[5] owing to the reference to schemata in its opening sentence.

---

[1] This is Leibniz's mode of stating the absolutist view of thought (cf. above, p. xxx ff.) to which, as we shall find, Kant gives much more adequate and incomparably deeper formulation in the *Dialectic*. Cf. pp. 430, 547 ff., 558 ff.

[2] Adickes, *K.* p. 272 *n.*, allows that the passage may be of earlier origin than the passages which precede and follow it.

[3] Pp. 214-15.

[4] As such it is commented on above, p. 410 ff.

[5] *Loc. cit.*

A 289-91 = B 346-9.   Table of the division of the conception of nothing.—This curious and ingenious classification of the various meanings of the term 'nothing' is chiefly of interest through its first division: "empty conception without object, *ens rationis.*"   The *ens rationis* can best be defined in its distinction from the fourth division: "empty object without conception, *nihil negativum.*"   The former is a *Gedankending*; the latter is an *Unding.*   The former indeed, though not contradictory, is mere fiction (*bloss Erdichtung*), and consequently must not be taken as falling within the field of the possible.   The latter is a concept which destroys itself, and which therefore stands in direct conflict with the possible. The *ens rationis* includes, Kant explicitly states,[1] the conception of noumena, "which must not be reckoned among the possibilities, although they must not for that reason be declared to be also impossible."   Kant must here be taking noumena in the positive sense.[2]   As usual Kant's attempt to obtain parallels for the four classes of category breaks down. The so-called *nihil privativum* and the *ens imaginarium* do not properly come within the denotation of the term 'nothing.' This is very evident in the examples which Kant cites.   Cold is as real as the opposite with which it is contrasted, while pure space and pure time are not negative even in a conventional sense.

[1] A 290 = B 347.   [2] Cf. above, p. 409 ff.

TRANSCENDENTAL LOGIC

DIVISION II

THE TRANSCENDENTAL DIALECTIC

INTRODUCTORY COMMENT UPON THE COMPOSITE ORIGIN AND CONFLICTING TENDENCIES OF THE DIALECTIC.

We have had constant occasion to observe the composite origin and conflicting tendencies of the *Analytic*. The *Dialectic* is hardly less composite in character, and is certainly not more uniform in its fundamental teaching.

The composite nature of the text, though bewildering to the unsophisticated reader, is not, however, without its compensations. The text, as it stands, preserves the record of the manifold influences which presided over its first inception, and of the devious paths by which Kant travelled to his later conclusions. It thus enables us to determine, with considerable accuracy, the successive stages through which it has passed in the process of settling into its present form. As we shall find, the sections on the antinomies contain the original argument, out of which by varied processes of supplementation and modification the other parts have arisen.

The conflict of doctrine has also its counter-advantages. The problems are impartially discussed from opposed standpoints; the difficulties peculiar to each of the competing possible solutions are frankly recognised, and indeed insisted upon; and the internal dialectic of Kant's own personal thinking obtains dramatic expression. We are thus the better enabled to appreciate the open-minded pertinacity with which Kant set himself to do justice to every significant aspect of his many-sided problems, and are consequently in less danger of simplifying his argument in any arbitrary manner, or of ignoring the tentative character of the solutions at which he arrives.

I shall first define the main lines of conflict, and shall then attempt to trace those conflicts to the considerations in which they have their source. The two chief lines of thought traceable throughout the *Dialectic* are represented by its negative and by its positive tendencies respectively. From one point of view, Reason is merely the understanding in its self-limiting, self-regulative employment, and the main purpose of the *Dialectic* is to guard against the delusive power of fictitious principles. From the other point of view, Reason is a faculty distinct from understanding, and its problems run parallel with those of the *Analytic*, forming no less important a subject of philosophical reflection, and no less fruitful a source of positive teaching. The one line of argument connects with Kant's more sceptical tendencies, the other with his deep-rooted belief in the ultimate validity of the absolute claims of pure thought.

When we approach the *Dialectic* from the standpoint of the *Analytic*, it is the negative aspect that is naturally most prominent. In the *Analytic* Kant has proved that all knowledge is limited to sense-experience, and that a metaphysical interpretation of reality is impossible. But as the human mind would seem to be possessed by an inborn need of metaphysical construction, this conclusion cannot obtain its due influence until the sources of the metaphysical tendency have been detected and laid bare. The *Dialectic* must yield *a psychology of metaphysics* as well as a *logic of illusion*.

But when, on the other hand, the problems of the *Dialectic* are viewed in their **distinction** from those of the *Analytic*, and their independent character is recognised, they appear in a perspective which sets them in a very different light. Reason is a faculty co-ordinate with understanding, and yields *a priori* concepts distinct in function, no less than in nature, from the categories. To mark this distinction Kant entitles the concepts of Reason Ideas. They demand both a metaphysical and a transcendental deduction. These requirements are fulfilled through their derivation from the three forms of syllogism, and by the proof that they exercise an indispensable function, at once limiting and directing the understanding. As limiting concepts, they condition the consciousness of those Ideal standards through which the human mind is enabled to distinguish between appearance and things in themselves. As regulative, they prescribe the problems which the understanding in its search for knowledge is called upon to solve.

These two tendencies, sceptical and constructive, are never, indeed, in complete opposition. Common to both, rendering possible the psychological explanation of the metaphysical impulse, which even the negative standpoint demands, is the doctrine of the regulative function of Ideal principles. This doctrine, which already appears in the *Dissertation* of 1770, was later developed into the Critical theory of transcendental illusion ; and by means of that theory Kant succeeded in bringing the two standpoints into a very real and vital connection with one another. At first sight it may seem to achieve their complete reconciliation, accounting for their distinction while rendering them mutually complementary ; and Kant's teaching may perhaps be so restated as to bear out this impression. But the harmony is never completely attained by Kant. Here, as in the *Analytic*, there is an equipoise of tendencies that persist in opposition.

Kant's mediating doctrine of transcendental illusion may first be stated. It rests upon a distinction between appearance and illusion. Appearance (*Erscheinung*) is a transcript in phenomenal terms of some independent reality ; and of such appearances we can acquire what from the human point of view is genuine knowledge. On the other hand, all professed insight into the nature of the transcendent or non-empirical is sheer illusion (*Schein*), and purely subjective. There are three species . of illusion, logical, empirical and transcendental. Logical illusion stands apart by itself. It is due merely to inattention or ignorance ; and vanishes immediately the attention is aroused. Empirical and transcendental illusion, on the other hand, have a twofold point of agreement, first, in being unavoidable, and secondly, in that they originate in our practical needs. We may know that the moon at its rising is no larger than in mid-heavens, that the ocean is no higher in the distance than at the shore ; this makes not the least difference in the perceptions as they continue to present themselves. That the illusions are adapted to our practical needs, and are consequently beneficial, is less often observed. Changes in the colour, form, and size of objects as they recede from us, the seeing of the parallel sides of a street as converging, enable us to achieve what would not otherwise be possible. By their means we acquire the power of compressing a wide extent of landscape into a single visual field, of determining distance, and the like. Their practical usefulness is in almost exact proportion to the freedom with which they depart from the standards of the independently real. Kant argues that, in these respects, transcendental illusion is analogous to the empirical. Just as the illusory characteristics of our perceptions are to be understood only in terms of their practical function, so the Ideas of pure Reason have always a practical bearing, and can only be explained and justified in terms of the needs which they satisfy. As theoretical enquirers, we accept all that affords us orientation in the attainment of knowledge; as moral agents, we postulate the conditions which are necessary for the realisation of the moral imperative. And as the Ideals of natural science are found (such is Kant's contention) to be in general form akin to those of the moral consciousness, they thus acquire a twofold footing in the mental life, maintaining their place there quite independently of theoretical proof. Though illusory, they are unavoidable; and though theoretically false,[1] they are from a practical point of view both legitimate and indispensable.

Kant, in developing this thesis, might profitably have pointed to still another respect in which the analogy holds between sense-experience and transcendental beliefs. The illusions of sense-perception come in the ordinary processes of experience to be detected as such by the mind. From the theoretical standpoint of the outside observer who compares the situation of one percipient with that of another, and so is enabled to cancel the differences which variety of situation carries with it, the useful illusions of ordinary experience are reduced to the level of appearance. In contradicting one another they reveal their subjective character, and also at the same time afford data for determining the objective conditions to which their subjectively necessary existence is causally due. In similar fashion the transcendental illusions result in contradictions, which compel the mind to recognise that the Ideals to which it is committed by its practical needs are of a subjective character, and can never legitimately be interpreted as representing the actual nature of the independently real.

The chief transcendental illusion, and ultimately the cause of all the others, consists in the belief that the Ideals of explanation which satisfy Reason must in general outline represent the nature of ultimate reality. What the individual seeks to discover he naturally believes to exist prior to the discovery. As practical beings, we regard the objects of sense-experience as absolute realities—they are the realities of practical life, and we are practical rather than theoretical beings—and the existing empirical sciences, conceived as Ideally completed, are therefore viewed as yielding an adequate representation of ultimate reality. But such a belief involves us in contradictions. The world of phenomena in space and time is endlessly relative. It can have no outer bounds or first

[1] Kant's commentators have frequently misrepresented this aspect of his teaching. Cf. below, pp. 498, 520-1, 527-37, 541-2, 543 ff., 555, 558-61.

beginning, and no smallest parts; and in the series of causal antecedents there can be no member that is not effect as well as cause. Viewed as representing a pre-existent goal, the Ideas of Reason are imaginary completions of the intrinsically and merely relative, and are in their very notion self-contradictory. All that is definite in their content conflicts with their absoluteness; and yet, as it would seem, only in their empirical reference can they hope for objective verification.

Such are the problems of the *Dialectic*, so far as they can be formulated in terms common to the two opposed standpoints. Their deeper significance, and the grounds of Kant's alternating treatment of them, only appear when he raises the further questions, what those Ideals of explanation which Reason prescribes really are, and how, if they conflict with the content of experience, it is possible that they should be conceived at all. To these questions Kant propounds both a sceptical and an Idealist answer. The former, in bare outline, may be stated as follows. The so-called Ideas are based upon experience and are derived from it. The understanding removes the limitations to which its pure concepts are subject in sense-experience, and proceeds to use them in their widest possible application, *i.e.* to things in general. As thus employed, they are without real significance, and are indeed self-contradictory. To form the Idea of the unconditioned, we have to omit all those conditions through which alone anything can be apprehended, even as possible. To construct the concept of absolute or unconditioned necessity, we have similarly to leave aside the conditions upon which necessity, as revealed in experience, in all cases depends; in eliminating conditions, we eliminate necessity in the only forms in which it is conceivable by us. Such Ideas are, indeed, simply *schematic forms*, whereby we body forth to ourselves, in more or less metaphorical terms, the concept of a *maximum*. They are imaginary extensions, in Ideal form, of the unity and system which understanding has discovered in actual experience, and which, under the inspiration of such Ideals, it seeks to realise in ever-increasing degree. If the understanding, as thus insisting upon Ideal satisfaction, be entitled Reason, the Ideas must be taken as expressing a subjective interest, and as exhausting their legitimate employment in the regulation of the understanding. Their transcendental deduction will consist in the proof that they are necessary to the understanding for the *perfecting* of its experience. They do not justify us in attempting to decide, in anticipation of actual experience, how far the contingent collocations and the inexhaustible complexities of brute experience are really reducible to a completely unified system ; but they quite legitimately demand that through all discouragements we persist in the endeavour towards their realisation. In any case, it is by experience that the degree of their reality has to be decided. We judge of things by the standard of that for which they exist, and not *vice versa*. As the sole legitimate function of the Ideas is that of inspiring the understanding in its empirical employment, they must never be interpreted as having metaphysical significance. As the Ideas exist solely for the sake of experience, it is they that must be condemned, if the two really diverge. We do not say "that a man is too long for his coat, but that the coat is too short for the man." [1] It is experience, not Ideas, which forms the criterion alike of truth and of reality.

Kant's teaching, when on Idealist lines, is of a very different character. Reason is distinct from understanding, and yet is no less indispensably involved in the conditioning of experience. All consciousness is consciousness of a whole which precedes and conditions its parts. Such consciousness cannot be accounted for by assuming that we are first conscious of the conditioned, and then proceed through omission of its limitations to form to ourselves, by means of the more positive factors involved in this antecedent consciousness, an Idea of an unconditioned whole. The Idea of the unconditioned is distinct in nature from all other concepts, and cannot be derived from them. It must be a pure *a priori* product of what may be named the faculty of Reason. Its uniqueness is what causes its apparent meaninglessness. As it is involved in all consciousness, it conditions all other concepts ; and cannot, therefore, be defined in terms of them. Its significance must not be looked for save in that Ideal, to which no experience, and no concept other than itself, can ever be adequate. That in this Ideal form it has a very real and genuine meaning is proved by our capacity to distinguish between appearance and reality. For upon it this distinction, in ultimate analysis, is found to rest. Consciousness of limitation presupposes a consciousness of what is beyond the limit ; consciousness of the unconditioned is prior to, and renders possible, our consciousness of the contingently given. The Idea of the unconditioned must therefore be counted as being, like the categories, though in a somewhat different manner, a condition of the possibility of experience. With it our standards both of truth and of reality are inextricably bound up. [2] The Ideas in which it specifies itself, so far from depending upon empirical verification, are the touchstone by which we detect the unreality of the sensible world, and by

[1] A 490=B 518.   [2] Cf. above, pp. 416-17.

which a truer reality, such as would be adequate to the Ideal demands of pure Reason, is prefigured to the mind.

These two standpoints are extremely divergent in their consequences. Each leads to a very different interpretation of the content of the Ideas, of their function in experience, and of their objective validity. On the one view, their content is merely empirical, and sense-experience is our sole criterion of truth and reality ; on the other, they have to be recognised as containing a pure *a priori* concept, and are themselves the standards by which even empirical truth can alone be determined. In the one case, they are Ideals projected by experience for its own empirical guidance ; they are built upon contingent experience, and depend upon it alike for the content which makes them conceivable and for their validity. In the other, they are presuppositions of experience, at once conditioning its possibility and revealing its phenomenal character. According to the sceptical view, Reason is concerned only with itself and its own subjective demands ; on the Idealist view, it is a metaphysical faculty, and outlines possibilities that may perhaps be established by practical Reason.

Such, in broad outline, are the central doctrines of the *Dialectic*. They constitute an extraordinarily stimulating and suggestive body of Critical teaching. In no other division of the *Critique* do the power and originality of Kant's thinking gain such abundant, forceful and illuminating expression. The accumulated results of the painstaking analyses of the earlier sections contribute a solidity and fulness of meaning, which render the argument extremely impressive, even to those who are out of sympathy with Kant's ultimate purposes. Its persistent influence, on sceptical no less than on Idealist lines, and often conveyed by very devious channels, can frequently be detected even in thinkers—Herbert Spencer is an instance—who would indignantly repudiate the charge of being indebted to such a source.

THE HISTORY AND DEVELOPMENT OF KANT'S VIEWS IN REGARD TO THE PROBLEMS OF THE *DIALECTIC*[1]

We may now proceed to consider the evidence in support of the early origin of the central portions of the *Dialectic*—the sections on the antinomies. As Benno Erdmann[2] has very

---

[1] Those readers who are not already well acquainted with the argument of the *Dialectic* may be recommended to pass at once to p. 441. What here follows presupposes acquaintance with the nature and purposes of the main divisions of the *Dialectic*.   [2] Introd. to *Reflexionen*, Bd. ii.

conclusively shown, preoccupation with the problem of antinomy was the chief cause of the revolution which took place
in Kant's views in 1769, and which found expression in his
Dissertation of 1770. It was the existence of antinomy which
led Kant to recognise the subjectivity of space and time.
That is to say, it led him to develop that doctrine of transcendental idealism which reappears in the concluding sections
of the *Aesthetic*, and which was recast and developed in the
Analytic. Already in the *Dissertation* it supplies the key for
the solution of the problems concerning infinity. The impossibility of completing the space, time, and causal series,
and the consequent impossibility of satisfying the demands
of the mind for totality, simplicity and unconditionedness,
do not, it is there maintained, discredit reason, but only serve
to establish the subjectivity of the sensuous forms to which
the element of infinitude is in all cases due.

Kant's thinking was, of course, diverted into an entirely
new channel (as his letter to Herz of February 21, 1772,[1] shows),
when he came to realise that the metaphysical validity or
invalidity of thought must be decided prior to any attempt to
discover a positive solution of such problems as are presented
by the antinomies. And when, owing to the renewed influence
of Hume, at some time subsequent to the date of the letter
to Herz, this new problem was recognised as being the
problem of *a priori synthesis*, all questions regarding the
nature of the absolutely real were made to take secondary
rank, yielding precedence to those of logical theory. When
the antinomy problems re-emerge, their discussion assumes
Critical form.

In three fundamental respects Kant's treatment of the
antinomies in the *Dissertation* differs from that of the *Critique*.
In the first place, the demand for totality or absoluteness is
not in the *Dissertation* ascribed to a separate faculty. Indeed
Kant's words would seem to show that at times he had inclined
to ascribe it merely to the free-ranging fancy or imagination.[2]
Secondly, as the various antinomies were traced exclusively
to the influence of space and time upon pure thought, they
were treated together, and no classification of them was
attempted. And lastly, though Kant's utterances are somewhat ambiguous,[3] the illusory character of the antinomies was
in the main viewed as being of a more or less *logical* nature.
That is to say, it was regarded as entirely preventable and as
" vanishing like smoke "[4] upon adoption of a true philosophical
standpoint.

---

[1] *W.* x. p. 123 ff. Cf. above, pp. 219-20.   [2] Cf. *Dissertation*, § 27 n.
[3] *Op. cit.* Cf. § 24 with § 27.   [4] *Op. cit.* § 27.

A number of the *Reflexionen* reveal the various tentative schemes, by trial of which Kant worked his way toward a more genuinely Critical treatment of the problems of infinity. The intellectual factors receive fuller recognition, and as a consequence a definite classification results. At some time prior to the discovery of the table of categories, Kant adopted a threefold division of what he names first principles or presuppositions—principles of substance-accident, of ground-consequence, and of whole-part. *Reflexion* ii. 578 is typical.

"Three *principia*: (1) in the field of the actual there is the relation of substance to accident (*inhaerentia*): (2) of ground to consequence (*dependentia*): (3) of parts and of composition (*compositio*). There are three presuppositions: of the subject, of the ground, and of the parts; of insition [Kant's own term], of sub-ordination, and of composition; therefore also three first *principia*: (1) subject, which is never a predicate; (2) ground, which is never a consequence; (3) unity, which is not itself composite."

There are numerous other *Reflexionen* to the same effect.[1] The resulting conceptions are defined both as limits[2] and as absolute totalities, and in *Reflexion* ii. 1252 are enumerated as follows:

"The first subject; the first ground; the first part. The subject which holds everything in itself; the ground which takes everything under itself; the whole which comprehends everything. The *totalitas absoluta* of reality, of series, of co-ordination."

The introduction of the terms 'absolute' and 'totality' indicate that Kant has also come to recognise the presence of a unique notion (equivalent to the "unconditioned" of the *Critique*), distinct in content from any of the three enumerated *principia*, but common to them all. From the very first Kant would seem to have appropriated for it the title Idea. *Reflexionen* ii. 1243, 1244, and 124 may be quoted:

"The Idea is single '(*individuum*), self-sufficient, and eternal. The divinity of our soul is its capacity to form the Idea. The senses give only copies or rather *apparentia*." "Idea is the repre-sentation of the whole in so far as it necessarily precedes the determination of the parts. It can never be empirically represented, for the reason that in experience we proceed from the parts through successive syntheses to the whole. It is the archetype (*Urbild*) of things, for certain objects are only possible through an Idea. Tran-scendental Ideas are those in which the absolute whole determines the parts in an aggregate or as series." "Metaphysics proper is the

---

[1] Cf. ii. 567, 571, 584, 585.   [2] Cf. ii. 1251 and 586.

application of transcendental philosophy to concepts supplied by Reason and necessary to it, to which, however, no corresponding objects can be given in experience. The concepts must therefore refer to the supersensible. That, however, can be nothing but the unconditioned, *for that is the sole theoretical Idea of reason*. [Not italicised in the original.] Metaphysics thus relates: (1) to that of which only the whole can be represented as absolutely unconditioned: (2) to things so far as they are in themselves sensuously unconditioned. The first part is cosmology, the second rational doctrine of the soul, pneumatology and theology."

At this stage, therefore, Kant would seem to have held that there is but one Idea strictly so called, and that the above three *principia* are merely specifications of it in terms of the concepts of substance-accident, ground-consequence, and whole-part. The classification thus obtained is in certain respects more satisfactory than that which is adopted in the *Critique*. It locates the cosmological argument with the causal category, and so would enable the conceptions of freedom or *causa sui*, and of Divine Existence, to be dealt with in their natural connection with one another. It also supplies, in the category of whole and part, a more fitting heading for those antinomy problems which deal with the unlimited and the limited, the divisible and the indivisible, the complex and the simple. The classification would, however, in separating the problem of the simple from that of substance, remain open to the same criticism as that of the *Critique*.[1]

This classification must, as we have stated, be of a date prior to Kant's discovery of the table of categories. That is quite clear from its ignoring the category of reciprocity, and from its combination of the other two categories of relation with the merely quantitative category of whole and part. For though the last is also entitled composition and co-ordination, it is conceived in these particular *Reflexionen* in exclusively quantitative terms. When Kant formulated the "metaphysical" deduction of the categories he was, of course, compelled to recast the classification, and did so in the only possible manner, consistent with his architectonic, by substituting the category of reciprocity for that of whole and part,[2] and by taking the new heading, obtained through combination of reciprocity with the Idea of the unconditioned, as equivalent to the Idea of Divine Existence. But this could not be done without dislocating the entire scheme. The

---

[1] Cf. below, pp. 458, 488 ff.

[2] In *Reflexionen* ii. 573, 576, and 582 we find Kant in the very act of so doing. *Compositio, co-ordinatio,* and *commercium* are treated as synonymous terms.

category of ground and consequence is deprived of its chief application, that expressed in the cosmological argument; and in order to provide a new content for it, Kant is compelled to force upon it the problems previously classified under the displaced category of whole and part. Even so, the problem of the *causa sui* cannot be eliminated, and reappears, partly as the problem of freedom, and partly as the modal problem of necessary existence.

The identification of the theological Idea with the category of reciprocity has a further consequence. It carries the problem of Divine Existence outside the sphere of the problems of infinity, and necessitates a very different treatment from that which it would naturally have received at Kant's hands, if developed in its connection with his own Critical teaching. He is driven to expound it in the extreme rationalistic form in which it had been formulated by Leibniz and Wolff, as a doctrine of the *Ens realissimum*.

Prior to the rearrangement, necessitated by recognition of the category of reciprocity, Kant would seem to have expected to bring the entire body of Wolffian metaphysics within the scope of a general doctrine of antinomy. The problems of the divisible and the indivisible, of the simple and the complex, leading as they do to discussion of the presuppositions underlying the Leibnizian monadology, concern spiritual as well as material substance. Similarly, the main problems of theology would have been treated in connection with the cosmological inference to a first cause, and with the discussion of the possibility of first beginnings in space and time.[1]

The sections in the *Critique* devoted to the antinomies reveal, in many ways, Kant's original design. It is especially noticeable in his discussion of the third and fourth antinomies. The problems of freedom and of necessary existence are by no means treated in merely cosmological fashion. Indeed Kant makes no pretence of concealing their psychological and theological implications. Even the first and second antinomies have obvious bearings of a similar character. But it is in the section entitled *The Interest of Reason in this Self-conflict*[2] that the broader significance of the antinomies

---

[1] The problem of freedom is first met with in Kant's *Lectures on Metaphysics* (Pölitz, edition of 1821, pp. 89, 330), but is not there given as an antinomy, and is treated as falling within the field of theology. In *Reflexion* ii. 585, also, it is equated in terms of the category of ground and consequence, with the concept of Divine Existence, the "*absolute* or *primum contingens (libertas)*." Upon elimination of theology, and therefore of the cosmological argument, from the sphere of antinomy, Kant raised freedom to the rank of an independent problem.

[2] A 462 = B 490.

finds its fullest expression. In its suggestive contrast of the two possible types of philosophy, Epicurean and Platonic, the argument entirely transcends the bounds prescribed to it by its cosmological setting. As we follow its comprehensive sweep, we can hardly avoid regretting that Kant failed to keep to his original plan, as here unfolded,[1] of expounding the self-conflict of Reason in the form of a broad judicial statement of the grounds and claims of the two opposing authorities which divide the allegiance of the human spirit, namely, the intellectual and the moral, science with its cognitive demands on the one hand, the consciousness of duty with its no less imperious prescriptions on the other. The materialist philosophies would then have been presented as inevitably arising when intellectual values are made supreme; and the Idealist philosophies as equally cogent when moral values are taken as primary and are allowed to determine speculative tenets. Against this background of conflicting dogmatisms the comprehensive and satisfying character of the Critical standpoint would have stood out the more clearly; and its historical affiliations, its debt to the sceptics and materialists, no less than to the Idealists, would have been depicted in more adequate terms. As it is, in the chapters on the *Paralogisms* and the *Ideal of Pure Reason* there is almost entire failure to recognise the possibility of a naturalistic solution of the problems with which they deal, and Kant so far succumbs to the outworn influences of his day and generation—the very influences from which the Critical philosophy, consistently developed, is a final breaking away—as to maintain, almost in the manner of the English Deists, of Voltaire and Rousseau, that God, Freedom, and Immortality are conceptions which the mind must necessarily form, and in the validity of which it must spontaneously believe. Kant is here, indeed, interpreting "natural reason" in the light of his own personal history. The Christian beliefs, in which he had been nurtured from childhood, and their rationalist counterparts in the Wolffian philosophy, had become, as it were, a second nature to him; and the resistance, which in his own person they had offered to the development of Critical teaching, he not unnaturally interpreted as evidence of their being imposed by the very structure of reason. He transforms the metaphysical sciences in their Wolffian form into inevitable illusions of the human mind.[2]

There is evidence that the theological problems were the first to be withdrawn from the sphere of the "sceptical

---

[1] Cf. below, pp. 498-9, 571 ff.　　[2] Cf. below, p. 454, with references in n. 1.

method,"[1] peculiar to the antinomies.   Thus *Reflexion* ii.
125[2] states that "metaphysics proper consists of *cosmologia
rationalis* and *theologia naturalis*"—rational psychology being,
as it would seem, still included within cosmology.[3]   What
the considerations were which induced Kant to claim similarly
independent treatment for rational psychology, we can only
conjecture.   For a time, while still holding to the bipartite
division, he would seem to have made the further change of
also separating psychology from cosmology, classing psychology and theology together as subdivisions of the rational
science of soul.

"[Metaphysics has two parts]: the first is cosmology, the second
rational doctrine of soul, pneumatology and theology."[4]

A main factor deciding Kant in favour of a dogmatic,
non-sceptical treatment of rational psychology may have
been the greater opportunity which it seemed to afford him
of connecting its doctrines with the teaching of the *Analytic*,
and especially with his central doctrine of apperception.
But to whatever cause the decision was due, it resulted in the
impoverishment of the second antinomy, through withdrawal
of the more important half of its natural content.   This
antinomy could no longer be made to comprehend a discussion of the logical bases of monadology, and of its professed
proofs of the simplicity and immortality of the soul.   Nothing
is left to it save the discussion of the monadistic theory of
matter (*somatologia pura*).[5]   This change has also, as already
noted, the unfortunate effect of precluding Kant from recognition of the physical application of the category of substance.
By the simple he means the substantial, and yet he may not
say so; his architectonic forbids.

I may hazard the further suggestion that Kant's interpretation of rational psychology in terms of the Critical
doctrine of apperception is of earlier date than his doctrine
of transcendental illusion.   For the chapter on the *Paralogisms* seems in its first form to have contained no reference
to that latter doctrine.[6]   The few passages which take account
of it, all bear evidence of being later intercalations.   This is
the more remarkable in that the Paralogisms can easily be
shown to be typical examples of transcendental illusion.
Indeed, neither the antinomies nor the theological Ideal
conform to its definition in the same strict fashion.

[1] A 507 = B 535.   Cf. below, pp. 481, 545-6.
[2] Cf. ii. 93, 94, 95, 1233, 1247.
[3] This is the view represented in *Reflexionen* ii. 94, 95.
[4] Cf. *Reflexionen* ii. 124.
[5] Cf. *Reflexionen* ii. 95.   [6] Cf. below, p. 457.

The problem as to whether the doctrine of transcendental illusion and the deduction of the Ideas from the three species of syllogism originated early or late, is largely bound up with the question as to when Kant finally adopted the terms *Analytic* and *Dialectic* as titles for the two main divisions of his *Transcendental Logic.* That Kant was at first very uncertain as to what the main divisions of his system ought to be, appears very clearly from the *Reflexionen.*[1] To his teaching as a whole he usually applies the title *Transcendental Philosophy,* and in *Reflexion* ii. 123 he enumerates the following subdivisions within it: *Aesthetic, Logic, Critique,* and *Architectonic.* By *Critique* Kant must here mean what in other *Reflexionen* he names *Discipline,* and which he finally named *Dialectic.* As thus identified with the *Discipline,* the *Dialectic* is at times viewed as a division of a *Methodology* or *Organon,* whose other divisions are entitled *Canon* and *Architectonic.*[2] This earlier scheme may therefore be represented as follows:

Transcendental Philosophy
- Doctrine of Elements
  - Aesthetic.
  - Logic.
- Doctrine of Methods (Methodology)
  - Critique = Discipline [corresponding to the Dialectic of the *Critique*].
  - Canon.
  - Architectonic.

The terms *Analytic* and *Dialectic* do not occur in these *Reflexionen,* and their adoption may therefore be inferred to synchronise with Kant's later decision to include the treatment of the metaphysical sciences within his *Logic*; and that decision was probably an immediate result of his having developed meantime a doctrine of transcendental illusion. The new scheme in its final form is therefore as follows:

Transcendental Philosophy or Critique of Pure Reason
- Doctrine of Elements
  - Aesthetic.
  - Logic
    - Analytic
      - of Concepts.
      - of Judgment.
    - Dialectic—of Reason.
- Doctrine of Methods (Methodology)
  - Discipline (retained but given a new and more general content).
  - Canon.
  - Architectonic.
  - History.

In thus transferring *Dialectic* from the *Methodology* to the *Doctrine of Elements,* Kant stands committed to the view that it contains positive teaching of a character analogous to that of the *Analytic,* with which it is now co-ordinated. As we have already noted, the fundamental opposition which runs

---

[1] Cf. ii. 86 ff.   [2] Cf. *Reflexionen* ii. 114-15.

through the entire *Dialectic* is due to the conflict between the older view of Reason as merely understanding in its transcendent employment, and this later view of it as a distinct faculty, yielding concepts with a positive and indispensable function, different from, and yet also analogous to, that exercised by the categories of the understanding.

Adickes, to whom students of Kant are indebted for a convincing demonstration of the constant influence of Kant's logical architectonic upon the content of the Critical teaching, would seem at this point to rely too exclusively upon that method of explanation. He contends that Kant's deduction of the. Ideas of Reason from the three species of syllogism is entirely traceable to this source, and is without real philosophical significance. That is perhaps in the main true. But it need not prevent us from appreciating the importance of the doctrines which Kant contrives to expound under guise of this logical machinery. We have already observed that prior to the discovery of this deduction Kant had recognised the connection between the concept of the unconditioned and the three Ideas through which it finds expression. As the forms of syllogism are differentiated in terms of the three categories of relation, the deduction does not interfere with Kant's retention of this classification of Ideas; while in connecting Reason as a faculty with reasoning as a logical process, an excellent opportunity is found for explaining the grounds and significance of the demand for unconditionedness, *i.e.* for completeness of explanation. This demand, as he has also come to recognise, lies open to question, and therefore calls for more precise definition.

The artificial character of the metaphysical deduction lies not so much in this derivation of the three Ideas of the unconditioned—unconditioned substance, unconditioned causality, unconditioned system—from the categorical, hypothetical, and disjunctive forms of syllogism respectively, as in the further equating of them with the Ideas of the Self, the World, and God. The Idea of unconditioned substance has many possible applications besides the use to which it is put in rational psychology. The Idea of an unconditioned causality may be conceived in psychological and theological as well as in cosmological terms; and as a matter of fact Kant himself frequently identifies it with the concept of freedom, as in the third and fourth antinomies, or when he enumerates the Ideas as being those of God, Freedom, and Immortality.[1] Similarly, the Idea of system is the inspiring principle of materialism,

---

[1] B 394 *n.* Immortality is here taken as representing the Idea of the soul as unconditioned substance.

and also finds in such philosophies as that of Spinoza much more adequate expression than in the *Ens realissimum* of the Wolffian School. But further comment is not, at this stage, really profitable. These are questions which can best be discussed as they emerge in the course of the argument.[1]

Kant carried his logical architectonic one stage further. Not satisfied with connecting the three Ideas of Reason with the categories that underlie the three species of syllogism, he also attempted to organise the various particular applications of each Idea in terms of the fourfold division of the table of categories. By the use of his usual high-handed methods he succeeded in doing so in the case of the psychological and cosmological Ideas. There are four paralogisms and four antinomies. But when the attempt failed in regard to the theological Idea, he very wisely abstained from either apology or explanation. That the failure was not due to lack of desire or perseverance appears from *Reflexion* ii. 1573, which would seem to be the record of an unavailing attempt to obtain a satisfactory articulation of the theological Ideal. Doubtless, had he been sufficiently bent upon it, he could have worked out some sort of fourfold division; but there were limits even to Kant's devotion to the architectonic scheme. It is difficult to see how any such arrangement could have been followed without serious perversion of the argument.

Adickes has suggested[2] that the distinction between the faculty of understanding and the faculty of judgment is subsequent to, and suggested by, Kant's successful tracing of the Ideas to a separate faculty of Reason. Some such distinction was demanded in order that the parallelism of transcendental and formal logic might be complete. This conjecture of Adickes is probably correct. It would seem to be supported by the internal evidence of the *Analytic of Principles*. As we have had occasion to note,[3] the doctrine of schematism, in terms of which the distinction between understanding and judgment is formulated, is late in date of origin.[4] This distinction is of the same artificial character as that between understanding and Reason; and though, like the latter distinction, it supplies Kant with a convenient framework for the arrangement of genuinely Critical material, it also tends to conceal the simpler and more inward bonds of true relationship.

[1] Cf. below, p. 454, with further references in *n.* 1.
[2] *Systematik*, pp. 115-16.   [3] Above, p. 334.
[4] This conclusion is supported by the evidence of the *Reflexionen*: they contain not a single reference to schematism.

TRANSCENDENTAL DIALECTIC

INTRODUCTION

I. Transcendental Illusion

Dialectic is a Logic of Illusion.[1]—The meaning which Kant attaches to the term dialectic has already been considered. The passage above quoted[2] from his *Logic* shows the meaning which he supposed the term historically to possess, namely, as being a sophistical art of disputation, presenting false principles in the guise of truth by means of a seeming fulfilment of the demands of strict logical proof. The incorrectness of this historical derivation hardly needs to be pointed out. Kant professes[3] to be following his contemporaries in thus using the term as a title for the treatment of false reasoning. But even this statement must be challenged. Adickes, after examination of a large number of eighteenth-century textbooks, reports[4] that in the six passages in which alone he has found it to occur it is never so employed. In Meier it is used as a title for the theory of probable reasoning,[5] and in Baumgarten it occurs only in adjectival form as equivalent to sophistical. This last is the nearest approach to Kant's definition. All historical considerations may therefore be swept aside. We are concerned only with the specific meaning which Kant thought good to attach to the term. He adapts it in the freest manner to the needs of his system. In A 61 = B 85, as in his *Logic*, he has defined it in merely negative fashion. He is now careful to specify the more positive aspects of the problems with which it deals. Though definable as the logic of illusion, the deceptive inferences with which it concerns itself are of a quite unique and supremely significant character. They must, as above noted,[6]

---

[1] A 293 = B 349.
[2] Pp. 173-4.
[3] Cf. A 61 = B 85.
[4] Adickes, *Systematik*, p. 77 ff.
[5] Cf. Kant's *caveat* in A 293 = B 349 against identifying dialectic with the doctrine of probable reasoning.
[6] Pp. 427-8.

be distinguished alike from logical and from empirical illusion They have their roots in the fundamental needs of the human mind, and the recognition of their illusory character does not render unnecessary either a positive explanation of their occurrence or a Critical valuation of their practical function as regulative ideals.

A 293 = B 349.—Regarding the connection between illusion and error cf. B 69, and above, pp. 148-53.

A 295 = B 352.—Logical, empirical, and transcendental illusion. Cf. above, pp. 13, 427-9, 437.

A 296 = B 352.—Kant here defines the terms transcendental and transcendent in a very unusual manner. The two terms are not, he states, synonymous. The principles of pure understanding are of merely empirical validity, and *consequently* are not of *transcendental* employment beyond the limits of experience. A principle is *transcendent* when it not only removes these limits, but prescribes the overstepping of them.

II. *Pure Reason as the Seat of Transcendental Illusion*[1]

(a) *Reason in General*

Reason, like understanding, is employed in two ways, formal or logical and real. The logical use of Reason consists in mediate inference, the real in the generation of concepts and principles. Reason is thus both a logical and a transcendental faculty, and we may therefore expect that its logical functions will serve as a clue to those that are transcendental. The argument which follows is extremely obscure. It is a foreshadowing in logical terms of a distinction which, as Kant himself indicates, cannot at this stage be adequately stated. The distinction may be extended and paraphrased as follows. Reason, generically taken as including both activities, is the faculty of principles, in distinction from understanding which is the faculty of rules.[2] Principles, properly so-called, are absolutely *a priori*. Universals which imply the element of intuition must not, therefore, be ranked as principles in the strict sense. They are more properly to be entitled rules. A true principle is one that affords knowledge of the particulars which come under it, and which does so from its own internal resources, that is to say, through pure concepts. In other words, it yields *a priori* synthetic knowledge, and yet does so independently of all given experience. Now, as the *Analytic* has proved, knowledge obtained through understanding, whether

---

[1] A 298 = B 355.   [2] Cf. above, p. 332.

in mathematical or in physical science, is never of this character. Its principles, even though originating in pure intuition or in the pure understanding, are valid only as conditions of possible experience, and are applicable only to such objects as can occur in the context of a sense-perception. That is to say, the understanding can never obtain synthetic knowledge through pure concepts. Though, for instance, it prescribes the principle that everything which happens must have a cause, that principle does not establish itself by means of the concepts which it contains, but only as being a presupposition necessary to the possibility of sense-experience. If, then, principles in the strict sense actually exist, they must be due to a faculty distinct from understanding, and will call for a deduction of a different character from that of the categories.

In the last paragraph but one of the section Kant indicates the doctrine which he is foreshadowing. The rules of understanding apply to appearances, prescribing the conditions under which the unity necessary to any and every experience can alone be attained. The principles of Reason do not apply directly to appearances, but only to the understanding, defining the standards to which its activities must conform, if a completely unified experience is to be achieved. Whereas the rules of understanding are the conditions of objective existence in space and time, principles in the strict sense are criteria for the attainment of such absoluteness and totality as will harmonise Reason with itself. Reason, determined by principles which issue from its own inherent nature, prescribes what the actual ought to be; understanding, proceeding from rules which express the conditions of possible experience, can yield knowledge only of what is found to exist in the course of sense-experience. The unity of Reason is Ideal; the unity of understanding is empirical. Principles are due to the *self-determination* of reason; the rules of understanding express the necessitated determinations of sense. The former demand a more perfect and complete unity than is ever attainable by means of the latter. Two passages from the *Lose Blätter* will help to define the distinction.

"There is a synthesis prototypon and a synthesis ectypon. The one . . . *simpliciter, a termino a priori,* . . . the other *secundum quid, a termino a posteriori.* . . . Reason advances from the universal to the particular, the understanding from the particular to the universal. . . . The first is absolute and belongs to the free or metaphysical, and also to the moral, employment of Reason."[1] "The principles of

---

[1] Reicke, i. p. 105.

the synthesis of pure Reason are all metaphysical. . . . [They] are principles of the subjective unity of knowledge through Reason, *i.e.* of the agreement of Reason with itself." [1]

The chief interest of this section lies in its clear indication of the dual standpoint to which Kant is committing himself by the manner in which he formulates this distinction between rules and principles. The indispensableness of the latter, upon which Kant is prepared to insist, points to the Idealist interpretation of their grounds and validity ; their derivation from mere concepts, without reference to or basis in experience, must, on the other hand, in view of the teaching of the *Analytic*, commit Kant to a sceptical treatment of their objective validity. In the above account, suggestions of the Idealist point of view are not entirely absent ; but, on the whole, it is the sceptical view that is dominant. The Ideas of Reason can be justified as necessary only for the perfecting of experience, not as conditions of experience as such. They express a subjective interest in the attainment of unity, not conditions of the possibility of objective existence.

"[Civil Laws] are only limitations imposed upon our freedom in order that such freedom may completely harmonise with itself ; hence they are directed to something which is entirely our own work, and of which we ourselves, through these concepts, can be the cause. But that objects in themselves, the very nature of things, should stand under principles, and should be determined according to mere concepts, is a demand which, if not impossible, is at least quite contrary to common sense [*widersinnisches*]." [2]

(b) The Logical Use of Reason [3]

In this subsection Kant introduces the distinction between understanding and judgment which he has sought to justify in A 130 ff. = B 169 ff. By showing that inference determines the *relation* between a major premiss (due to the understanding) and the condition defined in the minor premiss (due to the faculty of judgment), he professes to obtain justification for classifying the possible forms of reasoning according to the three categories of relation. The general remark is added that the purpose of Reason, in its logical employment as inference, is to obtain the highest possible unity, through subsumption of all multiplicity under the smallest possible number of universals.

---

[1] *Op. cit.* i. pp. 109-10.   [2] A 301-2 = B 358.   [3] A 303 = B 359.

(c) The Pure Use of Reason[1]

Kant here states the alternatives between which the *Dialectic* has to decide. Is Reason merely formal, arranging given material according to given forms of unity, or is it a source of principles which prescribe higher forms of unity than any revealed by actual experience? Further examination of its formal and logical procedure constrains us, Kant asserts, to adopt the latter position ; and at the same time indicates how those principles must be interpreted, namely, as subjective laws that apply not to objects but only to the activities of the understanding.

In the first place, a syllogism is not directly concerned with intuitions, but only with concepts and judgments. This may be taken as indicating that pure Reason relates to objects only mediately *by way* of understanding and its judgments. The unity which it seeks is higher than that of any possible experience ; it is a unity which must be constructed and cannot be given.[2]

Secondly, Reason in its logical use seeks the *universal* condition of its judgment ; and when such is not found in the major premiss proceeds to its discovery through a regressive series of prosyllogisms. In so doing it is obviously determined by a principle expressive of the peculiar function of Reason in its logical employment, namely, that for the conditioned knowledge of understanding the *unconditioned* unity in which that knowledge may find completion must be discovered. Such a principle is synthetic, since from analysis of the conception of the conditioned we can discover its relation to a condition, but never its relation to the *unconditioned*. That is a notion which falls entirely outside the sphere of the understanding, and which therefore demands a separate enquiry. How is the above *a priori* synthetic principle to be accounted for, if it cannot be traced to understanding? Has it objective, or has it merely subjective validity? And lastly, what further synthetic principles can be based upon it? Such are the questions to which Critical *Dialectic* must supply an answer. This *Dialectic* will be composed of two main divisions, the doctrine of "the transcendent concepts of pure Reason" and the doctrine of "transcendent and dialectical inferences of Reason."

[1] A 305 = B 362.

[2] The wording of the concluding sentence of the third paragraph (A 307 = B 363-4) is so condensed as to be misleading. "It [viz. the principle of causality] makes the unity of experience possible, and borrows nothing from the Reason. The latter, if it were not for this [its indirect] reference [through mediation of the understanding] to possible experience, could never [of itself], from mere concepts, have imposed a synthetic unity of that kind."

BOOK I

THE CONCEPTS OF PURE REASON[1]

The distinction here drawn between concepts obtained by reflection and concepts gained by inference is a somewhat misleading mode of stating the fact that, whereas the categories of understanding condition experience and so make possible the unity of consciousness necessary to all reflection, or, in other words, are conditions of the material supplied for inference, the concepts of Reason are Ideal constructions which though in a certain sense resting upon experience none the less transcend it. The function of the Ideas is to organise experience in its totality; that of the categories is to render possible the sense-perceptions constitutive of its content. The former refer to the unconditioned, and though that is a conception under which everything experienced is conceived to fall, it represents a type of knowledge to which no actual experience can ever be adequate.

Conceptus ratiocinati—conceptus ratiocinantes. When such transcendent concepts possess "objective validity," they are correctly inferred, and may be entitled *conceptus ratiocinati*. If, on the other hand, they are due to merely sophistical[2] reasoning, they are purely fictitious, *conceptus ratiocinantes*. This distinction raises many difficulties. Kant's intention cannot be to deny that the *conceptus ratiocinati* are "mere Ideas" (*entia rationis*)[3]—for such is his avowed and constant contention—or that the inference to them is dialectical and is based upon a transcendental illusion. Two alternatives are open. He may mean that they are only valid when the results of such inference are Critically reinterpreted, and when the function of the Ideas is realised to be merely regulative; or his intention may be to mark off the Ideas, strictly so-called, which are inevitable and beneficial products of Reason, from the many idle and superfluous inventions of speculative

---

[1] A 310 = B 366.
[2] *Schein des Schliessens* would seem to be here used in that sense.
[3] Cf. above, p. 424.

thought. Kant's concluding remark, that the questions at issue can be adequately discussed only at a later stage, may be taken as in the nature of an apology for the looseness of these preliminary statements, and as a warning to the reader not to insist upon them too absolutely. The participles *ratio-cinati* and *ratiocinantes* [1] are of doubtful latinity. The distinction of meaning here imposed upon them has not been traced in any other writer, and is perhaps Kant's own invention.[2]

SECTION I

IDEAS IN GENERAL [3]

Kant connects his use of the term Idea with the meaning in which it is employed by Plato. He urges upon all true lovers of philosophy the imperative need of rescuing from misuse a term so indispensable to mark a distinction more vital than any other to the very existence of the philosophical disciplines.

"[For Plato] Ideas are the archetypes of the things themselves, and not, like the categories, merely keys to possible experiences. In his view they issued from the Supreme Reason, and from that source have come to be shared in by human Reason. . . . He very well realised that our faculty of knowledge feels a much higher need than merely to spell out appearances according to a synthetic unity, in order to read them as experience. He knew that our Reason naturally exalts itself to forms of knowledge which so far transcend the bounds of experience that no given empirical object can ever coincide with them, but which must none the less be recognised as having their own reality and which are by no means mere fictions of the brain." [4]

Plato found these ideas chiefly, though not exclusively, in the practical sphere. When moral standards are in question, experience is the mother of illusion.

"For nothing can be more injurious or more unworthy of a philosopher than the vulgar appeal to so-called adverse experience. Such experience would never have existed at all, if those institutions had been established at the proper time in accordance with Ideas, and if Ideas had not been displaced by crude conceptions which, just because they have been derived from experience, have nullified all good intentions." [5]

---

[1] Cf. also A 669 = B 697 ; A 680 = B 709.
[2] Cf. Vaihinger, " Kant—ein Metaphysiker ?" in *Philosophische Abhandlungen* (Sigwart *Gedenkschrift*), p. 144.
[3] A 312 = B 368.   [4] A 313 = B 370.
[5] A 316-17 = B 373. The context of this passage is a defence of Plato's *Republic* against the charge that it is Utopian, because unrealisable.

Even in the natural sphere Ideas which are never themselves adequately embodied in the actual must be postulated
in order to account for the actual. Certain forms of existences "are possible only according to Ideas."

"A plant, an animal, the orderly arrangement of the cosmos—
probably, therefore, the entire natural world—clearly show that they
are possible only according to Ideas, and that though no single
creature in the conditions of its individual existence coincides with
the Idea of what is most perfect in its kind—just as little as does
any individual man exactly conform to the Idea of humanity, which
he actually carries in his soul as the archetype of his actions—yet
these Ideas are none the less completely determined in the Supreme
Understanding, each as an individual and each as unchangeable,
and are the original causes of things. But only the totality of
things, in their interconnection as constituting the universe, is completely adequate to the Idea."[1]

Though Kant avows the intention of adapting the term
Idea freely to the needs of his more Critical standpoint, all
these considerations contribute to the rich and varied meanings
in which he employs it.

Reflexionen and passages from the *Lectures on Metaphysics*
may be quoted to show the thoroughly Platonic character of
Kant's early use of the term, and to illustrate its gradual
adjustment to Critical demands.

"The Idea is the unity of knowledge, through which the manifold
either of knowledge or of the object is possible. In the former, the
whole of knowledge precedes its parts, the universal precedes the
particular; in the latter, knowledge of the objects precedes their
possibility, as *e.g.* in [objects that possess] order and perfection."[2]
"That an object is possible only through a form of knowledge is a
surprising statement; but all teleological relations are possible only
through a form of knowledge [*i.e.* a concept]."[3] "The Idea is
single (*individuum*), self-sufficient, and eternal. The divinity of our
soul is its capacity to form the Idea. The senses give only copies
or rather *apparentia*."[4] "As the Understanding of God is the
ground of all possibility, archetypes, Ideas, are in God. . . . The
divine *Intuitus* contains Ideas according to which we ourselves are
possible; *cognitio divina est cognitio archetypa*, and His Ideas are
archetypes of things. The [corresponding] forms of knowledge

---

[1] A 317-18 = B 374-5.
[2] *Reflexionen* ii. 1240. Cf. Schopenhauer: *World as Will and Idea* (*Werke*,
ii. p. 277: Eng. trans. i. p. 303): "The *Idea* is the unity that falls into multiplicity on account of the temporal and spatial form of our intuitive apprehension;
the *concept*, on the contrary, is the unity reconstructed out of multiplicity by
the abstraction of our reason; the latter may be defined as *unitas post rem*, the
former as *unitas ante rem*."
[3] *Lectures on Metaphysics* (Pölitz, 1821), p. 79.   [4] *Reflexionen* ii. 1243

possessed by the human understanding we may also entitle (in a comparative sense) archetypes or Ideas. They are those representations of our understanding which serve for judgment upon things."[1] "Idea is the representation of the whole in so far as it necessarily precedes the determination of the parts. It can never be empirically represented, because in experience we proceed from the parts through successive synthesis to the whole. It is the archetype of things, for certain objects are only possible through an Idea. Transcendental Ideas are those in which the absolute whole determines the parts in an aggregate or as series."[2] "The pure concepts of Reason have no *exemplaria*; they are themselves archetypes. But the concepts of our pure Reason have as their archetypes this Reason itself and are therefore subjective, not objective."[3] "The transcendental Ideas serve to limit the principles of experience, forbidding their extension to things in themselves, and showing that what is never an object of possible experience is not therefore a non-entity [*Unding*], and that experience is not adequate either to itself or to Reason, but always refers us further to what is beyond itself."[4] "The employment of the concept of understanding was immanent, that of the Ideas as concepts of objects is transcendent. But as regulative principles alike of the completion and of the limitation of our knowledge, they are Critically immanent."[5] "The difficulties of metaphysics all arise in connection with the reconciling of empirical principles with Ideas. The possibility of the latter cannot be denied, but neither can they be made empirically intelligible. The Idea is never a *conceptus dabilis*; it is not an empirically possible conception."[6]

Kant[7] appends the following 'Stufenleiter' (ladder-like) arrangement of titles for the various kinds of representation. Representation (*Vorstellung*) is the term which he substitutes for the Cartesian and Lockian employment of the term idea, now reserved for use in its true Platonic meaning. To entitle such a representation as that of red colour an idea is, in Kant's view, an intolerable and barbaric procedure; that representation is not even a concept of the understanding.

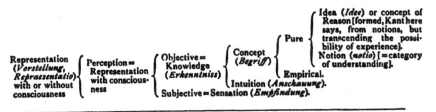

---

[1] *Lectures on Metaphysics*, pp. 308-9.   [2] *Reflexionen* ii. 1244.
[3] *Reflexionen* ii. 1254.   [4] *Reflexionen* ii. 1258.
[6] *Reflexionen* ii. 1259.   [5] *Reflexionen* ii. 1260.
[7] A 320 = B 376-7.

SECTION II

THE TRANSCENDENTAL IDEAS [1]

This section completes the metaphysical deduction of the Ideas. In the preceding sections on the logical and on the pure use of Reason, Kant has pointed out that Reason proceeds in accordance with the principle, that for the conditioned knowledge of understanding the unconditioned, in which it finds completion, must be discovered. This principle is synthetic, involving a concept which transcends the understanding; and as Reason in its logical use is merely formal, that concept must be due to Reason in its creative or transcendental activity. In the section before us Kant deduces from the three kinds of syllogism the three possible forms in which such an Idea of Reason can present itself. The deduction is, as already noted, wholly artificial, and masks Kant's real method of obtaining the Ideas, namely, through combination of the unique concept of the unconditioned with the three categories of relation. The deduction is based upon an extremely ingenious analogy between the logical function of Reason in deductive inference and its transcendental procedure in prescribing the Ideal of unconditioned totality. In the syllogism the predicate of the conclusion is shown to be connected with its subject in accordance with a condition which is stated in its universality in the major premiss. Thus if the conclusion be: Caius is mortal, in constructing the syllogism, required to establish it, we seek for a conception which contains the condition under which the predicate is given—in this case the conception "man"—and we state that condition in its universality: All men are mortal. Under this major premiss is then subsumed Caius, the object dealt with: Caius is a man. And so indirectly, by reference to the universal condition, we obtain the knowledge that Caius is mortal. Universality, antecedently stated, is restricted in the conclusion to a specific object. Now what corresponds in the synthesis of intuition to the *universality* (*universalitas*) of a logical premiss is *allness* (*universitas*) or *totality* of conditions. The transcendental concept of Reason, to which the logical procedure is to serve as clue, can therefore be no other than that of the totality of conditions for any given conditioned. And as totality of conditions is equivalent to the *unconditioned*, this latter must be taken as the fundamental concept of Reason;

[1] A 321 = B 377.

the unconditioned is conceived as being the ground of the synthesis of everything conditioned. But there are three species of relation, and consequently there are three forms in which the concept of Reason seeks to realise its demand for the unconditioned: (1) through categorical synthesis in one subject, (2) through hypothetical synthesis of the members of a series, and (3) through disjunctive synthesis of the parts in one system. To these three correspond the three species of syllogism, categorical, hypothetical, and disjunctive, in each of which thought passes through a regressive series of pro-syllogisms back to an unconditioned: the first to a concept which stands for what is always a subject and never a predicate; the second to a presupposition which itself presupposes nothing further; and the third to such an aggregate of the members of the division as will make that division complete. It may be observed that in this proof the threefold specification of the concept of the unconditioned is really obtained directly from the categories of relation, or at least from the judgments of relation, and not from the corresponding species of syllogism.

Totality and unconditionedness, when taken as equivalent, become synonymous with the *absolute*.[1] This last term, however, especially when taken as defining possibility and necessity, is ambiguous. The absolutely possible may signify either that which in itself, *i.e.* so far as regards its internal content, is possible; or else that which is in every respect and in all relations possible. The two meanings have come to be connected largely owing to the fact that the internally impossible is impossible in every respect. Otherwise, however, the two meanings fall completely apart. Absolute necessity and inner necessity are quite diverse in character. We must not, for instance, argue that the opposite of what is absolutely necessary must be inwardly impossible, nor consequently that absolute necessity must in the end reduce to an inner necessity. Examination will show that, in certain types of cases, not the slightest meaning can be attached to the phrase 'inner necessity.' As we possess the terms inner and logical to denote the first form of necessity, there is no excuse for employing the term absolute in any but the wider sense. That, Kant holds, is its original and proper meaning. The *absolute* totality to which the concept of Reason refers is that form of completeness which is in every respect unconditioned.

In A 326 = B 383 Kant's mode of statement emphasises the connection of the Ideas with the categories of relation. Reason, he claims, "seeks to extend the synthetic unity, which is

[1] A 323-4=B 380-1. Cf. below, pp. 480, 529, 559 60.

thought in the category, to the absolutely unconditioned." Such positive content as the Ideas can possess lies in the experience which they profess to unify; in so far as they transcend experience and point to an Ideal completion that is not empirically attainable, they refer to things of which the understanding can have no concept. It is necessary, however, that they should present themselves in this absolute and transcendent form, since otherwise the understanding would be without stimulus and without guidance. Though mere Ideas, they are neither arbitrary nor superfluous. They regulate the understanding in its empirical pursuit of that systematic unity which it requires for its own satisfaction.

In A 327-8 = B 383-4 one and the same ground is assigned for entitling the Ideas transcendental and also transcendent, namely, that, as they surpass experience, no object capable of being given through the senses corresponds to them. But a difference would none the less seem to be implied in the connotation of the two terms. In being prescribed by the very nature of Reason, they are transcendental; as over-stepping the limits of experience, they are transcendent. Kant's use of the terms subject and object in this passage is also somewhat puzzling. 'Object' is employed in the metaphysical sense proper only from the pre-Critical stand-point of the *Dissertation*, as meaning an existence apprehended through pure thought. The term 'subject' receives a corre-spondingly un-Critical connotation. The further phrase "the merely speculative use of Reason" is somewhat misleading, even though we recognise that for Kant speculative and theoretical are synonymous terms; we should rather expect "Reason in its legitimate or Critical or directive function." Kant's intended meaning, however, is sufficiently clear. When we say that a concept of Reason is an Idea merely, we have in mind the degree to which it can be *empirically* verified. We are asserting that it prescribes an Ideal to which experience may be made to approach, but which it can never attain. It defines "a problem to which there is no solution." In the practical sphere of morals, on the other hand, the Ideal of Reason must never be so described. Though only partially realisable, it is genuinely actual. Even those actions which imperfectly embody it none the less presuppose it as their indispensable condition. In two respects, therefore, as Kant points out, the statement that the transcendental concepts of Reason are merely Ideas calls for qualification. In the first place they are by no means "super-fluous and void." They supply a canon for the fruitful em-ployment of understanding. And secondly, they may perhaps be found to make possible a transition from natural to moral concepts, and so to bring the Ideas of practical Reason into connection with the principles of speculative thought. The reader may again note the genuinely Platonic character of Kant's use of the term Idea.

In A 330-1 = B 386-7 Kant returns to the problem of the metaphysical deduction, and analyses the nature of syllogistic reasoning.   The analysis differs from that of A 321 ff. = B 377 ff. only in emphasising that when a conclusion is given as valid the totality of the premises required for its establishment can be postulated as likewise given, and that when completely stated in the implied prosyllogisms the premises form a regressive series.   In this way Kant contrives to bring the logical process into closer connection with the transcendental principle, which he now definitively formulates as follows : When the conditioned is given, the series of conditions up to the unconditioned is likewise given.   The series of antecedent conditions may either have a first term or may be incapable of such.   In either case it has to be viewed as unconditioned, in the one case in virtue of its unconditioned beginning, in the other in its character as an unending and therefore unlimited series.   In one or other form Reason demands that the unconditioned be recognised as underlying and determining everything conditioned.[1]

SECTION III

SYSTEM OF THE TRANSCENDENTAL IDEAS [2]

The three Ideas of Reason, as derived from the three kinds of syllogism, are now brought into connection with the three possible relations in which representations are found to stand : first, to the thinking subject; secondly, to objects as appearances ; thirdly, to objects of thought in general.   Kant argues that the completed totalities towards which Reason strives are likewise three in number.   Reason seeks : (1) in regard to the subject known, as constituting the fact of inner experience, a representation of the self or soul that will render completely intelligible what is peculiar to the inner life ; (2) in regard to the object known, a conception of the completed totality of the world of phenomena, the cosmos ; (3) in regard to the ultimate synthesis of the subject known and the object known, such a conception of all existing things

[1] Regarding the *progressive series* from the conditioned to its consequences, cf. A 336-7 = B 393-4, A 410-11 = B 437-8, A 511 = B 539.   [2] A 333 = B 390.

as will render intelligible the co-operation of mind and external nature in one experience. In this way Kant professes to obtain transcendental justification for the threefold division of metaphysical science into rational psychology, rational cosmology, and rational theology. The absolute unity of the thinking subject is dealt with by psychology, the totality of all appearances by cosmology, and the Being, which contains the condition of the possibility of all that can be thought, by theology.

In thus proceeding, Kant is assuming that the concepts of unconditioned substance and of unconditioned necessity can be interpreted only in spiritualist and theological terms.[1] This assumption stands in direct conflict with what the history of philosophy records. The Absolute has frequently been materialistically defined, and, as Kant himself admits, we cannot prove that the thinking subject may not be naturalistically conditioned. Architectonic is again exercising its baleful influence. That the argument is lacking in cogency is indeed so evident that Kant takes notice of the deficiency,[2] and promises that it will be remedied in the sequel. This promise he is unable to fulfil. Such further reasons as he is able to offer are of the same external character.[3]

"Of these transcendental Ideas, *strictly speaking, no objective deduction, such as we were able to give of the categories, is possible.*"[4]   As Kant indicates by use of the phrase 'strictly speaking,' this statement is subject to modification. He himself formulates a transcendental deduction of the Ideas, as principles regulative of experience.[5] The deduction from the three forms of syllogism, which Kant here entitles subjective, ought properly to be named 'metaphysical.'[6]

---

[1] Cf. above, pp. 418. 436, 439-40; below, pp. 473-7, 520-1, 537, 543 ff., 575.
[2] Cf. A 335.
[3] Cf. A 337-8 = B 394-6 and note appended to B 394.
[4] A 336 = B 393.
[5] Cf. A 671 = B 699; above, pp. 426, 430, 436; below, pp. 552-4, 572 ff.
[6] On the difference between the ascending and the descending series, cf. A 331-2 = B 338 and A 410-11 = B 437-8.

BOOK II

THE DIALECTICAL INFERENCES OF PURE REASON[1]

CHAPTER I

THE PARALOGISMS OF PURE REASON[2]

As rational psychology fails to distinguish between appearances and things in themselves, it identifies mere apperception with inner sense; the self in experiencing the succession of its inner states is supposed to acquire knowledge of its own essential nature. " I, as thinking, am an object of inner sense, and am entitled soul," in contrast to the body which is an object of outer sense. Empirical psychology deals with the concrete detail of inner experience; rational psychology abstracts from all such special experiences, indeed from everything empirical, professing to establish its doctrine upon the single judgment, " I think." That judgment has already been investigated in its connection with the problem of the possibility, within the field of experience, of synthetic *a priori* judgments. It has now to be considered as a possible basis for knowledge of the self as a thinking being (*ein denkend Wesen*) or soul (*Seele*).

Following the guiding thread of the table of categories, but placing them in what he regards as being, in this connection, the most convenient order, Kant obtains a " topic " or classification of the possible rubrics for the doctrines of a rational psychology: (1) the soul is *substance*; (2) is *simple*; (3) is *numerically identical*; (4) stands in relation to *possible* objects in space. Now all those four doctrines are, Kant holds,

---

[1] The questions raised in the two introductory paragraphs (A 336-40= B 396-8) as to the content of the Ideas, their problematic character, and their possibility as concepts, are first adequately discussed in later chapters. The three new terms here introduced, Paralogism, Antinomy, and Ideal, can also best be commented upon in their own special context.

[2] A 341 = B 399.

incapable of demonstration. The proofs propounded by rational psychology are logically imperfect, committing the logical fallacy which is technically named paralogism.[1] The fallacy is not, however, of merely logical character. Had that been the case, it could never have gained such general currency. Certainly no metaphysical science, widely accepted by profound thinkers, could ever have come to be based upon it. The paralogism is transcendental in character, resting upon a transcendental ground. It represents an illusion which from any non-Critical standpoint is altogether unavoidable. Its dialectic is a natural dialectic, wrongly interpreted by the Schools, but not capriciously invented by them. The key to its proper treatment is first supplied by the results of the transcendental deduction. We are now called upon to apply these results in explanation of the occurrence of the paralogisms, and in judgment upon their false claims. Little that is really new is to be found in this chapter; but many of the established results of the *Analytic* receive interesting illustration, and are thereby set in a clearer light.

In rational psychology the " I think " is taken in its universal, or to use Kant's somewhat misleading term, problematic aspect, that is to say, not as a judgment expressive of the self's own existence but "in its mere possibility,"[2] as representing the self-consciousness of all possible thinking beings. As we cannot gain a representation of thinking beings through outer experience, we are constrained to think them in terms of our own self-consciousness. The " I think " is thus taken as a universal judgment, expressing what belongs to the conception of thinking being in general. The judgment is so interpreted by rational psychology, "in order to see what predicates applicable to its subject (be that subject actually existent or not) may flow from so simple a judgment."

In summarising what is directly relevant in the argument of the transcendental deduction, Kant emphasises that the I, as representation, is altogether empty of content.[3]

"We cannot even say that it is a conception, but only that it is a bare (*blosses*) consciousness which accompanies all conceptions. Through this I or he or it (the thing) which thinks, nothing further is represented than a transcendental subject of the thoughts $= x \ . \ . \ ."$

It is apprehended only in its relation to the thoughts which are its predicates; apart from them we cannot form any conception whatever of it, but can only revolve in a perpetual

---

[1] Cf. below, pp. 466, 470.　　[2] A 347.　　[3] A 345-6 = B 403-4.

circle, since any judgment upon it has already made use of its representation.[1]

The patchwork character of the *Critique*, the artificial nature of the connections between its various parts, is nowhere more evident than in this section on the *Paralogisms*. According to the definition given of transcendental illusion, we naturally expect Kant's argument to show that the *Paralogisms* rest upon a failure to distinguish between appearance and reality. As a matter of fact, the cause of their fallacy is traced in the first three *Paralogisms* solely to a failure to distinguish between the logical and the real application of the categories. The argument can indeed be restated so as to agree with the introductory sections of the *Dialectic*. But Kant's manner of expounding the *Paralogisms* shows that this chapter must originally have been written independently of any intention to develop such teaching as that of the sections to which, in the *Critique*, they are made to lead up.[2]

First Paralogism: of Substantiality.[3]—Save for the phrase 'subject in itself,' there is, in Kant's comment upon this *Paralogism*, not a word regarding the necessity of a distinction between appearance and reality, but only an insistence that the " I think " yields no knowledge of the thinking self. Consciousness of the self and knowledge of its underlying substance are by no means identical. The self, so far as it enters into consciousness, is a merely logical subject; the underlying substrate is that to which this self-consciousness and all other thoughts are due. It is in the light of this distinction that Kant discusses the substantiality of the subject. As expressive of the " I think," the category of substance and attribute can be employed only to define the relation in which consciousness stands to its thoughts; it expresses the merely logical relation of a subject to its predicates. It tells us nothing regarding the nature of the " I," save only that it is the invariable centre of reference for all thoughts. In order to know the self as substance, and so as capable of persisting throughout all change, and as surviving even the death of the body, we should require to have an intuition of it, and of such intuition there is not the slightest trace in the " I think." It " signifies a substance only in Idea, not in reality."[4] As Kant adds later,[5] the permanence and self-identity of the representation of the self justifies no argument to the permanence and self-identity of its underlying conditions. Inference from the nature of representation to the nature of the object represented

---

[1] Cf. A 354-5.   [2] Cf. above, p. 437.   [3] A 348.
[4] A 351.   [5] A 363-4.

is entirely illegitimate. In the equating of the two, and not, as the introduction to the *Dialectic* would lead us to expect, in a failure to distinguish appearance from reality, consists the paralogistic fallacy of this first syllogism.

Second Paralogism: of Simplicity.[1]—We may follow Adickes[2] in his analysis of A 351-62. (*a*) The original criticism, parallel to that of the first *Paralogism*, would seem to be contained in paragraphs five to nine. (*b*) The opening paragraphs, and (*c*) the concluding paragraphs, would seem, for reasons stated below, to be independent and later additions.

(*a*) The argument of the central paragraphs runs almost exactly parallel with the criticism of the first *Paralogism*, applying the same line of thought, in disproof of the assumed argument for the simplicity of the soul. It may be noted, in passing, that Kant here departs from his table of categories. There is no category of simplicity. The connection which he seeks to establish between the concept of simplicity and the categories of quality is arbitrary. It more naturally connects with the category of unity; but the category of unity is required for the third *Paralogism*. For explanation of the way in which he equates the concept of simplicity with the category of reality Kant is satisfied to refer the reader to the section on the second antinomy in which this same identification occurs.[3] Indeed the simplicity here dwelt upon seems hardly distinguishable from substantiality, and therefore it is not surprising that Kant's criticism of the second *Paralogism* should be practically identical with that of the first.[4] Since the " I," as logical subject of thought, signifies only a something in general, and embodies no insight into the constitution of this something, it is for that reason empty of all content, and consequently simple. "The simplicity of the *representation* of a subject is not *eo ipso* a knowledge of the simplicity of the subject itself. . . ." The second *Paralogism* thus, in Kant's view, falsely argues from the merely logical unity of the subject *in representation* to the actual simplicity of the subject *in itself*.

(*b*) One reason for regarding the first four paragraphs as a later addition is their opening reference to the introductory sections of the *Dialectic*, of which this chapter otherwise takes little or no account. This *Paralogism* is, Kant declares, "the Achilles of all the dialectical inferences in the pure doctrine of the soul," meaning that it may well seem a quite invulnerable argument.[5]

---

[1] A 351.　　　　　　　　　　　　　　　[2] *K.* 688 *n.*

[3] A similar criticism holds true of the conception of identity employed in the third *Paralogism*, and arbitrarily equated with the categories of quantity.

[4] Cf. A 355-6.

[5] It is very forcibly developed in Mendelssohn's " Phädon " (1767) (*Gesam-*

"It is no mere sophistical play contrived by a dogmatist in order to impart to his assertions a superficial plausibility (*Schein*), but an inference which appears to withstand even the keenest scrutiny and the most scrupulously exact investigation."

The second paragraph is a very pointed restatement of a main supporting argument of this second *Paralogism*. This argument well deserves the eulogy with which Kant has ushered it in. It is as follows. The unity of consciousness can not be explained as due to the co-operative action of independent substances. Such a merely external effect as that of motion in a material body may be the resultant of the united motions of its parts. But it is otherwise with thought. For should that which thinks be viewed as composite, and the different representations, as, for instance, of the single words of a verse, be conceived as distributed among the several parts, a multiplicity of separate consciousnesses would result, and the single complex consciousness, that of the verse as a whole, would be rendered impossible. Consciousness cannot therefore—such is the argument—inhere in the composite. The soul must be a simple substance.[1]

As there is no reference in this argument to the " I think," the criticism cannot be that of the first *Paralogism*, nor that of the central paragraphs of this second *Paralogism*. Kant's reply—as given in the third and fourth paragraphs—is in effect to refer the reader to the results of the *Analytic*, and is formulated in the manner of his *Introduction* to the *Critique*. The principle that multiplicity of representation presupposes absolute unity in the thinking subject can neither be demonstrated analytically from mere concepts, nor derived from experience. Being a synthetic *a priori* judgment, it can be established only by means of a transcendental deduction. But in that form it will define only a condition required for the possibility of consciousness; it can tell us nothing in regard to the noumenal nature of the thinking being. And, as Kant argues in the third *Paralogism*,[2] there may be a possible analogy between thought and motion, though of a different kind from that above suggested.

The entire absence of all connection between the argument of these paragraphs and the argument of those which immedi-

---

melte Schriften, 1843, ii. p. 151 ff.). This is a work with which Kant was familiar. Cf. below, p. 470.

[1] This is the argument which William James has expounded in his characteristically picturesque style. " Take a sentence of a dozen words, and take twelve men and tell to each one word. Then stand the men in a row or jam them in a bunch, and let each think of his word as intently as he will; nowhere will there be a consciousness of the whole sentence " (*Principles of Psychology*, i. p. 160).

[2] A 363 *n*. Cf. below, pp. 461-2.

ately follow upon them, at least suffices to show that this second *Paralogism* has not been written as a continuous whole; and taken together with the fact that the problem is here formulated in terms of the *Introduction* to the *Critique*, would seem to show that this part of the section is of comparatively late origin.

(c) The concluding paragraphs, which are of considerable intrinsic interest, also reflect an independent line of criticism. As the phrase "the above proposition"[1] seems to indicate, they were not originally composed in this present connection. They give expression to Kant's partial agreement with the line of argument followed by the rationalists, but also seek to show that, despite such partial validity, the argument does not lend support to any metaphysical extension of our empirical knowledge. In A 358 we have what may be a reference to the argument of the introductory sections of the *Dialectic*. The argument under criticism is praised as being "natural and popular," "occurring even to the least sophisticated understanding," and as leading it to view the soul as an altogether different existence from the body. The argument is as follows. None of the qualities proper to material existence, such as impenetrability or motion, are to be discovered in our inner experience. Nor can feelings, desires, thoughts, etc., be externally intuited. In view of these differences, we seem justified in asserting that the soul cannot be an appearance in space, and cannot therefore be corporeal. Kant replies by drawing attention to the fundamental Critical distinction between appearances and things in themselves.[2] If material bodies, as apprehended, were things in themselves, the argument would certainly justify us in refusing to regard the soul and its states as of similar nature. But since, as the *Aesthetic* has shown, bodies, as known, are mere appearances of outer sense, the real question at issue is not that of the distinction between the soul and bodies in space, but of the distinction between the soul and that something which conditions all outer appearances.

" . . . this something which underlies the outer appearances and which so affects our sense that it obtains the representations of space, matter, shape, etc., this something, viewed as noumenon (or better, as transcendental object), might yet also at the same time serve as the subject of our thoughts. . . ."[3]

Thus the argument criticised serves only to enforce the very genuine distinction between inner and outer appearances; it

---

[1] A 356. Cf. Adickes, *K.* p. 688 *n.*
[2] The argument is here in harmony with Kant's definition of transcendental illusion.   [3] A 358.

justifies no assertion, either positive or negative, as to the nature of the soul or as to its relation to body in its noumenal aspect. The monadistic, spiritualist theory of material existence remains an open possibility, though only as an hypothesis incapable either of proof or of disproof. We cannot obtain, by way of inference from the character of our apperceptive consciousness, any genuine addition to our speculative insight.

Third Paralogism: of Personality.[1]—Kant's criticism again runs parallel with that of the preceding *Paralogisms*. The fallacy involved is traced to a confusion between the numerical identity of the self *in representation* and the numerical identity of the subject *in itself*. The logical subject of knowledge must, as the transcendental deduction has proved, think itself as self-identical throughout all its experiences. This is indeed all that the judgment "I think" expresses. It is mere identity, "I am I." But from the identity of representation we must not argue to identity of the underlying self. So far as the unity of self-consciousness is concerned, there is nothing to prevent the noumenal conditions of the self from undergoing transformation so complete as to involve the loss of identity, while yet supporting the representation of an identical self.

"Although the dictum of certain ancient Schools, that everything in the world is in a flux and nothing permanent and abiding, cannot be reconciled with the admission of substances, it is not refuted by the unity of self-consciousness. For we are unable from our own consciousness to determine whether, as souls, we are permanent or not. Since we reckon as belonging to our identical self only that of which we are conscious, we must necessarily judge that we are one and the same throughout the whole time of which we are conscious. We cannot, however, claim that such a judgment would be valid from the standpoint of an outside observer. As the only permanent appearance which we meet with in the soul is the representation 'I' that accompanies and connects them all, we are unable to prove that this 'I,' a mere thought, may not be in the same state of flux as the other thoughts which are connected together by its means."[2]

And Kant adds an interesting illustration.[3]

"An elastic ball which impinges on another similar ball in a straight line communicates to the latter its whole motion, and therefore its whole state (*i.e.* if we take account only of the positions in space). If, then, in analogy with such bodies, we postulate substances such that the one communicates to the other representations together with the consciousness of them, we can conceive a whole series of

---

[1] A 361.   [2] A 364.
[3] William James's psychological description of self-consciousness is simply an extension of this illustration. Cf. *Principles of Psychology*, i. p. 339; quoted above, p. 278 *n*.

substances of which the first transmits its state together with its consciousness to the second, the second its own state with that of the preceding substance to the third, and this in turn the states of all the preceding substances together with its own consciousness and with their consciousness to another. The last substance would then be conscious of all the states of the substances, which had undergone change before its own change, as being its own states, because they would have been transferred to it together with the consciousness of them. And yet it would not have been one and the same person in all these states."[1]

The perversely Hegelian character of Caird's and Watson's manner of interpreting the *Critique* is especially evident in their treatment of the *Paralogisms*. They make not the least mention of this part of Kant's teaching.

Kant employs a further argument which would seem to show that at the time when these paragraphs were written the general tendency of his thought was predominantly subjectivist in character. There are, he implies, as many different times as there are selves that represent time.[2] The argument is as follows. As the "I think" is equivalent to "I am I," we may say either that all time of which I am conscious is in me, or that I am conscious of myself as numerically identical in each and every part of it. In my individual consciousness, therefore, identity of my person is unfailingly present. But an observer, viewing me from the outside,[3] represents me in the time of his own consciousness; and as the time in which he thus sets me is not that of my own thinking, the self-identity of my consciousness, even if he recognises its existence, does not justify him in inferring the objective permanence of my self.

The two concluding paragraphs seem to have been independently composed.[4] They contribute nothing of importance.

Fourth Paralogism : of Ideality.[5]—The main argument of this *Paralogism*, which contains the first edition refutation of idealism, has already been considered above.[6] We require, therefore, only to treat of it in its connection with the other *Paralogisms*, and to note some few minor points that remain for consideration. Its argument differs from that of the other *Paralogisms* in that the fallacy involved is traced, in agreement with the requirements of the introductory sections of

---

[1] A 363 n.

[2] A 362-3 and A 364. We must also, however, bear in mind that in this chapter Kant occasionally argues in *ad hominem* fashion from the point of view of the position criticised.

[3] Cf. A 353-4.

[4] Cf. Adickes, *K.* p. 695 n.

[5] A 366.

[6] P. 301 ff.

the *Dialectic*, to a failure to distinguish between appearances and things in themselves. Its connection with the table of categories is extremely artificial. In A 344 = B 402 the category employed is that of possibility, in A 404 and A 344 *n.* that of existence.[1] Kant's attempt to combine the problem here treated with that of the other *Paralogisms* can only be explained as due to the requirements of his architectonic.[2] This *Paralogism* does not concern itself with the nature of the soul. It refers exclusively to the mode of existence to be ascribed to objective appearances. None the less, Kant contrives to bring it within the range of rational psychology in the following manner. He argues[3] that rational psychologists are one and all adherents of empirical idealism. They confound appearances in space with things in themselves, and therefore assert that our knowledge of their existence is inferential and consequently uncertain. The errors of empirical idealism are thus bound up with the dogmatic assumptions of the rationalist position. They are traceable to its failure to distinguish between appearances and things in themselves. Such dogmatism may take the form of materialism or of ontological dualism, as well as of spiritualism.[4] All three, in professing to possess knowledge of things in themselves, violate Critical principles. If the chief function of rational psychology consists in securing the conception of the soul against the onslaughts of materialism,[5] that can be much more effectively attained through transcendental idealism.

"For, on [Critical] teaching, so completely are we freed from the fear that on the removal of matter all thought, and even the very existence of thinking beings, would be destroyed, that on the contrary it is clearly shown that if I remove the thinking subject the whole corporeal world must at once vanish, since it is nothing save appearance in the sensibility of our subject and a species of its representations."[6]

We do not, indeed, succeed in proving that the thinking self is in its existence independent of the "transcendental substrate"[7] of outer appearances. But as both possibilities remain open, the admission of our ignorance leaves us free to look to other than speculative sources for proof of the independent and abiding existence of the self.

Reflection on the Whole of Pure Psychology.[8]—This section affords Kant the opportunity of discussing certain problems

---

[1] The note to A 344 has evidently got displaced; it must, as Adickes points out, belong to A 404.
[2] Cf. above, pp. 320, 455.   [3] A 371-2.   [4] A 380-1.
[5] Cf. A 383.   [6] A 383.   [7] A 383.   [8] A 381.

which he desires to deal with, but is unable to introduce under the recognised rubrics of his logical architectonic.[1]   There are, Kant says, three other dialectical questions, essential to the purposes of rational psychology, grounded upon the same transcendental illusion (confusion of appearances with things in themselves), and soluble in similar fashion : (1) as to the possibility of the communion of soul and body, *i.e.* of the state of the soul during the life of the body ; (2) as to the beginning of this association, *i.e.* of the soul in and before birth ; (3) as to the termination of this association, *i.e.* of the soul in and after the death of the body.   Kant treats these three problems from the extreme subjectivist standpoint, inner and outer sense being distinguished and related in the manner peculiar to the first edition.   The contrast between mind and body is a difference solely between the appearances of inner and those of outer sense.   Both alike exist only in and through the thinking subject, though the latter

". . . have this deceptive property that, representing objects in space, they as it were detach themselves from the soul and appear to hover outside it."[2]

The problem, therefore, of the association of soul and body, properly understood, is not that of the interaction of the soul with other known substances of an opposite nature, but only

". . . how in a thinking subject outer intuition, namely, that of space, with its filling in of figure and motion, is possible.   And that is a question which no human being can possibly answer.   The gap in our knowledge . . . can only be indicated through the ascription of outer appearances to that transcendental object which is the cause of this species of representations, but of which we can have no knowledge whatsoever and of which we shall never acquire any conception."[3]

The familiar problem of the association of mind and body is thus due to a transcendental illusion which leads the mind to hypostatise representations, viewing them as independent existences that act upon the senses and generate our subjective states.   The motions in space, which are merely the expression in terms of appearance of the influence of the transcendental object upon "our senses,"[4] are thus wrongly

[1] The first four paragraphs are probably a later intercalation (Adickes, *K.* p. 708 *n.*), since they connect both with the introductory sections of the *Dialectic* and with the *Introduction* to the *Critique.*   Also, the opening words of the fifth paragraph seem to refer us not to anything antecedent in this section, but directly to the concluding passages of the fourth *Paralogism.*

[2] A 385.   [3] A 393.   [4] A 387.

regarded as the causes of our sensations. They themselves are mere representations, and, as Kant implies, are for that reason incapable of acting as causes. In this section, it may be noted in passing, there is not the least trace of the phenomenalist teaching, according to which spatial objects are viewed as acting upon the bodily sense-organs. Kant here denies all interaction of mind and body, and recognises only the interaction of their noumenal conditions. Appearances as such can never have causal efficacy. The position represented is pure subjectivism, and very significantly goes along with Kant's earlier doctrine of the transcendental object.[1]

The dogmatic character of the interaction theory appears very clearly, as Kant proceeds to point out, in the objections which have been made to it, whether by those who substitute for it the theories of pre-established harmony and occasionalism, or by those who adopt a sceptical non-committal attitude. Their objections rest upon exactly the same presupposition as the theory which they are attacking. To demonstrate the impossibility of interaction, they must be able to show that the transcendental object is not the cause of outer appearances; and owing to the limitations of our knowledge that is entirely beyond our powers. Failing, however, to draw a distinction between appearances and things in themselves, they have not realised the actual nature of the situation, and accordingly have directed their objections merely to showing that mind and body, taken as independent existences, must not be viewed as capable of interaction.

The Critical standpoint also supplies the proper formulation for the other two problems—a formulation which in itself decides the degree and manner of our possible insight in regard to them. The view that the thinking subject may be capable of thought prior to all association with the body should be stated as asserting

"... that prior to the beginning of that species of sensibility in virtue of which something appears to us in space, those transcendental objects, which in our present state appear to us as bodies, could have been intuited in an entirely different manner."[2]

The view that the soul, upon the cessation of all association with the corporeal world, may still continue to think, will similarly consist in the contention

"... that if that species of sensibility, in virtue of which transcendental objects (which in our present state are entirely unknown) appear to us as a material world, should cease, all intuition of them would not

---

[1] Cf. above, pp. 215-16.   [2] A 393-4.

for that reason be removed; but that it would still be possible that those same unknown objects should continue to be known [sic] by the thinking subject, though no longer, indeed, in the quality of bodies."[1]

Not the least ground, Kant claims, can be discovered by means of speculation in support of such assertions. Even their bare possibility cannot be demonstrated. But it is equally impossible to establish any valid objection to them. Since we cannot pretend to knowledge of things in themselves, a modest acquiescence in the limitations of experience alone becomes us.

The remaining paragraphs (A 396-405) contain nothing that is new. They merely repeat points already more adequately stated. A 401-2, which deals with the nature of apperception and its relation to the categories, has been considered above.[2] The argument that, as the self must presuppose the thought of itself in knowing anything, it cannot know itself as object, is also commented upon above.[3]

The statement[4] that the determining self (the thinking, das Denken) is to be distinguished from the determinable self (the thinking subject) as knowledge from its object, should be interpreted in the light of Kant's argument in the second and third Paralogisms, that the simplicity and self-identity of the representation of an object must not be taken as knowledge of simplicity or numerical identity in the object represented.

The analysis given in A 402-3 of the fallacy involved in the Paralogisms is, as Adickes has pointed out,[5] confused and misleading. Kant here declares that in the major premiss of each syllogism the assertion is intended in the merely logical sense, and therefore as applicable only to the subject in representation, but in the minor premiss and conclusion is asserted of the subject as bearer of consciousness, i.e. in itself. But were that so, the minor premiss would be a false assertion, and the false conclusion would not be traceable to logical fallacy. Kant gives the correct statement of his position in B 410-11.[6] The attempted justification of the fourfold arrangement of the Paralogisms with which the section concludes suffers from the artificiality of Kant's logical architectonic.

SECOND EDITION STATEMENT OF THE PARALOGISMS[7]

Except for the introductory paragraphs, which remain unaltered, the chapter is completely recast in the second edition. The treatment of the four Paralogisms which in the

---

[1] A 394.   [2] Pp. 326-7.   [3] Pp. 327-8.   [4] A 402. Cf. B 407.
[5] K. p. 717 n.   [6] Cf. below, p. 470.   [7] B 406 ff.

first edition occupied thirty-three pages is reduced to five. The problems of the mutual interaction of mind and body, of its prenatal character and of its immortality, the discussion of which in the first edition required some ten pages, are now disposed of in a single paragraph (B 426-7). The remaining twenty-two pages of the new chapter are almost entirely devoted to more or less polemical discussion of criticisms which had been passed upon the first edition. These had been in great part directed against Kant's doctrine of apperception and of inner sense, and so could fittingly be dealt with in connection with the problems of rational psychology. As Benno Erdmann has suggested,[1] B 409-14 and 419-21 would seem to be directed against Ulrich's[2] Leibnizian position and especially against his metaphysical interpretation of apperception. B 428-30 treats of the difficulties raised by Pistorius[3] in regard to the existence of the self. B 414-15 is similarly polemical, but in this case Kant cites his opponent, Mendelssohn, by name. Throughout, as in the alterations made in the chapter on *Phenomena and Noumena*, Kant insists more strongly than in the first edition upon the unknowableness of the self, and on the difference between thought and knowledge. The pure forms of thought are not, Kant now declares, concepts of objects, that is, are not categories,[4] but " merely logical functions." Though this involves no essential doctrinal change, it indicates the altered standpoint from which Kant now regards his problem. Its significance has already been dwelt upon.[5]

In formulating the several arguments of the four *Paralogisms*, Kant develops and places in the forefront a statement which receives only passing mention in A 352-3, 362, 366-7, 381-2, namely, that the truths contained in the judgments of rational psychology find expression in merely identical (*i.e.* analytic) propositions. This enables Kant to formulate both the *Paralogisms* and his criticisms thereof in much briefer and more pointed fashion. In each case the *Paralogism*, as he shows, substitutes a synthetic *a priori* judgment, involving an extension of our knowledge and a reference to the noumenal self, for the given judgment which, in so far as it is valid, is always a merely analytic restatement of the

---

[1] *Kriticismus*, p. 227 ; cf. p. 106 ff.
[2] A. H. Ulrich, *Institutiones logicae et metaphysicae* (1785).
[3] In his review of Kant's *Prolegomena* in the *Allgemeine Deutsche Bibliothek* (1784).
[4] Obviously by categories Kant here really means schemata. Cf. A 348, where Kant states that " pure categories . . . have in themselves no objctive, meaning. . . . Apart from intuition they are merely functions of a judgement without content." [5] Above, pp. 404 ff., 413 ff.

purely formal "I think." From the very start also, Kant introduces the distinctions of his own Critical teaching, especially that between thinking and intuiting, and that between the determining and the determinable self.

First Paralogism.—That the I which thinks must always *in thought* be viewed as subject and not as mere predicate, is an identical proposition. It must not be taken as meaning that the subject which underlies thought is an abiding substance. This latter proposition is of much wider scope, and would involve such data (in this case entirely lacking) as are required for the establishment of a synthetic *a priori* judgment.

Second Paralogism.—That the I of *apperception* and so of all *thought* is single and cannot be resolved into a multiplicity of subjects, is involved in the very conception of thought, and is therefore an analytic proposition. It must not be interpreted as signifying that the self is a simple substance. For the latter assertion is again a synthetic proposition, and presupposes for its possibility an intuition by the self of its own essential nature. As all our intuitions are merely sensuous, that cannot be looked for in the "I think."

"It would, indeed, be surprising if what in other cases requires so much labour to discover—namely, what it is, of all that is presented by intuition, that is substance, and further, whether this substance is simple (*e.g.* in the parts of matter)—should be thus directly given me, as if by revelation, in the poorest of all representations."[1]

We may here observe how the practice, adopted by Caird, of translating *Anschauung* by 'perception' has misled him into serious misunderstanding of Kant's teaching. It has caused him[2] to interpret Kant as arguing that we have no knowledge of the self because we can have no *sensuous* perception of it. Kant's argument rather is that as all human "intuition" is sensuous, we are cut off from all possibility of determining our noumenal nature. We are thrown back upon mere concepts which, as yielding only analytic propositions, cannot extend our insight beyond the limits of sense-experience. The term 'intuition' is much broader in meaning than the term 'perception'; it can also be employed as equivalent to the phrase '*immediate* apprehension.'[3] The grounds for Kant's contention that we have no intuition or immediate knowledge of the self are embodied in, and inspire

---

[1] B 408.
[2] *Critical Philosophy*, ii. p. 34. So also in Watson's *Kant Explained*, p. 244.
[3] Caird (*op. cit.* p. 35) takes account of Kant's conception of a possible intuitive understanding, but illegitimately assumes that by it he must mean a *creative* understanding. Cf. above, p. 408.

his doctrine of inner sense.[1] It may also be noted that in
B 412 Kant, speaking of the necessity of intuition for knowledge of the self, uses the unusual phrase 'a permanent
intuition'—a phrase which, so far as I have observed, he
nowhere employs in dealing with the intuition that conditions
the sense perception of material bodies.[2] Its employment
here may perhaps be due to the fact that its implied reference
is not to a given sensuous manifold but to some form of
immediate apprehension, capable of revealing the permanent
nature of the noumenal self.

Third Paralogism.—That I am identical with myself
throughout the consciousness of my manifold experiences, is
likewise an analytic proposition obtainable by mere analysis
of the "I think." And since that form of consciousness,
as stated in the criticism of the preceding *Paralogism*, is
purely conceptual, containing no element of intuition, no
judgment based solely upon it can ever be taken as equivalent
to the synthetic proposition that the self, as thinking being,
is an identical substance.

Fourth Paralogism.—This *Paralogism* is somewhat altered.
As noted above,[3] the problem dealt with in the first edition
concerns the outer world, and only quite indirectly the nature
of the self. In the second edition that argument is restated,[4]
and is more properly located within the *Analytic*. The
argument which now takes its place runs parallel with that
of the three preceding *Paralogisms*. The assertion that I
distinguish my own existence as a thinking being from other
things outside me, including thereunder my own body, is an
analytic proposition, since by *other* things is meant things
which I think as different from myself.

"But I do not thereby learn whether this consciousness of
myself would be at all possible apart from things outside me
through which representations are given to me, and whether,
therefore, I can exist merely as thinking being (*i.e.* without existing
in human form)."

In B 417-18 Kant points out that rational psychology, in
asserting that the self can be conscious apart from all
consciousness of outer things, commits itself to the acceptance of problematic idealism. If consciousness of outer
objects is not necessary to consciousness of self, there can

[1] Cf. above, p. 295 ff.
[2] Cf. B 415 *n*. In B xxxix. *n* (at the end), quoted above pp. 309-10, Kant
is careful to point out that the representation of something permanent is by no
means identical with permanent representation. [3] P. 463.
[4] Namely, as *Refutation of Idealism*, B 274 ff. Cf. above, p. 308 ff.

be no valid method of proving their existence.   In the fourth
Paralogism of the first edition, the inter-dependence of rational
psychology and empirical idealism is also dwelt upon, but
is there traced to a confusion of appearances with things in
themselves.[1]

B 410-11.—The correct formulation is here given of what
in the first edition[2] is quite incorrectly stated.[3]   A paralogism
is a syllogism which errs in logical form (as contrasted with
a syllogism erring in matter, *i.e.* the premisses of which are
false).   In the paralogisms of Rational Psychology, the
logical fallacy committed is that of ambiguous middle, or as
Kant names it, the *sophisma figurae dictionis*.   In the major
premiss the middle term is used as referring to real existence,
in the minor only as expressive of the unity of consciousness.

**Refutation of Mendelssohn's Proof of the Permanence of the
Soul.**[4]—Mendelssohn's argument is that the soul, as it does
not consist of parts,[5] cannot disappear *gradually* by dis-
integration into its constituent elements.   If, therefore, it
perishes, it must pass out of existence *suddenly*; at one
moment it will exist, at the next moment it will be non-
existent.   But, Mendelssohn maintains, for three closely connected reasons this would seem to be impossible.   In the
first place, the immediate juxtaposition of directly opposed
states is never to be met with in the material world.   Complete opposites, such as day and night, waking and sleeping,
never follow upon one another abruptly, but only through a
series of intermediate states.[6]   Secondly, among the opposites
which material processes thus bridge over, the opposition of
being and not-being is never to be found.   Only by a miracle
can a material existence be annihilated.[7]   If, therefore, empirical evidence is to be allowed as relevant, we must not
assert of the invisible soul what is never known to befall the
material existences of the visible world.   Thirdly—the only
part of Mendelssohn's argument which Kant mentions—the
sudden cessation of the soul's existence would also violate
the law of the continuity of time.[8]   Between any two
moments there is always an intermediate time in which the
one moment passes continuously into the other.

Kant's reply to this third part of Mendelssohn's argument
is that though the soul must not be conceived as perishing
suddenly, it may pass out of existence by a continuous
diminution through an infinite number of smaller degrees of

---

[1] Cf. above, pp. 457, 462-3.   [2] A 402.   [3] Cf. above, p. 466.
[4] B 413-15.   [5] *Gesammelte Schriften*, ii. p. 151 ff.
[6] *Op. cit.* p. 121 ff.   [7] *Op. cit.* pp. 128 ff., 168.
[8] *Op. cit.* p. 125 ff.

intensive reality; and in support of this view he maintains the very doubtful position that clearness and obscurity of representation are not features of the contents apprehended, but only of the intensity of the consciousness directed upon them.[1]

B 417-22.—Kant here points out that rational psychology, as above expounded, proceeds synthetically, starting from the assertion of the substantiality of the soul and proceeding to the proof that its existence is independent of outer things. But it may proceed in the reverse fashion, analytically developing the implications supposed to be involved in the " I think," viewed as an existential judgment, *i.e.* as signifying " I exist thinking." Kant restates the argument in this analytic form in order, as it would seem, to secure the opportunity of replying to those criticisms of his teaching in the first edition which concern his doctrine of apperception and his employment of the categories, especially of the category of existence, in relation to the self. What is new and important in these pages, and also in the connected passages in B 428-30, has been discussed above.[2]

B 419-20.—After remarking that simplicity or unity is involved in the very possibility of apperception, Kant proceeds to argue that it can never be explained from a strictly materialist standpoint, since nothing that is real in space is ever simple. Points are merely limits, and are not therefore themselves anything that can form part of space. The passage as a whole would seem to be directed against the Leibnizian teaching of Ulrich.[3]

B 426-7.—Kant makes a remark to which nothing in his argument yields any real support, namely, that the dialectical illusion in rational psychology is due to the substitution of an Idea of reason for the quite indeterminate concept of a thinking being in general. As is argued below,[4] the assumption which he is here making that the concept of the self is an *a priori* and ultimate Idea of pure Reason, cannot be regarded as a genuine part of his Critical teaching.

B 427-8 touches quite briefly upon questions more fully and adequately treated in the first edition. The scanty treatment here accorded to them would seem to indicate, as Benno Erdmann remarks,[5] that the problem of the interaction of mind and body which so occupied Kant's mind from 1747 to 1770 has meantime almost entirely lost interest for him. The problem of immortality remains central, but it is now approached from the ethical side.

---

[1] Regarding the value of the hypotheses propounded by Kant in his note to B 415, cf below, p. 543 ff. [2] P. 321 ff.
[3] Cf. above, p. 467. [4] Pp. 473-7. [5] *Kriticismus*, p. 226.

In **B 421** and **B 423-6** Kant draws from his criticism of the *Paralogisms* the final conclusion that the metaphysical problems as to the nature and destiny of the self are essentially *practical* problems. When approached from a theoretical standpoint, as curious questions to be settled by logical dialectic, their speculative proof

"... so stands upon the point of a hair, that even the schools preserve it from falling only so long as they keep it unceasingly spinning round like a top; even in their own eyes it yields no abiding foundation upon which anything could be built."[1]   "Rational psychology exists not as *doctrine*, ... but only as *discipline*. It sets impassable limits to speculative reason in this field, and thus keeps us, on the one hand, from throwing ourselves into the arms of soulless materialism, or, on the other hand, from losing ourselves in an unsubstantial spiritualism which can have no real meaning for us in this present life. But though it furnishes no positive doctrine, it reminds us that we should regard this refusal of Reason to give satisfying response to our inquisitive probings into what is beyond the limits of this present life as a hint from Reason to divert our self-knowledge from fruitless and extravagant speculation to its fruitful practical employment."[2]   "The proofs which are serviceable for the world at large preserve their entire value undiminished, and indeed, upon the surrender of these dogmatic pretensions, gain in clearness and in natural force. For Reason is then located in its own peculiar sphere, namely the order of ends, which is also at the same time an order of nature; and since it is in itself a practical faculty which is not bound down to natural conditions, it is justified in extending the order of ends, and therewith our own existence, beyond the limits of experience and of life."[3]

Then follows brief indication of the central teaching of the *Metaphysics of Ethics* and of the two later *Critiques*. Through moral values that outweigh all considerations of utility and happiness, we become conscious of an inner vocation which inspires feelings of sublimity similar to those which are aroused by contemplation of the starry firmament; and to the verities thus disclosed we can add the less certain but none the less valuable confirmation yielded by natural beauty and design, and by the conformity of nature to our intellectual demands.

"Man's natural endowments — not merely his talents and the impulses to employ them, but above all else the Moral Law within him — go so far beyond all utility and advantage which he may derive from them in this present life, that he learns thereby to prize the mere consciousness of a righteous will as being, apart from all advantageous consequences, apart even from the shadowy reward of

---

[1] B 424.   [2] B 421.   [3] B 424-5.

posthumous fame, supreme over all other values; and so feels an inner call to fit himself, by his conduct in this world, and by the sacrifice of many of its advantages, for being a citizen of a better world upon which he lays hold in Idea. This powerful and incontrovertible proof is reinforced by our ever-increasing knowledge of purposiveness in all that we see around us, and by a glimpse of the immensity of creation, and therefore also by the consciousness of a certain illimitableness in the possible extension of our knowledge and of a striving commensurate therewith. All this still remains to us, though we must renounce the hope of ever comprehending, from the mere theoretical knowledge of ourselves, the necessary continuance of our existence." [1]

IS THE NOTION OF THE SELF A NECESSARY IDEA OF REASON?

One point of great importance must be dwelt upon before we pass from the *Paralogisms*. Though the negative consequences which follow from the teaching of the objective deduction are here developed in the most explicit manner, Kant does not within the limits of this chapter, in either edition, make any further reference to the doctrine expounded in the introductory sections of the *Dialectic*,[2] viz. that the notion of the self as an immortal being is a necessary Idea of human Reason. The reader is therefore left under the impression that that doctrine is unaffected by the destructive criticism passed upon rational psychology, and that it still survives as an essential tenet of the Critical philosophy. And he is confirmed in this view when he finds the doctrine reappearing in the *Appendix* to the *Dialectic* and in the *Methodology*. The Idea of the self is there represented as performing a quite indispensable, regulative function in the development of the empirical science of psychology. Now it is one thing to maintain the existence of Ideal demands of Reason for unity, system and unconditionedness, and to assert that it is in virtue of these demands that we are led, in the face of immense discouragement and seeming contradictions, to reduce the chance collocations and bewildering complexities of ordinary experience to something more nearly approximating to what Reason prescribes. But it is a very different matter when Kant claims that in any one sphere, such as that of psychology, the unity and the unconditionedness must necessarily be of one predetermined type. He is then injecting into the Ideals that *specific* guidance which only the detail of experience is

---

[1] B 425-6. Cf. above, pp. lvi-lxi; below, p. 570 ff.
[2] The only approach to such a reference is in B 426-7, noted above, p. 471.

really capable of supplying. He is proving false to his own Critical empiricism, in which no function is ascribed to Reason that need in any way conflict with the autonomy of specialist research; and he is also violating his fundamental principle that the *a priori* can never be other than purely formal. Indeed, when Kant discloses somewhat more in detail what he means by the regulative function of the Idea of the self, the ambiguity of his statements reveals the unconsidered character of this part of his teaching. It is the expression only of a preconception, and has eluded the scrutiny of his Critical method largely because of the protective colouring which its admirable adaptation to the needs of his architectonic confers upon it. If, for instance, we compare the three passages in which it is expounded in the *Appendix* to the *Dialectic*, we find that Kant himself alternates between the authoritative prescription to psychology of a spiritualist hypothesis and what in ultimate analysis, when ambiguities of language are discounted, amounts simply to the demand for the greatest possible simplification of its complex phenomena. The passages are as follows.

"In conformity with these Ideas as principles we shall first, in psychology, connect in inner experience all appearances, all actions and receptivity of our mind, as if (*als ob*) the mind were a simple substance which persists with personal identity (in this life at least), while its states, to which those of the body belong only as outer conditions, are in continual change."[1]

" . . . in the human mind we have sensation, consciousness, imagination, memory, wit, power of discrimination, pleasure, desire, etc. Now, to begin with, a logical maxim requires that we should reduce, so far as may be possible, this seeming diversity, by comparing these with one another and detecting their hidden identity. We have to enquire whether imagination combined with consciousness may not be the same thing as memory, wit, power of discrimination, and perhaps even identical with understanding and Reason. Though logic is not capable of deciding whether a *fundamental power* actually exists, the Idea of such a power is the problem involved in a systematic representation of the multiplicity of powers. The logical principle of Reason calls upon us to bring about such unity as completely as possible; and the more appearances of this or that power are found to be identical with one another, the more probable it becomes that they are simply different manifestations of one and the same power, which may be entitled, relatively speaking, their *fundamental power*. The same is done with the other powers. The relatively fundamental powers must in turn be compared with one another, with a view to discovering their harmony, and so bringing

---

[1] A 672 = B 700. Cf. below, p. 554.

them nearer to a single radical, *i.e.* absolutely fundamental, power. But this unity of Reason is purely hypothetical. We do not assert that such a power must necessarily be met with, but that we must seek it in the interest of Reason, that is, of establishing certain principles for the manifold rules which experience may supply to us. We must endeavour, wherever possible, to bring in this way systematic unity into our knowledge."[1]

In the third of the *Appendix* passages these two views are confusedly combined. Kant is insisting that an Idea never asserts, even as an hypothesis, the existence of a real thing.

"[An Idea] is only the schema of the regulative principle by which Reason, so far as lies in its power, extends systematic unity over the whole field of experience. The first object of such an Idea is the ' I ' itself, viewed simply as thinking nature or soul. If I am to investigate the properties with which a thinking being exists in itself, I must interrogate experience. I cannot even apply any one of the categories to this object, except in so far as its schema is given in sense intuition. But I never thereby attain to a systematic unity of all appearances of inner sense. Instead, then, of the empirical concept (of that which the soul actually is), which cannot carry us far, Reason takes the concept of the empirical unity of all thought ; and by thinking this unity as unconditioned and original, it forms from it a concept of Reason, *i.e.* the Idea of a simple substance, which, unchangeable in itself (personally identical), stands in association with other real things outside it ; in a word, the Idea of a simple self-subsisting intelligence. Yet in so doing it has nothing in view save principles of systematic unity in the explanation of the appearances of the soul. It is endeavouring to represent all determinations as existing in a single subject, all powers, so far as possible, as derived from a single fundamental power, all change as belonging to the states of one and the same permanent being, and all appearances in space as completely different from the actions of thought. The simplicity and other properties of substance are intended to be only the schema of this regulative principle, and are not presupposed as the real ground of the properties of the soul. For these may rest on altogether different grounds of which we can know nothing. The soul in itself could not be known through these assumed predicates, not even if we regarded them as absolutely valid in regard to it. For they constitute a mere Idea which cannot be represented *in concreto*. Nothing but advantage can result from the psychological Idea thus conceived, if only we take heed that it is not viewed as more than a mere Idea, and that it is therefore taken as valid only

---

[1] A 649=B 677-8. Tetens in his *Philosophische Versuche* (1777) had devoted an entire chapter to this question. His term *Grundkraft* is that which Kant here employs. Cf. *Philosophische Versuche*, Bd. i., *Elfter Versuch* : " Concerning the fundamental power of the human soul." Incidentally Tetens discusses Rousseau's suggestion that this fundamental power consists in man's capacity for perfecting himself. Cf. Kant's *Lectures on Metaphysics* (Pölitz, 1821, p. 192 ff.).

in its bearing on the systematic employment of Reason in determining the appearances of our soul. For no empirical laws of bodily appearances, which are of a totally different kind, will then intervene in the explanation of what belongs exclusively to inner sense. No windy hypotheses of generation, extinction, and palingenesis of souls will be permitted. The consideration of this object of inner sense will thus be kept completely pure and unmixed, without employing heterogeneous properties. Also, Reason's investigations will be directed to reducing the grounds of explanation in this field, so far as may be possible, to a single principle. All this will be best obtained (indeed is obtainable in no other way) through such a schema, viewed as if (*als ob*) it were a real being. The psychological Idea, moreover, can signify nothing but the schema of a regulative principle. For were I to enquire whether *the soul in itself* is of spiritual nature, the question would have no meaning. In employing such a concept I not only abstract from corporeal nature, but from nature in general, *i.e.* from all predicates of a possible experience, and therefore from all conditions for thinking an object for such a concept: yet only as related to an object can it be said to have a meaning."[1]

The last passage would seem to indicate that Kant has still another and only partially avowed reason for insisting upon a *special* and *spiritualist* Idea, as regulative of empirical psychology. It is necessary, he would seem to argue, in order to mark off the peculiar nature of its subject matter, and to warn us against attempting to explain its phenomena in the mechanistic manner of physical science. But if that is Kant's intention, he has failed to formulate the position in any really tenable way. It is impossible to maintain, as he here does, that "no empirical laws of bodily appearances [can] intervene in the explanation of what belongs exclusively to inner sense."[2] Indeed, in the immediately following sentences, he very clearly indicates how completely such a position conflicts with his own real teaching. To think away the corporeal is to think away all experience. Experience is not dualistically divided into separate worlds. It is one and single, and the principle of causality rules universally throughout, connecting inner experiences of sense, feeling, and desire, with their outer conditions, organic and physical.[3] Thus Kant's retention of the Idea of the self is chiefly of interest as revealing the strength and tenacity of his spiritualist leanings. We may judge of the disinterestedness and courage of his thinking by the contrary character of his pre-conceptions.

[1] A 682-4 = B 710-12. A 771-2 = B 799 in the *Methodology* is similarly ambiguous, though tending to the spiritualist mode of formulation.
[2] Cf. above, pp. 275-6, 279 ff., 312 ff., 384-5, 464-5.
[3] Cf. end of B xxxix. *n.*, quoted above, pp. 309-10.

For even when they have been shown to be theoretically indemonstrable, they continue to retain by honorific title the dignity from which they have been deposed. The full force of the objections is none the less recognised.

"The simplicity of substance . . . is not presupposed as the real ground of the properties of the soul. For these may rest on altogether different grounds of which we can know nothing."

That, however, is only Kant's unbiassed estimate of the theoretical evidence; it is not an expression of his own personal belief.

CHAPTER II

THE ANTINOMY OF PURE REASON[1]

This introduction summarises the preceding argument, and distinguishes the new problems of *Antinomy* from those of the *Paralogisms*. In rational psychology the doctrines propounded are wholly on the side of "pneumatism"; in the antinomies a very different situation is disclosed. For though rational cosmology likewise expounds itself in a series of demonstrated theses, its teaching stands in irreconcilable conflict with the actual nature of appearances, as expressed through a series of antitheses which are demonstrable in an equally cogent manner.

SECTION I

SYSTEM OF THE COSMOLOGICAL IDEAS[2]

The first eight paragraphs of this section are of great textual interest. They must have been written at a time when Kant still intended to expound his entire criticism of metaphysical science in the form of a doctrine of antinomy. For they define the Ideas of Reason as exclusively cosmological,[3] and give a very different explanation of their origin from that which has been expounded in the preceding chapters. Evidently, therefore, this part of the section must have been written prior to Kant's formulation of the metaphysical deduction from the three species of syllogism. This is supported by the fact that the argument begins anew, just as if the matter had not previously been discussed; and that, though a new view of the nature of Reason is propounded, there is not the least mention of the more Idealist view which

[1] A 405 = B 432.　　　　　　　　　[2] A 408 = B 435.
[3] Cf. A 414 = B 441, where it is stated that there is no transcendental Idea of the substantial.

it displaces. Reason, Kant here teaches, is not a faculty separate from the understanding, and does not therefore produce any concept peculiar to itself. Reason is simply a name for the understanding in so far as it acts independently of sensibility, and seeks, by means of its pure forms, in abstraction from all empirical limitations, to grasp the unconditioned. "The transcendental Ideas are in reality nothing but categories extended to the unconditioned." The intelligible, as thus conceived by the understanding, expresses itself, as he later shows, in a series of theses; while the sensuous expresses its opposite and conflicting character in a series of antitheses.

Yet not all categories yield a concept of the unconditioned. That is possible only to those which concern themselves with a series of members conditioning and conditioned, and in reference to which, therefore, the postulate of an unconditioned would seem to be legitimate, viz. : (1) unconditioned quantity in space and time; (2) unconditioned quality (indivisibility and simplicity) of reality in space (matter); (3) unconditioned causality of appearances; (4) unconditioned necessity of appearances. As this arrangement is determined by the needs of Kant's architectonic, no detailed comment is here called for. Its consequences we shall have ample opportunity to consider later. As already noted, Kant's statement in A 414 = B 441, that "the category of substance and accident does not lend itself to a transcendental Idea," shows very clearly that, at the time when he composed this passage, he had not yet bethought himself of placing a separate and independent Idea at the basis of rational psychology. But as Kant here strives to follow the fourfold arrangement of the categories, the content of these paragraphs must either have been later .recast or have been composed in the interval between his discovery of the metaphysical deduction of the categories and his formulation of the corresponding deduction of the Ideas from the three forms of syllogism. It may also be observed that the derivation of the cosmological Idea from the hypothetical syllogism, which embodies only the category of causality, clashes with the above specification of it in terms of all four rubrics of category.

The remaining paragraphs (ninth to thirteenth) of this section must be of later date, as they are developed in view of the independent treatment of the theological Ideal.[1] (Adickes, in dating the ninth and tenth paragraphs with the preceding instead of with the concluding paragraphs, would seem to have overlooked this fact.) In order to justify the treatment of the Ideas of a first cause and of unconditioned necessity, as

[1] Cf. above, p. 434 ff.

cosmological, Kant now asserts that the antinomies concern only appearances—"our [cosmical] Ideas being directed only to what is unconditioned *among the appearances*,"[1] *and not to noumena*.[2]   His explanation of the nature of transcendental illusion, and of the antinomies in particular, as being due to a failure to distinguish between appearance and things in themselves, is thus ruthlessly sacrificed to considerations of architectonic.   Kant could not, of course, consistently hold to the position here adopted; but it causes him from time to time, especially in dealing with the third and fourth antinomies, to make statements which tend seriously to obscure the argument and to bewilder the careful reader.

Kant is far from clear as to the relation in which the concepts of the totality of conditions and of the unconditioned stand to one another.[3]   In A 322 = B 379 they would seem to be taken as exactly equivalent concepts.   In A 416-17 = B 443-5 they are apparently regarded as distinct, the former only leading up to the latter.   But discussion of this important point must meantime be deferred.[4]

SECTION II

ANTITHETIC OF PURE REASON [5]

"[Antithetic] is the conflict between two apparently dogmatic judgments [*Erkenntnisse*] to neither of which can we ascribe any superior claim to acceptance over the other, *i.e.* by Antithetic I mean a *thesis*, together with an *antithesis*."   "Transcendental Antithetic is an investigation of the antinomy of pure Reason, its causes and outcome."

The very existence of such antinomy presupposes a twofold condition : first, that it does not refer to a gratuitous but to an inevitable problem of human Reason, "one which it must necessarily encounter in its natural progress"; and secondly, that the thesis and the antithesis together generate a "natural and inevitable illusion," which continues to persist even after its deceptive power has been clearly disclosed.   Such conflict is caused by the fact that Reason seeks a unity which transcends

---

[1] A 419 = B 447.   [2] A 420 = B 447.
[3] A very curious sentence in Kant's letter to Schulze (*W.* x. pp. 344-5, quoted above, p. 199) seems to be traceable to this source.
[4] Cf. below, pp. 529, 559-60, and above, pp. 199-200, 433-4, 451.   For A 410-11 = B 439-40 on the difference between the ascending and descending series, cf. A 331-2 = B 387-8 and A 336-7 = B 393-4.
[5] A 420 = B 448.

the understanding, and which nevertheless is meant to conform to the conditions of the understanding. If the unity is adequate to the demands of Reason, it is too great for the understanding ; if it is commensurate with the understanding, it is too small for Reason.[1] The theses express the higher unity at which Reason aims ; the antitheses are the judgments to which the understanding is constrained by the nature of the appearances with which both it and Reason profess to deal. If we hold to Reason, we make assertions contradictory of the appearances ; while if we place reliance on the understanding, Reason condemns our conclusions.

This conflict is limited to those few problems above enumerated in which we are called upon to complete a given series.[2] Since totality, whether in the form of a first beginning of the series or as an actual infinity of the whole series, can never itself be experienced, these are problems in regard to which experience can be of no assistance to us. It can neither confirm nor refute any particular solution. The only possible method of deciding between the competing claims is to watch or even to provoke the conflict, in the hope that we may finally be able to detect some misunderstanding, and so to resolve the conflict to the satisfaction of both the litigants. Such is Kant's description of what he entitles his " sceptical method."[3]

Without here attempting a full discussion of the subject, it seems advisable to point out at the very start what Kant's exposition seriously obscures, namely, the real character of the evidence upon which the theses and the antitheses respectively rest. The latter are not correctly stated as transcending experience, and as therefore incapable of confirmation by it. The proofs which Kant offers of them are, indeed, of a non-empirical *a priori* character. They are formulated in terms of the dogmatic rationalism of the Leibnizian position, with a constant appeal to abstract principles. But, as a matter of fact, they can be much more adequately established —in so far as they can be established at all—through analysis of the spatial and temporal conditions of material existence.

---

[1] Cf. *per contra* A 486=B 514.

[2] The limitation of Kant's discussion to space, time, and causality is, of course, due to his acceptance of the current view that the concepts of infinity and continuity are derived from our intuitions of space and time. As we have already noted in discussing his intuitional theory of mathematical reasoning (above, pp. 40-1, 117 ff., 128 ff.), he fails to extend to mathematical concepts his own "transcendental " view of the categories, namely, as *conditioning* the possibility of intuitional experience. Such concepts as order, plurality, whole and part, continuity, infinity, are prior to time and space in the logical order of thought ; and to be adequately treated must be considered in their widest application.

[3] Cf. A 507=B 535, and above, p. 431 ff. ; below, pp. 501, 545-6.

As space and time are continuous and homogeneous, any
assertion which is true of a space or time however small is
likewise true of a space or time however large. Any space
consists of spaces, and must be regarded as itself part of a
larger whole.[1] Any time consists of parts which are themselves times, and is apprehensible only as following upon preceding times. It is by such considerations as these that we
are led to regard the material world as unlimited, as infinitely
divisible, and as having no first state.

Kant's method of demonstrating the theses—that the
world is limited, is finitely divisible, and has a first state—is no
less misleading. Here again his rationalistic arguments conceal the basis upon which the various theses really rest.
Their true determining ground is the demand of Reason for
some more satisfactory form of unconditionedness than that
which is found in the actual infinite. It is this demand which
has led philosophers to look around for proofs in support of
the theses, and to elaborate those rationalistic arguments
which Kant here reproduces. Thus the grounds of the antitheses are altogether different from those of the theses; and
in neither case are they properly represented by the arguments which Kant employs.[2]

The reasons why Kant in his detailed statement of the
antinomies has omitted, or at least subordinated, the above
considerations, are complex and various. In the first place,
this doctrine of antinomy was in several of its main features
already formulated prior to his development of the Critical
philosophy. It forms part of his *Dissertation* of 1770; and
at that time Kant was still largely in fundamental sympathy
with the Leibnizian ontology. Secondly, Kant is here professing to criticise the science of rational cosmology, and is
therefore bound to expound it in more or less current form.
And in the third place, he teaches that *the antinomies exist as
antinomies only when viewed from the false standpoint of dogmatic rationalism.* Had he eliminated the rationalistic proofs,

[1] Cf. Kant's posthumously published *Transition from the Metaphysical First
Principles of Natural Science to Physics* (*Altpreussische Monatsschrift, 1882*), pp.
279-80: "If we take in regard to space, not its definition, but only an *a priori*
proposition, *e.g.* that space is a whole which must be thought only as part of a still
greater whole, it is clear . . . that it is an irrational magnitude, measurable
indeed, but in its comparison with unity transcending all number." "If space is
something objectively existent, it is a magnitude which can exist only as part of
another given magnitude."

[2] Cf. Schopenhauer, *World as Will and Idea* (*Werke, Frauenstädt*, ii. pp. 585-6;
Eng. trans. ii. pp. 107-8). "I find and assert that the whole antinomy is
a mere delusion, a sham fight. Only the assertions of the antitheses really rest
upon the forms of our faculty of knowledge, *i.e.* if we express it objectively, on the
necessary, *a priori* certain, most universal laws of nature. Their proofs alone are

the conflict of the antinomies, in its strictly logical form, as the conflict of direct contradictories, would at once have vanished.   The general framework of this division of the *Dialectic* demanded a rationalistic treatment of both theses and antitheses, and Kant believed that the rationalistic proofs which he propounds in their support are unanswerable, so long as the dogmatic standpoint of ordinary consciousness and of Leibnizian ontology is preserved.   But even when that important limitation is kept in view, Kant fails to justify this interpretation of the conflict, and we must therefore be prepared to find that his proofs, *whether of theses or of antitheses*, are in all cases inconclusive.   I shall append to each of his arguments a statement of the reasons which constrain us to reject them as unsound.   We shall then be in a position to consider his whole doctrine of antinomy in its broader aspects, and in its connection with the teaching of the other main divisions of the *Dialectic*.

FIRST ANTINOMY

Thesis.—(*a*) The world has a beginning in time, and (*b*) is also limited in regard to space.

Thesis *a*.   Proof.—If we assume the opposite, namely, that the world has no beginning in time, and if we define the infinite as that which can never be completed by means of a successive synthesis, we must conclude that the world-series can never complete itself.   But the entire series of past events *elapses, i.e.* completes itself at each moment.   It cannot therefore be infinite.

Criticism.—This argument gains its plausibility from the illegitimate use of the term 'elapse' (*verfliessen*) as equivalent to 'complete itself.'   If it be really correct to define the infinite as that which can never be completed, the conclusion to be drawn is that the temporal series is always actually infinite, and that no point or event in it is nearer to or further from

---

therefore drawn from objective grounds.   On the other hand, the assertions and proofs of the theses have no other than a subjective ground, rest solely on the weakness of the reasoning individual; for his imagination becomes tired with an endless regression, and therefore he puts an end to it by arbitrary assumptions, which he tries to smooth over as well as he can; and his judgment, moreover, is in this case paralysed by early and deeply imprinted prejudices.   On this account the proof of the thesis in all the four conflicts is throughout a mere sophism, while that of the antithesis is a necessary inference of the reason from the laws of the world as idea known to us *a priori*.   It is, moreover, only with great pains and skill that Kant is able to sustain the thesis, and make it appear to attack its opponent, which is endowed with native power. . . .   I shall show that the proofs which Kant adduces of the individual theses are sophisms, while those of the antitheses are quite fairly and correctly drawn from objective grounds."

either its beginning or its end.[1]   We may select any point in the series as that from which we propose to begin a regress to the earlier members of the series, but if the series is actually infinite, it will be a regress without possibility of completion, and one therefore which removes all justification for asserting that at the point chosen a series has completed itself.   It has no beginning, and has no completion.   What it has done at each moment of the past it is still doing at each present moment, namely, coming out of an inexhaustible past and passing into an equally inexhaustible future.   Time is by its given nature capable of being interpreted only as actually infinite, alike in its past and in its future.   It cannot complete itself any more than it can begin itself.   The one would be as gross a violation of its nature as would the other.   The present exists only as a species of transition, unique in itself, but analogous in nature to the innumerable other times that constitute time past.   It is a transition from the infinite through the infinite to the infinite.   That we cannot comprehend how, from an infinitude that has no beginning, the present should ever have been reached, is no sufficient reason for denying what by the very nature of time we are compelled to accept as a correct description of the situation which is being analysed. The actual nature of time is such as to rule out from among the possibilities the thesis which Kant is here professing to be able to establish; time, being such as it actually is, can have no beginning.

What thus holds of time may likewise hold of events in time.   If time is actually infinite, no proof can be derived from it in support of the assumption that the world has had a beginning in time.

The phrase "by means of a successive synthesis" gives a needlessly subjectivist colouring to Kant's method of proof. The antinomy is professedly being stated from the realist standpoint, and ought not therefore to be complicated by any such reference.   This objection applies, as we shall find, still more strongly to Kant's proof of the second part of the thesis. The latter proof depends upon this subjectivist reference; the present proof does not.

Kant limits his problem to the past infinitude of time. The reason for this lies, of course, in the fact that he is concerned with the problem of creation.   The limitation is, however, misleading.

Thesis *b.*—The world is limited in regard to space.

Proof.—Assume the opposite, namely, that the world is

---

[1] Cf. F. Erhardt's *Kritik der Kantischen Antinomienlehre* (1888), a brief but excellent analysis of this section of the *Critique*.

an infinite, given whole of coexisting parts. A magnitude not given within the determinate limits of an intuition can only be thought through the synthesis of its parts, and its totality through their completed synthesis. In order, therefore, that we may be able to think as a single whole the world which fills all space, the successive synthesis of the parts of an infinite world must be regarded as completed, *i.e.* an infinite must be regarded as having elapsed in the enumeration of all coexisting things. This, however, is impossible. An infinite aggregate of actual things cannot therefore be viewed as a given whole, nor as being given as coexistent. Consequently the world of spatial existences must be regarded as finite.

Criticism.—From the impossibility of traversing infinite space in thought by the successive addition of part to part, Kant here argues that "an infinite aggregate of actual things cannot be viewed as a given whole," and consequently that the world cannot be infinitely extended in space. That is, from a *subjective impossibility of apprehension* he infers an *objective impossibility of existence*. But Kant has himself *defined* the infinite as involving this subjective impossibility; for in the proof of thesis *a* he has stated that the infinitude of a series consists in the very fact that it can never be completed through successive synthesis. Kant is therefore propounding against the *existence* of the infinite tne very feature which by definition constitutes its infinitude. The implication would seem to be that the concept of the infinite is the concept of that which *ex definitione* cannot exist, and that there is therefore a contradiction in the very idea of the actual infinite.

Deferring for a moment the further objections to which such procedure lies open, we may observe that Kant, in arguing from a subjective to an objective impossibility, commits the fallacy of *ignoratio elenchi*. For when the conditions of objective existence are recognised in their distinction from those of mental apprehension, the supposed contradiction vanishes, and the argument ceases to have any cogency. The use of the words 'given' and 'whole' is misleading. If space is infinite, it is without bounds, and cannot therefore exist as a whole in any usual meaning of that term. For the same reason it must be incapable of being given as a whole. Its infinitude is a presupposition which analysis of actually given portions of it constrains us to postulate, and has to be conceived in terms of the definition employed in thesis *a*. The given must always be conceived as involving what is not itself given and what is not even capable of complete construction. In terms of this presupposition an actual infinite, not given and not capable of construction, can be represented with entire consistency.

But to return to the main assumption upon which Kant's proof would seem to rest: it is all-important to observe that Kant does not, either in the *Critique* or in any other of his writings, assert that the concept of the actual infinite is inherently self-contradictory. This is a matter in regard to which many of Kant's critics have misrepresented his teaching. Kant's argument may, as we have just maintained, be found on examination to involve the above assertion; but this, if clearly established, so far from commending the argument to Kant, would have led him to reject it as invalid. The passage in the *Dissertation*[1] of 1770, which contains his most definite utterance on this point, represents the view from which he never afterwards departed. It may be quoted in full.

"Those who reject the actual mathematical infinite do so in a very casual manner. For they so construct their definition of the infinite that they are able to extract a contradiction from it. The *infinite* is described by them as *a quantity than which none greater is possible*, and the mathematical infinite as a multiplicity—of an assignable unit—than which none greater is possible. Since they thus substitute *maximum* for *infinitum*, and a greatest multiplicity is impossible, they easily conclude against this infinite which they have themselves invented. Or, it may be, they entitle an infinite multiplicity an *infinite number*, and point out that such a phrase is meaningless, as is, indeed, perfectly evident. But again they have fought and overthrown only the figments of their own minds. If, however, they had conceived the mathematical infinite as a quantity which, when related to measure, as its unit, is *a multiplicity greater than all number*; and if furthermore, they had observed that *measurability* here denotes only the relation [of the infinite] to the standards of the human intellect, which is not permitted to attain to a *definite conception of multiplicity* save by the successive addition of unit to unit, nor to the *sum-total* (which is called *number*) save by completing this progress in a finite time; they would have perceived clearly that what does not conform to the established law of some subject need not on that account exceed all intellection. An intellect may exist, though not indeed a human intellect, which perceives a multiplicity distinctly in one intuition [*uno obtutu*] without the successive application of a measure."

The concluding sentences of this *Dissertation* passage may be taken as Kant's own better and abiding judgment in regard to the question before us. We must not argue from the impossibility of mentally traversing the infinite to the impossibility of its existence. Indeed the essentials of the above passage are restated in the 'Observation' on this thesis.[1] Thus the concept of the actual infinite is not only, as a concept, perfectly self-consistent, it is also one which, in view of the nature of time and of space, we are constrained to accept as a correct representation of the actually given. The thesis of this first antinomy runs directly counter to admitted facts. That Kant is here arguing in respect to the world, and not merely in respect to space and time, does not essentially alter the situation. For if space and time are necessarily to be viewed as infinite, there can be no *a priori* proof—none, at least, of the kind here attempted—that the world-series may not be so likewise.

Antithesis.—(*a*) The world has no beginning in time; (*b*) has no limits in space. In both these respects the world is infinite.

In these antitheses Kant assumes that space and time are actually infinite, and from that assumption advances to the proof that this is likewise true of the world in its spatial and temporal aspects. This, by itself, ought to be sufficient evidence that Kant does not regard the actual infinite as an inherently impossible conception. As the antinomies are avowedly formulated from the realist, dogmatic standpoint of ordinary consciousness, Kant is also enabled to assume that if the world begins to be, it must have an antecedent cause determining it to exist at that moment rather than at another.

Antithesis *a*. Proof.—Let us assume the opposite, namely, that the world has a beginning. It will then be preceded by an empty time in which it was not. But in an empty time no becoming is possible, since no part of an empty time is distinguished from any other part in such a way as to make it a condition determining the existence of the world rather than its non-existence. The world must therefore be infinite as regards past time.

Criticism.—In this argument everything depends upon what is to be meant by the term 'world.' If Kant means by it merely the material world, the assumption of its non-existence does not leave only empty time and space. Other kinds of existence may be possible, and in these a sufficient cause of its first beginning may be found. The nature of creative action will remain mysterious and incomprehensible, but that is no sufficient reason for denying its possibility. If, on the other hand, Kant means by the world 'all that is,' the assumption of its non-existence is likewise the assumption of the non-existence of all its possible causes. That, however,

---

[1] Cf. A 431·2 = B 460·1 : ". . . the concept [of the infinite] is not the concept of a maximum; by it we think only its relation to any assignable unit, in respect to which it is greater than all number."

is for ordinary consciousness a quite impossible assumption, since it runs counter to the causal principle which is taken as universally valid. From this point of view the argument consists in making an impossible assumption, and in then pointing out the impossible consequence which must follow. By such a mode of argument no conclusion can be reached. Kant's decision ought rather to have been that, as time is actually infinite, the world may be so likewise, but that though *reality* must in some form be eternally existent, the *material world* cannot be proved to be so by any *a priori* proof of the kind here given.

Antithesis *b*. Proof.—Let us assume the opposite, namely, that the world is finite, existing in an empty limitless space. There will then be not only a relation of things *in space*, but also of things *to space*. But as the world is a totality outside of which no object of intuition can be found, the relation of the world to empty space is a relation to *no object*. Such a relation is nothing. Consequently the opposite holds; the world must be infinitely extended.

Criticism.—That Kant himself felt the inadequacy of this argument, when taken from the dogmatic standpoint, is indicated by the lengthy note which he has appended to it, and which develops his own Critical view of space as not a real independent object, but merely the form of external intuition. From the standpoint of ordinary consciousness space is a self-existent entity, and there is no insuperable difficulty in conceiving a relation as holding between it and its contents. The introduction of the opposed standpoint of the *Aesthetic* therefore runs directly counter to Kant's own intention of expounding the antinomies from the dogmatic standpoint which involves this realist view of space, and of showing that they afford, in independence of the arguments of the *Aesthetic*, an indirect proof of the untenableness of that belief.[1] The conclusion which ought to have been drawn is analogous to that above suggested for thesis *a*. As space is actually infinite, the material world may be so likewise; but that it actually is so, cannot be established by an *a priori* argument of the kind here attempted.

SECOND ANTINOMY

Thesis.—Every composite substance in the world consists of simple parts, and nothing anywhere exists save the simple or what is composed of it.

Proof.—Let us assume the opposite, namely, that substances

---

[1] Cf. Kant's statement in the *Observation* to this antithesis, A 431·3 = B 459-61.

do not consist of simple parts. If all composition be then removed in thought, no composite part, and (as there are no simple parts) also no simple part, and therefore nothing whatsoever, will remain. Consequently no substance will be given. Either, therefore, it is impossible to remove in thought all composition, or after its removal something that exists without composition, *i.e.* the simple, must remain. In the former case the composite would not itself consist of substances (with them composition is a merely accidental relation, and they must, as self-persisting beings, be able to exist independently of it). As this contradicts our assumption, only the latter alternative remains, namely, that the substantial compounds in the world consist of simple parts.

Criticism.—Kant here assumes, by his definition of terms, the point which he professes to establish by argument. The substance referred to, though never itself mentioned by name, is extended matter. Kant identifies it with 'composite substance.' Substance, he further dogmatically decides, is that which is capable of independent existence, and to which all relations of composition are therefore merely accidental. If these assumptions be granted, it at once follows that composition cannot be essential to matter, and that when all composition is thought away, its reality will be disclosed as consisting in simple parts. Kant, however, makes no attempt to prove that extended matter can be defined in any such terms. From the dogmatic point of view of ordinary consciousness, though not from the sophisticated standpoint of Leibniz, extension is of the very essence of matter ; and, as Kant himself believed,[1] the continuity of extension is such as to exclude all possibility of elimination of the composite. For he maintains that, however far division be carried, the parts remain no less composite than the whole from which the regress has started. On any such view the extended and the composite are not equivalent terms. The opposite of the composite is the simple ; the opposite of the extended is the non-extended. Kant is here surreptitiously substituting a Leibnizian metaphysics in place of the empirical reality which is supposed to necessitate the argument.

In the *Observation* on this thesis Kant shows consciousness

---

[1] Kant regarded the point as a limit, *i.e.* as a boundary (*Dissertation*, § 14, 4 ; § 15, C : " The simple in space is not a part but a limit " ; A 169-70 = B 211) ; whereas certain modern mathematicians take the point as one of the undefined elements. When the point is regarded in this latter manner, space may perhaps be satisfactorily defined as a set of points. In arguing for the antithesis, and in the passages just cited, Kant also assumes that, in the case of space, the properties of the class are determined by the properties of its elements. This questionable assumption is involved in his assertion that space can consist only of spaces.

of the defects of his argument. It does not apply to space, time, or change.

"We ought not to call space a *compositum* but a *totum*, because its parts are possible only in the whole, not the whole through the parts."[1]

As Kant further states, he is speaking only of the simples of the Leibnizian system. This thesis is "the dialectical principle of monadology." Again in the *Observation* on the antithesis, in commenting on the mathematical proof of the infinite divisibility of matter, Kant even goes so far as to declare that the argument of the thesis is based on an illegitimate substitution of things in themselves, conceived by the pure understanding, for the appearances with which alone the antinomy is concerned.[2]

". . . it is quite futile to attempt to overthrow, by sophistical manipulation of purely discursive concepts, the manifest, demonstrated truth of mathematics."

Antithesis.—No composite thing in the world consists of simple parts, and there nowhere exists in the world anything simple.

Proof.—Let us assume the opposite, namely, that a composite thing (as substance) consists of simple parts. As all external relation, and therefore all composition of substances, is only possible in space, space must consist of as many parts as there are parts of the composite that occupies it. Space, however, does not consist of simple parts, but of spaces. The simple must therefore occupy a space. Now as everything real which occupies a space contains in itself a manifold of constituents external to one another, and therefore is composite, and as a real composite is not composed of accidents (for without substance accidents could not be outside one another), but of substances, the simple would be a substantial composite, which is self-contradictory.

Criticism.—The Leibnizian standpoint is here completely deserted. Instead of proceeding to demonstrate the direct opposite of the thesis, Kant in this argument deals with the extended bodies of empirical intuition. The proof given ultimately reduces to an argument from the continuous nature of space to the continuous nature of the matter which occupies it. But as the thesis and the antithesis thus refer to different realities, the former to things in themselves conceived by pure understanding, and the latter to the sensuous, no antinomy

---

[1] A 438 = B 466.   [2] A 439-41 = B 467-9.

has been shown to subsist. Antinomy presupposes that both the opposing assertions have the same reference. Kant, as already noted, argues in the *Observation* to this antithesis that all attempts "made by the monadists" to refute the mathematical proof of the infinite divisibility of matter are quite futile, and are due to their forgetting that in this discussion we are concerned only with appearances.

"The monadists have, indeed, been sufficiently acute to seek to avoid this difficulty by not treating space as a condition of the possibility of the objects of outer intuition (bodies), but by taking these and the dynamical relation of substances as the condition of the possibility of space. But we have a concept of bodies only as appearances, and as such they necessarily presuppose space as the condition of the possibility of all outer appearance." [1]

How Kant, after writing these words, should still have left standing the proof which he has given of the thesis may be partially explained as due to the continuing influence of his earlier view,[2] according to which antinomy represents not a conflict between opposing views of the world of ordinary consciousness, but between the demands of pure thought and the forms of sensuous existence. That older view of antinomy here gains the upper hand, notwithstanding its lack of agreement with the general scheme of the *Dialectic*.

There is a further inconsistency in Kant's procedure which may perhaps be taken as indicating the early origin of this portion of the *Critique*. He presents the mathematical proof of the continuity of matter as conclusive. Yet in the *Metaphysical First Principles of Natural Science* (1786) he most emphatically states that "the infinite divisibility of matter is very far from being proved through proof of the infinite divisibility of space." [3]

Russell,[4] in discussing the thesis and antithesis on their merits, from the point of view of certain present-day mathematical theories, makes the following criticism of Kant's procedure.

"Here, again, the argument applies to things in space and time, and to all collections, whether existent or not. . . . And with this extension [5] the proof of the proposition must, I think, be admitted ; only that *terms* or *concepts* should be substituted for *substances*, and that, instead of the argument that relations between substances are accidental (*zufällig*), we should content ourselves with saying that relations imply terms and complexity implies relations."

---

[1] A 441 = B 469.　　　　[2] Developed in the *Dissertation* (1770).
[3] Zweites Hauptstück, Lehrsatz 4, Anmerkung 1. Cf. also Anmerkung 2.
[4] *Principles of Mathematics*, i. p. 460.　　　[5] Cf. above, p. 481 *n*. 2.

Russell further argues that Kant's assumption in the antithesis, that "space does not consist of simple parts, but of spaces," cannot be granted.   It

". . . involves a covert use of the axiom of finitude, *i.e.* the axiom that, if a space does consist of points, it must consist of some finite number of points.   When once this is denied, we may admit that no finite number of divisions of a space will lead to points, while yet holding every space to be composed of points.   A finite space is a whole consisting of simple parts, but not of any finite number of simple parts.   Exactly the same thing is true of the stretch between 1 and 2.   Thus the antinomy is not specially spatial, and any answer which is applicable in Arithmetic is applicable here also. The thesis, which is an essential postulate of Logic, should be accepted, while the antithesis should be rejected."

But, as above observed,[1] those mathematicians who adopt this view so alter the meaning of the term point that it would perhaps be equally true to say that the thesis, as thus interpreted by Russell, coincides with what Kant believes himself to be asserting in the antithesis.

THIRD ANTINOMY

Thesis.—Causality according to the laws of nature is not the only causality from which the appearances of the world can be deduced.   There is also required for their explanation another, that of freedom.

Proof.—Let us assume the opposite.   In that case everything that happens presupposes a previous state upon which it follows according to a rule.   That previous state is itself caused in similar fashion, and so on *in infinitum*.   But if everything thus happens according to the mere laws of nature, there can never be a first beginning, and therefore no completeness of the series on the side of the derivative causes. But the law of nature is that nothing happens without a cause *sufficiently* determined *a priori*.   If, therefore, all causality is possible only according to the laws of nature, the principle contradicts itself when taken in unlimited universality.   Such causality cannot therefore be the sole causality possible.   We must admit an absolute spontaneity, whereby a series of appearances, that proceed according to laws of nature, begins by itself.

Criticism.—The vital point of this argument lies in the assertion that the principle of causality calls for a *sufficient* cause for each event, and that such sufficiency is not to be

---

[1] P. 489 *n.*

found in natural causes which are themselves derivative or conditioned. As the antecedent series of causes for an event can never be traced back to a first cause, it can never be completed, and can never, therefore, be sufficient to account for the event under consideration. Either, therefore, the principle of causality contradicts itself, or some form of free self-originative causality must be postulated. This argument cannot be accepted as valid. Each natural cause is sufficient to account for its effect. That is to say, the causation is sufficient *at each stage*. That the series of antecedent causes cannot be completed is due to its actual infinitude, not to any insufficiency in the causality which it embodies.[1] To prove his point, Kant would have to show that the conception of the actual infinite is inherently self-contradictory; and that, as we have already noted, he does not mean to assert. His argument here lies open to the same criticism as we have already passed upon his argument in proof of the thesis of the first antinomy.

Antithesis.—There is no freedom; everything in the world proceeds solely in accordance with laws of nature.

Proof.—Let us assume the opposite. Free causality, *i.e.* the power of absolute origination, presupposes the possibility of a state of the cause which has no causal connection with its preceding state, and which does not follow from it. But this is opposed to the law of causality, and would render unity of experience impossible. Freedom is therefore an empty thought-entity (*Gedankending*), and is not to be met with in any experience.

[1] Cf. Schopenhauer, *World as Will and Idea* (*Werke, Frauenstädt*, ii. p. 590; Eng. trans. ii. pp. 111-12). "The argument for the third thesis is a very fine sophism, and is really Kant's pretended principle of pure reason itself entirely unadulterated and unchanged. It tries to prove the finiteness of the series of causes by saying that, in order to be *sufficient*, a cause must contain the complete sum of the conditions from which the succeeding state, the effect, proceeds. For the completeness of the determinations present *together* in the state which is the cause, the argument now substitutes the completeness of the series of causes by which that state itself was brought to actuality; and because completeness presupposes the condition of being rounded off or closed in, and this again presupposes finiteness, the argument infers from this a first cause, closing the series and therefore unconditioned. But the juggling is obvious. In order to conceive the state A as the sufficient cause of the state B, I assume that it contains the sum of the necessary determinations from the coexistence of which the state B inevitably follows. Now by this my demand upon it as a *sufficient* cause is entirely satisfied, and has no direct connection with the question how the state A itself came to be; this rather belongs to an entirely different consideration, in which I regard the said state A no more as cause, but as itself an effect; in which case another state again must be related to it, just as it was related to B. The assumption of the finiteness of the series of causes and effects, and accordingly of a first beginning, appears nowhere in this as necessary, any more than the presentness of the present moment requires us to assume a beginning of time itself."

Criticism.—We may first observe the strange relation in which the proof of the thesis stands to that of the antithesis. According to the former, freedom must be postulated because otherwise the principle of causality would contradict itself. According to the latter, freedom is impossible, and for the same reason. Now, as Erhardt has pointed out,[1] a principle cannot be reconciled with itself through the making of an assumption which contradicts it. That would only be the institution of a second contradiction, not the removal of the previous conflict. If the proof of the thesis be correct, that of the antithesis must be false; if the proof of the antithesis be correct, that of the thesis must be invalid. For though the thesis and the antithesis may themselves contradict one another, such conflict must not exist between the grounds upon which they establish themselves. If the reasons cited in their support are contradictory of one another, the total argument is rendered null and void. The supporting proofs being contradictory of one another, nothing whatsoever has been established. There will remain as a pressing and immediate problem the task of distinguishing the truth from among the competing alternatives; and until this has been done, the argument cannot proceed. The assumption of freedom either does or does not contradict the principle of causality. Antinomy is not the simple assertion that both A and not-A are true, but that A and not-A, though contradictory of one another, can both be established by arguments in which such contradiction does not occur.[2]

The proof given of the thesis would seem, as already noted, to be untenable. The principle of natural causality is not self-contradictory. What now is to be said regarding the proof of the antithesis? If the principle of natural causality be formulated as asserting that every event has an *antecedent* cause determining it to exist, then certainly free, spontaneous, or self-originating causality is excluded. Here, as in Kant's proof of the antithesis of the first antinomy, everything depends upon definition of the terms employed. It must be borne in mind that the antinomies are asserted to exist only on the dogmatic level. Critical considerations must not, therefore, be allowed to intervene. Now for ordinary consciousness the concept of causality has a very indefinite meaning, and a very wide application. Causation may be spontaneous as well as mechanical, spiritual as well as material. All possibilities lie open, and no mere reference to the concept of causal dependence suffices to decide between them. Free

[1] *Op. cit.* p. 24.
[2] For comment upon Kant's defence of his procedure cf. below, p. 496.

causality, so far as *dogmatic* analysis of the causal postulate can show to the contrary, may or may not be possible.[1] Kant has failed to establish the antithesis save by the surreptitious introduction of conclusions which presuppose the truth of his Critical teaching. This is especially shown in the emphasis laid upon 'unity of experience.' The further statement[2] that freedom means lawlessness is only true if Kant's teaching is mutilated by reduction merely to its assertion of the objective validity of the mechanistic principles of natural science. Kant is both running with the hare and hunting with the hounds.

Though this antinomy is chiefly concerned with the problem of freedom, *i.e.* of spontaneous origination *within* the world, the proof of the thesis refers only to the cosmological problem of a first cause.[3] The reasons of this oscillation we shall have occasion to consider in dealing with the fourth antinomy. The terms world and nature play the same ambiguous part as in the antithesis of the first antinomy; they tend to be employed in the narrower, mechanistic sense of Kant's own Critical teaching.

FOURTH ANTINOMY

As the proofs of the thesis and antithesis proceed on lines identical with those of the third antinomy, I shall omit detailed statement of them.[4] Kant again argues from the fact that every change has a condition which precedes it in time. There is no difference in the proofs themselves, but only in the nature of the inference which they are made to support. In the third antinomy they lead to the assertion and denial of free causality; in the fourth antinomy they lead to the assertion and denial of an absolutely necessary being. The assertion is required in order to save the principle of causality from self-contradiction; the denial is also necessary, and for the same reason. The illegitimacy of this procedure has already been pointed out.[5] Though the thesis and the antithesis will, if antinomy be assumed to represent an actual

---

[1] Cf. Kant's *Observation* on the thesis.

[2] A 451 = B 479.　　　　　　　　　　　[3] Cf. also A 451 = B 479.

[4] Cf. Schopenhauer, *op. cit.* p. 591; Eng. trans. p. 113. "The fourth conflict is . . . really tautological with the third; and the proof of the thesis is also essentially the same as that of the preceding one. Kant's assertion that every conditioned presupposes a complete series of conditions, and therefore a series which ends with an unconditioned, is a *petitio principii* which must simply be denied. Everything conditioned presupposes nothing but its condition; that this is again conditioned raises a new consideration which is not directly contained in the first."　　　　　　[5] Above, p. 494.

conflict, contradict one another, no such conflict is allowable in the grounds which profess to establish them. We must not assert, as *argument*, that both A and not-A are true.

In the *Observation* on the antithesis [1] Kant has himself taken notice of this " strange " situation.

" From the same ground on which, in the thesis, the existence of an original being was inferred, its non-existence is inferred, and that with equal stringency."

A necessary being is inferred to exist, because the past series of events cannot contain all the conditions of an event, unless the unconditioned is to be found among them. A necessary being is denied to exist, because the series of merely conditioned events contains all the conditions that there are. Kant's defence of this procedure is as follows:

" Nevertheless, the method of argument in both cases is entirely in conformity even with ordinary human reason, which frequently falls into conflict with itself from considering its object from two different points of view. M. de Mairan [2] regarded the controversy between two famous astronomers, which arose from a similar difficulty in regard to choice of standpoint, as a sufficiently remarkable phenomenon to justify his writing a special treatise upon it. The one had argued that *the moon revolves on its own axis*, because it always turns the same side towards the earth. The other drew the opposite conclusion that *the moon does not revolve on its own axis*, because it always turns the same side towards the earth. Both inferences were correct, according to the point of view which each chose in observing the moon's motion."

This example is not really relevant. In spite of Kant's assertion to the contrary, the point of view is one and the same in thesis and in antithesis. In both cases the absolutely necessary being is viewed as the first of the changes in the world of sense. To maintain that when thus viewed it both is and is not demanded by the law of causality, is as impossible as to assert that in one and the same meaning of our terms the moon both does and does not revolve on its own axis. That the proofs of the fourth antinomy are identical with those of the third is due to the fact that Kant, under the stress of his architectonic, [3] is striving to construct four antinomies while only three are really distinguishable. The third and fourth antinomies coincide as formulations of the problem whether or not the conditioned implies, and

---

[1] A 459 = B 487.

[2] Jean Jacques Dortous de Mairan (1678–1771), physicist and mathematician. In 1740 he succeeded Fontenelle as perpetual Secretary of the French Academy of Sciences.   [3] Cf. above, pp. 435, 495 *n.* 4.

originates in, the unconditioned. The precise determination of this unconditioned, whether as free causality or as a necessary being, or in any other way, is a further problem, and does not properly fall within the scope of the *cosmological* inquiries, which are alone in place in this division of the *Critique*.

The manner in which Kant, in treating of freedom, makes the transition [1] from the cosmological (or theological) unconditioned to the psychological is significant. The cosmological unconditioned is proved to exist by the argument of the thesis, and its existence is at once interpreted as establishing at least in this one case the actuality of free spontaneous causality. Kant remarks that this

" . . . transcendental Idea of freedom does not by any means constitute the entire content of the psychological concept of that name, which is mainly empirical, but only that of absolute spontaneity of action. . . . The necessity of a first beginning, due to freedom, of a series of appearances we have demonstrated only in so far as it is required for the conceivability of an origin of the world. . . . But as, after all, the power of spontaneously originating a series in time has thus been proved (though not understood), it is now permissible for us to admit within the course of the world different series as capable in their causality of beginning of themselves, and so to attribute to their substances a power of acting from freedom."

That each such successive series in the world can only have a relatively primary beginning, and must always be preceded by some other state of things, is no sufficient objection to such causality.

"For we are here speaking of an absolutely first beginning not in time, but in causality. If, for instance, I at this moment arise from my chair in complete freedom, without being necessarily determined thereto by the influence of natural causes, a new series, with all its natural consequences *in infinitum*, has its absolute beginning in this event, although the event itself is only, with regard to time, the continuation of a preceding series."

Thus Kant's proof of freedom in the thesis of the third antinomy is merely a corollary from his proof of the existence of a cosmological or theological unconditioned ; and further, this freedom is not, like the cosmological unconditioned, proved to exist, but only to be " admissible " as a possibility. Similarly in the antithesis, the only disproof of freedom is the disproof of unconditioned causality *in general*. The antinomy deals with the general opposition and relation between the contingent and the unconditioned.

[1] A 448-50 = B 476-8.

It is this same opposition exactly which constitutes the subject-matter of the fourth antinomy. The terms used are different, but their meanings are one and the same. For though Kant substitutes 'absolutely necessary being' for 'unconditioned causality,' the former is still conceived as belonging to the world of sense, as the unconditioned origin of its changes. And as Kant is careful to add, only the causal, cosmological argument can be employed to establish the existence of an absolutely necessary being; nothing can legitimately be inferred from the mere Idea. The verbal change is consequently verbal only; the argument of the fourth antinomy coincides in result no less than in method of proof with the argument of the third. It is impossible to define the unconditioned in any more specific fashion save by an enquiry which entirely transcends the scope of the argument that Kant is here presenting. Kant's procedure also lies open to the further objection that the conception of an absolutely necessary being, which he here introduces without preliminary analysis or explanation, is later shown by him[1] to be devoid of significance. He employs it, but precludes himself from either investigating it or from drawing any serviceable consequences from it. The situation is not without the elements of comedy. In order to seem to mark a real distinction between the fourth and the third antinomies, Kant has perforce to trespass upon the domain of theology; but as he is aware that the trespass is forbidden, he seeks to mitigate the offence by returning from the foray empty-handed. To such unhappy straits is he again reduced by his over-fond devotion to architectonic.

SECTION III

THE INTEREST OF REASON IN THIS SELF-CONFLICT[2]

This section, though extremely important, requires no lengthy comment. It is lucid and straightforward. It may be summarised as follows. The theses and the antitheses rest upon diverse and conflicting interests. The theses, though expressed in dry formulas, divested of the empirical features through which alone their true grandeur can be displayed, represent the proud pretensions of dogmatic Reason. The antitheses give expression to principles of pure empiricism. The former are supported by interests of a practical and

---

[1] Cf. above, p. 427 ff.; below, pp. 520-1, 527-37, 541 ff.   [2] A 462 = B 490.

popular character : upon them morals and religion are based. The latter, while conflicting with our spiritual interests, far exceed the theses in their intellectual advantages.   This explains

"... the zelotic passion of the one party, and the calm assurance of the other, and why the world hails the one with eager approval, and is implacably prejudiced against the other."

No legitimate objection could be raised against the principles of the empirical philosopher, if he sought only to rebuke the rashness and presumption of Reason when it boasts of *knowledge*, and when it represents as *speculative insight* that which is grounded only in *faith*.

"But when empiricism itself, as frequently happens, becomes dogmatic . . ., and confidently denies whatever lies beyond the sphere of its intuitive knowledge, it betrays the same lack of modesty; and that is all the more reprehensible owing to the irreparable injury which is thereby caused to the practical interests of Reason."

Each party asserts more than it knows.   The one allows our practical interests to delude Reason as to its inherent powers ; the other would so extend empirical knowledge as to destroy the validity of our moral principles.   Kant regards the opposition as being historically typified by the contrasted systems of Platonism and Epicureanism.   It befits us, as self-reflecting beings, to free ourselves, at least provisionally, from the partiality of those divergent interests, and by application of "the sceptical method," unconcerned about consequences, to penetrate to the primary sources of this perennial conflict.   As Kant states in the next section, the conflict is of such a character as to be genuinely resolvable.

This section must have been written, or at least first sketched, at the time when Kant still intended to bring his whole criticism of the metaphysical sciences within the scope of his doctrine of antinomy.[1]

SECTION IV

THE TRANSCENDENTAL PROBLEMS OF PURE REASON, IN SO FAR AS THEY ABSOLUTELY MUST BE CAPABLE OF SOLUTION [2]

There are sciences the very nature of which requires that every question which can occur in them must be completely

---

[1] Cf. above, pp. 434 ff., 479.   [2] A 476 = B 504.

answerable from what can be presumed to be known. This is true of the science of ethics. When I ask to what course of action I am committed in moral duty, the question must be answerable in terms of the considerations which have led to its being propounded. For there can be no moral obligation in regard to that of which we cannot have knowledge. We must not plead that the problem is unanswerable; a solution must be found. Kant proceeds to argue that this is no less true of transcendental philosophy.

". . . it is unique among speculative sciences in that no question which concerns an object given to pure Reason is insoluble for this same human Reason, and that no excuse of an unavoidable ignorance, or of the problem's unfathomable depth, can release us from the obligation to answer it thoroughly and completely. That very concept which puts us in position to ask the question must also qualify us to answer it, since, as in the case of right and wrong, the object is not to be met with outside the concept."

The third and fourth paragraphs would seem to be later interpolations. The section, like Section III., must have been written at the time when Kant still regarded the doctrine of antinomy as covering the entire field of metaphysics. Transcendental philosophy is identified with cosmology, as dealt with in the antinomies. But in the third paragraph the former is taken as a wider term. Also, in the first two paragraphs the problems of pure Reason are regarded as soluble because their objects are not to be met with outside the concepts of them; whereas in the third paragraph they are viewed as soluble because their object is given empirically. Again, in the second paragraph transcendental philosophy has been taken as unique among speculative [*i.e.* theoretical] sciences; in the fourth paragraph mathematics is placed alongside it.

Examination of this section as a whole (and the same is true of the immediately following section) justifies the conclusion that at the time when it was written Kant regarded the Ideas of Reason as having a purely and exclusively regulative function, and consequently as exhausting their inherent meaning in their empirical reference. He regards them as entirely lacking in metaphysical significance. They are invented by Reason for Reason's own satisfaction, and must therefore yield in their internal content the explanation of their existence, and must also supply a complete and thorough answer to all problems which are traceable to them. A dogmatic (*i.e.* ontological) solution of the antinomies is, as we have already found, impossible; the Critical solution considers the question subjectively,

" . . . in accordance with the foundation of the knowledge upon which it is based." [1] "For your object is only in your brain, and cannot be given outside it; so that you have only to take care to be at one with yourself, and to avoid the amphiboly which transforms your Idea into a supposed representation of an object empirically given and therefore to be known according to the laws of experience." [2]

Kant's argument in proof of this purely subjective interpretation of the Ideas consists in showing that they are not presented in any given appearances, and are not even necessary to explain appearances. The unconditioned, whether of quantity, of division, or of origination, has nothing to do with any experience, whether actual or possible.

"You would not, for instance, in any wise be able to explain the appearances of a body better, or even differently, if you assumed that it consists either of simple or of inexhaustibly composite parts; for neither a simple appearance nor an infinite composition can ever come before you. Appearances demand explanation only in so far as the conditions of their explanation are given in perception, [and the unconditioned can never be so given]." [3]

This standpoint, at once sceptical and empirical, is further developed in the next section.

SECTION V

SCEPTICAL REPRESENTATION OF THE COSMOLOGICAL QUESTIONS [4]

Applying the "sceptical method," [5] Kant argues that even supposing one or other party could conclusively establish itself through final refutation of the other, no advantage of any kind would accrue. The victory would be a fruitless one, and the outcome "mere nonsense." [6] The sole validity of the Ideas lies in their empirical reference; and yet this reference is one which proves them to be, when objectively interpreted, entirely meaningless. The cosmological Idea is always either too large or too small for any concept of the understanding. No matter what view is taken, the only possible object (viz. that yielded by experience) will not fit into it. If the world has no beginning, or is infinitely divisible, or has no first cause, the regress transcends all empirical concepts; while if the world has a beginning, is composed of

---

[1] A 484 = B 512.   [2] *Ibid.*   [3] A 483 = B 511.
[4] A 485 = B 513.   [5] Cf. above, p. 481; below, pp. 545-6.
[6] Kant plays on the double meaning of "sinnleeres"—"empty of sense" and "non-sense."

simple parts, and has a first cause, it is too small for the concepts through which alone it can be experienced. In other words, the cosmological Ideas are always either too large or too small for the empirical regress, and therefore stand condemned by sense-experience, which can alone impart relation to an object, *i.e.* truth and meaning to any concept. For, as Kant explicitly states, *we must not reverse this relation and condemn empirical concepts, as being in the one case too small, and in the other case too large for the Idea. Experience, not Ideas, is the criterion alike of reality and of truth.*

"The possible empirical concept is, therefore, the standard by which we must judge whether the Idea is mere Idea and thought-entity (*Gedankending*), or whether it finds its object in the world."[1]

When two things are compared, that for the sake of which the other exists is the sole proper standard. We do not say "that a man is too long for his coat, but that the coat is too short for the man."[2] We are thus confirmed in the view that the antinomies rest upon a false view of the manner in which the object of the cosmological Ideas can be given; and are set upon the track, followed out in the next section, of the illusion to which they are due.

This reduction of the Ideas to mere thought-entities is one of the two alternative views which, as we have already stated,[3] compete with one another throughout the entire *Dialectic.* We may, for instance, compare the above explanation of the conflict between the Ideas and experience with that given in A 422 = B 450. In the latter passage the antinomies are traced to a conflict between Reason and understanding. If the unity is adequate to the demands of Reason, it is too great for the understanding; if it is adequate to the understanding, it is too small for Reason. Kant does not here allow that the claims of Reason are *ipso facto* condemned through the incapacity of experience to fulfil them. On the contrary, he implies that it is through the Ideas that we come to realise the merely phenomenal character of everything experienced.

Our task, in this Commentary, is only to distinguish the passages in which those two conflicting tendencies appear, and to trace the consequences which follow from Kant's alternation between them. Discussion of their significance had best be deferred to the close of the *Dialectic*, where Kant dwells upon the regulative function of Reason. At present we need merely note that the main content of the above

[1] A 489 = B 517.　　[2] A 490 = B 518.　　[3] Above, p. 426 ff.

sections, in which the sceptical view is expounded, is of early date, prior to the working out of the *Paralogisms* and of the *Ideal.*

SECTION VI

TRANSCENDENTAL IDEALISM AS THE KEY TO THE SOLUTION OF THE COSMOLOGICAL DIALECTIC [1]

In this section subjectivism is dominant. The type of transcendental idealism expounded is that earlier and less developed form which connects with the doctrine of the transcendental object.[2] It shows no trace of Kant's maturer teaching. No distinction is drawn between representation and the objects represented. To the transcendental object, the "purely intelligible cause" of appearances in general, and to it alone, Kant ascribes "the whole extent and connection of our possible perceptions."[3] Appearances exist only in the degree to which they are constructed in experience. As they are mere representations, they cannot exist outside the mind. Independently of such construction, they may indeed be said to be given in the transcendental object, but they only become objects to us on the supposition that they can be reached through extension of the series of our actual perceptions. It is in this form alone, as conceived in a regressive series of possible perceptions, and not as having existed in itself, that even the immemorial past course of the world can be represented as real ;

". . . so that all events which have taken place in the immense periods that have preceded my own existence mean really nothing but the possibility of extending the chain of experience from the present perception back to the conditions which determine it in time."[4]

A similar interpretation has to be given to all propositions which assert the present reality of that which has never been actually experienced.

"In outcome it is a matter of indifference whether I say that in the empirical advance in space I can meet with stars a hundred times farther removed than the outermost now perceptible to me, or whether I say that they are perhaps to be met with in cosmical space even though no human being has ever perceived or ever will

---

[1] A 490 = B 518.   [2] Cf. above p. 204 ff.   [3] A 494 = B 522-3.
[4] A 495 = B 523.

perceive them. For even if they were given as things in themselves, without relation to possible experience,[1] they are still nothing to me, and therefore are not objects, save in so far as they are contained in the series of the empirical regress."[2]

The distinction between appearances and things in themselves must always, Kant observes, be borne in mind when we are interpreting the meaning of our empirical concepts ; and this is especially necessary when those concepts are brought into connection with the cosmological Idea of an unconditioned. The antinomies are due to a failure to appreciate this fundamental distinction, and the key to their solution lies in its recognition.

"It would be an injustice to ascribe to us that long-decried empirical idealism which, while it admits the genuine actuality of space, denies the existence of the extended beings in it . . ."[3]

This is in line with the passages from the *Prolegomena* commented upon above.[4]

SECTION VII

CRITICAL DECISION OF THE COSMOLOGICAL CONFLICT OF REASON WITH ITSELF[5]

Kant's argument is as follows. The antinomies rest upon the principle that if the conditioned be given, the entire series of all its conditions is likewise given. If the objects of the senses were independently real, there would be no escape from this assumption, and the dialectical conflict would consequently be irresolvable. Transcendental idealism, as above stated, reveals a way out of the dilemma. As appearances are merely representations, their antecedent conditions do not exist *as appearances*, save in the degree in which they are mentally constructed. Though the appearances are given, their *empirical* conditions are not thereby given. The most that we can say is that a regress to the conditions, *i.e.* a continued empirical synthesis in that direction, is *commanded* or *required*. The cosmological argument can thus be shown to be logically invalid. The syllogism, which it involves, is as follows :

If the conditioned be given, the entire series of all its conditions is likewise given.

---

[1] Cf. A 494 = B 522-3 : ". . . we can say of the transcendental object that it is given in itself prior to all experience."

[2] A 496 = B 524.   [3] A 491 = B 519.   [4] Pp. 305-7.   [5] A 497 = B 525.

The objects of the senses are given as conditioned.

Therefore the entire series of all their conditions is likewise given.

In the major premiss the concept of the conditioned is employed transcendently (Kant says transcendentally), in the minor empirically. But though the inference thus commits the logical fallacy of *sophisma figurae dictionis*, the ground of its occurrence, and the reason why it is not at once detected, lie in a natural and inevitable illusion which leads us to accept the sensible world in space as being independently real. Only through Critical investigation can the deceptive power of this illusion be overcome. Owing to its influence, the above fallacy has been committed by dogmatists and empiricists alike. It can be shown that in refuting each other

... "they are really quarrelling about nothing, and that a certain transcendental illusion has caused them to see a reality where none is to be found."[1]

The existence of antinomy, Kant further argues, presupposes that theses and antitheses are contradictory opposites, *i.e.* that no third alternative is possible. When opposed assertions are not contradictories but contraries, the opposition, to use Kant's terms, is not analytical but dialectical. Both may be false; for the one does not merely contradict the other, but makes, in addition, a further statement on its own account. Now examination of the illusion above described enables us to perceive that the opposites, in reference to which antinomy occurs, are of this dialectical character. *Theses and antitheses are alike false.* Since the world does not exist as a thing in itself, it exists neither as an infinite whole nor as a finite whole, but only in the degree in which it is constructed in an empirical regress. We must not apply "*the Idea of absolute totality, which is valid only as a condition of things in themelves,*"[2] to appearances. (The words which I have italicised mark the emergence of Kant's non-sceptical, non-empirical view of the nature and function of the Ideas of Reason.) Thus antinomy, rightly understood, does not favour scepticism, but only the "sceptical method," and indeed yields an indirect proof of the correctness of Critical teaching. This proof may be presented in the form of a dilemma. If the world is a whole existing in itself, it is either finite or infinite. But the former alternative is refuted by the proofs given of the antitheses, and the latter alternative by the proofs of the theses. Therefore the world cannot be a whole existing in itself. From this it follows that appearances are nothing

[1] A 501-2 = B 529-30.   [2] A 506 = B 534.

outside our representations; and that is what is asserted in the doctrine of transcendental idealism.

In A 499 = B 527 Kant uses ambiguous language,[1] which can be interpreted as asserting that in the regress there can be no lack of given conditions. Such a statement would presuppose positive knowledge regarding the unknown transcendental object.[2] The opposite, more correct, view is given in A 514-15 = B 542-3 and A 517 ff. = B 545 ff., though in the latter passage with a reversion to the above position.[3]

The earlier manuscripts, which Kant has so far been employing, probably terminate either, as Adickes suggests,[4] at the end of this section, or at the close of Section VIII., which is of doubtful date. Section IX. is certainly from a later period; it represents a more complex standpoint, in which Reason is no longer viewed as possessing a merely empirical function, and in which consequently the theses and antitheses are no longer indiscriminately denounced as being alike false. Under the influence of his later, more Idealistic preoccupations, Kant so far modifies the above solution as to assert *that in the case of the last two antinomies both theses and antitheses are true, when properly interpreted.*

SECTION VIII

THE REGULATIVE PRINCIPLE OF PURE REASON IN REGARD TO THE COSMOLOGICAL IDEAS [5]

The principle of pure Reason, correctly formulated, is that when the conditioned is given a regress upon the totality of its conditions is *set as a problem.* As such it is valid,

". . . not indeed as an *axiom* . . . but as a *problem* for the understanding . . ., leading it to undertake and to continue, according to the completeness in the Idea, the regress in the series of conditions of any given conditioned." [6]

It does not anticipate, prior to the regress, what actually exists as object, but only postulates, in the form of a rule, how the understanding ought to proceed. It does not tell us whether or how the unconditioned exists, but how the empirical regress is to be carried out under the guidance of a

---

[1] Cf. end of passage: "There can be no lack of conditions that are given through this regress."

[2] Cf. below, pp. 507-8.   [3] Cf. below, pp. 507-9.

[4] *K.* p. 414 *n.* The two last paragraphs of Section VII., which correct its argument, that of the Transcendental Aesthetic, are probably later additions.

[5] A 508 = B 536.   [6] *Loc. cit.*

mere Idea. Such a rule can be regulative only, and the Idea of totality which it contains must never be invested with objective reality. As the absolutely unconditioned can never be met with in experience, we know, indeed, beforehand that in the process of the regress the unconditioned will never be reached. But the duty of seeking it by way of such regress is none the less prescribed.

Kant proceeds to give a somewhat bewildering account of the familiar distinction between *progressus in infinitum* and *progressus in indefinitum*, and to draw a very doubtful distinction between the series in division of a given whole and the series in extension of it.[1] The illustration from the series of human generations is an unfortunate one; the discovery that it began at some one point in the past would not necessarily violate any demand of Reason. Such a series is not comparable with those of space, time, and causality.[2] The only important result of this digression is the conclusion that whatever demand be made, whether of regress *in infinitum* or of regress *in indefinitum*, in neither case can the series of conditions be regarded as being given as infinite in the object.

"The question, therefore, is no longer how great this series of conditions may be in itself, whether finite or infinite, for it is nothing in itself; but how we are to carry out the empirical regress, and how far we should continue it."[3]

We have already noted[4] Kant's ambiguous suggestion in A 499 = B 527, that in the empirical regress there can be no lack of given conditions. The statement, thus interpreted, is illegitimate. The most that he can claim is that, were further sensations not forthcoming, we should still have to conceive those last obtained as being preceded by empty space and time, and as lacking in any experienced cause. Under such circumstances we should experience neither finitude nor unconditionedness, but only incapacity to find a content suitable to the inexhaustible character of the spatial and temporal conditions of experience, or in satisfaction of our demand for causal antecedents. In A 514-15 = B 542-3 Kant shows consciousness of this difficulty, but in dealing with it he adopts a half-way position which still lies open to objection. He recognises that, since no member of a series can be empirically given as absolutely unconditioned, a higher member is always *possible*, and that the search for it is therefore prescribed; none the less he asserts that in regard to

---

[1] As to the distinction between the ascending and the descending series, cf. above, pp. 453 *n.*, 484.
[2] Cf. A 522 = B 549-50.   [3] A 514 = B 542.   [4] Above, p. 506.

given wholes we are justified in taking up a very different position, namely, that the regress in the series of their internal conditions does not proceed, as in the above case, *in indefinitum*, but *in infinitum, i.e.* that in this case more members *exist and are empirically given* than we can reach through the regress. In given wholes we are commanded to *find* more members; in serial extension we are justified only in *inquiring* for more. This half-way position is a makeshift, and is in no respect tenable.   The evidence for the infinite extensibility of space and time is as conclusive as for their infinite divisibility.   And when we consider sensuous existence under these forms, it is just as possible that the transcendental object may, beyond a certain point, fail to supply material for further division, as that it may fail to yield data for further expansion.   What Kant asserts of the latter, that further advance must always remain as a possibility, and for that reason must always call for the open mind of further inquiry, without any attempted anticipatory assertion either *pro* or *contra*, alone represents the true Critical standpoint.   The cessation of data may really, however, be due to an increase in the subtlety of the conditioning processes that incapacitates them from acting upon our senses;[1] by indirect means this disability may be overcome.   Reason, in its conception of an unconditioned, prescribes to us a task that is inexhaustible in its demands. We have no right to lay down our intellectual arms before any barrier however baffling, or to despair before any chasm however empty and abrupt.

SECTION IX

THE EMPIRICAL EMPLOYMENT OF THE REGULATIVE PRIN-CIPLE OF REASON IN REGARD TO ALL COSMOLOGICAL IDEAS [2]

SOLUTION OF THE FIRST AND SECOND ANTINOMIES

Statement.—The fundamental fact upon which, as Kant has already stated, the regulative principle of Reason is based, is that it is impossible to experience an absolute limit.   It is always *possible* that a still higher member of the series may be found; and that being so, it is our duty to search for it. But as we are here dealing with possibilities only, the regress is *in indefinitum*, not *in infinitum*.

[1] Cf. A 522 = B 550.   [2] A 515 = B 543.

" . . . we must seek the concept of the quantity of the world only according to the rule which determines the empirical regress in it. This rule says no more than that however far we may have attained in the series of empirical conditions, we should never assume an absolute limit, but should subordinate every appearance, as conditioned, to another as its condition, and that we must then advance to this condition. This is the *regressus in indefinitum*, which, as it determines no quantity in the object, is clearly enough distinguishable from the *regressus in infinitum*."[1]

We are acquainted only with the rule, and not with the whole object. Any assertion, therefore, which we can make, must be dictated solely by the rule, and be an expression of it. Neither the thesis nor the antithesis of the first antinomy is valid; there is a third alternative. The sensible world is neither finite nor infinite in extent; it is infinitely extensible, in terms of the rule.

Unfortunately Kant is not content to leave his conclusion in this form. He complicates his argument, and bewilders the reader, by maintaining that this is a virtual acceptance of the antithesis, in that we assert negatively, that an absolute limit in either time or space is empirically impossible;[2] and affirmatively, that the regress goes on *in indefinitum*, and consequently has no absolute quantity.

Kant also repeats the argument of the preceding section in regard to given wholes.[3] When the problem is that of subdivision, the regress starts from a given whole, and therefore from a whole whose conditions (the parts) are given with it. The division is, therefore, *in infinitum*, and not merely *in indefinitum*. This does not, however, he argues, mean that the given whole consists of infinitely many parts. For though the parts are contained in the intuition of the whole, yet the whole division arises only through the regress that generates it. It is a *quantum continuum*, not a *quantum discretum*.[4] This argument has been criticised above.[5] Kant here ignores the possibility that the parts of matter, though extended, may be physically indivisible, or that they may be centres of force which control, but do not occupy, a determinate space.

---

[1] A 519-20 = B 547-8.
[2] When Kant adds (A 521 = B 549), "and therefore absolutely also," he inconsistently reverts to the position ambiguously suggested in A 499 = B 527. Cf. above, p. 506.
[3] A 523-6 = B 551-4.
[4] The assertion of infinite divisibility is not applicable, Kant states (A 526-7 = B 554-5), to bodies as organised, but only to bodies as mere occupants of space. Organisation involves distinction of parts, and therefore discreteness. How far organisation can go in organised bodies, experience alone can show us.
[5] P. 508.

REMARKS ON THE DISTINCTION BETWEEN THE MATHE-MATICAL-TRANSCENDENTAL AND THE DYNAMICAL-TRANSCENDENTAL IDEAS [1]

Statement.—Kant again [2] introduces the distinction between the mathematical and the dynamical. The mathematical Ideas synthesise the homogeneous, the dynamical may connect the heterogeneous. In employing the former we must therefore remain within the phenomenal; through the latter we may be able to transcend it. The way is thus opened for propounding, in regard to the third and fourth antinomies, a solution in which the pretensions of Reason no less than those of understanding may find satisfaction. Whereas both the theses and the antitheses of the first and second antinomies have to be declared false, those of the third and fourth antinomies *may both be true*—the theses applying to the intelligible realm, and the antitheses to the world of sense.

Comment.—When the distinction between the mathematical and the dynamical is thus extended from the categories to the Ideas, its validity becomes highly doubtful. Space and time are certainly themselves homogeneous, and the categories of quality and quantity, in so far as they are mathematically employed, may perhaps be similarly described. But when the term is still further extended, to cover the pairs of correlative opposites with which the first two antinomies deal, those, namely, between the limited and the unlimited, the simple and the infinitely divisible, Kant would seem to be making a highly artificial distinction. The first two antinomies deal not with space and time as such, but with the sensible world in space and time; and within this sensible world, even in its quantitative aspects, qualitative differences have to be reckoned with. Common sense does, indeed, tend to assume that the unlimited and the simple must, like that which they condition, be in space and time, and so form with the conditioned a homogeneous series. But this assumption ordinary consciousness is equally disposed to make in regard to a first cause and to the unconditionally necessary.

Kant further attempts [3] to distinguish between the mathematical and the dynamical by asserting that the dynamical antinomies are not concerned with the quantity of their object, but only with its *existence*. He admits, however, that in all four cases a series arises which is either too large or too small for the understanding; and that being so, in each case the problem arises as to the *existence* of an unconditioned.

---

[1] A 528 = B 556.   [2] Cf. above, pp. 345-7.   [3] A 535-6 = B 563-4.

The artificiality of Kant's distinction becomes clear when we recognise that the opposed solutions, which he gives of the two sets of antinomies, can be mutually interchanged. As the sensible world rests upon intelligible grounds, both the theses and the antitheses of the first two antinomies may be true, the former in the intelligible realm and the latter in the sensuous. Similarly, both the theses and antitheses of the third and fourth antinomies may be false. In the sensible world, about which alone anything can be determined, the series of dynamical conditions forms neither a finite nor an infinite series. There is a third alternative, akin to that of the antitheses, but distinct in character from it, namely, that the series is infinitely extensible. Kant's differential treatment of the two sets of antinomies is arbitrary, and would seem to be due to his having attempted to superimpose, with the least possible modification, a later solution of the antinomies upon one previously developed. In the earlier view, as we have already had occasion to observe, Reason has a merely empirical application. Its Ideas are taken as existing "only in the brain." Only their empirical reference can substantiate them, or indeed give them the least significance. And as they are by their very nature incapable of empirical embodiment, all assertions which involve them must necessarily be false. Later, Kant came to regard Reason as having its own independent rights. Encouraged by his successful establishment of the objective validity of the categories, progressively more and more convinced of the importance of the distinction, which that proof reinforced, between appearances and things in themselves, and preoccupied with the problems of the spiritual life, his old-time faith in the absolute claims of pure thought reasserted itself., Through Reason we realise our kinship with noumenal realities, and through its demands the nature of the unconditioned is foreshadowed to the mind. The theses and antitheses, which throughout the entire history of philosophy have competed with one another, may both be true. Their perennial conflict demonstrates the need for some more catholic standpoint from which the two great authorities by which human life is controlled and directed, the intellectual and the moral, may be reconciled. Neither can be made to yield to the other ; each is supreme in its own field. The distinction between appearances and things in themselves, recognition of which is the first step towards an adequate theory of knowledge, and without which the nature of the intellectual life remains self-contradictory and incomprehensible, itself affords the means of such a reconciliation. The understanding is the sole key to the world of appearance, the moral imperative to the realm of things in themselves. Reason with its demand for the unconditioned mediates between them, and enables us to realise our dual vocation.

This radical alteration of standpoint was bound to make the employment of manuscript representing the earlier and more sceptical attitude altogether unsatisfactory; and only Kant's constitutional unwillingness to sacrifice what he had once committed to paper can account for his retention of the older expositions. He allows his previous treatment of the first two antinomies to remain in its sceptical form, and, by means of the distinction between the mathematical and the dynamical, develops his newer, more Idealist view exclusively in reference to the third and fourth antinomies. That it is no less applicable to the others, we have already seen.

Though the Idealist view, *as here expounded*, may be thus described, relatively to the sceptical view of Reason, as later, that is not to be taken as meaning that it represents the latest stage in the development of Kant's Critical teaching. It seems to belong to the period prior to that in which the central sections of the *Analytic* were composed. The evidence [1] for this consists chiefly in its subjectivist references to the nature of appearances. It would seem to be contemporary with Kant's doctrine of the transcendental object.

SOLUTION OF THE THIRD ANTINOMY [2]

Statement.—As appearances are representations only, they must have a ground which is not itself an appearance ; [3] and though the effects of such an intelligible cause appear, and accordingly are determined through other appearances, its causality is not itself similarly conditioned. Both it and its causality lie outside the empirical series ; only the effects fall within the realm of experience. And that causality, not being subject to time, does not require to stand under another cause as its effect. In this way Kant derives from his transcendental idealism an explanation of the possibility of an action being at once free and causally determined. This explanation he takes as applying either to a first cause of the whole realm of natural phenomena or to a finite being regarded as a free agent. The proof of the possibility of this

---

[1] Cf. A 537 = B 564-5 ; also A 546 = B 574-5, in which Kant asserts that man knows himself not only through the senses but " also through pure apperception, and indeed in actions and inner determinations which cannot be reckoned as impressions of the senses." Such statements would seem to show that, at the time of writing, Kant had not yet developed his doctrine of inner sense.

[2] A 532 = B 560.   [3] A 536-7 = B 564-5.

metaphysical, or, as Kant entitles it, "transcendental freedom," removes what has always been the real difficulty that lay in the way of "practical freedom." The conception of freedom is a transcendental Idea which can neither be derived from experience nor verified by it. It is created by Reason for itself;[1] and reveals the *possibility* that in this third antinomy both thesis and antithesis may be true. The alternatives—"every effect must arise from nature," and "every effect must arise from freedom"—are not exclusive of one another. They may be true of one and the same event in different relations.[2] The event may be free in reference to its intelligible cause, determined as an existence in space and time. Were appearances things in themselves, freedom and causality would necessarily conflict: by means of the above ontological distinction freedom can be asserted without any diminution in the scope allowed to the causal principle. All events, without a single possible exception, are subject to the law of natural determination; and yet every event may *at the same time* proceed from a free cause.

POSSIBILITY OF HARMONISING CAUSALITY THROUGH FREEDOM WITH THE UNIVERSAL LAW OF NATURAL NECESSITY[3]

Statement.—The above conclusion is so seemingly paradoxical that Kant devotes this and the following section to its further elucidation. How can events be both free and determined? The answer lies in recognition of the two-sided character of every natural existence. It is, in one aspect, mere appearance; in another, it has at its foundation a transcendental object. It is an appearance of the latter, and for its complete comprehension this latter must be taken into account. Now there is nothing to *prevent* us from attributing to the transcendental object a causality which is not phenomenal. Such causality may make the appearance just that appearance which it is. In the world of sense every efficient cause must have a specific empirical character, since only so can it determine one effect rather than another according to the universal and invariable law expressive of its nature. We must similarly allow to the transcendental object an intelligible character, and trace to it all those appearances which as members of the empirical series stand to one another in unbroken causal connection. This transcendental object, owing to its intelligible character, is not in time. Its act

---

[1] A 533=B 561.   [2] A 536=B 564.   [3] A 538=B 566.

does not either arise or perish, and is not, therefore, subject to the law of empirical determination which applies only to the changeable, *i.e.* to events subsequent upon previous states. Such supersensuous causality can find no place in the series of empirical conditions, and though it can be conceived only in terms of the empirical character which is its outcome, the difference between it and natural causality may be as complete as that which subsists between the transcendental and the empirical objects of knowledge. In its empirical character the action is a part of nature, and enters into a causal nexus which conforms to universal laws.[1] All its effects are inevitably determined by antecedent natural conditions. In its intelligible character, however, this same active subject must be considered free from all influence of sensibility and from all determination through natural events. In so far as it is a noumenon, there can be no change in it, and therefore nothing which is capable of explanation in terms of natural causes. Even its empirical effects are not traceable to it as events in time. For as events these effects are always the results of antecedent empirical causes. What is alone due to noumenal causality is that empirical character in virtue of which appearances are what they are, and owing to which they stand in specific and necessary causal relations to one another.

" . . . the empirical character is *permanent*, while its effects, according to variation in the concomitant, and in part limiting conditions, appear in changeable forms."[2]

Empirical causality is itself in its specific nature conditioned by an intelligible cause.[3]

EXPLANATION OF THE RELATION OF FREEDOM TO NECESSITY OF NATURE [4]

Statement.—No single appearance can be exempted from the law of natural causality. For it would then be placed outside all possible experience, and would be for us a fiction of the brain, or rather could not be conceived at all. Nothing, therefore, *in nature* can act freely or spontaneously. But while thus recognising that all *events* without exception are

---

[1] Cf. Kant's *Uebergang von der metaph. Anfangsgründe der Naturwissenschaft zur Physik* (*Altpreussische Monatsschrift* (1882), pp. 272-3).
[2] A 549 = B 577. Italics not in Kant.
[3] In A 540 = B 568 a different and less satisfactory view finds expression.
[4] A 542 = B 570.

empirically conditioned, we may, as already pointed out, regard empirical causality as itself an effect of a non-empirical and intelligible power.[1] In events there may be nothing but nature, and yet nature itself, or perhaps even some of the existences composing it, may rest upon powers of a noumenal order.   Kant proceeds to show that such an hypothesis is not only allowable, but is indispensable for understanding the distinguishing features of human life in its practical aspect.

Man is a natural existence, and his activities are subject to empirical laws.   Like all other objects of nature, he has an empirical character, and in virtue of it takes his place as an integral part of the system of nature.   But man is unique among all natural existences in that he not only knows himself as a sensible existence, but also, through pure apperception, becomes aware of himself as possessing faculties of a strictly intelligible character.[2]   Such are the faculties of understanding and Reason, especially the latter in its practical employment. The "ought" of the moral imperative expresses a kind of necessity and a form of causation which we nowhere find in the world of nature.   The understanding can know in nature only what actually is, has been, or will be.   Nothing natural can be other than it is in the particular relations in which it is found.   Moral action transcends the natural in that it finds its cause, not in an appearance or set of appearances, but in an Ideal of pure Reason.   Such action must indeed be possible under natural conditions, but such conditions do not determine its rightness, and consequently cannot determine its causality.

"Reason . . . does not here follow the order of things as they present themselves in appearance, but frames to itself with perfect spontaneity an order of its own according to Ideas, to which it adapts the empirical conditions, and according to which it declares actions to be necessary even although they have never yet taken place, and perhaps never will take place.   And at the same time Reason also presupposes that it can itself have causality in regard to all these actions, since otherwise no empirical effects could be expected from its Ideas."[3]

If such action of pure Reason be admitted to be possible, it will have to be viewed, purely intelligible though it be, as also possessing an empirical character, *i.e.* as conforming to the system of nature.   Its empirical consequences will be the effects of antecedent appearances, and will empirically determine by natural necessity all subsequent acts.   In this empirical character, therefore, there can be no freedom.   Were our

[1] A 544 = B 572.   [2] A 546-7 = B 574-5.   [3] A 548 = B 576.

knowledge of the circumstances sufficiently extensive, every human action, so far as it is appearance, could be predicted and shown to be necessary. How, then, can we talk of actions as free, when from the point of view of appearances they must in all cases be regarded as inevitable? The solution is that which has already been given of the broader issue. The *entire* empirical character, the whole system of nature, is determined by the intelligible character. And the former results from the latter, not empirically, and therefore not according to any temporal, causal law. It does not arise or begin at a certain time. The intelligible character conditions the empirical series *as a series*, and not as if it were a first member of it.

"Thus what we have failed to find in any empirical series is disclosed as possible, namely, that the condition of a successive series of events may itself be empirically unconditioned."[1]

The intelligible character lies *outside* the series of appearances. "Reason is the *abiding (beharrliche)* condition of all free actions. . . ."[2] Freedom ought not, therefore, to be conceived only negatively as independence of empirical conditions, but also positively as the power of originating a series of events. The empirical series is in time. Reason, which is its unconditioned condition, admits of nothing antecedent to itself; it knows neither before nor after. The series is the immediate effect of a non-temporal reality.

In illustration of his meaning, not, as he is careful to add, with the profession of thereby confirming its truth, Kant points out that moral judgment upon a vicious action is not determined in view of the inheritance, circumstances and past life of the offender, but is passed just as if he might in each action be supposed to begin, quite by himself, a new series of effects. This, in Kant's view, shows that practical Reason is regarded as a cause completely capable, independently of all empirical conditions, of determining the act, and that it is present in all the actions of men under all conditions, and is always the same. To explain why the intelligible character should in any specific case produce just this particular empirical character, good or bad,

". . . transcends all the powers of our Reason, indeed all its rights of questioning, just as if we were to ask why the transcendental object of our outer sensuous intuition yields intuition in *space* only and no other."[3]

---

[1] A 552 = B 580.   [2] A 553 = B 581.   [3] A 557 = B 585.

In conclusion Kant states that his intention has not been to establish the reality of freedom, not even to prove its possibility. Freedom has been dealt with only as a transcendental Idea; and the only point established is that freedom is, so to speak, a *possible possibility*, in that it is *not contradicted* either by experience or by anything that can be proved to be a presupposition of experience.

Comment.—Adequate comment upon this section is difficult for many reasons. The section is full of archaic expressions from the earlier stages of Kant's Critical teaching. Secondly, the section anticipates a problem which is first adequately dealt with in the second *Critique*. And lastly, but not least, the discussion of freedom in connection with a cosmological antinomy leads Kant to treat it in the same manner as the general antinomy, and in so doing to ignore the chief difficulty to which human freedom, as an independent problem with its own peculiar difficulties, lies open. For it is comparatively easy to reconcile the universality of the causal principle with the unconditionedness of the transcendental ground upon which nature *as a whole* is made to rest. It is a very different matter to reconcile the spontaneous origination of *particular* causal series, or the freedom of *particular* existences, such as human beings, with the singleness and uniformity of a natural system in which every part is determined by every other. Self-consciousness, with the capacity which it confers of constructing rational ideals, certainly, as Kant rightly contends, creates a situation to which mechanical categories are by no means adequate. But the mere reference to the conceivability of distinct causal series, having each a pure conception as their intelligible ground, does not suffice to meet the fundamental difficulty that, on Kant's own admission, each such separate series must form an integral part of the unitary system of natural law. In only one passage does Kant even touch upon this difficulty. Speaking [1] of Reason's power of originating a series of events, he adds that while nothing *begins* in Reason itself (as it admits of no conditions antecedent to itself in time), the new series must none the less have a beginning in the natural world. But the proviso, which he at once makes, indicates that he is aware that this statement is untenable. For he adds the qualification that though a beginning of the series, it is never an absolutely first beginning. In other words, it is not a beginning in any real sense of the term. As the argument of his next paragraph shows, it is the entire system of nature,

[1] A 553-4 = B 581-2.

and not any one series within it, which can alone account, in empirical terms, for any one action.

It is open to Kant to argue, as he has already done,[1] that the transcendental object conditions each separate appearance as well as all appearances in their totality, and that the specific empirical character of each causal series is therefore no less noumenally conditioned than is nature as a whole. But this does not suffice to meet the difficulty—how, if all natural phenomena constitute a single closed system in which everything is determined by everything else, a moral agent, acting spontaneously, can be free to originate a genuinely new series of natural events. We seem constrained to conclude that Kant has failed to sustain his position. A solution is rendered impossible by the very terms in which he formulates the problem. If the spiritual and the natural be opposed to one another as the timeless and the temporal, and if the natural be further viewed as a unitary system, individual moral freedom is no longer defensible. Only the " transcendental freedom " of the *cosmological* argument can be reckoned as among the open possibilities.

As regards the character of the Critical doctrine which underlies this section, we need only note that the statement in A 546-7 = B 574-5, that man knows himself through pure apperception as "a purely intelligible object,"[2] does not conform to Kant's final teaching. The section can be dated through its unwavering adherence to the subjectivist doctrine of the transcendental object.[3]

SOLUTION OF THE FOURTH ANTINOMY [4]

Statement.—A solution the same in principle as that of the third antinomy is adopted. Both thesis and antithesis may be true, the latter of the world of sense and the former of its non-empirical ground. All things sensible are contingent, but the contingent series in its entirety may nevertheless rest upon an unconditionally necessary being. The unconditioned, since it is outside the series, does not require that any one link in the series should be itself unconditioned. " Reason proceeds by one path in its empirical use, and by yet another path in its transcendental use," *i.e.* it limits itself by the law of causality in dealing with appearances, lest in losing the thread of the empirical conditions it should fall into idle and empty speculations ; while, on the other hand, it limits that law to appearances, lest it should wrongly declare that what is useless for

---

[1] Cf. A 537-41 = B 565-9 and A 544 = B 572.
[2] Cf. A 566 = B 594.   [3] Cf. above, p. 204 ff.   [4] A 559 = B 587.

the explanation of appearances is therefore impossible in itself. This does not prove that an absolutely necessary being is really possible, but only that its impossibility must not be concluded from the necessary contingency of all things sensuous.

Comment.—Kant's method of distinguishing[1] this conclusion from that of the preceding antinomy is again artificial. " Necessary being " is not in conception more *extramundanum* than "unconditioned cause." If Kant's distinction were valid, the argument of the fourth antinomy would no longer be cosmological ; it would coincide with the problem of the *Ideal of Pure Reason.*

CONCLUDING OBSERVATION ON THE WHOLE ANTINOMY OF PURE REASON[2]

Statement.—When we seek the unconditioned entirely beyond experience, our Ideas cease to be cosmological ; they become transcendent. They separate themselves off from all empirical use of the understanding, and create to themselves an object, the material of which is not taken from experience, and which is therefore a mere thing of the mind (*blosses Gedankending*). None the less the cosmological Idea of the fourth antinomy impels us to take this step. When sensuous appearances, as merely contingent, require us to look for something altogether distinct in nature from them, our only available instruments, in so doing, are those pure concepts of things in general which contingent experience involves. We use them as instruments in such manner as may enable us to form, through analogy, some kind of notion of intelligible things. Taken in abstraction from the forms of sense, they yield that notion of an absolutely necessary Being which is equivalent to the concept of the theological Ideal.

CONCLUDING COMMENT ON KANT'S DOCTRINE OF THE ANTINOMIES

We may now, in conclusion, briefly summarise the results obtained in this chapter. Kant fails to justify the assertion that on the dogmatic level there exist antinomies in which both the contradictory alternatives allow of cogent demonstration. His proofs are in every instance invalid. The real nature of antinomy must, as he himself occasionally intimates, be defined in a very different manner, namely, as a conflict between the demand of Reason for unity and system, and

[1] A 561 = B 589.   [2] A 565 = B 593.

the specific nature of the conditions, especially of the spatial and temporal conditions, under which the sensuous exists. In this wider form it constitutes a genuine problem, which demands for its solution the fundamental Critical distinction between appearances and things-in-themselves, and also a more thoroughgoing discussion than has yet been attempted of the nature of Reason and of the function of its Ideas. It is to these connected questions that Kant devotes his main attention in the remaining portions of the *Dialectic*, so that in passing to the *Ideal of Pure Reason* he is not proceeding to the treatment of a new set of problems, but to the restatement and to the more adequate solution of the fundamental conflict between understanding and Reason.

The observations which closed our comment upon the *Paralogisms* are thus again in order. The teaching of the sections on the *Antinomies*, no less than that of those on the *Paralogisms*, is incomplete, and if taken by itself is bound to mislead. The Ideas of an unconditioned self and of an unconditioned ground of nature have thus far been taken as at least conceptually possible, and as signifying what may perhaps be real existences. These Ideas are in certain of the remaining sections of the *Dialectic* called in question. They are there declared to be without inherent meaning. They are useful fictions—*heuristische Fiktionen*—and in their psychological nature are simply *schemata* of regulative principles. Their theoretical significance consists merely in their regulative and limitative functions. They must not be regarded, even hypothetically, as representing real existences. In the practical (*i.e.* ethical) sphere they do indeed acquire a very different standing. But with that the *Critique of Pure Reason* is not directly concerned. The reader may therefore be warned not to omit the chapter on the *Ideal of Pure Reason*, on the supposition that it embodies only a criticism of the Cartesian and teleological proofs of God's existence. It is an integral part of Critical teaching, and carries Kant's entire argument forward to its final conclusions. Only in view of the new and deeper considerations, which it brings to light, can his treatment even of the *Antinomies* be properly understood. Its main opening section (Section II.) is, indeed, among the most scholastically rationalistic in the entire *Critique*; but in the later sections it unfolds, with a boldness and consistency to which we find no parallel in the treatment of the *Paralogisms* and of the *Antinomies*, the full consequences of the more sceptical of Kant's alternating standpoints. It disintegrates the concepts of the unconditioned, which have hitherto been employed without analysis and without question; and upon their elimination from among the legitimate instruments of Reason, the situation undergoes entire transformation, the two points of view appearing for the first time in the full extent of their divergence and conflict. For Kant's Idealist view of Reason and of its Ideas still continues to find occasional statement, showing that he has not been able decisively to commit himself to this more sceptical interpretation of the function of Reason; that he is conscious that the Idealist view alone gives adequate expression to certain fundamental considerations which have to be reckoned with; and that unless the two views can in some manner be reconciled with one another, a really definitive and satisfactory solution of the problem has not been reached.   When, therefore, we speak of Kant's final conclusions, we must be taken as referring to the twofold tendencies, sceptical and Idealist, which to the very last persist in competition with one another. The greater adequacy of Kant's argument in the chapter on the *Ideal of Pure Reason* and in the important *Appendix* attached to the *Dialectic* consists in its forcible and considered exposition of both attitudes. Most of the sections on the *Antinomies* must, as we have seen, be dated as among the earliest parts of the *Critique*. Their teaching is correspondingly immature. The chapter on the *Ideal* and the *Appendix*, on the other hand, were among the latest to be written, and contain, together with the central portions of the *Analytic*, our most authoritative exposition of Kant's Critical principles.

CHAPTER III

THE IDEAL OF PURE REASON

SECTIONS I AND II

THE TRANSCENDENTAL IDEAL [1]

THE statements of the first section cannot profitably be commented upon at this stage; they are of a merely general character.[2] I pass at once to Section II., which, as above stated, is quite the most archaic piece of rationalistic argument in the entire *Critique*. It is not merely Leibnizian, but Wolffian in character. For Kant the Wolffian logic had an old-time flavour and familiarity that rendered it by no means distasteful; and he is here, as it were, recalling, not altogether without sympathy, the lessons of his student years. They enable him to render definite, by way of contrast, the outcome of his own Critical teaching.

As Kant here restates the Wolffian notion of the *Ens realissimum* in such fashion as is required to make it conform to his deduction of the theological Idea from the disjunctive syllogism, a preliminary statement of the more orthodox formulation will help to set Wolff's doctrine in a clearer light. In so doing, I shall follow Baumgarten, whose *Metaphysica* Kant used as a class text-book. Briefly summarised Baumgarten's statement is as follows.[3] The *Ens perfectissimum* is that Being which possesses as many predicates, *i.e.* perfections, as can possibly exist together in a single thing, and in which every one of its perfections is as great as is anywhere possible. This most perfect Being must be a real Being, and its reality must be the greatest possible. It is that in which the most and the greatest realities are. But all realities are

---

[1] A 567 = B 593.
[2] For Kant's comparison of his Ideas with those of Plato, cf. above, pp. 447-9.
[3] §§ 803 ff. in 5th edition (Halle, 1763).

522

affirmative determinations, and no denial is a reality.   Accordingly no reality can contradict another reality, and all realities can exist together in the same thing.   The *Ens perfectissimum*, in possessing all the realities that can exist together, must therefore possess all realities without exception, and every one of them in the highest degree.   The notion of an individual existence that is at once *perfectissimum* and also *realissimum* is thus determinable by pure Reason from its internal resources.   It is the ground and condition of all other existences ; all of them arise through limitation of its purely positive nature.

Kant seeks to justify his metaphysical deduction of the *Ideal* from the disjunctive syllogism, by recasting the above argument in the following manner.   Since everything which exists is completely determined, it is subject to the principle of complete determination, according to which one of each of the possible pairs of contradictory predicates must be applicable to it.   To be completely determined the thing must be compared with the sum total of all possible predicates. Although this idea of the sum total of all possible predicates, through reference to which alone any concept can be completely determined, seems itself indeterminate, we find nevertheless on closer examination that it individualises itself *a priori*, transforming itself into the concept of an individual existence that is completely determined by the mere Idea, and which may therefore be called an Ideal of pure Reason. That is proved as follows.   No one can definitely think a negation unless he founds it on the opposite affirmation. A man completely blind cannot frame the smallest conception of darkness, because he has none of light.   All negations are therefore derivative ; it is the realities which contain the material by which a complete determination of anything becomes possible.   The source, from which all possible predicates may be derived, can be nothing but the sum total of reality.   And this concept of the *omnitudo realitatis* is the Idea of a Being that is single and individual.   As all finite beings derive the material of their possibility from it, they presuppose it, and cannot, therefore, constitute it.   They are imperfect copies (*ectypa*), of which it is the sole Ideal. The Idea is also individual.   Out of each possible pair of contradictory predicates, that one which expresses reality belongs to it.   By these infinitely numerous positive predicates it is determined to absolute concreteness ; and as it therefore possesses all that has reality, not only in nature but in man, it must be conceived as a personal and intelligent Primordial Being.   The logical Ideal, thus determining itself completely by its own concept, appears not only as ideal but also as real, not only as logical but also as divine.

Kant so far anticipates his criticism of the ontological argument as to give, in the remaining paragraphs of this second section, a preliminary criticism of this procedure. For the purpose for which the Ideal is postulated, namely, the determination of all finite and therefore limited existences, Reason does not require to presuppose an existence corresponding to it. Its mere Idea will suffice.

"All manifoldness of things is only a correspondingly varied mode of limiting the concept of the highest reality which forms their common substratum, just as all figures are only possible as so many different modes of limiting infinite space."[1]

This relation is not, however, that of a real existence to other things but of an Idea to concepts. The Idea is a mere fiction, necessary for comprehending the limited, not a reality that can be asserted, even hypothetically,[2] as given along with the limited. None the less, owing to a natural transcendental illusion, the mind inevitably tends to hypostatise it, and so generates the object of rational theology.

Comment.—The explanation of this illusion, which Kant proceeds to give in the two concluding paragraphs, is peculiarly confusing. Though the concept of an all-comprehensive reality may, he argues, be required for the definition of sensible objects, such a concept must not for that reason be taken as representing a real existence. The teaching of the section on *Amphiboly* is here entirely ignored; and the reader is bewildered by the assumption, which Kant apparently makes, that something analogous to the Leibnizian Ideal is a prerequisite of possible experience.

These last remarks indicate the kind of criticism to which the argument of this section lays itself open. In expounding the teaching of the Leibnizian science of rational theology, Kant strives to represent its Ideal as being an inevitable Idea of human Reason; and in order to make this argument at all convincing he is constrained to treat as valid the presupposed ontology, though that has already been shown in the discussion of *Amphiboly* to be altogether untenable.[3] Limitation is not merely negative; genuine realities may negate one another. Though the objects of sense presuppose the entire system to which they belong, the form of this presupposition is in no respect analogous to that which Wolff would represent as holding between finite existences and the

---

[1] A 578 = B 606.   [2] A 580 = B 608.   [3] Cf. above, p. 418 ff.

Ens realissimum. The passage in the *Analytic*[1] in which Kant directly controverts the above teaching is as follows:

"The principle, that realities (as pure assertions) never logically contradict each other . . . has not the least meaning either in regard to nature or in regard to any thing-in-itself. . . . Although Herr von Leibniz did not, indeed, announce this proposition with all the pomp of a new principle, he yet made use of it for new assertions, and his followers expressly incorporated it in their Leibnizian-Wolffian system. According to this principle all evils, for instance, are merely consequences of the limitations of created beings, *i.e.* negations, because negations alone conflict with reality. . . . Similarly his disciples consider it not only possible, but even natural, to combine all reality, without fear of any conflict, in one being, because the only conflict which they recognise is that of contradiction, whereby the concept of a thing is itself removed. They do not admit the conflict of reciprocal injury in which each of two real grounds destroys the effect of the other—a process which we can represent to ourselves only in terms of conditions presented to us in sensibility."

Thus the Ideal which Kant here declares to be a necessary Idea of Reason is denounced in the *Analytic* as based on false principles peculiar to the Leibnizian philosophy, and as "without the least meaning in regard either to nature or to any thing in itself." The teaching of the *Analytic* will no more combine with this scholastic rationalism than oil with water. The reader may safely absolve himself from the thankless task of attempting to render Kant's argumentation in these paragraphs consistent with itself. Fortunately, in the next section, Kant returns to the standpoint proper to the doctrine he is expounding, and lays bare, with remarkable subtlety and in a very convincing manner, the concealed dialectic by which the conclusions of this metaphysical science are really determined.[2]

SECTION III

THE SPECULATIVE ARGUMENTS IN PROOF OF THE EXISTENCE OF A SUPREME BEING[3]

Statement.—Though the Ideal is not arbitrary, but is presupposed in every attempt to define completely a finite concept, Reason would feel hesitation in thus transforming what is merely a logical concept into a Divine Existence, were it

[1] A 272-4 = B 328-30.
[2] Cf. Kant's distinction between distributive and collective unity in A 582-3 = B 610 with A 644 = B 672.   [3] A 583 = B 611.

not that it is impelled from another direction to derive reality from such a source.   All existences known in experience are contingent, and so lead us (owing to the constitution of our Reason) to assume an absolutely necessary Being as their ground and cause.   Now when we examine our various concepts, to ascertain which will cover this notion of necessary existence, we find that there is one that possesses outstanding claims, namely, that Idea which contains a therefore for every wherefore, which is in no respect defective, and which does not permit us to postulate any condition.   The concepts of the Ideal and of the necessary alone represent the unconditioned ; and as they agree in this fundamental respect, they must, we therefore argue, be identical.   And to this conclusion we are the more inclined, in that, by thus idealising reality, we are at the same time enabled to realise our Ideal.

This line of argument, which starts from the contingent, is as little valid as that which proceeds directly from the Ideal.   But since these arguments express certain tendencies inherent in the human mind, they have a vitality which survives any merely forensic refutation.   Though the conclusions to which they lead are false, they are none the less inevitably drawn.   Our acceptance of them is due to a transcendental illusion which may be detected as such, but which, like the ingrained illusions of sense - experience, must none the less persist.

Comment.—The opening paragraph of Section V[1] is the natural completion of the above analysis.   The ontological argument, in *starting* from the concept of the *Ens realissimum*, inverts the natural procedure.   It is "a merely scholastic innovation," and would never have been attempted save for the need of finding some necessary Being, to which we may ascend from contingent existence.   It maintains that this necessary Being must be unconditioned and *a priori* certain, and accordingly looks for a concept capable of fulfilling this requirement.   Such a concept is supposed to exist in the Idea of an *Ens realissimum*, and this Idea is therefore used to gain more definite knowledge of that which has been previously and independently recognised, namely, the necessary Being.

"This natural procedure of Reason was concealed from view, and instead of ending with this concept, the attempt was made to begin with it, and so to deduce from it that necessity of existence which it was only fitted to complete.   Thus arose the unfortunate ontological proof, which yields satisfaction neither to the natural and healthy understanding nor to the more academic demands of strict proof."[2]

---

[1] A 603=B 631.   [2] A 603·4=B 631-2.

To return to Section III.: Kant breaks the continuity of his argument, and anticipates his discussion of the cosmological proof, by stopping to point out the illegitimacy of the assumption which underlies the first step in the above argument, namely, that a limited being cannot be absolutely necessary. Though the concept of a limited being does not contain the unconditioned, that does not prove that its existence is conditioned. Indeed each and every limited being may, for all their concepts show to the contrary, be unconditionally necessary.[1] The above argument is consequently inconclusive, and cannot be relied on to give us any concept whatever of the qualities of a necessary Being. But this is a merely logical defect, and, as already noted, it is not really upon logical cogency that the persuasive force of the argument depends.

In conclusion Kant points out that there are only three possible kinds of speculative (*i.e.* theoretical) proofs of the existence of God: (1) from definite experience and the specific nature of the world of sense as revealed in experience; (2) from indefinite experience, *i.e.* from the fact that any existence at all is empirically given; (3) the non-empirical *a priori* proof from mere concepts. The first is the *physico-theological* or *teleogical* argument, the second is the *cosmological*, and the third is the *ontological*. Kant finds it advisable to reverse the order of the proofs, and to begin by consideration of the ontological argument. This would seem to indicate that the 'scholastic innovation' to which he traces the origin of the ontological proof has more justification than his remarks appear to allow.

SECTION IV

THE IMPOSSIBILITY OF AN ONTOLOGICAL PROOF[2]

Statement.—Hitherto Kant has employed the concept of an absolutely necessary Being without question. He now recognises that the problem, from which we ought to start, is not whether the existence of an absolutely necessary Being can be demonstrated, but whether, and how, such a Being can even be conceived. And upon analysis he discovers that the assumed notion of an absolutely necessary, *i.e. unconditioned* Being is entirely lacking in intelligible content. For in eliminating all conditioning causes—through which alone the understanding can conceive necessity of existence—we

---

[1] Cf. below, pp. 533, 536.   [2] A 592 = B 620.

also remove this particular kind of necessity. A verbal definition may, indeed, be given of the Idea, as when we say that it represents something the non-existence of which is impossible. But this yields no insight into the reasons which make its non-existence inconceivable, and such insight is required if anything at all is to be thought in the Idea.

"The expedient of removing all those conditions which the understanding indispensably requires in order to regard something as necessary, simply through the introduction of the word *unconditioned*, is very far from sufficing to show whether I am still thinking anything, or not rather perhaps nothing at all, in the concept of the unconditionally necessary."[1]

The untenableness of the concept has been in large part concealed through a confusion between logical and ontological necessity, that is, between necessity of judgment and necessity of existence. The fact that every proposition of geometry must be regarded as absolutely necessary was supposed to justify this identification. It was not observed that logical necessity refers only to *judgments*, not to *things* and their relations, and that the absolute necessity of the judgment holds only upon the assumption that the conditioned necessity of the thing referred to has previously been granted. If there be any such thing as a triangle, the assertion that it has three angles will follow with absolute necessity; but the existence of a triangle or even of space in general is contingent. In other words, the asserted necessity is only a form of logical sequence, not the unconditioned necessity of existence which is supposed to be disclosed in the Idea of Reason. All judgments, so far as they refer to existence, as distinct from mere possibility, are hypothetical, and serve to define a reality that is only contingently given. In adopting this position, Kant is in entire agreement with Hume. The contradictory of a matter of fact is always thinkable. There has, Kant claims, been no more fruitful source of illusion throughout the whole history of philosophy than the belief in an absolute necessity that is purely logical.[2] In the ontological argument we have the most striking instance of such rationalistic exaggeration of the powers of thought.

Comment.—Had this criticism of the Idea of unconditioned necessity been introduced at an earlier stage in Kant's argument, much confusion would have been avoided. It involves the thorough revisal of his criticism of the third and fourth antinomies, as well as of the whole account hitherto given of the function of Reason and of its metaphysical dialectic. The

[1] A 593 = B 621.   [2] Cf. A 4-5 = B 8-9; A 735-8 = B 763-6.

principle, that if the conditioned be given, the whole series of conditions up to the unconditioned is likewise given, must no longer be accepted as a basis for argument. Indeed the very terms in which Reason has so far been defined, as the faculty of the unconditioned, become subject to question. In that definition the term unconditioned has tacitly been taken as equivalent to the unconditionally necessary, and on elimination of the element of necessity, it will reduce merely to the concept of totality, which is a pure form of the understanding. Those parts of the *Dialectic*, which embody the view that Reason is simply the understanding transcendently employed, will thus be confirmed; the alternative view of Reason as a separate faculty will have to be eliminated. But these are questions which Kant himself proceeds to raise and discuss.[1] Meantime he applies the above results in criticism of the ontological argument.

Statement.—In an identical judgment it is contradictory to reject the predicate while retaining the subject. But there is no contradiction if we reject subject and predicate alike, for nothing is then left that can be contradicted. If we assume that there is a triangle, we are bound to recognise that it has three angles, but there is no contradiction in rejecting the triangle together with its three angles. The same holds true of an absolutely necessary Being. 'God is omnipotent' is an identical and therefore necessary judgment. But if we say, 'There is no God,' neither the omnipotence nor any other attribute remains; and there is therefore not the least contradiction in saying that God does not exist. The only way of evading this conclusion is to argue that there are subjects which cannot be removed out of existence. This, however, would only be another way of asserting that there exist absolutely necessary subjects, and that is the very assertion which is now in question, and which the ontological argument undertakes to prove. Our sole test of what cannot be removed is the contradiction which would thereby result; and the only possible instance which can be cited is the concept of the *Ens realissimum*. It remains, therefore, to establish the above criticism for this specific case.

At the start Kant points out that absence of internal contradiction, even if granted, proves only that the *Ens realissimum* is a *logically* possible concept (as distinguished from the *nihil negativum*[2]); it does not suffice to establish the possibility of the object of the concept. But for the sake of argument Kant allows this initial assumption to pass. The argument to be disproved is that as reality comprehends

---

[1] Cf. above, pp. 427-8, and references there given.   [2] Cf. above, p. 424.

existence, existence is contained in the concept of *Ens realissimum*, and cannot therefore be denied of it without removing its internal possibility. The really fundamental assumption of this argument is that existence is capable of being included in the concept of a *possible* being. If that were so, the assertion of its existence would be an analytic proposition, and the proof could not be challenged. (The assumption is partly concealed by alternation of the terms reality and existence; in their actual employment they are completely synonymous.) As the above assumption thus decides the entire issue, Kant sets himself to establish, in direct opposition to it, the thesis, that every proposition which predicates existence is synthetic, and that in consequence its denial can never involve a logical contradiction. Existence can never form part of the content of a conception, and therefore must not be regarded as a possible predicate. What logically corresponds to it in a judgment is a purely formal factor, namely, the copula. The proposition, 'God is omnipotent,' contains two concepts, each of which has its object—God and omnipotence. The word 'is' adds no new predicate, but only serves to posit the predicate in its relation to the subject. Similarly, when we take the subject together with all its predicates (including that of omnipotence), and say, 'God is' or 'there is a God,' we attach no new predicate to the concept of God, but only posit the subject in itself with all its predicates as being an object that stands in relation to our concept. In order that the proposition be true, the *content* of the object and of the concept must be one and the same. If the object contained more than the concept, the concept would not express the object, and the proposition would assert a relation that does not hold. Or to state the same point in another way, the real must not contain more content than the possible. Otherwise it would not be the possible, but something different from the possible, which would then be taken as existing. A hundred real thalers do not contain the least coin more than a hundred possible thalers. Though my financial position is very differently affected by a hundred real thalers than by the thought of them only, a conceived hundred thalers are not in the least increased through acquiring existence outside my concept.

Kant presents his argument in still another form. If we think in a thing every kind of reality except one, the missing reality is not supplied by my saying that this defective thing exists. On the contrary, it exists with the same defect with which I have thought it. When, therefore, I think a Being as the highest reality, without any defect, the question still remains whether it exists or not. For though, in my concept, nothing may be lacking of the possible real *content* of a thing in general, something is still lacking in its relation to my whole state of thinking, namely, knowledge of its existence; and such knowledge can never be obtained save in an *a posteriori* manner. That is owing to the limitations imposed by the conditions of our sense-experience. We never confound the existence of a sensible object with its mere concept. The concept represents something that may or may not exist: to determine existence we must refer to actual experience. As Kant has already stated, the actual is always for us the accidental, and its assertion is therefore synthetic. A possible idea and the idea of a possible thing are quite distinct.[1] A thing is known to be possible only when presented in some concrete experience, or when, though not actually experienced, it has been proved to be bound up, according to empirical laws, with given perceptions. It is not, therefore, surprising that if we try, as is done in the ontological argument, to think existence through the pure category, we cannot mention a single mark distinguishing it from a merely logical possibility. The concept of a Supreme Being is, in many respects, a valuable Idea, but just because it is an Idea of pure Reason, *i.e.* a mere Idea, we can no more extend our knowledge of real existence by means of it, than a merchant can better his position by adding a few noughts to his cash account.

There are many points of connection between this section and the first edition *Introduction*; and in view of these points of contact Adickes has suggested[2] that the considerations which arose in the examination of the ontological argument may have been what brought Kant to realise that the various problems of the *Critique* can all be traced to the central problem of *a priori* synthesis.

SECTION V

THE IMPOSSIBILITY OF A COSMOLOGICAL PROOF OF THE EXISTENCE OF GOD[3]

Statement.—Kant, as already noted, views the ontological proof as 'a mere innovation of scholastic wisdom' which restates, in a quite unnatural form, a line of thought much more adequately expressed in the cosmological proof. To

[1] Cf. above, p. 392 ff.   [2] *K.* p. 475 *n.*   [3] A 603 = B 631.

discover the natural dialectic of Reason we must therefore look to this latter form of argument. It is composed of two distinct stages. In the first stage it makes no use of specific experience: if *anything* is given us as existing, *e.g.* the self, there must exist an absolutely necessary Being as its cause. Then, in the second stage, it is argued that as such a Being must be altogether outside experience, Reason must leave experience entirely aside, and discover from among pure concepts what properties an absolutely necessary Being ought to possess, *i.e.* which among all possible things contains in itself the conditions of absolute necessity. The requisite enlightenment is believed by Reason to be derivable only from the concept of an *Ens realissimum*, and Reason therefore at once concludes that this concept must represent the absolutely necessary Being.

Now in that final conclusion the truth of the ontological argument is assumed. If the concept of a Being of the highest reality is so completely adequate to the concept of necessary existence that they can be regarded as identical, the latter must be capable of being derived from the former, and that is all that is maintained in the ontological proof. To make this point clearer, Kant states it in scholastic form. If the proposition be true, that every absolutely necessary Being is at the same time the most real Being (and this is the *nervus probandi* of the cosmological proof in so far as it is also theological), it must, like all affirmative propositions, be capable of conversion, at least *per accidens*. This gives us the proposition that some *Entia realissima* are at the same time absolutely necessary Beings. One *Ens realissimum*, however, does not differ from another, and what applies to one applies to all. In this case, therefore, we must employ simple conversion, and say that every *Ens realissimum* is a necessary Being. Thus the cosmological proof is not only as illusory as the ontological, but also less honest. While pretending to lead us by a new road to a sound conclusion, it brings us back, after a short circuit, into the old path. If the ontological argument is correct, the cosmological is superfluous; and if the ontological is false, the cosmological cannot possibly be true.

But the first stage of the cosmological argument, that by which it is distinguished from the ontological, is itself fallacious. A whole nest of dialectical assumptions lies hidden in its apparently simple and legitimate inference from the contingent to the necessary. To advance from the contingent to the necessary, from the relative to the absolute, from the given to the transcendent, is just as illegitimate as the opposite process of passing from Idea to existence. The necessity of thought, which is in both cases the sole ground of the inference, is found on examination to be of merely subjective character. No less than three false assumptions are involved in this inference. In the first place, the principle that everything must have a cause, which can be proved to be valid only within the world of sense, is here applied to the sensible world as a whole; and is therefore employed in the wider form which coincides with the fundamental principle of the higher faculty of Reason. We assume, that if the conditioned be given, the totality of its conditions *up to the unconditioned* is given likewise. No such principle can be granted. As it is synthetic, it could be established only as a condition of the possibility of experience. But no such proof is offered: the principle is based upon a purely intellectual concept. Secondly, the inference to a first cause rests on the kindred assumption that an infinite series of empirical causes is impossible. That conclusion can never be drawn, even within the realm of experience. How, then, can we rely upon it in advancing beyond experience? Certainly, no one can prove that the empirical series is infinite, but just as little can we establish the opposite. In discussing the third and fourth antinomies Kant has shown that the existence of a first cause or of an absolutely necessary Being, though possible (or rather, possibly possible), is never demonstrable. Thirdly—as has been shown in A 592-3 = B 620-1—in inferring to an unconditioned cause, it is blindly assumed that the removal of all conditions does not at the same time remove the very concept of necessity. Our only notion of necessity is derived from experience, and therefore depends on those finite conditions which the argument would deny to us. The concept of unconditioned necessity is entirely null and void.

The fourth defect, which Kant enumerates, refers to the second stage of the cosmological argument, and has already been considered. He ought also to have mentioned a still further assumption underlying its first stage, namely, that a concept which represents a limited being, as, for instance, that of matter, cannot represent necessary existence. This also is an assumption which it cannot justify. This objection Kant has himself stated in A 586 = B 614 and A 588 = B 616.[1]

Comment. — We are apt to overlook the wider sweep which Kant's criticism takes in this section, owing to his omission to notify the reader that he is here calling in question a principle which he has hitherto been taking for

---

[1] Cf. above, p. 527. The concluding paragraphs A 613-14 = B 641-2 can best be treated later in another connection. Cf. below, p. 536.

granted, namely, the principle in terms of which he has in the opening sections of the *Dialectic* defined the faculty of Reason, that if the conditioned be given the totality of conditions up to the unconditioned is given likewise. The first step in his rejection of this principle occurs as merely incidental to his criticism of the ontological argument. It is there shown that the concept of the unconditionally necessary is without meaning. Now, in this present section, he calls in question the principle itself. It must be rejected not only, as stated in the third of the above objections, because the concept of the unconditioned, which tacitly implies the factor of absolute necessity, is without real significance, but also for two further reasons—those above cited in the first and second objections. How very differently the problems of the *Dialectic* appear, and how very differently the Ideas of Reason have to be regarded, when this principle, and also the concept of the unconditioned of which it is the application, are thus called in question, will be shown in the sequel.

DISCOVERY AND EXPLANATION OF THE TRANSCENDENTAL ILLUSION IN ALL TRANSCENDENTAL PROOFS OF THE EXISTENCE OF A NECESSARY BEING [1]

Statement.—We do not properly fulfil the task prescribed by Critical teaching in merely disproving the cosmological argument. We must also explain its hold upon the mind. If it is, as Kant insists, more natural to the mind than the ontological, and yet, as we have just seen, is more fallacious; if it has not been invented by philosophers, but is the instinctive reasoning of the natural man, it must rest, like all dialectical illusion, upon a misunderstanding of the legitimate demands of pure Reason. *Reason demands the unconditioned, and yet cannot think it.*

"Unconditioned necessity, which we so indispensably require as the last bearer of all things, is for human Reason the veritable abyss. . . . We can neither help thinking, nor can we bear the thought, that a Being—even if it be the one which we represent to ourselves as supreme amongst all Beings—should, as it were, say to itself: 'I am from eternity to eternity, and outside me there is nothing save what is through my will; *but whence am I?*' All support here fails us; and *supreme* perfection, no less than the *least* perfection, is unsubstantial and baseless for the merely speculative Reason. . . ." [2]

We are obliged to think something as necessary for all

---

[1] A 614 = B 642.   [2] A 613 = B 641.

existence, and yet at the same time are unable to think anything as in itself necessary—God as little as anything else.

The explanation [1] of this strange fact must be that which follows as a corollary from the limitation of our knowledge to sense-experience, namely, that our concepts of necessity and contingency do not concern things in themselves, and cannot therefore be applied to them in accordance with either of the two possible alternatives. Each alternative must express a subjective principle of Reason; and the two together (that something exists by necessity, and that everything is only contingent) must form complementary rules for the guidance of the understanding. These rules will then be purely heuristic and regulative, relating only to the formal interests of Reason, and may well stand side by side. For the one tells us that we ought to philosophise as if there were a necessary first ground for everything that exists, i.e. that we ought to be always dissatisfied with relativity and contingency, and to seek always for what is unconditionally necessary. The other warns us against regarding any single determination in things (such, for instance, as impenetrability or gravity) as absolutely necessary, and so bids us keep the way always open for further derivation. In other words, Reason guides the understanding by a twofold command. The understanding must derive phenomena and their existence from other phenomena, just as if there were no necessary Being at all; while at the same time it must always strive towards the completeness of that derivation, just as if such a necessary Being were presupposed. It is owing to a transcendental illusion or subreption that we view the latter principle as constitutive, and so think its unity as hypostatised in the form of an *Ens realissimum*. The falsity of this substitution becomes evident as soon as we consider *that unconditioned necessity, as a thing in itself, cannot even be conceived, and that the " Idea " of it cannot, therefore, be ascribed to Reason save as a merely formal principle, regulative of the understanding in its interpretation of given experience.* [2]

Comment.—The reader may observe that, when Kant is developing this sceptical view of the Ideal of Reason, the explanation of dialectical illusion in terms of transcendental idealism falls into the background. The illusion is no longer traced to a confusion between appearances and things in themselves, but to the false interpretation of regulative principles as being constitutive. When it is the cosmological problem with which we are dealing, the two illusions do, indeed, coincide. If we view the objects of sense-experience as things in themselves, we are bound to regard the Ideal completion of the natural sciences as an adequate representation of ulti- mate reality.   But in Rational Theology, which is professedly directed towards the definition of a Being distinct from nature and conditioning all finite existence, it is not failure to dis- tinguish between appearance and things in themselves, but the mistaking of a merely formal Ideal for a representation of reality, that is alone responsible for the conclusions drawn.

In A 617-18 = B 645-6 Kant makes statements which con- flict with the teaching of A 586 = B 614 and A 588 = B 616. In the latter passages he has argued that the concept of a limited being may not without specific proof be taken as contradictory of absolute necessity.   He now categorically declares that the philosophers of antiquity are in error in regarding matter as primitive and necessary; and the reason which he gives is that the regulative principle of Reason forbids us to view extension and impenetrability, "which together constitute the concept of matter," as ultimate principles of experience.   But obviously Kant is here going further than his regulative principle will justify.   It demands only that we should always look for still higher principles of unity, and so keep open the way for possible further deriva- tion; it does not enable us to assert that such will actually be found to exist.   Notwithstanding the Ideal demands of the regulative principle, matter may be primordial and neces- sary, and its properties of extension and impenetrability may not be derivable from anything more ultimate.

In this connection we may raise the more general question, how far the Ideal demand for necessity and unity in know- ledge and existence can be concretely pictured.   Kant gives a varying answer.   Sometimes—when he is emphasising the limitation of our theoretical knowledge to sense-experience— he reduces the speculative Idea of Divine Existence to a purely abstract maxim for the regulation of natural science. When the Ideal occupies the mind on its own account, and so attracts our attention away from our sense-knowledge, it is an unreality, and perverts the understanding; it yields genuine light and leading only as a quite general maxim within the sphere of natural science.   From this point of view necessary Being, even as an Ideal, can by no means be identi- fied with a personal God.   It signifies only the highest possible system and unity of the endlessly varied natural phenomena in space and time, and can be approximately realised in the most various ways.   Its significance is entirely cosmological. It is an Ideal of positive science, and signifies only sys- tematic unity in the object known.   In being transformed from a scientific ideal into a subject of theological enquiry, it has inevitably given rise to dialectical illusion. At other times,—when he is concerned to defend the concept of Divine Existence as at least possible, and so to prepare the way for its postulation as implied in the moral law, or when he is seeking, as in the *Critique of Judgment*, to render comprehensible the complete adaptation of phenomenal nature in its material aspect to the needs of our understanding—Kant insists that we are ultimately compelled, by the nature of our faculties, to conceive the Ideal of Reason as a personal God, as an Intelligence working according to purposes. Only by such a personal God, he maintains, can the demands of Reason be genuinely satisfied.

These two interpretations of the Ideal of Reason are in conflict with one another; and so far as the *Critique of Pure Reason* is concerned, a very insufficient attempt is made to justify the frequent assertion that the Idea of God is *the* Ideal of Reason, and not merely one possible, and highly problematic, interpretation of it. If the Idea of God is a necessary Idea, it cannot be adequately expressed through any merely regulative maxim. It demands not only system in knowledge but also perfection in the nature of the known. It is not a merely logical Ideal such as might be satisfied by any rational system, but an Ideal which concerns matter as well as form, man as well as nature, our moral needs as well as our intellectual demands. If Kant is to maintain that the only genuine function of theoretical Reason is to guide the understanding in its scientific application, he is debarred from asserting that a concrete interpretation of its regulative principles is unavoidable. And he is also precluded by his own limitation of all knowledge to sense-experience from seeking to define by any positive predicate the transcendent nature of the thing in itself.

Such justification as Kant can offer in support of his assertion that the Idea of God, of Intelligent Perfection, is an indispensable Idea of human Reason, is chiefly based upon the teleological aspect of nature which is dealt with in the physico-theological proof. Mechanical science implies only the cosmological Idea: teleological unity presupposes the theological Ideal. Further enquiry, then, into the necessity of the Idea of God as a regulative principle, and its dangers as a source of dialectical illusion, we must defer until we have examined the one remaining argument.[1]

---

[1] Cf. below, pp. 541-2, 552 ff.

SECTION VI

THE IMPOSSIBILITY OF THE PHYSICO-THEOLOGICAL PROOF [1]

Statement.—The teleological proof starts from our definite knowledge of the order and constitution of the sensible world. The actual world presents such immeasurable order, variety, fitness, and beauty, that we are led to believe that here at least is sufficient proof of the existence of God. Kant's attitude towards this argument is at once extremely critical and extremely sympathetic. Though he represents it as the oldest, the clearest, and the most convincing, he is none the less prepared to show that it contains every one of the fallacies involved in the other two proofs, as well as some false assumptions peculiar to itself. It possesses overpowering persuasive force, not because of any inherent logical cogency, but because it so successfully appeals to feeling as to silence the intellect. It would, Kant declares, be not only comfortless, but utterly vain to attempt to diminish its influence.

"[The mind is] aroused from the indecision of all melancholy reflection, as from a dream, by one glance at the wonders of nature and the majesty of the universe. . . ." [2]

Meantime, however, we are concerned with its merely logical force. We have to decide whether, as theoretical proof, it can claim assent on its own merits, requiring no favour, and no help from any other quarter. On the basis of empirical facts the argument makes the following assertions. (1) There are everywhere in the world clear indications of adaptation to a definite end. (2) As this adaptation cannot be due to the working of blind, mechanical laws, and accordingly cannot be explained as originating in things themselves, it must have been imposed upon them from without; and there must therefore exist, apart from the sensible world, an intelligent Being who has arranged it according to ideas antecedently formed. (3) As there is unity in the reciprocal relations of the parts of the universe as portions of a single edifice, and as the universe is infinite in extent and inexhaustible in variety, its intelligent cause must be single, all-powerful, all-wise, *i.e.* God.

Now, even granting for the sake of argument the admissibility of these assertions, they enable us to infer only an intelligent author of the purposive form of nature, not of its matter, only an architect who is very much hampered by the

---

[1] A 620 = B 648.   [2] A 624 = B 652.

inadaptability of the material in which he has to work, not a
Creator to whose will everything is due.   To prove the
contingency of matter itself, we should have to establish the
truth of the cosmological proof.

But the assumptions implied even in the demonstration
that God exists as a *formative* power, are by no means
beyond dispute.   Why may not nature be regarded as giving
form to itself by its blindly working forces?   Can it really be
proved that nature is a work of art that demands an artificer
as certainly as does a house, or a ship, or a clock?   Kant's
argument is at this point extremely brief, and I shall so far
digress from the statement of it, which he here gives, as to
supplement it from his other writings.   Even so-called dead
matter is not merely inert.   By its inherent powers of gravity
and chemical attraction it spontaneously gives rise to the
most wonderful forms.   When Clarke and Voltaire, in their
enthusiasm over Newton's great discovery, asserted that the
planetary system must have been divinely created, each planet
being launched in the tangent of its orbit by the finger of God,
just as a wheel must be fixed into its place by the hand of
the mechanician, they under-estimated the organising power of
blind inanimate nature.   As Kant argued in his early treatise,[1]
the planetary system can quite well have arisen, and, as it
would seem, actually has come into existence, through the
action of blindly working laws.   The mechanical principles
which account for its present maintenance will also account
for its origin and development.   But it is when we turn
to animate nature, which is the chief source from which
arguments for design are derived, that the insufficiency of the
teleological argument becomes most manifest.   As Kant
points out in the *Critique of Judgment*, the differentia
distinguishing the living from the lifeless, is not so much
that it is organised as that it is self-organising.   When,
therefore, we treat an organism as an analogon of art we
completely misrepresent its essential nature.[2]   In regarding
it as put together by an external agent we are ignoring its
internal self-developing power.   As Hume had previously
maintained in his *Dialogues on Natural Religion*,[3] the facts

[1] *Universal Natural History and Theory of the Heavens* (1755).

[2] *Critique of Judgment*, §§ 64, 65. Cf. below, p. 557.

[3] Hamann completed his translation of Hume's *Dialogues on Natural Religion*
on August 7, 1780 (cf. Hamann's *Werke*, vi. 154 ff.) : and Kant, notwithstanding
his being occupied in finishing the *Critique*, read through the manuscript.   It
is highly likely that this first perusal of Hume's *Dialogues* not only confirmed
Kant in his negative attitude towards natural theology, but also enabled him to
define more clearly than he otherwise would have done, the negative consequences
of his own Critical principles.   The chapter on the *Ideal*, as we have already
observed (above, pp. 434-5, 527-9, 531), was probably one of the last parts of the

of the organic world not only agree with the facts of the inorganic world in *not* supporting the argument of the teleological proof, but are in direct conflict with it.

But to return to Kant's immediate statement of the argument. Setting the above objection aside, and granting for the present that nature may be regarded as the outcome of an external artificer, we can argue only to a cause adequate to its production, *i.e.* to an extraordinarily wise and wonderfully powerful Being. Even if we ignore the existence of evil and defect in nature, the step from great power to omnipotence, and from great wisdom to omniscience, is one that can never be justified on empirical grounds.[1]   Since the Ideas of Reason, and above all the completely determined, individual Ideal of Reason, transcend experience, experience can never justify us in inferring their reality.   The teleological argument can, indeed, only lead us to the point of admiring the greatness, wisdom, and power of the author of the world. In proceeding further it abandons experience altogether, and reasons, not from particular kinds and excellencies of natural design, but from the contingency of all such adaptation to the existence of a necessary Being, exactly in the manner of the cosmological argument.   And it ends by assuming, in agreement with the ontological proof, that the only possible necessary Being is the Ideal of Reason.   Thus after committing a number of fallacies on its own account, the teleological argument itself endorses all those that are involved in the more *a priori* proofs.   The teleological argument rests on the cosmological, and the cosmological on the ontological, which therefore would be the only proof possible, were the proof of a completely transcendent proposition ever possible at all.   The strange fact that the convincing force of the arguments thus varies inversely with their validity shows, Kant maintains, that we are correct in concluding that they do not really depend upon their logical cogency, and merely express, in abstract terms, beliefs deep-rooted in the human spirit.

Critique to be brought into final form.   It does not seem possible, however, to establish in any specific manner the exact influence which Hume's *Dialogues* may thus have exercised upon the argument of this portion of the *Critique*. When Schreiter's translation of the *Dialogues* appeared in 1781, Hamann, not unwilling to escape the notoriety of seeming to father so sceptical a work, withdrew his own translation.

[1] This is the main point of Hume's argument in Section XI. of his *Enquiry concerning the Human Understanding*.

SECTION VII

CRITICISM OF ALL THEOLOGY BASED ON SPECULATIVE PRINCIPLES OF REASON [1]

A 631-3 = B 659-66.—On the distinction between "theist" and "deist," cf. *Encyclopædia Britannica*, vii. p. 934:

"The later distinction between 'theist' and 'deist,' which stamped the latter word as excluding the belief in providence or in the immanence of God, was apparently formulated in the end of the eighteenth century by those rationalists who were aggrieved at being identified with the naturalists."

A 633-4 = B 661-2.—Kant here does no more than indicate that by way of practical Reason it may be possible to postulate, though not theoretically to comprehend, a Supreme Being. On the distinction between postulates and hypotheses, cf. A 769 ff. = B 797 ff., and below, p. 543 ff. Cf. also p. 571 ff.

A 634 = B 662.—On relative necessity, cf. below, pp. 555, 571 ff.

A 635-9 = B 663-7 only summarises points already treated.

A 639-42 = B 667-70.—Kant concludes by declaring that the Ideal, in addition to its regulative function, possesses two further prerogatives. In the first place, it supplies a standard, in the light of which any knowledge of Divine Existence, acquired from other sources, can be purified and rendered consistent with itself. For it is "an Ideal without a flaw," the true crown and culmination of the whole of human knowledge.

"If there should be a moral theology . . . transcendental theology . . . will then prove itself indispensable in determining its concept and in constantly testing Reason which is so often deceived by sensibility, and which is frequently out of harmony with its own Ideas." [2]

And secondly, though the Ideal fails to establish itself theoretically, the arguments given in its support suffice to show the quite insufficient foundations upon which all atheistic, deistic, and anthropomorphic philosophies rest.

Comment.—These concluding remarks cannot be accepted as representing Kant's true teaching. The Ideal, by his own showing, is by no means without a flaw. In so far as it involves the concept of unconditioned necessity, it is meaningless; it is purely logical, and therefore contains no indication of

[1] A 631 = B 659.   [2] A 641 = B 669.

real content ; it embodies a false view of the nature of negation, and therefore of the relation of realities to one another. In short, it is constituted in accordance with the false, un-Critical principles of Leibnizian metaphysics, and is found on ex-amination to be non-existent even as a purely mental entity. Reduced to its proper terms, it becomes a mere schema regulative of the understanding in the extension of experience, and does not yield even a negative criterion for the testing of our ideals of Divine Existence. The criterion, which Kant really so employs, is not that of an *Ens realissimum*, but the concept of an Intuitive Understanding, which, as he has indicated in the chapter on *Phenomena and Noumena*,[1] is our most adequate Ideal of completed Perfection. This latter is not itself, however, a spontaneously formed concept of natural Reason, and does not justify the assertion that the Idea of God is a necessary Idea of the human mind. In attempting to defend such a thesis, Kant is unduly influenced by the almost universal acceptance of deistic beliefs in the Europe of his time.[2] His criticism of the Ideal of Reason and of rational theology is much more destructive, and really allows that theology much less value, even as natural dialectic, than he is willing to admit.[3] Architectonic forbids that the extreme radical consequences of the teaching of the *Analytic* should be allowed to show in their full force. These shortcomings are, however, in great part remedied in the elaborate *Appendix* which Kant has attached to the *Dialectic*.

[1] Cf. above, p. 407 ff., and below, p. 552 ff.
[2] Cf. above, p. 454, with further references in *n.* 1.   [3] Cf. above, pp. 536-7.

APPENDIX TO THE TRANSCENDENTAL DIALECTIC

THE REGULATIVE EMPLOYMENT OF THE IDEAS OF PURE REASON [1]

Before we proceed to deal with this *Appendix* it will be of advantage to consider the section in the *Methodology* on *the Discipline of Pure Reason in regard to Hypotheses.*[2] That section affords a very illuminating introduction to the problems here discussed, and is extremely important for understanding Kant's view of metaphysical science as yielding either complete certainty or else nothing at all. This is a doctrine which he from time to time suggests, to the considerable bewilderment of the modern reader.[3] In discussing it he starts from the obvious objection, that though nothing can be known through Reason in its pure *a priori* employment, metaphysics may yet be possible in an empirical form, as consisting of hypotheses, constructed in conjectural explanation of the facts of experience. Kant replies by defining the conditions under which alone hypotheses can be entertained as such. There must always be something completely certain, and not only invented or merely "opined," namely, the *possibility* of the object to which the hypothesis appeals. Once that is proved, it is allowable, on the basis of experience, to form opinions regarding its reality. Then, and only then, can such opinions be entitled hypotheses. Otherwise we are not employing the understanding to explain; we are simply indulging the imagination in its tendency to dream. Now since the categories of the pure understanding do not enable us to invent *a priori* the concept of a dynamical connection, but only to apprehend it when presented in experience, we cannot by means of these categories invent a single object endowed with a new quality

---

[1] A 642 = B 670.   [2] A 769-82 = B 797-810.
[3] A xiv, B xxiii-iv, and *Reflexionen* ii. 1451 : "In metaphysics there can be no such thing as uncertainty." Cf. above, pp. 10, 35.

not empirically given; and cannot, therefore, base an hypothesis upon any such conception.

"Thus it is not permissible to invent any new original powers, as, for instance, an understanding capable of intuiting its objects without the aid of senses; or a force of attraction without any contact; or a new kind of substance existing in space and yet not impenetrable. Nor is it legitimate to postulate any other form of communion of substances than that revealed in experience, any presence that is not spatial, any duration that is not temporal. In a word our Reason can employ as conditions of the possibility of things only the conditions of possible experience; it can never, as it were, *create* concepts of things, independently of those conditions. Such concepts, though not self-contradictory, would be without an object." [1]

This does not, however, mean that the concepts of pure Reason can have no valid employment. They are, it is true, Ideas merely, with no object corresponding to them in any experience; but then it is also true that they are not hypotheses, referring to imagined objects, supposed to be possibly real. They are purely problematic. They are heuristic fictions (*heuristische Fiktionen*), the sole function of which is to serve as principles regulative of the understanding in its systematic employment. Used in any other manner they reduce to the level of merely mental entities (*Gedankendinge*) whose very possibility is indemonstrable, and which cannot therefore be employed as hypotheses for the explanation of appearances. Given appearances can be accounted for only in terms of laws known to hold among appearances. To explain natural phenomena by a transcendental hypothesis—mental processes by the assumption of the soul as a substantial, simple, spiritual being, or order and design in nature by the assumption of a Divine Author—is never admissible.

". . . that would be to explain something, which in terms of known empirical principles we do not understand sufficiently, by something which we do not understand at all." [2]

And Kant adds that the wildest hypotheses, if only they are physical, are more tolerable than a hyperphysical one. They at least conform to the conditions under which alone hypothetical explanation as such is allowable. "Outside this field, to form opinions, is merely to play with thoughts. . . ." [3]

A further condition, required to render an hypothesis acceptable, is its adequacy for determining *a priori* all the consequences which are actually given. If for that purpose supplementary hypotheses have to be called in, the force of

---

[1] A 770-1 = B 798-9.　　　[2] A 772 = B 800.　　　[3] A 775 = B 803.

the main assumption is proportionately weakened. Thus we can easily explain natural order and design, if we are allowed to postulate a Divine Author who is absolutely perfect and all-powerful. But that hypothesis lies open to all the objections suggested by defects and evils in nature, and can only be preserved through new hypotheses which modify the main assumption. Similarly the hypothesis of the human soul as an abiding and purely spiritual being, existing in independence of the body, has to be modified to meet the difficulties which arise from the phenomena of growth and decay. But the new hypotheses, then constructed, derive their whole authority from the main hypothesis which they are themselves defending.

Such is Kant's criticism of metaphysics when its teaching is based on the facts of experience hypothetically interpreted. In regard to transcendent metaphysics, there are, in Kant's view, only two alternatives.[1] Either its propositions must be established independently of all experience in purely *a priori* fashion, and therefore as absolutely certain; or they must consist in hypotheses empirically grounded. The first alternative has in the *Analytic* and *Dialectic* been shown to be impossible; the second alternative he rejects for the above reasons.

But this does not close Kant's treatment of metaphysical hypotheses. He proceeds to develop a doctrine which, in its fearless confidence in the truth of Critical teaching, is the worthy outcome of his abiding belief in the value of a "sceptical method."[2] As Reason is by its very nature dialectical, outside opponents are not those from whom we have most to fear. Their objections are really derived from a source which lies in ourselves, and until these have been traced to their origin, and destroyed from the root upwards, we can expect no lasting peace. Our duty, therefore, is to encourage our doubts, until by the very luxuriance of their growth they enable us to discover the hidden roots from which they derive their perennial vitality.

"External tranquillity is a mere illusion. The germ of these objections, which lies in the nature of human Reason, must be rooted out. But how can we uproot it, unless we give it freedom, nay, nourishment, to send out shoots so that it may discover itself to our eyes, and that we may then destroy it together with its root? Therefore think out objections which have never yet occurred to any opponent; lend him, indeed, your weapons, or grant him the most favourable position which he could possibly desire. You have

---

[1] Cf. A 781-2 = B 809-10. 　　　[2] Cf. above, pp. 481, 501.

nothing to fear in all this, but much to hope for; you may gain for yourselves a possession which can never again be contested."[1]

In this campaign to eradicate doubt by following it out to its furthermost limits, the hypotheses of pure Reason, "leaden weapons though they be, since they are not steeled by any law of experience," are an indispensable part of our equipment. For though hypotheses are useless for the establishment of metaphysical propositions, they are, Kant teaches, both admirable and valuable for their defence. That is to say, their true metaphysical function is not dogmatic, but polemical. They are weapons of war to which we may legitimately resort for the maintenance of beliefs otherwise established. If, for instance, we have been led to postulate the immaterial, self-subsistent nature of the soul, and are met by the difficulty that experience would seem to prove that both the growth and the decay of our mental powers are due to the body, we can weaken this objection by formulating the hypothesis that the body is not the cause of our thinking, but only a restrictive condition of it, peculiar to our present state, and that, though it furthers our sensuous and animal faculties, it acts as an impediment to our spiritual life. Similarly, to meet the many objections against belief in the eternal existence of a finite being whose birth depends upon contingencies of all kinds, such as the food supply, the whims of government, or even vice, we can adduce the transcendental hypothesis that life has neither beginning in birth nor ending in death, the entire world of sense being but an image due to our present mode of knowledge, an image which like a dream has in itself no objective reality. Such hypotheses are not, indeed, even Ideas of Reason, but simply concepts *invented* to show that the objections which are raised depend upon the false assumption that the possibilities have been exhausted, and that the laws of nature comprehend the whole field of possible existences. These hypotheses at least suffice to reveal the uncertain character of the doubts which assail us in our practical beliefs.

"[Transcendental hypotheses] are nothing but private opinions. Nevertheless, we cannot properly dispense with them as weapons against the misgivings which are apt to occur; they are necessary even to secure our inner tranquillity. We must preserve to them this character, carefully guarding against the assumption of their independent authority or absolute validity, since otherwise they would drown Reason in fictions and delusions."[2]

---

[1] A 777-8 = B 805-6.   [2] A 782 = B 810.

We may now return to A 642-68 = B 670-96. The teach-ing of this section is extremely self-contradictory, waver-ing between a subjective and an objective interpretation of the Ideas of Reason. The probable explanation is that Kant is here recasting older material, and leaves standing more of his earlier solutions than is consistent with his final conclusions. We can best approach the discussion by con-sidering Kant's statements in A 645 = B 673 and in A 650 ff. = B 678 ff. They expound, though unfortunately in the briefest terms, a point of view which Idealism has since adopted as fundamental. Kant himself, very strangely, never develops its consequences at any great length.[1] The Idea, which Reason follows in the exercise of its sole true function, the systematising of the knowledge supplied by the under-standing, is that of a unity in which the thought of the whole precedes the knowledge of its parts, and contains the con-ditions according to which the place of every part and its relation to the other parts are determined *a priori*. This Idea specialises itself in various forms, and in all of them directs the understanding to a knowledge that will be that of no mere aggregate but of a genuine system. Such concepts are not derived from nature ; we interrogate nature *according to them*, and consider our knowledge defective so long as it fails to embody them. In A 650 = B 678 Kant further points out that this Idea of Reason does not merely direct the under-standing to search for such unity, but also claims for itself objective reality. And he adds,

" . . . it is difficult to understand how there can be a logical principle by which Reason prescribes the unity of rules, unless we also presuppose a transcendental principle whereby such systematic unity is *a priori* assumed to be necessarily inherent in the objects."

For how could we treat diversity in nature as only dis-guised unity, if we were also free to regard that unity as contrary to the actual nature of the real ?

" Reason would then run counter to its own vocation, proposing as its aim an Idea quite inconsistent with the constitution of nature."[2]

Nor is our knowledge of the principle merely empirical, deduced from the unity which we find in contingent experience. On the contrary, there is an inherent and necessary law of Reason compelling us, antecedently to all specific experience, to look for such unity.

---

[1] Cf. above, pp. 97-8, 102, 390-1, 426 ff., 447 ff.　　　[2] A 651 = B 679.

" . . . without it we should have no Reason at all, and without Reason no coherent employment of the understanding, and *in the absence of this no sufficient criterion of empirical truth.* In order, therefore, to secure an empirical criterion we are absolutely compelled to presuppose the systematic unity of nature as objectively valid and necessary." [1] "It might be supposed that this is merely an economical contrivance of Reason, seeking to save itself all possible trouble, a hypothetical attempt, which, if it succeeds, will, through the unity thus attained, impart probability to the presumed principle of explanation. But such a selfish purpose can very easily be distinguished from the Idea. For in the latter we presuppose that this unity of Reason is in conformity with nature itself; and that, although we are indeed unable to determine the limits of this unity, Reason does not here beg but command." [2]

This last alternative, that Reason is here propounding a tentative hypothesis, in order by trial to discover how far it can be empirically verified—an alternative which Kant in the above passage rejects as unduly subjective, and as consequently failing to recognise the objective claims and *a priori* authority of the Ideas of Reason,—is yet a view which he himself adopts and indeed develops at considerable length in this same section. This, as already stated, affords evidence of the composite character and varying origins of the material here presented.

The *Dissertation* of 1770 gives a purely subjectivist interpretation of the regulative principles, among which, from its pre-Critical standpoint, it classes the principle of causality and the principle of the conservation of matter.

"[We adopt principles] which delude the intellect into mistaking them for arguments derived from the object, whereas they are commended to us only by the peculiar nature of the intellect, owing to their convenience for its free and ample employment. They therefore . . . rest on *subjective* grounds . . . namely, on the conditions under which it seems easy and expeditious for the intellect to make use of its insight. . . . These rules of judging, to which we freely submit and to which we adhere as if they were axioms, solely for the reason that *were we to depart from them almost no judgment regarding a given object would be permissible to our intellect*, I entitle *principles of convenience.* . . . [One of these is] the popularly received canon, *principia non esse multiplicanda praeter summam necessitatem*, to which we yield our adhesion, not because we have insight into causal unity in the world either by reason or by experience, but because we seek it by an impulse of the intellect, which seems to itself to have advanced in the explanation of phenomena only in the degree in which it is granted to it to descend from a single principle to the greatest number of consequences." [3]

---

[1] *Loc. cit.* Italics not in text.　　[2] A 653=B 681.　　[3] *Dissertation*, § 30.

This, in essentials, is the view which we find developed in A 646-9 = B 674-8. Reason is the faculty of deducing the particular from the general. When the general is admitted only as *problematical*, as a mere idea, while the particular is certain, we determine the universality of the rule by applying it to the particulars, and then upon confirmation of its validity proceed to draw conclusions regarding cases not actually given. This Kant entitles the *hypothetical* use of Reason. Reason must never be employed constitutively. It serves only for the introduction, as far as may be found possible, of unity into the particulars of knowledge. It seeks to make the rule *approximate* to universality.[1] The unity which it demands

". . . is a *projected* unity, to be regarded not as given in itself, but as a problem only. This unity aids us in discovering a principle for the manifold and special employment of the understanding, drawing its attention to cases which are not given, and thus rendering it more coherent."[2]

The unity is merely logical, or rather methodological.[3] To postulate, in consequence of its serviceableness, real unity in the objects themselves would be to transform it into a transcendental principle of Reason, and to render

". . . the systematic unity necessary, not only subjectively and logically, as method, but objectively also."[4]

The above paragraphs are intercalated between A 645 = B 673 and A 650-63 = B 678-91, in which, as we have already seen, the directly opposite view is propounded, namely, that such principles are *not* merely hypothetical, *nor* merely logical. In all cases they claim reality, and rest upon transcendental principles; they condition the very possibility of experience; and may therefore be asserted to be *a priori* necessary and to be objectively valid. To quote two additional passages:

". . . we can conclude from the universal to the particular, only if universal qualities are ascribed to things as the foundation upon which the particular qualities rest."[5] "The foundation of these laws [cf. below, pp. 550-1] is not due to any secret design of making an experiment by putting them forward as merely tentative suggestions. . . . It is easily seen that they contemplate the parsimony of

---

[1] The extremely un-Critical reason which Kant here (A 647-B 675) gives for its necessarily remaining hypothetical is the "impossibility of knowing all possible consequences." This use of the term hypothetical is also confusing in view of Kant's criticism of the hypothetical employment of Reason in A 769 ff. = B 797 ff.

[2] A 647 = B 675. [3] *Loc. cit.* and A 649 = B 677.
[4] A 648 = B 676. [5] A 652 = B 680.

fundamental causes, the manifoldness of effects, and the consequent affinity of the parts of nature, as being in themselves both rational and natural. Hence these principles carry their recommendation directly in themselves, and not merely as methodological devices."[1]

Thus, in direct opposition to the preceding view of Reason's function as hypothetical, Kant is now prepared to maintain that the maxims of Reason are without meaning and without application save in so far as they can be grounded in a transcendental principle.[2]

Let us follow Kant's detailed exposition of this last thesis. The logical maxim, to seek for systematic unity, rests upon the transcendental principle that the apparently infinite variety of nature does not exclude identity of species, that the various species are varieties of a few genera, and these again of still higher genera. This is the scholastic maxim: *entia praeter necessitatem non esse multiplicanda.* Upon this principle rests the possibility of concepts, and therefore of the understanding itself. It is balanced, however, by a second principle, no less necessary, the transcendental law of specification, namely, that there must be manifoldness and diversity in things, that every genus must specify itself in divergent species, and these again in sub-species. Or as it is expressed in its scholastic form: *entium varietates non temere esse minuendas.* This principle is equally transcendental. It expresses a condition no less necessary for the possibility of the understanding, and therefore of experience. As the understanding knows all that it knows by concepts only, however far it may carry the division of genera, it can never know by means of pure intuition, but always again by lower concepts. If, therefore, there were no lower concepts, there could be no higher concepts;[3] the gap existing between individuals and genera could never be bridged; or rather, since neither individuals nor universals could then be apprehended, neither would exist for the mind. As the higher concepts acquire all their content from the lower, they presuppose them for their own existence.

"Every concept may be regarded as a point which, in so far as it represents the standpoint of a spectator, has its own horizon. . . . This horizon must be capable of containing an infinite number of points, each of which again has its own narrower horizon; that is, every species contains sub-species, according to the principle of specification, and the logical horizon consists exclusively of smaller

---

[1] A 660-1 = B 688-9.   [2] A 656 = B 684.   [3] A 656 = B 684.

horizons (sub-species), never of points which possess no extent (individuals)."[1]

Combining these two principles, that of *homogeneity* and that of *specification*, we obtain a third, that of *continuity*. The logical law of the *continuum formarum logicarum* presupposes the transcendental law, *lex continui in natura*. It provides that homogeneity be combined with the greatest possible diversity by prescribing a continuous transition from every species to every other, or in other words by requiring that between any two species or sub-species, however closely related, intermediate species be always regarded as possible. (The paragraph at the end of A 661 = B 689, with its proviso that we cannot make any definite empirical use of this law, is probably of later origin; it connects with the concluding parts of the section.) That this third law is also *a priori* and transcendental, is shown by the fact that it is not derived from the prior discovery of system in nature, but has itself given rise to the systematised character of our knowledge.[2]

The psychological, chemical, and astronomical examples which Kant employs to illustrate these laws call for no special comment. They were taken from contemporary science, and in the advance of our knowledge have become more confusing than helpful. The citation in A 646 = B 674 of the concepts of " pure earth, pure water, pure air " as being " concepts of Reason " is especially bewildering. They are, even in the use which Kant himself ascribes to them, simply empirical hypotheses, formulated for the purposes of purely physical explanation ; they are in no genuine sense universal, regulative principles.

In passing to A 663-8 = B 691-6 we find still another variation in the substance of Kant's teaching. He returns, though with a greater maturity of statement, and with a very different and much more satisfactory terminology, to the more sceptical view of A 646-9 = B 674-7.[3] The interest of the above principles, Kant continues to maintain, lies in their transcendentality. Despite the fact that they are mere Ideas for the guidance of understanding, and can only be approached asymptotically, they are synthetic *a priori* judgments, and would seem to have an objective, though indeterminate, validity. So far his statements are in line with the preceding paragraphs. But he proceeds to add that this objective validity consists exclusively in their heuristic function. They differ fundamentally

---

[1] A 658 = B 686. [2] A 660 = B 688.
[3] The opening paragraphs of the section, A 642 5 = B 670-3, may be of the same date as the concluding paragraphs.

from the dynamical, no less than from the mathematical, principles of understanding, in that no schema of sensibility can be assigned to them. In other words, their object can never be exhibited *in concreto*; it transcends all possible experience. For this reason they are incapable of a transcendental deduction.[1] They are among the conditions indispensably necessary to the possibility, not of each and every experience, but only of experience as systematised *in the interest of Reason*. In place of a schema they can possess only what may be called the *analogon* of a schema, that is, they represent the Idea of a *maximum*, which the understanding in the subjective interest of Reason—or, otherwise expressed,[2] in the interest of a certain possible perfection of our knowledge of objects—is called upon to realise *as much as possible*. Thus they are at once *subjective* in the source from which they arise, and also *indeterminate* as to the conditions under which, and the extent to which, they can obtain empirical embodiment. The fact that in this capacity they represent a *maximum*, does not justify any assertion either as to the degree of unity which experience on detailed investigation will ultimately be found to verify, or as to the noumenal reality by which experience is conditioned.

In A 644-5 = B 672-3 Kant employs certain optical analogies to illustrate the illusion which the Ideas, in the absence of Critical teaching, inevitably generate. When the understanding is regulated by the Idea of a *maximum*, and seeks to view all the lines of experience as converging upon and pointing to it, it necessarily regards it, *focus imaginarius* though it be, as actually existing. The illusion, by which objects are seen behind the surface of a mirror, is indispensably necessary if we are to be able to see what lies behind our backs. The transcendental illusion, which confers reality upon the Ideas of Reason, is similarly incidental to the attempt to view experience in its greatest possible extension.

ON THE FINAL PURPOSE OF THE NATURAL DIALECTIC OF HUMAN REASON[3]

This section is thoroughly unified and consistent in its teaching. Its repetitious character is doubtless due to Kant's personal difficulty either in definitively accepting or in altogether rejecting the constructive, Idealist interpretation of the function of Reason. He at least succeeds in formulating a view which, while not asserting anything more than is

---

[1] Cf. *per contra* A 669-70 = B 697-8.   [2] A 666 = B 694.   [3] A 669 = B 697.

required in the scientific extension of experience, indicates the many possibilities which such experience fails to exclude. As the Ideas of Reason are not merely empty thought-entities (*entia rationis ratiocinantis*[1]), but have a certain kind of objective validity (*i.e.* are *entia rationis ratiocinatae*[2]), they demand a transcendental deduction.[3] What this deduction is, and how it differs from that of the categories, we must now determine. Its discovery will, Kant claims, crown and complete our Critical labours.

Kant begins by drawing a distinction between representing *an object absolutely*, and representing *an object in the Idea*.

"In the former case our concepts are employed to determine the object, in the latter case there is in truth only a schema for which no object, not even a hypothetical one, is directly given, and which only enables us to represent to ourselves indirectly other objects in their systematic unity, by means of their relation to this Idea."[4]

An Idea is only a schema (Kant in terms of A 655 = B 693 ought rather to have said *analogon* of a schema) whereby we represent to ourselves, as for instance in the concept of a Highest Intelligence, not an objective reality but only such perfection of Reason as will tend to the greatest possible unity in the empirical employment of understanding.

With this introduction, Kant ushers in his famous "*als ob*" doctrine. We must view the things of the world *as if* they derived their existence from a Highest Intelligence. That Idea is heuristic only, not expository. Its purpose is not to enable us to comprehend such a Being, or even to think its existence, but only to show us how we should seek to determine the constitution and connection of the objects of experience. The three transcendental Ideas do not determine an object corresponding to them, but, *under the presupposition of such an object in the Idea*, lead us to systematic unity of *empirical* knowledge. When they are thus strictly interpreted as merely regulative of empirical enquiry, they will always endorse experience and never run counter to it. Reason, which seeks completeness of explanation, must therefore always act in accordance with them. Only thereby can experience acquire its fullest possible extension. This is the transcendental deduction of which we are in search. It establishes the indispensableness of the Ideas of Reason for the completion of experience, and their legitimacy as regulative principles.

We may here interrupt Kant's exposition so far as to

[1] Cf. above, pp. 446-7.
[3] Cf. *per contra* A 663·4 = B 691·2.
[2] Cf. A 681 = B 709.
[4] A 670 = B 698.

point out that this argument does not do justice to the full force of his position. The true Critical contention—and only if we interpret the passage in the light of this contention can the proof be regarded as transcendental in the strict sense—is that the Ideas are necessary to the possibility of each and every experience, involved together with the categories as conditions of the very existence of consciousness. They are not merely regulative, but are regulative of an experience which they also help to make possible.[1] They express the standards in whose light we condemn all knowledge which does not fulfil them ; and we have consequently no option save to endeavour to conform to their demands. In other words, they are not derivative concepts obtained by merely omitting the restrictions essential to our empirical consciousness, but represent a presupposition necessarily involved in all consciousness. Some such restatement of the argument is demanded by the position which Kant has himself outlined in A 645 = B 673 and in A 650 ff. = B 678 ff. Unfortunately he does not return to it. The more sceptical view which he has meantime been developing remains dominant. The deduction is left in this semi-Critical form.

A 672-6 = B 700-4 give a fuller statement of the "*als ob*" doctrine. In psychology we must proceed *as if* the mind were a simple substance endowed with personal identity [2] (in this life at least), not in order to derive explanation of its changing states from the soul so conceived, but to derive them from each other in accordance with the Idea. In cosmology and theology (we may observe the straits to which Kant is reduced in his attempt to distinguish them) we ought to consider all phenomena both in their series and in their totality *as if* they were due to a highest and all-sufficient unitary ground. In so doing we shall not derive the order and system in the world from the object of the Idea, but only extract from the Idea the rule whereby the understanding attains the greatest possible satisfaction in the connecting of natural causes and effects.

---

[1] I may here guard against misunderstanding. Though the Ideas of Reason condition the experience which they regulate, this must not be taken as nullifying Kant's fundamental distinction between the regulative and the constitutive. Even when he is developing his less sceptical view, he adopts, in metaphysics as in ethics, a position which is radically distinct from that of Hegel. Though the moral ideal represents reality of the highest order, it transcends all possible realisation of itself in human life. Though it conditions all our morality, it at the same time condemns it. The Christian virtue of humility defines the only attitude proper to the human soul. In an exactly similar manner, the fact that the Ideas of Reason have to be regarded as conditioning the possibility of sense-experience need not prevent us from also recognising that they likewise make possible our consciousness of its limitations.   [2] Cf. above, pp. 473-7.

In A 676-7 = B 704-5 Kant resorts to still another distinction—between *suppositio relativa* and *suppositio absoluta*. This distinction is suggested by the semi-objectivity of principles that are merely regulative. Though we have to recognise them as necessary, such necessity does not justify the assertion of their independent validity. When we admit a supreme ground as the source of the order and system which the principles demand, we do so only in order to think the universality of the principles with greater definiteness. Such supposition is relative to the needs of Reason in its *empirical* employment: not absolute, as pointing to the existence of such a being in itself.

" This explains why, in relation to what is given to the senses as existing, we require the Idea of a primordial Being necessary in itself, and yet can never form the slightest concept of it or of its absolute necessity." [1]

This last statement leads to the further problem to which Kant here gives his final solution, how if, as has been shown in the *Dialectic*, the concepts of absolute necessity and of unconditionedness are without meaning, the Ideas of Reason can be entertained at all, even mentally. What is their actual content and how is it possible to conceive them? Kant's reply is developed in terms of the semi-Critical subjectivist point of view which dominates this section. The Ideas are mere Ideas. They yield not the slightest concept either of the internal possibility or of the necessity of any object corresponding to them. They only seem to do so, owing to a transcendental illusion. On examination we find that the concepts which we employ in thinking them as independently real, are one and all derived from experience. That is to say, we judge of them after the analogy of reality, substance, causality, and necessity in the sensible world. [2]

"[They are consequently] *analoga* only of real things, not real things in themselves. We remove from the object of the Idea the conditions which limit the concept of the understanding, but which at the same time alone make it possible for us to have a determinate concept of anything. What we then think is, therefore, a something of which, as it is in itself, we have no concept whatsoever, but which we none the less represent to ourselves as standing in a relation to the sum-total of appearances analogous to that in which appearances stand to one another." [3]

---

[1] A 679 = B 707.   [2] A 678 = B 706.
[3] A 674 = B 702. Cf. A 678-9 = B 706-7.

They do not carry our knowledge beyond the objects of possible experience, but only extend the empirical unity of experience. They are the schemata of regulative principles. In them Reason is concerned with nothing but its own inherent demands; and as their unity is the unity of a system which is to be sought only in experience,[1] qualities derived from the sensible world can quite legitimately be employed in their specific determination. They are not inherently dialectical; their demands have the rationality which we have a right to expect in the Ideals of Reason. When Critically examined, they propound no problem which Reason is not in itself entirely competent to solve.[2] It is to their misemployment that transcendental illusion is due. In the form in which they arise from the natural disposition of our Reason they are good and serviceable.[3]

To the question what is the most adequate form in which the regulative schema can be represented,[4] Kant gives an answer which shows how very far he is from regarding the Leibnizian *Ens realissimum* as the true expression of the Ideal of Reason. It is through the employment of teleological concepts that we can best attain the highest possible form of systematic unity.

"The highest formal unity . . . is the *purposive* unity of things. The *speculative* [*i.e.* theoretical] interest of Reason makes it necessary to regard all order in the world *as if* it had originated in the purpose of a Supreme Reason. Such a principle opens out to our Reason, as applied in the field of experience, altogether new views as to how the things of the world may be connected according to teleological laws, and so enables it to arrive at their greatest systematic unity. The assumption of a Supreme Intelligence, as the one and only cause of the universe, though in the Idea alone, can therefore always benefit Reason and can never injure it."[5]

For so long as this assumption is employed only as a regulative principle, even error cannot be really harmful. The worst that can happen is that where we expected a teleological connection, a merely mechanical or physical one is met with. If, on the other hand, we leave the solid ground of experience, and use the assumption to explain what we are unable to account for in empirical terms, we sacrifice all real insight, and confound Reason by transforming a concept, which is anthropomorphically determined for the

---

[1] A 680 = B 708.
[2] As above noted (pp. 499 ff.), when we find Kant thus insisting upon the completely soluble character of all problems of pure Reason, the sceptical, subjectivist tendency is dominant.
[3] A 669 = B 697.　[4] Cf. above, pp. 536-7, 541-2.　[5] A 686-7 = B 714-15.

purposes of empirical orientation, into a means of explaining order as non-natural and as imposed from without on the material basis of things.

This is a point of sufficient importance to call for more detailed statement. Hume in his *Dialogues* points out that the main defect in the teleological proof of God's existence is its assumption that order and design are foreign to the inherent constitution of things, and must be of non-natural origin. The argument is therefore weakened by every advance in the natural sciences. It also runs directly counter to the very phenomena, those of animal life, upon which it is chiefly based, since the main characteristic of the organic in its distinction from the inorganic is its inner wealth of productive and reproductive powers. With these criticisms Kant is in entire agreement. From them, in the passage before us, he derives an argument in support of a strictly regulative interpretation of his "*als ob*" doctrine. The avowed intention of the teleological argument is to prove *from nature* the existence of an intelligent supreme cause. If therefore its standpoint be held to with more consistency than its own defenders have hitherto shown, it will be found to rest upon the regulative principle, that we must study nature as if an *inherent* order were *native* to it, and so seek to approach by degrees, in proportion as such *natural unity* is empirically discovered, the absolute perfection which inspires our researches. But if we transform our Ideal into an instrument of explanation, beginning with what ought properly to be only our goal, we delude ourselves with the belief that what can only be acquired through the slow and tentative labours of empirical enquiry is already in our possession.

"If I begin with a supreme purposive Being as the ground of all things, the unity of nature is really surrendered, as being quite foreign and accidental to the nature of things, and as not to be known from its own general laws. There thus arises a vicious circle: we are assuming just that very point which is mainly in dispute."[1]

Such a method of argument is self-destructive, since if we do not find order and perfection in the nature of things, and *therefore in their general and necessary laws*, we are not in a position to infer such a Being as the source of all causality.

To the question whether we may not interpret natural order, once it has been discovered by empirical investigation, as due to the divine will, Kant replies that such procedure is allowable only on the condition that it is the same to us

---

[1] A 693=B 721. Cf. above, p. 539.

whether we say that God has wisely willed it or that nature has wisely arranged it.   We may admit the Idea of a Supreme Being only in so far as it is required by Reason as the regulative principle of all investigation of *nature*;

" . . . and we cannot, therefore, without contradicting ourselves, ignore the general laws of nature in view of which the Idea was adopted, and look upon the purposiveness of nature as contingent and hyper-physical in its origin.   For we were not justified in assuming above nature a Being of those qualities, but only in adopting the Idea of it in order to be able to view the appearances, according to the analogy of a causal determination, as systematically connected with one another." [1]   "Thus pure Reason, which at first seemed to promise nothing less than the extension of knowledge beyond all limits of experience, contains, if properly understood, nothing but regulative principles. . . ." [2]

CONCLUDING COMMENT ON THE DIALECTIC

I may now summarise Kant's answer to the three main questions of the *Dialectic*: (1) Whether, or in what degree, the so-called Ideas of Reason are concepts due to a faculty altogether distinct from the understanding, and how far, as thus originating in pure Reason, they allow of definition; (2) how far they are capable of a transcendental deduction; (3) what kind of objective validity this deduction proves them to possess.

These questions are closely interconnected; the solution of any one determines the kind of solution to be given to all three.   Kant, as we have found, develops his final position through a series of very subtle distinctions by which he contrives to justify and retain, though in a highly modified form, the more crudely stated divisions between Ideas and categories, between Reason and understanding, upon which the initial argument of the *Dialectic* is based.

The answer amounts in essentials to the conclusion that understanding, in directing itself by means of Ideals, exercises a function so distinct from that whereby it conditions concrete and specific experience, that it may well receive a separate title; that the Ideas in terms of which it constructs these Ideals, though schematic (*i.e.* sensuous and empirical in content), are not themselves empirical, and so far from being merely extended concepts of understanding, express transcendental conditions upon which all use of the understanding rests.

[1] A 699-700 = B 727-8.   [2] A 701 = B 729.

Now if this position is to be justified, Kant ought to show that the fundamental Idea of Reason, that of the unconditioned, is altogether distinct from any concept of the understanding, and in particular that it must not be identified with the category of totality, nor be viewed as being merely the concept of conditioned existence with its various empirical limitations thought away. Needless to say, Kant does not fulfil these requirements in any consistent manner. The *Critique* contains the material for a variety of different solutions; it does not definitively commit itself to any one of them.

If the argument of A 650 ff. = B 678 ff. were developed, we should be in possession of what may be called the Idealist solution. It would proceed somewhat as follows. Consciousness as such is always the awareness of a whole which precedes and conditions its parts. Such consciousness cannot be accounted for on the assumption that we are first conscious of the conditioned, and then proceed to remove limitations and to form for ourselves, by means of the more positive factors involved in this antecedent consciousness, an Idea of the totality within which the given falls. The Idea of the unconditioned, distinct from all concepts of understanding, is one of the *a priori* conditions of possible experience, and is capable of a transcendental deduction of equal validity with, and of the same general nature as, that of the categories. It is presupposed in the possibility of our contingently given experience.

As this Idea conditions all subordinate concepts, it cannot be defined in terms of them. That does not, however, deprive it of all meaning; its significance is of a unique kind; it finds expression in those Ideals which, while guiding the mind in the construction of experience, also serve as the criteria through which experience is condemned as only phenomenal.

But this, as we have found, is not a line of argument which Kant has developed in any detail. The passages which point to it occur chiefly in the introductory portions of the *Dialectic*; in its later sections they are both brief and scanty. When he sets himself, as in the chapter on the *Ideal of Pure Reason* and in the subsequent *Appendix*, to define his conclusions, it is a much more empirical, and indeed sceptical, line that he almost invariably follows. There are, he then declares, strictly no pure, *a priori* Ideas. The supposed Ideas of unconditionedness and of absolute necessity are discovered on examination to be without the least significance for the mind. The Ideas, properly defined, are merely schemata of regulative principles, and their whole content reduces without remainder to such categories as totality, substance, causality, necessity, transcendently applied. As *Ideas*, they are then without real meaning; but they can be employed by analogy to define an Ideal which serves an indispensable function in the extension of experience. From this point of view, the transcendental deduction of the Ideas is radically distinct from that of the categories. The proof is not that they are necessary for the possibility of experience, but only that they are required for its perfect, or at least more complete, development. And as Kant is unable to prove that such completion is really possible, the objective validity of the Ideas is left open to question. They should be taken only as heuristic principles; the extent of their truth, even in the empirical realm, cannot be determined by the *a priori* method that is alone proper to a *Critique of Pure Reason.*

The first view is inspired by the fundamental teaching of the *Analytic*, and is the only view which will justify Kant in retaining his distinction between appearance and things in themselves. All that is positive in the second view can be combined with the first view; but, on the other hand, the negative implications of the second view are at variance with its own positive teaching. For when the Ideas are regarded as empirical in origin no less than in function, their entire authority is derived from experience, and cannot be regarded as being transcendental in any valid sense of that term. In alternating between these two interpretations of the function of Reason, Kant is wavering between the Idealist and the merely sceptical view of the scope and powers of pure thought. On the Idealist interpretation Reason is a metaphysical faculty, revealing to us the phenomenal character of experience, and outlining possibilities such as may perhaps be established on moral grounds. From the sceptical standpoint, on the other hand, Reason gives expression to what may be only our subjective preference for unity and system in the ordering of experience. According to the one, the criteria of truth and reality are bound up with the Ideas; according to the other, sense-experience is the standard by which the validity even of the Ideas must ultimately be judged. From the fact that Kant should have continued sympathetically to develop two such opposite standpoints, we would seem to be justified in concluding that he discerned, or at least desiderated, some more complete reconciliation of their teaching than he has himself thus far been able to achieve, and that no solution which would either subordinate the Ideal demands of thought, or ignore the gifts of experience, could ever have been definitively accepted by him as satisfactorily meeting the issues at stake. The Idealist solution is that to which his teaching as a whole most decisively points; but he is as conscious of the difficulties which lie in its path as he is personally convinced of its ultimate truth. His continuing appreciation of the value of sceptical teaching is a tacit admission that the Idealist doctrines, in the form which he has so far been able to give to them, are not really adequate to the complexity of the problems. As further confirmation of the tentative character of Kant's conclusions in the *Critique of Pure Reason*, we have his own later writings. In the *Critique of Judgment*, published nine years later, in teaching less sceptical and more constructive, though still delicately balanced between the competing possibilities, and always, therefore, leaving the final decision to moral considerations, Kant ventures upon a restatement of the problems of the *Dialectic*. To this restatement both of the above tendencies contribute valuable elements.

APPENDIX A[1]

TRANSCENDENTAL DOCTRINE OF METHODS

CHAPTER I

THE DISCIPLINE[2] OF PURE REASON

KANT is neither an intellectualist nor an anti-intellectualist. Reason, the proper duty of which is to prescribe a discipline to all other endeavours, itself requires discipline; and when it is employed in the metaphysical sphere, independently of experience, it demands not merely the correction of single errors, but the eradication of their causes through "a separate negative code," such as a Critical philosophy can alone supply. In the *Transcendental Doctrine of Elements* this demand has been met as regards the *materials* or *contents* of the Critical system; we are now concerned only with its *methods* or *formal conditions*.[3]

This distinction is highly artificial. As already indicated, it is determined by the requirements of Kant's architectonic. The entire teaching of the *Methodology* has already been more or less exhaustively expounded in the earlier divisions of the *Critique*.

SECTION I

THE DISCIPLINE OF PURE REASON IN ITS DOGMATIC EMPLOYMENT

In dealing with the distinction between mathematical and philosophical knowledge, Kant is here returning to one of the

---

[1] Nearly all the important points raised in the *Methodology*, and several of its chief sections, I have commented upon in their connection with the earlier parts of the *Critique*. Also, the *Methodology* is extremely diffuse. For these reasons I have found it advisable to give such additional comment as seems necessary in the form of this Appendix.

[2] On Kant's use of the terms 'discipline' and 'canon,' cf. above, pp. 71-2, 170, 174, 438. [3] Cf. above, p. 438.

main points of his *Introduction* to the *Critique*.[1] His most exhaustive treatment of it is, however, to be found in a treatise which he wrote as early as 1764, his *Enquiry into the Clearness of the Principles of Natural Theology and Morals.* The continuing influence of the teaching of that early work is obvious throughout this section, and largely accounts for the form in which certain of its tenets are propounded.

". . . one can say with Bishop Warburton that nothing has been more injurious to philosophy than mathematics, that is, than the imitation of its method in a sphere where it is impossible of application. . . ."[2]

So far from being identical in general nature, mathematics and philosophy are, Kant declares, fundamentally opposed in all essential features. For it is in their methods, and not merely in their subject-matter, that the essential difference between them is to be found.[3] Philosophical knowledge can be acquired only through *concepts*, mathematical knowledge is gained through the *construction* of concepts.[4] The one is discursive merely; the other is intuitive. Philosophy can consider the particular only in the general; mathematics studies the general in the particular.[5] Philosophical concepts, such as those of substance and causality, are, indeed, capable of application in transcendental synthesis, but in this employment they yield only empirical knowledge of the sensuously given; and from empirical concepts the universal and necessary judgments required for the possibility of metaphysical science can never be obtained.

The exactness of mathematics depends on definitions, axioms, and demonstrations, none of which are obtainable in philosophy. To take each in order.

I. **Definitions.**—To define in the manner prescribed by mathematics is to represent the *complete* concept of a thing. This is never possible in regard to empirical concepts. We are more certain of their denotation than of their connotation; and though they may be *explained*, they cannot be defined. Since new observations add or remove predicates, an empirical concept is always liable to modification.

"What useful purpose could be served by defining an empirical concept, such, for instance, as that of water? When we speak of

---

[1] A 4-5 = B 8-9.
[2] *Untersuchung: Zweite Betrachtung, W.* ii. p. 283.
[3] Kant here disavows the position of the *Untersuchung* in which (*Erste Betrachtung*, § 4) he had asserted that mathematics deals with quantity and philosophy with qualities.
[4] For comment upon this distinction, cf. above, pp. 131-3, 338-9.
[5] *Untersuchung: Erste Betrachtung*, § 2.

water and its properties, we do not stop short at what is thought in the word water, but proceed to experiments. The word, with the few marks which are attached to it, is more properly to be regarded as merely a designation than as a conception. The so-called definition is nothing more than a determining of the word." [1]

Exact definition is equally impossible in regard to *a priori* forms, such as time or causality. Since they are not framed by the mind, but are *given* to it, the completeness of our analysis of them can never be guaranteed. Though they are known, they are known only as problems.

"As Augustine has said, 'I know well what time is, but if any one asks me, I cannot tell.' " [2]

Mathematical definitions *make* concepts; philosophical definitions only explain them. [3] Philosophy cannot, therefore, imitate mathematics by beginning with definitions. In philosophy the incomplete exposition must precede the complete; definitions are the final outcome of our enquiry, and not as in mathematics the only possible beginning of its proofs. Indeed, the mathematical concept may be said to be given by the very process in which it is constructively defined; and, as thus originating in the process of definition, it can never be erroneous. [4] Philosophy, on the other hand, swarms with faulty definitions, which are none the less serviceable.

"In mathematics definition belongs *ad esse*, in philosophy *ad melius esse*. It is desirable to attain it, but often very difficult. Jurists are still without a definition of their concept of Right." [5]

II. **Axioms.**—This paragraph is extremely misleading as a statement of Kant's view regarding the nature of geometrical axioms. In stating that they are self-evident, [6] he does not really mean to assert what that phrase usually involves, namely, absolute *a priori* validity. For Kant the geometrical axioms are merely descriptions of certain *de facto* properties of the given intuition of space. They have the merely hypothetical validity of all propositions that refer to the contingently

---

[1] A 728 = B 756.
[2] *Untersuchung: Zweite Betrachtung*, W. ii. p. 283.
[3] *Untersuchung: Erste Betrachtung*, § 1, W. ii. p. 276: "Mathematics proceeds to all its definitions by a *synthetic* procedure, philosophy by an analytic procedure."
[4] In the *Untersuchung* Kant's statements are more cautious, and also more adequate. Cf. *Erste Betrachtung*, § 3, W. ii. p. 279: "In mathematics there are only a few but in philosophy there are innumerable irresolvable concepts. . . ."
[5] A 731 n. = B 759 n.
[6] The phrases which Kant employs (A 732-3 = B 760-1) are: "*unmittelbargewiss*," "*evident*," "*augenscheinlich*." Cf. above, pp. xxxv-vi, 36 ff., 53.

given. For even as a pure intuition, space belongs to the realm of the merely factual.[1] This un-Critical opposition of the self-evidence of geometrical axioms to the synthetic character of such "philosophical" truths as the principle of causality is bound up with Kant's unreasoned conviction that space in order to be space at all, must be Euclidean.[2] Kant's reference in this paragraph to the propositions of arithmetic is equally open to criticism. For though he is more consistent in recognising their synthetic character, he still speaks as if they could be described as self-evident, *i.e.* as immediately certain. The cause of this inconsistency is, of course, to be found in his intuitional theory of mathematical science. Mathematical propositions are obtained through intuition; those of philosophy call for an elaborate and difficult process of transcendental deduction. When modern mathematical theory rejects this intuitional view, it is really extending to mathematical concepts Kant's own interpretation of the function of the categories. Concepts condition the *possibility* of intuitional experience, and find in this conditioning power the ground of their objective validity.[3] Here, as in the *Aesthetic*,[4] Kant fails adequately to distinguish between the problems of pure and applied mathematics.

III. **Demonstrations.**—Kant again introduces his very unsatisfactory doctrine of the construction of concepts:[5] and he even goes so far as to maintain, in complete violation of his own doctrine of transcendental deduction, that where there is no intuition, there can be no demonstration. Apodictic propositions, he declares, are either *dogmata* or *mathemata*; and the former are beyond the competence of the human mind. But no sooner has he made these statements than he virtually withdraws them by adding that, though apodictic propositions cannot be established directly from concepts, they can be indirectly proved by reference to something purely contingent, namely, possible experience. Thus the principle of causality can be apodictically proved as a condition of possible experience. Though it may not be called a *dogma*, it can be entitled a *principle*! In explanation of this distinction, which betrays a lingering regard for the self-evident maxims of rationalistic teaching, Kant adds that the principle of causality, though a principle, has itself to be proved.

"... it has the peculiarity that it first makes possible its own ground of proof, namely, experience...."[6]

---

[1] Cf. above, pp. 118, 142, 185-6.
[2] Cf. above, pp. 38-42, 93-4, 118-20, 133.
[5] Cf. above, p. 131 ff.
[2] Cf. above, p. 117 ff.
[4] Cf. above, pp. 111-12, 114-15.
[6] A 737 = B 765.

This, as we have noted,[1] is exactly what mathematical axioms must also be able to do, if they are to establish their objective validity.

SECTION II

THE DISCIPLINE OF PURE REASON IN ITS POLEMICAL EMPLOYMENT

This section contains an admirable defence of the value of scepticism.

" Even poisons have their use. They serve to counteract other poisons generated in our system, and must have a place in every complete pharmacopeia. The objections against the persuasions and complacency of our purely speculative Reason arise from the very nature of Reason itself, and must therefore have their own good use and purpose, which ought not to be disdained. Why has Providence placed many things which are closely bound up with our highest interests so far beyond our reach, that we are only permitted to apprehend them in a manner lacking in clearness and subject to doubt, in such fashion that our enquiring gaze is more excited than satisfied? It is at least doubtful whether it serves any useful purpose, and whether it is not, indeed, perhaps even harmful to venture upon bold interpretations of such uncertain appearances. But there can be no manner of doubt that it is always best to grant Reason complete liberty, both of enquiry and of criticism, so that it may be without hindrance in attending to its own proper interests. These interests are no less furthered by the limitation than by the extension of its speculations ; and they will always suffer when outside influences intervene to divert it from its natural path, and to constrain it by what is irrelevant to its own proper ends." [2]   " Whenever I hear that a writer of real ability has demonstrated away the freedom of the human will, the hope of a future life, and the existence of God, I am eager to read the book, for I expect him by his talents to increase my insight into these matters." [3]

---

[1] Cf. above, pp. 36 ff., 117 ff., 128 ff., 565·6.   [2] A 743·4 = B 771·2.
[3] A 753 = B 781.   In A 745 = B 773 Kant's mention of Hume can hardly refer to Hume's *Dialogues* (cf. above, pp. 539-40 *n.*).   Kant probably has in mind Section XI. of the *Enquiry*.   The important discussion of Hume's position in A 760 ff. = B 788 ff. has been commented upon above, p. 61 ff.   With Priestley's teaching (A 745·6 = B 773·4) Kant probably became acquainted through some indirect source.   The first of Priestley's philosophical writings to appear in German was his *History of the Corruptions of Christianity*.   The translation was published in 1782.   In A 747·8 = B 775·6 Kant quite obviously has Rousseau in mind.

SECTION IV[1]

THE DISCIPLINE OF PURE REASON IN REGARD TO ITS PROOFS [2]

This section merely restates the general nature and requirements of transcendental proof. The exposition is much less satisfactory than that already given in the *Analytic* and *Dialectic*. The only really new factor is the distinction between apagogical and direct proof. The former may produce conviction, but cannot enable us to comprehend the grounds of the truth of our conviction. Also, outside mathematics, it is extremely dangerous to attempt to establish a thesis by showing its contradictory to be impossible.[3] This is especially true in the sphere of our Critical enquiries, since the chief danger to be guarded against is the confounding of the subjectively necessary with the independently real. In this field of investigation it is never permissible to attempt to justify a synthetic proposition by refuting its opposite. Such seeming proofs can easily be secured, and have been the favourite weapons of dogmatic thinkers.

"Each must defend his position directly, by a legitimate proof that carries with it transcendental deduction of the grounds upon which it is itself made to rest. Only when this has been done, are we in a position to decide how far its claims allow of rational justification. If an opponent relies on subjective grounds, it is an easy matter to refute him. The dogmatist cannot, however, profit by this advantage. His own judgments are, as a rule, no less dependent upon subjective influences; and he can himself in turn be similarly cornered. But if both parties proceed by the direct method, *either* they will soon discover the difficulty, nay, the impossibility, of showing reason for their assertions, and will be left with no resort save to appeal to some form of prescriptive authority; *or* the *Critique* will the more easily discover the illusion to which their dogmatic procedure is due; and pure Reason will be compelled to relinquish its exaggerated pretensions in the realm of speculation, and to withdraw within the limits of its proper territory—that of practical principles."[4]

---

[1] Section III., on *The Discipline of Pure Reason in Regard to Hypotheses*, has been commented on above, pp. 543-6.   [2] A 782 = B 810.

[3] Even in mathematics the indirect method is not always available. Cf. Russell. *Principles of Mathematics*, i. p. 15.   [4] A 794 = B 822.

CHAPTER II

THE CANON[1] OF PURE REASON

SECTION I

THE ULTIMATE END OF THE PURE USE OF OUR REASON[2]

The problems of the existence of God, the freedom of the will, and the immortality of the soul have, Kant declares, little *theoretical* interest. For, as he has already argued, even if we were justified in postulating God, freedom, and immortality, they would not enable us to account for the phenomena of sense-experience, the only objects of possible knowledge. But the three problems are also connected with our *practical* interests, and in that reference they constitute the chief subject of metaphysical enquiry.[3] The practical is whatever is possible through freedom ; and the decision as to *what we ought to do* is the supreme interest of pure Reason in its highest employment.

". . . the ultimate intention of Nature in her wise provision for us has indeed, in the constitution of our Reason, been directed to our moral interests alone."[4]

This is the position which Kant endeavours to establish in his *Foundations of the Metaphysics of Morals*, and in the *Critique of Practical Reason*. The very brief outline which he here gives of his argument is necessarily incomplete ; and is in consequence somewhat misleading. He first disposes of the problem of freedom ; and does so in a manner which shows that he had not, when this section was composed, developed his Critical views on the nature of moral freedom. He is for the present content to draw a quite un-Critical

---

[1] Cf. above, p. 563 *n.* 2.   [2] A 797 = B 825.
[3] Cf. *Critique of Judgment, W.* v. p. 473 ; Bernard's trans. p. 411 : "*God, freedom,* and *immortality* are the problems at the solution of which all the preparations of Metaphysics aim, as their ultimate and unique purpose."
[4] A 800-1 = B 829.

distinction between transcendental and practical freedom.[1]
The latter belongs to the will in so far as it is determined by
Reason alone, independently of sensuous impulses. Reason
prescribes objective *laws of freedom*, and the will under the
influence of these laws overcomes the affections of sense.
Such practical freedom can, Kant asserts, be proved by experience to be a natural cause. Transcendental freedom,[2]
on the other hand, *i.e.* the power of making a new beginning
in the series of phenomena, is a problem which can never be
empirically solved. It is a purely speculative question with
which Reason in its practical employment is not in the least
concerned. The canon of pure Reason has therefore to deal
only with the two remaining problems, God and immortality.
Comment upon these assertions can best be made in connection with the argument of the next section.[3]

SECTION II

THE IDEAL OF THE HIGHEST GOOD, AS A DETERMINING
GROUND OF THE ULTIMATE END OF PURE REASON [4]

Reason in its speculative employment transcends experience, but solely for the sake of experience. In other words,
speculative Reason has a purely empirical function. (This is
the explanation of the somewhat paradoxical contention, to
which Kant has already committed himself, that the problems
of God and immortality, *though seemingly speculative in
character*, really originate in our practical interests.) But
pure Reason has also a practical use; and it is in this latter
employment that it first discloses the genuinely metaphysical
character of its present constitution and ultimate aims. The
moral consciousness, in revealing to us an Ideal of absolute
value, places in our hands the only available key to the
mysteries of existence. As this moral consciousness represents the deepest reality of human life, it may be expected
to have greater metaphysical significance than anything else
in human experience; and since the ends which it reveals
also present themselves as *absolute* in value, and are indeed
the only absolute values of which we can form any conception,
this conclusion would seem to be confirmed.

Happiness has natural value; morality, *i.e.* the being

---

[1] The statement in A 801 = B 829 that morals is a subject foreign to transcendental philosophy is in line with that of A 14-15 = B 28, and conflicts with the
position later adopted in the *Critique of Practical Reason*. Cf. above, p. 77.
[2] A 803 = B 831-2.   [3] Cf. below, pp. 571-5.   [4] A 804 = B 832.

worthy to be happy, has absolute value. The means of attaining the former obtain expression in prudential or pragmatic laws that are empirically grounded. The conditions of the latter are embodied in a categorical imperative of an *a priori* character. The former *advise* us how best to satisfy our natural desire for happiness; the latter *dictates* to us how we must behave in order to deserve happiness.

Kant's further argument is too condensed to be really clear, and if adequately discussed would carry us quite beyond the legitimate limits of this *Commentary*. I shall therefore confine myself to a brief and free restatement of his general position. The Critical teaching can be described as resulting in a new interpretation of the function of philosophy.[1] The task of the philosopher, properly viewed, does not consist in the solution of *speculative* problems; such problems transcend our human powers. All that philosophy can reasonably attempt is to analyse and define the situations, cognitive and practical, in which, owing to the specific conditions of human existence, we find ourselves to be placed. Upon analysis of the cognitive situation Kant discovers that while all possibilities are open, the theoretical data are never such as to justify ontological assertions.[2] When, however, he passes to the practical situation, wider horizons, definitely outlined, at once present themselves. The moral consciousness is the key to the meaning of the entire universe as well as of human life. Its values are the sole ultimate values, and enable us to interpret in *moral* terms (even though we cannot comprehend in any genuinely *theoretical* fashion) the meaning of the dispensation under which we live. The moral consciousness, like sense-experience, discloses upon examination a systematic unity of presupposed conditions. In the theoretical sphere this unity cannot be proved to be more than a postulated Ideal of *empirical* experience; and it is an Ideal which, even if granted to have absolute validity, is too indefinite to enable us to assert that ultimate reality is spiritual in character, or is teleologically ordered. The underlying conditions, on the other hand, of practical experience have from the start a purely noumenal reference. They have no other function than to define, in terms of the moral consciousness, the ultimate meaning of reality as a whole. They postulate[3] a universe in which the values of spiritual experience are supported and conserved.

[1] Cf. above, p. lvi.
[2] These statements are subject to modification, if the distinction (not clearly recognised by Kant, but really essential to his position) between immanent and transcendent metaphysics is insisted upon. Cf. above, pp. liv-v, 22, 56, 66-70.
[3] Cf. above, p. 541.

But the main difference in Kant's treatment of the two situations, cognitive and practical, only emerges into view when we recognise the differing modes in which the transcendental method of proof is applied in the two cases. The *a priori* forms of sensibility, understanding, and Reason are proved by reference to possible experience, as being its indispensable conditions. In moral matters, however, we must not appeal to experience. The actual is no test of the Ideal; "what is" is no test of what ought to be. And secondly, the moral law, if valid at all, must apply not merely within the limits of experience, but with absolute universality to all rational beings. The moral law, therefore, can neither be given us in experience, nor be proved as one of the conditions necessary to its possibility. Its validity, in other words, can be established neither through experience nor through theoretical reason.

Though such is Kant's own method of formulating the issue, it exaggerates the difference of his procedure in the two *Critiques*, and is very misleading as a statement of his real position. In one passage, in the *Critique of Practical Reason*,[1] Kant does, indeed, assert that the moral law requires no deduction. It is, he claims, a *fact* of which we are *a priori* conscious: so far from itself requiring proof, it enables us to prove the reality of freedom. Yet in the very same section he argues that the deduction of freedom from the moral law is a credential of the latter, and is a sufficient substitute for all *a priori* justification. According to the first statement we have an immediate consciousness of the validity of the moral law; according to the second statement the moral law proves itself indirectly, by serving as a principle for the deduction of freedom. The second form of statement alone harmonises with the argument developed in the third section of the *Foundations of the Metaphysics of Morals*, and more correctly expresses the intention of Kant's central argument in the *Critique of Practical Reason*. For the difference between the two transcendental proofs in the two *Critiques* does not really consist in any diversity of method, but solely in the differing character of the premises from which each starts. The ambiguity of Kant's argument in the second *Critique* seems chiefly to be caused by his failure clearly to recognise that the moral law, though a form of pure Reason, exercises, in the process of its transcendental proof, a function which exactly corresponds to that which is discharged by possible experience in the first *Critique*. Our consciousness of the moral law is, like sense-experience, a given fact. It is *de*

---

[1] *W.* v. pp. 47-8; Abbott's trans. (3rd edition) p. 136.

facto, and cannot be deduced from anything more ultimate than itself.[1] But as given, it enables us to deduce its transcendental conditions. This does not mean that our immediate consciousness of it *as given* guarantees its validity. The nature of its validity is established only in the process whereby it reveals its necessary implications. The objects of sense-experience are assumed by ordinary consciousness to be absolutely real; in the process of establishing the transcendental conditions of such experience they are discovered to be merely phenomenal. The pure principles of understanding thus gain objective validity as the conditions of a given experience which reveals only appearances. Ordinary consciousness similarly starts from the assumption of the absolute validity of the moral law. But in this case the consciousness of the law is discovered on examination to be explicable, *even as a possibility*, only on the assumption that it is due to the autonomous activity of a noumenal being. By its existence it proves the conditions through which alone it is explicable. Its mere existence suffices to prove that its validity is objective in a deeper and truer sense than the principles of understanding. *The notion of freedom, and therefore all the connected Ideas of pure Reason, gain noumenal reality as the conditions of a moral consciousness which is incapable of explanation as illusory or even phenomenal.* Since the consciousness of the moral law is thus noumenally grounded, it has a validity with which nothing in the phenomenal world can possibly compare. It is the one form in which noumenal reality directly discloses itself to the human mind.[2]

Obviously the essential crux of Kant's argument lies in the proof that the moral consciousness *is* only explicable in this manner, as the self-legislation of a noumenal being. Into the merits of his argument we cannot, however, here enter; and I need only draw attention to the manner in which it conflicts with the statement of the preceding section, that the possibility of transcendental freedom is a purely speculative question with which practical Reason is not concerned. The reality of freedom, as a form of noumenal activity, is the cardinal fact of Kant's metaphysics of morals. For though our consciousness

[1] Cf. *Critique of Practical Reason*, *W*. v. pp. 31-7; Abbott's trans. p. 120.
[2] Cf. *Critique of Practical Reason*, *W*. v. p. 43; Abbott's trans. p. 132: "The moral law, although it gives no *view*, yet gives us a fact absolutely inexplicable from any data of the sensible world, or from the whole compass of our theoretical use of reason, a fact which points to a pure world of the understanding, nay, even defines it *positively*, and enables us to know something of it, namely, a law."

of the moral law is the *ratio cognoscendi* of freedom, transcendental freedom is the *ratio essendi* of the moral law.[1]

"With this faculty [of practical Reason], transcendental freedom is also established; freedom, namely, in that absolute sense in which speculative Reason required it, in its use of the concept of causality, in order to escape the antinomy into which it inevitably falls, when in the chain of cause and effect it tries to think the *unconditioned*. . . Freedom is the only one of all the Ideas of the speculative Reason of which we *know* the possibility *a priori* (without, however, understanding it), because it is the condition of the moral law which we know."[2] "[Freedom] is the only one of all the Ideas of pure Reason whose object is a thing of fact and to be reckoned among the *scibilia*."[3] "It is thus very remarkable that of the three pure rational Ideas, God, freedom, and immortality, that of freedom is the only concept of the supersensible which (by means of the causality that is thought in it) proves its objective reality in nature by means of the effects it can produce there; and thus renders possible the connection of both the others with nature, and of all three with one another so as to form a Religion. . . . The concept of freedom (as fundamental concept of all unconditioned practical laws) can extend Reason beyond those bounds within which every natural (theoretical) concept must inevitably remain confined."[4]

Thus freedom is for Kant a demonstrated fact, and in that respect differs from the Ideas of God and immortality, which are merely problematic conceptions, and which can be postulated only as articles of "practical faith."

This brings us to the final question, upon what grounds Kant ascribes validity to the Ideas of God and immortality. At this point in his argument Kant introduces the conception of the *Summum Bonum*. Reason, in prescribing the moral law, prescribes, as the final and complete end of all our actions, the *Summum Bonum*, *i.e.* happiness proportioned to moral worth. *Owing to the limitations of our faculties*, the complete attainment of this supreme end is conceivable by us only on the assumption of a future life wherein perfect worthiness may be attained, and of an omnipotent Divine Being who will apportion happiness in accordance with merit.

"[This Divine Being] must be omnipotent, in order that the whole of nature and its relation to morality . . . may be subject to his will; omniscient, that he may know our innermost sentiments and their moral worth; omnipresent, that he may be immediately

---

[1] Cf. *Critique of Practical Reason*, in note to Preface.
[2] *Op. cit.*, Preface, at the beginning, Abbott's trans. pp. 87-8. Cf. also the concluding pages of Book I., *W.* v. pp. 103-6, Abbott, pp. 197-200.
[3] *Critique of Judgment*, *W.* v. p. 468; Bernard's trans. p. 406.
[4] *Op. cit.* p. 474; Bernard's trans. p. 413.

present for the satisfying of every need which the highest good demands ; eternal, that this harmony of nature and freedom may never fail, etc."[1]

The moral ideal thus supplies us with a ground[2] for regarding the universe as systematically ordered according to moral purposes, and also with a principle that enables us to infer the nature and properties of its Supreme Cause.   In place of a demonology, which is all that physical theology can establish, we construct upon moral grounds a genuine theology.

The concepts thus obtained are, however, anthropomorphic; and for that reason alone must be denied all speculative value.   This is especially evident in regard to the Idea of God.   Owing to our incapacity to comprehend how moral merit can condition happiness, we conceive them as *externally* combined through the intervention of a supreme Judge and Ruler.   As Kant indicates,[3] we must not assert that this represents the actual situation.   He himself seems to have inclined to a more mystical interpretation of the universe, conceiving the relation of happiness to virtue as being grounded in a supersensuous but necessary order that may, indeed, be bodied forth in the inadequate symbols of the deistic creed, but which in its true nature transcends our powers of understanding.   So far as the Ideas of God and immortality are necessary to define the moral standpoint, they have genuine validity for all moral beings ; but if developed on their own account as speculative dogmas, they acquire a definiteness of formulation which is not essential to their moral function, and which lays them open to suspicion even in their legitimate use.

These considerations also indicate Kant's further reason for entitling the *Summum Bonum*, God and immortality, Ideas of *faith*.   Though they can be established as presuppositions of the moral situation in which we find ourselves, such demonstration itself rests upon the acceptance of the moral consciousness as possessing a supersensuous sanction ; and that in turn is determined by features in the moral situation not deducible from any higher order of considerations.

---

[1] A 815 = B 843.

[2] Cf. *Critique of Practical Reason*, *W.* v. pp. 143-4 *n.* ; Abbott's trans. p. 242 : "It is a duty to realise the *Summum Bonum* to the utmost of our power, therefore it must be possible, consequently it is unavoidable for every rational being in the world to assume what is necessary for its objective possibility.   The assumption is as necessary as the moral law, in connexion with which alone it is valid."

[3] Cf. *Critique of Practical Reason*, *W.* v. p. 142 ff. ; Abbott's trans. p. 240 ff. ; *Critique of Judgment*, *W.* v. pp. 469-70 ; Bernard's trans. pp. 406-8.

"Belief in matters of faith is a belief in a pure practical point of view, *i.e.* a moral faith, which proves nothing for theoretical, pure, rational cognition, but only for that which is practical and directed to the fulfilment of its duties; it in no way extends speculation. . . . If the supreme principle of all moral laws is a postulate, the possibility of its highest Object . . . is thereby postulated along with it."[1] "So far, as practical Reason has the right to yield us guidance, we shall not look upon actions as obligatory because they are the commands of God, but shall regard them as divine commands because we have an inward obligation to them. . . . Moral theology is thus of immanent use only. It enables us to fulfil our vocation in this present world by showing us how to adapt ourselves to the system of all ends, and by warning us against the fanaticism and indeed the impiety of abandoning the guidance of a morally legislative Reason in the right conduct of our lives, in order to derive guidance directly from the Idea of the Supreme Being. For we should then be making a transcendent employment of moral theology; and that, like a transcendent use of pure speculation, must pervert and frustrate the ultimate ends of Reason."[2]

SECTION III

OPINING, KNOWING, AND BELIEVING [3]

Kant first distinguishes between conviction (*Ueberzeugung*) and persuasion (*Ueberredung*). A judgment which is objectively grounded, and which is therefore valid for all other rational beings, is affirmed with conviction. When the affirmation is due only to the peculiar character of the subject, the manner in which it is asserted may be entitled persuasion. Persuasion is therefore "a mere illusion."[4] Conviction exists in three degrees, opinion, belief, and knowledge. In opinion we are conscious that the judgment is insufficiently grounded, and that our conviction is subjectively incomplete. In belief the subjective conviction is complete, but is recognised as lacking in objective justification. In knowledge the objective grounds and the subjective conviction are alike complete.

After pointing out that opinion is not permissible in judg-

---

[1] *Critique of Judgment*, *W.* v. pp. 369-72; Bernard's trans. pp. 407-10. Cf. note in same section: "It is a trust in the promise of the moral law; not, however, such as is contained in it, but such as I put into it, and that on morally adequate grounds."

[2] A 819 = B 847.　　　　　　　　　　　　　　　[3] A 820 = B 848.

[4] The distinction is less harshly drawn in Kant's *Logic*, *Einleitung*, ix (Hartenstein), viii. p. 73; Eng. trans. p. 63: "Conviction is opposed to persuasion. Persuasion is an assent from inadequate reasons, in respect to which we do not know whether they are only subjective or are also objective. Persuasion often precedes conviction."

ments of pure Reason,[1] Kant develops the further distinction between *pragmatic or doctrinal belief* and *moral belief.* When a belief is contingent (*i.e.* is affirmed with the consciousness that on fuller knowledge it may turn out to be false), and yet nevertheless supplies a ground for the employment of means to certain desired ends, it may be called *pragmatic* belief. Such belief admits of degree, and can be tested by wager or by oath.[2] What may be called *doctrinal belief* is analogous in character, and is taken by Kant, in somewhat misleading fashion, as describing our mode of accepting such doctrines as the existence of God and the immortality of the soul.[3] They are adopted as helpful towards a contingent but important end, the discovery of order in the system of nature. This account of the nature of Ideas is in line with Kant's early view of them as *merely* regulative. Taken in connection with his repeated employment of the term 'moral sentiments' (*moralische Gesinnungen*), it tends to prove that this section is early in date of writing.

In *moral belief* the end, the *Summum Bonum*, is absolutely necessary, and as there is only one condition under which we can conceive it as being realised, namely, on the assumption of the existence of God and of a future life, the belief in God and immortality possesses the same certainty as the moral sentiments.

"The belief in a God and another world is so interwoven with my moral sentiment that as there is little danger of my losing the latter, there is equally little cause for fear that the former can ever be taken from me."[4]

As I have just suggested, this basing of moral belief upon subjective sentiments, which, as Kant very inconsistently proceeds to suggest, may possibly be lacking in certain men, marks this section as being of early origin. But in concluding the section, in reply to the objection that, in thus tracing such articles of faith to our "natural interest" in morality, philosophy admits its powerlessness to advance beyond the ordinary understanding, Kant propounds one of his abiding convictions, namely, that in matters which concern all men without distinction nature is not guilty of any partial distribution of her gifts, and that in regard to the essential ends of human nature the highest philosophy cannot advance beyond what is

[1] Cf. above, pp. 10, 543. Cf. *Fortschritte* ; *Werke* (Hartenstein), viii. p. 561.
[2] Cf. *Logic, loc. cit.* Cf. *Foundations of the Metaphysics of Morals, W.* iv. pp. 416-17 : Abbott's trans. pp. 33-34.
[3] Regarding Kant's distinction in A 827 = B 855 between Ideas and hypotheses cf. above, p. 543 ff. Cf. also *Critique of Judgment, W.* v. pp. 392 ff., 461 ff. ; Bernard's trans. pp. 302 ff., 395 ff.   [4] A 829 = B 857. Cf. Appendix C.

revealed to the common understanding.[1]   The reverence which
Kant ever cherished for the memory of his parents, and for
the religion which was so natural to them, must have pre-
disposed him to a recognition of the widespread sources of
the spiritual life.   But Kant has himself placed on record
his sense of the great debt which in this connection he also
owed to the teaching of Rousseau.

"I am by disposition an enquirer.   I feel the consuming thirst
for knowledge, the eager unrest to advance ever further, and the
delights of discovery.   There was a time when I believed that this
is what confers real dignity upon human life, and I despised the
common people who know nothing.   Rousseau has set me right.
This imagined advantage vanishes.   I learn to honor men, and
should regard myself as of much less use than the common labourer,
if I did not believe that my philosophy will restore to all men the
common rights of humanity."[2]

The sublimity of the starry heavens and the imperative of
the moral law are ever present influences on the life of man ;
and they require for their apprehension no previous initiation
through science and philosophy.   The naked eye reveals the
former ; of the latter all men are immediately aware.[3]   In
their universal appeal they are of the very substance of human
existence.   Philosophy may avail to counteract the hindrances
which prevent them from exercising their native influence ; it
cannot be a substitute for the inspiration which they alone
can yield.

[1] Cf. Kant's Preface to the *Critique of Practical Reason*, *W.* v. p. 8 *n.* :
Abbott's trans. p. 93 *n.*   "A reviewer who wanted to find some fault with this
work—[the *Foundations of the Metaphysics of Morals*]—has hit the truth better,
perhaps, than he thought, when he says that no new principle of morality is set
forth in it, but only a *new formula*.   But who would think of introducing a new
principle of all morality, and making himself as it were the first inventor
of it, just as if all the world before him were ignorant what duty was, or had been
in thorough-going error ?   But whoever knows of what importance to a mathematician a formula is, which defines accurately what is to be done to work out a
problem, will not think that a formula is insignificant and useless which does the
same for all duty in general."   Cf. *Fortschritte, Werke* (Hartenstein), viii. p. 563.
[2] *Fragmente aus dem Nachlasse, Werke* (Hartenstein), viii. p. 624, already
quoted above, p. lvii.   Cf. also *op. cit.* p. 630.
[3] Cf. *Critique of Practical Reason*, Conclusion, *W.* v. pp. 161-2 : Abbott's
trans. p. 260.

CHAPTER III

THE ARCHITECTONIC OF PURE REASON [1]

Adickes [2] very justly remarks that "this is a section after Kant's own heart, in which there is presented, almost unsought, the opportunity, which he elsewhere so frequently creates for himself, of indulging in his favourite hobby." The section is of slight scientific importance, and is chiefly of interest for the light which it casts upon Kant's personality. Moreover the distinctions which Kant here draws are for the most part not his own philosophical property, but are taken over from the Wolffian system.

The distinctions may be exhibited in tabular form as follows : [3]

---

[1] A 832 = B 860.   [2] *K.* p. 633 *n.* · Cf. above, p. xxii.

[3] Cf. Adickes, *K.* p. 635 *n.*, and Vaihinger, i. p. 306. In this table *Critique* is distinguished from the *System* of pure Reason (cf. above, pp. 71-2). The transcendental philosophy of pure Reason of this table corresponds to the *Analytic* of the *Critique*, and to "pure natural science" in the absolute sense (cf. above, pp. 66-7). The rational physics of this table corresponds to the *Metaphysical First Principles of Natural Science.*

[TABLE

579

KNOWLEDGE

- **Historical or empirical** (*cognitio ex datis*).
  - Empirical physiology.
  - Empirical anthropology.
- **Rational** (*cognitio ex principiis*).
  - Mathematics, based on the construction of concepts.
  - Philosophical[1] (based on pure concepts):—metaphysics in the widest sense.
    - Propaedeutic: Critique.
    - System of pure reason, both practical and speculative: metaphysics in the wider sense.
      - Metaphysics of morals, i.e. of all that ought to be.
      - Metaphysics (in a more limited sense) of nature,[2] i.e. of all that is.
        - Transcendental philosophy of pure reason: ontology.[3]
        - Physiology of pure reason.
          - Immanent.
            - Rational physics.
            - Rational psychology.
          - Transcendent.
            - Cosmology
            - Theology
            - Metaphysics in the most limited sense.

[1] When Kant in A 840 = B 868 takes philosophy as including empirical knowledge he contradicts the spirit, though not the letter of his own preceding statements. In his *Introduction to Logic* (Hartenstein, viii. p. 22, Abbott's trans. p. 12) the empirical is identified with the historical.

[2] *Fortschritte, Werke* (Hartenstein), viii. p. 554.

[3] *Op. cit.* p. 520.

Kant further distinguishes between the "scholastic" and the "universal" or traditional meaning of the term philosophy.[1] In the former sense philosophy is viewed from the point of view of its *logical* perfection, and the philosopher appears as an *artist* of Reason.[2] Philosophy in the broader and higher sense is "the science of the relation of all knowledge to the essential ends of human Reason."[3] The philosopher then appears as the *lawgiver* of human Reason. Of the essential ends, the *ultimate* end is man's moral destiny; to this the other essential ends of human Reason are subordinate means. For though the legislation of human Reason concerns nature as well as freedom, and has therefore to be dealt with by a philosophy of nature, *i.e.* of *all that is*, as well as by a philosophy of morals, *i.e.* of *that which ought to be*, the former is subordinate to the latter in the same degree in which in human life knowledge is subordinate to moral action. Whereas speculative metaphysics serves rather to ward off errors than to extend knowledge,[4] in the metaphysics of morals "all culture [*Kultur*] of human Reason"[5] finds its indispensable completion.

Empirical psychology is excluded from the domain of metaphysics. It is destined to form part of a complete system of anthropology, the pendant to the empirical doctrine of nature.[6]

[1] *I.e.* between the conception of philosophy as *Schulbegriff* and as *Weltbegriff* (*conceptus cosmicus*). He explains in a note to A 839 = B 868 that he employs these latter terms as indicating that philosophy in the traditional or humanistic sense is concerned with "that which must necessarily interest every one." I have translated *Weltbegriff* as '*universal* concept.' By *conceptus cosmicus* Kant means 'concept shared by the whole world,' or 'common to all mankind.'

[2] Cf. Kant's *Logic, Introduction*, § iii. : Abbott's trans. pp. 14-15 : "In this scholastic signification of the word, philosophy aims only at *skill*; in reference to the higher concept common to all mankind, on the contrary, it aims at *utility*. In the former aspect, therefore, it is a doctrine of skill; in the latter a doctrine of wisdom; it is the lawgiver of reason; and hence the philosopher is *not* a *master of the art of reason*, but a *lawgiver*. The master of the art of reason, or as Socrates calls him, the *philodoxus*, strives merely for speculative knowledge, without concerning himself how much this knowledge contributes to the ultimate end of human reason : he gives rules for the use of reason for all kinds of ends. The practical philosopher, the teacher of wisdom by doctrine and example, is the true philosopher. For philosophy is the Ideal of a perfect wisdom, which shows us the ultimate ends of all human reason."

[3] A 839 = B 867.   [4] A 851 = B 879.   [5] A 850 = B 878.

[6] A 848-9 = B 876-7. Cf. above, pp. 237, 311 *n.*, 312 *n.*, 384-5, 473-7, 554.

CHAPTER IV

THE HISTORY OF PURE REASON [1]

This title, as Kant states, is inserted only to mark the place of the present chapter in a complete system of pure reason. The very cursory outline, which alone Kant here attempts to give, merely repeats the main historical distinctions of which the *Critique* has made use. The contrast between the sensationalism of Epicurus and the intellectualism of Plato has been developed in A 465 ff. = B 493 ff.[2] The contrast between Locke and Leibniz is dwelt upon in A 43 ff. = B 60 ff. and A 270 ff. = B 326 ff. Under the title 'naturalist of pure Reason' Kant is referring to the 'common sense' school, which is typically represented by Beattie.[3] In his *Logic*[4] Kant gives a fuller account of his interpretation of the history of philosophy.

[1] A 852 = B 880.   [2] Cf. A 313 ff. = B 370 ff., above, pp. 498-9.
[3] Cf. above, pp. xxviii-xxix.
[4] *Einleitung*, § iv. : Abbott's trans. pp. 17-23.

APPENDIX B

A MORE DETAILED STATEMENT OF KANT'S RELATIONS TO HIS PHILOSOPHICAL PREDECESSORS [1]

THE development of philosophy, prior to Kant, had rendered two problems especially prominent—the problem of sense-perception and the problem of judgment. In the one we have to deal with the question of the interrelation of mind knowing and objects known; in the other with the connection holding between subject and predicate in the various forms of judgment. In the one we enquire how it is possible to know reality; in the other we seek to determine the criterion of truth. These two problems are, as Kant discovered, inseparable from one another; and the logical is the more fundamental of the two. Indeed it was Hume's analysis of the judgment involved in the causal principle that enabled Kant to formulate his Critical solution of the problem of perception. In this Appendix I propose to follow these problems as they rise into view in the systems of Descartes and his successors.

Galileo's revolutionary teaching regarding the nature of motion was the immediate occasion of Descartes' restatement of the problem of perception. That teaching necessitated an entirely new view of the nature of matter, and consequently of the interrelation of mind and body. Questions never before seriously entertained now became pressing. The solutions had to be as novel as the situation which they were designed to meet.

These new problems arose in the following manner. According to the medieval view, motion may properly be conceived on the analogy of human activity. It comes into being, exhausts itself in exercise, and ceases to be. It is a fleeting activity; only its " material " and " formal " conditions have any permanence of existence. According to Galileo's

---

[1] Supplementary to pp. xxv-xxxiii. Throughout I shall make use of my *Studies in the Cartesian Philosophy*, and may refer the reader to them for further justification of the positions adopted.

teaching, on the other hand, motion is as different from human activity as matter is from mind. It is ingenerable and indestructible. We know it only through the effect which in some incomprehensible fashion it produces in those bodies into which it enters, namely, their translation from one part of space to another. That this translatory motion is called by the same name as the power which generates it, doubtless in some degree accounts for the fact that our understanding of the one tends to conceal from us our entire ignorance of the other.[1] We have only to reflect, however, in order to realise that motion is completely mysterious in its intrinsic dynamical nature. We cannot, for instance, profess to comprehend, even in the least degree, how motion, though incapable of existing apart from matter, should yet be sufficiently independent to be able to pass from one body to another.

Descartes, following out some of the chief consequences of this new teaching, concluded that matter is passive and inert, that it is distinguished neither by positive nor by negative properties from the space which it fills, and that it is to motion that all the articulated organisation of animate and inanimate nature is due. Descartes failed, indeed, to appreciate the dynamical character of motion, and by constantly speaking as if it were reducible to the translatory motion, in which it manifests itself, he represented it as known in all its essential features. None the less, the rôles previously assigned to matter and motion are, in Descartes' system, completely reversed. Matter is subordinated to motion as the instrument to the agency by which it is directed and shaped. On the older view, material bodies had, through the possession of formative and vital forces, all manner of intrinsic powers. By the new view these composite and nondescript existences are resolved into two elements, all the properties of which can be quantitatively defined—into a matter which is uniform and homogeneous, and into motion whose sole effect is the translation of bodies in space. Matter is the passive and inert substance out of which motion, by its mere mechanical powers, can produce the whole range of material forms.

This revolutionary change in the physical standpoint involved restatement of the philosophical issues. But the resulting difficulties were found thoroughly baffling. Though Descartes and his successors were willing to adopt any hypothesis, however paradoxical, which the facts might seem to demand, their theories, however modified and restated, led only deeper into a hopeless *impasse*. The unsolved

[1] For recognition of this distinction, cf. Herbert Spencer, *Principles of Psychology*, vol. i., 3rd ed., pp. 620-3.

problems of the Cartesian systems formed the discouraging heritage to which Kant fell heir. If matter is always purely material, and motion is its sole organising power, there can be no real kinship between body and mind. The formative and vital forces, which in the Scholastic philosophy and in popular thought serve to maintain the appearance of continuity between matter and mind, can no longer be credited. Motion, which alone is left to mediate between the opposites, is purely mechanical, and (on Descartes' view) is entirely lacking in inner or hidden powers. The animal body is exclusively material, and is therefore as incapable of feeling or consciousness as any machine made by human hands. The bodily senses are not 'sensitive'; the brain cannot think. Mental experiences do, of course, accompany the brain-motions. But why a sensation should thus arise when a particular motion is caused in the brain, or how a mental resolution can be followed by a brain state, are questions to which no satisfactory answer can be given. The mental and the material, the spiritual and the mechanical, fall entirely apart.

The difficulties arising out of this incomprehensibility of the causal interrelations of mind and body are not, however, in themselves a valid argument against a dualistic interpretation of the real. The difficulties of accounting for the causal relation are, in essential respects, equally great even when the interaction is between homogeneous existences. The difficulties are due to the nature of causal action as such, not to the character of the bodies between which it holds. This, indeed, was clearly recognised by Descartes, and was insisted upon by his immediate successors. The transference of motion by impact is no less incomprehensible than the interaction of soul and body. If motion can exist only in matter, there is no possible method of conceiving how it can make the transition from one discrete portion of matter to another. Causal action is thus a problem which no philosophy can pretend to solve, and which every philosophy, whether monistic or dualistic, must recognise as transcending the scope of our present knowledge.

It is in another and more special form that Descartes' dualism first reveals its fatal defects, namely, in its bearing upon the problem of sense-perception. Descartes can solve the problem of knowledge only by first postulating the doctrine of representative perception. That doctrine is rendered necessary by his interpretation of the dualism of mind and body. Objects can be known only mediately by means of their action upon the sense-organs, and through the sense-organs upon the brain. The resulting brain states are in themselves merely forms of motion. They lead, however, in a manner which Descartes never professes to explain,[1] to the appearance of sensations in the mental field. Out of these sensations the mind then constructs mental images of the distant bodies; and it is these mental images alone which are directly apprehended. Material bodies are invisible and intangible; they are knowable only through their mental duplicates. Thus, according to the doctrine of representative perception, each mind is segregated in a world apart. It looks out upon a landscape which is as mental and as truly inward as are its feelings and desires. The apparently ultimate relation of mind knowing and object known is rendered complex and problematic through the distinction between mental objects and real things. Mental objects are in all cases images merely. They exist only so long as they are apprehended; and they are numerically and existentially distinct in each individual mind. Real things are not immediately perceived; they are hypothetically inferred. To ordinary consciousness the body which acts on the sense-organ is the object known; when reflective consciousness is philosophically enlightened, the object immediately known is recognised as a merely mental image, and the external object sinks to the level of an assumed cause.

The paradoxical character of this doctrine is accentuated by Galileo's distinction between primary and secondary qualities.[2] Those physical processes, which are entitled light and heat, bear no resemblance to the sensations through which they become known. The many-coloured world of ordinary consciousness is an illusory appearance which can exist only in the human mind. We must distinguish between the sensible world which, though purely mental, appears, through an unavoidable illusion, to be externally real, and that very different world of matter and motion which reveals its independent nature only to reflective thinking. In the latter world the rich variety of sensuous appearance can find no place. There remain only the quantitative, mechanical properties of extension, figure and motion; and even these have to be interpreted in the revolutionary fashion of physical science.

The doctrine of representative perception cannot, however, defend successfully the positions which it thus involves. It wavers in unstable equilibrium. The facts, physical and physiological, upon which it is based, are in conflict with the conclusions in which it results. This has been very clearly

---

[1] Cf. *Studies in the Cartesian Philosophy*, pp. 80-2, 106-7.
[2] This distinction is due to Galileo, though the terms "primary" and "secondary" were first employed by Locke.

demonstrated by many writers in recent times.[1] The conflict manifested itself in the period between Descartes and Kant only through the uneasy questionings of Locke and Berkeley. The problem, fundamental though it be, is almost completely ignored by Spinoza, Leibniz, and Wolff.

Stated in modern terms, the inherently contradictory character of the doctrine consists in its unavoidable alternation between the realist attitude to which it owes its origin, and the idealist conclusion in which it issues. Such oscillation is due to the twofold simultaneous relation in which it regards ideas as standing to the objects that they are supposed to represent. The function of sensations is cognitive; their origin is mechanical. As cognitive they stand to objects in a relation of inclusion; they reveal the objects, reduplicating them in image before the mind. Yet in their origin they are effects, mechanically generated by the action of material bodies upon the sense-organs and brain. As they are effects mechanically generated, there is no guarantee that they resemble their causes; and if we may argue from other forms of mechanical causation, there is little likelihood that they do. They stand to their first causes in a relation of exclusion, separated from them by a large number of varying intermediate processes. There is thus a conflict between the function of sensations and their origin. Their origin in the external objects is supposed to confer upon them a representative power; and yet the very nature of this origin invalidates any such claim.

This irreconcilability of the subjectivist consequences of the doctrine with its realist basis was seized upon by Berkeley. To remove the contradiction, he denied the facts from which the doctrine had been developed. That is to say, starting from its results he disproved its premises. Arguing from the physical and physiological conditions of perception Descartes had concluded that only sensations can be directly apprehended by the mind. Berkeley starts from this conclusion, and virtually adopts it as an assumption which cannot be questioned, and which does not call for proof. Since, he contends, we know only sensations, the assertion that they are due to material causes is mere hypothesis, and is one for which there may be no valid grounds. As Descartes himself had already suggested, there is a second possible method of interpreting the relevant facts. There may exist an all-

---

[1] I have dealt with Avenarius' criticism in "Avenarius' Philosophy of Pure Experience" (*Mind*, vol. xv. N.S., pp. 13-31, 149-160); with Bergson's criticism in "Subjectivism and Realism in Modern Philosophy" (*Philosophical Review*, vol. xvii. pp. 138-148); and with the general issue as a whole in "The Problem of Knowledge" (*Journal of Philosophy*, vol. ix. pp. 113-128).

powerful Being who produces the sensations in our minds from moment to moment; and provided that they are produced in the same order as now, the whole material world might be annihilated without our being in the least aware that so important an event had taken place. Since we can experience only sensations, any hypothesis which will account for the order of their happening is equally legitimate. The whole question becomes one of relative simplicity in the explanation given. The simpler analysis, other things being equal, must hold the field.

Berkeley reinforces this argument by pointing to the many embarrassing consequences to which Descartes' dualism must lead. We postulate bodies in order to account for the origin of our sensations, and yet are unable to do so by their means. The dualistic theory creates more difficulties than it solves, without a single counter-advantage, save perhaps—so Berkeley argues—that it seems to harmonise better with the traditional prejudices of the philosophic consciousness.

If we grant Berkeley his premises, the main lines of his argument are fairly cogent, however unconvincing may be his own positive views. The crux, however, of the Berkeleian idealism lies almost exclusively in the establishment of its fundamental assumption, that only ideas (*i.e.* images) can be known by the mind. This assumption Berkeley, almost without argument, takes over from his predecessors. It was currently accepted, and from it, therefore, he believed that he could safely argue. It rests, however, upon the assumption of facts which he himself questions. In rejecting the Cartesian dualism he casts down the ladder by which alone it is possible to climb into his position. For save through the facts of physics and physiology there seems to be no possible method of disproving the belief of ordinary consciousness, that in perception we apprehend independent material bodies. And until that belief can be shown to be false and ungrounded, the Berkeleian idealism is without support. It cannot establish the fundamental assumption upon which its entire argument proceeds. Thus, though Berkeley convincingly demonstrates the internal incoherence of the doctrine of representative perception—the inconsistency of its conclusions with the physical and physiological facts upon which alone it can be based—he cannot himself solve the problem in answer to which that doctrine was propounded. His services, like those of so many other reformers, were such as he did not himself foresee. In simplifying the problem, he prepared the way for the more sceptical treatment of its difficult issues by Hume.

At this point, in the philosophy of Hume, the problem of

perception comes into the closest possible connection with the logical problem, referred to above. The question, how mind knowing is related to the objects known, is found to depend upon the question, how in certain crucial cases predicates may legitimately be referred to their subject. This logical problem arises in two forms, a narrower and a wider. The narrower issue concerns only the principle of causality. With what right do we assert that every event must have a cause? What is the ground which justifies us in thus predicating of events a causal character? Obviously, this logical question is fundamental, and must be answered before we can hope to solve the more special problem, as to our right to interpret sensations as effects of material bodies. Hume was the first to emphasise the vital interconnection of these two lines of enquiry.

The wider issue is the generating problem of Kant's *Critique*: How in a judgment can a predicate be asserted of a subject in which it is not already involved? In other words, what is it that in such a case justifies us in connecting the predicate with the subject? Though this problem was never directly raised by any pre-Kantian thinker, not even by Hume, it is absolutely vital to all the pre-Kantian systems. Thus Descartes' philosophy is based upon a distinction, nowhere explicitly drawn but everywhere silently assumed, between abstract and fruitful ideas. The former contain just so much content and no more; this content may be explicitly unfolded in a series of judgments, but no addition is thereby made to our knowledge. The latter, on the other hand, are endowed with an extraordinary power of inner growth. To the attentive mind they disclose a marvellous variety of inner meaning. The chief problem of scientific method consists, according to Descartes, in the discovery of these fruitful ideas, and in the separation of them from the irrelevant accompaniments which prevent them from unfolding their inner content. Once they are discovered, the steady progress of knowledge is assured. They are the springs of knowledge, and from them we have only to follow down the widening river of truth.

Descartes professed to give a complete list of the possible fruitful ideas. They are, he claimed, better known than any other concepts. They lie at the basis of all experience, and no one can possibly be ignorant of them; though, owing to their simplicity and omnipresence, their philosophical importance has been overlooked. When, however, Descartes proceeded to classify them, he found that while such ideas as space, triangle, number, motion, contain an inexhaustible content that is progressively unfolded in the mathematical sciences, those ideas, on the other hand, through which we conceive mental existences,—the notions of mind, thought, self—do not by any means prove fruitful upon attentive enquiry. As Malebranche later insisted, we can define mind only in negative terms; its whole meaning is determined through its opposition to the space-world, which alone is truly known. Though it is the function of mind to know, it cannot know itself. And when we remove from our list of ideas those which are not really fruitful, we find that only mathematical concepts remain.[1] They alone have this apparently miraculous property of inexhaustibly developing before the mind. Scientific knowledge is limited to the material world; and even there, the limits of our mathematical insight are the limits of our knowledge.

Malebranche believed no less thoroughly than Descartes in the asserted power and fruitfulness of mathematical concepts. Under the influence of this belief, he developed, as so many other thinkers from Plato onwards have done, a highly mystical theory of scientific knowledge. It is a revelation of eternal truth, and yet is acquired by inner reflection, not laboriously built up by external observation. It comes by searching of the mind, not by exploration of the outer world. But Malebranche was not content, like Descartes, merely to accept this type of knowledge. He proceeded to account for it in metaphysical terms. The fruitfulness of mathematical ideas is due, he claimed, to the fundamental concept of extension in which they all share. This idea, representing, as it does, an infinite existence, is too great to be contained within the finite mind. Through it the mind is widened to the apprehension of something beyond itself; we know it through consciousness of its archetype in the mind of God. It is the one point at which consciousness transcends its subjective limits. Its fruitfulness is due to, and is the manifestation of, this divine source. The reason why we are condemned to remain ignorant of everything beyond the sphere of quantity is that extension alone holds this unique position. It is the only fruitful idea which the mind possesses, and other concepts, such as triangle, circle, or number, are fruitful only in proportion as they share in it. We can acquire no genuine knowledge even of the nature of the self. Being ignorant of mind, we cannot comprehend the self which is one of its modes. It is as if we sought to comprehend the nature of a triangle, in the absence of any conception of space. Were

---

[1] On Descartes' failure to distinguish between the mathematical and the dynamical aspects of motion, cf. above, p. 584.

we in possession of the archetypal idea of mind, we should not only be able to deduce from it those various feelings and emotions which we have already experienced, and those sensations of the secondary qualities which we falsely ascribe to the influence of external objects, but we should also be able to discover by pure contemplation innumerable other emotions and qualities, which entirely transcend our present powers. And all of these would then be experienced in their ideal nature, and not, as now, merely through feeble and confused feeling. If mathematicians destroy their bodily health through absorption in the progressive clarification of the mysteries of space, what might not happen if the archetypal idea of mind were revealed to us? Could we attend to the preservation of a body which would incessantly distract us from the infinite and overwhelming experiences of our divine destiny?

This romantic conception of the possibilities of rational science reveals more clearly than any other Cartesian doctrine the real bearing and perverse character of the rationalistic preconceptions which underlie the Cartesian systems. The Cartesians would fain make rational science, conceived on the analogy of the mathematical disciplines, coextensive with the entire realm of the real. This grotesque enterprise is conceived as abstractly possible even by so cautious a thinker as John Locke. His reason for condemning the physical sciences as logically imperfect is that they fail to conform to this rationalistic ideal. Hence those sentences which sound so strangely in the mouth of Locke, the sensationalist.

"It is the contemplation of our abstract ideas that alone is able to afford us general knowledge."[1] "The true method of advancing knowledge is by considering our abstract ideas."[2] "[Did we know the real essence of gold] it would be no more necessary that gold should exist, and that we should make experiments upon it, than it is necessary for the knowing of the properties of a triangle, that a triangle should exist in any matter: the idea in our minds would serve for the one as well as for the other."[3] "In the knowledge of bodies, we must be content to glean what we can from particular experiments, since we cannot, from a discovery of their real essences, grasp at a time whole sheaves, and in bundles comprehend the nature and the properties of whole species together."[4]

Locke's empirical doctrine of knowledge is thus based upon a rationalistic theory of the real. It is not, he holds, the constitution of reality, but the *de facto* limitations of our

[1] *Essay concerning Human Understanding*, IV. vi. 16.
[2] *Op. cit.* IV. xii. 7.   [3] *Op. cit.* IV. vi. 11.   [4] *Op. cit.* IV. xii. 12.

human faculties which make empirical induction the only practicable mode of discovery in natural science. Indeed, Locke gives more extreme expression than even Descartes does, to the mystically conceived mathematical method. Being ignorant of mathematics, and not over well-informed even in the physical sciences, Locke was not checked by any too close acquaintance with the real character and necessary limits of this method; and he accordingly makes statements in that unqualified fashion which seldom fails to betray the writer who is expounding views which he has not developed for himself by first-hand study of the relevant facts.

But though the unique character of mathematical knowledge thus forced itself upon the attention of all the Cartesian thinkers, and in the above manner led even the most level-headed of Descartes' successors to dream strange dreams, no real attempt was made (save in the neglected writings of Leibniz) to examine, in a sober spirit, the grounds and conditions of its possibility. In the English School, Locke's eulogy of abstract ideas served only to drive his immediate successors to an opposite extreme. Both Berkeley and Hume attempted to explain away, in an impossible manner, those fundamental differences, which, beyond all questioning, profoundly differentiate mathematical from empirical judgments.[1] It is not surprising that Kant, who had no direct acquaintance with Hume's *Treatise*, should have asserted that had Hume realised the bearing of his main teaching upon the theory of mathematical science, he would have hesitated to draw his sceptical conclusions. Such, however, was not the case. Hume's theory of mathematical reasoning undoubtedly forms the least satisfactory part of his philosophy. He did, however, perceive the general bearing of his central teaching. It was in large degree his ignorance of the mathematical disciplines that concealed from him the thorough unsatisfactoriness of his general position, and which prevented him from formulating the logical problem in its full scope—the problem, namely, how judgments which make additions to our previous knowledge, and yet do not rest upon mere sensation, are possible. He treated it only as it presents itself in those judgments which involve the concept of causality.[2] But this analysis of causal judgments awoke Kant from his dogmatic slumber, and so ultimately led to the raising of the logical problem in its widest form:—how synthetic *a priori* judgments, whether mathematical, physical, or metaphysical, are possible.

[1] Cf. above, pp. 27-8.
[2] Though the concept of substance is also discussed by Hume, his treatment of it is quite perfunctory.

Hume discussed the causal problem both in regard to the general principle of causality and in its bearing upon our particular judgments of causal relation. The problems concerned in these two discussions are essentially distinct. The first involves immensely wider issues, and so far as can be judged from the existing circumstantial evidence,[1] it was this first discussion, not as has been so often assumed by Kant's commentators the second and more limited problem, which exercised so profound an influence upon Kant at the turning-point of his speculations. In stating it, it will be best to take Hume's own words.

"To begin with the first question concerning the necessity of a cause: 'Tis a general maxim in philosophy, that *whatever begins to exist*, must have a cause of existence. This is commonly taken for granted in all reasonings, without any proof given or demanded. 'Tis supposed to be founded on intuition, and to be one of those maxims, which though they may be deny'd with the lips, 'tis impossible for men in their hearts really to doubt of. But if we examine this maxim by the idea of knowledge above explain'd we shall discover in it no mark of any such intuitive certainty; but on the contrary shall find, that 'tis of a nature quite foreign to that species of conviction." [2]

The principle that every event must have a cause, is neither intuitively nor demonstratively certain. So far from there existing a *necessary* connection between the idea of an event as something happening in time and the idea of a cause, no connection of any kind is discoverable by us. We can conceive an object to be non-existent at this moment, and existent the next, without requiring to conjoin with it the altogether different idea of a productive source.

This had been implicitly recognised by those few philosophers who had attempted to give demonstrations of the principle. By so doing, however, they only reinforce Hume's contention that it possesses no rational basis. When Hobbes argues that as all the points of time and place in which we can suppose an object to begin to exist, are in themselves equal, there must be some cause determining an event to happen at one moment rather than at another, he is assuming the very principle which he professes to prove. There is no greater difficulty in supposing the time and place to be fixed without a cause, than in supposing the existence to be so determined. If the denial of a cause is not intuitively absurd in the one case, it cannot be so in the other. If the first demands a

---

[1] Cf. above, pp. xxv ff., 61 ff.
[2] *Treatise on Human Nature* (Green and Grose), i. p. 380.

proof, so likewise must the second. Similarly with the arguments advanced by Locke and Clarke. Locke argues that if anything is produced without a cause, it is produced by nothing, and that that is impossible, since nothing can never be a cause any more than it can be something, or equal to two right angles. Clarke's contention that if anything were without a cause, it would produce *itself*, *i.e.* exist before it existed, is of the same character. These arguments assume the only point which is in question.

"When we exclude all causes we really do exclude them, and neither suppose nothing nor the object itself to be the causes of the existence, and consequently can draw no argument from the absurdity of these suppositions to prove the absurdity of that exclusion." [1]

The remaining argument, that every effect must have a cause, since this is implied in the very idea of an effect, is "still more frivolous."

"Every effect necessarily presupposes a cause; effect being a relative term, of which cause is the correlative. But this does not prove that every being must be preceded by a cause; no more than it follows, because every husband must have a wife, that therefore every man must be married." [2]

The far-reaching conclusion, that the principle of causality has no possible rational basis, Hume extends and reinforces through his other doctrines, viz. that synthetic reason [3] is merely generalised belief, and that belief is in all cases due to the ultimate instincts and propensities which *de facto* constitute our human nature. The synthetic principles which lie at the basis of our experience are non-rational in character. Each is due to a 'blind and powerful instinct,' which, demanding no evidence, and ignoring theoretical inconsistency for the sake of practical convenience, necessitates belief.

"Nature by an absolute and uncontrollable necessity has determined us to judge as well as to breathe and feel." [4] "All these operations are a species of natural instincts, which no reasoning or process of the thought and understanding is able either to produce or to prevent." [5]

Reason is "nothing but a wonderful and unintelligible instinct in our souls." [6] It justifies itself by its practical uses,

---

[1] *Op. cit.* p. 383. [2] *Loc. cit.*

[3] For justification of the phrase "synthetic reason," I must refer to my articles in *Mind*, vol. xiv. N.S. pp. 149-73, 335-47, on "The Naturalism of Hume."

[4] *Treatise* (Green and Grose), i. pp. 474-5.

[5] *Enquiry concerning Human Understanding* (Green and Grose), p. 40.

[6] *Treatise*, p. 471.

but can afford no standard to which objective reality must conform.

It is from this point of view that Hume states his answer to the problem of perception. Our natural belief in the permanence and identity of objects, as expressed through the principle of substance and attribute, leads us to interpret the objects of sense-perception as independent realities. We interpret our subjective sensations as being qualities of independent substances. Our other natural belief, in the dynamical interdependence of events, as expressed through the principle of causality, leads, however, to the opposite conclusion, that the known objects are merely mental. For by it we are constrained to interpret sensations, not as objective qualities, but only as subjective effects, expressive of the reactions of our psycho-physical organism. The Cartesian problems owe their origin to the mistaken attempt to harmonise, in a theoretical fashion, these two conflicting principles. The conflict is inevitable and the antinomy is insoluble, so long as the two principles are regarded as objectively valid. The only satisfactory solution comes through recognition that reason is unable to account, save in reference to practical ends, even for its own inevitable demands. The principle of substance and attribute and the principle of causality co-operate in rendering possible such organisation of our sense-experience as is required for practical life. But when we carry this organisation further than practical life itself demands, the two principles at once conflict.

Kant shows no interest in this constructive part of Hume's philosophy; and must, indeed, have been almost entirely ignorant of it, since it finds only very imperfect expression in the *Enquiry*, and is ignored in Beattie's *Nature of Truth*. Accordingly, Kant does not regard Hume as offering a positive explanation of knowledge, but rather as representing the point of view of thoroughgoing scepticism. But even had he been acquainted at first hand with Hume's *Treatise*, he would undoubtedly have felt little sympathy with Hume's naturalistic view of the function of reason. His training in the mathematical sciences would have enabled him to detect the inadequacy of Hume's treatment of mathematical knowledge, and his strong moral convictions would have led him to rebel against the naturalistic assumptions which underlie Hume's entire position. The Berkeley-Hume comedy is thus repeated with reversed rôles. Just as Berkeley's anti-materialistic philosophy was mainly influential as a step towards the naturalism of Hume, and as such still survives in the philosophies of

John Stuart Mill, Herbert Spencer, Huxley, Mach and Karl Pearson, so in turn Hume's anti-metaphysical theory of knowledge was destined to be one of the chief contributory sources of the German speculative movement.

We may now turn to Hume's treatment of the narrower problem—that of justifying our *particular* causal judgments. Hume's attitude towards this question is predetermined by the more fundamental argument, above stated, which precedes it in the *Treatise*, but which is entirely omitted from the corresponding chapters of the *Enquiry*. As the general principle of causality is of an irrational character, the same must be true of those particular judgments which are based upon it. Much of Hume's argument on this question is, indeed, merely a restatement of what had already been pointed out by his predecessors. There is no necessary connection discoverable between *any* cause and its effect. This is especially evident as regards the connection between brain states and mental experiences. No explanation can be given why a motion in the brain should produce sensations in the mind, or why a mental resolution should produce movements in the body. Such sequences may be empirically verified; they cannot be rationally understood. That this likewise holds, though in less obvious fashion, of the causal interrelations of material bodies, had been emphasised by Geulincx, Malebranche, Locke, and Berkeley. The fact that one billiard ball should communicate motion to another by impact is, when examined, found to be no less incomprehensible than the interaction of mind and body. Hume, in the following passage, is only reinforcing this admitted fact, in terms of his own philosophy.

"We fancy that were we brought on a sudden into this world we could at first have inferred that one billiard ball would communicate motion to another upon impulse; and that we needed not to have waited for the event, in order to pronounce with certainty upon it. Such is the influence of custom, that, where it is strongest, it not only covers our natural ignorance, but even conceals itself, and seems not to take place merely because it is found in the highest degree." [1]

Nor are we conscious of any causal power within the self. When Berkeley claims that mind has the faculty of producing images at will, he is really ascribing to it creative agency. And such creation, as Malebranche had already pointed out, is not even conceivable.

"I deny that my will produces in me my ideas, for I cannot even conceive how it could produce them, since my will, not being able

---

[1] *Enquiry* (Green and Grose), pp. 25-6.

to act or will without knowledge, presupposes my ideas and does not make them." [1] "Is there not here," Hume asks, "either in a spiritual or material substance, or both, some secret mechanism or structure of parts, upon which the effect depends, and which, being entirely unknown to us, renders the power or energy of the will equally unknown and incomprehensible?" [2]

But the fact that Hume thus restates conclusions already emphasised by his predecessors will not justify us in contending (as certain historians of philosophy seem inclined to do) that in his treatment of the causal problem he failed to make any important advance upon the teaching of the Occasionalists. Hume was the first to perceive the essential falsity of the Cartesian, rationalistic view of the causal nexus. For Descartes, an effect is that which can be deduced with logical necessity from the concept of its cause. The Occasionalists similarly argued that because natural events can never be deduced from one another they must in all cases be due to supernatural agency; like Descartes, they one and all failed to comprehend that since by an effect we mean that which follows *in time* upon its cause, and since, therefore, the principle of causality is the law of *change*, the nature of causality cannot be expressed in logical terms. Hume was the first to appreciate the significance of this fundamental fact; and an entirely new set of problems at once came into view. If causal connection is not, as previous thinkers had believed, logical in character, if it does not signify logical dependence of the so-called effect upon its cause, its true connotation must lie elsewhere; and until this has been traced to its hidden source, any attempted solution of metaphysical problems is certain to involve many false assumptions. The answer that is given to the problem of the origin and content of the causal concept must determine our interpretation alike of sense-experience and of pure thought.

The problem presents on examination, however, a most paradoxical aspect. As Hume has already shown, every effect is an event distinct from its cause, and there is never any connection, beyond that of mere sequence, discoverable between them. We observe only sequence; we assert necessary connection. What, then, is in our minds when this latter assertion is made? And how, if the notion of necessitated connection cannot be gained through observation of the external events, is it acquired by us? Hume again propounds

[1] *Éclaircissement* sur chap. iii. pt. ii. liv. vi. *de la Recherche*: tome iv. (1712) p. 381.   [2] *Enquiry*, p. 57.

a naturalistic solution. Causation, *i.e. necessitated* sequence in time, is not in any sense a conception; it is not a comprehended relation between events, but a misunderstood feeling in our minds. We cannot form any, even the most remote, conception of how one event can produce another. Neither imagination nor pure thought, however freely they may act, are capable of inventing any such notion. But nature, by the manner in which it has constituted our minds, deludes us into the belief that we are in actual possession of this idea. The repeated sequence of events, in fixed order, generates in us the feeling of a tendency to pass from the perception or idea of the one to the idea of the other. This feeling, thus generated by custom, and often in somewhat confused fashion combined with the feeling of 'animal nisus,' which is experienced in bodily effort, is mistaken by the mind for a definite concept of force, causality, necessary connection. As mere feeling it can afford no insight into the relation holding between events, and as merely subjective can justify no inference in regard to that relation. The terms force, causality, necessitated sequence in time, have a practical value, as names for our instinctive, natural expectations; but when employed as instruments for the *theoretical* interpretation of experience, they lead us off on a false trail.

This is one of the fundamental points upon which Hume reveals a deeper speculative insight than either Malebranche, Geulincx, or Locke. Though these latter insist upon our ignorance of the relation holding between events, they still assume that causation and natural necessity are concepts which have a quite intelligible meaning; and in consequence they fail to draw the all-important conclusion, that the general principle of causality has neither intuitive nor demonstrative validity. For that is the revolutionary outcome of Hume's analysis of the notion of necessitated connection. The principle of causality is a synthetic judgment in which no connection is discoverable between its subject and its predicate. That is the reason why it is neither self-evident nor capable of being established upon more ultimate grounds.

As has already been stated, the wider problem concerning the *principle* of causality is developed only in the *Treatise*; the problem regarding the *concept* of causality is discussed both in the *Treatise* and in the *Enquiry*. An appreciation of the wider problem is required, however, in order to set this second problem in its true light, for it is only through its connection with the wider issue that Hume's reduction of the concept of causality to a merely instinctive, non-rational expectation acquires its full significance. Hume's analysis then amounts, as Kant was the first to realise, to an attack upon the objective validity of all constructive thinking. Not only rationalism, but even such metaphysics as may claim to base its conclusions upon the teaching of experience, is thereby rendered altogether impossible. The issue is crucial, and must be honestly faced, before metaphysical conclusions, no matter what their specific character may be, whether *a priori* or empirical, can legitimately be drawn. If we may not assert that an event must have some cause, even the right to enquire for a cause must first be justified. And if so fundamental a principle as that of causality is not self-evident, are there any principles which can make this claim?

The account which we have so far given of Hume's argument covers only that part of it which is directed against the rationalist position, and which was therefore so influential in turning Kant on to the line of his Critical speculations. But Hume attacked with equal vigour the empiricist standpoint; and as this aspect of his teaching, constituting as it did an integral part of Kant's own philosophy, must undoubtedly have helped to confirm Kant in his early rationalist convictions, we may profitably dwell upon it at some length. In opposition to the empiricists, Hume argues that experience is incapable of justifying any inference in regard to matters of fact. It cannot serve as a basis from which we can inductively extend our knowledge of facts beyond what the senses and memory reveal. Inductive inference, when so employed, necessarily involves a *petitio principii*; we assume the very point we profess to have proved.

The argument by which Hume establishes this important contention is as follows. All inductive reasoning from experience presupposes the validity of belief in causal connection. For when we have no knowledge of causes, we have no justification for asserting the continuance of uniformities. Now it has been shown that we have no experience of any necessary relation between so-called causes and their effects. The most that experience can supply are sequences which repeat themselves. In regarding the sequences as causal, and so as universally constant, we make an assertion for which experience gives no support, and to which no amount of repeated experience, recalled in memory, can add one jot of real evidence. To argue that because the sequences have remained constant in a great number of repeated experiences, they are therefore more likely to remain constant, is to assume that constancy in the past is a ground for inferring it in the future; and that is the very point which demands proof. In drawing the conclusion we virtually assume that there is a necessary connection, *i.e.* an absolutely constant relation, between events. But since no *single* experience of causal sequence affords ground for inferring that the sequence will continue in the future, no number of repeated experiences, recalled in memory, can contribute to the strengthening of the inference. It is meaningless to talk even of likelihood or probability. The fact that the sun has without a single known exception arisen each day in the past does not (if we accept the argument disproving all knowledge of necessary connection) constitute *proof* that it will rise to-morrow.

"None but a fool or a madman will be unaffected in his expectations or natural beliefs by this constancy, but he is no philosopher who accepts this as in the nature of evidence." [1]

Since, for all that we know to the contrary, bodies may change their nature and mode of action at any moment, it is vain to pretend that we are scientifically assured of the future because of the past.

"My practice, you say, refutes my doubts.[2] But you mistake the purport of my question. As an agent, I am quite satisfied in the point; but as a philosopher, who has some share of curiosity, I will not say scepticism, I want to learn the foundation of this inference. No reading, no enquiry has yet been able to remove my difficulty or give me satisfaction in a matter of such importance. Can I do better than propose the difficulty to the public, even though, perhaps, I have small hopes of obtaining a solution? We shall at least, by this means, be sensible of our ignorance, if we do not augment our knowledge." [3]

Kant was the first, after thirty years, to take up this challenge. Experience is no source of evidence until the causal postulate has been *independently* proved. Only if the principle of causality can be established prior to all specific experience, only if we can predetermine experience as necessarily conforming to it, are empirical arguments valid at all. Hume's enquiry thus directly leads to the later, no less than to the earlier form of Kant's epoch-making question.[4] In its earlier formulation it referred only to *a priori* judgments; in its wider application it was found to arise with equal cogency in connection with empirical judgments. And as thus extended, it generated the problem: How is sense-experience, regarded as a form of *knowledge*, possible at all? [5] By

[1] *Enquiry*, p. 32.
[2] This is the objection upon which Beattie chiefly insists.
[3] *Op. cit.* pp. 33-4.   [4] Cf. above, pp. 39 ff., 54, 222 ff., 241, 286-9.
[5] How far Hume's criticism of empiricism really influenced Kant in his appreciation of this deeper problem, it seems impossible to decide. Very prob-

showing that the principle of causality has neither intuitive nor demonstrative validity, Hume cuts the ground from under the rationalists; by showing that sense-experience cannot by itself yield conclusions which are objectively valid, he at the same time destroys the empiricist position. In this latter contention Kant stands in complete agreement with Hume. That the sensuously given is incapable of grounding even probable inferences, is a fundamental presupposition (never discussed, but always explicitly assumed) of the Critical philosophy. It was by challenging the sufficiency of Hume's other line of argument, that which is directed against the· rationalists, that Kant discovered a way of escape from the sceptical dilemma. The conditions of experience can be proved by a transcendental method, which, though *a priori* in character, does not lie open to Hume's sceptical objections. Each single experience involves rational principles, and consequently even a single empirical observation may suffice to justify an inductive inference. Experience conforms to the demands of pure *a priori* thought; and can legitimately be construed in accordance with them.

We may now pass to the philosophy in which Kant was educated. It gave to his thinking that rationalist trend, to which, in spite of all counter-influences, he never ceased to remain true.[1] It also contributed to his philosophy several of its constructive principles. Only two rationalist systems need be considered, those of Leibniz and of Wolff. Kant, by his own admission,[2] had been baffled in his attempts (probably not very persevering) to master Spinoza's philosophy. It was with Wolff's system that he was most familiar; but both directly and indirectly, both in his early years and in the 'seventies, the incomparably deeper teaching of Leibniz must have exercised upon him a profoundly formative influence. In defining the points of agreement and of difference between Hume and Leibniz,[3] we have already outlined Leibniz's general view of the nature and powers of pure thought, and may therefore at once proceed to the relevant detail of his main tenets.

Upon two fundamental points Leibniz stands in opposition to Spinoza. He seeks to maintain the reality of the contingent

---

ably Kant proceeded to it by independent development of his own standpoint, after the initial impulse received on the more strictly logical issue.

[1] The assertion, by Kuno Fischer and Paulsen, of an empirical period in Kant's development, has been challenged by Adickes, B. Erdmann, Riehl, and Vaihinger.

[2] Cf. B. Erdmann's *Kriticismus*, p. 147; *Critique of Judgment*, W. v. p. 391 (Bernard's trans. p. 301).

[3] Above, pp. xxx-iii.

or accidental. These terms are indeed, as he conceives them, synonymous with the actual. Necessity rules only in the sphere of the possible. Contingency or freedom is the differentiating characteristic of the real. This point of view is bound up with his second contention, namely, that the real is a kingdom of ends. It is through divine choice of the best among the possible worlds that the actual present order has arisen. There are thus two principles which determine the real: the principle of contradiction which legislates with absolute universality, and the principle of the best, or, otherwise formulated, of sufficient reason, which differentiates reality from truth, limiting thought, in order that, without violating logic, it may freely satisfy the moral needs. Leibniz thus vindicates against Spinoza the reality of freedom and the existence of ends.

Though Leibniz agrees with Spinoza that the philosophically perfect method would be to start from an adequate concept of the Divine Being, and to deduce from His attributes the whole nature of finite reality, he regards our concept of God as being too imperfect to allow of such procedure. We are compelled to resort to experience, and by analysis to search out the various concepts which it involves. By the study of these concepts and their interrelations, we determine, in obedience to the law of contradiction, the nature of the possible. The real, in contradistinction from the possible, involves, however, the notion of ends. The existence of these ends can never be determined by logical, but only by moral considerations. The chief problem of philosophical method is, therefore, to discover the exact relation in which the logical and the teleological, the necessary and the contingent, stand to one another.

The absence of contradiction is in itself a sufficient guarantee of possibility, i.e. even of the possibility of real existence. How very far Leibniz is willing to go on this line is shown by his acceptance of the ontological argument. The whole weight of his system rests, indeed, upon this proof. The notion of God is, he maintains, the sole concept which can determine itself in a purely logical manner not only as possible but also as real. If we are to avoid violating the principle of contradiction, the *Ens perfectissimum* must be regarded as possessing the perfection of real existence. And since God is perfect in moral as in all other attributes, His actions must be in conformity with moral demands. In creating the natural order God must therefore have chosen that combination of possibilities which constitutes the best of all possible worlds. By means of this conceptual bridge we are enabled to pass by pure *a priori* thinking from the logically possible to the factually real.

Pure logical thinking is thus an instrument whereby ultimate reality can be defined in a valid manner. *Pure thought is speculative and metaphysical in its very essence.* It uncovers to us what no experience can reveal, the wider universe which exists eternally in the mind of God. Every concept (whether mathematical, dynamical, or moral), provided only that it is not self-contradictory, is an eternal essence, with the intrinsic nature of which even God must reckon in the creation of things. When, therefore, we are determining the unchanging nature of the eternally possible, there is no necessary reference to Divine existence. The purely logical criterion suffices as a test of truth. Every judgment which is made in regard to such concepts must express only what their content involves. All such judgments must be analytic in order to be true.

When, however, we proceed from the possible to the real, that is to say, from the necessary to the contingent, the logical test is no longer sufficient; and only by appeal to the second principle, that of sufficient reason, can judgments about reality be logically justified. Whether or not the principle of sufficient reason is deducible, as Wolff sought to maintain, from the principle of contradiction, is a point of quite secondary importance. That is a question which does not deserve the emphasis which has been laid upon it. What is chiefly important is that for Leibniz, as for Wolff, both principles are principles of analysis. The principle of sufficient reason is not an instrument for determining necessary relations between independent substances. The sufficient ground of a valid predicate must in all cases be found in the concept of the subject to which it is referred. The difference between the two principles lies elsewhere, namely, in the character of the connection established between subject and predicate. In the one case the denial of the proposition involves a direct self-contradiction. In the other the opposite of the judgment is perfectly conceivable; our reason for asserting it is a moral (employing the term in the eighteenth-century sense), not a logical ground. The subject is so constituted, that in the choice of ends, in pursuit of the good, it must by its very nature so behave. The principle of sufficient reason, which represents in our finite knowledge the divine principle of the best, compels us to recognise the predicate as involved in the subject—as involved through a ground which inclines without necessitating. Often the analysis cannot be carried sufficiently far to enable us thus to transform a judgment empirically given into one which is adequately grounded. None the less, in recognising it as true, we postulate that the predicate is related to the subject in this way. There are not for Leibniz two methods of establishing truth, sense-perception to reveal contingent fact, and general reasoning to establish necessary truth. A proposition can be accepted as true only in so far as we can at least *postulate*, through absence of contradiction and through sufficient reason, its analytic character. It must express some form of identity. The proposition, Caesar crossed the Rubicon, is given us as historical fact. The more complete our knowledge of Caesar and of his time, the further we can carry the analysis; and that analysis if completely executed would displace the merely factual validity of the judgment by insight into its metaphysical truth. Thus experience, with its assertions of the here and now about particulars inexhaustibly concrete, sets to rational science an inexhaustible task. We can proceed in our analysis indefinitely, pushing out the frontiers of thought further and further into the empirical realm. Only by the Divine Mind can the task be completed, and all things seen as ordered in complete obedience to the two principles of thought.

Leibniz, in propounding this view, develops a genuinely original conception of the relation holding between appearance and reality. Only monads, that is, spiritual beings, exist. Apart from the representative activity of the monads there are no such existences as space and time, as matter and motion. The mathematical and physical sciences, in their present forms, therefore, cannot be interpreted as revealing absolute existences. But if ideally developed, they would emancipate themselves from mechanical and sensuous notions; and would consist of a body of truths, which, as thus perfected, would be discovered to constitute the very being of thought. Pure thought or reason consists in the apprehension of such truths. To discover and to prove them thought does not require to issue out beyond itself. It creates this conceptual world in the very act of apprehending it; and as this realm of truth thus expresses the necessary character of all thought, whether divine or human, it is universal and unchanging. Each mind apprehends the same eternal truth; but owing to imperfection each finite being apprehends it with some degree of obscurity and confusion, fragmentarily, in terms of sense, and so falls prey to the illusion that the self stands in mechanical relations to a spatial and temporal world of matter and motion.

Leibniz supports this doctrine by his theory of sense-

THE PHILOSOPHY OF LEIBNIZ

experience as originating spontaneously from within the individual mind. Thereby he is only repeating that pure thought generates its whole content from within itself. Sense-experience, in its intrinsic nature, is nothing but pure thought. Such thought, owing to the inexhaustible wealth of its conceptual significance, so confuses the mind which thus generates it, that only by prolonged analysis can larger and larger portions of it be construed into the conceptual judgments which have all along constituted its sole content. And in the process, space, time, and motion lose all sensuous character, appearing in their true nature as orders of relation which can be adequately apprehended only in conceptual terms. They remain absolutely real as objects of thought, though as sensible existences they are reduced to the level of mere appearance. Such is the view of thought which is unfolded in Leibniz's writings, in startling contrast to the naturalistic teaching of his Scotch antagonist.

As already indicated, Kant's first-hand knowledge of Leibniz's teaching was very limited. He was acquainted with it chiefly through the inadequate channel of Wolff's somewhat commonplace exposition of its principles. But even from such a source he could derive what was most essential, namely, Leibniz's view of thought as absolute in its powers and unlimited in its claims. How closely Wolff holds to the main tenet of Leibniz's system appears from his definition of philosophy as "the science of possible things, so far as they are possible." He thus retains, though without the deeper suggestiveness of Leibniz's speculative insight, the view that thought precedes reality and legislates for it. By the possible is not meant the existentially or psychologically possible, but the conceptually necessary, that which, prior to all existence, has objective validity, sharing in the universal and necessary character of thought itself.

As Riehl has very justly pointed out,[1] Wolff's philosophy had, prior even to the period of Kant's earliest writings, been displaced by empirical, psychological enquiries and by eclectic, popular philosophy. Owing to the prevailing lack of thoroughness in philosophical thinking, "Problemlosigkeit" characterised the whole period. The two exclusively alternative views of the function of thought stood alongside one another within each of the competing systems, quite unreconciled and in their mutual conflict absolutely destructive of all real consistency and thoroughness of thought. It was Kant who restored rationalism to its rightful place. He reinvigorated the flaccid tone of his day by adopting in his writings, both

[1] *Philosophischer Kriticismus*, 2nd ed. p. 209.

early and late, the strict method of rational science, and by insisting that the really crucial issues be boldly faced. In essentials Kant holds to Wolff's definition of philosophy as "the science of possible things, so far as they are possible." As I have just remarked, the possible is taken in an objective sense, and the definition consequently gives expression to the view of philosophy upon which Kant so frequently insists, as lying wholly in the sphere of pure *a priori* thought. Its function is to determine prior to specific experience what experience must be; and obviously that is only possible by means of an *a priori*, purely conceptual method. His *Critique*, as its title indicates, is a criticism of pure reason by pure reason. Nothing which escapes definition through pure *a priori* thinking can come within its sphere. The problem of the "possibility of experience" is the problem of discovering the conditions which *necessarily* determine experience to be what it is. Kant, of course, radically transforms the whole problem, in method of treatment as well as in results, when in defining the subject-matter of enquiry he substitutes experience for things absolutely existent. This modification is primarily due to the influence of Hume. But the constant occurrence in Kant's philosophy of the term "possibility" marks his continued belief in the Idealist view of thought. Though pure thought never by itself amounts to knowledge—therein Kant departs from the extreme rationalist position—only through it is any knowledge, empirical or *a priori*, possible at all. Philosophy, in order to exist, must be a system of *a priori* rational principles. Nothing empirical or hypothetical can find any place in it.[1] Yet at the same time it is the system of the *a priori* conditions only of experience, not of ultimate reality. Such is the twofold relation of agreement and difference in which Kant stands to his rationalist predecessors.

[1] Cf. above, pp. lv-vi, lxi, 543 ff.

APPENDIX C

KANT'S "OPUS POSTUMUM"

UNTIL the appearance in 1920 of Adickes' elaborate and careful study[1] of the manuscripts which compose what is now usually entitled Kant's *Opus Postumum*,[2] students of Kant have been dependent upon the sections published by Reicke in the *Altpreussische Monatsschrift* (1882–1884). Not only, however, are these latter incomplete, but the parts omitted have frequently been those which are most important. Also, the sections reproduced have been altered and added to in a very arbitrary manner. Reicke's part in the work consisted in copying, partly with his own hand and partly with the co-operation of others, the selected portions. After a single collation with the originals, the copies were edited by E. Arnoldt,[3] whose method of procedure was as follows:

"Arnoldt then prepared the sheets for the press, and did so—it is unbelievable but true!—without acquainting himself with the manuscripts which were available in his immediate neighbourhood. In the editing he left out much,—in its place (at least in great part) inserting dashes. Further he extended the punctuation and altered the text through numerous conjectures, without in any way indicating, either through a general note or by special indication, where these changes have been made. His intention was, on the one hand to have Kant appear before the public in as worthy a manner as [to himself] seemed possible, and yet on the other to allow the character of the manuscripts to show itself, *i.e.* through the retention of misguided statements."[4]

[1] Erich Adickes, *Kants Opus Postumum, dargestellt und beurteilt* (Berlin, 1920).
[2] Following Reicke, I have above (pp. 275 *n.*, 283 *n.*, 482 *n.*, 514 *n.*) entitled it the *Transition from the Metaphysical First Principles of Natural Science to Physics*. Kant so entitles it in his letter to Garve (September 21, 1798; *W.* xii. p. 257). This, however, is only one among the many other titles to which he inclined, according as this or that part of the work was most preoccupying his attention. Cf. below, pp. 608 *n.* 2, 610 *n.* 2.
[3] Arnoldt, at his own request, was not named as co-editor, as he regarded the copying as being the most exacting part of the work!
[4] Adickes, pp. 13-14.

In the reprinted passages the omissions amount to more than 13,800 words ; and these occur, Adickes tells us, just in those very sections which are the most important, and for the proper understanding of which every clause and every word is more or less significant. We have to bear in mind that the manuscripts were not intended for immediate publication, but are Kant's private notes, in which, with frequent failure and at best with only comparative success, constantly restating and modifying, with words and sentences crossed out, and with notes added on the margins, as suggestions occurred to him, he endeavoured to arrive at a satisfactory formulation of certain new positions to which he was tentatively feeling his way. Considering that Arnoldt, while making his own interpolations, alterations, and omissions, was ignorant of the originals, it is perhaps surprising that Reicke's text is not even less reliable than it proves to be. As Adickes testifies :

"I have several times found that passages which, in Reicke's text are insoluble riddles, lost their terrors, and became clear and intelligible, immediately I was in position to peruse them in the manuscript." [1]

Adickes has succeeded in dating the twelve main sections as begun not later than 1797. His dating of the various sections as relatively earlier or later, and of the earliest of them as belonging to the years 1797–1798, is important for several reasons. In the first place, it finally disposes of the view, rashly sponsored by Kuno Fischer,[2] and repeated by others, that the *Opus Postumum* is a work of Kant's senility, revealing in painful fashion, amidst endless repetitions, and with only occasional flashes of genuine insight, his failing efforts to follow out a continuous train of thought. This, indeed, is in some degree true, though much less so than appears on superficial study, of what are usually numbered the seventh and the first sections. These sections were, as Adickes quite conclusively demonstrates, the last to be written, the seventh falling within the year 1800, and the first in the period between December 1800 and Kant's death in 1804—the major part probably being written in 1801 and its last passages in 1803. Even in these sections increasing age shows itself

---

[1] Adickes, p. 3.

[2] Shortly after Reicke's publication of selections from the *Opus Postumum*, Pastor C. E. A. Krause of Hamburg purchased the original manuscripts from Kant's heirs ; and while upholding their value against Kuno Fischer's ill-informed attacks, himself took an almost equally exaggerated view, eulogising the *Opus Postumum* as being "Kant's greatest work" I In 1884 Krause published his *Immanuel Kant wider Kuno Fischer*, in reply to Kuno Fischer's *Das Streber- und Gründertum in der Litteratur* (1884).

mainly in Kant's failure to co-ordinate his more complex lines of thought. Since all the remainder of the twelve sections can, however, be assigned to the years between 1797 and the early months of 1800, when Kant was publishing his *Metaphysische Anfangsgründe der Rechtslehre*, his *Streit der Fakultäten*, and his *Anthropologie in pragmatischer Hinsicht*, and composing letters which show no sign of weakening mental powers, whatever defects these sections may exhibit must be otherwise explained than by any alleged senility in their author. As a matter of fact, the repetitions, and the extremely disjointed character of the text, are more or less such as we find in the already published *Lose Blätter*, dating from Kant's most active period. They represent his usual method of composition; and the most that can be said is that with the passage of years Kant came more and more to depend, for the development of his thoughts, upon the processes of actual writing—passing, almost momentary conjectures finding their way on to paper, as well as those formulations to which he could give his more deliberate approval.[1] Also, just as in his earlier works—most notably in the *Critique of Pure Reason*—he still, even in these last years, alternates between competing methods of developing his thought, seeking, as he has himself said,[2] to test his doctrines by trial of their opposites. Frequently, too, as we shall have occasion to observe, he states the particular point to which he is at the moment directing attention with all possible emphasis, leaving the necessary qualifications temporarily aside. This indeed explains how Vaihinger [3]—to whom students of Kant owe so great a debt—has been able to allege that Kant in his last years, as represented by the *Opus Postumum*, had so far departed from his earlier views, or, as Vaihinger maintains, so successfully clarified them, as to become a pupil of Zoroaster, and—much in the manner of Nietzsche, who was writing his *Also sprach Zarathustra* in the very years in which parts of Kant's *Opus Postumum* first saw the light—to hold that all our concepts of noumenal being, including that of Divine Existence, are but fictions, and that they are justified only as they inspire human effort in the realising of its self-prescribed ideals.

If this interpretation of Kant's final teaching were correct, it would, in the view of most of Kant's readers, indicate a mental and moral instability, to account for which the

---

[1] Their editing, to be satisfactory, would demand an exact reprint, with all the alterations and marginal notes, including the words and sentences which Kant has crossed out: his first thoughts are at times more illuminating, as a clue to his meaning, than the more cautious, less self-revealing terms which he substitutes.

[2] Cf. above, p. xxiii.

[3] *Die Philosophie des als ob* (2nd edition, 1913), p. 721 ff.

enfeeblement of age might reasonably be postulated. The evidence, however, carefully studied, points to very different conclusions. Kant's newly acquired interest in Zoroaster [1] was indeed so great that in 1802 he contemplated including that name in the title of his work.[2] But, as we should have expected, the sources of his interest are hardly those of Nietzsche. Kant in his eighties, as he appears in the *Opus Postumum*, is quite capable of revising, and on evidence shown of modifying, his older teaching. He remains astonishingly flexible in all save his most fundamental philosophical convictions, concentrating his attention on those features of his teaching which had been most called in question by his pupils and younger contemporaries; and in regard to them developing very novel views, fittingly, though not always successfully, expressed by means of certain newly devised terms. Thus he discusses the fundamental and very far-reaching issues which underlie his much-challenged and, considering his other doctrines, very difficult and obscure *Refutation of Idealism*. That refutation, as involving a realist view of the world both of science and of ordinary experience, can, as he now explicitly recognises, only be defended through a doctrine of double affection; and this doctrine he proceeds to develop in great detail. Secondly, Kant restates that part of his teaching which, more than any other, had been questioned and very generally rejected by his contemporaries and by the more independent among his own pupils—his doctrines in regard to the existence and nature of things in themselves. In this connection he also discusses the Idea of God, and in so doing acknowledges the inadequacy of his professedly practical, but really theoretical, proof of God's existence, advocating in its place a proof of a more consistently moral character.

But I have still to mention the chief item in the programme which Kant sets before himself. The *Opus Postumum* is designed to serve as a *Transition from the Metaphysical First Principles of Natural Science to Physics*.[3] In order that this transition be made in accordance with Critical principles, Kant now proposes to extend the sphere of those tran-

---

[1] Due presumably to the appearance of Kleuker's translation (1st edition, 1776; 2nd edition, 1786) of Anquetil Du Perron's work: " *Zend-Avesta, Zoroaster's lebendiges Wort, worin die Lehren und Meinungen von Gott, Welt, Natur und Menschen, imgleichen die Zeremonien des heiligen Dienstes der Persen usf. aufbehalten sind.*"

[2] Two of the titles thus suggested by Kant are: " *Zoroaster: oder die Philosophie im Ganzen ihres Inbegriffs unter einem Prinsip susammengefasst* "; "*Zoroaster: das Ideal der physisch und zugleich moralisch praktischen Vernunft in Einem Sinnen-Objekt vereinigt.*"

[3] Cf. above, p. 607 n. 2.

scendental considerations whereby in the *Critique of Pure Reason* and in the *Metaphysical Foundations of Natural Science* the constitution of physical nature has been determined in a strictly *a priori* manner. That is to say, Kant has meantime, since the publication of the latter treatise in 1786, come to believe that the transcendental method is capable of a much wider application than he had then thought feasible. Not merely the general form of nature but the possible types both of physical energy and of secondary qualities can, he now maintains, be anticipated and systematised in accordance with the *a priori* principles of understanding. Accordingly the table of categories is again brought into action, affording Kant in his last years yet another opportunity of indulging in his favourite pastime, the elaboration of new and ingenious applications of his architectonic.

These attempts to anticipate, on *a priori* grounds, the outcome of sense perception and of scientific enquiry are, it need hardly be said, from the start doomed to failure. If the table of categories, as we have to recognise, cannot justify even the more moderate demands of Kant's formal requirements in the *Critique*, it is still less fitted to predetermine the possible modes of energy or the possible types of secondary qualities. But the mere fact that Kant should even attempt to do so is highly significant of his altered perspective at this period; and, in passing, I may indicate the general lines upon which this new deduction is made to proceed.

The deduction opens with an analysis of the concept of motion or moving force. In respect of *origin*, motion is either inherent (congenital) or communicated (impressed); in respect of *direction* either attractive or repulsive; in respect of *place* either progressive or oscillatory; and finally, in respect of the *filling* of space, it must either fill empty pores in a body and so be coercible, or penetrate throughout it and so be incoercible. This fourfold division, in order to establish its claim to be at once necessary and exhaustive, must rest on an *a priori* principle; and what higher sanction could it have than the fourfold division of the table of categories! No satisfactory method of establishing connection between the fourfold division of the categories and the above four pairs of alternatives can, indeed, be devised; and even supposing that could be done, the four pairs of alternatives cannot be shown to be exhaustive of the types of physical force with which the natural sciences deal. Belief in the adequacy of his architectonic tides Kant, however, over all such difficulties; and while he describes the pairs of opposites ever anew, in the most varying terms, the fourfold division remains a constant feature in all his lists.[1] The difficulties become yet more patently insuperable and the enterprise even more grotesquely ill-devised—to extract from formal categories a reason for our having five, and only five, senses![2] —when Kant proceeds by similar methods to prove on strictly *a priori* grounds that only six types of secondary qualities are empirically possible. Though this part of Kant's new teaching is developed in the *Opus Postumum* with remarkable patience and ingenuity, it is, as Adickes justly concludes, entirely worthless.[3]

But this being so, why, it may be asked, even allowing for Kant's unreasoning affection for his logical architectonic, does he set himself so impossible a task? Why does he persist in an endeavour which, however the material be recast, ends only in failure? The answer to this question supplies what would seem to be the key to the understanding of the *Opus Postumum* as a whole. Taken in its entirety, it deals with three apparently unconnected problems: the doctrine of double affection, the principles of natural science, the nature and extent of our knowledge of noumenal realities. The first-named problem, however, when properly appreciated, by itself—the other contributory factors will be noted later— largely accounts for Kant's preoccupation with the other two; and it likewise explains how Kant came to depart from his earlier position in regard to the strictly formal character of the legislation which the understanding prescribes to the phenomenal world in space and time. Why the doctrine of double affection is so fundamental in Kant's system,[4] and why, while being so, it had yet to wait until Kant's last years for any precise and explicit formulation, are the two main questions to which I shall endeavour to give an answer.[5]

The fact that Kant's doctrine of double affection, though not formulated in the *Critique of Pure Reason*, has all along been fundamental in his theory of knowledge, goes far to account for the very strange circumstance that competent students of Kant have hitherto ranged themselves in opposing camps:

"Fischer and Krause [6] are representatives of the two opposed ways

---

[1] Kant enumerates, in these lists, at least thirteen different pairs of opposites, and his professed reduction of the thirteen to four is nowhere shown.

[2] Kant sometimes counts the senses as six in number, taking heat as a vital sense.

[3] Cf. Adickes, p. 343 ff.   [4] Cf. above, pp. 270 ff., 312 ff., 373-4, 415-17.

[5] The publication of Adickes' promised work, "*Kants Lehre von der doppelten Affektion unseres Ich als Schlüssel zu seiner Erkenntnistheorie,*" has, unfortunately, been delayed by war-conditions.

[6] Pastor C. E. A. Krause, not the better-known K. C. F. Krause. Cf. above, p. 608 *n.* 2.

of interpreting the Kantian Philosophy which from the nineties of the eighteenth century up to our own time have challenged one another ever anew. The one party, to which Johann Schulze (recognised by Kant himself as the best interpreter of his works[1]) and many other Kantians of the eighteenth century, and in recent times Kuno Fischer, Paulsen, B. Erdmann, and Riehl—to name only a few—belong, allows that Kant, in accordance with the indubitable wording of his writings, postulated things in themselves as existing independently of us and as affecting us, but on the other hand is for the most part inclined to deny the possibility of an affection through phenomenal objects.

"The other party, from Maimon and Fichte to Krause and the Marburg School,[2] desires to free Kant from the alleged contradiction and absurdity of regarding things in themselves as self-subsisting and as acting upon us, and appealing from the letter of his writings to their supposed spirit, leaves to him only an affection through phenomenal objects, and in these objects finds the immediate and last cause of the sensations. But while it frees Kant from certain contradictions, it either involves him in others yet more grievous, or must place a very forced interpretation upon his words.

"There is only one way of escape from this dilemma: in accordance with Kant's express assertions, we must hold with Vaihinger that Kant intended to assert an affection of the self through things in themselves, as well as its affection through phenomenal objects. Only from this standpoint can the inconsistencies and contradictions with which the two parties mutually make play against one another be shown to vanish."[3]

Kant's *Opus Postumum* gives welcome confirmation of the correctness of Vaihinger's view, which has been followed in the body of this *Commentary*. In the *Critique of Pure Reason*, when arguing on phenomenalist lines, Kant has maintained that on the basis of transcendental idealism an empirical realism can be established; but nowhere does he face the difficulties which such a position involves. In one set of passages[4] he refers us to things in themselves as the primary, external conditions of sense-experience; in yet another set of passages[5] it is physical stimuli which are cited as the causes of our sensations. Nowhere does he explain how, if objects be appearances, conditioned by mental processes, they can also be causes, initiating and yielding material for these processes. The latter assertions are extorted from

---

[1] Cf. above, p. 129 *n*. 5.
[2] The School of Cohen and the Neo-Kantians, among whom may be counted Windelband and Rickert. Green, Caird, and the Hegelians generally, belong to this second group.
[3] Adickes, p. 18.
[4] Cf. above, pp. 217-18, 275 ff., 314 ff., 373-4.
[5] *Ibid.*

him, in part by the empirical evidence, very difficult to question or otherwise interpret, supplied by the physical and physiological sciences, and in part by the exigencies of his own method of refuting idealism of the Berkeleian and Cartesian types. That refutation, in the form in which it is stated in the second edition of the *Critique*, demands the drawing of a distinction between our representations and the objects which they disclose; and as he quite evidently means us to conclude, the allowing of independent existence to the latter. That these independent existences have causal efficacy is likewise, for similar reasons, postulated in certain other sections of the *Critique*.[1] All of these admissions, however, appear more by way of implication than by explicit avowal and defence; their compatibility with his other doctrines he does not even attempt to discuss, save in the most general manner as bearing on the question of subjective idealism *versus* empirical realism; and even in this connection, the latter position is developed, not in terms of itself, but mainly by refutation of its supposedly sole alternative. Now however, in the *Opus Postumum*, the situation is dramatically altered: the difficulties which have hitherto been kept in the obscurer background occupy the centre of the stage. The two-level doctrine, which in the *Critique* emerges as the distinction between empirical and noumenal reality, reappears in a much more definite form as the distinction between a quite literal interpretation of the teaching of the natural sciences on the one hand and the transcendental idealism which yields the key to the generating problem of the Critical philosophy on the other; and as a consequence the doctrine of double affection becomes the main subject of argument and exposition. Even when it is not itself under consideration, it is, as we shall find, all-determining, in deciding the kind of hypotheses and conclusions which, on other, at first sight seemingly unconnected issues, are being propounded.

Kant's treatment of the doctrine of double affection is lengthy and elaborate, but only his main points immediately concern us; and of these I shall give first a more general and then a more detailed statement. In Kant's view the ultimate source of all spontaneity and agency lies in things in themselves. As regards the self in itself, this spontaneity is shown in its production *out of itself* of forms which are peculiar to itself, namely, time, space, and the categories. Through these forms, by means of its synthetic activities, it posits the phenomenal world. Even the very notion of the thing in itself as object is formed by it on the analogy of the unity of apperception, as

[1] Cf. above, pp. 313-21, 373-4.

prescribing to the mind the task of so unifying the contents of its knowledge that all existences in space, including thereunder the empirical self, can be conceived as constituting a single unitary system. The self has thus set itself into the given, and has quite literally "made itself its own object." It is the "possessor and originator" (*Inhaber und Urheber*[1]) of the entire phenomenal world.

Things in themselves are likewise a source of spontaneity and agency. They affect the self in itself, and thereby generate the material (*Stoff*), the noumenal manifold, so to speak, upon which the self stamps its own very specific imprint. How much has to be allowed to the subjective factors remains, however, somewhat uncertain. Kant quite obviously halts indecisively between alternative views. Sometimes he seems to imply that the internal, timeless relations in which things in themselves stand to one another are translated by the self into time and space, and so have still to be thought as being the source of the causal, dynamical capacities which, in terms of the subjective categories, we ascribe to all physical existences. Just as the known, empirical self is not a second existence, separate from the transcendental self, but, on the contrary, has to be viewed as retaining the spontaneity, the active capacity for self-expression, which is the fundamental feature of its noumenal counterpart, the self in itself, so empirical objects in their interactions will mirror the potencies which they phenomenally represent. At other times, and more usually, things in themselves, in the course of Kant's exposition, pass entirely into the background; the co-existences and sequences, *i.e.* this and that happening as here and now, rather than elsewhere or at some other time, are presumably still to be regarded as determined by the unknown things in themselves—as to this Kant, for obvious reasons, maintains a discreet silence—but in all other respects the system of physical nature is viewed as being determined by the inherent constitution and self-imposed demands of the transcendental self. If we take the phenomenal world as comprising the empirical self in its psychical as well as in its physical aspect, Kant's ultimate position is indeed a curiously inconsistent blending of the two views. The empirical self and the physical entities with which it stands in dynamical interaction in space are treated as meeting, so to speak, on a level of equality. They have the same relative degree of independent existence, and the same relative capacity of initiating change. But when their relation to their noumenal conditions comes up for consideration, this equality is no longer upheld. The

---

[1] Cited by Adickes, p. 662.

empirical self continues to be regarded as the representative of the transcendental self, and as capable of exercising identically the same synthetic functions, and so as reconstructing out of the given sensuous manifold a world identical in its physical, non-sensuous features with that which has been already constructed by the noumenal self. On the other hand, all the fundamental characteristics of the physical entities— their having this and that fundamental type of moving energy —no less than their strictly formal features, are traced to the noumenal self. Kant's phenomenalism thus becomes markedly lopsided; and this not through any inadvertence or arbitrary choice, but for reasons which, however unsatisfactory, are quite unavoidable.

In my ignorance of Kant's actual methods of argument in the unpublished sections of the *Opus Postumum*, I ventured, in this *Commentary*,[1] to conjecture that his doctrine of double affection would lead him to conclude that on the phenomenal level "the problem of knowledge proper, namely, how it is possible to have or acquire knowledge, whether of a motion in space or of a sensation in time does not arise"; and that in treating this latter problem, in which we are referred to noumenal conditions, the negative consequences of his *Objective Deduction*, as drawn in the section on the *Paralogisms*, would receive fuller recognition. These conjectures prove to be mistaken.[2] Kant proceeds on quite other lines. In the first place—I may perhaps be pardoned for expecting the contrary —he equips the empirical self not only with consciousness, but with a complete transcendental outfit of mental forms and synthetic processes, and by these means proceeds to supply an answer to the question how the empirical self, by means of its given sensations, can acquire knowledge of the independent existences to which these sensations are due. And secondly, so far is Kant from hesitating to conceive the noumenal conditions of experience as consisting in a noumenal self, that on the contrary all other noumenal conditions withdraw into the background, and the self, virtually conceived as an all-powerful creator, originates from its own internal resources the world which it is then (we must not say subsequently) in position to contemplate. Things in themselves are indeed

---

[1] Above, p. 275. For reasons indicated below (pp. 633-4), I have left my original statements unaltered.

[2] On the other hand, the views above adopted (pp. 204-19) in regard to Kant's early doctrine of the transcendental object seem to be confirmed by the *Opus Postumum*. Though Adickes has employed the phrase "transcendental object" in the heading of one of his sections (pp. 669-89), in none of the passages cited is it used by Kant himself. It is quite obviously incompatible with his recognition, so very explicit in the *Opus Postumum*, of the *threefold* distinction between representation, the empirical object, and the thing in itself.

assumed to affect the noumenal self, and thereby to supply, or perhaps alternately to stimulate the self to supply, a noumenal manifold; but this manifold is so subserviently plastic to the self's requirements that nothing really precise and specific[1] is thereby determined. Consequently, the phenomenal world thus generated is, to all intents and purposes, viewed as an emanation from the self, creatively produced, but modelled on no previously existent pattern, ideal or real. Kant's old-time watchwords—that all order and system in nature are due to the mind, that transcendental idealism, especially the doctrine of the ideality, *i.e.* subjectivity, of time and space, is the key to the solution of the Critical problems, that the mind can only anticipate what it has itself predetermined—are not only held to, but receive even more emphatic endorsement throughout the *Opus Postumum* than in those sections of the *Critique* which are earliest in date of writing.

Yet this need not be taken as signifying that Kant has at last ceased to oscillate between subjectivism and phenomenalism, and has definitely decided in favour of the former. What it does apparently mean is that Kant has succumbed to the malign influence of his own unfortunate manner of distinguishing between appearance and reality by the method of antagonism, as contrasted types of existence.[2] He is now maintaining that between the self in itself and things in themselves knowledge, as a form of contemplation, is impossible. Noumenally regarded, knowledge is only possible as a relation holding between the mind and that which stands related to it as a creature to its creator.[3] Hence Kant's insistence that physical nature, even on its material side, as regards its possible types of moving forces, is predetermined by the intrinsic constitution of the self. On the other hand, phenomenally regarded, the knowledge which the empirical self acquires of physical entities in space is knowledge in the strictest sense of the term; it is the apprehension by the self of actual, independent existences. The world thus known is a phenomenal world, but the knowledge that we have of it is knowledge which allows of a genuinely realistic attitude in the explanation both of its coming about and of its validity once it has been acquired. Further, the first view of experience is, Kant maintains, necessary in order to establish the second: the only method of justifying our knowledge of

[1] As above noted, Kant's teaching in this regard is somewhat uncertain: we can hardly avoid regarding it as intentionally obscure.

[2] Cf. above, pp. liv, 416-17, 558-61.

[3] This, as above noted (p. 160), is a view which is also found in the *Critique of Pure Reason*.

physical entities is to show that their existence is pre-conditioned by those very *a priori* forms through which alone they can be apprehended. Short of such demonstration, we cannot bridge the gulf which lies between the sensations, which alone are immediately experienced by the empirical self, and the independent existences which its empirical judgments profess to define.

Thus, in regard to Kant's final positions, as revealed in the *Opus Postumum*, whatever else be doubtful, two points at least are abundantly clear: first, that he definitely commits himself to a realist view of the physical system in space and time, and of the manner in which we acquire knowledge of it; and secondly, that he is willing to go almost any lengths in the way of speculative hypotheses regarding the noumenal conditions of our sense-experience, if only thereby the difficulties which stand in the way of this empirical realism can be successfully dealt with. The one requirement upon which he insists is that the hypotheses adopted be compatible with the solution given to the generating problem of the Critical philosophy, how synthetic *a priori* judgments are possible. In the *Opus Postumum*, as in the *Critique of Pure Reason*, transcendental idealism is the ultimate foundation upon which his realist account of the natural world is based. Neither his subjectivist principles nor his realist inclinations are sacrificed: the two are segregated on different levels. But ultimately it is still subjectivist principles, working on the deeper (or obscurer) level, which supply Kant with his answer to the fundamental problem: how the self-transcendence involved in knowledge, realistically interpreted, can be possible. The self can be a knower only if it be a creator. An untenable method of distinguishing appearance and reality, backed by a subjectivism of the most extreme type, are the foundations upon which Kant is attempting to erect a realist view of the natural world! His phenomenalism, that is to say, is in direct conflict with many of the purposes which have inspired it.[1]

With these somewhat general, introductory remarks, I may now pass to a more detailed statement of Kant's doctrines. Since the nature of noumenal affection can be determined only by way of speculative hypotheses, and since these hypotheses are devised exclusively in order to account for the possibility of our sense experience and of the scientific knowledge which

---

[1] Beyond the corrections above indicated (p. 616), I have not found reason to alter in any essential way the criticisms passed in the first edition of this *Commentary* (above, pp. 281-4, 316-17) upon the defects of Kant's phenomenalism. Study of the *Opus Postumum* serves only to underline these defects, and would seem to show that when the path by which he has himself sought to remedy these defects is followed to the end, it turns out to be an *impasse*.

is based thereon, they can best be understood when approached by way of these latter. If, therefore, we first consider Kant's doctrine of empirical affection, and note the points at which, taken in and by itself, it fails to account for the knowledge which experience does actually yield, we shall be in a position to define quite precisely the requirements which the doctrine of noumenal affection must be made to satisfy.

Kant's doctrine of empirical affection, *i.e.* affection of the empirical self, is as follows. The empirical self, like the empirical object, is conceived as exercising a certain spontaneity, whereby it reacts, and that in a twofold manner, when affected by physical stimuli. Kant seems to have begun by distinguishing between the self in its physical and the self in its psychical aspect. In a few passages, all of which Adickes dates as among the earliest to be written, the self in its physical aspect, in so far as it is equivalent to the brain, is taken as being an integral part of the unitary system of reciprocally acting bodies, and therefore as responding with counter-movements. These brain-motions are of a purely material character, and do not in their mode of origin differ from the reactions of other physical bodies.[1] Secondly, the self responds to the mechanical stimulus in a purely psychical manner; in the exercise of its moving forces (*bewegende Kräfte*) it affects itself, and in so doing posits, and in positing apprehends, sensations characterised by this and that secondary quality. Each sensation is an "*Aktus der Autonomie*." The empirical self, in being affected, has affected itself.

This initial theory Kant proceeded to modify in one important respect, namely, in his manner of conceiving the origin of the brain-motions.[2] He seems almost at once to have concluded that the empirical self cannot be regarded in a dual manner, as being psychical and yet also the physical brain. He therefore distinguished between the self and the brain, and set the latter in subordination to the former. Consequently, his more deliberate teaching, as represented by all the later passages, is that the physical stimulus, taken as completing itself in and through certain brain-processes, exhausts itself in its psychical effect upon the self, and that the self thereupon responds in a twofold manner, by bringing into existence certain other brain-motions, and by positing its

---

[1] Kant conceived (cf. above, pp. 351, 373-4, 379-80) physical entities as centres of force, not in the Cartesian manner as externally endowed with motion. The empirical self is, however, more than physical; and among its moving forces Kant in the *Opus Postumum* enumerates " understanding and desire " (*Verstand und Begehren*).

[2] Cf. Adickes, p. 257 ff.

sensations. Kant, we may presume, conceived that in the former precisely those amounts of energy are produced anew which have been expended in generating the self-affection. On this view the empirical self, as a self and not merely as a name for the body, acquires the same relative independence and autonomy as physical entities. It has its own "moving forces," and among these Kant enumerates understanding and desire (*Verstand und Begehren*). It acts upon the body, and not merely the body upon it; and such control of the body it manifests no less in sense-perception than in voluntary movements.

But in addition to these two sets of activities Kant endows the empirical self with a third set, namely, those synthetic activities whereby sensations are interpreted into perceived objects. In these activities likewise, the self affects itself; they are involved in the positing of "sensations *with consciousness*." To them is due the sensuous apprehension of the independent world within which the physical stimuli fall.

"The perception of the object is the consciousness of the moving force of the subject itself, not in so far as it is affected, but in so far as it affects itself, *i.e.* by means of the understanding brings the manifold of appearance under a principle of its combination,—a principle which is the ground of the possibility of experience, *i.e.* of the systematic connection of the perceptions."[1]

The existences defined by the natural sciences are not, Kant is here maintaining, endowed, as are the objects of our immediate experience, with the secondary qualities. That only comes about through their action upon the empirical self, and so through the resulting apprehension of them in sensuous terms. Acting upon the bodily sense organs, they give rise to a purely sensuous manifold; and it is out of this manifold, not in itself spatially or temporally ordered, that the empirical self, through its intuitional forms and intellectual categories, elaborates those sense-experiences which form the sole basis of any possible, further knowledge. Only later, by reflection upon the world thus apprehended, in the light of evidence obtained through the more indirect processes of scientific enquiry, does the empirical self learn to discount the secondary qualities and to define the physical existences in their true, independent nature.

Clearly, Kant is no longer regarding the empirical self, in the manner of the *Critique of Pure Reason*, as the known and embodied; it is here represented as both active and conscious; and we are left wondering what rôle, if any, is left for the

[1] Cited by Adickes, p. 269.

transcendental self and for its affection by things in themselves. Has not Kant, on the basis of a scientific realism, worked his way round to a position which must render him sceptical as to the need for assuming either a transcendental self (viewed, that is, in any *ontological* fashion) or things in themselves? That such was by no means Kant's intention, and that this is not in the least how he interpreted the outcome of these novel doctrines, becomes at once clear when we recognise, as we must, that if only the empirical self and its activities could be appealed to in explanation of experience, Kant's answer to his fundamental problem—how synthetic *a priori* judgments are possible—would be undermined. He would be maintaining that the self, in interpreting its sensations through space, time, and the categories, acquires knowledge of independent existences; and yet how this should be possible would only be explicable on the assumption of a pre-established harmony between mental forms and that which is known by their means. Now, as hitherto, Kant rejects such a solution as unphilosophical. He continues to maintain, indeed with increased emphasis, that only on a basis of transcendental *idealism* can any such *realistic* interpretation of empirical existence be upheld. Should the above explanation of our sense-experience be capable of no supplementation, and so have to justify itself in terms of itself, not realism, but scepticism, would be the inevitable outcome. If sensations alone are immediately apprehended, and if all else be apprehensible only through the additions which the mind itself makes thereto, then, in the absence of all transcendental justification of the latter, there can be no assured knowledge of the independently real. The independently real will have to be recognised as equivalent to the realm of things in themselves, and therefore as not accessible by any possible experience or by any inference based thereon.

This is obvious, immediately we recognise how thoroughgoing (in its own strange way) is the realism which Kant is professing to establish. Empirical selves and empirical objects have, he is teaching, such completeness of reality that by their interactions they can bring into existence a set of further phenomena, which, save for their interactions, would never come about, namely, the sensations of the secondary qualities.[1] And, on Kant's view, only these

---

[1] " Metaphysically considered," material bodies are appearances; "for physics they are the things in themselves (*die Sachen an sich selbst*) which affect the senses (*den Sinn*)." (Cited by Adickes, p. 239.) Kant varies greatly in his use of the phrases *Erscheinung von der Erscheinung, indirekte, mittelbare Erscheinung, Erscheinung der zweiten Ordnung, Erscheinung vom zweiten Range* (cf. above, p. 283 *n.* 2, and Adickes, p. 298 ff.). In the main they are defined

sensations are immediately present (so to speak) to the mind; all else is added in the process of their apprehension. The empirical self, interpreting the sensations in accordance with forms determined by its own intrinsic nature, sets them into space and time, and uniting them in terms of the categories, thereby acquires experience of the dynamical, space-time world to which they are due. In other words, starting from the empirically given sensations, it is through synthetic *a priori* judgments that we transcend them, and in transcending them apprehend their independently existing physical causes. How such apprehension, as a form of reliable experience, should be possible, calls for that type of deduction, *i.e.* justification, which, as Kant believed, only a transcendental idealism, resting on his "Copernican hypothesis," can supply. As he therefore argues, a realist doctrine of empirical affection requires, as its necessary supplement, an idealist doctrine of noumenal affection. Only through the self's timeless conditioning of its time-space world can sense-experience—the sole source of scientific knowledge—itself rank as a comprehensible occurrence.

Now so long as Kant was occupied, in the period 1770–1796, in the absorbing and strenuous task of finding an answer to the question, how experience, theoretical, moral, and aesthetic, is possible, we can understand why he should be content to justify our scientific judgments by maintaining that they apply only to appearances which are mind-dependent, no distinction being yet drawn between dependence on the empirical and dependence on the noumenal self. Since objects must conform to the conditions under which alone experience is possible, knowledge is not of independently existing realities, but only of appearances; the objects can be known only in so far as they have been *made* in the process of their apprehension. When, however, this task

---

in terms of the contrast between the physical and the metaphysical view of reality. What from the physical standpoint is thing in itself (*Sache an sich selbst*) is from the metaphysical standpoint only appearance. Both the material existences themselves, as complexes of moving forces, and their systematic ordering rest on the self-affection of the self, and are therefore appearances. The appearances of these appearances are the sensations, *i.e.* the secondary sense-qualities. In those other passages, however, in which Kant confines his view to the standpoint of the empirical self, the above phrases are employed in a very bewildering manner, in at least two quite distinct senses. As a rule the term appearance then denotes the sensations, *i.e.* the *a posteriori*, secondary sense-qualities. They are viewed as *direct* appearances, *i.e.* as being the sense-data beyond which the empirical self advances to the corresponding, underlying physical agents. The latter are the indirect or mediate appearances arrived at as the outcome of the ordering, objectivising activities of the empirical self. But the terms are also occasionally employed in the reverse manner, and therefore more in harmony with the meaning assigned to them from the metaphysical standpoint.

was completed, and Kant's mind, at greater leisure, could play more freely upon the situation thus disclosed, he very soon came to appreciate that this solution fails to do justice to certain of the facts for which it professes to account, and especially to the body of empirical knowledge accumulated in the physical and physiological sciences. That in his own thinking Kant gave a quite literal interpretation to the teaching of these sciences is shown by his abiding interest in all speculations regarding the infra-microscopic structure of physical happenings. I need only refer in this connection to his speculations regarding the constitution of matter, as developed in the *Metaphysical Principles of Natural Science*, and to his elaboration of an "aether" theory of gravitation, cohesion, etc., in the *Opus Postumum*. That when not plainly interdicted by any supposed consequences of his metaphysical doctrines he gave an equally literal interpretation to the teaching of the physiological sciences is shown by the statement made in the first edition of the *Critique of Pure Reason*,[1] that our sensations are due to physical stimuli acting on the sense organs and brain, and by his appreciation of Sömmering's theory[2] that the brain-processes corresponding to the analytic and synthetic activities of the mind consist in the resolution of the water in the brain cavities into its chemical components upon the impact of sense stimuli and their recombination when the stimuli cease. Clearly, Kant felt himself to be quite definitely committed to some interpretation of physical nature which would enable him to accept the results of the natural sciences more or less at their face value, without any such high-handed restatement as Berkeleian subjectivism is constrained to adopt. And presumably it is because Kant thus finds himself proceeding on genuinely realist lines that he feels constrained in the *Opus Postumum* to ask that very question which he has so tantalisingly refused to raise in the *Critique* itself—to the consequent ranging, as above noted,[3] of his bewildered commentators into two opposed camps—how if, as he argues in his *Refutation of Idealism*, objects are distinct existences from the representations through which they are known, the principles of a transcendental idealism can still be upheld. Kant's method of reply, as already noted, is to establish his subjectivist principles so securely in their noumenal

---

[1] A 28-9. In the second edition Kant substituted for the paragraph in which this statement occurs a briefer passage of a non-committal character. As to Kant's probable reason for making this change, cf. above, pp. 120-2. Cf. also p. 275.

[2] *Werke* (Hartenstein), vi. p. 457 ff.

[3] Above, pp. 612-13.

functioning that in relation to the phenomenal order they enjoy all rights of eminent domain. Briefly outlined, the resulting doctrine of noumenal affection is as follows:

The self in itself, Kant now unequivocally teaches, "makes" its object by a "self-positing of itself as object."

"Space and time are not things but only modes of representation. . . . Their positing contains only that which is *made (gemacht)*, not anything that is *given*."[1] "Space and time are not indirect, mediate, derivate, but direct, immediate, primitive intuitions, through which the subject affects itself as appearance, and therefore represent their object as limitless. The complex of the representations which are contained in this intuition is the progress *in infinitum*. The object [of that complex] is neither ideal (*idealistisch*) nor real (*realistisch*); for it is not in any way *given*, but only *thought* (*non dari, sed intelligi potest*)."[2] "That a space *is* cannot be perceived. I *posit* a space. . . ."[3] "The subject which makes itself the *sense*-representation of space and time, is itself in this act likewise object. Self-intuition."[4] "The subject posits itself in the pure intuition and makes itself its object (*macht sich zum Objekt*)."[5] "Space and time are not objects, but determinations of the subject through itself, whereby it affects itself as object in the appearance, and as thing [*i.e.* self] in itself = *x* is determining ground of itself."[6] "All my faculty of representation (*facultas repraesentativa*), which consists of intuition and conception, begins with the consciousness of itself. . . . Our sense-intuition is not, in the first place, perception; for a [metaphysical] principle precedes . . . the positing of itself and the being conscious of this positing (*Position*). The form[s] of this positing of the manifold as connected throughout are the pure intuitions which are entitled space and time."[7] "Space and time are not things which exist outside the representation, and which as apprehensible are given; they are that which the faculty of representation makes for itself."[8]

These are a selection from the passages of like tenor cited by Adickes. They illustrate Kant's fundamental contention that

". . . the principle of the ideality of space and of time is the key to the Transcendental Philosophy, according to which synthetic and *a priori* knowledge can be extended only in so far as the objects of the senses are represented as appearances, and according to which the thing itself is no existing being but as = *x* is merely a principle."[9] "According to the principle of Transcendental Philosophy [*i.e.* of] the possibility of synthetic *a priori* judgments, [what comes first] is

---

[1] Cited by Adickes, p. 635.
[2] Cited by Adickes, p. 618 *n*.   [3] Cited by Adickes, p. 635.   [4] *Loc. cit.*
[5] Cited by Adickes, p. 636.   [6] Cited by Adickes, p. 638.
[7] *Loc. cit.*   [8] Cited by Adickes, p. 639.
[9] Cited by Adickes, pp. 673-4.

not the act of the apprehension of the manifold given in intuition (*apprehensio simplex*), but the principle of the autonomy whereby the self makes itself its object as given in appearance, [*i.e.* as] phenomenal object."[1] "The principle of the ideality of intuition underlies all our knowledge of things outside us, *i.e.* we do not apprehend objects as in themselves given (*apprehensio simplex*), but the subject makes for itself (invents)[2] the manifold of the object of the senses, so far as its form is concerned. . . ."[3]

In line with the use of the very strong term "*fingit*" Kant likewise speaks of space and time as original and primitive products of the *imagination*.

"[The representation of space and time] is an act of the subject itself and a product of the faculty of imagination (*Einbildungskraft*), which however is not derived (*repraesentatio derivativa*), but is original"[4] "Space and time are products (but primitive products) of our own faculty of imagination, and therefore are self-made intuitions since the subject affects itself, and thereby is appearance, not thing in itself."[5]

This general point of view Kant extends to the categories.

". . . the categories are not existing things [meaning, presumably, not inherent to them], but acts (*Actus*) through which the subject, for the sake of possible experience, posits itself *a priori* and constitutes itself as an object." "The subject posits itself through synthetic propositions *a priori* [and] through the forms of sensuous intuition, space and time, since the subject exercises forces (*Kräfte*) whereby [as thing in itself] it affects itself and determines itself to appearances."[6]

Thirdly, Kant extends this standpoint to include the concept of the thing in itself.

"The object in itself or noumenon is a mere *Gedankending* (*ens rationis*), in the representation of which the subject posits itself" (*Theätet*).[7] "Space and time are products, but primitive products, of our own faculty of imagination, and therefore are self-made intuitions, since the subject [the self in itself] affects itself, and the appearance is not therefore thing in itself. The material (*Das Materiale*), the thing in itself = x, is the mere representation of the self's own activity,"[8] *i.e.* the thought of its own unity, represented as that which has to be sought in the unity of the experienced. The thing in itself = x, in its distinction from appearance, is "not itself a separate object, but only a special relation (*respectus*), for the

---

[1] Cited by Adickes, p. 641.　　　　[2] *Schafft sich selbst* (*fingit*).
[3] Cited by Adickes, p. 645.　　　　[4] Cited by Adickes, p. 639.
[5] Cited by Adickes, p. 654.　　　　[6] Cited by Adickes, p. 645.
[7] Cited by Adickes, p. 654. For the reference to *Theätet* cf. below, p. 632.
[8] *Loc. cit.*

constituting of the self as object," *i.e.* (as Adickes interprets this and similar passages) in order to set its transcendental unity of apperception over against itself in objective form in the unity of the single objects and of the whole of nature.[1]

Lastly, in order to complete the doctrine of noumenal affection, Kant ought to have advanced yet one stage further, and to have extended the process of self-positing so as to derive from the inherent constitution of the self the possible types of moving forces in nature, and the possible types of secondary qualities which the empirical self can experience in reaction upon these forces. Only so can Kant hope to establish his view of nature as being an emanation, due in all its features to the creative activities of the noumenal self; and only so can he succeed in offering transcendental justification of the synthetic processes whereby the empirical self, working on the basis of its given sensations, proceeds to a knowledge of the moving forces to which they are due. This latter type of knowledge—such is Kant's thesis in the *Opus Postumum*—can be possible only if, and in so far as, the empirical self repeats upon the sense-data, in the way of interpretation, *a priori* synthetic activities, identical in type with those which, in their creative character, have brought the world of moving forces into being. This thesis is, however, developed in any detail only in those sections of Kant's manuscript in which, working on the empirical level, and with the results of the physical sciences in view, he endeavours to establish some kind of necessary connection between the table of categories and the various types of moving forces; and, as we have already noted,[2] all Kant's many and persevering attempts to carry out this programme prove abortive. But clearly, if on the empirical level no connection can be discerned between the factors in our sense-experience which are admittedly *a priori* and those more specific factors for which *a.priori* justification is sought, there can be no hope of doing so when the discussion is transferred to the much more conjectural realm of noumenal existence. We need not therefore be surprised that this aspect of Kant's doctrine of noumenal affection receives at his hands but scanty attention, and that he propounds it in such obscure and quite general terms as the following :

"That [*i.e.* The thought that] there is something outside myself [in space or as the thing in itself], is a product of myself. I make myself. Space cannot be perceived. Nor can even the moving force in space be perceived, since it cannot be represented as actual

---

[1] *Loc. cit.*   [2] Above, pp. 611-12.

unless there be a body which exercises it [and that body too must be posited by the self]. We make everything ourselves."[1]

In thus continuing to *postulate* that the *a priori* in nature is coextensive with all the main structural features of the natural order, and that it even extends to the secondary qualities, Kant is falling back upon mere assertion, and is leaving a gap in the argument just at the very point at which further explanation is most required.

Two further points of general interest regarding the *Opus Postumum* call for notice—(1) the nature of Kant's secondary motives in expounding his new doctrines in the above terms, and (2) his discussion of the nature and validity of the Idea of God.

(1) The many passages in which Kant deals with the concept of the thing in itself, one and all agree in their strong subjectivist colouring. It is a *Gedankending*, an *ens rationis*. In its representation, the self posits, not any independent reality, but only itself. It is entertained for the sake of experience, and is not known to exist either as its object or as its ground.

"The thing in itself is not another object, but another mode whereby [the self] makes itself its own object." "Not *objectum noumenon*, but the act of the understanding which makes the sense-intuition as mere phenomenon, is the intelligible object" [meaning, as Adickes suggests, takes over, for transcendental philosophy, the rôle of the intelligible object].[2] "The thing in itself is a *Gedankending (ens rationis)* of the connection of this manifold whole into the unity to which the self constitutes itself."[3] "The object in itself = x is the sense-object in itself, not, however, as another object, but as another mode of representation."[4] "The correlate of the thing in appearance is the thing in itself, is the subject which I make into the object" [*i.e.* whereby the subject makes itself its own object, by reading its own unity into the given].[5]

This attitude, together with Kant's new phrases, *sich selbst setzen, sich selbst bestimmen, sich selbst aufstellen, sich selbst schaffen, sich selbst konstituieren, sich selbst afficieren*, and especially the frequently recurring variations in the phrase *sich selbst machen*, are in line with, and give expression to, his insistence upon the spontaneity and, as it were, self-creative character of the noumenal self; and constantly they suggest the somewhat similar teaching which in these very years, 1796–1803, was being upheld by Beck and by Fichte.

---

[1] Cited by Adickes, p. 648; cf. also pp. 755-7.
[2] Cited by Adickes, p. 651.   [3] Cited by Adickes, pp. 651-2.
[4] Cited by Adickes, p. 653.   [5] Cited by Adickes, p. 652.

Jacob Sigismund Beck, one of Kant's ablest pupils, in fulfilment of his ambition to give, in a manner compatible with the expression of his own personal views, a systematic exposition of his Master's teaching, published in 1793–1794 the two volumes of his *Erläuternder Auszug aus den kritischen Schriften des H. Prof. Kant*. After this preliminary, more purely expository work, Beck proceeded to recast Kant's teaching in a yet more independent manner. His *Einzig-möglicher Standpunkt, aus welchem die kritische Philosophie beurteilt werden muss* appeared in 1796, and in it many of those very questions with which Kant occupies himself in the *Opus Postumum*, especially those which bear on the doctrine of double affection, are very explicitly discussed. How remarkably he anticipated some of Kant's later views can best be shown by quotation of the following passage :[1]

"If I be asked, how I have come to the representation of the object which I see before me, I reply that the object affects me. The object which I see or touch produces a sensation in me by means of the light or of its impenetrability. Yet at the same time I can also say that the understanding synthesises originatively (*synthesiert ursprünglich*) in the generation of the originative-synthetic objective unity; that in this originative representing I posit a permanent, wherein I represent to myself the time itself, that I posit a something (cause), through which the change of my own subjective state, namely, that I was without this representation and that I had this representation, receives its time-determination. In these statements we are very far from contradicting ourselves. What has to be noted is this: the transcendental thesis, that the understanding originatively posits a something, first gives significance and meaning to the empirical thesis, that the object affects me. For the former is the concept of the originative representing, wherein all the meaning of our concepts must be grounded. Indeed the concept of my understanding, as a faculty in me, even the concept of the 'I' first acquires significance and meaning from this originative positing."

But even more significant of Beck's influence in concentrating Kant's attention upon these particular problems, and incidentally upon the problem as to the extent and character of our apprehension of things in themselves, is Beck's remarkably interesting letter of 20th June 1797,[2] a date, it will be observed, within the period of the *Opus Postumum*. He draws Kant's attention to the now famous passage in Jacobi's dialogue, *David Hume über den Glauben, oder Idealismus und Realismus* :[3]

---

[1] Cited by Adickes, p. 611.   [2] *W*. xii. pp. 162-71.
[3] Published 1787. The passage occurs in an Appendix to the dialogue, vol. ii. of Jacobi's *Werke* (1815), p. 304.

"I must confess that this circumstance [viz. that objects make impressions on the senses] has been a stone of stumbling to me (*mich nicht wenig aufgehalten hat*) in my study of the Kantian Philosophy, so that time and again I have been compelled to retrace my steps and to restart the *Critique of Pure Reason* ever anew, since I was always finding myself bewildered in that without this presupposition I could not make entry into the system, and that with this presupposition I could not remain in it."

What, Beck asks Kant, is his reply to this criticism? Beck himself, for reasons which he assigns, definitely holds to the doctrine of empirical affection. The only objects which are known in terms of the categories are physical existences, and they alone, therefore, can be viewed as the causes of our sensations. When an absolute employment is made of the categories, we delude ourselves with the belief that we have concepts of things in themselves, and so fall into error. The concept of the thing in itself is not, he declares, accessible to theoretical philosophy; it belongs exclusively to the moral domain.

Though, unhappily, Kant's reply to this letter has not survived, in the immediately following year similar criticisms were pressed upon him, even more pointedly, by another correspondent, a friend of Beck's, J. H. Tieftrunk. Whence, Tieftrunk enquires,[1] the manifold of sensation?

"Apperception gives only the *degree* (*Grad*), *i.e.* the unity of the synthesis of the perception, and so rests on spontaneity, and is determination of the material of sensibility in accordance with a rule of apperception. Whence then the material? From sensibility? But whence does sensibility have it? From the objects which affect it? But what is that which affects it? What are the objects? Are they things in themselves or—[*sic*]?"

Though spontaneity and receptivity are, Tieftrunk proceeds, two distinct sources of knowledge, they are faculties of one and the same mind, and therefore in correspondence with one another.

"If it be further asked, what affects the mind?—I reply that it affects itself, since it is at once receptivity and spontaneity. . . . But whence is that which sensibility gives out of its own depths, out of itself? Whence has arisen the material and empirical, as such, when I abstract from that which it has become through the influence of spontaneity in accordance with the forms of sensibility? Does sensibility supply it purely out of its own depths, or do things in themselves, which are separate and distinct from the sensibility, give rise to it? I reply: *everything* which sensibility gives—both matter and form—is determined by its nature to be just that for us which

---

[1] *W.* xii. pp. 215-16; the letter is of the date 5th November 1797.

it is for us. . . . Apart from sensibility and understanding there is neither inner nor outer. . . . But since we cannot avoid asking : what then, independently of all conditions of our sensibility (as regards both form and matter) and of apperception, is the final ground of representations, the answer is : this last ground is for our understanding nothing but a thought of negative character, *i.e.* one to which no object corresponds, but which as a mere thought is not only admissible but necessary, since theoretical reason does not in thinking find itself absolutely limited to what is for us possible experience, and since practical reason can yield grounds for allowing reality to such a thought, though only in its practical bearing. In regard to things in themselves, of which we have only a negative concept, we cannot say : they *affect*, because the concept of affection expresses a real relation between *knowable* beings (*Wesen*), and for its employment it is required that the things so related be given and positively determined. Nor consequently can we say : things in themselves introduce representations of themselves into the mind ; for the problematic concept of them is itself only a relating point of representations of the mind, a *Gedankending*. We can know nothing at all save appearances, but in recognising this we at the same time in the thought posit a something which is not appearance, and so through mere logical position leave as it were an empty space for practical knowledge." [1]

We have Kant's reply to this letter ; but again, unfortunately, Kant under pressure, as he states, of manifold engagements, does not deal with all of Tieftrunk's questions, and passes over just that question to which we should most wish to have his answer, viz. regarding the source of the material of sensibility. He does indeed speak of the subject as being affected by the object in accordance with its own special constitution, and of the object as therefore being apprehended as it *appears* to us, indirectly, not as it is in itself. This, however, is merely an evasion of Tieftrunk's main question, and does not take us beyond the letter of the *Critique*. Tieftrunk has stated the question so pointedly that Kant cannot have failed to appreciate its importance ; and his omission to give a more explicit answer may be taken as signifying that he had none ready ; but since this is a problem with which, as the manuscripts of his *Opus Postumum* show, he was in this very year occupying himself, we may reasonably conjecture that Beck's and Tieftrunk's criticisms have contributed thereto. For the present, Kant contents himself with the following statement of his general position :

" . . . objects of the senses (of the outer as well as of the inner sense) can never be known by us save as they appear to us, not as

---

[1] *W.* xii. pp. 216-17.

they are in themselves. It likewise follows that supersensible objects are not for us objects of our theoretical knowledge. But the Idea of them cannot be dispensed with, at least as problematic (*quaestionis instar*). For the sensible would then be without its counterpart, the supersensible, and that would point to a logical defect in the division. The latter must be regarded as being transcendent for theoretical knowledge, and as belonging to pure, practical knowledge, freed from all empirical conditions, and its place (*Stelle*) as not, therefore, being entirely empty." [1]

Fichte adopted a position very similar to that of Beck, but expounded it in a manner which involved a much more pronounced divergence from orthodox Critical teaching. His *Grundlage der gesamten Wissenschaftslehre* appeared in 1794, and his supplementary expositions in the immediately following years. So that already, in the period during which Kant was preparing his *Opus Postumum*, Fichte's Philosophy was the dominant philosophical influence throughout Germany. [2] Though Kant never professed to have studied Fichte's writings with any thoroughness or care, he was more or less conversant with their tendency and main watchwords through intercourse with friends and through the literary journals. [3] When, therefore, we observe how Kant proceeded to transform his old-time doctrine of noumenal affection into a doctrine of self-positing, and to employ a new set of phrases which one and all suggest a type of position closely akin to that for which Beck and Fichte were standing, it is difficult to avoid drawing the conclusion that his choice of terminology was in part determined by his desire to show, in opposition to Beck's theoretical scepticism and to Fichte's absolute idealism, that though the principles of transcendental idealism, when consistently developed, allow of, and indeed demand, some such type of teaching, they do not require, and cannot justify, any departure from the strict letter of the Critical Philosophy —at least not when the teaching of the first *Critique* is supplemented, as he now professes to supplement it, by a more adequate *a priori* deduction of the order of nature, and by more explicit recognition of the two-fold source of "sensory" affection.

There are three other contemporary writers whose influence is discernible in the *Opus Postumum*—G. E. Schulze, D. Tiedemann, and Lichtenberg. Schulze published anonymously in 1792 his *Anesidemus oder über die Fundamente der von dem Herrn Professor Reinhold in Jena gelieferten*

---

[1] *IV*. xii. p. 224.
[2] Cf. Adamson, *Fichte* (Blackwood Philosophical Series), p. 52.
[3] Cf. *W*..xii. p. 241.

Elementarphilosophie.[1] In this work Schulze attacks Kant's teaching in regard to things in themselves, dwelling upon the inconsistency of combining the assertion of their unknowableness with a doctrine of noumenal affection. He himself holds that hitherto no proof either of the existence or of the non-existence of things in themselves, and no professedly final delimitation of human knowledge has been successfully achieved. Yet his position is not definitely sceptical. He refuses so to anticipate the future as to class these problems as ultimately insoluble.

Tiedemann, on the other hand, upholds a pre-Kantian type of dogmatism. His philosophy, as expounded in his *Theätet oder über das menschliche Wissen: ein Beitrag zur Vernunftkritik* (1794), is eclectic ; it combines, in a quite naïve manner, empirical and rationalist elements. He propounds a new conceptual proof of the substantiality and simplicity of the soul, and maintains that things in themselves are knowable— acting upon our organisation, they give rise to sensations which in their extension, figure, motion, force, etc., reveal the actual, independent nature of things in themselves. Kant's idealism he denounces as being indistinguishable from the most extreme subjectivism.

Kant's numerous references, in the *Opus Postumum*, to these two writers show a very strange twofold characteristic. In the first place, as so often happens in his criticisms of other thinkers, he adopts a very external and for the most part quite unjustifiable interpretation of their teaching. He represents both as doubting, and even as denying, the reality of the corporeal world, and so as standing for an idealism of the most extreme " egoistic " and sceptical type. In the second place, in the passages in which he challenges their teaching, the subjectivism of his own doctrine of noumenal self-positing receives the most emphatic expression.

"The object in itself, noumenon, is a mere *Gedankending, ens rationis*, in whose representation the subject posits itself. Theätet [*sic*]."[2] "Space is not a *Begriff* (*conceptus*) but *Anschauung* (*intuitus*). As such it is something inhering in the subject not existing outside the subject, and is a whole of a special kind in that it can be represented only as part of a yet greater whole, and therefore as infinite. It is a characteristic of the object which can belong to it only as appearance (quality of the subject) wherein the thinking subject posits itself, and neither an Anesidem nor a Theätet (idealist or egoist) can say anything contrary thereto. . . ."[3] "The first act of thinking contains a principle of the ideality of the object

---

[1] It was reviewed by Fichte in 1794.
[2] Cited by Adickes, p. 616.   [3] Cited by Adickes, pp. 617-18.

in me and outside me as appearance, *i.e.* of the self-affecting subject in a system of the Ideas which contain merely the formal [factors] of the advance to experience in general (Änesidem), *i.e.* the transcendental philosophy is an idealism."[1]

The only satisfactory explanation of this very strange combination of unsympathetic criticism with elaboration of a position so remarkably similar to that criticised would seem to be the explanation given above, in regard to Kant's adoption of the terminology of Beck and Fichte. Kant is not, as might at first sight appear, retreating in face of the attacks. He is stealing the enemy's thunder before assaulting their positions. Either, as Adickes suggests, he is entertaining the hope, by a more careful restatement of his fundamental Critical tenets, to bring about reunion of the diverging groups of his disciples, or else he is striving to show that within the scope of his own system even the most extreme assertions urged against it find their place and relative justification, or at least that the new terminology allows of being so interpreted. He could also point out that this terminology is simply a variation upon that which he has himself employed in the *Critique of Pure Reason*, and especially of the assertion there made, though not developed in any detail, that: "The 'I think' expresses the *actus* whereby I determine my existence."[2] As Adickes persuasively argues: "Had Kant succeeded in completing the *Opus Postumum* and in publishing it in or about 1800, it would without doubt have made an altogether different impression than in 1884 or to-day. Though it could not have reversed what had meantime happened, and could hardly have directed the further developments into other channels, yet it is highly probable that it would have ushered in a surprisingly rich renaissance of his School. Precisely that which nowadays repels us in the *Opus Postumum*, the extravagance of its apriorism and formalism, the extension of the transcendental method over to the content of experience, would probably have then had the contrary effect.[3]

If, on the other hand, we endeavour to estimate the intrinsic philosophical value of the *Opus Postumum*, the verdict must be of a very different character. Under pressure, or as we may perhaps more correctly say, under sanction, of the prevailing tendencies of the time, especially as expressed through the dominating influence of Fichte, Kant in these last years has allowed his *Privat-meinungen* regarding the

[1] Cited by Adickes, p. 625.
[2] B 157 *n.* In this passage we find the term "*setzen*" as well as the term "*bestimmen*," and the sentence: "*Doch macht diese Spontaneität, dass ich mich Intelligenz nenne.*"
[3] Adickes, p. 669.

noumenal activities of the self, as a free and active agent, to obtain expression in a manner out of harmony with the more carefully defined positions of his own best period. For there are certain fairly obvious, and indeed unanswerable, criticisms to which his new teaching lies exposed. How can Kant, while insisting, as he does, that the concept of the thing in itself is a self-posited *ens rationis*, and *not* the thought of any independently existing object, still continue to supplement his doctrine of empirical affection by a doctrine of noumenal affection? How, if all the categories — he is even more explicit as to this in the *Opus Postumum* than in the *Critique of Pure Reason*—be purely formal functions of unity, and therefore meaningless save in their application to an intuitively given material, can they be used to define things in themselves as affecting the self in itself?

Here I find difficulty in accepting Adickes' contention that Kant was able to follow his recalcitrant disciples in their denial of any theoretical knowledge of things in themselves just because he had himself come to assign so large a rôle to the empirical self. If my interpretation, as above given, of Kant's new teaching be correct—it is based upon the evidence which Adickes himself supplies—the doctrine of empirical affection rests upon, and indispensably presupposes, the supplementary doctrine of noumenal affection. The empirical self can empirically apprehend only what the transcendental self has itself determined. We must therefore have the right to postulate, not only that things in themselves affect the self in itself, but also—a much more definite and precise assumption—that the self in itself is capable of creatively producing, out of a manifold which though given is also sufficiently plastic, that phenomenal world wherein the empirical self and physical entities subsist and interact. As I have emphasised, the doctrine of empirical affection by itself, when not thus supported, so far from affording a solution of the problems of knowledge, would have to fall back upon a pre-established harmony wherein the *a priori* additions would be supposed to have been so adjusted that they can be relied upon to reconstruct what is independently real.

Adickes is indeed able, in support of his view, to point to Kant's frequent references, in passages written in the years 1801-1803, to Lichtenberg,[1] whom Kant speaks of as a well-informed though independent disciple, and who did thus combine an empirical realism with denial of all theoretical

---

[1] G. C. Lichtenberg (1742-1799), physicist and satirical writer. Kant's references are all to the second volume of his *Vermischte Schriften* (edited in nine volumes, 1800-1805, by L. Chr. Lichtenberg and Fr. Fries), which was published in 1801. Cf. Adickes, pp. 149-50, 833.

apprehension of things in themselves. Under the influence of Lichtenberg's enthusiastic references to Spinoza, Kant even goes so far as to depict Spinoza, Schelling, and Lichtenberg as typifying three stages in the development of his own transcendental philosophy: "System of transcendental idealism through Schelling, Spinoza, Lichtenberg—as it were three dimensions: the present, the past, and the future."[1] But these references occurring in that part of Kant's manuscript which fall within the years 1802–1803 are part of the evidence pointing to his increased mental enfeeblement, and are of little weight. If we may judge by the lengthy quotations which Adickes gives[2] from Lichtenberg's work, the latter can have had no real appreciation of what was really fundamental in Kant's system. He was a physicist by profession, and as his attempt to combine, in a confused, eclectic manner, the teachings of Spinoza and of Kant would seem to show, he was really only an amateur in the field of philosophy. His doctrine of knowledge is merely a very usual type of subjectivism, backed by a belief in the existence of unknowable things in themselves. He has no more really genuine understanding of what is fundamental in Kant's Critical teaching than had, say, Schopenhauer, who, some years later, in making his own independent contribution, also laid claim to unpartisan discipleship.[3]

That Kant unwaveringly held to a belief in the existence of things in themselves, and yet likewise denied all possibility of theoretical knowledge[4] of them, cannot be questioned by any student of the *Critique of Pure Reason*; and it is no less clearly the teaching of the *Opus Postumum*. There is, indeed, in the latter work, not only a still greater insistence upon the merely problematic character of the concept of the thing in itself, but also, what is very noticeable, a *complete* absence of any suggestion of what I have entitled the Idealist, or absolutist, view of the nature and function of the Ideas of Reason, and therefore of what is now universally recognised as the only feasible method of justifying the distinction, if it is to be tenable at all, between reality and its appearances, namely, not by way of opposition and contrast, but as a distinction between a whole and the subordinate existences which it conditions.[5] Kant's failure in the *Critique* to show how his distinction between Ideas and categories bears upon

---

[1] Cited by Adickes, p. 764.   [2] Adickes, pp. 834-9.
[3] Cf. above, pp. 366 n., 407 n.
[4] Allowing, that is, for the very definite meaning which he assigns to the term "knowledge," and also for his absolutist view of the function of Reason. Cf. above, pp. lv-lvi, 416, 430.
[5] Cf. above, pp. liv, 414-17, 429-31, 520-1, 558-61.

the distinction between phenomena and things in themselves is, as I have argued, in the body of the *Commentary*,[1] largely due to the predominance throughout the *Dialectic* of his sceptical view of Reason. This sceptical view prevails throughout the *Opus Postumum*, so much so that the contrasting absolutist view—so far as Adickes' quotations disclose—is never, even once, directly stated, though it continues, of course, to be implied in some of the terms employed. But obviously, if the absolutist view of Reason is to be eliminated, the doctrines of noumenal self-positing and of noumenal affection are, *a fortiori*, still less tenable. When, therefore, in the *Opus Postumum* Kant professes, as regards the self in itself, to have knowledge beyond what his Critical principles justify, and so to be able to extend the jurisdiction of his architectonic to the content as well as to the form of experience, the effect is merely to underline the abiding deficiencies of his general teaching. So far as its treatment of these particular problems is concerned, the *Opus Postumum* is mainly valuable as showing how dissatisfied Kant had become with much that is fundamental in his theory of knowledge.

As regards the nature and grounds of his distinction between things in themselves and appearances, the attitude from which Kant never departed, and beyond which—his Idealist view of Reason notwithstanding—he never succeeded in advancing, is adequately presented in the passage already quoted.[2]

"[On the mental origin of the forms of intuition] is grounded the central proposition: objects of the senses (of the outer as well as of the inner) can never be known by us save as they appear to us, not as they are in themselves. It likewise follows that supersensible objects are not for us objects of our theoretical knowledge. But the Idea of them cannot be dispensed with, at least as problematic (*quaestionis instar*). For the sensible would then be left without its counterpart, the supersensible, and that would point to a logical defect in the division. The latter must be regarded as being transcendent for theoretical knowledge, and as belonging to pure, practical knowledge, freed from all empirical conditions, and its place (*Stelle*) as not, therefore, being entirely empty."

(2) The passages dealing with the Idea of God occur almost exclusively[3] in the section which dates from the years 1800–1803, and like the other passages to which I have just been referring, show the extent to which Kant's mind was then preoccupied with Lichtenberg's teaching as expounded in the second volume of his *Vermischte Schriften*. As already

---

[1] Above, pp. 560-1.   [2] Above, pp. 630-1.
[3] For the few references which occur in other sections, cf. Adickes, p. 843.

stated,[1] this volume appeared in 1801. Kant's advance copy, received quite possibly in 1800, is still extant, with his marginal notes.

Kant adopts towards the Idea of God the same attitude as towards the concept of things in themselves, namely, that God undeniably exists, but that in the theoretical domain nothing whatsoever can be established in regard to His reality. These are also Lichtenberg's two main theses. In addition, Lichtenberg dwells at length upon the favourite theme of the Eighteenth Century Deists, that man has no special duties towards God. This Deism is indeed partially modified by Lichtenberg's Spinozistic leanings; but what it thereby gains in depth, it loses in clarity. The following passages are cited by Adickes[2] from Lichtenberg's work:

"There is absolutely no other way of worshipping God than by fulfilling those duties, and by acting in accordance with those laws which reason has prescribed. That there is a God can, in my view, signify only that I feel myself, the freedom of my will notwithstanding, constrained to do right. What further need have we for a God? That He exist [?]. When this further need is made explicit, we are brought, I believe, to Kant's contention: our *heart* does indeed recognise a God, but to make this comprehensible to reason is indeed difficult, if not altogether impossible." "The belief in a God is instinct; it is as natural to men as going upon two legs, but in many men suffers modification, and in others is entirely suppressed. Ordinarily, however, it is there, and is indispensable to the inward completion of the faculty of knowledge." "Religion is really the art whereby, through the thought of God, without any other aid, we provide ourselves with comfort and courage in all our evils, and with strength to stand out against them."

That Kant must already, of his own accord, and in analogy with his treatment of the Idea of the thing in itself, have been inclining to similar teaching is shown by three passages[3] in the earlier, so-called tenth and eleventh, sections which were written (August 1799 to April 1800) prior to Kant's reading of Lichtenberg's work. But these tendencies were quite evidently reinforced, and the methods of statement in part determined, by Lichtenberg's teaching, as is shown by the following passages, all of which are taken from manuscripts of the years 1800–1803:

"The mere idea of God is at the same time a postulate of His existence. To think the Idea and to believe is an identical act."[4]

---

[1] Above, p. 634 *n*.   [2] Pp. 837-8.
[3] Cited by Adickes, pp. 828-9. Only the following need be quoted: "God over us, God beside us, God in us. 1. Power and fear. 2. Presence and worship (innermost adoration). 3. Following of his duty as shadow to the light."   [4] Cited by Adickes, p. 776.

The thought of Him is at the same time the belief in Him and in His personality."[1] On the other hand, the concept of God "is not that of a substance, *i.e.* of a thing which exists independently of my thinking, but the Idea (*Selbstgeschöpf, Gedankending, ens rationis*) of a Reason that constitutes itself into a *Gedankending,* and which propounds synthetic *a priori* judgments in accordance with the principles of Transcendental Philosophy. It is an Ideal of which, since the concept is transcendent, we do not and cannot ask whether such an object exists."[2] "The question : Is there a God? We cannot prove such an object of thought to be a substance outside the subject."[3] God is "the product of our own Reason," "the Ideal of a substance which we ourselves make." To this extent, we are "subjective self-creators."[4] "The proposition : there is a God (for Himself), can be established neither through pure reason nor from empirical sources of knowledge." "It is not Nature in the world that leads to God, *e.g.* through its beautiful ordering, but reversewise." "If we should represent God in accordance with His works, how should we judge Him? *Homo homini lupus.* He reveals His infinite understanding, but not in moral fashion."[5] "God is not a thing subsisting outside me; but my own thought. It is absurd to ask whether a God exists."[6] But Kant, as if to guard himself against misunderstanding, adds that the thought of God is "no invention, *i.e.* no arbitrarily made concept (*conceptus factitius*) but necessarily given (*datus*) to Reason."[7]

In extension of this position, Kant now rejects as being untenable, and as being illegitimately theoretical, the proof of God's existence upon which he has relied in the *Critique of Practical Reason,* namely, by reference to the *Summum Bonum.* Though Kant nowhere, in explicit terms, avows this change of standpoint, or at least does not do so in any passage quoted by Adickes, the whole tenor of his argument is towards substituting a proof of a more strictly moral character, all the emphasis being laid upon the direct relation in which the Idea of God stands to the moral imperative. This new proof Kant tentatively formulates in at least three distinguishable forms.[8]

(1) In one set of passages Kant maintains that the religious interpretation of all duties as divine commands is not a supplementary, later interpretation, but is, for every moral being, immediately and necessarily given together with the apprehension of the duties, *i.e.* the categorical imperative leads directly to God, and affords surety of His reality.

[1] *Loc. cit.*
[2] Cited by Adickes, p. 791.
[3] Cited by Adickes, p. 791.
[4] Cited by Adickes, p. 793.
[5] Cited by Adickes, p. 786.
[6] Cited by Adickes, p. 789.
[7] Cited by Adickes, p. 800.
[8] Adickes, drawing a further distinction within the first formulation, distinguishes four forms. Cf. p. 802 ff.

"In the morally practical Reason lies the categorical imperative, to regard all human duties as divine commands."[1] "The realism of the Idea of God can be proved only through the duty-imperative."[2] "Beings must be thought which, although they exist only in the thoughts of the philosopher, yet in these have morally practical reality. These are God, the world-all, and man as subjected in the world to the duty-concept according to the categorical imperative, which as categorical is also a principle of freedom."[3] "A being which is capable of holding sway over all rational beings in accordance with laws of duty (the categorical imperative), and is justified in so doing, is God. But the existence of such a being can be *postulated* only in a practical reference, namely [in view of] the necessity of so acting as if in the knowledge of all my duties as divine commands (*tanquam non cæu*) I stood under this awful but also at the same time salutary guidance and surety. Accordingly the *existence* of such a being is not postulated in this formula; such postulating would be self-contradictory."[4]

The concluding sentence is far from clear; comparison of it with other passages[5] shows that Kant intends to signify that the certainty obtained of God's existence is a certainty of practical belief, not of theoretical demonstration.

(2) In a second set of passages, Kant makes no reference to the existence of God but only to the Idea of God. But in these passages also, duties are alleged to be apprehensible only as divine commands.

"The categorical imperative of the command of duty is grounded in the Idea of an *imperantis*, who is all-powerful and holds universal sway (formal). This is the Idea of God."[6] "What constrains us to the Idea of God? No empirical concept; no metaphysic. What presents this *a priori* concept is Transcendental Philosophy, the concept of duty."[7] "The imperative of duty proves to men their freedom, and at the same time conducts them to the Idea of God."[8]

(3) In yet another set of passages Kant suggests that God Himself, and not merely the Idea of God as a trans-subjective Being, is immanent in the human spirit.

"God is not a being outside me, but merely a thought in me. God is the morally practical self-legislative Reason. Therefore only

---

[1] Cited by Adickes, p. 802.
[2] Cited by Adickes, pp. 788-9.
[3] *Loc. cit.*
[4] Cited by Adickes, pp. 802-3. This is one of the passages which Vaihinger (*Philosophie des als ob*, 2nd ed., p. 726) cites in justification of his equating Kant with Nietzsche (cf. above, p. 609). As Adickes points out (p. 803), Vaihinger mistranslates the last sentence by taking the last clause as referring, not to the postulating, but to existence.
[5] Cf. those cited by Adickes, p. 803 ff.
[6] Cited by Adickes, p. 808.
[7] *Loc. cit.*
[8] *Loc. cit.*

a God in me, about me, and over me."[1]) "The proposition:
There is a God says nothing more than: There is in the human
morally self-determining Reason a highest principle which determines
itself, and finds itself compelled unremittingly to act in accordance
with such a principle."[2] "God can be sought only in us."[3]
"There is a God, namely, in the Idea of the morally practical
Reason which [determines] itself to a continuous oversight as well
as guidance of the actions according to *one* principle, like to a
Zoroaster."[4]

Kant's reading of the *Zend-Avesta*,[5] and also his reading
of Lichtenberg's eulogies of Spinoza, are here in evidence.

"Similarly to the Zoroastrian principle of intuiting all things in
God, and of dictating how they should be (like Lichtenberg) and
the capacity of thought as inner intuition to develop *out of itself.*"[6]

Many of the passages are directed against the view of God
as a substance.

"Cosmotheology. It is an object of the morally practical
Reason, which contains the principle of all human duties as being
divine commands, and yet does not require us to assume a special
substance existing outside man."[7] "There is a Being (*Wesen*) in
me, which though distinct from me stands to me in relations of
causal efficacy, and which, itself free, *i.e.* not dependent upon the law
of nature in space and time, inwardly directs me (justifies or
condemns), and I, as man, am myself this Being. It is not a
substance outside me; and what is strangest of all, the causality is
a determination to action in freedom, and not as a necessity of
nature."[8] "God must be represented not as substance outside me,
but as [the] highest moral principle in me. But indirectly as a
power in me (gods do not exist) [it] is the Ideal of power and
wisdom in *one* concept; if it is [represented as the Ideal?] outside
me, it is the determining ground of my [? its] omnipresence."[9]
"The Idea (not concept) of God is not the concept of a substance.
The personality which we ascribe to it, which is also bound up with
the singleness of its object (not a plurality of gods" [passage ends
abruptly].[10] "The Idea of that which human Reason itself makes
out of the World-All is the active representation of God. Not as a
special personality, *substance outside me* but as a thought in me."[11]

Clearly Kant's views have undergone considerable change
since the writing of the *Critique of Practical Reason*. God is
no longer viewed as a Being who must be postulated in order

---

[1] Cited by Adickes, p. 819.
[2] *Loc. cit.*   [3] *Loc. cit.*   [4] Cited by Adickes, p. 730.
[5] Cf. above, pp. 609-10.   [6] Cited by Adickes, p. 730.
[7] Cited by Adickes, p. 824.   [8] Cited by Adickes, pp. 824-5.
[9] Cited by Adickes, p. 826.   [10] Cited by Adickes, pp. 826-7.
[11] Cited by Adickes, p. 827.

to make possible the coincidence of virtue with happiness. God speaks with the voice of the categorical imperative, and thereby reveals Himself in a direct manner. But as the passages above quoted also show, this new point of view is suggested merely; it is nowhere developed in a systematic manner; and even as thus suggested, it is formulated in at least three diverse ways.

INDEX

Absolute. *See* Unconditioned

Absolutist aspect of human consciousness, xxxvii–xl, lvii, lviii–lix, lix–lxi, 270–1, 274, 282, 285–7, 331 *n.*, 423 *n.*

Actuality, 391 ff.

Adamson, Robert, xxiv *n.* 15

Addison, 156

Adickes, E., xxviii–xxx, 76, 169, 200, 202, 215 *n.*, 233 *n.*, 234, 304, 363, 376, 397, 406 *n.*, 423, 439–40, 441 464 *n.*, 466, 479, 579 *n.*, 601 *n.*

Affinity, objective, 224, 253–7, 266–7

"Als ob" doctrine, 524, 553 ff.

Analogy, Kant's use of the term, 356–8

Analytic and synthetic judgment, xxv ff., xlii–liii, xliv, 28 ff., 37 ff., 59–60, 65; existential judgment, 530–1; distinction perhaps suggested by examination of ontological argument, 531. *See* Judgment

Analytic and synthetic methods, 44 ff., 111, 117 *n. See* Transcendental method

Analytic, distinguished from the *Dialectic,* 172–4, 438–42

Anthropologic, Kant's, 81 *n.*, 100 *n.*

Antinomies, lii, liii, 432, 478 ff., 519–20

Appearance, Kant's views regarding, xliii–xliv, li–lii, lvii–lviii, 18–22, 83–5, 120–2, 147 ff., 205 ff., 215 ff., 279–84, 293 ff., 301 ff., 312 ff., 321 ff., 330–1, 372–3, 404 ff., 427 ff.; criticism of Leibnizian view of, 143–6; criticism of Locke's view of, 146–7; ideality of, 147 ff.; outer and inner appearances reduce to relations, 147–8; appearance and illusion, 148 ff.; causal efficacy of appearances, 216, 217–18, 351, 373–4; distinction between appearance and reality based not on categories of understanding but on Ideas of Reason, lvii–lviii, 217–18, 326 *n.*, 331, 390–1, 414–17, 426–31, 473–7. 511–12, 519–21, 541–2, 558–61, Appendix C

Apperception, and memory, 251; in what sense original, xli, xlviii–l, liv–lv, 260–3, 461–2, 472–7; transcendental unity of, liv–lvi, 207 ff., 212, 250–3, 260–3, 270, 277–9, 322 ff., 455 ff., 473–7; absent from the animal mind, lii–liv; objective unity of, 270–1, 274, 282, 285–7; and inner sense, 295–8; 331 ff., 512 *n. See* Self

A priori, Kant's views regarding the, xxxiii–xxxiv, xl–xliii, lvi–lix, 1–2, 39–40, 42, 54 ff.; problem of *a priori* synthetic judgment, 26 ff, 39–40, 43 ff.; its validity merely *de facto,* xli–xlii, xlix–l, 30, 57, 118, 142, 185–6, 257–9, 291, 391–2, 393, 400–1, 411; the faculties in which it originates, xlviii–xlix, liv–lvi, 1–2, 50–1, 237–8, 263 ff., 391–2, 393, 398, 563–5; semi-Critical view of the, 188–9, 232, 263–4. *See* Understanding, Reason

Aquinas, 73

Architectonic, xxx, 34, 100, 184, 332–6, 340–1. 342, 343, 345, 347, 390, 392, 394, 419 ff., 434, 437, 439–40, 440, 454, 463, 464, 474, 479–80, 496, 498, 542, 563, 579, Appendix C

Aristotle, l, 196, 198, 390. *See* Logic

Arithmetic, 32, 40–1, 65–6, 128 ff., 337–8, 347, 566

Association, and judgment, xli–xlii, lii–liv; and consciousness, xlvii–xlix; rests on objective affinity, 253–7, 266–7

Attributive judgment, Kant's exclusive emphasis upon, 37–8, 180–1, 197

Augustine, St., 73, 110, 565

Avenarius, 587 *n.*

Axioms, Kant's view of, 50, 127, 348, 565–7

Augustine, Robert, xvi

Bacon, Francis, 4–5, 74

Bain, A., 86 *n.*

643

metaphysical and practical validity of the Ideas, 570–6; concluding comments on Kant's views of the, 558–61; condition distinction between appearance and reality, lvii–lvii, 217–18, 326 n., 331, 391, 414–17. 426–31, 473–7, 511–12, 519–21, 541–2, 558–61. *See* Deduction of Ideas

Illusion, and appearance, 148 ff.; Berkeley regards objects of outer sense as, 157, 307–8; inner experience not illusory, 323–4; transcendental, 13, 427–9, 437, 456 ff., 480, 552, 555

Imagination, may be the common root of sensibility and understanding, 77, 225, 265; productive, 224 ff., 264 ff., 337, 348, 375–6

Immanent and transcendent metaphysics. *See* Metaphysics

Immortality, problem of, 569 ff.

Incongruous counterparts, 161 ff.

Infinitude, of space, 105 ff.; of time, 124 ff.; Kant's view of, 483 ff.; distinction between *in infinitum* and *in indefinitum*, 507 ff.

Inner Sense, xlix, n., 148, 291 ff., 360, 464, 468–9; and apperception, 321 ff., 512 n.

Intuition, Kant's doctrine of pure, 40 ff., 79–80, 118–20, 128 ff., 167–8, 468–9; intuition and conception, 38–42, 93–98, 105–9, 118–20, 126, 128–34, 165–6, 167–8. 194, 390–1, 564–6; formal intuition and form of intuition, 109, 114–16

Intuitive understanding, Kant's view of, 160, 291, 408 ff., 468 n. 542

Jacobi, 300

Jakob, xxxvi n.

James, William, xv, 86, 377–8, 459 n., 461 n.

Janitsch, 155, 156

Jones, Sir Henry, 36

Judgment, Kant's doctrine of the, xli–xlii, xliv, xlvii–l lii–liv, 177 ff., 192 ff., 286 ff.; the fundamental activity of the understanding, xli–xlii, xliii, xlvii–xlviii, 133, 181–2, 288, 332, 370; *a priori* and empirical, 27–8; analytic and synthetic, xxv ff., 28 ff., 37 ff. 59–60; judgment 7 + 5 = 12, 65; relational types ignored by Kant, 37 ff.; Kant's attributive view of, 37–8, 180–1, 197; as assertion of contingency, 139 ff., 55, 286–9; Kant's distinction between judgments of perception and

judgments of experience, 288–9; existential, 527–31

Knowing and thinking, distinction between, lix–lx, 20, 25, 290–1, 331, 404 ff. *See* Categories

Knowledge, the narrow meaning assigned to term by Kant, lix–lx, lxiv, 25

Knützen, 161

Kuehn, Manfred, xxiii n. 5

Lambert, xxix n., xxxv, xxxix, 74, 138, 150, 193

Lange, F., 23

Lectures on Metaphysics, Kant's, 261 275 n., 299, 448–9, 475 n.

Lectures on the Philosophy of Religion Kant's, 261

Leibniz, Kant's relation to, xxxvii–xl, xl, xliii, li, lv–lvi, lix; his absolutist view of thought, xxx–xxxii; anticipates Kant's phenomenalism, 21–2; his rejection of empiricism, 27, 58; his pre-established harmony, 28; regards synthetic judgments as always empirical, 30; his conceptual atomism, 38; Kant probably influenced by the *Nouveaux Essais* of, 92, 186; referred to by Kant, 112; Kant's relation to, 140–1; Kant's criticism of his interpretation of sensibility and appearance, 143–6; his view of space, 161 ff.; Kant influenced by the spiritualism of, 208–9, 343. 260–1, 263; his subjectivism and doctrine of *petites perceptions*, 272–3, 298–9, 306; his alternative views of the reality of the material world, 298–9: continuing influence of his rationalism on Kant, 394–5, 398–9, 418 ff.; his view of the possible as wider than the actual, 401–2; antinomies formulated by Kant from the standpoint of the Leibnizian rationalism, 481 ff.; Kant's formulation of the ontological argument Leibnizian, 522 ff., 556; contrast between Locke and, 146–7, 421, 582; on mathematical method, 592; the philosophical teaching of, 601–6; on the nature of sense-experience, 604–5; influence on Kant, 605–6

Limiting concepts, Ideas as, 408, 413–17, 436 ff. *See* Ideas of Reason

Locke, xxiii, n. 12, xxxix, xlvi, li, 15; Kant's criticism of his view of appearance, 146–7; Kant's restatement of his distinction between primary and secondary qualities, 120–2, 146, 149 ff., 306; subjectivism of, 272, 306; on